D0345168

FOR EARTH'S SAKE

David R. Brower
Help!

FOR EARTH'S SAKE

The Life and Times of

DAVID BROWER

PEREGRINE SMITH BOOKS

SALT LAKE CITY

First edition

95 94 93 92 91   10 9 8 7 6 5 4 3 2 1

This is a Peregrine Smith Book, published by Gibbs Smith, Publisher, P.O. Box 667, Layton, Utah 84041

Design by J. Scott Knudsen, Park City, Utah

Manufactured in the United States of America

Library of Congress Cataloging-in-Publication Data

Brower, David Ross, 1912–
For earth's sake: the life and times of David Brower/David R. Brower.
p. cm.
ISBN 0-87905-013-6
1. Brower, David Ross, 1912– .
2. Conservationists–United States–Biography. 3. Environmentalist–United States–Biography. I. Title.
QH31.B859A3 1990
333.7′2′092–dc20
[B] 89-26605
CIP

The paper used in this publication meets the minimum requirements of American National Standard for Information Sciences–Permanence of Paper for Printed Library Materials, ANSI Z39.48-1984 ♾

*For the only person,
necessarily excluding myself,
who could possibly have put
up with me for forty-six and
a half years—Anne*

Contents

FOREWORD

I VIEW DAVID BROWER as the most important environmental activist our country has produced in the twentieth century. He is a modern-day Thoreau, an American original. Consistent with his life thus far, this unconventional man has produced an unconventional autobiography. This volume and its companion, to be published by our company in the near future, will become the definitive record of his life and thought so far. The book carries much that the contemporary reader and future generations will find of value. It is a full record. It contains both new writing and writings from the earlier periods of David's career, begun in the 1930s.

David's greatest gift, I feel, is that of inspiring others to take action, both by his example and his compelling spirit. He calls us to be bold in our own lives and reminds us over and over again, "Boldness has genius, power, and magic in it." I hope David's book becomes an active agent in our world society—a tool for passing the courage for boldness and magic.

GIBBS M. SMITH

PREFACE

IF NOT FOR ANYTHING ELSE, I ought to be remembered for my strawberry waffles. John McPhee mentioned them in *Encounters with the Archdruid* but he never had a sample of what I would call my ultimate product—which has evolved to include grated apple, carrot, zucchini, oat bran, eggs, and Lea & Perrins all skillfully baked in a Belgian waffle iron. A round one, of course; if it is not round, the waffles are aesthetically incorrect when buried with strawberries and whipped cream, or augmented with a preserve made from our own resident and delectable plums. The further requirement is that they be eaten on a Saturday or Sunday morning in the company of an exciting assortment of good friends, including an exciting assortment of children and grandchildren (two).

I go into all this detail because I have found this institutional breakfast essential to my progress in the environmental movement. Without my forty-six years of waffling, I should surely have burned out several times by now instead of not at all. By coincidence, Anne, a remarkably patient wife, editor, and English major, has been at those breakfasts for those same forty-six years.

I have other virtues, of course. I know no one who can procrastinate better, or demonstrate greater mastery of creative sloth. I have accomplished all manner of unimportant work simply because responsibility required me to do something essential instead, and it didn't get done.

Crucial though these qualities have been, they pale when compared to what will be the subject of my dissertation one of these days: *The Joy of Rationalizing.*

What rationalization has done for me will be apparent throughout this book. For example, people who rationalize well will never think of themselves as lazy or shiftless. A long period of goofing off will instead be perceived as a proper allowance of time for creativity or meditation or trying to find out who one is.

In an autobiography, for instance, competent rationalizers will draw as heavily as possible on material already written, knowing that only by doing so will they reveal how their thoughts evolved—and how well they wrote before their other obligations became easier, more interesting, and more glamorous than writing.

I began rationalizing the moment a publisher asked if I wanted to write my autobiography. To do so, I would have to look back. Looking back would be fatal. Preferring to avoid fatality, I reasoned that if I looked back only half the time, and ahead the rest, all would be well. Thus, from 1982 to 1986 or so, I took care to look ahead, and looked back so seldom that the publisher demanded a return of the nice advance I had received and given to Friends of the Earth.

Three people, knowing my proclivities, offered to ghost my story for me, but I thought I would not need ghostwriters unless the book were to be written posthumously. I'd rather do it myself, as soon as possible, preferably later. To people asking how I was doing I repeated a favorite story. At a cocktail party in Stonington, Connecticut, I was told that one of the guests, a writer from *The New Yorker,* was writing his autobiography.

Stepping up to him I said, "I understand you are writing your autobiography."

"That's right."

"Have you reached the climax?"

Notice how well I handle conversation. It may have been a touch tactless, but I was asking from the heart. What really happens to a person who undertakes to write the story of his life? Is everything downhill from there? Is there life after autobiography?

So I went back to planning conferences, making speeches, traveling to important places, eating strawberry waffles, and goofing off.

Sensing this inner struggle, Gibbs Smith said, why don't we just call it *My Story So Far*? And go ahead and use your old forewords.

All I had then to do was draw on my thirty years' experience in trying to design books to come up with a way to distinguish, in the mixture of old writings and new, between now and then. I think I have, now and then.

In the course of all this work and procrastinating on behalf of a book, I have fallen further behind than usual in everything else, and have decided to try to keep in shape for another twenty years or so in order to catch up. I will need a lot of help.

First, I must tell you about the help I have had with this opus:

Acknowledgments

Robert Bender, when he was with William Morrow and Co., suggested that I write an autobiography, Perry Knowlton arranged for a nice contract and advance (which went to Friends of the Earth), Mr. Bender moved to Simon and Schuster, and the editor who succeeded him, after looking eighteen months at material I had submitted a year or two late, is reported to have said, "What could I tell him that would not be discouraging?" Anne and I paid back the advance we had never received.

Anne unsuccessfully warned Gibbs Smith not to give me any advance, but to wait until I produced something. Stephen Lyons, who edited two books for Friends of the Earth before deserting print media for electronic, revised the outline Hugh Nash, editor for the Sierra Club and FOE, had generously prepared for me not to follow. Steve put a month of valiant effort, in between rewarding jobs, trying to get me to write enough, but not too much, in a way his mother would understand. He left me with instructions that were designed to arouse me from my creative sloth, the opening line of which was "Start with one Tanqueray martini," and continuing with a host of sensible suggestions, which I took to heart if not to paper as often as I should have. Tom Turner, long the editor of FOE's *Not Man Apart,* tried to help by interviewing me at length (Kenneth Brower had earlier tried to do so at short), and Jerry Emory assiduously transcribed thousands of words of that interview, as well as a series of essentially autobiographical talks I had given, at Ron Hayes's urging, in delightful or historic spots at which our party paused on a thirteen-day trip through the Grand Canyon in 1977. I began sorting through mountains of material I had written or wanted to write about, and fled from those mountains at every opportunity. Robert Browning took time from some of his work on the Mark Twain papers at the Bancroft Library to try to make sense of what I was fleeing from, but could not stop the flight.

Gibbs Smith waited. Madge Baird, his editorial director, waited.

Then she began a series of weekly telephone calls from Utah to check on my progress. Alan Weaver, of Sierra Club Books, coaxed me with further pleading, in person and by telephone.

Gibbs Smith waited more, earning but not receiving an award for patience beyond understanding. We both serve on the Sierra Club Publications Committee, and I began to dread attending its meetings empty-handed.

Then the good news. Through no fault of mine, the Sierra Club suffered a budget crunch severe enough to cause Alan Weaver to lose his assistant, Bill Travers. At a dinner following the February 1989 meeting of the Publications Committee, Alan suggested that Bill could put what I had written and was about to write into the Zenith lap-top computer I had purchased to be compatible with Gibbs Smith, Inc.'s computer but had not learned to operate. Alan called Bill, who joined the meeting, agreed to try, and succeeded. Without my knowing it, Bill had, as a teaching assistant for a wilderness class at the University of California, San Diego, been instrumental in getting me to address the class twice. He liked what he heard, liked wilderness, liked climbing and skiing, kept my nose to Radio Shack Model 80 (which I can operated fast but not well), raised good questions about what I was producing, and four days before his marriage on August 19, 1989, shipped off to Utah, hard copy and disks, a manuscript about half as long as *War and Peace*. It would have been fully as long had there been more peace to write about.

About a third of the way through this final siege—on May 1—Anne and I celebrated our forty-sixth wedding anniversary. She had not read the manuscript yet, so we may very well celebrate our forty-seventh, between the publication of volumes one and two. John De Graff kindly let us use the title of his documentary, and I hope no one reads too much hubris into the title or accepts it all at face value, since I have an agenda that will fill the twenty-year extension I have asked for.

I owe special thanks to Heather Bennett for skillfully improving what she was confronted with, and extraordinary thanks to those who put up with me in the trying and joyful days you are about to share.

To the Sierra Club and to Friends of the Earth, my thanks for permission to reprint some of the articles, forewords, and photographs originally published in their books and periodicals, 1935-1989; specific sources are given within the text. "It Couldn't be Climbed" originally appeared in the *Saturday Evening Post,* February 1940. The other half of the book is from my Radio Shack Model 80 and its extra memory chip, giving it a capacity of about twenty thousands words. It was periodically cleared to make room for more, initially by MCI mail, telephoned from wherever I was to Earth Island, San Francisco, and picked up by Bill Travers on my Zenith computer, usually 5 feet away from the Model 80. I finally found a 5-foot cable that cut MCI out of the loop, in about a tenth of the time. One of these days I may learn to talk to the Zenith myself–perhaps by 1992, the Sierra Club's hundredth birthday and my eightieth. Don't count on it.

DAVID R. BROWER
September 19, 1989

CHAPTER 1

AWAKENING

FOUNDER'S ROCK AND STRAWBERRY CREEK

FREDERICK LAW OLMSTED *père,* and Frederick Law Olmsted, *fils,* were indeed as Carl Russell said, two fires of one genius, and both of them made a substantial impact on my thinking about landscape. The father, whom I wasn't born soon enough to know, made the first impact. In his park-designing spree, in addition to his work on Central Park and his caveat about what ought to happen in Yosemite, he looked over San Francisco's East Bay, urged that the regional parks be set aside in the Oakland and Berkeley hills, and hoped that their streams would be edged with parks from the piedmont to the bay. For the time being that hope is lost, with one small exception. An important part of Strawberry Creek can still breathe, even as it did when salmon once spawned in it, on the campus of the University of California, its plan the result of an Olmsted recommendation. It was on Strawberry Creek that I built my first of several dams and on a handsome, lichen-covered rock between the North and South forks of Strawberry Creek that I made my first climb.

Founder's Rock is not nearly so high as it used to be when I could not reach the Campanile drinking fountain with my mouth and had to turn the handle by standing on tiptoe and reaching up, drinking from the scalloped edge of the collecting basin just under the fountain. At that height I found Founder's Rock quite impressive, and my boyhood chum, Douglas Morris, and I worked out several routes. They were not death-defying, but they felt good. Founder's Rock was just a block above the Mechanical Drawing Building (now bearing the name "Naval Architecture") where my father was an instructor and there were vast areas of blackboard for a six-year-old to decorate between classes. I don't mind laying claim to the first ascent of Founder's West Face. I did it at six, almost long ago enough in

1918 to eliminate other claimants, and long ago enough for the west side to have been a face.

The campus was a wonderful playground. Initially, the dams on Strawberry Creek were the best part. In summer, the flow of the creek was minimal and easily controlled. Rocks, leaves, sticks, and mud were all we needed to back up a fairly impressive pool, and we were often successful enough, when things worked right, to dry up the stream below. But not for long, because the best part of building a dam was rupturing it and watching the flood surge downstream. In the rainy season there was far too much water to manage, and we would dash the six blocks from our house at 2232 Haste Street in the heaviest rains to see how high the wild creek was rising on its banks.

Tragedy struck Strawberry Creek when engineers, architects, and builders explored the Hayward Fault and chose its intersection with Strawberry Creek as the site for the California Memorial Stadium.

That was back in the days when you could get a stadium for a mere million dollars. My father was a stadium subscriber. For a hundred dollars, I think it was, you could get tickets for the next twenty California-Stanford Big Games. They promised to put the subscriber's name on the seat he bought twenty chances to occupy, but they never got around to the carving. That, however, was not the tragedy. What was sad was the capture and entombment of Strawberry Creek and the creation of Tightwad Hill. The original slope was sluiced away with hydraulic-mining technology, long after it was made illegal in California because of the severe environmental impact. (The Sacramento River, before the hydraulic days, had been navigable all the way to Red Bluff.) Mud sluiced from the hill settled behind a cofferdam and became the stadium floor. The tragedy was that only part of the mud stayed there. The rest of it became an uncelebrated, disastrous environmental impact on my creek, and it was no longer any fun to build a dam on it, or even possible. The pristine streambed became a muddy sludge into which our feet sank six inches or so. It was a mess. We had to look elsewhere for our fun, putting rocks on the Southern Pacific track at the corner of Haste and Ellsworth to see what kind of powder the red electric trains could crush them to, or putting a penny across a gap in the track to start the wigwag signal going, now and then leaving pennies there because the train would flatten them out so nicely.

The tragedy of Strawberry was alleviated a little when Cal beat Stanford in 1922 as we watched, from freshly created Tightwad Hill, the first Big Game played in the new Memorial Stadium. The first football game I ever watched was played on old California Field in 1918, where the new Hearst Gym for Women is, replacing the Maybeck beauty on College Avenue that turned Berkeley's sky red the night it burned. I crashed that game. The Wonder Team was playing, they told me, but what they were playing I didn't know. My athletic skill did not exist. There were other priorities. It had been six years since my mother had taught me how to play the piano. I liked it, and liked to practice, which got in the way of ball playing. I had lessons, briefly, at the Cora W. Jenkins School of Music, an easy streetcar ride away. I memorized her composition, "The Wind," and taught it to Barbara, my daughter, fifty years later. I learned a little bit about performing before a very small public at occasional recitals—but far preferred to play for my mother.

She lost the ability to watch me a few days after my brother Joseph was born. She had returned from the hospital but was not recovering well at all. Very quickly her sight left her as we watched, and her sense of smell, too. She had long before lost the hearing in one ear and a mastoidectomy a month before I was born did not help. Years later the diagnosis was that she suffered an inoperable brain tumor.

In the nineteen and a half years that remained for her after her blinding, she was valiant in what she tried to do, in the absence of two and a half of her senses. She could walk well—her growing up on a ranch in Two Rock Valley, in Sonoma County, gave her that ability, and her love of hills—and I took her on some of her longest walks after she lost her sight. The longest were to the summit of Grizzly Peak, at the upper edge of Strawberry Creek's watershed, also the upper edge of the Berkeley campus. Her devotion to religion deepened, and she regularly attended our nearby Presbyterian church, where her raptness led the minister at her funeral service to describe her, quite aptly, as radiant. She could do some housework, learned to type a little, could play the phonograph and radio, make her way upstairs and downstairs (in a three-story house), and enjoy conversation. It was important to leave things where she left them so she could find them. It was especially necessary to make certain that doors were either wide open or completely closed. She took some terrible bangs when we forgot. When she walked confidently forward with her hands spread to touch whatever was coming next, a door left ajar would be between her hands and her forehead would find it. It still hurts.

She could play the piano—the Ludwig upright she and I both learned on, still operable, although too soft of touch and shedding its ivories—and I liked to listen to her playing. I can still see her, when I played—the easy compositions of Rachmaninoff and Liszt, or more often, my own—stopping whatever she was doing, listening attentively, with a pleased smile. So I played a lot, reluctant only because the temperature in the parlor was so low it made my fingers stiff.

Playing the piano, helping with cooking, washing, ironing, gardening, housework, apartment restoration as necessary between tenants in the ten Haste Street apartments that helped sustain us, and being the chief baby-sitter for my younger brother—all these encroached heavily on the time that my contemporaries could devote to athletics. I must confess (though there is no one now to hear it) that I lacked enthusiasm for any of these chores except the piano and Joe. I would have preferred being outdoors with my peers.

By 1923, Joe was four. I was his twelve-year-old surrogate father, and was beginning to wonder how soon he would be embarrassed by my ignorance of the traditional male sports. The Berkeley fire of September 17 made it possible for me to learn something about football. It burned the Rubel house across the street on LeRoy Avenue from the Hillside School, which suffered the same fate. The Rubels rented interim housing on Regent Street, around the corner from Willard Junior High, and I was shortly out on that street—even though it was several blocks from my home—with Don Rubel, my new classmate, and a football.

My neighbors and I also played on the street, Haste Street when there was not too much traffic, or more often on South Atherton, only a block long and usually free of traffic though inhabited by one irate householder who did not like it when a bobbled pass or misdirected punt sent a football into her garden. She would often call the police. When the officer drove up—it was usually the same one—we would all walk over to his car to make it easy for him. He would remonstrate, we would duly move two blocks away to the vacant lot at Dwight Way and Fulton, and not return to South Atherton for a day or two. One of those South Atherton days provided a different interruption. When we were quiet between plays, we heard a rumble that seemed to emanate from all over, followed by a general raising of windows and sticking out of heads. It had been an earthquake, scary enough to those indoors, but of no impact on us, except for the strange sound.

When I was eight, walking home one day on South Atherton, I happened to look up at the sky and saw a brilliant object streak across it, leaving what I would now call a vapor trail. The object itself glowed red and tapered to a point in front. I described it excitedly when I got into the house, but there were no other witnesses and my parents must have thought I imagined it. I didn't. My first UFO mystifies me still.

South Atherton provided one further service. Its lack of traffic helped me belatedly learn to ride a bike. It was my brother Ralph's, which he in essence donated to me. I made up for my late learning by riding long and hard with delight. I never equaled my father's achievement—he had bicycled across the Sierra to work for a summer at a paper mill on the Truckee River at Floriston—but I introduced Ralph's bike to every conceivably bikable trail in Strawberry Canyon, and there were miles of such trails. The excitement was riding down the old Fish Ranch Road, single-lane and unpaved. The New Departure coaster brake overheated on the long descent. My speed was not quite sane considering that I had to stay in the middle of the road, between the parallel ruts, or be thrown for a loop if I drifted into one of them.

The road was almost as bad where I first encountered an old Model T Ford. I was not quite a teenager, but on the trail-like roads of my cousins' farm in Two Rock Valley, where no one could object, I learned to drive and to contribute my bit to the dismemberment of America. I admired the amazing design of the Model T. There were three pedals underfoot, where only two are now, or only one if you choose to be energy-intensive and drive an automatic transmission.

But before you worry about those, set the hand brake, which puts the transmission into neutral, adjust the spark, on the left side of the steering wheel and within a finger's reach, and the throttle, on the right side, and get out in front and put the crank in its slot just below the radiator. Do not grasp the crank handle with your thumb around it unless you want a broken thumb if the engine kicks back. Align your thumb with your forefinger and give a vigorous twirl. If you have been living right, the engine will start.

Get in. If you want to back up, release the hand brake as you engage the middle pedal, and back you lurch. If you want to stop, press the left pedal. More likely, you will want to go forward, so press down smoothly on the right pedal as you release the hand brake, apply some throttle with your right hand, and take off. Adjust the spark to taste. If you want to stop *fast,* press all three pedals.

Something frightening and ennobling happened to me when I released the right pedal and felt the Model T shift at once from low gear to high. Sixty-three years later, as I shift into high and start down Euclid Avenue, having just turned into the steep block leading down to the Berkeley campus, I momentarily feel, as I did in 1924, that the car is in control and I am not. But there is no panic now. If I need to stop in a hurry, one pedal will suffice. No foot-groping for three.

It must have been in 1926 that I learned how to drive on pavement. First it was Dad's 1921 Willys-Knight, and I now apologize to it for what it went through at my hands. Next came a 1930 Ford, which should apologize to me. Dad thought it so bad that he talked me into buying a 1934 Plymouth coupe, which established a 3:25 record from Yosemite to Berkeley before there were freeways. One day, just south of Mono Lake, it overheated so badly that the engine kept running after the ignition was turned off, and it was time for Plymouth II, also 1934, then the 1938 Plymouth that I sold when I went to war. The 1939 Buick I bought to get home from Colorado after the war was succeeded by the only car I didn't love, which should be nameless. No. It was a 1947 Mercury, bought new from an old high-school friend, and its front end wasn't ever right. On to the 1948 Pontiac, hydromatic, and 1950 and 1952 stick-shift Buicks bought from a stepbrother and driven home from Flint, Michigan, in record time. I thought that the stick shifts could be improved on, and they were, in the Power Glide 1956 Chevy wagon which we loved a lot. The children wanted to bury it in our front lawn, with due ceremony. But the front lawn was gone by 1961, when we picked up our VW bus at the factory in Germany. We drove it all over Europe, shipped it to Montreal and drove it home and ever after until, with its fourth engine, it was stolen from our driveway. We already had our 1968 Volvo, which now has gone two hundred sixty thousand miles on the original rings. They do not quite provide the compression they once did, however, and the car is too precious to take out of town and far from friendly service. A 1983 Toyota wagon, also stick shift, takes the long trips.

That makes thirteen cars of my (our) own, all but one of them loved, and how will we ever save the earth from the greenhouse effect (first identified, by the way, in 1896) if such love affairs cannot be broken up?

Perhaps the pavement that breeds all these cars should be broken up, and roads returned to what the Fish Ranch Road was like, or the Lincoln Highway, all as part of the transition back to trails. You could travel trails with no fossil fuels at all, no greenhouse gases, no highway deaths, and with flat stomachs. Which is what I did in the Strawberry Creek watershed, afoot or on Ralph's bike.

Ralph made another permanent gift to me—his United States Geological Survey topographic map, Concord quadrangle. From it I learned to read contours, and later to draw them. I was most interested in the Strawberry Creek watershed, my butterfly-hunting, bicycling, and hiking private wilderness—most of it the undeveloped part of the Berkeley campus. Wildcat Creek and Siesta Valley, just east of the Strawberry watershed, were tempting but forbidden territory, being an important part of our water supply. A road crossed the Wildcat Creek drainage but one was not supposed to leave the road. It seemed senseless to put Siesta Valley off limits because there was development below it, and above the San Pablo reservoir. On Ralph's map what is now Orinda was called Bryant, and the map showed one building there.

The part with no buildings or roads was what I liked best. The map did not show the trails. So I projected it with the family's primitive magic lantern, traced the contours on a much enlarged scale, and carefully put in all the trails. My map still exists somewhere in our garage—one of those two-car attics—but most of the trails no longer exist. They were kept open, in their short lifetimes, by a University of California tradition of trail clearing, once a year, by the student body. I never participated. I just helped wear the trails, not clear them. The highest development, then, was the men's swimming pool a short distance up Strawberry Canyon. At the mouth of the canyon was the last farm in Berkeley—the University Farm Dairy, with its barn, cows, and the certified raw milk our family subscribed to, four quarts a day, in returnable glass bottles.

But certified milk was not an adequate gross local product from the Strawberry Creek resource. The barn was not compatible with the stadium. The forest of Monterey pine was not compatible with the Berkeley fire (the eucalyptus survived, though we didn't think it would), nor was Berkeley, so a fire lookout tower was built on Grizzly Peak, to be followed by the extension of Grizzly Peak Boulevard, forever and hopelessly scarring the wild hills and the experience of wildness there. And World War II brought the invasion of my hills by nuclear technology. The splitting of atoms was the last straw. Cyclotron, bevatron, ancillary roads and structures, the Lawrence Hall of Science, and there went the hills of home. The shore of the bay receded, clarity of the air along with it, bridges crossed the bay and the Golden Gate, the Indian shellmounds no longer told of how long how many people had lived here without having to trammel the place, and San Francisco forgot how to sit lightly on the land. But all was not lost. Except for a military excrescence or two, Mount Tamalpais hardly noticed the change. The state park and the water district kept it open. Angel Island kept its cool, the remnants of Ellis Island West hardly interfering with its profile, and its summit, Mount Livermore, still providing a most favorable sweep of a most favorable, favored place, where military territoriality kept hills open enough to be eligible for protection in the Golden Gate Headlands National Recreation Area. Although Mr. Olmsted's hope for a Strawberry Creek piedmont-to-bay park was clobbered by the city and maimed by the university, it was kept almost intact in an extraordinary chain of regional parks. They pay tribute to restraint, where what is important is what is left open, and not covered by what Ansel Adams called the White Cliffs of Doelger (after a San Francisco developer). They are what still make the San Francisco Bay Area a nice place to look upon, and Berkeley a nice place to have begun in and still be in.

I am glad that for my beginnings there were blanks on the map in Strawberry's upper reaches, there were many butterflies there, there was an open-space program on the Berkeley campus, and there were quiet streets and vacant lots. A tall skinny lad could learn a lot about what goes on in wild places, a lad whose fingers would learn to guide a football on a journey long enough to make a new kid on the block gasp, or invent and run through a cadenza that would make a mother smile.

SIERRA TRAILS 1918–1932

ONE OF THE THINGS we forget to do is to look. Here we are, with the remarkable gift of eyes, exquisite organs that can take light and make it mean something to us. But how often we simply take eyes for granted! What's new? There's the scene—the hill, the street, the smiling face—and what of it?

You don't take eyes for granted if you grew up with a mother who lost her sight when you were eight. You begin not only to look more carefully for yourself, but also to look for her, to see for her what she once saw and loved, to make your description of what you see for her as real as you can, and to find your reward in her response as she couples your words with what she remembers from when light meant something to her eyes.

We went to the Sierra when she could no longer see the places she could remember from earlier years—years in which my father and she took their children into a Sierra quite unlike what we have now.

Before there was Interstate 80 there was U.S. 40. Before that there was the Lincoln Highway. Its predecessor, when our family's 1916 Maxwell took it on, was a one-lane dirt road, and it is fair to call it the experiencing of a Sierra trail.

Our first day in that summer of 1918 got us to the public campground almost within downtown Sacramento. We hit the motor trail in the Sierra foothills and made it to a campsite just outside Colfax next night. There are many night sounds I should like to hear again, but the one I want to hear most is the lonely, long, well-quilled whistle of the Mallet calling to its mate.

The Mallet is simply the most beautifully impressive steam locomotive ever created. How did an engineer quill a whistle? He had to have a steam locomotive, not a diesel, and know how to feather the whistle's aperture to slide into a lower note, especially on the last blast, letting it trail off into the dusk—certainly one of the most beautiful of sounds of the night, and long gone. The Mallet had more driving wheels than I was prepared to count at age six. The cab was placed so that the engineer could see where he was going, not where he had been; it was up front, with the boiler behind. There were three Mallets in a long freight train—one at each end and one in the middle—as the train made its way up the Sierra grade, from Roseville over the top to Truckee, where engines were changed.

The Mallet was not calling to its mate, of course; the engineer was simply announcing the train's approach to a crossing with the two long blasts, a short, and a long, or was letting forth with four long complaints at being blocked by a red signal.

I didn't know all that at the time, nor does it matter any more, but it was a wonderful voice in the Sierra night. I'll not be satisfied until we have run out of the abundance of oil and are required to replace the plethora of automobiles, dashing hither and yon aimlessly, with the authority of a railroad train that knows where it is going and why, headed by a Mallet that knows what to say.

Our Maxwell did not threaten the Mallet and would not have worried a horse very much. We got over Donner Pass and down to the campground at Donner Lake the next day. On the fourth day of our journey we paused to look at Emerald Bay, Lake Tahoe's most beautiful cove. Ralph and I were more interested in playing chipmunk on the roadside granite boulders than in looking at scenery. Chipmunks had fascinated us all day as they played hide-and-seek beneath the Maxwell's wheels. At our speed, and with theirs, they were in no danger. The best way to admire their skills was to imitate them with our own comparatively awkward rock-scrambling.

And in the evening of the fourth day we rested. We were at the Nevada line on the south end of Lake Tahoe. It had taken us twenty-four hours to cover the distance that now takes an hour. And, where Harrah's Club and surrounding city would one day be, we were alone. We made camp.

Our kitchen was the side of the camping box my father made to fit on the starboard running board, an automobile appendage that was not to be eliminated for a decade or two. The side opened out to reveal utensils and supplies. Our bedroom consisted of a ground sheet and blankets laid out on the ground, our parents sleeping on the outer edges of a three-children sandwich. That was security!

My mother, as long as she had her sight and sense of smell, was an excellent camp cook. I liked most of what she prepared, but had no use then for carrots, parsnips, cottage cheese, or buttermilk. (I can still leave buttermilk alone.)

At the south end of Lake Tahoe in the late teens there were two structures at the California-Nevada boundary—a pier at what was then called Lakeside and a combination store and post office. A steamer went round Lake Tahoe once a day and would pause at our pier for mail and an occasional passenger.

What I have described is now a small city, complete with Harrah's Club, shops, motels, gas stations, and a daily gridlock in summer. No trace remains of the campground that served us so well.

That enormous change is not matched at Echo Lake, only a few miles southwest of our former Tahoe campground and about a thousand feet higher. At Echo Lake in the early twenties we had a tiny pier, a combination store and post office, several widely spaced summer cabins along the bluff overlooking Tahoe and on the shores of Lower and Upper Echo Lakes, and a simple national-forest campground. That was then.

With the addition of a few cabins, that is still the situation at Echo. What causes the difference? The property at the south end of Tahoe was privately owned. At Echo Lake we were in the Eldorado National Forest. The combination of the cabin owners and the Forest Service provided mutual oversight. The Forest Service would allow the cabin owners to do no wrong, and the cabin owners reciprocated. Together, the overseers kept the place remarkably the way it was over a span of some sixty years.

There are few places I can remember that have changed so little in that span of time.

Change has its virtues. I do not miss the one-lane dirt road, and I certainly like what Dr. Salk did for our children and what instant replay does for football. But the south end of Lake Tahoe doesn't exhibit any virtue that I would like to see propagated. I should like to see the Tahoe-Echo comparison brought to the attention of anyone who is in danger of being persuaded that privatization of public lands is a good idea. My mother was spared the trauma of looking at today's south end, or even of hearing about it.

An unreasonable lapse of time brought us to Mono Lake. Los Angeles had not yet plotted against the streams that feed the lake, without which it subsides, so we had no reason to worry. We were to cross Tioga Pass, and thanks to the children's piling out of the car and my mother's pushing it, we got over the steepest part of the Lee Vining Canyon grade, just short of the waterfall, now rarely seen, below Ellery Lake. At the pass we stopped for an ascent of Gaylor Peak, a minor, pleasant summit of metamorphic rock lying just west of the north-south pass. The "we" did not include me, however. At the age of six, I had no interest in the climb.

Later, after we had stopped in Yosemite Valley and the family had gone up the trail to Vernal and Nevada falls, I rebelled at the bridge across the Merced River from which the first view of Vernal Fall burst forth. It wasn't today's sturdy bridge. It was a big log, flattened on top, with a rail along one side, and I would have none of it. My sister Edith gave up the rest of the trip to baby-sit with her younger brother.

The young mountaineer did no better the next day at the base of Sentinel Dome. Perhaps I was a bit mountain sick. Whatever the excuse, the rest of the family climbed the dome. I climbed into the Maxwell and slept.

It was hot on the old Big Oak Flat Road as we headed home from Yosemite, and beside an attractive pool we stopped and my father, in the raw, practiced his sidestroke—so far as I know, the only stroke he used. No traffic bothered us.

One further night we were camped out somewhere in a meadow alongside a high stretch of road. I remember the security we children felt sleeping on the ground with our parents flanking us, and I remember the little train. No Mallet this time. Just the small train that supported some dastardly work I then knew nothing about—the building of the O'Shaughnessy Dam and the imminent drowning of the national park's other yosemite, Hetch Hetchy Valley.

Two years passed. We were camped at Lower Echo Lake, near the pass just west of the south end of Lake Tahoe. I was still apprehensive about mountain-climbing as we waited for Dad to return from his solo ascent of Echo Peak. The peak was a rugged-looking one to us. It was after dark, and he wasn't back yet.

He finally got back all right, but it had been a more difficult scramble down the west side of the peak than he had counted on. That didn't speed my own mountain assurance.

Things weren't much better six years later in 1926, when we were trying out the new All-Year Highway to Yosemite Valley – one that avoided the high elevations of the Big Oak Flat and Wawona roads by ascending the canyon of the Merced River. We went to Glacier Point and took the Eleven-Mile Trail down to the valley. At Glacier Point there is a sturdy rail to cling to as you look down to the valley three thousand feet directly below. There is no rail at the edge of Panorama Cliff, however, and the Eleven-Mile Trail passes by that cliff. Not right by it, but a good three hundred feet back from it. I still felt uneasy about that distant exposure, hardly imagining that in eleven years I would be making the first ascent of it, with Morgan Harris my climbing companion.

I was still not quite a mountaineer in 1929. This time, butterfly net in hand, I was willing to climb Gaylor Peak to check it out for butterflies, but unwilling to cross a small snowfield, for fear there might be concealed crevasses there. Though I had been reading about mountaineering, glaciers and all, I was not yet ready for the real thing.

The next year valor overcame discretion. The city of Berkeley operated three summer camps, and Echo Lake Camp needed a clerk. I could type well enough and got the job – and much more. The camp director Lynn Barrett, his wife, three cooks, a maintenance man, five people to help in the kitchen and dining room, and a clerk were the staff that served the hundred or so guests who gathered on the bluff overlooking Lake Tahoe and half a mile from Lower Echo. Mere clerking was dull, so I would help out in the kitchen at dishwashing time. It wasn't the dishes I liked, but Betty Hillier, and the singing as we worked the dishes over – singing with fairly good harmony. I knew about chords by then and could sing – or try to – any of the four parts that were missing. At Summit House, at a nickel a record, there was a chance to dance – for me a chance to learn how. The melody and lyrics still spin through my memory.

Some of the guests also wanted to take trips. Motorboats took us up Lower Echo, through the channel, and on to Kleeberger's Landing at the far end of Upper Echo. From there we walked to Desolation Valley, Mount Ralston, Lake-of-the-Woods, Angora Peak, and on occasion to Mount Tallac, and to peaks named Dick, Jack, and Pyramid.

Betty Hillier led the first trip to Desolation Valley and got lost. Up stepped the young man who had explored Strawberry Canyon and vicinity for butterflies and had even made a contour map of the area—with the topographic map of the Desolation Valley. He spotted on the map exactly where we were, and we were no longer lost. Whereupon he became the guide for that summer and the next two. Many, many trips. Six times up Pyramid. Across the Tahoe Valley to Freel and Job's Sister. Thirteen times up Ralston, pioneering routes back to camp along the Ralston Ridge. A one-day forty-two-miler to Tallac, Dick, Jack, and Pyramid, with a midnight return. All that and much, much more. It was heady stuff. And for the first year, Betty Hillier put up with it. I was not her first love, but she was mine. The mountains were all right.

Coming home from Echo in the summer of 1931, Ralph, who had joined the crew, and I returned by way of the Tioga Road and paused in Tuolumne Meadows. There Dad met us. In the 1921 Willys-Knight touring model complete with tonneau windshields for the wind shy who rode in the back seat, Dad left Berkeley shortly after midnight and, by the next noon, having parked the Willys in Tuolumne Meadows, was on the summit of Mount Lyell, Yosemite's highest peak, with two sons beside him.

Mount Lyell was not an easy peak in those days. For one thing, it was a fifteen-mile walk and climb from Tuolumne Meadows. There was the glacier. At the top of the glacier, the bergschrund and the chimney, a fair scramble for anyone, and Dad was fifty-two and hadn't climbed a mountain since Echo Peak.

Lyell has an airy summit. It gives you a little of the feeling of flying. Going down takes less effort but more nerve than going up. For one thing, your eyes are near your hands on the ascent but not near your feet on the descent. Dad was unflappable but not untiring. Ralph and I had been out in the mountains all summer, Dad not at all. We tore on ahead, euphoric, and darkness came but Dad did not. I went back a few miles. He was coming right along, but at a pace he could manage. This time I stayed with him. At ten that night a tired father, deserving it well, hit the sack.

Then there was the summer of thirty-two, and turnabout. This time Joseph Brower joined his father and two older brothers—before an Echo Lake summer, not after one. We thought we would take a look at Mount Whitney from the Lone Pine side. Owens Valley, at that point, is one of the deep ones. Lone Pine's elevation is thirty-five hundred feet, Mount Whitney's, 14,495.811. Round the difference to eleven thousand feet and you will understand why we were glad the road went up from Lone Pine to Hunter's Flat, at eight thousand feet. Six and a half thousand to go, and we were on our way. At twelve thousand five hundred I was in the highest of spirits. I suppose I was also sentimental, because I was singing "I love you, California," and loving the song. Just about one hundred more feet of climbing and I was out of it, vomiting. My head ached. I sprawled on a warm friendly rock, out-and-out mountain sick. Knowing that rest would fix me, Dad and Ralph went on, Dad the farthest. He made the pass before turning around. We were spread out on the eastern slope of Mount Whitney in chronological order, and I was grateful that Joe hadn't passed me. None of us would escape free. We had all been exposed to more snow than our unprotected epidermis would put up with. You never saw such sunburn! Faces swollen, blistered, peeling—skip the details. We were learning.

From hot to cold. The Willys-Knight again, but this time no family. It was George Rockwood, Bill Van Voorhis, and I, and we were trying our winter skills in Yosemite, early in 1931 and early in 1932, also. It was trying because we had no skills. Wrong footgear, no adequate camping equipment, no parkas, no ropes—and just as well since we knew nothing about using ropes. But we were eager. Up the Yosemite Falls Trail, across to North Dome, down through Indian Canyon, slogging through not-too-deep snow, enjoying the days well enough, if not the nights. We were inventive, but too inventive. Having no tents, and not having budgets that would accommodate us in the hotels, we made camp under the Cascade Creek bridge, a little below the valley. We were quite comfortable, but our campfire made smoke, which the rangers discovered, following which they discovered and removed the source—us. This happened two winters in a row. George and Bill agreed on one stipulation, and all three of us on a second. The second, "Rangers are no damned good." The first, "He who follows a Brower never follows a trail."

Butterflies

"Butterfly Is a Stupid Word," the Spaniard said; "*mariposa* is so much more beautiful." "I much prefer *farfalla,*" the Italian countered. The woman from Paris said, "*papillon*, of course." The Japanese suggested, "I like the softness of *chocho-san.*" The German bristled and demanded, "What's the matter with *schmetterling?*"

Monarch! is what Al Furer shouted, naming the queen of butterflies, and we were off in mad pursuit, nets in hand. We had not seen or caught a monarch before, but knew well from Holland's *Butterfly Book* what one looked like. It was a difficult chase. Monarchs can fly very well, with good evasive maneuvers when alarmed. But we succeeded, and this monarch would never winter on a eucalyptus tree on Bolinas Mesa. We killed it, mounted it, and displayed it proudly.

In 1924, Al and his brother Fred were tenants in our apartment house on Haste Street, newly arrived in Berkeley from Honolulu via the

SS *Lurline,* sugarboat ancestor of the Matson Line's most elegant liner. When Al wasn't practicing "Ase's Tod" on his violin, he and his brother were out chasing butterflies. I joined the chase.

By the next year the monarch had been joined by tiger, zebra, western, and pipevine swallowtails, mourning cloaks, blues, hairsteaks, skippers, checkerspots, peacocks, silverspots, California sisters, tortoise shells, angle wings, red admirals, Lorquin's admirals, painted and West Coast ladies, hunter's butterflies, pine whites, orange tips, and sulfurs. I caught and killed them all mercilessly, mounted them, added labels giving their vital statistics in the smallest letters I could print with a crowquill pen, and displayed them in neat cases that cost a dollar fifty each – not easy money to find in the 1920s in a poor household. One of my proudest finds was an extraordinarily beautiful sport of the common checkerspot that swarmed the Berkeley Hills in late May and early June. I drew a good representation of it with colored pencils, and that illustration is all that is left of the collection. Because I failed to take proper precautions, museum beetles reduced it all to dust.

If I were to do it all over again, I would settle for collecting butterflies with a camera – still, 16-mm, or video – rather than dashing madly about with a net. It is just the right challenge for anyone who would be patient, deliberate, and slow-moving. I'll do it just as soon as I retire.

When the summer ended and the Furers returned to Honolulu, I discovered that collecting butterflies was a very lonely hobby, and certainly looked askance at. As I wandered net in hand through the Berkeley Hills in search of new species or variations, I would try to anticipate the sidelong glances of the occasional passersby with a simple device. I would whistle assorted popular tunes, to prove that I was not totally oddball. I knew most of them. My favorite then was the now-forgotten "What Does It Matter?" by Irving Berlin. I may have succeeded in my ruse, but probably received backward rather than sidelong glances. I didn't dare check.

Embarrassed as I was by what I imagined others thought of my *farfalla* folly, I was fascinated by what it taught me. It was my introduction to an understanding of ecosystems. If your eyes are alert to butterflies, the alertness is catching. Questions arise and answers are sought. What are the ranges of the various species? When are they out? At how great a distance can you identify them by their flight pattern? What flower attracts them? What predators do they attract? What food-plant fit for her eggs is the female able to identify unfailingly as she flies over the diverse wild gardens? Can you successfully raise her caterpillars at home? I tried. And there were plenty of suggestions in the *Butterfly Book* about the care and feeding of caterpillars.

The Holland book was great, but most of its butterflies were strange ones. What I needed was what John Adams Comstock produced – a big beautiful book full of color illustrations, *Butterflies of California.* It cost twenty-five dollars, far beyond my means, but I was able to persuade the Berkeley Public Library to buy it. I took it out endlessly. In one of its brief periods on the shelves, Robert Wind borrowed it, found the name of the usual usurper, and looked me up. He was so well organized a collector that I felt outclassed, and my enthusiasm for lepidoptera waned. But not until we had collected together, finding a species that has subsequently been wiped out, I am sure, by developers. I still loved collecting well enough to hate developers and what they were prepared to do to what they call raw land and I call wildness. I lost touch with Robert Wind until I discovered him in his import shop on Cannery Row in Monterey. He had found a supply of *Butterflies of California* and I am still kicking myself for not having bought at least one each for home and office, whenever I run short of nostalgia.

I suppose that the most important lesson I learned from butterflies was taught me by the Western swallowtail, which went by the name *Papilio zelicon* when I was in my butterfly phase. My first recollection of its caterpillar is of an unfortunate individual I discovered when I was playing with Douglas Keith Morris, one of my favorite friends, disapproved of by my parents for reasons I never understood. Perhaps it was because I did strange things under his influence. For example:

The caterpillar was feeding on parsley in Douglas's garden. It was minding its own business and was quite handsome – green with bands of black and yellow – and almost two inches long. I touched it. It arched its back and extended two glistening orange horns toward my finger. They shot out from just behind its head. They had not been visible before I alarmed it, and now it alarmed me. So I cut it in half, which proved fatal. As I learned later, the caterpillar was merely using its standard chemical defense against predators. The horns emitted an odor disagreeable to birds and their ilk. My ilk was too big to be affected, but I have never killed another for defending itself.

Parsley is an alternative food-plant. The Western swallowtail prefers anise, and California proliferates anise in the wild. The state should swarm with these swallowtails. It doesn't. They are not rare; neither are they common. They are uncommonly beautiful, however, and for that reason I undertook to raise some at home.

The eggs are easily recognizable, so I started with eggs. Shortly the tiny caterpillars emerged, black with a yellow band across the middle at first, becoming the handsome green, yellow, and black models after the fourth or fifth instar, as I remember it.

Finally, after a lot of patient feeding, caterpillars become chrysalids. The penultimate act of the caterpillar is to seek a hiding place, fashion silken anchorage for its rearmost stubs, then put itself on belay, weaving a band of perhaps a hundred silken strands that the caterpillar can lie back upon. After a brief intermission, the final act begins. The caterpillar sheds its skin one last time, revealing a tan chrysalis, its shape suggesting the form of the butterfly that will shortly be created within. There are two points where the antennae will be, and two shieldlike plates protecting the imminent wings. Touch the chrysalis and it will shake itself a little – its only defense.

Then comes the day!

The chrysalis has darkened, its translucence almost revealing the black body and dark unexpanded wings within. A crack appears and an antenna pops out. The crack widens and out pops another. A bit of exertion and the head is free, then the six legs, one after another, pawing for footholds, finding them, drawing the butterfly out, moving it to a twig it can hang under. The abdomen is distended, full of a fluid with a purpose. It must be pumped into the unexpanded wings, filling all the veins, extending the wings to full size. In about thirty minutes the wings are no longer limp. The fragrance explains why they are called flying flowers. A few openings and closings of the wings provide the test, and a beautiful creature is airborne and free.

In my backyard laboratory, the other chrysalids were getting the message. As each split and allowed the first antenna to come out, I lent a helping hand. Very gently I widened the split so that the butterfly could emerge without so much strain. They came out one by one and crawled to convenient twigs. But what was supposed to happen next never did. No fluid moved from abdomen to wings. The abdomen remained distended, the wings stayed shriveled, and the poor things began running around helplessly until they died.

Freeing them, I had denied them their freedom. A few decades later I would be informed by Nancy Newhall's lines in *This Is the American Earth,* in counterpoint with the Ansel Adams photograph of the Tuolumne River and the snow-clad summits of Mounts Dana and Gibbs, in Yosemite National Park.

What,to continue their renewal,
do air, water, life require of Man?
Only that below the snows and glaciers of peaks, the alpine meadows
and trees at timberline . . . face storms and meltings undisturbed
and here no mouse, nor eagle,
no wolf nor antelope, snake nor butterfly
be hindered from his errand.

Or hers. No errands at all, alas, for those swallowtails.

One of the most remarkable errands of all is a butterfly migration. If you happen to encounter a migration, what drives it? Holland wrote about mourning cloak migrations. He hypothesized that a phenomenon known as red rain may have been the droppings of a multitude of mourning cloaks flying overhead. My own two encounters with migrations were in the Sierra. One was a surge of California tortoise shells. Automobile radiators were covered so thickly with them that cars overheated. I witnessed the other migration from what I named "Feather Peak" when I made the first ascent of it in 1933. It was a first white human ascent, I am reasonably sure. But I was not alone on the summit. Preceding me up the western slope to the summit ridge was a horde of painted ladies, driven upward not by the wind, but by their own determination. Upon hitting the summit ridge there on the Sierra crest, they kept their elevation, more than twelve thousand feet, and headed toward Nevada and out of sight.

Why? No answer then, and I still wonder what causes the occasional migration, a rare phenomenon. Equally hard to explain is the annual migration of monarchs. Knowing what I now know about this, I hope I can be forgiven for every monarch I destroyed in my lepidopterous ardor. Nancy Newhall awakened in me a renewed sense of wonder with her simple line about a butterfly's errand. Our son Bob clinched it one evening when he was about fourteen. While we were talking in the kitchen I automatically, unthinking and annoyed, wiped a tiny moth out of existence with a sweep of my hand. "But, Dad," Bob protested, "that was his only chance!"

I haven't got over that yet, and that was thirty years ago. Had Bob been around thirty-two years earlier, I would have thought twice about catching a unique orange tip in the Berkeley Hills, the only one of its kind ever recorded and thus an endangered species, which I straight-away killed and later sold for ten dollars to a Mr. Jean Gunder, in Pasadena, who named it after me. A camera allows a trophy hunter to live and let live, and be happier for it. This is still where ethics begin in many religions, if not all. Unto others as unto self. George Dyson, builder and historian of the baidarka, a seagoing canoe, stated his ethical goal well: "to find freedom, without taking it from someone else." To which I would add that no natural law requires that "else" to be human.

I am content now to marvel at monarchs. A monarch egg laid on milkweed east of the Rockies, as far north as Canada, contains a map and the ability to read it, that far outdoes run-of-the-mill miracles in nature. It is a more complicated map than the one included in monarch eggs laid west of the Rockies. Each egg, given a lot of luck, will become a caterpillar that will mature to form a chrysalis from which an adult will emerge and in due course head south to winter in a remote forest in Mexico. Then, in the spring, the monarch will return to its birthplace, where the female, once fertilized, will deposit a new batch of eggs near her birthplace, each with that map in it. Monarchs born west of the Rockies have less get up and go. They settle for winter quarters in a few dozen special sites on the California coast, of which Pacific Grove is most famous. An impressive itinerary nonetheless, and let no one interrupt it!

TOUCH FOOTBALL

ONE OF THE FURER BROTHERS' friends from Hawaii was Hamilton MacCaughey, who lived in the Thousand Oaks section of Berkeley. Son of Vaughn MacCaughey, who would one day be Western Representative of the National Audubon Society, Ham was moderately interested in butterflies, but more interested in football. He actually owned one. He would later own an automobile agency in Reno and be deeply interested in efforts to protect the superb scenic resources of Maui. A football was then far stranger to me than a monarch. I caught passes awkwardly one embarrassing afternoon, but hadn't the foggiest idea how to pass a spiral or kick one. This to me was most dismal failure. Clearly I had spent too much time on music and butterflies.

Why hadn't my father helped me get acquainted with other sports? Ross J Brower had had his own problems. What was then called inflammatory rheumatism had hit him in high school and he hadn't reached his ultimate height, five-seven and a half in a family of six-foot-plussers, until he was in college. Undeterred, he married Mary Grace Barlow, who was just short of five-eleven, but he couldn't pass a football. There were no baseball paraphernalia around the house. I had negligible speed—3:12 for the half-mile. I was fair in the standing broad jump. That summed it up. In the world of my contemporaries, if you were no good in sports you were no good period.

That wasn't all. I was self-conscious about my teeth, with reason, until Swiss-made substitutes were installed in 1956. I got into tooth trouble when I was fourteen months old. My mother turned her back briefly when she was window shopping at the Red Front, a long-gone store at Shattuck and Kittredge, in downtown Berkeley. I managed to climb up in my baby carriage and tip it over backward. I tried to bite my way through the handle. The handle won. I lost three front baby teeth.

The gap was no problem until after I was six. Kids are supposed to have missing front baby teeth. But not second teeth. My front replacements were slow to arrive and when they arrived some enamel was missing. Poor occlusion led to orthodonture, generously financed by my mother's half-sister, Elizabeth MacNeil. No one then knew much about porcelain caps, and the Browers couldn't afford them anyway. My defense was to smile minimally. In my early twenties I barely afforded a gold substitute for the missing enamel. Gold was not all that great up front, but it was an improvement, and half-smiles were permissible. But the improvement hadn't occurred in 1924, and other problems arose. Most of the childhood diseases were out of the way, but not mumps. It hit me in the ninth grade, and I was two weeks out of school for mumps on one side, then two more for the other side. Impetigo followed and, as it pursued its course,

I had an argument with our hot water heater. Gas had accumulated somehow, and when I lit a match, the heater blew up in my face.

However little my father taught me about sports, he made up for it in what he taught me about patience. His was a superb example as he gently picked the debris out of my eyes. Just as gently, and frequently, he ministered to my impetigo lesions. And with still further patience he tutored me in algebra.

I had by now missed months of school, and was inclined to miss more than I needed to, concluding prematurely that I would have to repeat the low-ninth. The excuse was partly due to contagion and partly to my rapidly growing ability to rationalize. I consequently spent a lot of "recovery" time in the hills checking out butterflies and bicycle trails (on Ralph's bicycle—I never bought one of my own). In the course of all this I had my first experience with migraine—a half-hour period of impaired vision followed by mild headache and nausea. Sixty-three years later I would still be having unpredictable and unexplained brief bouts with the half-interrupted vision.

I was a mess. But I didn't lose the semester. When I at last was persuaded to return, my father's patience paid off. An algebra problem was put on the blackboard and Bessie Maine asked any student to volunteer to solve it. Although it was my first day back after two months' absence, I volunteered, went up to the board, and succeeded.

That was an important schoolroom success. I had done well in grammar school, skipping the high-second, high-third, and low-fifth. I had been in the fast-track group for the first two years of junior high, but after my long absence I seemed to be headed nowhere. The blackboard feat put me back in the scholastic running.

Enter Donald Madison Rubel, classmate and nine months my senior. I encountered Don first in 1923 at Willard Junior High. In our shared advisory room I sat next to Jim MacKay, and Don was in the corner behind me, out of conversation range. I remember him as a sturdy boy in gym, a good athlete, and good-humored—even up to being witty, as when on one occasion, I forget quite which, he stood up rigidly at attention and said, "I am a Russian rouble," to everyone's delight.

We also attended the same Sunday School, at the First Presbyterian Church in Berkeley, and there I got better acquainted with him. But our friendship grew when he and I, probably at his insistence, joined the Pioneers, the local YMCA's equivalent of the Boy Scouts, and therefore a little more religious than the Scouts.

Our Pioneer motto came from Luke 2:52—"And Jesus increased in wisdom and stature, and in favor with God and man." Jimmy Whipple was our troop leader, and would remind us from time to time about the motto, and would begin each meeting with a prayer. I don't remember what we did at meetings, but we played basketball (I was poor at it and Don good), had a chance to swim in the Y pool, and took trips. One of the most memorable was to Point Richmond, where we camped out and slept on the ground by the foggy shore. I don't know about Don, but I had one blanket, and it was not enough.

The other most memorable occasion was a trip to Muir Beach, in Marin County, where we slept in comfort in a cabin, played Run, Sheep, Run! joyfully in the dark of the night (I forget the rules), played on the beach and swam in the ocean, and where, in the beachside inn, Don and I took turns playing the piano.

We also took turns on the Steinway when the Rubel's new house was built. I was a frequent guest there. Don and his twin sister Dorothy played much better than I. They could read music at a proper speed while I drifted into memorizing a piece as fast as possible, and then into improvising and composing. My early compositions did not impress Don, and I had no chance to try my later ones on him. I think he would have approved of some of them.

Don had not failed to notice what a lousy athlete I was and thought he could do something about it. Although I could neither pass nor kick a football, he put me in at right guard on the Regent Street Varsity. It was a sandlot team, drawn from the neighborhood, that played on such grassy fields as existed before UC Berkeley jammed them with buildings. It took me a while to learn that my duties consisted of something more than trying to tackle the guard playing opposite me. Jud Van Meter got quite annoyed with my determined violation of the rules and Don straightened me out. Things got better, and I became hero for a moment when I recovered my first fumble. Don saw to it that I got better and better. We meanwhile got closer and closer, and he became far and away my best friend, especially when we entered Berkeley High.

In 1928 Don wanted very much to be on the Berkeley Bees, the one hundred thirty-pound junior team, and I'll not forget his struggle to lose the five pounds he had to lose to qualify. He starved and sweated until he got down to the limit. He was fast enough to be a good back, but Frank Gross put him in at guard, and he was very good at it. The team was very good too, having gone undefeated for many years.

Although by this time I was, thanks to Don, getting quite good at passball, our name then for touch tackle, I was too strung out – skinny is the word (oh, to be skinny again!) – to make the team, but I did make manager. What with the team and our music, Don and I were pretty close to inseparable.

His home world was vastly different from mine. His father was quite successful in Agricultural Extension, and there was enough money in the family for the new house, the Steinway grand, and the Dodge Senior Six, augmenting the Dodge Victory Six Don's father drove for the university. Our family was poor, my father having lost his job as instructor in mechanical drawing when they closed the department, my mother having been blind since 1920, and the apartment rentals we depended upon fluctuating then the way they haven't ever fluctuated since.

Don's letting me share his world, and bringing out the athletic ability I would never otherwise have found, did something for me that nothing else did. Day after day at Berkeley High, I waited at the gym for Don to emerge from the academic building, walking erect, head held high, even tilted back a bit, as he headed for football practice.

I don't think either of us knew it, but I loved him.

My father insisted that I enter Cal in January 1929, right after Don and I had graduated. Don's parents properly withheld pressure, and Don entered the following August. I had thought I wanted to major in entomology, but would have shifted to agricultural economics, following Don's example, if my attendance at Cal had not turned out to be so fitful. Don helped me get a summer job with him at Merco-Nordstrom Valve Company, invited me to lunch at his fraternity (that didn't work out), and disapproved of my first love because of something he knew about her that I never found out. He duly finished his education and I am still working on mine.

In any event, our paths diverged, not to cross for a few decades. It was in the prolonged absence, sparked by such recollections as these, that I realized how much Don had done for me.

When we first met again he was in Washington, D.C., holding a high office in the Department of Agriculture, an admirer of Secretary Orville Freeman. I did not share that admiration because Mr. Freeman presided over the U.S. Forest Service, which by then had spent some three decades disagreeing with me. So Don and I remembered our football days and companions.

Unfortunately Don had lived too far away from Haste Street to join our neighborhood passball sessions, but he contributed to them beyond belief. My next-door neighbor George Rockwood also played on the Regent Street Varsity. We had a routine in which either he or I would appear in front of the other's door with a football to say, "How about getting a game started?" There were always enough neighbors to round up, and we needed only two more as a minimum to oppose us. Anyone added to our side could be matched with the same number on the other side. George and I were the critical mass.

Don, with a simple act, coached us into being unbeatable for years. He sketched out a basic play on which we could build another ten. It looked like this:

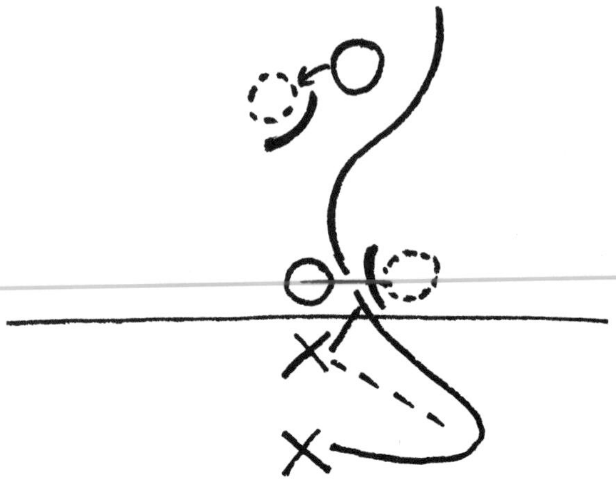

The idea was that the offensive back would run laterally, say to the right, and receive the ball on the run. The offensive center would check the opposing center momentarily to let the ball carrier pass him and cut back. The defensive back would have started to the right to tag the runner and the offensive center would block so as to keep him going in that direction. The offensive runner, having cut back, would run past the safety on the left and score.

This is exactly what happened the first time we tried it. The variations called for a forward pass to the center, who would run left and deep, or for the runner to cut back immediately upon receipt of the ball, or to pass short and receive an instant lateral, or to lateral to the center, who had fallen back to pass deep to the original runner, who had run like hell in the confusion and was comfortably behind the defense. We would either pass or run, depending upon the situation and the terrain.

I was usually the passer. I could pass accurately and far, or drill a bullet in if that was called for. I had also developed a devastating underhanded pass that could go fifty yards and float farther than the defense expected. If I had to run, I had to depend upon being tricky, not upon speed. Change of pace was my best trick.

George could pass well, but not quite so well. I learned to catch almost as well as he, even one-handed. George could catch passes that the defense thought were hopelessly overthrown simply because George never gave up. If he really wanted to, he could probably have outsped the football.

Our favorite third man for the team was Bill Van Voorhis, expatriate Texan, who was six-feet-four. In my early years in high school I disliked

Neighborhood friends playing touch football. Photograph by David R. Brower.

him, thanks to his unending joy in dunking me in the swimming pool. He was bigger, being a Texan, and a good swimmer for the same reason. It was not fair. But once he got into our passball act, all was forgiven. All I had to do was pass a high one. His leap was not up to a present day slammer's, but high enough. What was more important, it didn't matter how many people tried to interrupt his catch. If he got his fingers on the ball, it made no difference if a man tugged on each arm. He held on to it.

This went on for years. We would play passball until it got so dark the ball would hit the receiver before he could see it. I was very pleased with my success, and greatly enjoyed impressing people who had not played with me before by uncorking a sixty-five-yarder when appropriate. When a pass defender could be heard to utter a "Jeee-suuus!" or equivalent I glowed.

Such skill as I was developing splashed over into sandlot football. There I learned that the most important thing to do was to run into a defender as hard as I could, which softened his resistance, or to tackle as hard as I could, which softened the runner. My happiest moment was on West Field, where the Life Sciences Building now stands on the Berkeley campus. I was back to punt. My punt was blocked. I caught it and ran for a touchdown.

Years later it did my ego no harm at Officers' Candidate School at Fort Benning, Georgia, when I played touch football opposite an all-American footballer and impressed even him.

All the foregoing could be long forgotten by most people, but not by someone who at twelve could not pass or kick a spiral. And most of it would probably have bored Don Rubel. It bored my sons. They learned early how to handle the other end of their father's sixty-five-yarders, and soon were matching them.

So much for pride. How about the inevitable fall? It came in about 1930 when Bill's younger brother, Coerte, formed a team with Barrett Ely and a third man (blond, deep-set eyes, dark eyebrows, a good six feet). They went after us. They were fast. They could pass and catch well. And they lateral-passed us silly. With too many consecutive losses, we began to lose interest in the game, though I vowed to keep it up until I reached fifty. When I was about forty-two I was playing touch on the Tilden Park playfield. Phil Berry, twenty-five years younger, faster, and with enough drive to become Sierra Club president some fifteen years later, ran me down after I had caught a pass. He didn't settle for tagging me, but gave me a massive shove from behind that knocked me on my face and wrenched my back.

It was time to seek other diversions.

FITFULLY AT UCB

FOR FIFTY YEARS, dreams have been putting me back in the classes at the University of California in Berkeley that I last actually attended in 1931, and I am getting tired of them. They all end up the same way. After a brave start, I seem to forget to go to classes and go on a guilt trip instead.

There are other recurrent dreams, too. In one I start on a climb that seems only moderately difficult, but in no time at all the rock begins to get crumbly and the exposure more and more horrendous. If and when I do fall, I am grateful to have learned long ago how to turn a fall into a delightful hang-gliding experience. And I keep dreaming that I am smoking again—just one cigarette that really won't count against me. But then I realize that it does count against me, and the whole record of not having succumbed to cigarettes since May 1, 1959, has gone up in smoke.

It is with great relief that I wake up from the smoking dream, delight from the flying experience, and regret from the university failure.

Rationalization still comes easy. I did continue my university education at the University of California Press. There were manuscripts from many fields—zoology, paleontology, geology, music, sociology, anthropology, film, botany, geomorphology, mathematics, medicine, and even mountaineering (my own field)—that required my learning a smattering about each of the subjects in the process of trying to clarify the writing and organization. I was at the press from 1941 to 1952, with time out for World War II. My army training included writing and editing about mountaineering in addition to all I had to learn about ordinary infantry matters. I was even the director of a school in the army reserve.

Anne periodically tries to make me feel better about my academic shortcomings. She knows no other sophomore dropout who has nine honorary degrees. She tells me that I have been able to do many of the things I have done because I didn't get enough education to know that they were impossible.

And I occasionally say that I am a graduate of the University of the Colorado River.

But I still didn't finish college, and I wish I had.

Yes, there was the Great Depression and there was no money in the family and I had to work. That's an excuse. I started in January instead of with my friends in August. That's an excuse. I didn't like my major, entomology, but no courses were available in January anyway. I passed the Subject A English test (with an entomological essay) but failed the agility test, much to my embarrassment. That's no excuse, but it probably had more to do with my dropping out than the others. Let's not talk about it.

Starting in the off-season, I picked up some courses that were to be useful–pomology, forestry, bacteriology, botany, some more chemistry–but they just opened doors that I should like to have gone through. Maybe next time.

Early Jobs

Joe Pennell, Our Foreman, had already picked up Don Rubel and, thanks to Don, picked me up too at Haste and Fulton on our way to Merco-Nordstrom Valve Company, an Emeryville plant that manufactured valves ranging from half an inch to thirty-six inches. For the summer of twenty-nine I learned what assembly lines were like. Blowing surplus grease off small valves with compressed air all day, or setting an adjustment nut at a valve base, was not fascinating at all. The place was noisy enough that I could sing all day and be heard by no one, which helped. Clocks were to watch.

There were earlier jobs that I also saw fit to leave out of my resumes. I had Berkeley *Daily Gazette* route thirteen, and then route two, delivering papers on my oversize skate coaster. On September 17, 1923, I sat on the *Gazette* roof while waiting for papers and watched the Berkeley fire wreak its havoc north of the university campus and head toward the campus itself. Our house was only four blocks from the south side, and my father and brother were on our roof, watching for the burning shingles that were dropping out of the searing north wind. What a sense of relief when the wind changed from north to west! The change caught a few houses that had been missed, but the campus was saved, and much more. In 1926 I entered Berkeley High, and became a paid lab assistant in physics, being far better in physics than I was in algebra. Constance Binnie Abbot saw to it that I repeat Algebra 3 and 4. She had no tolerance for procrastinators, and I was playing passball when I should have been doing my algebra homework. Being manager of the Berkeley Bee football team paid off in popularity, but not academically.

Ted Grindle, before he married my sister, got me a summer job delivering telegrams for Western Union. Thanks to Berkeley's hills it did wonders for my leg muscles.

Also through Ted, I became a clerk at Alberta Candy Company, later to be Bunte Brothers, Western Branch Corporation, where I learned to type, having alleged that I already knew how when I took the job. The piano had trained my fingers well enough that I got away with it, learning how before they noticed. I did sales recapitulation sheets and worked slowly up to pricing clerk and billing clerk, learning the intricacies of the Burroughs Moon Hopkins accounting machine. Somehow I had enough mechanical aptitude to fix it when I jammed it. I was also house salesman, dealing with any retail customers or jobbers who dropped by the factory. All too often I helped myself to the plant's sweet products. Most of my body could handle all this better than my teeth did.

Having learned how to operate the Moon Hopkins, I worked for a time billing freight shipments for Valley Express on the midnight shift. Both this and the candy company job were in San Francisco, so I commuted daily on the Southern Pacific red trains and the accompanying ferry service across the bay. For twenty-one cents I could get from home to work within a few minutes of the time it now takes BART to cover the distance for a dollar eighty-five. I wish we had known enough to complain more effectively when they decided to spend thirty-five million dollars to remove the rails from the lower deck of the Bay Bridge and thus destroy a mass transit system that has not been equaled by the two billion dollars spent so far on the BART system.

If I had been willing to continue commuting between Berkeley and San Francisco, I might have stayed with one firm long enough to advance and get stuck there. The commuting I became accustomed to, however, was between Berkeley and the Sierra. Perhaps it was just that I preferred spending my birthdays in high places instead of in the fogbound Berkeley of July. It was far more fun to look from Mount Ralston, alongside Echo Lake, across the state to Mount Diablo than to look at Diablo from Grizzly Peak. I would like to do it right now. But there's that brown opacity that floods California's Great Valley in summer. Opaque doesn't have many good connotations. Ansel Adams would agree. He met with Ronald Reagan once in the White House and found him opaque, adding that "the light passes through in neither direction."

CHAPTER 2

MOUNTAINEERING

WILDERNESS OFF TRAIL

ECHO LAKE AND DESOLATION VALLEY, Mount Lyell, an attempt, at least, on Mount Whitney—these were fine, but not enough. One of the guests at the Berkeley Echo Lake Camp told me that since I liked mountains so much I should check out the Sierra Club. I should not have forgotten who he was because he made such a difference. Following his advice, I visited the office in Mills Tower, met Virginia Ferguson, the club's sole employee, chatted briefly, and shortly became known to her as the young man who kept coming in to buy back issues of the *Sierra Club Bulletin*. I read each annual magazine cover to cover. The accounts of exploration and climbs were what I liked best, together with the photographs, especially those by Ansel Adams.

George Rockwood and I undertook a seven-week backpack trip in the Sierra in 1933, inspired by those old bulletins. The trip cost each of us three dollars a week.

It was just as well it cost me no more, because twenty-one dollars was just what I had been paid for three months' work the preceding spring on the Two Rock Valley farm of cousins on my mother's side, Walter and Fanny Foster and their five children. There I had learned all about feeding chickens, gathering eggs, a little about shearing sheep, milking cows, and saddling horses (I put the cropper up front on my first attempt, but heard no horses laughing, just cousins), a little more about disking and harrowing, and more about how harrowing it was to dehorn and neuter livestock. My greatest achievement was being able to teach Pet, one of the work horses, to whinny at my approach and let me put my arm around her neck and stroke her. She would attempt to bite any and all of my cousins whenever given a chance.

It was disappointing to be paid so little for so much, but I was in good shape. There had been lots of exercise in the open air, and plenty of opportunity, in the frequent solitude, to sing all the current Bing Crosby pieces with a fairly good Crosby imitation—I could even break my voice tearfully the way Bing did in "Many Happy Returns of the Day."

Twenty-one dollars was more than George and I got for the next job. We felled and cut up eucalyptus for several weeks in what was to become Tilden Regional Park, just east of Berkeley, and for this we got only the wood, which we traded for food. This was 1933, and the Great Depression was still in force. Walter Foster was getting a mere six cents a pound for his lambs, and Clarence Saunders's chain store was advertising a special on carrots at one cent a bunch.

With the food we got from trading, and twenty-one dollars apiece, we started out. My father kindly drove us to Big Pine Creek. En route we left a cache of food under a cabin at Mammoth Lakes. Big Pine Creek was gateway to the Palisades, the Sierra's most rugged summits. Somehow I had arranged to bring a butterfly net along, and found myself wildly pursuing the rarest butterflies I knew of. *Papilio pergamus* specimens would bring seven dollars for a female, three for a male. I learned this from an obscure advertisement Jean Gunder, the Pasadena man who bought my orangeless orange-tip butterfly, ran often in an obscure magazine. Here at last were many pergamus swallowtails. I had no wish to sell them, but wanted specimens anyway. I had never before tried to run over talus watching a butterfly instead of my feet. Somehow I caught some swallowtails without shredding myself in the talus.

I was less careful but luckier two days later on one of the Palisades, The Thumb. We had camped at the first lake on the South Fork of Big Pine Creek and found all the peaks too formidable except for The Thumb. George wanted to go no farther than the bottom of the couloir leading to the summit. I went up the couloir a short distance, then started swarming up its east wall. One block on the wall was just waiting for me. I grabbed the top of it with both hands, which didn't faze it, but when I put my knee against it and drew myself up, it came free. I would have followed its plunge to the couloir had there not been a tiny ledge above me that I could grab frantically with two fingers of my left hand. It and they held and I was spared a sheer seventy-five-foot fall and subsequent roll that I doubt I would have survived. "Are you OK?" George asked as the rock hurtled past him. "OK," I said, and settled my nerves as I sat for a few moments on the arête immediately above.

Norman Clyde, whom I met at dinner at Glacier Lodge two nights later listened to my story and told me about three-point suspension: in a tough place, you move only one limb at a time, first making sure that the other three are secure.

This advice served me well when I climbed the North Palisade from the glacier soon thereafter, using a sharp granite rock for an ice ax, and relying on basketball shoes when I should have had nailed boots. The rock climb from the North Palisade's U-notch was one on which I later preferred having a rope for security, but in 1933 I climbed it solo with nothing for protection but Norman Clyde's advice about three-point suspension.

From Norman, George and I had learned of a knapsacker's route across the Palisades rampart. It was between Mount Winchell and Agassiz Needle and I dubbed it "Agassizjoch," having read about such places in a mountaineering book. It was an easy crossing, made notable by our mistaking the sound of a golden eagle's dive for a rock avalanche.

Norman had also suggested two ways we could cross Glacier Divide, once we had followed the John Muir Trail over Muir Pass to the lower end of Evolution Lake. En route we had camped at Darwin Bench, one of my two favorite campsites in the entire Sierra Nevada, and then chose one of Norman's knapsack passes, dubbing it "The Keyhole," because that is what we passed through on our way to the Piute Creek drainage and our timberline camp at Golden Trout Lake.

At campfire we had a visitor, a young man camped nearby who was traveling the Sierra in the opposite direction from ours. He had started on his trip with his brother, Noel, who had lost interest. Hervey Voge was continuing by himself. We traded information about routes and I told of my climbs. Hervey strongly advised that I join the Sierra Club and get some instruction from the rock-climbing section of the San Francisco Bay Chapter. That would turn out to be important advice.

I would profit even more from later encounters with the man George and I were talking to a day later. We were coming off Pilot Knob and headed toward the Sierra Club late June camp in Hutchinson Meadow, and here was this bearded type, camera and tripod over his shoulder, coming up through the timberline forest. "You must be Ansel Adams," I said. He agreed. Neither of us knew who I was. The conversation was brief. I spoke of my admiration for his work. He complained about the early morning cumulus clouds; they were still too fuzzy to photograph. Then he went up, and we went down to pick up a second breakfast at the Sierra Club camp before leaving the trail at French Canyon to head into an area where, to quote Mrs. Malaprop, the hand of man had not set foot.

On the bench above French Canyon, as we crossed the stream at the head of what George named "Wet Lake" (good enough humor for us at the time, and in keeping with George's question, "Why does the sun only shine in the daytime, and not at night when we need it?"), the water turned white with the thrashing about of huge trout. By means I shall not reveal we caught an eighteen-inch golden trout, steaks from which vastly improved our menu. I made first recorded ascents of two nearby peaks, one of which Norman Clyde claimed he had climbed first. If so, he left no record, unusual for Norman. I'm sure he was on an adjacent peak. We crossed what we named "Shallow Lake Pass," well marked by sheep droppings, and descended to Lake Italy where we camped above timberline, using willow twigs for firewood. George stayed in camp while I, in one full day, traversed Bear Creek Spire, Mount Dade, and Mount Abbot. We then crossed the Abbot-Gabb knapsack pass, picked up our food cache at

Mammoth, ate royally at Lake Mary Lodge in exchange for my piano playing, and ended up our seven weeks by racing each other over Mounts Gibbs and Dana and dropping down to Tuolumne Meadows, where my brother Ralph and his bride, Dorothy, picked us up.

The new alignment of the Tioga Road had been carved out and graveled, and I noted with regret that the road engineers had shown no sensitivity in whacking away at the north end of the Lembert Dome ridge. (Fifty-six years later the ugly scar still shows no sign of recovery.) Before descending to Yosemite Valley we climbed the most beautiful of the summits in the Tuolumne Meadows region—John Muir's favorite, too—Cathedral Peak. I would probably never again be in as good shape. I was twenty-one, tan, lean, able to shame a horse at mealtime, and ready to take the three-thousand-foot ascent to Glacier Point via the Ledge Trail in just over an hour. This would not make the *Guinness Book of World Records,* but it suited me just fine.

FAR FROM THE MADDING MULES

THE SEVEN SUMMER WEEKS in 1933 led to a brief note that the editor Francis Farquhar accepted for the annual magazine number of the *Sierra Club Bulletin.* Hervey Voge, indeed, talked me into joining the Sierra Club to learn how to climb more safely than he thought I had. On Berkeley and Mount Diablo rocks and in Pinnacles National Monument we climbed often, either with the club's rock-climbing section or by ourselves. Over small glasses of Angelica or Tokay—we were learning about wine and were young enough to prefer it sweet—we planned carefully for a 1934 "Knapsack Survey of Sierra Routes and Records." It was a nice name, and we should probably have sought a grant to help finance our effort. The ten weeks were filled with much delight, a little anguish, and some of our fondest memories.

Back at Bunte Brothers candy works in the fall of 1934, I was again commuting from Berkeley to San Francisco—a pleasant routine in those days. I liked to ride the old red Southern Pacific electric line from Haste Street in Berkeley to the Oakland Mole. The ferries were the best part. The old *Sacramento* provided a wonderful display, behind upper deck inside windows, of the marvelous steam-driven machinery that operated the walking beam and paddlewheels. The *Berkeley,* screw-driven and addled, lacked the precision of the *Sacramento,* and gave the pilings of the Oakland and San Francisco ferry slips frequent cause to groan loudly, and once or twice to snap. Unless it was raining, I usually rode on the front deck, a wilderness experience of sorts, with a good wind to face, nothing to block the view, and a chance to be bolder than the passengers cowering in the warmth of the cabin or safely out of the wind on the rear deck.

In the fall of 1934, however, I chose to cower inside myself, and to write about Hervey's and my seventy Sierra days of knapsacking and climbing. There was half an hour a day for scribbling in my childish longhand. I worked the manuscript over and over, typed it up, and Francis Farquhar, after showing me what good editing can cut out, published "Far from the Madding Mules" in the 1935 annual magazine of the *Sierra Club Bulletin*. Our Sierra trip was immortalized and my ego trip had begun.

"Is There Any Sugar left for my cornmeal?"

"No, there's no sugar, and there isn't any milk either—until we reach North Lake. You'll just have to get along with the bacon grease we fried our last onion in. . . ."

"What! Aren't those beans done yet? Why they've been cooking over the embers all day, since we left this morning."

"Yes, and we've been gone ten hours. You would insist on bringing beans. Oh well, pass some over. I am going to eat, at any cost. . . ."

And thus, during the summer of 1933, did George Rockwood and I so thoroughly enjoy our seven weeks' knapsacking trip that no sooner was it over than I began to plan for another. In May 1934, it was time to go again. Unhappily, George was detained by work and a sense of responsibility to it; but Hervey Voge, whom we had met in Humphreys Basin in 1933, was well acquainted with knapsacking, and had long since planned to be with us. So on May 18, having shipped provisions for forty-eight days ahead of us to Glacier Lodge (on Big Pine Creek) and to Independence, Hervey and I loaded an additional twenty-five days' supplies into the car, and left Berkeley at ten in the evening. All night we drove, passing the Yosemite Aspen Valley ranger station at six the next morning. It was yet quite early, even in this dry year, for Tioga Road travel, and the road was still moist, the roadside trees fresh. We glided among the tall fir and pine columns of the cool forest, reveling in the fragrance of it. At the pass we left nine days' food, then dropped into Mono Basin, turning south to make our next two caches at the end of the Mammoth Lakes road and at ten thousand five hundred feet on Rock Creek. At Independence, after a short stop for perishables and the provisions shipped ahead from Berkeley, we made our final turning into the Sierra, ascending the spectacular road to Onion Valley.

Here, on the following morning, the food was divided into three groups, two of which were cached. The third, with our equipment, was tied to the packboards, and late that afternoon we started up the south fork of Independence Creek—a shortcut to Center Basin. The pace was slow and none too steady; but it was good to feel the rocks under foot and to smell the lodgepole pines once more; good to wet again our knees and noses as we drank from the streams among the cyclamen and grasses. It was good, too, to rest. At length we came to a little lake, at ten thousand three hundred feet elevation, and camped just above beside a granite apron, among lodgepole and foxtail pines. Water was close by, and kettles of it soon were heating above a pine-bough fire in a little rock fireplace. Our summer had really started.

With an eight days' supply of food we crossed the saddle between University Peak and "Peak 12,910," dropping down to a timberline camp at eleven thousand three hundred feet in Center Basin. One day we devoted to acclimatizing ourselves, and climbed Center Peak, where we found no record of an ascent since the first in 1898. Another day we crossed Junction Pass into the cliffbound canyon to the south, and followed the fork of Shepherd Creek a short distance toward Shepherd Pass. There, amid the moraine masses that covered the canyon floor, we cached several days' food for subsequent use. To complete the circuit of University Peak, we returned the next day to Onion Valley by Kearsarge Pass, experiencing our first bit of late spring weather. At ten forty-five in the morning snow began to fall. Hervey three days previously had forecast this storm; but he had given the starting hour at eleven, not ten forty-five, and had predicted rain, not snow. I can never forgive him these blunders.

With replenished supplies we started from Onion Valley a second time. Crossing Kearsarge Pass, we followed down Bubbs Creek to Junction Meadow, whence we went up East Creek to East Lake. Above this lake, on the west side of the floor of the canyon, is a huge granite cave, an assurance of shelter in the event of a storm. Four peaks fell to our attack during our stay, but they only fell along with much snow. Snow was falling heavily as we traversed Mount Brewer, and flurried another day on "Peak 12,610." From East Lake we had hoped to trace Clarence King's route to and from Mount Tyndall, but the snow fell so discouragingly that it was decided to look for the footsteps of Mr. King another year. So on Memorial Day we packed to Harrison Pass and passed the afternoon on Mount Stanford.

From Harrison Pass there were delightful miles of descent into the Kern Basin. How pleasingly this basin contrasts with the severity of the Kings-Kern Divide – its long inclines, its broad hollows filled with lakes and meadows, its somber distant aspect of ridges and forest, all blending in soothing tranquillity with the late afternoon diffusion of sunlight! We marched into the evening, past the beaten remains of trees that spoke of a once kindlier climate, into a last stand of lodgepoles, the highest on Tyndall Creek. Sonorously, a hermit thrush gave cheer to the efforts of this forest to survive. We paused to camp and give him audience, while from the broad canyon of the Kern arose a chill night breeze, and the pines

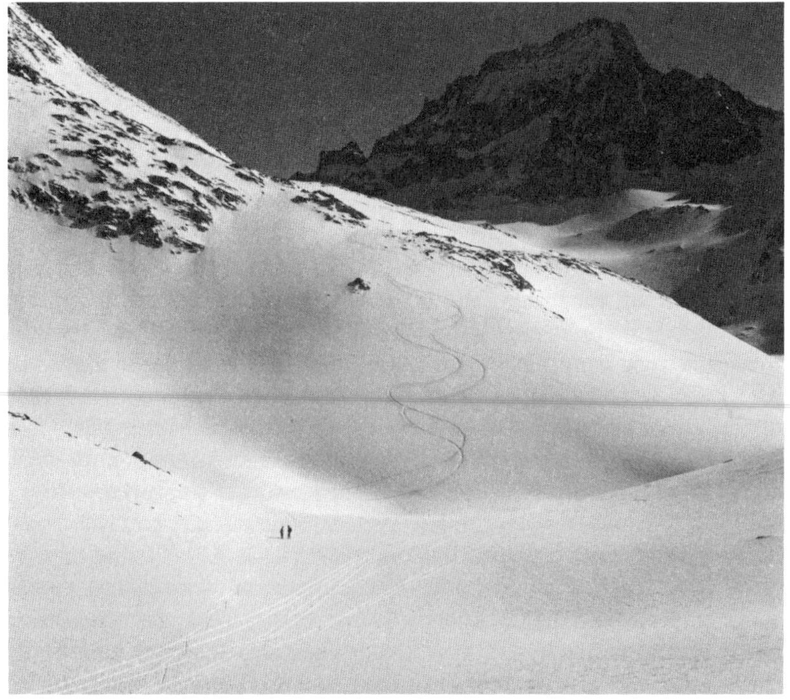

Winter ascent of Bear Creek Spire, 1941. Photo by David R. Brower.

responded to the throbbing roar of the creek below. Intangible in shadow, the peaks appeared closer, as if they, too, were listening to the ethereal Sierran fugue.

Although much activity had been planned for our Kern sojourn, our desires were somewhat appeased by the first day's effort – a moonlight ascent of Mount Tyndall, breakfast after sunrise on Mount Williamson, lunch on Mount Barnard, a second lunch at Wales Lake, and a ten-mile walk back to camp. Next day we crossed Foresters Pass, adding en route what was apparently the first ascent of "Peak 13,826."

Hardly were we settled once more in the headwaters of Kings River when a new storm set in, and snow fell for about twenty-four hours in the next forty-eight. We camped in a light stand of lodgepole under East Vidette; but as the storm was obviously not intending to leave, we did, and after a night's camp below Bullfrog Lake, crossed Kearsarge Pass and returned to our cache at Onion Valley.

Already our trip had enlightened us to this extent: that we could leave the beaten path, and that snowstorms could be either enjoyed on their own account or rendered innocuous by song. Next we were to prove that a flashlight in the knapsack is superfluous – at least, we didn't have one. We had crossed Glen Pass and were camping in Sixty Lakes Basin. We were returning from an ascent of Mount Clarence King and stood watching the brilliance of a sunset over the mists and clouds that gathered around the peak. The evening chill urged that we hasten, simultaneously inactivating our attempts to do so. But with some struggle and two rope-downs we descended a thousand feet of icy rock to the notch south of our peak before the stars had all come out. To the east lay our camp, far below chutes, granite bluffs, lakeshore meadow, and talus. A steep snow slope led down another five hundred feet. Ahead were the bluffs of a granite step, the holds becoming more obscure in the steadily increasing darkness. At first we could see the route dimly; but soon we were sounding the blackness, tossing rocks into the foreground. If, after a second in the air, a rock still whistled, we were discouraged from further progress in that direction. To the north a little stream cascaded, and hoping that there would be no high falls in the course of it, we crossed over on some ledges, and followed it down successfully to a meadow. We staggered forward, one foot stepping high, the other in an unseen pocket perhaps a foot below. Occasionally we could hear a stream gurgling, and found that we could avoid stepping into it by holding to the willows and feeling for the water with our hands. Then, as we poked around what might have been any one of the sixty lakes, what a surprise it was to stumble right into camp. A fire was soon lit, but only for heat and for cooking – we didn't need the light!

From Sixty Lakes Basin we marched three days, over Pinchot Pass and Mather Pass to Palisade Creek. Then, by crossing the notch between Middle Palisade and The Thumb, we were able to descend the South Fork of Big Pine Creek to Glacier Lodge and our next cache. For the first time in two weeks Hervey could look at another face.

Here, also, was our first experience with a mule on a trail. Although confirmed knapsackers, we had deemed it advisable to have our two-hundred-twenty-pound cache moved up the North Fork trail to a camp at Fifth Lake, at an altitude of ten feet. Old Jiggs, our mule, was most lovable, but he was quite unaware that we were running the trip. He was thirsty in the middle of each ford, famished at the sight of every wisp of grass, and susceptible to *wanderlust* each time we rested; but these faults were as nothing. His racial idiosyncrasy of one single forward speed on ups, downs, and levels was, however, most exasperating. On an uphill stretch he was usually resting his head upon my packboard, pushing, and blowing sweet words in my ear. Then, as the trail dropped, my customary step-out would be suddenly curbed as I reached my rope's end, and there was definite indication that nothing I might do would change matters. By the time we reached Fifth Lake I was thoroughly subjugated to the desires of the dumb animal, and a much faster uphill climber than I had ever desired to be.

The following evening, June 14, quite unaffected by the report at Glacier Lodge that he had been lost, Norman Clyde arrived in our camp, immediately dubbing it "The Palace Hotel." One look at his towering pack suggested a retaliating analogy, for surely he was bearing a "Coit Memorial" pack. We were not particularly surprised to see him, as we had intended to climb together in the Palisade Group. The real surprise came at dinner, when he not only took several dozen eggs intact from his pack, but was able to manage a second helping of a "knock 'em dead mulligan" of rice, corned beef, and chili powder, cooled with hot cocoa. We had figured that only the most hardy could manage such menus, and had forgotten that there was at least one person in the Sierra as hardy as we. After dinner we considered climbs in the region, lamenting the "snow-cluttered" condition of the north and northeast faces. One climb, it was decided, was sufficiently unhampered by the new snow—Agassiz Needle, by the east face and north arête.

Next morning we started, with Norman Clyde bearing the brunt of the work as leader. He chose the route, and cut or cleared the steps with his ice ax, while we took a day off. The actual climbing was not difficult, but might well have been so had we digressed from the route followed. The party worked smoothly together, and it was only natural that we should reach the summit. What seemed unnatural, however, was the balmy weather when we arrived there. Where were the clouds, the singing rocks, the snow flurries? What should one do on a peak when not confronted with the urgent need for shelter? We could only pause to absorb the sun and scene and to sign the Sierra Club register. And here, indeed, is the answer to all who question climbing with a "why do they do it?" Who, once having enjoyed it, does not long for the deep satisfactions of beholding a panorama from a vantage-point, access to which has cost something in effort and training; of knowing that here is a frontier still; of being aloof, and yet in close communion; of being awed by the great, but remaining proud of the success of the organized effort of the small? Consider, also, the intellectual pleasures of geological or biological inquiry; the diabolical sport of rolling rocks down upon no one (one hopes) below; the reminiscence of topographical acquaintance; the aesthetic enjoyment of the pictures of harsh cliffs, towering clouds, and graceful trees, and the softest mottling of color and light and shadow.

It took two more climbs to convince us that our efforts were best saved until the snow was off the shelves. One of these was the traverse of Mount Sill, from the great notch of North Palisade over into the South Fork of Big Pine Creek, whence camp was reached by the notch between Mount Sill and Peak 13,500. The second climb was a traverse of Temple Crag, up two chutes on the north face, and down by the Buck Mountain (Peak 12,840) saddle. On neither of these climbs did a drop of rain fall. We were treated only to thunder, lightning, mist, hail, and snow. The storm on Temple Crag, the third storm in four days at Fifth Lake, instigated a move to lower country. We didn't mind the storms, for they were confined to daytime; but the snow melted very slowly on the fourteen-thousand-foot peaks.

Three days of marching, loafing, and fishing brought us to a base camp for Devil's Crags, at ten thousand feet, on the south fork of Rambaud Creek. One afternoon was devoted to reconnaissance from Rambaud Peak, where Hervey made a diagram of the chutes and notches of the Crags, which became most useful. For the next three days there followed our most interesting mountaineering. We climbed ten of the low Crags and explored nine of the chutes. We climbed both roped and ropeless, and roped down in severe places. Norman spent long periods with his ice ax, cutting steps for the party. We basked in the sun and chilled in the wind. Hervey built enormous cairns, and we left little registers. Each night we returned to one of our happiest camps—on a meadow-shelf, shaded by hemlocks and pines, with colorful cliffs, and graced by a lakelet, flower-bordered with cassiope-bells and cyclamen.

When, at last, we had climbed all previously unclimbed Devil's Crags, we moved camp to Dusy Basin. The peaks were now yellow in smoke-filtered sunlight, for a forest fire was burning in some lower region. We could barely distinguish the peaks of the Black Divide across Le Conte Canyon. The next afternoon we returned to the "Palace Hotel," where mail was waiting for us. Welcome in mine was a package from George Rockwood—a birthday present of a carton of candy bars. He well remembered what had, the previous summer, been an easily absorbed addition to supposedly well-balanced rations.

June 29 was to be our last day of climbing in the Palisade region, and we proposed to make a full day of it. We were unable to get away from camp before eight, but this was our usual procedure, far more comfortable than three-in-the-morning lantern-light starts. We enjoyed the sunny walk up the trail and over the Palisade Glacier, and settled down to climbing in the chute leading to the notch between North Palisade and Thunderbolt Peak. Ropeless climbing took us to the summit block of Thunderbolt, a belayed shoulder stand to the top. Then, turning back, we kept to the ridge, traversing the two peaks of the North Palisade, and continued southeast into the great notch. The sun set as we returned to the glacier and the amber summer alpenglow tinged the peaks about us. We were thankful not to be in camp, fussing over kettles and campfires, and regretted that there were so many below who chose not to see sunsets from high places, among them many mountaineers. Secretly, I wondered if on many a morning, while I was struggling to keep the tang *in* the air and *out* of the sleeping bag, someone, thousands of feet above, was not regretting that I was choosing not to witness sun*rises* from high places. If he were, I wish he wouldn't.

It was time to bid Norman Clyde good-bye, for a while, at least. In his company we had learned much of safety and precaution, and of the use of the ice ax, both for mountaineering and for domestic purposes. We had gathered bits of geological and botanical nomenclature, and we had heard stories and anecdotes about the Sierra, and about those who love it and those who live too close to appreciate its attributes. Moreover, we had become acquainted with Clyde's technique of establishing "boulevards" up the precipitous sides of peaks, particularly in the Palisade group. But on July 1 our schedule called for northerly progress, so once again we crossed our Jigsaw Pass (a mile north of Agassiz Needle) to Bishop Pass and Dusy Basin.

On July 2 we reached Muir Shelter, carrying seven days' supply of food, regular equipment, and quite a supply of firewood, planning to stop at the hut two nights, and wishing to leave untouched such wood as might be there. As we closed the door behind us a long-threatening thunderstorm broke loose in earnest. The wind became a gale, and the hail rattled against the little window, but the walls were of stone, over a foot thick, and quite unyielding. We lit a fire, cooked supper over the fireplace grate, and the room warmed with the smoke that was buffeted down the chimney. When the storm had subsided we stepped out into the fresh wind to absorb colorful bits of a most glorious sunset. Tremendous towering banks of nimbus opened up and shone pure white or breathed their last foreboding in gray-blacks, until the sun sank behind some unnamed peak with a blaze of sunset gaudiness, presently to subside into a peaceful delicacy of color—a spectacle perhaps to be equaled or surpassed, but never duplicated.

From the hut we made a one-day trip into the mismapped basin of Goddard and Disappearing creeks. From Scylla and Charybdis much cartographic error was obvious, several lakes being omitted. One lake in particular captured our attention. On the map it appeared to drain into Goddard Creek. Actually the only drainage was into Disappearing Creek, by *two* outlets. This comment is made for the purpose of correction and not in disparagement of the remarkable topographic work done more than twenty-five years ago by George R. Davis, of the U.S. Geological Survey. In many respects his Mount Goddard quadrangle is one of the finest maps ever made of rough country. [Francis Farquhar edited this erudition into a twenty-three-year-old's carping.]

Another day took us through the snowless Evolution Basin to a camp at eleven thousand one hundred feet on the Darwin fork of Evolution Creek, from which, as a base, we traversed Mount Darwin from north to west. In two more marches we crossed Glacier Divide into Humphreys Basin, the Pilot Knob ridge into French Canyon, Pine Creek Pass, and another pass (for knapsackers only) from Pine Lake directly into Morgan Creek, where we followed an old tractor road to our cache on Rock Creek, in Little Lakes Valley. Norman Clyde arrived the same afternoon from Glacier Lodge, and made camp ahead of us.

While not engaged in guarding our provisions against the depredations of Belding ground squirrels we explored the neighboring peaks—Bear Creek Spire, by the east face and north arête, Abbot, from the glacier, and Mount Dade. Then we moved into Pioneer Basin with its supposedly unclimbed peaks—Huntington, Morgan, Hopkins, and Crocker. We were not very much surprised to find on the southerly peak of Mount Huntington the record of a previous ascent, but were astonished at the discovery that the climber was a Basque—perhaps the only sheepherder who ever climbed a peak and left a notation of his act of indiscretion. But, other than the benchmark on Mount Stanford, no additional record was found that day in a search of the ridge as far north as Mount Morgan. It was sunset as Norman and I—Hervey was left favoring an ankle on Stanford—reached Mount Morgan. We traversed Stanford again at 9:00 P.M. and made our way by starlight down the southwest side, frustrating Hervey's rescue plans by reaching camp shortly after midnight.

The ascent of Hopkins and Crocker ended our Pioneer Basin days. Hervey and I undertook an involved departure from the trail, crossing the northeast shoulder of Mount Crocker and descending a chute into McGee Creek—one of the best knapsack climbs in the Sierra. Our next passes—the first, west of "Peak 12,309," the second, north of "Peak 12,292"—were much easier, and connected with the Duck Lake trail to our Mammoth Lakes cache. Steady travel took us over Mammoth, Agnew, and Donohue passes to Tuolumne Meadows; then north with the second two weeks of the Sierra Club Outing party into Matterhorn Canyon. Very exclusively, we camped two miles above the commissary.

By starting early in the morning of July 24 we were able to get on and off the Doodad before the trampling multitudes arrived, but we were less fortunate on the West Tooth, where ours was the third ascent of the day. These peaks, about as difficult as any we had climbed, were the only ones of the sixty-two climbed since May 21 on which we had been preceded this year.

At campfire that night it was decided that something must be done. Our earliest plans had called for an ascent of Matterhorn Peak, and now we were faced with the problem of finding space at the top. Then we recalled having read at Mammoth Lakes of a lunar eclipse scheduled to start at two the next morning. Our *chef d'œuvre* would be the first ascent of Matterhorn Peak by the light of a partially eclipsed moon.

The starting hour, midnight, arrived after we had slept but three hours. While I was trying to convince myself that I was doing the right thing on the correct night, Hervey was out and ready to go. I even retained my incredulity until the eclipse started. We stumbled very little, for the eclipse was not total, and long before it reached its height the eastern sky had brightened. While we were yet a few feet below the summit the sun rose, and we witnessed the phenomenon of seeing the sun cast, simultaneously, our shadows and the shadow of the earth.

As we were finishing breakfast back in camp, a Sierra Club party led by Norman Clyde filed by. When we mentioned our climb, it transpired that none of those in the party, nor, indeed, any of the hundred or more Sierra Club members in camp, had known of the eclipse. A little later in the morning the newlywed Mr. and Mrs. Leonard passed our camp on the way to their headquarters on Blacksmith Creek. It had been over two months since we had seen them, and there was much to discuss. Inevitably, we reached the subject of the eclipse. Leonard ventured, "It must have been especially beautiful, with the moon full!" We all laughed as we remembered our elementary astronomy. What a sight an eclipsed *new* moon would be!

Months before, while deep in the plans for this summer of Sierra knapsacking, we had asked ourselves how long we might climb before the sport would pall on us. We came close to the answer in the Sawtooth region. We had just climbed the West Tooth. The entire ridge presented excellent climbing, particularly the traverse of the Three Teeth. But there on the West Tooth, with the Middle Tooth almost within touching distance, our interest subsided. Although it was still early in the afternoon, we roped down from the ridge and returned to camp.

Was ten weeks, then, the limit? Could the Sierra offer only a transitory enjoyment, merely a temporary escape? Had the rudimentary life toppled from its exalted pedestal in our lives?

The final answer must be an individual one. After Hervey Voge and I had returned to Tuolumne Meadows, and had parted to go to our respective homes, as I rode down, down, and out into the hot valley, my individual answer took form with pangs of regret. By the time I reached Berkeley the answer was certain:

This person was not coming home—he had just left it!

***Sierra Club Bulletin*, 1935**

I had left my wilderness home indeed. Although I would not leave it for long, I would never again be so self-reliant in the wild for so long, or see so few people there, or be so totally absorbed in exploring and enjoying and so unconcerned with protecting the wildness that had made the experience possible. In our Sierra backpacking, George, Hervey, and I saw no one but each other for weeks at a time. A fact that amazes me still is that in all my seventy-seven years I have never been totally alone in the wild for more than the thirty hours of my unsuccessful solo attempt to climb Mount Clark, in Yosemite. A Samivel cartoon shows a person alone in the Alps saying: "Solitude at last! How much nicer it would be if there were only someone to talk to about it." I became so exhausted on that attempt that I imagined during the following night, when I fell asleep, too tired to continue, that there was someone with me. But we didn't talk.

Back at Muir Pass, in the hut the Sierra Club built there honoring John Muir, there is a register, with room in it for passersby to sign their names. Hervey and I wrote rather more than that, electing to catalog all the peaks we had climbed by that date of the sixty-five we would climb that summer. I am not sure that Hervey should share the blame. A subsequent passerby, who knew Hervey because he, Dan Luten, was a chemist too, and would be my next-door neighbor and conservation coach, made his entry under ours: "All the above could be performed with the energy contained in one pint of Texaco Fire Chief gasoline."

This ended five full summers in the Sierra—three at Echo, with tiny touches of wilderness added, and two in the High Sierra, one of the three places in the Lower Forty-Nine where you could then get more than ten miles from a road. Only two remain—one in Sequoia National Park and the other in the Bob Marshall Wilderness in Montana. The energy I expended certainly awakened me to wilderness and enabled me to go to some places on the map that White Man had not visited before, and Red Man probably had no interest in. I had added several names to help clutter the map. But I had not yet understood what wilderness means or what the threats were to the last vestige of it. I was low and slow on the learning curve. Lots of input. Hardly any data processing. In any event, I hadn't started abusing the language with such terms.

Mount Waddington: An Unfinished Story

The Climbs Hervey Voge and I made in the summer of 1934 led to our being invited to attempt Mount Waddington, British Columbia's most notorious unclimbed summit. Hervey couldn't get away from Harvard, where he was a National Research Fellow in 1935, and I could not get away from Yosemite in 1936, when Sierra Club people, including Hervey, would make a second try.

I was too poor to go in 1935, but it was arranged that I would write dispatches from the expedition for the North American Newspaper Alliance (NANA), for which I would be paid three hundred dollars in advance. This covered the seaplane fare for our party of eight from Vancouver to Knight Inlet and back. The rest of the group kindly agreed to ask no more of me than that.

NANA didn't get much news for its money. There was little time to write at the beginning, and once we were on the Franklin Glacier there was no way to get news out. I simply stored it up in my head and in scattered notes. For a few months after the trip, in my spare time in Yosemite, I put the story together for myself.

I was twenty-three at the time, pleased that my account of the previous Sierra summer had been published in the *Sierra Club Bulletin,* full of the excitement of my first and only expedition, and feeling very literary. Perhaps this was a sublimation of my having been invited to join an expedition to K-2, in the Karakoram, which I could not afford.

High on Mount Waddington's Dais Glacier I celebrated my twenty-third birthday, and would not have a more exceptional celebration until my seventy-fifth, perhaps ten feet above sea level in Berkeley. The Waddington story does reveal that mountains were getting to me. Their mark was never erased.

In the Rugged and Unmapped mountain wilderness that is the Coast Range of British Columbia, myriad peaks tower into the sky. Deep mantles of ice scintillate in the sun of the occasional fair day; black and jagged crags shred the spray of the sea of cloud and mist that seldom ceases to roll in from the Pacific. Monarch of the peaks, and most challenging and defiant of all North American peaks that had remained unclimbed in 1935, is Mount Waddington. It is in the heart of the range that parallels the Pacific shores of Canada for five hundred miles, presenting a wonderland of tremendous snowfall and glaciation, of dense virgin forests, of long fjords and canyons seldom penetrated beyond the silt-laden river deltas, and of peaks that are all but unknown. The mountain is hardly two hundred miles northwest of the skyscrapers of Vancouver, B.C. The base of it had been reached often from west, south, and east, by invigorating backpacking through magnificent forest and glacier-floored corridors. Yet, in 1935, thirteen years since the discovery of Waddington, the efforts of twenty-five climbers, in thirteen attempts to reach the summit, had failed.

What might possibly have caused such a sequence of failures? The peak is not too high, being topped in elevation by many peaks in the United States. It is not far from civilization. Had the climate been too severe, the faces and ridges too forbidding, or were the climbers who attempted it insufficiently skilled? Several San Francisco members of the Sierra Club asked themselves these questions when the first accounts of failure were noticed, then proceeded to unearth some of the answers on the shelves of the club's library. Before long one thing was decided definitely: that we would have to investigate the peak and its problems at close range.

By reading and rereading the sizeable collection of mountaineering-journal articles about the Coast Range, we could piece together Mount Waddington's story. We found it very recent, brief, unfinished, and teeming with interest. The peak is the highest in Canada south of the Alaskan border ranges—even higher than Mount Robson, long thought to be the monarch of Canada. Yet neither its height nor presence were appreciated until 1922. A surveyor photographed it that year from Mount Good Hope,

Mount Waddington Expedition members, 1935. Left to right: Don Woods, Jules Eichorn, Farnie Loomis, Dave Brower, Bestor Robinson, Bob Ratcliff, Jack Riegelhuth, Dick Leonard. Photograph with self-timer by Dick Leonard.

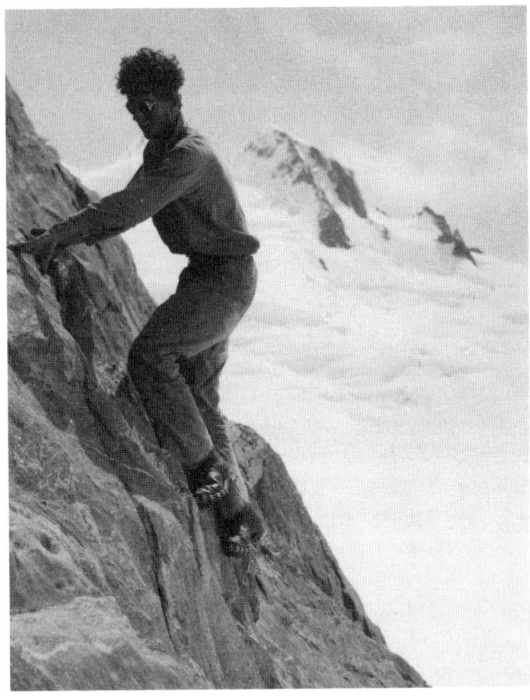

Dave on Mount Waddington, 1935, wearing tricouni-nailed boots.

Mount Waddington, British Columbia. Photograph by David R. Brower, 1935.

to the southeast. Previously there had been only vague reports of a mysterious peak, of dark precipices towering far above the ice-covered summits surrounding them; but stormy skies had combined with inaccessibility to delay bringing the rumors to earth. Thus "Mystery Mountain" early became an apt description of the peak, and is still widely used. "Waddington" officially replaced this when, by triangulation, some of the mystery was removed with the determination of the altitude as 13,260 feet. With the lure of superior height added to the natural appeal of terra incognito, a real challenge was born. First to respond was W. A. Don Munday, a Vancouver alpinist. With his wife, herself an excellent climber and packer, he obtained his first glimpse in 1925, when on a Vancouver Island peak fifty miles distant. The following year they approached from Bute Inlet and the Homathko Valley. The nearest they came to Mount Waddington was the base of Spearman Peak, which left two miles to go. Before they returned to their camp they had been traveling thirty-one hours, during twenty-four of which the party of five was roped together.

They were back in 1927 with two months for the attack, but again, in three attempts, were stopped short of the goal. On the third of these attempts they left a bivouac at 5:00 A.M., advanced steadily to twelve thousand seven hundred feet on the west ridge of Waddington's lower snow summit, and were caught in a terrific storm. Don Munday described it in the 1928 *Canadian Alpine Journal*:

"The full fury of the storm smote us, the wind nearly pinning us to the rocks; lightning and thunder now came simultaneously, flash following flash so closely that the alternate brilliance and blackness left us almost blinded; rain, hail, and snow lashed us in turn. Our ice axes buzzed with blue fans of flame up to three inches in length for nearly three hours. A dancing fringe of flame around the brim of my hat made a beacon of me when the storm was not too thick, the flame of my ice ax being of less guidance to the others because jutting rocks around us glowed with similar weird lights. The snow on our clothing shone with ghostly light . . .

"The storm showed no signs of abating, so we went on down, dropping from rock to rock in a way we would not have dared in broad daylight."

At their bivouac, which they reached at 2:30 A.M., water was pouring over their provisions and equipment. A kettle had caught four inches of rain. There they shivered under a tarpaulin until daylight, when they descended the Franklin Glacier to their base camp, which was reached thirty-nine sleepless hours after the start of the climb.

Another of that summer's many storms continued without interruption for a week—or, to be exact, six days and seven nights.

Back again in 1928, the Mundays reached the snow summit of Waddington, elevation approximately thirteen thousand two hundred feet. Still separating them from success was a notch four hundred feet deep in the knife-edged ridge; beyond rose the final rock tower, a spire dropping at a frightful angle three thousand feet to the western glaciers, which in turn cascaded ten thousand feet down toward the Pacific. "No mountain yet attempted in Canada," Munday decided, "has such a well-guarded summit." It was evening when they topped the snow summit, and there was nothing to do but to retrace their steps.

In 1933 Mr. and Mrs. Munday, Henry S. Hall, of Boston, the American Alpine Club secretary, and Hans Fuhrer, a Swiss guide who had adopted the Canadian Rockies, joined forces. It was hoped that the combination of the several abilities that had conquered in the Alps, the Andes, the Caucasus, and the Canadian and American Rockies, would be too much for the Coast Range. The party came into the region from the Homathko Valley, devoting most of the time to reconnaissance. The result of their only attempt on Waddington was the first ascent of Mount Combatant, third highest peak of the region, on the summit of which they spent the night. It was a mild evening, for the temperature dropped only to twenty-two degrees. The summit tower of their intended goal, just across from Mount Combatant, appeared to them more impossible than ever. The most likely approach seemed to be over the snow summit.

With this thought in mind, the same party was on that summit just thirteen months later. It was two o'clock in the afternoon. The weather was still perfect after six days without storm. Nevertheless, an hour later they were starting back to their camp, having deliberately passed up the peak in good weather, simply feeling, as Hall expressed it, that they wished to live longer.

The year 1934 brought two other attempts; one outstandingly fine, the other a tragedy.

In the first party Roger and Ferris Neave, Campbell Secord, and Arthur Davidson (packing), all young men of Winnipeg, spent nineteen days between the Homathko Valley and their base camp, relaying eighty-pound packs, even constructing a bridge across Nude Creek, where the white water of the "creek" was seventy-five feet from bank to bank. From base camp the Neaves and Secord, with only a sleeping bag for shelter, pushed on up the Tiedemann glacier, spending four nights out in the open en route. When on the fifth day one of the storms suddenly cleared in the afternoon, they started for the peak, prepared to climb all night. Unfortunately the respite was brief, for a driving snowstorm stopped them at the base of the rock tower. They returned to the sleeping bag late that evening.

Next morning, they started again in the storm and for ten hours they fought a good battle, scraping holds on the snow-covered ledges, chipping them on the ice-glazed cliffs of the tower. With mitts and ropes frozen stiff, they forged on, using a route that would at least have been very difficult in perfect weather. Snow fell continually. Finally only five hundred feet separated them from the cherished objective, but that five hundred feet was far worse than the distance already covered; their time was up, and they turned back. In spite of rushed rappels it was dark when they reached the glacier—so dark that Ferris Neave didn't know he had reached the bergschrund until part of its upper lip broke under his foot and dropped far into the darkness. Having thus found it, the men spent the night in an ice cave hung on the upper wall. With the return of daylight they descended to the now completely buried sleeping bag, over which snow was still falling. Their sleeping bag became thoroughly soaked and the danger from avalanches increased. They retreated.

In the fair weather just preceding the storm that repulsed the Winnipeg party, and unaware of that party's presence in the region, Alec Dalgleish, Eric Brooks, Neal Carter, and Alan Lambert of Vancouver had come up the Franklin Glacier, to attempt Waddington from the southwest. Leaving Icefall Point late on June 25, they traveled through the night and climbed from the Buckler Glacier to a steep rock buttress by nine the next morning. Dalgleish, after a fifty-foot lead, was stopped. Lambert unroped and climbed up to discuss the chance of continuing. They decided to retreat and he climbed back down. Dalgleish descended to within thirty feet above the others. Suddenly, with no cry or exclamation, he fell. Brooks pulled in some of the slack rope over a rock belay before the terrific jerk of the fifty-foot fall nearly upset him. He held on, but the taut rope, sliding down a sharp edge of rock, was severed. Dalgleish fell seven hundred feet further down the snow slope. Had Dalgleish not been roped, Carter later said, he might have fallen clear of the rock to the snow, and the fatal pendulum-swing against the gully wall, occurring when the rope suddenly became taut, would have been averted. But the mountain gave no odds. A man perhaps slightly fatigued, an unguarded moment, and tragedy followed swiftly.

These are highlights of the story of the "Mountain of Mystery" that led us to form a Sierra Club expedition to Waddington. Bestor Robinson, Sierra Club director and member of the American Alpine Club, the first of our group attracted by the mountain, was naturally enough the leader. He combined desire, drive, and stamina with experience in many North American ranges and the Alps, as well as a wife and four youngsters, thoughts of whom would certainly dispel any tendencies toward reckless climbing—by himself, or the rest of us. Richard Leonard, Jules Eichorn, Robert Ratcliff, Jack Riegelhuth, Don Woods, and I were all Sierra Club members. We welcomed William F. ("Farnie") Loomis from the Harvard Mountaineering Club.

Five of us, including me, had not yet set foot on a major glacier. But then, Waddington had ten times defeated those who understood glacier problems. The base of the peak had been attained often, but whenever the weather had permitted further attack it had been the final tower—a rock-climb—that had cooled the ardor of the attempt. We felt we were strong on rock-climbing, of a technical sort not yet used to advantage on Waddington. It involved the use of rope, piton, carabiner, and a special love of standing upon next to nothing. We learned rock-climbing during several years' training in the Sierra and various rock parks in the vicinity of San Francisco and Boston. What snow- and ice-craft we knew came from our skiing, and mountaineering literature.

Climaxing months of preparation, we drove in three well-loaded automobiles the twelve hundred miles to Vancouver, and on June 24 hurried through last-minute purchases, and boarded two seaplanes that were to save ninety-seven percent of the time ordinarily required for the round trip by steamer to Knight Inlet.

For what finer introduction to this northland realm of forested ranges and meandering fjords could one ask than to fly above the island patterns of the Inland Passage? The vast forest domain, broken only by scattered lakes, stretched from snowline to surf, covering even cliffs, where scattered ledges sustained the towering and tenacious spruce and fir. Far below, on waters burnished by the afternoon sun, tugs had forests in tow—raft after massive raft of immense logs, bound for mills to the south. In untouched stands on the rugged slopes, new growth struggled through mossy, vine-wreathed remains of trees that once had been new. In just such forest we, too, would soon be struggling.

Finally, almost touching the cloud ceiling that hid the high peaks from view, the planes rushed through a narrow pass, where on either side forested summits peered in the windows. Ahead was Knight Inlet, its winding gorge flooded with smooth, green water. Dropping four thousand feet in a swift descent, we skimmed just above the surface, close to colorful cliffs and dashing cascades, for the thirty miles to the head of the inlet. At the rapidly growing delta of the Franklin and Kliniklini rivers, we joined the first plane, already unloading. We stripped below the waist to get ourselves and provisions ashore. As Dick Leonard put it, our climb began two feet below sea level as we waded ashore. The Franklin River's reputed thirty-three degrees gave us a chilly reception. With everything ashore, less than three hours after they had been loaded, we watched the planes gather speed, rise with dripping pontoons, and wheel southward to vanish into the distance. For a while the drone of the motors lingered, then that was gone, and the silence of a remote wilderness descended about us.

Our sleep was broken often in the strange surroundings, especially by the ubiquitous and all-too-easily-felt no-see-ums, that have all the talents of mosquitos and are too small to be impeded by mosquito netting. We started early up the river. Let no more be said of the luxuriance, the devil's club and lesser undergrowth, and the many-tiered disintegrating down-timber of the British Columbia rain forest than that our six-mile struggle through the forest with the sixty- to ninety-pound packs lasted thirteen hours. Our speed was not seriously below average, ours was the easiest approach to Waddington, and we had gained only five hundred feet in elevation. The rock-littered terminus of the thirty-mile-long Franklin Glacier was in sight, so close above our camp that the nearby trees had not matured since the retreating glacier had bared their sustaining soil. Slightly upstream the canyon floor and the lower four hundred feet of its walls were unforested, evidence of a great decrease in the glacier's volume within a generation.

All the next day we climbed the glacier, pausing often to examine more closely the many features of the glacier–moraines, sand-cones, glacier-tables, crevasses, and surface streams. Of these the streams seemed especially interesting. Some acquire considerable volume, thereby eroding canyons in the ice. Others may slip from sight for short distances to reappear below, leap in fascinating waterfalls, pause in enchanting cobalt-blue lakelets–unbelievably blue; but very few streams reach the end of the glacier on the surface, roaring instead down circular moulins, or glacial mills, to disappear into shadowy depths. Many moulins were abandoned; new upstream crevasses intercepted the torrents that carved them. What an adventure it would be to work one's way down their icy walls, to explore the midnight-blue caverns of the heart of the glacier! And now and then, from far below, many hundred feet beneath the surface, may be heard the distant rumble of the gathering Franklin River, as it rushes down to meet the light of day.

Proceeding up the glacier we met our first crevasses in an outside lane, where the glacier rounded a corner. Keeping to the inside we found the surface a veritable boulevard, the heavy packs alone slowing our pace. At its junction with the Confederation Glacier, the Franklin was broken into a labyrinth of crevasses, largely parallel in direction, separating islands of ice only too rarely connected. The snow here had not melted completely, and we roped up. The leader, sounding with his ice ax, determined where the innocent-looking snow patches concealed crevasses. The rest of us followed exactly in his footsteps. Now and then a slight difference in pounds of man per square inch of boot would mean that someone would drop in to his knee or hip, through a snow-bridge over which the others had passed securely. Such incidents were amusing, thanks to our prompt and proper use of the rope.

When we passed the junction it was evening, with just enough twilight for our brief climb up the lateral moraine to a forest, lakelet, and grassy campsite. We cooked over open fires, demonstrating our various skills in fire and fireplace building, then quietly relaxed on heather beds to gaze at the stars. This evening was doubly enjoyed, for we knew others like it were soon to be denied. Future cooking would be on tiny kerosene-burning Primus stoves, which would either go or wouldn't, leaving no chance for argument or competition. The stars couldn't last for long. We had all read enough about Waddington weather to know that.

The third day from the beach was a light one, bringing us to the main icefall, where the Franklin, thousands of feet in depth, cascades nearly one thousand feet in a wild confusion of chasms and tottering towers of blue ice. Here further progress on the glacier, if possible, would have been too hazardous, so we left it. We chose a route up the northwest side of the canyon to Icefall Point, a low ridge the glacier sweeps around into the gorge we had ascended. Here, at timberline, would be our base camp; food and equipment would be left there for subsequent use. The next day was intended to take us high into clouds that hovered over the Dais Glacier, obscuring Waddington, to a high climbing camp just under the final cliffs.

Instead it brought a continuation of the wet snow and rain brought in early the night before by a southerly wind that swept across the icefall. It blurred the distant peaks, engulfed them in a dreary gray, until, in final conspiracy, darkness joined the dripping clouds and drove us in for shelter that was soon saturated—tents, sleeping bags, and clothing alike. Our waterproofing, we explained to ourselves, was designed for the freezing temperature and dry snow of higher altitudes. Rationalization afforded us little comfort.

Our itinerary called for relaying of supplies during bad weather, so back we went to Knight Inlet. Jules Eichorn, with a bruised hip, remained with Don Woods to take care of camp, particularly to dry things out. The rest of us returned the twenty miles to the beach that day, thoroughly soaked by incessant rain. The forest was, if anything, more soaked than we were, and it took the combined wet-woodcraft of all six of us to convert a portion of the dripping forest into a comfortable night's accommodation. A *zeltsack* (a large sheet of waterproofing for emergency bivouacs) made a fine lean-to. A few of us knew where tinder hides during rains, and with this to dry and ignite the wet wood, we had a blazing fire under way. Fire, health, and song weathered the storm, but we wondered about the future. No firewood grows on the upper Franklin Glacier.

Three days later we were all at Icefall Point again, ready for a ten-day attack on the peak. The weather gods took their cue, and another southerly gale swept across the region. This second snowfall was milder. While it continued we moved half the supplies up the glacier. Icefall Camp, with its struggling pioneer trees that had anchored our tents, was behind us. We entered an arctic realm of rock and ice, where winter and Waddington rule undisputed. The storm quietly ended. Through its last flurries we could glimpse the mountain, a giant of ice and rock towering eight thousand feet above us. The lesser peaks, Mounts Cavalier, Jester, Squire, and Halberdier, seemed to bow in homage to its majesty. We, thanks to the weight of the packs, bowed too as we turned up the Dais Glacier. A mile and a half high we decided to camp. The site was secure and sheltered, free of the deteriorating stress that plagues high, exposed campsites.

First we packed down the snow on the area for the tents, then sounded for nearby crevasses and marked them with warning flags. Duralumin pegs and ice ax poles held up our quadrangle of four-by-five-by-seven-foot tents, their entrance flaps all facing a central court. Ropes, food, and utensils went into one tent. On the floors of the others we placed extra waterproofing, then double sleeping bags and personal belongings, and finally Bestor Robinson and Bob Ratcliff in one, Dick Leonard, Jules Eichorn, and Jack Riegelhuth in the second, Farnie Loomis, Don Woods, and me in the third. I recall no great excess of enclosed space for either turning or breathing. The theory was that anyone who was tired enough would sleep anyway. The theory was applied and worked.

July 3 marked our first attempt on the mountain. At 3:00 A.M. we awoke to find the sky clear. Hurriedly we breakfasted and collapsed the tents and started up the Dais Glacier, fully equipped to have two groups attempt two routes simultaneously, each prepared to spend a night high on the mountain in an emergency. Progress was rapid; the tricouni nails on our boots bit well into the icy crust as we climbed the icefall of the Epaulette Glacier that dropped three thousand feet from the foot of Waddington's tremendous south face. The rope, our lifeguard when we crossed the snow-bridges over crevasses, comforted us as we crawled or squirmed across frail arches, especially when just three or four feet of snow separated us from the deep, shadowy caverns beneath.

We advanced to the highest crevasses on the glacier—the bergschrund; and, using a snow-bridge formed by repeated avalanches, climbed above the typically overhanging upper lip. We formed two ropes: Jules, Bestor, and Dick on the first; Jack, Farnie, and I on the other. We proceeded together a short distance, prepared to take separate routes up the face. The first rope was to try the steep two-thousand-foot face leading directly to the summit; the second was to go further southwest to a steep four-hundred-foot snow couloir cut by avalanches' erosion, then traverse Waddington's south arête.

The weather moved first. Borne by a freezing gale, clouds had been advancing from the Pacific, long since obscuring the lower Franklin Canyon. Now heavy mists enshrouded us, snow began to fall, visibility dropped to nothing. Considering it futile to attempt so difficult a climb without at least knowing where we were headed, we turned around; nor did we regret the decision to retreat. Back in camp it snowed all that Wednesday night, all day Thursday, and by Friday evening, when the storm abated, the uninterrupted fifty-four-hour fall had deposited new snow to a depth of two feet in the higher regions. The Fourth of July had come and passed, celebrated by our unfurling a small American flag from the top tent pole. We had hoped to sail it on the peak that day.

If the snowy days were warm, the nights were certainly not so; and we several times blessed the heat-conserving system of sleeping two and three in one sleeping bag. As we relaxed upon our beds of ice, waiting for sleep to follow lethargy, there was much to discuss and sing about, so that our diminutive quadrangle of tents in the midst of an immense and bleak snowy waste hummed contentedly. Robinson knew several of the poems of Robert W. Service, and in low, dramatic inflection would repeat these stories of the far north, of shootings and cremations, which could hardly have found better setting.

Mount Waddington, six thousand feet above, was not seen for two days. Then on the second of the stormy evenings, as we were quieting down to the discussion stage, Eichorn happened still to be outside. His sudden cry, "Say! Look at it now!" rudely invaded our torpor, and sounded too sincere to be disregarded. We found him gazing high into the clouds, at a chance aperture in the cloud ceiling. Gleaming far above us, in an evanescent aura of sunset rosy-amber, was the very summit, a marvel of delicate and warm color that tinged the new snow and cold, untrodden stone. With the base obscured by cloud and shadow, it seemed ethereally detached from the earth, as unassailable as a vision. It vanished as we watched, fading before the color was gone behind the gossamer curtains of mist and gray enveloping flurries of snow. We had crawled out reluctant, but did not regret having done so. The glimpse itself had been brief, but its splendor epitomized our reasons for being there. This was not a forsaken wasteland; it was an earthly haven for the spirit of roving; and whether the peak was climbed or not we knew that sometime we would have to come back.

We scanned the south face with binoculars. Up that terrific cliff there were still two routes that might go, if enough of the new snow would only clear. It was still worth another try, particularly since we could not afford to wait for a moderate stretch of fair weather. Early on the morning of July 7, four days after the first attempt, the second was under way. The recent snow had not consolidated, and was crusted so superficially that on each step, just as there appeared to be enough support for a forward thrust of the foot, the crust would collapse, and we would break through nearly to our knees. Later, on the forty-degree snow slope below the chosen four-hundred-foot couloir, we sank to our hips. Troubles had just begun. As we crossed the bergschrund an almost continuous avalanche poured from a couloir to our right, and we were not completely reassured by the deduction that our couloir, being much the shorter, did not offer as excellent an avalanche source. The angle of its slopes neared fifty degrees, and the recent snow lay loosely over old snow packed to the consistency of ice.

This demanded the tedious work of cutting steps through the surface layer into the safe snow beneath, instead of merely kicking in with the toes, perhaps to start a disastrous surface peel.

Eichorn, in the lead, cut steps with veteran rapidity; but even rapid step-cutting is slow progress. Cautiously belaying around the ice axes, and with but one man moving at a time, we followed Jules's zigzag course up the couloir. Our ropes were in the order of the first attempt, with Don Woods and Bob Ratcliff in support. Again we were prepared to push forward, fully equipped, on two fronts. We reached the top of the couloir, Jules drove a piton into a crack, snapped in both a carabiner and the rope with which Bestor was belaying him, led up a delicate pitch to steep rock covered with thin ice, climbed to a sloping, snow-covered ledge, drove in another piton, and anchored himself. Bestor and Dick were belayed up to him in turn. Leading the second rope I came up to them. It was not yet time to diverge on two routes.

Dick changed lead with Jules, advanced upward, and was placing his second piton when a particularly loud crash and shower of icicles overhead changed a mild concern to tense anxiety. The crash was merely a repetition of the occurrence of the past hour, during which the sun, now overhead, had melted and released huge sheets of ice from the rock a thousand feet above, sending fragments showering and ricocheting around us. It was apparent that the previous day's thaw and subsequent night's chill had covered the face with more ice that would soon be falling. We were in one of the most obvious paths, and the increasing frequency of discharge was demanding more than mere unrelaxing alertness. If it were only possible to get out of the line of fire we could continue. To our left the route ran into a hopeless face; to the right–our intended egress in reconnaissance–all ledges sloped steeply outward, each covered with loose new snow to a depth of from two to three feet, ever ready to launch itself over the five-hundred-foot face to the glacier below. To clear off holds on all these ledges and still have time to approach the summit was a remote possibility, even if the remainder of the route chanced to be in perfect condition. To advance would mean a night spent somewhere on the face, with zeltsacks, stoves, and food for protection. But would that protection afford ample margin of safety against storm? This question was important, for clouds were forming again. Clouds, clouds! Would they never leave? Might we not trust our existence to luck and continue? Again the vote was to retreat.

The route by which we must return was now less safe than the ledge upon which we stood. The sun was softening the already unstable surface snow in the couloir, and an avalanche there was imminent. We descended with all possible speed compatible with safety, roping down the difficult higher portion, "fielding" from there down: Dick would glissade down the slope, braking his speed with his ice ax. The other two belayed around their buried axes until all the rope was out. Then Dick, anchoring, would belay Jules in the same procedure with Bestor's assistance. In this way one person was always moving rapidly, yet safely. We hurried down, the rattling of ice and loosened rock becoming steadily more ominous. In the couloirs on either side avalanches hissed down, to drop with a deep thudding roll to the lower lips of the bergschrunds beneath. Quickly roping down over our own 'schrund we belayed Bestor as he jumped, and were soon out on the open, gradual, safer slopes.

Waddington had displayed a few simple defensive weapons, and they had been quite enough. We were immensely relieved as we stepped back out of range. Two attempts, aptly armed with strategy and equipment, had failed. And we had hardly touched the rock.

Bombardment of the south face by falling rock and ice continued to demonstrate forcefully that a route up the face, until cleared of both snow and ice, was out of the question. There was little chance that we would see the three or more successive fair days required to clear it. Our last chance was to climb the snow summit. Just below its peak, high on the snow terrace above the hanging Angel Glacier, where Munday, Hall, and Fuhrer had declined further attempt, we must camp and push on.

That night, back at Dais Glacier Camp, the barometer fell sharply; after midnight snow was again swirling down on our little tents. By morning there were eight inches of new snow, and the fall continued methodically until nightfall. A perfect day followed. We sat on a rocky sun-porch just above the camp, drying things out, noticing how the progress of the sun across the sky was marked by avalanches. Only the shadows could delay the loosening of the new snow masses from the peaks around us at the rate of a slide every few minutes. The shadows failed that night. Enormous masses of snow and ice lay piled below the thousand-foot tracks from which loud thundering startled us.

At five o'clock on the morning of July 10 we began moving camp to the Angel Glacier snow terrace. The weather was good, but morning cirrus clouds foretold bad weather. Consequently, we left tiny flags to mark our course among the crevasses and seracs of the north icefall of the Dais. Too soon the sun reached the slopes, proceeding to transform the slight crust to corn snow—a wet, large-grained variety with dangerously little cohesion. We at first sank to our knees, and later, as the slope steepened, almost to the hips, a tremendous waste of the energy our ultimate attack on the rock tower would require. Here was a real test for our duralumin snowshoes, and they worked. The metal edges cut into the slope and we rarely sank much over a foot. With little interruption we advanced to the ridge crest, and paused to melt snow and make tea in a spot sheltered from the fresh southerly wind.

A few steps further along the ridge we could look for the first time into the labyrinth of deep glacier-floored canyons of the northern and eastern approaches. Toward the snow summit the ridge was truly Himalayan in character. Snow, hundreds of feet of it, had piled on this leeward side, there to be transformed into glacier by its own tremendous weight. All these glaciers were the progeny of the ever-advancing clouds that had come in from the Pacific, had settled on the range, to drop their snow burden for uninterrupted centuries. The snow, compacted into crystal ice, still at least appeared to be clouds, slipping down the range slopes, slowly creeping through the canyons, toward the ancestral waters of the Pacific. Our route followed a very broad shelf on the north side of the ridge. Above it were the steep, heavily mantled, deeply crevassed slopes that had launched the devastating ice avalanches. We wound our way through their massive debris blocks. Below its peaceful terrace the Angel Glacier formed an overhanging ice wall hundreds of feet in height. The imperceptible motion of the glacier inexorably forces this wall too far over the precipice supporting it, until the wall collapses, releasing enormous masses of ice to shatter the cliffs, and thunder down to the Scimitar Glacier, five thousand feet below. We were spared such cataclysms.

We found a level spot partly protected from wind and least exposed to avalanches. Bestor went ahead in search of a better site but found none. Here we pitched the highest camp ever established in the Provinces. Bestor's aneroid barometer read 12,550 feet. The snow summit, however, determined as 13,200 feet by comparison with the triangulated altitude of the rock tower, was still 1,000 feet above us. The aneroid readings were either high, the barometric pressure low, or, as suggested by the persistent readings of Munday and Hall, the elevations of the region are higher than shown. The triangulation stations were twenty to twenty-five miles distant, and employed by J. T. Underhill in a survey of the Klinaklini River Valley in 1927, at which time an exact height of Waddington was of minor importance.

At 6:00 P.M. Bestor, Jules, Farnie, Don, and I set out on snowshoes for the snow summit. Dick, Bob, and Jack stayed behind to cope with camp, fully realizing that an expected turn in the weather might prevent another ascent in the morning. Dick deserved more than anyone else to go to the highest point the expedition was to reach. His effort and ingenuity had been outstanding from the expedition's earliest plans until now. He offered to remain behind.

For two hours, and at top speed, the rest of us plodded upward through the wintry powder snow. Finally the summit was just above us, its slope so steep and windswept that we forsook snowshoes and brought the ice axes into play. Eichorn led, and as he cut up over the final 'schrund we could begin to appreciate the airiness of our position, rather sensing what was to come. As he reached the top he exclaimed, "My God, look at that!"

We quickened our steps. Soon our conquest of the snow summit appeared insignificant in comparison. Our insecure footing of wind-packed snow fell away abruptly on all sides of us; and far below, from one of the most severe sides, arose a narrow knife-edge of rock, smothered everywhere under several feet of ice-feathers, sublimed from the winds of the north Pacific. Rising from the glacier-filled cirques, thousands of feet below on either side, were the slopes of this knife-edge, terrifically steep and covered with ice. All this was in shadow, for the sun, at eight o'clock, was very low. Towering into the evening alpenglow was the awe-inspiring culmination of it all—austere, untouchable, defiant, brooding over the tempest of a surging sea of clouds closing in beneath us. Its long and pointed shadow extended far toward the southeast, witness to the actuality of what otherwise seemed unreal.

It was late, and the rising wind, well below freezing, urged that we hurriedly conclude all photography and reconnaissance. Before we started down a possible hope of success appeared. Fixed ropes could be left to the notch below us after we had roped down. Then, with a full day, with full reserve strength, with the safeguard of many pitons, there was hope. From our position the rock tower involved the ascent of no more than five hundred feet of arête, protected by overhangs and ice, but apparently of much less severity in average angle than Yosemite Valley's two Cathedral Spires, up which Bestor, Dick, and Jules had found the routes.

That evening back in camp we cooked our supper in the tents (try three men, a Primus stove, and victuals in a four-by-five-by-seven-foot tent sometime), and slipped into the sleeping bags for a short rest, preparatory to the final try. Out in the night the wind dropped its temperature and picked up speed. The swirl of clouds from below rose to join forces, and a blizzard was upon us. Driving particles of snow found every aperture in the tents and drifted in. The gale, sweeping down from the snowfields above, snapped and cracked the fabric until it seemed that the frail sheets of cotton and balloon silk would shred at the next stress. Constant anxiety forbade sleep. To be shorn of protection in such a storm would have been desperate. The Mundays and Hall had been hard put when a storm ruined their tents at seven thousand feet. We were a mile higher.

Fortunately those who had set up the camp had known what they were doing. The duralumin tent pegs had been pressed deeply into packed snow, and enough slack had been left in the ropes to permit flapping, and still to prevent tearing. With dawn the wind had died and it was snowing quietly. Dick, Bob, and Jack started after a quick breakfast, hoping that, while the rock tower was now out of the question, they might at least reach the snow summit. Our tracks of the night before had been of the diameter of our snowshoes, and nearly a foot deep. There was no sign of them, and visibility in the heavy snowfall was so poor that Jack on his end of the rope could barely see Dick on the other. It was still possible to continue; but Dick, foreseeing that this heavy new fall would very shortly mean very serious avalanche danger on our route back to the Dais Glacier, suggested that the attempt be abandoned at once.

As we retraced the course of our old but now entirely obscured footprints, we were thankful for the little red flags that now guided so faithfully through the obscurity, down across the Angel Glacier shelf, back up to the ridge crest. Here we found that the storm had actually not subsided, but that the wind had merely shifted from south to west; for a blast of snow particles met us, stinging faces, coating our beards with ice. The men ahead and behind were just vague shadows. Someone found the spot where we had sipped tea the day before, marked by a flag as the place to turn down into the couloir, but otherwise a mere eddy in the horizontal swirl of snow. Down we turned, fielding when necessary, keeping close to the rock walls when the avalanche exposure was too great. We made good time, only to lose it below with the route. Too soon we headed for the open glacier, suddenly to be stopped by the precipitous upper lip of a broad crevasse. Up again, around, and down to the west, the snow now so soft that a downward thrust of a snowshoe would loosen a tiny avalanche that would slide several feet—tiny, but of ill omen. As we traversed one steep slope we used particular care to avoid too great a severance of the surface tension of the snow. Footsteps had to be far apart, and we followed the leader's with precision.

As we dropped below the storm a long-awaited red flag appeared ahead, marking the last of the blind crevasses. A few more minutes found us seated at our campsite, unroped, rubbing circulation back into frost-numbed feet, then raiding the commissary.

We were now in full retreat, and Waddington relented, giving us two days of cloudless skies. Back to Icefall Point and trees; down the mighty Franklin, whose source was now so familiar; into the forest, where serenity quieted our disappointment. This was a region of wonders other than mere unclimbed peaks.

At the beach July 14 dawned, the third of the cloudless days. Almost before we had finished breakfast a distant drone announced the return of our planes. Soon they were circling overhead, where the pilots saw the smoke from our fire, and landed at the edge of the delta. Just before we were whisked southward to Vancouver, to enormous prepared meals, and to friends, the planes swung high above the still water of Knight Inlet. Revealed to the northeast was Mystery Mountain, still challenging and defiant, and surely a monarch of the myriad peaks, thin icy mantles scintillating in the sun, that towered into the British Columbia sky.

Thus ended what turned out to be just another attempt on Waddington. Our story yields no climax. It is unfinished. We may liken these several attempts to the waves that beat against a rock shore. They rise in a grand crescendo of aspiration, only to break in futility. But finally the waves win.

Sand.

***Dave Brower's Notes, unpublished,* 1935**

The final paragraph was the shortest I would ever write, or should I say overwrite. I liked it very much at the time. A little melodrama never hurt anyone. Besides, to me at that time, a peak that had been climbed would rate, on a scale of one to ten, hardly more than a one. An unclimbed peak, especially if many attempts on it had failed, rated the full ten.

Whenever the weather permits and a commercial airliner flies me anywhere near Mount Waddington, I look hard for an old if somewhat hostile friend. From what others tell about the Franklin River approach and the devastated forests, destroyed fisheries, and retreating glacier, I'll settle for viewing Mystery Mountain from afar, and urging national park protection for what is left.

Mount Waddington remained a ten after our failure to climb it in 1935, and after the 1936 Sierra Club expedition repeated our failure. Bill House and Fritz Weisner, American Alpine Club climbers from the east, gave the Sierra Club men first chance, then dared climb an ice couloir the Sierrans thought was too fraught with objective danger—the avalanches, falling rock, and falling ice the mountain may unleash. It becomes subjective danger when you ask for it by deliberately getting in the way. Bill and Fritz did and made the first ascent, brilliantly.

Beyond the Skiways

It Was After My Summer excitement on Mount Waddington that Bunte Brothers finally wearied of my wanderings. The candy business wasn't doing too well anyway. My first attempt to find other work succeeded. There was a Moon Hopkins calculating and printing machine in the accounting department of the Yosemite Park & Curry Company, and if I could live in Yosemite Valley while operating it, why not? The work was dull but Yosemite certainly was not. And Waddington's glaciers helped me visualize and understand the work of the Sierra glaciers that had given Yosemite Valley its magnificence.

While I was working in the accounting office there was an accident on Half Dome. The Yosemite rangers had a difficult time in the rescue effort. Oliver Kehrlein, who provided some public-relations service for the YP&C Co., later told the National Park Service that they could have saved themselves a lot of trouble if they had called on Dave Brower's knowledge of rock-climbing to help in the rescue. The Park Service did not respond, but Oliver found others who would. He asked me: "Do you want to keep

David Brower, Kenneth Adam, Kenneth Davis, Hervey Voge, 1937, first winter ascent of Mount Clark, Yosemite. Photograph with self-timer by by David R. Brower.

running that machine in the accounting department, or are you ready for a real challenge? The company is looking for a new publicity manager."

I thought I was ready. Stanley Plumb, the advertising manager, became my boss. He was anxious to have me photograph Yosemite visitors who had society-page potential with Half Dome in the background. The photograph and brief story were to go to the visitor's local paper. This would help increase travel to Yosemite and improve the company's bottom line.

There were two problems. First, I was more interested in photographing scenery than people. On my initial mission, covering visitors on a horseback ride and outdoor breakfast, I forgot to pull the slide on the

Graflex I had never used before and ended up with nothing. I did better with a Rolleiflex and still better with a Zeiss Super Ikonta B I bought when I failed to persuade the company to buy one. Second, I was not anxious to see Yosemite more crowded than it already was, and my heart was not in my work. If the eminent visitors had shown interest in climbing Yosemite's cliffs, it would have been different. I found it no problem, however, to go skiing at Badger Pass every day in winter, looking for a chance to photograph notables or anyone else on the ski slopes.

Marian Moreing was my loyal supporter in the effort to get out many of the photo-stories Stanley Plumb wanted, but not enough went out. Stories about the valley, its High Sierra, Yosemite glaciers, and Yosemite history were more interesting than accounts of visitors. Ansel Adams patiently shared my troubles. I got to know him very well because it was his photographs we used when we really wanted people to know what the valley was all about.

The best of my photographs of visiting notables in Yosemite was of Helen Hayes, smiling as she pointed out a Yosemite cliff to her daughter. It was a beautiful print, with all the right values in it. Why? Because Ansel Adams made the print, getting everything there was in it out of my negative.

Stanley Plumb, his patience exhausted, let me know in October 1937 that my position had been discontinued. He helped me find interim odd jobs, and brought me back for the summer of 1938 to sell tickets for Yosemite trips in Camp Curry and occasionally to provide the narration for valley tours. There were no public-address systems on the buses so I was able to develop voice and command that would eventually prove to be valuable in my duties in the U.S. Mountain Troops. Only once did my voice give out on a valley tour. It was probably a relief to the tourists, who thereupon could look at the scenery without having to hear about it, especially about all the places people had climbed that I was more interested in than they were.

Between Waddington and Shiprock I was privileged to spend all but a few winter days on skis, for the most part on the slopes at Badger Pass in Yosemite. It was part of my work. I broke the monotony of it "beyond the skiways," the title of an article I wrote for the 1938 *Sierra Club Bulletin*.

"SKI-MOUNTAINEERING" IS A CUMBERSOME TERM, but no other term so aptly describes the grand sport that results when skiing and mountaineering are combined. The ski-mountaineer's recipe, complex but not exacting, is this: find out how to handle skis reasonably well, gather winter equipment together, learn how to use it, find some trusted friends to carry most of it, then try to beard Old Man Winter in his den—out beyond the skiways. Out there one will find the timberline country, where temperatures are more invigorating, where snows are persistently drier and more powdery, where broad open slopes are tracked only by one's chosen friends, where surroundings are rugged, yet marvelously adapted to ski-mountaineering. In such terrain even the most blasé of resort skiers have been temporarily overcome with reverence. They have learned that the christy is more than a matter of accurately synchronizing the advance of the inside ski and the outside shoulder; it is a symbol of ski control that broadens winter horizons.

Perhaps a few tales of recent winter exploits will suggest how ski-mountaineering, with proper preparation, is really an inimitable way to enjoy the Sierra snows.

Mount Lyell

Mount Lyell, highest peak in Yosemite National Park, has been climbed without great difficulty during summer months by hundreds of people; but until March 1936 the peak had remained inviolate in winter. Three attempts had failed. In 1934 a party was driven to retreat by a blizzard, after having reached a twelve-thousand-four-hundred-foot pass at the headwaters of the Maclure Fork of the Merced. A year later an attempt was stopped short of this point by a sub-zero, fair-weather blizzard of wind-whipped powder snow. A third attempt was made in January 1936, but again the weather guarded the peak with nine successive days of storm.

February 29, 1936, at Happy Isles, in Yosemite Valley, Bestor Robinson, Lewis F. Clark, Boynton S. ("Bunco") Kaiser, Einar Nilsson, and I started the fourth attempt. With fifty-pound packs containing sleeping bags, tents, rope, ice axes, emergency equipment, food, and clothing, we followed the course of the Merced Canyon trail to Merced Lake ranger station. The next night, in a rising wind, we established high camp at "Hell Hole"—nearly two thousand feet above Bernice Lake and timberline. Camping on snow, we again discovered, had pleasures all its own.

By the time sleeping bags, knapsacks, and men had been piled inside the two tiny tents the congestion was quite cozy. Sole evidence of the wind outside was the powder that sifted through every available aperture, to the syncopated accompaniment of flapping tent fabric. Having snow inside was an advantage, since it was no longer necessary to reach outside to get it for melting over our Primus stoves. Bestor, Lewis, and Bunco prepared the soup on their stove. Einar and I improvised an entrée of chocolate, cheese, and oatmeal—Bestor had left the macaroni at Merced Lake. With everything ready, dinner was served: a momentary lull in the gale was awaited, tent flaps were unzipped, victuals passed frantically so that we could rezip before the next snow-laden gust. The wind usually won.

By morning the wind had developed into a hurricane. Our next game, upon leaving camp, was to see who could stand up longest. On one occasion Lewis was upset by an errant gust, although he had braced against it with ski poles. Long snow-banners were torn from ridges and peaks to be flung far to leeward, and to avoid following suit while crossing the first spur of Mount Maclure, we dismounted and crawled, digging in hands and toes for anchorage. Bestor had forecast summit weather in which it would be possible to hold up a match and watch it burn!

Four hours later we were on the summit of Mount Lyell, with Bestor doing just that. We had left the wind far below the Lyell Glacier bergschrund, and in comparative comfort our rope of five had followed Bunco's lead up the final sixty-five-degree pitch of snow and rock. As we settled down for a summit siesta the Sierra Nevada, from the Tuolumne to the Kaweahs, was revealed. We could now understand why Spanish explorers had called this "One Great Snowy Range of Mountains." The entire range had an alpine aspect that we had never fully appreciated in forest-belt ski country. Even after the seven-thousand-foot descent in afternoon and moonlight to the ranger station, and the next day's nineteen-mile journey to Yosemite Valley, we were still thinking of that view—of those incomparable north slopes, powder that lasts for months, square miles without a tree, the High Sierra above timberline—winter paradise, earmarked for the ski-mountaineer.

Mount Clark

With Mount Lyell climbed, the next year found Kenneth Adam, Kenneth Davis (the rock-climbing section is overrun with Kenneths), Hervey Voge, and me looking for a new objective; accordingly, we left our snow camp on the Starr King Plateau February 21, headed for Mount Clark. Crossing the confusion of canyons in the Illilouette Basin took more time than we had anticipated, and it was quite late when we left our skis at eleven thousand feet to traverse the steep snow slope east of the summit with rope and ice ax. While waiting for Hervey to kick steps in the wind-packed powder, we contemplated the schuss into a tiny lake a thousand feet directly beneath and were relieved not to be on skis at the moment. We climbed too soon to the southeast arête, a mistake that King and Gardiner seem to have made during their dramatic first ascent in 1866. So we returned to the snow slope and traversed over snow-covered ledges to the right. A short vertical chimney, a bit of scrambling, and we were on top.

The sun was setting, and our anxiety to return to our skis before dark prevented giving due attention to the alpenglow along the Sierra crest. But perhaps nothing was lost, since to have remained would have meant losing a finer experience. We returned to our skis just in time to whip down through a scrubby timberline slalom and out upon a broad open space before the western glory had faded. For luxurious minutes our skis carried us effortlessly toward the fiery western sky. The smarting of cold wind on faces, the mad rush of air past tingling ears, the now somber peaks shooting skyward, the transition to amber and then to silver as the full moon rose and cast our racing shadows before us on the snows – these of the many sensations that whirled through our minds during that memorable descent will live longest. Details of the remaining trip back through the moonlight – shadows we thought were holes, holes we thought were shadows, the long traverse across the western cirque, the uncertainties of the route, the final arrival at our two forlorn tents, food, sleep – these are still chronologically stored in our minds. But minds have a limited capacity for chronological details. For each new detail we ask our minds to store, another is crowded out. Deep impressions are lodged more firmly. They are not easily loosened to be taken out and described. That is why accounts of ski descents never reflect satisfactorily the inward experiences of the skier.

Mount Starr King

In summer, the ascent of the dome of Starr King by either of the two usual routes is a pleasant climax to a half-day's travel on and off trails – provided one knows rope technique moderately well. In winter, the north route, covered deep with snow, while doubtless easy enough, is nevertheless full of hidden dangers. Consequently, Joe Specht and I chose the south route, drove to Mono Meadow, skied down into Illilouette Creek, then, by climbing twenty-five hundred feet, arrived on the southeast saddle of Starr King. Here a long-threatening sky greeted us with a flurry of snow. We would have to change to tennis shoes for the final friction climb, and while tennis shoes are not uncomfortable in a snowstorm, the low coefficient of friction is decidedly so. We had already waited for several sunny days to clear the south face of previously fallen snow. So prospects above were dismal. Below, the open slopes up which we had toiled looked most inviting. A few moments' run would return us to the creek before our morning tracks from Mono Meadow were obliterated. Starr King was after all a rock-climb, not a ski-mountaineering objective. The ascent would be safe enough, but another time would be better. Having observed all this, we parked our skis and started up.

The cracks and the open chimneys relied upon for tensile and cross-pressure holds in summer climbs were filled with snow, and it was necessary to find an alternative, relying on friction alone upon rock, much of which was wet as well as smooth. Arrival on the summit was more than a victory over snow and rock. I had met Joe Specht in August 1935, through mutual interest in an ascent of Starr King. We had looked at the mountain almost daily. Now, at last, we had been able to synchronize our free time to make the ascent – March 9, 1937.

The Palisades

Driven farther afield than most early-season snow-seekers, Arthur Blake, Morgan Harris, and I arrived January 5, 1938, at Glacier Lodge, on Big Pine Creek. Joined by Norman Clyde, we carried sixty-pound packs to eleven thousand feet on the North Fork, where there was promise of good skiing in the deep-powder snow.

January 8, during an attempt on the North Palisade, Norman, Morgan, and I were stopped just above the bergschrund below the U-notch. Temperature was the most troublesome difficulty, for we were in sunshine less than half an hour. Air temperature was estimated as close to zero. At the bergschrund it was necessary to change from ski boots to frozen climbing boots. We soon concluded, therefore, that to continue might mean frozen feet, as well as a long descent after dark. So we retreated, with the situation thoroughly rationalized, and enjoyed the matchless slopes of smooth, dry powder that blanketed the Palisade Glacier. A safe winter ascent from the glacier will probably require a milder temperature, full knowledge of avalanche hazards on steep faces and couloirs, complete snow- and rock-climbing equipment, including roomy, tricouni-nailed ski boots.

Mount Winchell was climbed two days later in a partial spirit of retaliation for the repulse. Norman, Morgan, and I took skis to twelve thousand nine hundred feet and continued with tricounis, rope, and ice axes up the east ridge. The entire upper arête was well exposed to sun and was quite clear. It was also fully exposed to wind, which seemed inordinately cold throughout the climb. Confirmation of the temperature came at the summit, where we noticed that water poured into a tin cup had either to be drunk at once or chipped out with a pocket knife. But, even with such a cold reception, we could enjoy the cloudless sky, the snowy expanse of peaks from Whitney to Ritter, the contrast of snowless ranges toward coast and desert.

A leisurely descent, part of which was roped, brought us to our skis. During moments of the run back to camp, when we were not fighting breakable crust or lowering skis with rope and ice ax—that is, during those moments when we glided swiftly and almost noiselessly down perfect slopes of powder—we became aware of the great improvement skis are making in mountaineering. Not very long ago, the attainment of a summit was the climax of the climber's day. Now there are two climaxes. Hail to the schuss!

***Sierra Club Bulletin*, 1938**

The winter-summit climax on North Palisade had to wait four years, when Raffi Bedayn, Fred Kelley, and I camped on the Palisade Glacier during Easter week and, minus Raffi, temporarily ill, made the first winter ascent early in spring.

Some exciting mountaineering was to intervene, and a certain amount of out-of-the-ordinary jobs as well. When the Yosemite days ended in the summer of 1938, I worked briefly in a photographic dark room, checked county records about hopgrowers' financial habits, and edited some 16-mm films, making use of what I had learned in the Yosemite publicity department. Fortunately I was still living with my parents and could get by financially, if only barely.

Early in 1939 my Sierra Club friends found part-time work for me in the Sierra Club office in Mills Tower, San Francisco. This was in part thanks to the article I had written for the *Sierra Club Bulletin* ("Far from the Madding Mules") which led Francis Farquhar to add me to the club's editorial board in 1935. I had joined the club in 1933, with Richard M. Leonard as my sponsor. Marjory Bridge, who later married Francis Farquhar, put me on my first club committee that autumn – a committee to catalog climbing localities in the San Francisco Bay Area. The committee mapped and described the climbs on Cragmont, Indian, and Pinnacle rocks, Grizzly Caves, Miraloma Rocks, the East Peak of Mount Tamalpais, and Pine Canyon on Mount Diablo, all of them sites where climbing history was being made. Altogether, the mix of climbing, mapping, writing, and after-climb dinner parties was congenial and rewarding.

Whatever else I was supposed to do in the club office, there was a battle going on and I concentrated on it. It was the campaign to establish Kings Canyon National Park. Not included in the paid duties was the opportunity to start a newsletter for the San Francisco Bay Chapter of the club. It was named *The Yodeler* by Charlotte Mauk, and I was its first editor.

The seventy-five dollars per month bought the club my full time, not just the half the budget called for. This was augmented pleasantly in the summer of 1939 when Dick Leonard added me as an assistant manager to the Sierra Club High Trip. We traveled in the region to be encompassed in Kings Canyon National Park. I borrowed a Bell & Howell 16-mm camera from Richard Stith, for whom I had worked briefly in Hollywood, and went to work on the first Sierra Club film, *Sky-Land Trails of the Kings*. The film would have a role in the park battle.

Shiprock reconnaissance party, including friends from the Colorado Mountain Club.

SHIPROCK

THAT SUMMER'S CHALLENGES in leading and filming lifted my spirit nicely, and it was soon to rise higher still. As Sierrans on Mount Waddington, we had been proved short on experience with snow and ice. Perhaps we had better get back to rock. Shiprock in 1939 rated a full ten, having turned back a dozen attempts. Shiprock sails magnificently, though at a standstill, in the New Mexico quadrant of the Four Corners, near a town of the same name on the banks of the San Juan River. The slopes of Shiprock are about as gradual as the bow of an ocean liner. Their steepness should mean that the rock is sound and stable. But their angles do not tell the truth. The rhyolitic breccia may be sound inside, but if you are climbing its outside, which is all that is available, you had better press the handholds against the ship. If you pull out on them instead, they will let you down.

On the west side of Shiprock there is a sound-rock exception, the prominent intrusion of basalt up which many parties started their attempts, but which disappears beneath the fragile breccia all too soon. On this kind of rock the early attempts crumbled.

In 1939 we had read about the most recent of those attempts in "A Piece of Bent Iron," an article in the *Saturday Evening Post* in which Robert Ormes described his near-tragedy when he fell from the North Tower of Shiprock. His life was saved by the belayer below him.

It was our turn to try the rock and avoid the fall. Bestor Robinson would write about the attempt for the *Sierra Club Bulletin,* and I was given the opportunity, if our attempt should succeed, to write all about it and submit to the *Saturday Evening Post* the story of my only climb that made its way into *Who's Who.*

I submitted it, along with some thirty photographs of the climb taken by various members of the party. The *Post* remained silent. The silence was broken by a letter from a friend in Southern California, who asked if I had any photographs of the climb that he might send along, together with a note on our climb, to someone on the *Post* staff who had asked for it. I responded with a telegram to the *Post* saying that photographs and a full-length article were already lying on someone's desk in Philadelphia, and would someone please look them up.

Shortly thereafter I received a letter from Wesley Winans Stout, editor of the *Post:*

"Do you think that you could condense this into not more than fifteen pages of the same wordage, eliminating everything except how you came to go, who you were and how you did it? If you could retell your story with a good deal more economy, we could use it as a one-pager. We should have to ask you to do this reasonably soon and to send us the Kodachromes.

"Is Bedayan an Armenian or Syrian by descent, as his name suggests? And how old was each of you?

"We shall keep the other pictures until we have heard from you."

From my Yosemite days I knew Frank J. Taylor, who had written frequently for the *Post,* and who had also collaborated with Horace Albright in the book *Oh Ranger!* What, I asked Frank, did the letter mean? Frank replied, "You've sold an article."

Untypically, I wasted little time and sent the duly condensed article, together with our eighteen good kodachromes, on November 30, adding a postscript to my letter of transmittal:

"Robinson has just received a note from Robert L. M. Underhill, an outstanding mountaineering authority of the Appalachian and American Alpine clubs, who states in regard to Shiprock ascent, 'Finest thing ever done in rock-climbing on our continent.' We are not displeased."

When the galley proof arrived I was bold enough to challenge some of the *Post*'s editing. They had changed my "New Mexico desert" to "New Mexican desert" and I commented: "This is meant more as a place-name than as an adjective modifying 'desert.' Believe should remain as is."

Then I got still bolder. The *Post* had changed my *Navajo* to *Navaho* so I wrote:

"I imagine I am only batting my head against the stone mass of typographical consistency to point out that this is a Spanish word, with the Spanish phonetic-derivation carrying over into common usage in the English. I noted the *Post*'s spelling *Navaho* in the Ormes article, but failed to find that spelling confirmed anywhere in Navajo-land. I have today checked with Mr. and Mrs. Dane Coolidge (he a writer on the Southwest), of Berkeley, who agree that *j* is right and *h* is wrong. The *h* might be simpler. It might be well to change San Jose and La Jolla to San Hosay and La Hoya. We in the West and Southwest would never permit it, however. I hope the *Post* will mend its ways."

In 1939 the Sierra Club was paying me as much as was available – half pay for full time – and it did not go very far. So I was ready for the great day when the club's faithful assistant secretary, Virginia Ferguson, opened a letter to me from the *Post*, out of which fell their check to me for five hundred dollars.

In early February 1940 the *Post* published the article, "It Couldn't Be Climbed," but failed to spell "Navajo" correctly:

EVEN THE SQUAWKING, circling crows would have been hard put to find landing space on those awful western precipices of Shiprock. Yet a man was climbing there. On the weathered, crumbling skeleton of the ancient volcanic relic, he balanced delicately over empty space.

Dead-tired, he clung to microscopic knobs. Without warning, a foothold collapsed, sent him hurtling toward the New Mexico desert, a sickening fourteen hundred feet below. It was too late to be frightened. He could only wonder where he would first strike the cliff, to rebound into oblivion. Then –

Silently, his fall stopped short. He dangled, head down, from a rope tied around his waist. Fifteen feet above him was a thin, wedgelike spike of iron, now bent – a piton he had previously driven into a narrow binding crack. His companions paid out slack, and down he came, his rope slipping pulley-fashion through an oval-shaped carabiner that had been hooked into an eye in the spike and snapped shut. Two little pieces of modern mountaineering equipment had done their duty. The climber had been ten feet above his piton and carabiner when he fell. Yet he, and the young fellows tied to his rope, had lived to tell the tale.

Bob Ormes wrote the story of this fall in *The Saturday Evening Post* for July 22, 1939. He confessed that the tumble had discouraged his further desire to climb Shiprock. The fall and the story did another thing. They crystallized the desires of other climbers to investigate the number one climbing problem of the continent.

The impregnability of Shiprock was becoming notorious. The fantastic shape and the weird setting had long made the mountain a famous landmark. Party after party of climbers, each, perhaps, better organized than its predecessor, came from afar. From the security of the level New Mexico desert they scanned the two-thousand-foot walls. They tried to climb, failed, and concluded that it couldn't be climbed. But no explanation would satisfy the climbers to follow. Each failure only increased the challenge. In the *Post,* Ormes had written: "A sudden fear came over us that some other party . . . Canadians, Appalachian or Sierra Club members would capture first honors, instead of us who lived within a few hundred miles of it."

Bestor Robinson, Raffi Bedayan, John Dyer, and I, as climbers in the Sierra Club, were glad to learn that we had been feared. Then we, too, began to fear intervention by still more distant climbers.

Correspondence with Ormes and his Colorado friends produced charts of the offensive plays they had tried–photographs and paragraphs illustrating the difficulties of Shiprock. Their equipment, technique, and strategy had been good. So was the route–as far as it went. The men? We could only guess, but to conduct so thorough a campaign they must have been good. What did we have that they didn't? We thought we had something different, untried except in short practice climbs–equipment never before used, as far as we knew. With a versatile party of climbers, we could try it on the Ship.

Bestor Robinson, forty-one, was long on experience. His training grounds had been the Alps, Rockies, Sierra Nevada, mountains of Lower California, and the Canadian Coast Mountains. He had led two expeditions to Mount Waddington in British Columbia, had joined an attempt on Kates Needle in Alaska. His particular right to rock-climbing fame arose with his participation in the first ascents of the two Cathedral Spires in Yosemite Valley. Like soldiers, climbers are sympathetic to the advantages of good food. So Mrs. Robinson, taking leave of the four children, joined the party as base-camp cook. She had trodden many a summit herself and was reconciled to her husband's role of human fly.

Similar to Robinson in weight and power was Raffi Bedayan, twenty-four, partner in his father's grocery. Of Armenian descent, he was one of the most enthusiastic climbers ever to have joined Sierra Club ranks, and was equally interested in skiing and in the conservation ideals of the club. His flair for difficult leads had been proved in Yosemite. But the ease with which he held falls in practice sessions put him in the anchor-man class. Proper anchoring, or belaying, would be essential for safe climbing on Shiprock.

With two anchor men on deck, it was necessary to find a lightweight climber. John Dyer, twenty-nine, organic chemist, weighed one hundred thirty-five. He was an analytical, methodical climber, always happiest where the hand- and footholds were most doubtful. Dyer had had much experience with the unsound type of volcanic rock found at Shiprock.

Robinson's description of me—"long, lean, and lanky"—may suggest why I went along: to reach the handholds others couldn't. With somewhat more than one hundred fifty ascents of walls and rock climbs in the High Sierra and Yosemite Valley in my twenty-seven years, I still liked to climb and refused to stay home.

Thirty hours and twelve hundred miles from Berkeley, California, by car, we pulled up as near to Shiprock as we cared to venture on a rainy night and retired into two tiny tents.

When Bestor's yodel announced the break of day, I made the mistake of drawing back a tent flap for a peek to the west. Awful vertical cliffs, a cluster of needles thrust through the early-morning velvet of the desert plain, met my startled eyes, and I recoiled into my bag, hoping the whole thing was a nightmare. Then a car sped up on the adjacent road. Robinson strolled over to meet three men we had been expecting from Colorado. Mel Griffith had been with Bob Ormes on Shiprock. With him were two companions also well acquainted with the climb. They had just completed a six-hour drive from Montrose, Colorado, to give us, firsthand, the benefit of their experience with our common opponent.

We followed the Coloradans along two parallel ruts through sparse bunch grass and greasewood, across a shallow wash, past a watering trough, government-built for Navajo cattle, then two miles farther to the very foot of the peak. In the shelter of some large boulders that had fallen from the east cliffs, we made camp, while Mrs. Robinson turned to breakfast.

After breakfast we walked around the base of the great rock, Griffith giving us a climbing history of each of the faces. Here, one man had fallen while climbing by himself and had spent several weeks in the hospital. Over there, other parties had tried and tried again but had hardly left the desert floor. At the top of that basalt gully, the Colorado parties had reached their highest point, but not Shiprock's. From that lofty tower, Ormes had fallen. The thing was tantalizing. Everywhere we could see climbable pitches—up gullies, across ledges, along sharp ridges. But, unfortunately, none of the pitches connected into a route to the top.

Griffith and his companions passed the baton on to the Sierra Club in the relay against Shiprock and started back to Montrose. How soon must we pass the baton along? We had just four days in which to endeavor to carry it to the top.

The route situation, as we now saw it, was briefly this: Shiprock culminated in three high pinnacles—the north and south towers, and between them the much-sought summit tower. All were completely isolated from the desert, except the north tower, the base of which could be attained only by a basalt gully on the west. The summit tower, in turn, could be approached only from the east—from a bowl at the top of a deep gully honeycombed with overhangs. No one had yet entered even the gully, not to mention the bowl. Griffith, Ormes, and party had hoped to climb over the north tower and rope down into the bowl, but the tower would have none of it. They saw another possibility—a steep chimney dropping northeast from the base of the north tower. Climbing a crag, they looked down this chimney, then concluded it would only drop them down among the caves of the honeycomb gully. Those caves were reserved exclusively, they knew, for birds in good physical condition. "But our not having actually explored that chimney," Griffith had said, "has kind of stuck in my craw ever since."

Monday morning found us at the base of the north tower, from which Ormes had fallen. We had, figuratively, stood upon the shoulders of the Colorado men to reach this point and could now fairly evaluate their climbing ability. Apparently, our predecessors not only knew how to talk and write about climbing, but they could climb too. We would be the last to admit that we couldn't climb as high on the north tower as had the Coloradans. We might well be able to climb higher. But now the frowning overhangs of the tower convinced us that we didn't want to climb it at all, if we could help it.

Not yet ready for the drive back through Arizona's desert wild flowers, I started down the chimney that was "sticking in Griffith's craw." The first hundred feet was a walk. The next hundred was a jump. Jumping is frowned upon in better mountaineering circles, especially downward jumps of such length. We would have to rope down from two pitons that could be driven into cracks above the jump. It would not be enough merely to tie a rope to the pitons and slide down. It must also be safe to come back up. This could be accomplished, of course, by climbing the rope hand over hand. But such procedure would leave no margin of safety. The slightest slip would result in a fall that might easily prove fatal.

Rock engineer Robinson invented an elevator. A short piece of rope was tied to both pitons, which were thus mutually supporting. To the lower end of the rope a carabiner was tied to serve as a pulley. Into the carabiner Robinson snapped the center of a two-hundred-seventy-foot rope. This afforded one hundred thirty-five feet of doubled rope, which reached well beyond the bottom of the jump. Winding the rope around hip and chest in the approved manner, I slid down, reassured by the knowledge that there was the equivalent of a block and tackle to get me back up the cliff when a return became necessary. Leaving Bedayan in a penetrating cold wind, Robinson and Dyer soon joined me. Together we made our way down from the end of the rope. We dropped underneath a series of chock stones jammed between the narrowing chimney walls, then crept gingerly down a gravel-greased funnel and out into an amphitheater at its base. Raffi was not particularly happy to have been left. But we didn't know what was ahead, and he could conveniently protect our return with an upper belay.

About an hour later we were still trying to discover exactly what was ahead, and Raffi was still shivering in the wind. Relenting, we signaled him down, carefully crossed the amphitheater, and served lunch in a spot less exposed to the October winds from the distant, snow-clad San Juans. Being on the east side, we could now yodel to Florence Robinson.

"Where . . . are . . . you?" her answer came faintly. And the diminutiveness of the speck from which the call came suggested the reason for her question. If we could barely make her out, she probably could not see us at all. Looking up, we paused to refresh our memory of the tremendous scale of the cliffs ahead.

Except for being cold, our amphitheater was quite comfortable. It was safe to move about without the rope. But caution was ever advisable. The floor tipped steeply to the east, and a dislodged stone would, after a quick roll, plunge over the honeycomb overhangs of the tremendous eastern gully. After a few muffled crashes, fragments of the same stone would emerge on the desert, a hundred floors below.

To continue, we must return to the foot of our elevator chimney, then, somehow, traverse under the north tower to the bowl under the summit tower. From there, a short and supposedly easy climb would bring us to the homestretch. We would then be on the right side of the north tower without having to climb over it and rope down, and we would also have a known route back to camp.

There were, however, some complications. We still had to get around the north tower, and it presented an unbroken face five hundred feet high. Any traverse around it would be fully exposed to the honeycomb gully, where stones rattled so ominously. We couldn't see much hope of making that traverse. You don't walk out, willy-nilly, on an unbroken face. You first look for something to walk upon. We looked for a long time.

Mountaineering is just a business of climbing from one stymie to another. Every properly written mountaineering book must picture several impossible pitches, which eventually are climbed through superhuman effort. The pitch that looked impossible now confronted us. We weren't giving up yet.

We knew a cliff always shows its worst face to an observer looking across at it. Foreshortening, on the other hand, lends enchantment. So I started down toward the honeycomb gully for an optimist's view of the north tower. Harboring no desire to take after the loose rocks occasionally dislodged, I accepted a belay from Robinson. I wasn't nervous. Anyone can become accustomed to high, exposed places – the state of acrophobia soon becomes monotonous. Nevertheless, the gully was steep, it was a long way to slip, and the breccia I was walking on was a poor excuse for rock. A climber must be allowed to make more than one mistake. Otherwise, experience could never teach him anything. Firmly planted at the upper end of my rope, Robinson was the guarantee against any overoptimistic tendencies on my part.

Cautiously working down, then ascending a tiny, unstable pinnacle that separated two upper forks of the honeycomb gully, I stopped to look up. I was surprised to discern a very usable route. One portion of the tower wasn't so steep as the rest. A shelving ledge led around a corner to a previously unseen and very respectable shelf. Then on around the corner there was another little pitch that could be overcome by a shoulder stand. Next, and separating the end of the highway from easy going above, was a thirty-foot unknown. It was a chance, at least. I climbed back to Bestor, and we laid plans for a traverse.

Traversing is merely going sideways. A fall from a traverse is more easily held, naturally, than the fall of a leader from above. Accordingly, the leader on a traverse is willing to make fairly long leads, taking a chance on the pendulum swing resulting from a mistake. So, with few misgivings, I took out eighty feet of rope before slowing down to see what I had got into.

I was traveling over a slope with an average angle of about sixty degrees. This was too steep for friction alone. Under the best conditions ordinary crepe-soled basketball shoes such as we were wearing will slip on a slope exceeding fifty degrees. The angle of the traverse, then, required relying upon small protuberances that diminished the angle, even if only for a width of half an inch or so. In such situations every instinct demands that you hug the rock and clutch for handholds. To do so, however, is just a mild form of suicide. Leaning toward the rock tends to force the feet off the minute holds. So one must stand vertically, relying for salvation upon balance, augmented by touch aiding balance with the fingertips of one hand. If there is any peculiar ability required of those who would climb the steep places, it is this sort of balance – inherent in every person who can walk upright on a sidewalk. Practice adapts balance to steeper and steeper slopes, and finally to cliffs.

Brower on the main mast of Shiprock, New Mexico, leading the first ascent. Photograph by Bestor Robinson.

So I had taken out eighty feet of rope. That, I concluded, was enough for the present. Balance climbing does not allow much margin for errors in judgment, and a mistake would send me swinging over the gully with a turning radius of eighty feet. I scouted around for a piton crack.

None of the cracks were worth ten cents on the dollar, but one of them had to do. I drove in a piton and snapped in my rope and carabiner. The resulting protection was far from bombproof, but it was a relief. Provided that the piton didn't come out too easily when and if I fell, my turning radius would be comfortingly shortened. I made for a small but reassuring shelf, twenty feet away, drove in two more pitons to anchor me to the shelf, and settled down to belay Robinson over to me.

With Robinson fastened to the little shelf and ready to belay the next steps of the journey, things looked easier. The remaining portion of the traverse was somewhat downgrade. I rounded the corner, arrived on the shelf that I had imagined was respectable from my "Optimist's Point," far below. It was respectable only in the sense that it was not despicable. Its saving grace was the tiny patch of grass that grew there. Even this simple bit of vegetation was a friendly relief from the lifeless rock. The shoulder-stand pitch was just ahead. Rather than await the arrival of someone's shoulder to stand upon, I drove a piton into a convenient crack and used it. Things were getting a bit exciting now. Beyond was the thirty-foot unknown pitch, still hidden by a recess in the face. If that pitch were easy, we could then enter the summit-tower bowl, so far not even threatened by the many climbers who had previously challenged Shiprock. With a last push on the piton I squirmed up to the next ledge, pulled in the remaining length of rope coming from Robinson, and carefully crossed the ledge to look at the crucial pitch hidden around the corner.

It was a thirty-foot double overhang!

I have never had any particular love for overhangs, and this was no exception. An overhang means that balance climbing is no longer possible. The arms must come into play—and strenuously—just to hold one into the rock. We had climbed one overhang to reach the base of the north tower. That had been child's play compared to what was now ahead. There wasn't a hold on the face that couldn't be peeled off with a ten-pound pull. Below and ahead of my ledge were the overhangs of the honeycomb gully. Thirty feet above me the top overhang rounded gradually into a shelf which we believed was a walk. Here, then, was the next stymie. A sudden movement of my hand alarmed a tiny lizard not three feet from me. It scampered over the first overhang and halfway up the second, effortlessly.

We had come too far, now, to give up without a struggle. I summoned a second climber for consultation, and soon Dyer joined me on the shelf. Johnny, the light man, would be the goat of this pitch. What did he think of it?

Studying it thoughtfully, Dyer concluded almost to himself, "Well, it's certainly worth a try—tomorrow."

I glanced at my watch. It was quarter past four—an hour and a quarter till dark. With an introductory yodel, I sent a message down to commissary. "We're coming down to dinner." Circumstances dictated an after remark: "We may be a little late."

Our subsequent moves were without military parallel. We retreated and consolidated our position as we went. A fixed rope was left along the traverse to speed things up on the next day. We left another fixed rope below our chimney elevator. Then we tackled the elevator itself, soon to appreciate fully Bestor's engineering. I tied into one end of the double rope. Bestor, Raffi, and I pulled the other. The carabiner we had tied to the pitons was better than a pulley, for the greater friction of the carabiner made it easier to hold the height gained with each heave.

With one man up the elevator, an additional belay from above could now be offered to the other passengers, and we moved quickly. A fiery sunset greeted our arrival at the base of the north tower, and darkness soon covered our descent of the basalt gully. But we were unconcerned, having made many descents in the dark before now. Florence was out to meet us with a flashlight, sensing that we had neglected to take ours with us. But we didn't need light. Just food.

By the next afternoon we had again gathered beneath the double overhang. The ledge upon which we held our council of war was none too spacious, and it sloped just a bit too much into the honeycomb gully. The surface was covered with scree—tiny fragments of rock—which rolled treacherously underfoot. We voted unanimously that there should be dependable anchorage to the ledge before any leader could risk the overhang. But there were no cracks on the entire ledge at all adequate for good anchorage. Had we been equipped only with pitons, safety would have demanded retreat.

This, then, was the spot to inaugurate the use of the bizarre mountaineering equipment we had brought along—expansion bolts. We took time out to place the first.

A compressed-air drill would have burrowed into the soft rock in seconds. Such drills are not, however, easily adapted to knapsacks. We had to be content with the slow process of pounding a star drill into the breccia with a piton hammer. This took nearly half an hour. Next, the special half-inch eyebolt and skirt were inserted in the two-inch hole. Tightening of the bolt expanded the skirt and held the bolt in the hole. A carabiner was snapped into the eye of the bolt. Now, by running the rope through this carabiner to the leader, the belayer could hold a severe fall securely.

But how did we know that the expansion bolt would not pull right out of the hole into which we had placed it so easily? It was one thing for a bolt to withstand the dead weight of an electric sign. That's about all the bolts are manufactured for. But we might subject the bolt to a greater strain, especially if any of the party were to duplicate Bob Ormes' dive.

We had wondered about this question in Berkeley long before now. There, during many of the Sierra Club rock-climbing section's weekly practice sessions, we had contrived a test. An expansion bolt was placed above an overhanging cliff, about twenty feet high, with a landing field of soft earth beneath it. A climber would tie into the rope and snap it into the expansion bolt with a carabiner. While a man below played the part of Bill House and belayed the rope, the climber would repeat Bob Ormes' fall, on a smaller scale. Two, three, four, and on up to ten feet of slack rope would be taken up before takeoffs. The bolt withstood the shock. Of course, we could have shocked the bolt too much had we not previously learned certain refinements in technique while holding similar falls with pitons. Any weight, stopped infinitely quick, exerts an infinite force. It is up to the man below actually to help the rope run through the carabiner before he stops it. This precludes the sudden jerk that might bring the piton out. We knew this from practice, for we had not only jerked pitons out but had sprung open carabiners and snapped ropes in test falls, where each accident was something to laugh about. Expansion bolts had passed adequate tests with honors. We were ready to proceed.

A shallow, narrow crack led over the top of the first overhang. Standing on Bedayan's shoulders, Robinson began pounding pitons into the crack with a vengeance. Dyer belayed. I paid out a secondary belay, and at the same time photographed the progress with three cameras—black-and-white stills, color stills, and color motion pictures.

Four pitons went in. Robinson threaded the two ropes through alternate carabiners in each piton. To each successive piton he also tied a rope sling, to be used as a foothold while he worked on the piton above. It took no little concentration to avoid a hopeless entanglement of ropes, hardware, and climbers. Twice Bestor came down to rest, for this was exhausting work. Assured that the pitons, having already withstood Robinson's two hundred pounds, would hold him, Dyer took over. From the top rope sling he could reach over the first overhang. Placing one more piton at the end of his reach, he was able to draw himself up. While all the pitons would now hold from two hundred to four hundred pounds, they could hardly be expected to hold a fall of any distance. Tests had proved that even an eight-foot fall can develop a thousand-pound strain if the belayer applies but a slight amount of excessive friction. Safety on the remaining overhang would require something better than those pitons. Again an expansion bolt came to the rescue. Having placed the second, Dyer snapped his rope into it and lowered himself to our ledge. It was already four o'clock, and time to return to camp. Our day's effort had resulted in a net advance of just twelve feet.

This would never do. We were spending too much time commuting between camp and the double overhang. It was nice to have home-cooked dinners every night, but it was hard on climbing progress. So the third morning we arrived on our ledge equipped to stay there all night, if necessary. In our packs were food for four or five meals, three pints of water, extra clothing, cameras, and other knickknacks a rock engineer considers standard equipment. I even wore my pajamas under my jeans and parka. We were prepared to meet our most consistent climbing companion—the cold wind, blowing constantly, as capricious desert zephyrs do, from all directions at once.

We had been saving Dyer. Back into the fray he went. Working on the upper overhang for an hour, he pounded in pitons, snapped and unsnapped carabiners, tied foot slings, and fought his way up the remaining eighteen feet. As the friction became too great through one line of carabiners, he started a second rope through others. Several times he cautioned us to be ready for a fall, but this was no cause for alarm. We merely got the cameras ready. He couldn't have fallen more than ten feet if he had jumped. Finally he inched his way over the top.

"What does it look like, Johnny?" we asked, as if the question had been rehearsed.

With an introductory "pretty good," he gave a complete description. There was still a fifteen-foot pitch, about forty degrees, covered with scree, but not with holds. It was climbable, but he would first want to place one more expansion bolt to safeguard further progress. Beyond was a small cave, an ideal belay position.

Three-quarters of an hour later I had joined him. Belayed by Dyer, I walked out to an exposed point, yodeled victoriously to Florence, and looked above us. It was little more than a walk up into the summit-tower bowl, and we were soon there. In a cave at the east base of the north tower—we were now two days from the west base—we cached surplus supplies and food, near and within us, respectively. Robinson prescribed a water-conservation program—light meals, minimum exertion, and minimum perspiration. Our scant three pints of water must be diluted with abstinence.

With sudden elation I discovered a package of fruit drops in a long-unused parka pocket. Opening the package, I magnanimously extended it.

"Here, Bestor, have one. Quick energy, you know."

He reached out, but some thought stayed his hand. In the faraway look in his eye I could perceive that profound calculations were going on. He was taking his water conservation seriously. How desiccating would the sugar be? Would plasmolysis leave his mouth dry? Would the extra energy lead to extra exertion and thus to further perspiration?

But perhaps, at last, his mouth watered at the sight of the lemon drop. It must not water in vain.

"Well, all right," Robinson condescended. "I'll have one."

For a moment I considered asking him how much water he had lost while all his profound thinking transpired.

But on to the summit tower! We were close beneath it now—the optimist's viewpoint. Things looked encouraging. Robinson and Bedayan started off to scout the north face; Dyer and I preferred first to look at the sharp south arête. The tower looked so grim from each approach that all of us soon reversed our preferences. Robinson, standing under the arête, thought it climbable. I, looking across at it from halfway up the south tower, maintained that it was not.

I was wrong. But to prove it we first traversed a narrow, four-hundred-foot ledge under the summit to the base of the north face.

Splitting this face was a wide crack that might provide the means of cracking the summit defenses. About an hour and seven pitons later I had reached the end of my rope. The crack continued another twenty feet to easy shelves, a scramble from the summit. But the crack chose to overhang just above my head. This was a crack far too wide for pitons—wide enough, perhaps, to be climbed. But I didn't know how. There was the added disadvantage that were I to drop anything from the worst part of that overhang—and I had myself in mind—it would strike first just about where we started climbing three days ago. That was too much ground to lose all at once. I deemed it better to learn to climb such cracks back in Berkeley, with a rope above, not below, were I to slip. What about our expansion bolts? I had some, but they were a safeguard, not a panacea for all climbing difficulties. It's one thing to place them for anchorage to a shelf. It's another matter to stand on next to nothing and to try to place them on an overhang to supply the handholds Nature forgot.

No one else seemed anxious to try the crack either, since the sun was setting. The shadow of Shiprock, stretching to the eastern horizon, was a magnificent sight, but it foretold imminent darkness. It was time to rope down.

Back to the cave, a frugal supper, embers of a greasewood campfire slowly dying. In the shelter of the somber cliffs towering on three sides of us, we found the night perfectly still. Far out across the desert flickered many a tiny flame. Navajos enjoying a perfect desert evening? It seemed hardly possible. The desert had appeared lifeless during the day, save for scattered groups of grazing cattle. These fires could not designate settlements. There were none. Occasionally the pinpoints of warm red would flare up, then slowly deepen in color, returning once again to a faint warm glow. They were throbbing stars that had fallen—they were signal fires—they marked the course of the meandering San Juan. Thus we conjectured, wondering also what the Navajos must have thought of our campfire, just beneath the invincible summit of Shiprock.

Before long the congestion of four men in a tiny two-man tent was in itself warming. The mattress of gravel was softened by drowsiness. We slept almost soundly. The sun slipped slowly around the opposite side of Shiprock, then found us again in our lofty crow's-nest. With a few raucous calls to notify our ground crew that we were up and doing, we started to work on the south arête, which I had proclaimed unclimbable the night before.

Our immediate problem this time was a forty-foot overhang. Again Robinson laid a foundation of direct-aid pitons. Again Dyer scampered over them, continuing where Bestor had left off—up a series of insecure cracks, out from under the overhang to the foot of a smooth, holdless face. His highest pitons were behind flakes that could almost be pried off by hand—

terribly insecure. Dyer had traversed beyond the overhang, but he was now hanging over something worse—the west face. The honeycomb gully had been bad enough, with its reverberating rock avalanches. Stark gully walls formed a stern frame for the view of the eastern desert. But the west face—stones don't crash there. Throw one off. For thirteen seconds there is a maddening silence. Then the stone explodes. There is no echo to the explosion. There is nothing from which an echo could come. There is no foreground. You sail above the desert, and the nearest object, to all appearances, is the horizon.

Dyer was unperturbed. He knew he couldn't climb the twelve-foot pitch ahead of him on nonexistent holds. So he threw a rope over a knob on the ridge. Bedayan, on the opposite side, anchored the rope through a piton. We had the mountain tied together, and Dyer with it. Speedily he made his way up the rope and settled on a distressingly small platform marking the top of the forty-foot overhang. There was nothing reliable to which he could anchor until he had placed another expansion bolt. For the fourth time this simple device had justified its mountaineering debut, and we could proceed safely.

There was a small overhang ahead, but we were beginning to like such opposition. Two pitons helped me over that. A slanting, grass-covered ledge, a tunnel under some jumbled blocks, a bit of back-and-knee—easy pitches sped us onward. I hurried up a simple friction slab, through a little alcove floored with blocks of debris. Blue sky filled a notch just overhead.

Climbing up and looking through, I called back to the party, "Never mind the hardware. Bring the register."

This was the top!

The weather was fine. The view was perfect. There were ideal platforms for candid camerists and cinematographers. There was room on the topmost crag for all of us, and a cairn besides. We were not at all worried about the route back. But some factor of an ideal climax was, to me at least, missing. What was it? Why didn't I experience that elation that had previously marked an arrival on an untrodden summit? This had been a far better climb than any of us had ever made.

That was it! The process of climbing had, in itself, been the climax. Each victorious solution of a particular problem—finding we could rope down our chimney and still get back up, connecting the inadequate holds of the friction traverse, watching Johnny disappear over the fantastic overhangs—each success had been climactic. The lure of that summit was magnetic. Yet, somehow, four days of concentration on a single, lofty objective had stolen the surprise at its attainment. It was so disconcerting that I put the wrong date in the Sierra Club register that we placed just below the summit block. I must go up and change it.

Raffi Bedayan was more practical. After we had concluded our several rope-downs, our last trip up the elevator, and had collected equipment to stow in the car, Raffi remembered something.

"Sonuvagun!" he exclaimed. "I forgot to leave my card!"

BEDAYAN'S GROCERY
San Francisco
We deliver anywhere

***Saturday Evening Post,* February 1940**

My parents, my sister, and my two brothers were properly pleased with our success on Shiprock, but my mother did not live to enjoy her son's success in the *Post*. I know she would not have enjoyed one of the things my temporary fame led to—the inquiry into my willingness to endorse Camel cigarettes, which I had by then been smoking for five years. The ad agency met with me, took one look, and withdrew the offer. I was spared the temptation of thus selling a bit of my soul, which would have distressed not only my parents, but my mountaineering colleagues as well.

Disappointed, but also a little relieved, I went on about my mountaineering, which included a first winter ascent of Dunderberg, a handsome metamorphic summit a few miles northwest of Mono Lake and just outside the eastern boundary of Yosemite National Park. Fritz Lipmann, Fred Kelley, and I succeeded, and spent the following evening in the lodge at Conway Summit. We were joined by one other traveler, an Austrian mountaineer living in Southern California. Somehow I helped the conversation about mountains drift to Shiprock and wondered if he had happened to see an article about the first ascent in the *Saturday Evening Post*.

"I saw it and read it," he replied; "but it was so miserably written!"

It would be another fifteen years before I rose to such literary heights. I had been asked to write an article about Sierra Club High Trips, and found the time to do so when partly laid up with mononucleosis. I dictated the article, had it transcribed, and submitted all twenty-two thousand five hundred words of it to *National Geographic* magazine. In June 1954, after a little prodding, the *Geographic* published it, minus fifteen thousand of those words. I was happy to spend the seven hundred fifty dollars (ten cents a word) I was paid on an addition of two rooms to our then seven-year-old house in Berkeley, where our six-member family was crowding our two bedrooms. The money pleased me enough to help me forget the words on the cutting-room floor. I later asked the editor who cut me how she went about it. Simply by removing those parts, she said, where there was no action.

Having miserably written about so much inaction, I developed terminal writer's block. Whatever else I may have achieved since has been strongly motivated by my determination to do anything to avoid putting words together. Forty-eight years after the Shiprock climb I was asked what else I remembered about the climb and put a few more words together for Eric Bjørnstad's book, *Desert Rock* (1988):

"When my father took me desert camping in Nevada in 1929, I learned that a garbage can full of water in the back seat of our 1921 Willys-Knight was good to have, and to use sparingly, while we looked futilely for a hoped-for ledge of silver ore.

"So I was ready for the real, if scarce, ledges of Shiprock with only a small canteen of water, to be refilled only at day's end–at the end of two days after our third-night bivouac.

"The Colorado team, who generously walked us around the old volcanic neck to help us avoid sticking our necks out as far as they had in their unsuccessful attempt, assured us that we would find no springs or even damp spots anywhere on the peak. Bestor and Raffi Bedayn [his later spelling] gave us our dry-climb instructions: 'Stay in the shade whenever possible; exert as little as you can and avoid unnecessary sweating.'

"We got by fine, even after losing water insensibly in occasional brisk winds–one blast of which sent my hat over the brink. (It landed neatly on a ledge of our return route.)

"I did something else right, in addition to losing my hat so skillfully, on that Columbus Day, 1939. I had caught cold on the long drive to Shiprock. I left it near the top. Subsequent climbers have not found it.

"So if you are sniffling and have run out of Vitamin C, go climb Shiprock!"

One more postscript:

Kenneth Brower, in an article about Navajo country for the *Atlantic* in early 1989, cited the climb of Shiprock in his introduction and later corresponded with an *Atlantic* reader. She described the Navajo reaction to the climb in a letter dated October 12, 1989, exactly fifty years after the first ascent. She wrote:

> I was the teacher and community worker at Cove Day School at the time the Shiprock was first climbed. It did excite the Navajo of Cove and Red Rock very much to see their sacred Tsebitai (Shiprock) [climbed]. Some Red Rock Indians alerted my Cove Indians. My Indians wanted to know who and why and who gave permission for the intrusion. A few of my Navajo as I remember, Jimmy Boatman, an Old Policeman, both old and respected, thought of evil spirits. Some thought it was a warning of evil-to-come. I do remember about eight or ten men had a short 'sing' to protect us–from what I never knew. I remember they hung my Coleman lantern outside for light for the two or three hour sing.
>
> Later that week we heard some *white* men did it. I was told some Red Rock Indians had watched from the Hogback (the ridge running from the monolith to the south for several miles) while on horseback. I do know there was no resentment–but more curiosity than anything else and surprise at accomplishment. Much talk went on in our dining room and meetings for weeks. To the Navajo who hadn't seen

the "light" or "something" the story was unfolded and got longer and wider.

My stay among the Navajo was a wonderful experience, both personally and professionally. I learned Navajo and only used an interpreter when reading a Government directive that had to have a witness. I enjoyed my life and work on the Reservation. The older Navajo would come into my kitchen and sit on the floor to drink coffee and eat bread. They told folk tales! I collected these tales and got them published in the *Southern Folklore Journal*. I would be "snowed in" for weeks and I had plenty of time to write, which I did. I believe *many* years ago there was a nice write-up about this *first* climb of the sacred Shiprock in the *Saturday Evening Post*. I'm 81 now and my memory is duller than in 1939. Maybe I need a good "Navajo Sing." . . .

Sincerely,
Mildred Lee Adair

P.S. Many folktales have Shiprock in them.

For a little more about Shiprock, see the section about Dick and Doris Leonard in chapter 5.

Lost Arrow

There Are Plenty of other climbs to remember, but I'll settle for the way I remembered one of them as I sat comfortable and secure outside a room at Yosemite Lodge in May 1988:

On May 15 Yosemite Falls should be at their peak, but I am afraid that, even though there are four days to go, the peak has already passed. This is not a big snow year. It is a sad snow year, with less than half the water resting in the High Sierra snowpack than ought to be there.

But small is still beautiful. I have moved the little patio table just outside our Yosemite Lodge room in Hemlock Cottage far enough that I can see what I am hearing. I can't see it all by any means. A small maple tree just a few steps away intercepts some of the view. Two incense cedars frame it on the left. A third cedar and two yellow pines are the right-hand frame. A dogwood in full bloom hides Laurel Cottage. And finding its way behind all the intervening foliage is Upper Yosemite Fall, all fourteen hundred thirty feet of it, hitting the ledge just below its lip, and arcing out for the big plunge, to lose itself in its own mist about where John Muir found his way out on a ledge I want no part of to see how wet and powerful the upper fall was.

There were big thunderheads over the Sierra as we drove up the Merced Canyon, and the sky is now completely overcast and it is a little hard to see what I want to see. Let me move my table a little farther out so that my lap computer can record what I want to see.

That's better. Now I can see all the Upper Fall, and off to the right the awesome Lost Arrow.

The sun was shining there, fifty years ago. The fall was booming away as usual. Dick Leonard and I were at one of the best places to see it from. Some four hundred fifty feet up on the first attempt to climb the Lost Arrow. It was frightening enough that we had no deep wish to reach the summit, which is narrow and far too curvy. If you were to start sliding off that curve you would not stop until you had dropped about fifteen hundred feet, and the face is sheer enough that you'd probably not bounce against it more than once as you fell. You would have committed your last error, and that is the alternate name Dick Leonard had given the Lost Arrow. The Last Error. We had just about reached the First Error – about four hundred fifty feet up the most gradual part of the chimney that separates the whole structure from the main face of Yosemite Point. We had used a lot of pitons to get as far as we did, quite a few of them for direct aid. We didn't plan to go much higher. We'd save that for Anton Nelson and John Salathé, who would spend five days and nights in the chimney and on the ascent of the final detached spire.

The First Error is as far as we had any wish to go, but as an excuse we'll say we ran out of time. To get to the broad ledge of the First Error I had to place a piton high enough up the chimney to allow me to make a leaping rope traverse from the chimney to the ledge.

Because it was fifty years ago, we had no nylon rope. Our rope was sisal, a less expensive fiber than Manila hemp, and we had not yet found how superior nylon is and sisal isn't because Dick hadn't invented nylon rope yet. So it's gung ho, swing out as far as you can to the left, and make a running leap to the right, out into space, and up, up and away – to the First Error ledge. It helps the spirit to yodel as you leap.

I did. Doris Leonard, waiting patiently at the base of the climb and watching Yosemite Fall for amusement, heard the yodel, looked up, did not know I was making a rope traverse, and thought instead that I had started a four-hundred-fifty-foot fall. The illusion cost her her lunch.

The rope traverse succeeded and we descended as good climbers do. No fall. Just deliberate rappels, glad that we had made a first ascent of a kind, pleased indeed that the illusion was only an illusion, and scrambled back down to the valley to replace Doris's lunch.

The Upper Yosemite Fall kept on booming. The photograph I made of it is one of my favorites, perhaps because it looks a little like the image Ansel Adams made of it when the fall was in the same mode.

But now it is fifty years later. The fall is going through its spring excitement. The light from the overcast sky has a grandeur of its own. The grand show is eternal, as Muir would have it. "God's power for man's use" was the way an advertisement once had it, with the Upper Fall as the illustration. It made Ansel furious. It would have made John Muir as furious. And if any ad man ever does that again, I hope you will be furious, too.

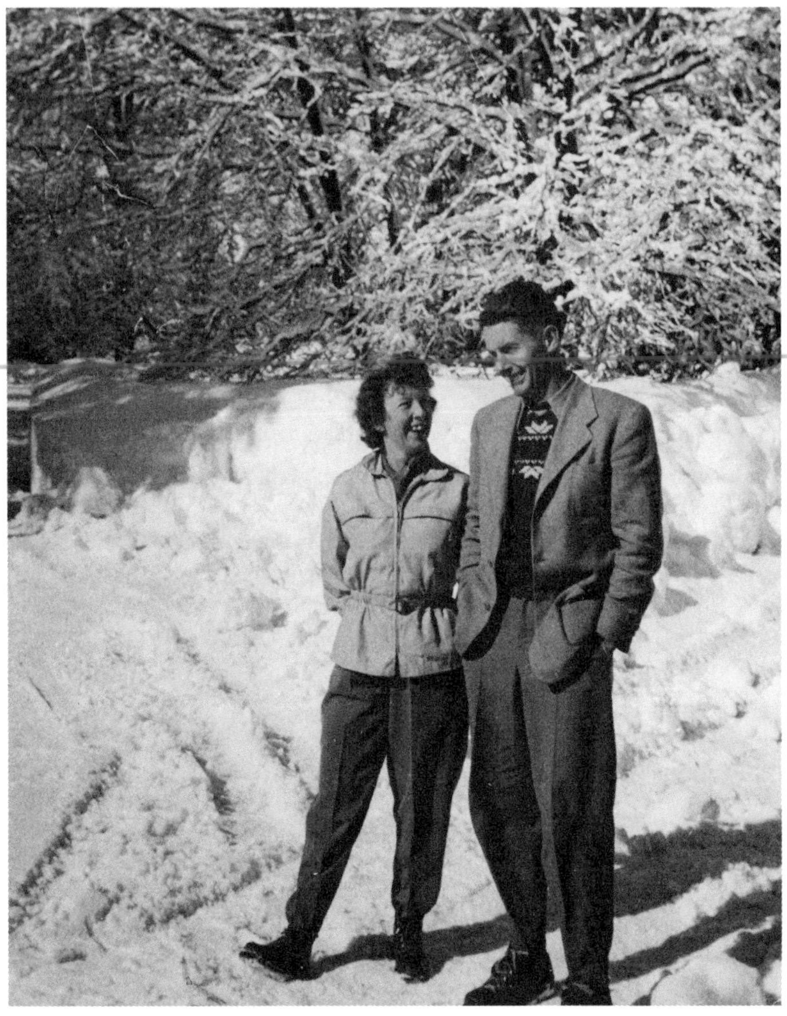

Dave and Anne in Yosemite, about 1947. Photo by Joseph Brower.

Right now the booming and crashing goes on. White water leaps out, contrasting nicely with the dark wet cliff behind it, water comets racing each other into oblivion in the common, surging mist, the whole thing properly untrammeled. No concrete plugs, no transmission towers and lines—nothing but wildness.

Let's drink to that!

After Shiprock and less difficult climbs my life began to shape up. The die was cast in May 1941. The brother of Francis Peloubet Farquhar was

Samuel Thaxter Farquhar, manager of the University of California Press. "There is an opening for an editor at the press," Francis told me. "Go over and see Harold Small about it."

On the way into Harold Small's office I strode rather brusquely past the young woman in the outer office who was one of the editors and whose outer office I was about to share. Her name was Anne Hus and she has not, after forty-six years, forgiven me for the insensitivity I showed that day.

She did, however, marry me two years later, a few days after I had become a second lieutenant in the U.S. Mountain Troops, and she has put up with me ever since.

CHAPTER 3

WAR

GETTING INTO WAR

ONE WOULD HARDLY consider that a several-day snow-camping trip in Little Lakes Valley, at timberline on the east side of the Sierra Nevada, was related to war. Or that testing something new to climbing, a high-stretch nylon rope, would have anything to do with combat. Or that zippered sections of totally waterproofed nylon (one section of which could house one sleeping bag in the snow, or four sections of which could accommodate at least four people in a mountain snowstorm) would in any way contribute to an Allied victory in World War II. But we thought so. And at least one of us, Dave Brower, rather hoped that such contributions would be all that was expected of him for the war effort.

That wasn't the way it worked out. But thanks to the Sierra Club's cooperation with Charles Minot ("Minnie") Dole and the National Ski Patrol System in the organization of a unit of United States Mountain Troops, and thanks to Bestor Robinson's having joined the staff of the U.S. Quartermaster General in the devising of military mountain equipment, and thanks to his having persuaded Dick Leonard to join him there, I was able to enlist in the U.S. Army before my draft board put me wherever some unknown person's whim would order me. Dick arranged that the first item in my 201 file, which was to contain my military biography, was a telegram from the Adjutant General to the effect that David R. Brower was to go to Camp Carson, Colorado, for basic training as a private in the mountain troops, following which he would attend The Infantry School (TIS) at Fort Benning, Georgia, following which, if successful, he would return to the mountain troops as a brand-new second lieutenant.

Strangely enough, that is what happened, but not without some moments of suspense and some months of anxiety. October 12, 1942, put my life as a civilian on hold. At thirty, I was a good ten years older than most of the men then going into service, and I feared that my ability to absorb further schooling was long gone. I had become a fairly heavy smoker and was apprehensive of having to run a mile every day before breakfast in the mountain troops. I certainly didn't think that an editor would mix very well with the troops, or that my editing ability would be of any value. And when my first day's service got me to the Presidio of Monterey and assigned to KP duty, along with my backpacking and touch-football associate, George Rockwood, who by coincidence arrived at the Presidio the same day, I was not cheered. Nor cheered further that first evening when another man, too long deprived of drink and fully into hallucination, awoke in the middle of the night screaming that the barracks was adrift and someone had damned well better tie the building up fast.

The train ride to Colorado, to a lonely man coming down with a cold, was an improvement. So was Camp Carson itself, even though the impact of human feet gave the surface of the camp only two alternatives—dust on the move or mud sticking to boots. I was heartened to discover, sharing the floor of the barracks I was assigned to, two men—Jake Nunnemacher of Wisconsin and Paul Harlow, of Richmond, California—who had read *Manual of Ski Mountaineering,* which I had edited for the University of California Press. We had instant rapport, as fellow privates. In headquarters, Captain John Woodward, of Washington, a friend of some of my skiing associates who had been assigned to the Eighty-seventh Mountain Infantry at Fort Lewis (or more appropriately, on Mount Rainier) had heard of me and brought me immediately to headquarters to work on a mountain-training manual.

All was almost roses. But one night the order had gone out to the company to cubicularize. Flu was abroad. To minimize risk of its spreading, bunks were to be arranged so that the head and foot ends would alternate. Thus my head would be about four feet away from my neighbor's feet instead of from his sneezing head—it would be, that is, if I had known about the order. Being at headquarters, I didn't. My sentence was to mop the barracks floor, and no excuses.

We were only temporarily at Carson, waiting for the completion of Camp Hale, in the valley of the Eagle River (its channel "will be obliterated," the planning map said), containing Pando, Colorado, across Tennessee Pass from Leadville. The Denver and Rio Grande Railroad took us there in the course of a night, the route twisting to and fro enough to put me at Camp Hale permanently disoriented. To this day Tennessee Pass remains north of Hale in my mind, even though the map knows better. The camp was not quite complete, but enough so for us. The heating system in the barracks was still a mystery, and I remember the night our ink froze on our shelves, and a day when the indoor temperature was ninety degrees at a time when the outdoors, into which we were moved for early-morning vigorous calisthenics, was thirty-five below zero. The hospital got a lot of pulmonary business out of that—lungs suffering from freezing because flatland lieutenants knew too little about mountains.

I was named squad leader, and named Paul Harlow assistant leader. On our floor were two Harvard men, one from Yale, and overall an educational background that would lead Lieutenant Colonel Robert C. Works, when I was under his command, to observe much later that we had men serving as corporals in the mountain troops who would be captains in any other infantry outfit. For my own amusement, I tried to see how fast I could field-strip and reassemble my M-1 rifle. Most of the others on the floor joined the contest. Having had a head start, I kept the lead. I can't believe now how fast I was then. It was just a matter of avoiding any lost motion. The rifle would flow apart and flow back together. Our other amusement came from our weekend opportunities to ski on Cooper Hill, just above Tennessee Pass. I had never been expert in downhill and never learned about skiing on narrow trails through the forest. We had better slopes to ski on in California. Paul Harlow and I became much better than we really were simply by following Jake Nunnemacher down the forest aisles of Cooper Hill, doing what he did much faster than we would otherwise have dared. I received some basic training—learned to fire the M-1 reasonably well, the carbine somehow as an expert, and refreshed my knowledge of first aid. Sierra Club ski-mountaineering training had given us "second aid" as well—things you would need to know if you were a day or so from any help. And of course there was close-order drill. I did not like it. I remember standing obediently in formation and wondering, from time to time, looking down at my feet, why I was such a wimp that I would not move them until someone ordered me to do so. Was I my own man or wasn't I? I wasn't.

I spent much less time on such drill than the others, however, because there was much further work on the mountain-training manual. My formal basic training suffered; so much so that when it came time for me to appear before the Camp Hale OCS board to see if I qualified for the Officer Candidate School, I did not know the answers to many questions. The president of the board intervened. "Private Brower has been assisting us in headquarters on the training manual," he explained, and answered the first question for me, as well as all the following questions I was not up to answering. It was a relief to have a friend in a high place. And why was he a friend? For one reason: because the president of the board was Major Paul Lafferty, who had snow-camped with us when he was a captain and we were testing army equipment in Little Lakes Valley.

Nine years later, in 1952, Fort Benning would be a pleasant place to visit when I dropped by for two weeks of active duty as Major Brower. It was something else in January 1943 for Officer Candidate Brower. My last formal schooling had ended not at all successfully twelve years earlier in Berkeley. Would this old brain, after more than thirty years' service, be able to absorb what an infantry officer needs to know in the heady business of killing or being killed? Probably not, but give it the old school try.

If anyone would like to know what it was like for me, there are the almost daily letters I wrote to Anne Hus. In my own protracted way, I proposed to her by mail as I rode the train to Columbus, Georgia, continuing the proposal with delight once I was astride my Fort Benning bunk – all this on the portable Royal my father lent me. The best news at Fort Benning came in the almost daily blue envelope I received from Anne at mail call.

Belmore Browne, who made the first ascent of Mount McKinley and became an advisor to the Air Corps (it would be a Force later) found that he had to keep reminding military types that "wars are fought outdoors," probably because there was so much indoors at West Point and Annapolis. He was a mountaineer, and so was I. Thanks to mountain experience I had been assigned to mountain troops and, I still hoped, would be reassigned there, instead of to regular infantry. Since the United States, unlike many European nations, had never had mountain troops, there was a great deal of mountaineering knowledge absent from conventional military thinking. I took some delight, therefore, in sharing my special knowledge in class whenever I thought it would be helpful. Perhaps you can see what is coming, but I was not prepared for it. I took sick leave on my bunk only once, and was lying there recovering from a cold, trying to sleep but not quite succeeding, in part because of some conversation going on in the upper floor where a few classmates of mine were doing bunk fatigue. I wasn't trying to eavesdrop, but was on the alert when I heard my name, followed by the line: "Brower! That turd! He's always asking questions." Which is how I learned, at least for the rest of my Benning days, that being a wizard, even if you don't think you are trying to be one, wins no respect. It was a timely shock. There were no more questions. Thanks to that bit of unintended enlightenment I apparently fared better. Near the end of the three months, students were required to rank their classmates. I learned to my surprise that I was ranked first, but not because I was a wizard. Maybe it was the touch football.

Or maybe it was the song, "A Ballad of OC 221," that I wrote and sang for the class at Fort Benning:

(With judicious juggling and using alternate choruses, this may be sung to the tunes of "Solomon Levi" or the "Rambling Wreck from Georgia Tech.")

A BALLAD OF OC 221

1.
The school solution's mighty nice
For Georgia's gentle sands
We hear they've used it once or twice
In brave New Guinea stands

But when the chips are really down and we're in rough terrain
We Benning boys will gather 'round
And join in this refrain:

CHORUS (Solomon Levi)
Hail the school solution, the good old GI way
Hail the school solution, we Benning Boys must say
It worked one time on the red-scarred hill
And under the lone pine tree
But brother, when I'm in battle will
The damned thing work for me?

OR, (Rambling Wreck)
Oh hail to our institution, boys, the good old GI way
The good old school solution that we used from day to day
It works around Columbus
It solves the worst G-T
Oh we hope to hell it works for us
When we're across the sea.

2.
Our first attempts at sounding off
We must admit were weak
We'd wheeze and stammer, gasp and cough
But rarely really speak
At last we got some real advice
A captain passed it out
And now we simply spread our legs
And swing our balls and shout.

3.
As if the course weren't hard enough
For any man to bear
A lot of songs of mountain stuff
Are always in the air
With songs of Oolah, songs of Sven
And mountain infantry
Oh how blissful it will be again
When they've gone back to ski.

4.
We've learned just what's in every book
Each paragraph and page

So that we'll know just where to look
When bitter battles rage
And if the answer doesn't fit
We'll find there this refrain:
"It all depends upon the sit-
uation and terrain."

5.
We ride in vans from class to class
And when the ride is through
The hardboard seats have made our ass-
es tired and black and blue
We've doubled-timed through Jungle Jim
And Hand to Hand as well
Before we'll go through that again
We'll see you first in Hell.

6.
We've learned to storm Ochillees's banks
And Chatahoochee's too
We've cracked up simulated tanks
And slopped through Dixie Dew
Logistics, tactics, and supply
Battalions in attack
Oh at these we never bat an eye
We know they'd bat it back.

7.
Curves in your hair are known as curls
They look nice on a few
It's curves that make the Petty girls
We'd like to make some, too
The architects and painters say
A curve is nice to see
Oh but mother when in hell will they
Stop throwing curves at me.

8.
Our days and nights are never free
Our bars seem far away
We struggle with the S-O-P
T-O and T-R-A
We've studied hard, we've studied late
But now we'll have some fun
For soon the Board will decimate OC 221.

As promised by the adjutant general in October 1942, new Second Lieutenant Brower was assigned to the mountain troops with a slight delay en route. That let me travel by train back home in late April 1943, as had been planned by mail, to marry Anne Hus on May 1. It was wartime, I explain, trying to forget the many amenities that were substantially ignored. Anne won't let me.

The wedding was at her home, presided over by Berkeley Judge Oliver Young, with Morgan Harris, my constant Yosemite climbing companion, as best man, the wedding being delayed until a meeting of the Sierra Club board of directors had ended. We left Berkeley late in the afternoon, I paused in Carmel to say hello and good-bye to George Rockwood and his wife June, then drove as far as King City, to spend our wedding night, with no advance reservation, in an old motel that happened to have space. The next evening we spent just over the Arizona border, the third in a tent in the rain alongside Shiprock, and the rest is best forgotten. With great courage she found a place to live in Denver, then another, and I commuted from Camp Hale and my assignment to the 86th Mountain Regiment as often as I could. I was very poor at mixing the roles of husband and new lieutenant, and I can think of endless ways to do better next time.

At Camp Hale, my old 87th Mountain Regiment, containing many old and new friends, including Paul Harlow, was ordered to take the island of Kiska from the Japanese. The Japanese left before they arrived. There was no reason, as we saw the 87th leave, to think they would be so lucky. As I watched Paul leave, I was well aware that I might not see him again. Wars are like that.

Shortly before the war I had composed a melody on my accordion that was waiting for words, and I came up with some. In an article in the *American Ski Annual* about mountain troop songs, Charles Bradley gave the song high praise. His brother Richard recorded it as I played it years later on the piano, and wrote the music, which the Air Force Band later played at a memorial service at Cooper Hill. So far as I know, that was never recorded. But here are the words (probably my best in years of undisciplined composition):

MOVING OUT

Evening falls and gloomy black
Crowds the western sky;
Down along the waiting track
Soldiers say good-bye;

Trained together, day by day,
Now one moves along;

The other slowly turns away,
Sadly sings this song:

You'll soon be moving out to fight,
Your training days are through;
It's anybody's guess where you will land.
I wish, as I'm alone tonight,
That I were going too,
Soldiering with you the way we planned.
Until our trails shall cross again,
And battle cries are still,
When lights of friendly life shine as before,
You'll share the zeal of fighting men,
Fighting with a will,
'Til the happy day you're home once more.

Just tonight I shook your hand,
Saw you on your way,
Hoped that you would understand
Words I didn't say.

Days together, all too brief,
Now have reached an end,
Leaving me a common grief–
Parting with a friend.

The times we mopped the barracks floor,
The talks we had at mess,
Those few and fleeting days we had to ski,
The times you beat my rifle score,
Or I took you at chess–
All were fun to guys like you and me.
But now we've got that job to do.
Those days are gone for now.
Better days must come, but who knows when?
Keep your thumbs up, smile some, too,
Sweat it out somehow,
'Til Fortune lets me shake your hand again.

June 1943 – Paul Lafferty was the intervenor in the right place at the right time once more. After my initial assignment to F company, 86th, I was assigned to the 10th Reconnaissance Cavalry Troop, a horseless outfit the name of which was all that was militarily available for our Mountain Training Center. We kept Camp Hale's rocks busy with climbing instructors and students.

In October 1943 we were moved to the West Virginia Mountain Maneuver Area to teach at Seneca Rock Assault Climbing School until the following June. [For more about our Seneca days, see the obituaries of Art Argiewicz and Dick Emerson, and GI Climbs.] The order closing our school was a severe blow to officers and enlisted instructors at Seneca. We were to be scattered all over the compass. We were grim.

At maneuver headquarters in Elkins we assembled around the pay telephone, got our coins together, and I went to work calling everyone I knew who might conceivably see how foolish it was to dismember what we had put together. I talked to Minnie Dole, Dick Leonard, Bestor Robinson for about two hours altogether – long enough to make us wonder if the coin box would accept more largesse. I kept at it, and was still at it when one of the men, who had gone inside, came out beaming. "The orders have been changed. We're all going to Camp Swift."

Bastrop, Texas, just outside Austin, was where it was, and mountainous it wasn't. We mountain troops were there to get leveled out, to learn what war would be like if you didn't have a bit of mountain defilade to hide in or height to observe from. On his arrival there, Captain David Rosendale, our 86th Mountain Infantry adjutant, exclaimed, "What a glorious expanse of sky!" I arrived in July after an eleven-day delay en route, having traveled from Washington, where Anne was editing in the Historical Branch of G-2 in the Pentagon. She was now four months pregnant with Kenneth. We paused in California, where she would live with her parents, my assignment to combat being imminent. So I was not in the best shape on arrival in Austin. It was the hottest day of the year, and in Austin, with its high humidity, that was bad news. I was immediately assigned as a platoon leader in Company I, 3d Battalion, 86th Mountain Infantry, and that night we were sent out to bivouac, a twenty-five-mile march away from our barracks. I had given up smoking throughout basic training and Fort Benning, but had picked it up again at Hale, rationalizing that I needed to smoke so that I would know when my men needed to smoke. As we started on that twenty-five-mile march I was not sure I had made the right decision. Somehow I held up – much better than on a later wearing night when, after twenty-four hours without sleep, I went out on night patrol. In the course of it, and for the only time in my life, I fell asleep while walking. I think I usually avoid hallucinations. That night I had enough for all time.

But what about Paul Lafferty? He was now a major, and commander of the 3d Battalion. Knowing of my lack of line training, and my year's devotion to teaching ten thousand men how to climb rocks, he had pulled me out of I Company and made me the battalion intelligence officer. As S-2, I was in command of that night patrol. Patrol leaders are not supposed to go to sleep while walking, and are not supposed to be as unaware as I was of what the patrol was supposed to find out. All Paul did this time was to assign me to something within my capabilities, and then somehow understand my failure to use them in my first test.

ARTUR ARGIEWICZ, JR.

AS THE TENTH MOUNTAIN DIVISION, from early February to early May 1945, fought its way across the North Apennines, the Po Valley, and into the Alps at Lake Garda, all too many of my friends who were platoon leaders, and good ones at that, didn't get a chance to go home again.

This was also true of men who were not platoon leaders. One of them, killed in action at age twenty-two, was a friend whose contribution I tried to explain in the *Sierra Club Bulletin* in 1945:

CASUALTIES IN THE TENTH MOUNTAIN were high for the short time—one hundred thirty days—it was in the line in northern Italy. Casualties would be high in any division given the job that was given the Tenth in the final months, especially if the division were to do that job with the battle skill attributed to the Tenth in the many commendations accorded it. That success, the result of combination of leadership, training, and individual skill, was of course costly—and the cost was paid by men who had come to the mountain troops from Alabama and Texas, with no love for mountains or any part of them, and by men who had traveled the mountain trails with you and me. Many Sierra Club members will remember Jack Benson, Rus Lindsey, and Art Argiewicz—Jack from the ski trails, Rus from Norden and rock-climbing, Art from four High Trips. They will remember others who died on battlefronts or in training, still others who must carry the mark of battle along with them now. That is, I hope they will remember—not with sackcloth, not with tears, but just by contemplating, a little, that what these men gave, willingly or not, has contributed toward an opportunity still to travel the trails.

To assess the contribution of each of these men is something I'm not prepared to attempt. But I know well that Art Argiewicz accomplished, against odds that should have discouraged a young man, things peculiarly reflecting skills that were enhanced by his contact with the Sierra Club. It so happened that he was the eighth man in the division to be killed in action. His death occurred in the confusion of a patrol skirmish at Quercicola, near Monte Belvedere, when he was leading his half of a squad to reinforce a strong point which was being infiltrated by a German patrol. His war was over while the front was still "static," before the division had been committed in an attack. He was then a private, first class. But his influence on the training of the mountain troops was to serve the division well on Riva Ridge during a major attack launched within a few days and may well continue to affect such mountain training as is carried on in years to come.

It would be hard for a soldier to understand how a private first class could influence an army training program; harder still, perhaps, for Sierra Club friends to appreciate how the influence could stem from a bespectacled lad with misfitting parka who had mischievously led lard fights in the 1938 High Trip commissary.

Without his glasses Art could hardly recognize a friend at fifteen feet, yet somehow he enlisted in the army, in late 1942. He wanted to be in the mountain troops. There he felt his rapidly increasing skill in the analysis of rock-climbing methods and equipment could be most useful, and there he landed, just as the snows were nearing their greatest depth at Camp Hale. If he had not already been regimentation's harshest opponent, he was soon to be. As he was put through such basic training as Hale could afford, and taught the agonies of the GI snowplow on Cooper Hill, he must have begun to wonder why he had chosen to enlist. But not for long. The Ground Forces established mountain maneuver areas in Virginia and West Virginia, and combed the personnel at Hale to find men who could best flash the light of mountain knowledge before selected flatland divisions to whom mountains were dark and foreboding. Art was among those chosen, and was flown to Virginia to teach rock-climbing—designated by the army as assault climbing. The training grounds were rocky, and covered by the soot of many years' accumulation from the trains that passed under the cliffs, but he grew on them. He had been well nurtured in Sierra Club lore of rock-climbing, but now his rapid growth of climbing skill, teaching ability, and supervising capacity left many of the old masters uncomfortably behind. His became one of the voices most heeded at meetings of instructors that determined what was to be taught. And he was as well heeded by students out on the rocks. Already sympathetic to their distaste for formal methods of army training, he was well suited to help in the outline of a course of instruction that was not "GI"—a course in which soldiers who didn't want any part of rock-climbing, put more on their own responsibility than the army would ordinarily have put them, would soon have their skilled instructors shuddering at the abandon with which they took to holdless pitches and nauseating overhangs. These soldiers would never, had they been asked, admit to any affinity for rock-climbing, but you didn't have to ask them. And they came, as soldiers most likely to become good specialists in climbing, from five flatland divisions.

Skill with his subordinates was possibly exceeded by Art's flair for maneuvering superiors with ideas different from his own into the realization of any absurdity of their argument. In a way he was still harassing his teachers as he had done in high school. But there was a friendly, if mischievous, smile in his manner as he did it, and the teachers learned. A lieutenant who had made a six- or seven-page outline of the course presented it to several of the instructors for remarks. The others may have found a moot point or two. I don't remember. But Art wrote twenty pages of caustic comment. What if he did throw away the pages, and present his case orally, with a concession here and there to diplomacy? He had still made himself known as the man who asked "why?" at the right times. For every error he caught or procedure he smoothed out, his superiors before long found another themselves, in anticipation of his scrutiny. I speak on this subject from an intimate knowledge, having long had to ask myself, before presenting a new idea on climbing to anyone, "What part of this will Argiewicz tear to pieces?" I was not, however, perpetrator of the outline that inspired the twenty pages of comment. Art always wrote for me at greater length. My revenge, of course, could be swift. "Sergeant Argiewicz," I would say (and the "sergeant" was just for company) "how would you like to work out a new thirteen-day schedule, including a new tactical problem for dessert that will really teach them something?" He would not, however, take off immediately and obediently produce such a schedule. Chances are he would present one, complete to a half-hourly breakdown, that he had already conceived in a hotel room in Petersburg during a weekend pass.

Several thousand men learned then, as well as a two-week concentrated course would permit, how to handle themselves in rugged terrain, day or night, with or without the rock-climber's gadgets. To what use this knowledge was put in combat, or will be put in civilian climbing by those who survived, it is too early to conclude. Even a careful perusal of the division histories of the Tenth, 28th, 35th, 45th, 75th, and 95th divisions might not reveal the full impact of this training. Whatever its ultimate value, however, Art put his best into it, and his fellow instructors, and his superiors who knew his work, appreciated it.

The mountain-training program ended. Art had said to me, "If I go back into regular line-outfit army life again, I'll withdraw so far into my shell it will make a turtle look like an extrovert." And he smiled a pleased smile as he realized how good a line he had composed. But although he did return to a line outfit, and suffered two harsh bits of injustice in being returned ahead of his fellow instructors and in being reduced in grade for failure to perform a job he was not permitted to perform, he did not go into that shell. In the closing days at Camp Swift, Army Ground Forces sent the manuscript for the new field manual, *Mountain Operations,* to division headquarters for final approval. I had dabbled with parts of the manual since 1942, and was asked for suggestions. I could do no better than call on Art, did, and the caustic comments began to appear again. He singled out the inconsistencies, found the gaps, wrote the correct doctrine, conceived new tactical training problems, posed for improved diagrams, edited my editing of his work, worked until two and three in the morning for ten days–AGF was in a hurry. Finally the portion on military rock-climbing, one-third of the manual, was reorganized, reillustrated, and rewritten, and was published essentially unchanged. The printed books reached the mountain troops just before they pushed off for the Po Valley flatlands, but at a time when mountain fighting of extreme difficulty was expected in the Alps. Art never saw it. He was not to know what impact his clear flow of thought and action, in a channel through which the Sierra Club started him, was to have on such mountain-training program as the army chose to continue. He would, I'm sure, be embarrassed but pleased to have Sierra Club members know it, and to remember his story should they happen again to see a fifteen-year-old, bespectacled lad lobbing lard in a High Trip commissary, or hear him yodeling from Cragmont Cliffs.

***Sierra Club Bulletin,* 1945**

The Apennines

When We Arrived in Naples on the previous Christmas Eve, with plans for an orderly transition from being troops in training to troops in combat, the Italian spin-off of the Battle of the Bulge had swept down the Italian west coast and we were rushed north to the Pisa plain to resist it. Our first taste of real war came when, in the course of an evening conditioning march along a railroad right-of-way, the men–singing "Lili Marlene" as they marched–managed to set off some German mines, and so did the medics who came to their rescue. The war had now become lethal to our outfit. Seven medics were killed. One of the injured medics was Robert Allen. He recovered and I have met him many times since in his Kendall Foundation role of dispensing relief to the Sierra Club and Friends of the Earth. His war ended early.

Mine went on and, fortunately, sent me from Pisa back to Pozzuoli, just north of Naples, for a refresher course in German strategy and tactics.

The Tenth Mountain's first and most famous combat achievement was well under way in late February 1945. Our rock-climbing background and training paid off in the surprise night attack on Riva Ridge, the Germans' key observation point from which on previous occasions they had directed the artillery fire that repulsed all attempts to take Monte Belvedere, which now could fall to the Tenth. Our 3d Battalion, 86th, was in reserve and now moved forward toward the final objective, Monte della Torraccia. Respectfully behind our forward elements, a battalion of the

85th Mountain Regiment, I climbed to the top of a gentle knoll facing the enemy to see what I could see. My only achievement en route was to get into an argument with Lieutenant Colonel John Hay, our own battalion commander, about where we were on his contour map. I won.

Atop the knoll I looked forward and saw nothing. Settling into a shallow slit trench I looked up. Immediately above me was a ragged little tree, leafless as it had to be in February. I looked to the rear, across a snowy little swale. Behind me I heard the *wump*! of a 75-mm howitzer, followed by a slight tick sound as the howitzer shell's casing brushed against a branch above me. I saw the rapidly diminishing dark circle of the rear of the shell as its sped beyond me to explode in a geyser of snow on the far side of the swale. Had the nose of the shell, containing the fuse, hit my branch instead, I would not have seen the geyser or anything else. It occurred to me that I need not remain in that slit trench any longer. I got up and walked, not sauntered, back to the battalion command post. I was now on borrowed time.

The 85th Regiment unit, which held the position in front of us, had dug in for the night in the woods forward of my knoll. "My troops are tired," their battalion commander, Lieutenant Colonel Stone, had said, and he ordered them to rest there in the shelter of the woods. Sometime in the night German patrols sensed where the battalion was, fired signal flares into the sky on both flanks, and German artillery plastered the area. Had the troops not dug in under the trees, casualties would have been light. Direct hits on foxholes are rare. But treebursts make direct hits unnecessary and casualties were horrendous.

The 2d Battalion, 85th, was hit too heavily to continue, and in the early morning hours the men of the 3d Battalion, 86th, filed past where I was at the battalion CP (command post), to pass through the beleaguered 85th and prepare for a dawn attack on Torraccia. As Sergeants Leo Healy and Dick Emerson, my closest friends from climbing school at Hale and West Virginia, passed, I shook their hands and wished them luck, not expecting to see them alive again. One word describes my own feeling at the onset of that first attack. Dread.

The attack was enormously successful. Jack Hay had insisted on heavy artillery preparation. The foxhole parapets of the German Mittenwald Mountain Battalion could absorb fire from a 30-caliber machine gun. But our heavy weapons company carried 50-caliber guns for which the parapets, and the men behind them, were no match. Torraccia was ours. The impregnable German North Apennine line had been penetrated. We could have pushed on immediately into the Po Valley because there was no further in-depth German defense. But there was also no in-depth support for continuing the attack. We had exceeded the expectations of the higher echelons. We were ordered to reorganize ourselves on what need not have been our final objective if the Italian theater generals had known how good our mountain division, fresh in the battlefield, would be.

We had hardly begun reorganizing when the Germans launched their night counterattack. This was no surprise. The Germans always tried to recover what they had just lost. A heavy artillery preparation was sent our way to soften us. Some three thousand rounds hit our position. The battalion CP in which we were huddled was a hastily assembled pile of sandbags thinly roofed. I had retreated to it from the slit trench dug—with a trenching tool scarred by enemy shrapnel—by Operations Sergeant Wilbur Vaughan and his assistant, Ted Rand, upon the taking of Torraccia. Arriving late as rear-echelon S-2, I had no time to dig and they invited me in, to lie in the shade, had there been any, of a battered leafless tree.

As the shells came in I was glad to get out of that shade, but uncertain of the identity of the incoming shells. If they were mortar shells, our position in defilade would not protect us, and it was easy to expect the shell that would penetrate the thin roof and end our war. My intelligence sergeant, Ernie Mareske, was dug in with his squad on the front of the slope, looking for enemy action, particularly for flash-bang data. Seeing the flash of enemy artillery in the night sky, he would read the azimuth to it and would time the shell's flight from flash to bang, thus giving him the distance, as well as the compass reading, to the offending gun. From these data he could give us the good news. "These are 75s, not mortars."

Those of us in the CP could thus lower our expectations, but the men in roofless foxholes could not. When the incoming artillery was at its highest intensity Jack Hay went outside and shouted, "Stay in your holes, men; we'll tell you when to move."

They stayed, and were spared what shrapnel does to men above ground and fleeing—a flight that would come naturally in a shell storm such as we were experiencing.

In the attack, Leo Healy had picked up a piece of shrapnel in his leg right at the start, as well as an undetermined bit of blast damage to his head from a shell that landed too close. He passed by me at the rear battalion CP, two prisoners in tow, as he headed for a hospital in Livorno. Duke Watson, our officer-in-charge when we closed Seneca, was leading I Company in the Torraccia assault and was severely (though not mortally) wounded and was carried out on the shoulder of his good friend, Ralph Bromaghin. Ralph, who repeatedly twitted Duke about his rosy complexion ("Duke, your face flushes like a toilet"), was also the spirit behind the Tenth Mountain's reputation as the most songful of U.S. military units. He was a morale man's morale man. When dawn came the next day Ralph was standing in his slit trench warming up his C-ration breakfast on a mountain stove. As a shell came whistling in and exploded I heard him call, "Medic! Medic!" and stepped out to learn the bad news. Those were his last words.

When the artillery preparation was over, the ground attack began—a frontal assault. One of our first captives was a German lieutenant, complete with a very good German reversible parka, the white side out, since there was still snow around us. There was a big pocket on the white side and a similar one on the tan side within, containing the lieutenant's field order and battle map. Proper procedure required moving prisoners swiftly to the rear, where trained intelligence people could debrief them. I knew of no one in higher echelons in the immediate rear who would have picked up what I learned in Pozzuoli. Moreover, we had good German language assistance right there on the line in I Company. Indeed, the Tenth Mountain was full of language help—climbers of French, Austrian, German, and Italian ancestry had flocked to the ski troops—and I called for it. I did not send our captured lieutenant to the rear. Our German-speaking corporal looked at the map and field order and couldn't make sense out of it. Time was wasting. I directed myself to concentrate. After all, what had I been to Pozzuoli for? Suddenly the map and field order told me what I needed to know. Our prisoner had been leading a platoon attacking our forward position frontally, but the main thrust would come up a ravine on our left flank. I told Jack Hay and he requested a massive concentration of artillery on the ravine. The concentration came promptly; the flank attack never showed up.

Our battalion's achievement was but part of what led to a commendation on February 25, 1945, to the officers and men of the Tenth from Major General George P. Hays, their commander:

> In your first assigned mission you had the following difficult tasks:
>
> a. Concentrate in a valley overlooked on three sides by the enemy, over an inadequate road net, without being discovered by the enemy.
>
> b. Seize by night assault the precipitous mountain range on your left consisting of mountains Mancinello, Serrassiccia, Cappel Busso, and Pizzo Campiano.
>
> c. Assault by night the enemy strong defensive line including the strong points of Mt. Gorgelesco, Mt. Belvedere, Valpiana, and the fortified towns of Corona, Pola, and Rocca Corneta.
>
> d. Hold the areas seized against counterattacks and capture the successive objectives northeast of Mt. Gorgelesco to include the final objective—Mt. Torraccia. A total advance from left to right of some eighteen thousand meters.
>
> You accomplished all of your assigned missions with magnificent dash and determination. You caught the enemy completely by surprise by your movement at night up precipitous slopes through his heavily mined areas and by your destruction of his dugouts and bunkers. You overran and defeated elements of eight different enemy battalions (parts of two divisions, plus two separate battalions), from which you captured approximately four hundred prisoners of war. You accomplished these results with remarkably low casualties, in comparison with results achieved. By your action you have won the confidence and admiration of all troops within the theater and the highest praise of your Corps, Army, Army Group, and Deputy Theater commanders.

As your Division Commander I am very proud of you and salute your courage, determination, fighting spirit, and the professional workmanship you have displayed in all your action.

The Italian front remained static until mid-April. Once again the 3d Battalion, 86th, was in reserve, but only briefly. Our unit was soon committed. I was riding forward in my S-2 jeep (an unusual break) when I heard my name called out from a file of men from the 87th. It was Jake Nunnemacher, the first man I had encountered at Carson in October 1942. I had not seen him since Camp Hale. We had time to exchange a few words. The feeling of dread was mutual, but I would be lucky. Just a few hours later he was killed.

Pursuit in the Alps

Once Again, to the surprise of higher headquarters, it was the Tenth that broke through, dropping out of the Apennines into the Po Valley, moving rapidly as a division combat patrol. The enemy was ahead of us, on both sides, and to the rear. We moved so swiftly that the Germans were in great confusion. At one point, their trucks brought supplies to us, instead of their own troops. Our own friends mistook us too, three U.S. P-38s strafing our motorized column. Hastily launched smoke-grenade signals told the next group of three who we were and they spared us. Buildings we bivouacked in and among at Bomporto were totally demolished by artillery soon after we left. We crossed the Po, liberated Verona, raced on to Lake Garda, and took Torbole and Riva, at its head—which I described in an article in the 1945 *Sierra Club Bulletin* that was part of my never-published war book:

Our First View of the Lake of Garda and the Alps around it came on the cold, stormy dawn of April 28, 1945, when our battalion of mountain troops first touched its hundred-mile shoreline. Through a drenching, all-night rain the 87th and 85th Mountain infantries had taken turns pursuing the fleeing Wehrmacht up the east shore from the Po Valley, and just before dawn the 86th passed through the forward elements of the 85th at a small group of resortlike villas known as Navene. Our eight-hour shift in the lead was coming up. At least it was supposed to be eight hours.

At Navene we found that the shoreline of Italy's largest lake was beginning to get rugged; gray granite cliffs and steep brushy slopes dropped sharply to the black, very deep, rough water, and rose more than seven thousand feet to the snow-covered bordering peaks. Along the east shore it became increasingly difficult for a highway to cling to the mountainside. About a mile north of the town was the first of a series of seven tunnels which led through the rocky buttresses to Torbole and Riva, larger towns at the north end of the lake. The first of those tunnels was now demolished, at least at its entrance, for the Germans had effectively halted the progress of the 85th by blasting the tunnel, as well as some minor bridges that led toward it. Preparatory to following the 86th's 2d Battalion, the 3d Battalion moved off the road and dispersed. Artillery and tanks moved up into position to fire on the enemy across the lake. The battalion CP was set up for the moment in a villa that had, until a day or two before, housed high German antiaircraft officers. It still housed—but not for long—a large hero-worshippers' portrait of Hitler. From the beach around the villa point we could have enjoyed our first close-up of the Alps, stormy though it was; but German shells began to whoosh over the point, to kick up fountains of water just beyond its far side. When our counterbattery fire put an end to this, we could still not settle down to enjoy either the villa or the scene.

The situation was not a happy one. We were committed to attack along Garda's east shore, where the ruggedness of the terrain multiplied the strength of each defending enemy soldier by ten. The highway, our main avenue of approach, was entirely too much an avenue for enemy defensive fires and demolitions. Word came down to the battalion that higher headquarters were considering a flanking action to the right of the highway. A trail led from Malcesine almost to the summit of the high escarpment east of the lake, then worked north, up and down, along the slopes of the ridge to a point above Torbole, at the head of the lake.

Wasn't this situation just what we were asking for? Hadn't we, as mountain troops, been trained and equipped for just such terrain? Shouldn't we be able to effect complete surprise by attacking along a route that the enemy—especially a disorganized enemy, few in number—would have to assume could defend itself? There were some who would answer yes to all these questions. But there were more who would answer no. Ironically, I remembered the training years that had gone before. At Camp Hale, and in West Virginia, in orientation lectures in which we tried to point out to mountain-troop and flatland GIs why we were giving them mountain training, one of my standard examples had been this: as the fighting in Italy moves northward, men are going to be needed for invasion routes across the Alps, or at least for flank protection when the Allied armies do a column right or column left to bypass the Alps. Some big gear in Washington will thumb through the files and say, "Aha! The Tenth (or the 28th, the 45th, 35th, 77th, or 95th) Division has been at Camp Hale (or West Virginia). They know all about mountain fighting. We'll use them." We could all laugh easily at that purported humor. We realized, first, how little we knew about mountains and how sadly unprepared we would be, after hardly more than a faltering mountain-training program in lesser American mountains, for the ever so much more thoroughly mountain-trained Germans fighting in the ever so much more rugged Alps. And in the second place, we were sure that the big gears knew of our shortcomings, and that such a horrible predicament could never happen to us.

So here we were, mountain troops, fighting in the Alps at last. But where was our mountain equipment? Presumably, it was back in Naples. Higher echelons weren't interested in mountain equipment, anyway. The equipment and clothing with us were no different from the ordinary flatland GI's equipment, right down to the last shred of underwear—except that even most of the flatland apparel had been left behind when we jumped off, and we hadn't had so much as a change of underwear for about a month and a half. Ropes, mountain boots, sleeping bags? Why ask about those? We hadn't yet captured enough German blankets to give more than one man in ten a blanket to his name. The Tenth Mountain was less well equipped for mountains than were the flatland men who had suffered so many needless casualties from weather and terrain on Attu! Yet the Alpine weather and snows above Lake Garda could be fully as severe.

How about the time element? Hastily calculating from my own mountain experience, I estimated that in good weather, with no snow on the trail, one man, who knew a little about mountains and was properly dressed for them but otherwise climbing free of load, could have covered the high route to Torbole in about seventeen hours. How would a battalion fare? The weather was not at all good; an unknown amount of snow covered the upper slopes. We may have had many men who knew a little about mountains when we hit Italy, but the division's four thousand casualties had included too many of the original mountain men. We utterly lacked proper clothing and equipment. A battalion column would be four miles long, hard to control, and flank protection for the column would be all but forbidden by the steepness of the slopes on either side of the trail. Without mules, we could hardly hope to secure such close artillery support as might be necessary. And finally, far from being free of loads, the men would have to carry weapons and ammunition. That would be bad enough for riflemen. Heavy weapons men would have tougher sledding still.

The road and the right flank were out. The left-flank route remained—the choppy waters of Garda, breaking against the lakeshore cliffs beneath the highway, fully exposed to all artillery fire the enemy could bring to bear. It must have been a difficult decision to make; it was certainly an unprecedented decision: the Tenth Mountain Division would conduct an amphibious operation in the Alps!

Just about at this time, an ironical, terrible smirk crept over the face of Fate with a capital *F*. A few hundred miles south of us, the highest echelons, seated in the comfortable splendor of the royal summer palace at Caserta, had fixed their names to the papers terminating German resistance in Italy and southern Austria. But at Lake Garda neither we nor the

Germans knew it. The speed of our advance had been just about as hard on our own communications as it had been on theirs.

Perhaps more through fortune than foresight, a covey or flight of "ducks" (amphibious trucks), attached to the division at the time of the Po crossing, was still with us, having been used to augment six-by-sixes in the motor march to Lake Garda; the ducks would have enough freeboard for the choppy lake water. So Malcesine became a port of embarkation for the men of the 2d Battalion. They boarded the ducks, which thereupon headed up the lake to bypass the demolished tunnels, staying close to the shore for what protection it might afford. No sooner had the flight of ducks become a fleet than the Germans replied with their only defense—antiaircraft artillery. Garda had been a hot spot for Allied airmen who flew bombing runs across the Alps, and the 88s that had harassed them were now depressed to blast the ducks out of the water. They cut loose from their positions in Riva and Torbole, with time fire that burst in angry black flak-puffs over the ducks, and with point-detonation shells that shot geysers high in the air above the ducks and their burden of mountaineers. Some shells blasted the cliffs above the fleet, and falling rocks were added to the flying fragments. The ducks moved farther offshore. The firing gained in intensity.

To those of us back at Malcesine who watched the scene, swearing at the Krauts, sweating out the 2d Battalion men as they moved steadily on through falling rock, flak, and geysers, straining to pick out enemy gun positions as counterbattery targets, it seemed as if the Tenth Mountain's first amphibious attack could only be annihilated. Men couldn't live out there. Then the word came back that there had been no casualties—and that it was our turn. Not daring to expect such amazing luck, we took off, some twenty-five men to each bobbing target. Our first ducks were untouched, but later loads were less fortunate.

Bypassing the first two tunnels, as had the 2d Battalion, we landed on a tiny beach in a cove, scrambled up the steep slope to the highway, and moved into the shelter of the third tunnel, which was free of demolitions. Meanwhile, the 2d Battalion had moved up the road nearly a mile and had set up a defensive position for the night. Under cover of darkness we passed through their position and set up our own well beyond it. Here the slope to the east was less severe, and although traversing it would not be easy, we welcomed the opportunity to deploy the battalion. Companies I and K would make the traverse; L Company would continue along the highway.

Whatever remnant of the night had been left for sleep was made as uncomfortable as possible by the continuing light drizzle. But a dark, cloudy, drizzly night on a steep, slippery, and rocky mountainside was luxury compared to what was coming up.

On Lake Garda, Italy, being shelled. Dave is in the middle. Photo by Walter Neuron.

Now the weather cleared. Observation was excellent—altogether too much of an advantage to the defending forces. The delay along the road which had been brought about by expert German demolition work gave the enemy a chance to organize his defense. But time had worked against us. Lack of sleep was beginning to show. Because of the rain, a late start, and the irregular motion of the trucks, the men had not slept too well during the move from Bussolengo, in the Po Valley. Most of the following night they had been moving toward the forward defensive position, digging in to improve that position, and getting ready to move out for the dawn attack. In fact, none of the men had enjoyed a full night's sleep since the Po River was crossed, and that had been the only good night since the final push began in the Apennines, fifteen long, demanding days from this spot on Garda's shore. Nor had there been time to eat properly. The men were worn.

But the attack continued. L Company men moved ahead through another tunnel, short and free of demolitions. But they couldn't get out of it. The north end was covered by machine-gun fire from an embrasure carved out of the solid granite just to one side of the entrance to the next tunnel. M Company men moved up a 50-caliber machine gun to seal off the embrasure with far more deadly fire than it could return. Under this cover, riflemen spurted forward, tossed grenades through the doorway in the wall of the next tunnel which connected with the embrasure room. Two of its occupants staggered out into the tunnel to die; another six lay where they were. The tunnel was ours, and the advance elements of L Company moved quickly through the black interior, to stumble over a pile of debris in the far end.

This was the Tunnel of the Dead, and Death had not left it. The first American troops to reach the far end had already seen too much horror to absorb any of the horror that met them there. Possibly it pleased them at the time. The debris was not all inorganic; it was a shambles. Apparently a rear-guard crew of about twenty Germans – it was not now possible to discern exactly how many – had been hand-moving a 20-mm antiaircraft gun to a new defensive position to their rear, where they could keep it depressed and continue to fire on infantry, not aircraft. The gun carrier was loaded with ammunition. Somehow they ran afoul of their own demolitions, likewise intended for us. Their war ended quickly, if not prettily. The explosion set fire to their own ammunition and to them. Pieces of men were scattered as far as fifty feet out of the tunnel. Part of the massive rock roof of the tunnel collapsed and fell to the floor, but there was too little rock to complete the burial or to extinguish the smoldering.

The L Company men moved forward over the debris, on toward the seventh – and last – tunnel, which curved, its far end being lined up directly on Torbole. The Germans did not intend to have L Company get out of this one, either, and fired machine-gun and pom-pom (20-mm antiaircraft bursting shells) fire into their end of it. Too many ricochets reached for our end, and L Company stopped.

The heavy weapons company men moved to the debris-filled mouth of tunnel number six to plan what relief they could for L Company. Major Bill Drake, now our battalion commander (Lieutenant Colonel John Hay was regimental executive officer at this point), was there. With him was Major John Seamans, now 2d Battalion commander, reconnoitering for a relief of our battalion. To complete the battalion staff representation, the tunnel-end party included Lieutenant Jim Church, M Company commander, Captain Barrett Ely, H Company CO, Lieutenant Ernie Field, 3d Battalion S-3, and Lieutenant Doug Butterwick, the battalion's antitank officer. Then there was the artillery forward observer, and Regular Army Sergeant Davis, one of the best machine-gun men in the business, plus about half of M Company. Some of the men were in the tunnel. Others were spread out in front. Suddenly, a few airbursts from the German 88s at Riva rent the air overhead and drove all the men into the tunnel for protection.

The battalion CP, where I was at that moment, was quite comfortably situated behind tunnel number five at the only point nearby from which radio contact could be had with the traversing companies and L Company. It was sunny, shrubs and annuals around us were showing their springtime greenery, and a few men went down to the lake to fill their canteens with mountain water. An ominous message came back from the battalion commander's radio operator.

"Send up all the litter teams you can get!" Captain Ev Bailey, now the battalion executive officer, relayed the message to the aid station, farther back along the road.

Soldiers don't pale easily. But Lieutenant Butterwick, who came running back to our CP about then, was pale. A piece of shell fragment an inch across had ripped into, but had not entered, the top of his steel helmet, and was still embedded there, although he didn't know it.

"Major Drake's been hit," he said to Bailey, "and wants you to take over. They got a direct hit inside the tunnel."

The details came later. The airbursts had driven everyone into the tunnel. Then a one-in-a-thousand shot hit the jackpot, and burst some fifty feet inside the tunnel. Those who were not hit with shell fragments or rock splinters were at least temporarily stunned or deafened. Some thought that another demolitions charge had gone off inside the tunnel. Others thought that an airburst had detonated in midair between the tunnel walls. Before the smoke and dust cleared there was the terrible sound of many moans. Men in agony screamed, "Medic! Medic!" It was a long time before the medics and litter teams arrived to salvage the living. The final toll was seven dead [including Barrett Ely, with whom I had long ago played touch football] and forty-four wounded. For one shell.

It was imperative to get some of the injured men back to complete medical aid as soon as possible. With help from the walking wounded, the litter teams moved them to comparative safety behind a buttress some distance back along the road. But engineers had not yet been able to repair the demolished road to Malcesine, and the remaining route of evacuation had to be by water. As one man in the battalion, Private First Class Ross, wrote, "The Germans had the water beyond the protecting rock ridge registered in and it was only with great difficulty that ducks could move in and out with ammo and supplies. Consequently, fast assault boats, powered with outboard motors, were called up. They were just large enough to hold two litters and the one-man crew, and were manned by an engineer outfit that did a superb job in keeping the old motors going as the small craft bounced from wave to wave. Several of them stalled, but the engineers always managed to get them started again before enemy artillery could zero in."

Devastating though the shell in the tunnel had been, the attack went on. By that night Companies I and K relieved the pressure on the far end of the last tunnel, and L Company fought its way into town. The battalion CP was set up among the German corpses in tunnel number six, and experienced great difficulty in maintaining communications. Only radio was available, and although well outside the tunnel, it was too well shielded by cliffs. Artillery men hand-moved their pack 75s into the tunnel, but had no targets to fire on. The will to attack seemed to be disintegrating into a stupor. In the rear echelons of the battalion the third sleepless night was beginning to tell. However, adrenalin distilled in fear was meanwhile keeping the forward elements well awake.

Excerpts from some of the front-line riflemen's accounts show that a staggering sort of progress survived that day's pandemonium. My closest friend in the mountain troops, Staff Sergeant Dick Emerson, third platoon guide for Company I, was a cool observer and participant in what turned out to be I Company's only fiasco:

"Early in the morning the men were wakened and the advance was continued (without time for eating). The day was off to a bad start. We moved in a long traverse of the mountain wall above the lake, on trail part of the time, but mostly in the tall thick brush. The pace was moderate, but the going was rough, what with the heavy loads of ammo and weapons. Finally, around noon, I Company, rounding the shoulder of the mountain, looked down on Torbole and called a halt.

"Up to this time very few I Company men knew the scheduled plan of attack, including many of the NCOs. I Company was to lead off, with K in reserve. Our position on the hill was excellent for observation and cover. Lieutenant Elufson, the acting company commander, and the four platoon leaders, with NCOs, observed and chose the likely route. It entered the town from above and behind, through a corridor of olive trees with a rock wall on either side. (Both these rock walls, it was found later, were well fortified.)

"Leading down the mountainside diagonally toward the town was a trail. The second platoon led off single file. The third, then the first, and finally the weapons platoons followed. As soon as the second platoon started down, it was fired on by long-range sniper fire. Immediately the platoon leader radioed back, 'We're pinned down by sniper fire.' Only two shots had been fired! Machine-gun sections were moved up to give covering fire. They opened up, spraying likely positions below—but the company didn't advance. Technical Sergeant Staley was given command of the second platoon. Again the covering fire started and the second and third platoons moved down the slope. Snipers picked at each man as he displaced forward. Generally the shots missed by a good six feet.

"By this time the sun was getting low. Radio contact with the second platoon was lost, so Lieutenant Rivers, of the Third, went down with his radio man to regain contact and find out what the trouble was. The radio man was hit on the way. About then the Jerries were seen to drag up a howitzer some fifteen hundred yards away and drop shells directly on the trail, inflicting casualties with each shell. Word was sent for the knee mortar to be brought up as a counter. The weapons platoon lieutenant had no knee mortar, so he sent the three mortar crews down the trail, mortars and all. Several were hit by the sniper because they presented too slow a target with their burdens. The mortars were never used.

"An order then came to withdraw. The second platoon was already down the mountain, and the third almost. The second was in a good covered position and would have suffered coming back up, but could not advance alone. The third was brought back up to help the first as support for K Company, which was now going to bypass I Company on a more direct route down. The second platoon was left where it was, with Lieutenant Rivers and a machine-gun section. They were not to move until dawn.

"Back on top again, Lieutenant Walucz took over the third platoon and I Company moved down behind K. Throughout the day I Company had plenty of spirit, but severely lacked leadership." Before dawn this battalion of mountain troops was to have run the gamut of infantry fighting. Already they had patrolled in camouflage whites and on skis in the Apennine snows, had fought their way down out of the Apennines while being supplied by mule, had walked through Po Valley farmlands, been cheered by liberated Italians, had ridden in motorized task force columns, had been strafed, had crossed a river in assault boats, captured a city, in the Alps had gone amphibious, and now had about accomplished a flanking action on a steep mountain slope. But they had not yet tangled with tanks. Staff Sergeant Faulkner, who was with the company now about to lead, describes the renewed attack:

"Finally the word came back that K Company was to go down the mountainside to take Torbole. Meanwhile the good old Air Corps was giving Jerry a hard time by dropping bombs and strafing, which enabled us to go down the slope undetected and without taking any casualties. We then had to cross a large, barren, rock-studded plateau in order to enter the outskirts of town. Three snipers spotted us, and they, plus two men with burp guns, pinned us down. By rushing from rock to rock we made it to a grove of trees and there organized our next plan of attack.

"Staff Sergeant Holbrook of the first squad in the third platoon nearly jumped into a foxhole with a Jerry, but he spotted him in time. It was from this Jerry that we got our information about what was in Torbole. He told us that there were three tanks in town and about eighty men from different outfits. We sent him back to the rear and started down the rest of the way into town.

"By this time it was dark; we had lost contact with the second platoon and most of the weapons platoon. We cleared out the first house we came to, which was used as a company CP and aid station.

"Part of the town was burning, so it enabled us to watch the streets more easily. All at once we heard a clatter of tanks and several loud reports. Everyone began to head for the hospital, a large building down by the lake's shore; but the two lieutenants got together and decided we could stop a counterattack more easily in the village square. So everyone took off like a herd of turtles to the village square.

"The counterattack started about ten at night and lasted until 4:30 next morning. It was pretty nerve-racking in those buildings, where you never knew where one of those tanks would roll around a corner and open up on the building you were in."

The 1st Battalion did have trouble, but finally took Nago. Meanwhile, however, neither K Company nor the 3d Battalion were through yet. Another man from K Company tells the rest of the story:

"Torbole had been a very pretty place, the kind you see pictured on Italian tourist posters, a clear blue lake, a small clean town on the shore, steep mountains, and a ruined castle on a promontory above the town. Torbole now, however, was the scene of fighting for a day. Formal gardens had shell craters in them, trees were shattered, and shops had been blown open and the merchandise scattered in the street. Although the search disclosed no live Germans, it did turn up a surprising number of souvenirs.

"Regimental headquarters moved up to town that morning, and supplies and artillery began coming up on ducks and by sailboat. Once again shells fell in the town as the Germans attempted to hit the vehicles and vessels moving in and out of the small Torbole harbor. Most of the shells landed harmlessly in the water, but occasionally one would land on the road along the shore. One of these killed Regimental Sergeant Major Evans and Colonel Darby, famous as a leader of the Rangers, who had just been transferred to the Tenth Mountain Division as assistant commandant."

By that evening the 3d Battalion, following the 2d, had settled into and around a three-hundred-year-old villa just vacated by German officers; the quarters were comfortable, and to add to the luxury, an issue of clean clothing was begun there. L Company, in response to a dramatic partisan note from the town of Arco, which ended, "We cannot hold out much longer," moved north five miles on the morning of May 2 and took the town without incident. Meanwhile, the issuing of equipment continued, and sleeping bags were included. There were higher, colder mountains to the north, and preliminary plans were being discussed for a further attack along the high Alpine ridges leading toward the Germans' last-ditch "Redoubt." With one eye on these higher mountains and their fortunately unoccupied, all-but-impregnable prepared emplacements on the slopes we had already passed, we strolled around the streets of Riva to see what we could, while we might, of one of Italy's most beautiful resort cities.

Riva and Torbole, to judge from the red crosses on almost all buildings, had been used largely as a hospital area. In addition, however, we found underground factories, the most extensive of them being devoted to the manufacture of airplane parts. On the shore of the lake an astounding discovery was made. We had already seen ducks, assault boats, and sailboats on the lake. There had been a steam-driven ship there as early as 1828, and a boat propelled by the harnessed power of a horse going around the deck in circles had antedated the steamer. Consequently we should not have been surprised to find in a lakeshore shed an almost completed submarine. It was very small, but it would seem to indicate that the Lake of Garda was to have been the last home of the Italian navy. Clearly the Tenth Mountain Division could achieve nothing finer. It had captured the navy intact!

Odd information had been filtering down from higher headquarters for some time. Back in the Apennines we had been told twice that at a certain time on a certain evening a German plane would fly over the lines and was not to be fired on. On another occasion we were told to be on the lookout for a German who would come to our lines and give a certain name. He was to be sped to the rear. Then, on April 30, we heard that there was to be no further air support in the theater. Two days later we had been ordered not to fire on Germans who looked as if they didn't want to fight. Arco had fallen without a shot.

At about 1700 on May 2, in the battalion CP at San Alessandro, the phone rang. They wanted "Blue 6," the battalion commander, and Captain Everett Bailey answered. He listened intently, as usual.

"What?" he asked, in a rather unmilitary manner. And the message was repeated to him. He smiled and grabbed my arm. "Dave, the war is over in Italy!"

Four days too late.

***Sierra Club Bulletin,* 1945**

The war story I like most to tell came about after the war in Italy had ended. From our battalion CP in San Alessandro, just up from Riva, we headed on our next mission. We were part of a regimental task force that was to proceed through Bolzano and Merano to Passo di Resia, on the Austrian-Italian border, and await further orders there. Lieutenant Colonel John Hay commanded the regimental task force. I had known him first as Major Hay, our Third Battalion CO, and would trade war stories with him much later, when I was a major, and he out of habit kept referring to me as lieutenant. What I remembered of our Italian campaign, and what he remembered, were so different you would think we were in different wars together. In a sense we were. For one thing, he had the perspective of a West Pointer, which I didn't. For another, he was to go on with his military career and become a lieutenant general. When I learned this I was more pleased than surprised. He was a hell of a good military leader. But I gave him good advice while I could still call him Jack.

Our task force was a column of vehicles four miles long. He was at the head of it and I was a good three miles behind, but in radio contact. We wound slowly up the Alpine road, passing the German troops who needed to retreat no longer and who were still armed. They were not smiling at us, much less waving the way Italians would, but I sensed that they were as glad as we were that their next move would be to POW camp in the Po Valley.

Our pace was governed by the slowest vehicle, and night fell soon after we had passed Merano. Out of habit we turned on our blackout lights. The idea behind blackout lights is that they are not to be seen by the enemy you are moving toward. By strange coincidence, this means that they are also not seen by the highway, which in turn means that the highway cannot look back at you and tell you where it is. It would be better to train fireflies to do their on-and-off act along the route ahead of you. Or to have a blind man in the lead. In short, driving blackout is no fun.

We were now about to travel the final miles to Passo di Resia on a road that meandered several miles up a broad meadow, each meander visible from the pass in daylight, but now not visible to our various drivers. I called our commander on the radio. "Jack, the war is over. Why the hell are we driving with blackout lights?" He granted that I had a point. He gave the order to turn on the normal headlights. Our four-mile-long meandering task force lit up.

The task force commander was not, of course, at the ultimate head of the column. As in all operations, there was a point, the small group of men who lead with their chins, and who arrived at the pass to find that its German defenders had not heard that the war was over. They had their hands on the lanyards ready to blow us away. Their forward positions had reported our approach. Then our lights came on. Fortunately, they assumed we knew something they didn't know, and didn't fire.

If my happiest recollection of World War II is Bailey's saying the war is over, my second happiest is the accidental role I played in letting the defenders of Passo di Resia know it was over.

What I would most like to forget is what happened as we were crossing the Po Valley. We were moving as rapidly as we could, delayed only by small centers of resistance, the smallest of which were the snipers. The mission of the sniper is not an enviable one. He is the one left behind to delay his opponent as best he can and thus give his unit time to retreat with minimum loss. If he fails, his unit suffers. If he succeeds, he is fair game for the opponent.

A sniper who had delayed us by killing one of our men was brought back, after capture, to the battalion S-2, me. The man who brought him back was the buddy of the man he had killed, but nevertheless did bring him back, hands over the head, prisoner-style, as required by the rules.

If I had judged the situation well I'd have said something like: "Good job, fella. We'll take care of this son of a bitch." And I would have said it without dawdling. But I didn't. Suddenly our man turned on the sniper and fired, killing him. We looked at his papers and the photos of his children,

Dave Brower on the upright, Po Valley at the end of World War II, 1945. Photograph by Wilbor Vaughan.

and I'll not be able to forget his last look at us—which would not have been his last look had I made an instant decision and acted upon it.

GI Climbs

THE TENTH'S COMMANDING GENERAL, George Hays, had told us on arrival in Italy that there would be bad times and good times. The bad were over, and I wrote about some of the good:

IN THOSE LAST DAYS OF FIGHTING in the Alpine foothills, along the shores of Lake Garda, there were few men in the Tenth Mountain Division who were not slightly awed by the abrupt and towering walls that rose seven thousand feet above the lake on either side. True, they were perhaps impressed more by the elaborate—and happily unoccupied—fortifications high on the slopes than by any academic problems in mountaineering. But with the final dash through Merano, and under the ten-thousand-foot wall of the Ortler and its glaciers, up to the border at

Passo di Resia, climbing fever struck. Surrounded by snowfields, cliffs, glaciers, and warehouses full of captured German mountain-troop equipment, our own Mountain Troops were more than ready to direct their mountain training toward other than military ends. Some military rock-climbing, glacier, and ski schools were set up, and instructors and pupils could refresh themselves on technique, whether at Trafoi, under Palla Bianca, near Passo del Predil in the Julian Alps, or on the Obersterpasterzenboden on Austria's highest peak, the Gross Glockner. They were then ready for busmen's holidays when weekends, free time, and occasional jeep transportation rolled around. Accounts of the climbing accomplishments of Sierra Club members in the division are not very well documented. During the period of occupation, members in different regiments were widely scattered, good telephone communication was not to be had, and it was hard to keep track of the men who had so often been less than a rope's length away.

But we could turn to *The Yodeler* belatedly to learn what had happened, and read "of Lieutenant Raffi Bedayn's eight-day leave, during which he had hoped to climb the Matterhorn, but was forestalled by bad weather and so turned to Mont Blanc," and his report that "the skiing is average, with some fair nine-thousand-foot runs off Monte Rosa. Mont Blanc was an interesting climb."

In a later *Yodeler,* Milton Hildebrand supplied some missing facts on this account, and added notes on his own climbs:

"A week ago Sunday I climbed Austria's Gross Glockner with Charlie Hanks. It was the second ascent of the mountain for Charlie, but he went up to act as my guide. It is a nice climb . . . rather easy, but required a little care.

"Last Sunday I followed Raffi's example and climbed Mont Blanc from Courmayeur. . . . (He) had a good day and tracks to follow, but made the round trip, an ascent of nearly 11,000 feet, in one day without a guide – a stunt which brought some rather favorable comment from veterans in the area. I did it the conventional way. I was without a competent climbing partner, so I joined a party of South Africans. We left the road in the afternoon and climbed to the Gouella Hut at 10,200, where we watched the clouds swirl and change and kept our fingers crossed. The stars came out about midnight and at 3:30 A.M. we started up the Mont Blanc glacier. There were three ropes in the party, each led by a guide who carried a candle lantern. We wound our way through the crevasses, and dawn found us on the narrow ridge. There the wind lashed snow-banners past our legs and it was bitter cold. Two men remained in the Vallot Hut, at 14,450 feet, while the rest of us pushed on to the summit."

Dolomites

Subsequently I learned that Charlie Hanks had also climbed the Piccola Cima (Kleine Zinne), of the Tre Cime di Lavaredo, one of the famous peaks of the Dolomites. This was getting into some of the country I knew. For on a Saturday evening in early June most of the instructors of the 86th's 3d Battalion climbing school had assembled in the little hotel under the Tre Cime with ambitious plans. Some of the men had been interested in the Comici route on the north face of the Grande Cima—a route that involved days of class-six climbing as well as the leader's hauling pitons up in a bucket whenever his stock ran low. But the class-five route on the Piccola north face looked better. Six of us started to look at it more closely, cutting up the hard snow of the couloir northwest of the peak, looking for a take-off for the vertical face, but continuing to the Grande-Piccola notch before finding such a route. Blocked only by a little barbed wire and an old machine-gun position, relics of World War I, the route led from the notch up over a broken but exceedingly steep face. The guidebook called it class three, which according to American standards required only a rope—just in case. Not being too sure that the Italians had our standards in mind when they numbered the route, we also took along hammers, pitons, and carabiners.

It was just as well. Ledges, scree-slopes precariously perched, and easy chimneys led back and forth, across and up the face nicely. But one of our three ropes of two consisted of two of the best instructors from the old Seneca Assault Climbing School in West Virginia—Dick M. Emerson, of Salt Lake City, and Leo A. Healy, of Boston. They somehow got off the route and onto a class-six variation of their own. Richard F. Weber and I, on another rope, were happy to have carabiners along, for there were three old pitons along the route, one of which was of assistance in getting us up an overhanging chimney, worn smooth, seemingly by too much use. All of us were quite content to rappel, and not climb, down from the airy summit.

Il Cervino

Raffi Bedayn had gone little farther than the Col du Lion on the Italian side of the Matterhorn—Il Cervino, to the Italians. Thanks to similarly bad weather Ernest K. Field, of the 86th, one of the ablest Colorado climbers, had not been able to reach that point. Expecting to fare no better than Bedayn or Field, Emerson, Healy, and I were yet almost irresistibly drawn to the Matterhorn when our turn for a rest leave came up in early July. We forsook the Glacier School, added a trailer to my S-2 jeep, threw in extra rations, extra gasoline, and climbing gear, and with Private First Class Frank Carriera, of Oakland, at the wheel, took off.

None of us had toured Italy before the war, and therefore couldn't very well compare our mode of travel with that of peacetime tourists. But we could well imagine that we were enjoying something distinctive. There were no crowds at the mountain hotels—military transport was about the only means of travel available. Outwardly, at least, the Italians seemed to welcome us. The mountains were well rested. We could not, of course, particularly enjoy Italian cooking. Their food was scarce, and although we sometimes let Italians cook and share our rations, we still felt we had mastered the cookery better than they. There was no gas rationing to worry about. We had merely to ask at each "Pet Depot" where the next gasoline dump was, count the miles and our gallons of gas, and drive on. To cross a border we had but to stop, exchange salutes, and continue. At Breuil the guides, by now accustomed to military traffic, told us the Matterhorn was impossible without guides. But once I had found a guide who understood my French (somewhat more fluent than my Italian or their English) and had shown him our climbing gear, nylon rope inclusive, we experienced only the most pleasant cooperation. We were shown the route, step by step, on a photograph of the mountain. In perfect weather we started out that afternoon for the Abruzzi refuge, high above the Col du Lion.

Late the next afternoon we were back at the hotel. We had reached the hut, enjoyed the night there, had found not too much new snow on the route, had followed that route to an elevation some eight hundred feet below the summit, which meant we had climbed seventy-two hundred of the eight thousand feet that the summit rose above Breuil. And the weather had remained perfect. But there, at fourteen thousand one hundred fifty feet, Leo had become acutely mountain sick. We turned back, now well aware of the size of the mountain. We were willing to concede a lot to those who had first ascended by this route, unaided by fixed ropes and nail scratches. Possibly those very ropes added to the unfriendly impression the mountain gave us. They were white with age, badly frayed at crucial points, and were anchored at the top with too little regard for physics—the simple, unnuclear variety. But it is a big mountain. You climb for hours, and it still rises more hours above you. The exposure—the thousands of feet of precipice plunging to the glaciers below—is, and I can think of no better word, classical.

Charmoz-Grèpon

Since Sierra Club climbers seemed to fare better in the Mont Blanc region, we next headed for Chamonix. Italy's lowland tourist meccas had been chosen as rest centers for the mountain troops. Chamonix was the rest center for an air defense command. The management accepted us as transients, specifying only that we not attempt to climb without guides. Each of us had a room with private bath in the Majestic Hotel, each room containing a double bed in which we could sleep equally comfortably crosswise or normally oriented. To infantrymen this was so elegant that it was a wonder we ever did get out of bed and climb. But we did, guideless. It was necessary only to give the rest center's commanding officer a slightly exaggerated account of our mountaineering proclivities. We had intended to be modest, but when I stated, "We're from the Mountain Troops," he asked only, "What are you doing over here?" I went on, detailing the mountain training we had given six divisions, the manual we had helped write, the skiing we had done, the civilian mountaineering, and added an alphabetical list of the American mountaineering clubs whose techniques we were familiar with. I never did ask him what part of my speech turned the trick, but he gave us the key to the Alps under his command, and turned his recreation department over to us. That included the counsel of some of the region's expert guides, and we ended up with a choice of adventures: (1) We could ski. This would entail borrowing skis, riding the completed portion of the Aiguille du Midi téléphérique eight thousand feet above the valley, next riding the uncompleted part up another three thousand feet, finally skiing down the Val Blanc to the Mer de Glace, thence down among its crevasses to the Hotel Montanvers, and back to Chamonix by cog railroad. (2) We could climb. Since we had shown an interest in the Aiguille du Grèpon, we were presented with a sketch, annotated in French and English, of the Charmoz-Grèpon traverse, class-four.

It was a hard choice to make. Skiing in France in July would have given us a wedge into any postwar skiing conversation. But that incomplete téléphérique gave us pause. A mechanized ascent of eleven thousand feet might very well have its pleasures; but the man who would ride that last three thousand feet suspended on a hair-thin, half-inch cable, seated only on a board with a capacity of two, not including feet, would also have his anxieties. We would climb.

Our reconnaissance had already been started over wine glasses when we procured our chart from the guides. We completed it July 17 with a morning's ride by téléphérique to Le Brévant, five thousand feet above Chamonix and across the valley from the Grèpon. That afternoon we rode the cog railway to Montanvers. We had planned on a quiet afternoon at the hotel, a fair night's rest, and an early start for our climb. But to a group of ex-GI climbing instructors, the climb was almost an anticlimax; for the train unloaded us in the middle of a climbing class being given a small unit of the Chasseurs Alpins—the French mountain troops. I must now defend what we were about to do. Dick Emerson, Leo Healy, and I had long worked as a team in military climbing instruction. Almost twice a month, for many of our months in West Virginia, we had put on climbing demonstrations, the most sensational part of which had been the holding of piton falls. Leo would climb up a thirty-five-foot cliff to a carabiner through which his rope ran back down to Dick. He would then gather in about twenty feet of slack and jump, relying upon Dick to stop his fall, pulleywise, from below. Mere stopping of the fall became so routine that I would place an X on the cliff and have Dick stop Leo so precisely that his feet would strike

Dick Emerson and Leon Healy on the summit of the Grèpon. Photograph by David R. Brower.

the mark—which was three feet above the ground. My part in the demonstration was to give the lecture—and to insist that the mark be at least three feet high. I go into this detail merely to show why we by now had become exhibitionists.

We immediately noticed that our French counterparts were using what we believed to be incorrect knots, as well as the unsafe shoulder belay (wrongly, at that), that their rappelling procedure was slow, that their pitons were driven insecurely in poor places, that their carabiners were hooked incorrectly, and that they were teaching party climbing with four on a rope. We sputtered quietly for a while, then retired to the hotel, changed to sneakers, and returned with nylon rope and hardware. Leo started it. Timidly he asked if he might try to rappel. With some misgivings, not being too sure he knew how, they acquiesced. He climbed into the army hasty rappel (rope only around one leg) and vanished in one sizzling bound. From then on the show was ours.

The Frenchmen took such presumptuous behavior far better, I'm afraid, than we would have. The aftermath was that they supplied some missing details on our route and wanted badly to buy the sneakers right off our feet.

Next morning we found that, perhaps through the efforts of a guides' association, the trails were unmarked. We do not care to admit how much time we wasted in the Alplands looking for the best way to the Glacier des Nantillons. There we put on crampons, and, since the weather was balmy and unthreatening, I put mine on sneakers, saved the weight of another pair of climbing boots, and got along very well. The region was so similar, in all but scale, to the Sawtooth Ridge country in northern Yosemite that I felt quite at home, and as we left the glacier and started scrambling over the fine granite, I made the mistake of asking aloud, "When does the climbing begin?" Almost immediately we had to begin looking for pitons. I added one in the ice chimney, both for protection in leading over ice in sneakers and to confound those who would follow along the route. It is an angle piton, invented by Dick Leonard for the American army and unique, I am sure, on the Mont Blanc massif. The traverse of the Charmoz arête was what we, too, would have called class four, adding, "with short class-five pitches." The rock was splendid, the exposure was exhilarating, the route was intricate; our rope of three was notably slower than two ropes of two would have been. Leo led the famous Mummery Crack expertly. Bringing up the rear, I noticed that, although puffing, I had had far more holds for my left leg and hand than Mummery's description—"clinging to slight discolorations in the rock"—had revealed. We agreed that the "Rue à Bicyclette" was no place for even a Wallenda's bicycle. Dick gave the lie to the name of the "A Cheval" pitch, climbing it cleanly with a lie-back. And at 1700 we were on the summit.

Our diagram served us well during the descent, with one exception. One of the short rappels along the ridge ended in a dilemma. We could climb down an iced chute to a platform that seemed to lead back to our arête; or we could climb up on a horrible chockstone bridging a nightmarish couloir that plunged with altogether too much decision five thousand feet down to the Mer de Glace. Naturally, we chose the iced chute. Leo went down first, to report, rather indefinitely, "it doesn't look too good." I had known Leo's optimism well enough to want nothing to do with any pitch that didn't look damned good to him. The chockstone still looked bad, but wrapping rope around rocks, climbing and sliding in a very unmilitary manner, I got on the chockstone, found there was nothing to it, and that it indeed was our route.

When we were on the glacier below, watching the blood-dripping icicles in a crimson sérac sunset, we turned to look back at Leo's platform. It was narrow, short, snow-covered, and sloped outward badly above a thousand-foot smooth precipice.

Midnight and moonlight brought us back to the hotel, and we lazily sauntered down the trail next morning to Chamonix, to stray among the edelweiss-filled windows of the souvenir shops, and bemusedly to wander past the circle swings and Ferris wheel of the portable carnival, brought to Chamonix for those who don't know who de Saussure is or what he is pointing at from his statue in the square of this little town beneath the thirteen-thousand-foot, glacier-spangled façade of Mont Blanc.

***Sierra Club Bulletin,* 1945**

DICK EMERSON

IN 1983, I HAD THE SAD TASK of recalling good climbing times, and many others, for the *American Alpine Journal*. Dick Emerson was my closest friend in the war:

DICK EMERSON AND I MET almost forty years ago and shared the U.S. Mountain Trooper's war. Thirteen years his senior, I am unprepared to write the inclusive dates after his name and to face his leaving before I did.

Dick's high points in mountaineering I shared only vicariously. In the Himalaya, his high point on Masherbrum was the highest camp, where his stomach rebelled and forced him to stay there alone while others spent the day and the entire night reaching the summit and struggling back down to camp. On his approach to Everest's West Ridge, his stomach again lowered his expectations, but this time not out where he could spend a day overlooking the world at its highest. Instead he bivouacked by secret plan, secure and snug within a crevasse, safely out of the tempest of one of the wildest Himalayan storms on record. He climbed back out of his fortress when the night and the winds relented, astonishing friends who had not expected to see him again, much less alive.

Lesser highs, in altitude if not in achievement, were in the postwar Tetons, where as a National Park Service climbing ranger he participated in rescues so scary you'd rather not hear about them, and in climbs that were a delight to read about.

It was the skill of his writing and telling that let me share his postwar climbing world, in which he carried on far beyond where I left off—at the bergschrund under the north face of the Grand Teton in 1956, which he and Phil Berry thereupon ascended. His other world I shared through an unbroken friendship; this let me be on hand for his wedding in Wyoming, watch his postwar winning of his Ph.D., witness his skill as a parent, and enjoy the excellence of his photography. Out of everyone's twelve thousand slides, a hundred made it into the Sierra Club book, *Everest: The West Ridge;* seventeen were Dick's, and they are revealing of what mountains and mountain people meant to him. He and his camera got along very well together, and I am anxious to try to find out what Professor Emerson, social anthropologist, had in mind in the mixing of photographs, research, and prose to explain for us about the Inhabitated Wilderness of the western end of the Himalaya chain. He and Pat went there again and again. At the year's beginning, the material to be interpreted was awaiting the organizer, there on the desk to which he did not return.

Dick Emerson's consuming and informing curiosity began early, but I know of it only from his vivid accounts, with or without martinis. The last one, without, was in his last October and was most detailed. In May 1943 he first crossed my ken, an enlisted man at Camp Hale, Colorado, when I returned there, a brand-new second lieutenant and husband, to join the Mountain Training Center. There were barracks and streets where the Eagle River had been before the army engineers marked it for obliteration, and, at the east end of C Street, there were rocks. On these we tested potential climbing instructors, and Dick tested superior, which was as high as you could get. He rapidly rose to instructor supervisor at Hale, and taught the officer classes at Seneca and Champe Rocks in the West Virginia Mountain Maneuver Area. Altogether, our group of climbers gave assault climbing courses to elements of five army divisions, teaching about ten thousand army men for a hundred thousand climbing days all told, with few (although some very hairy) accidents, and no deaths.

Dick's skill as a balance climber and teacher was exemplary. He added a keen idea of how things ought to be designed, whether courses or equipment, and vastly improved the look and function of two of the army pitons. He also devised routes which led, at Champe Rock, to the only occasion on which Lieutenant Brower gave Corporal Emerson an order. For several months I had pretty much been his teacher, and here he was now, within view of his class, probing unprotected a lead on a most exposed face—a face I myself wanted nothing to do with and certainly didn't want him falling from, or tempting unprotected, gung-ho students to experiment with. Moving to where he (but no one else) could see my gesture, I waggled a finger to beckon him down. Perhaps because his better judgment welcomed the excuse, he came down, smoothly and unperturbed, and added a smile I've seen a thousand times.

Back at Camp Hale, Leo Barrieau (now Healy), Dick, and I became a trio and kept in touch ever after. Whenever two or three of us got together, the intervening time would be flooded out. We were a little older, but remembering well, and had a flood of mental videotapes, in full color, that we could play for each other. One of our favorites was of Seneca days and the spectacular demonstration we put on several times at Jenningstown Gap for the non-Seneca troops engaged in run-of-the-mill mountain maneuvers. The astonishing thing was not that our belays never failed, but that when, after our hair-raising demonstration, we asked for volunteers from the flatlands troop, a horde of them would line up to tie in and jump off. Perhaps, we thought quietly, they wanted to avoid combat duty.

We didn't avoid it. Christmas 1944 found us in Naples, and into the North Apennines campaign. At San Alessandro, just above Riva, we learned on May 3 that our war was over. For the survivors, the three months following the end of our war were joyous. Our regiment set up climbing schools, we ski-raced, and used every possible excuse for excursions to the far corners, rewarded with decades of borrowed time.

A cardiac arrest as Dick slept, perhaps triggered by the stress of a malignancy I had always thought him far too rugged to incur or put up with, took away the years that ought to have remained for him, just before Christmas and the wedding planned for his daughter, Leslie, and Randy Udall. On January 2, for his part in the eulogy, Randy selected some words of Dick's that were some of his finest, of special meaning to me, and good medicine, I think, for anyone who cares about mountains. Back in 1960 I had asked Dick to write about the Masherbrum expedition for the *Sierra Club Bulletin,* and he did a craftsman's job. I had only one useful editorial suggestion to make. When Nick Clinch and Jawed Akbar headed for the top, and Willi Unsoeld and George Bell were far below and out of sight, there Dick was, alone. "What was all that solitude like?" I asked him. "Could you add a paragraph or a page and tell us about it?" He did, and the *Bulletin's* passage also occupies a page of the Everest book. Randy found it there and excerpted it:

"It did not come all at once, that sense of consuming solitude. At first it was just a matter of resting passively, amidst spectacular scenery, but this steadily changed into a peculiarly mixed sensation of aroused relaxation: poised and attentive, infinitely at ease. After so much effort, to sit there, totally alone at twenty-five thousand feet, surrounded by a still and motionless world of rock and ice and blue-black sky—was satisfying in a very special way. It was not the euphoria of altitude. It was the exhilaration of wilderness. . . . I raised my goggles for an unobstructed view of Beauty."

Dick looked and saw very well, far more sensitively than his detached manner would ever let you think. He also heard the sound and caught the aroma and flavor. He felt the mountain, underfoot and at his fingertips, respected it, and moved there with an assurance I have never seen surpassed. "We never grow tired of each other, the mountain and I," Li Po wrote long ago. I think that Dick, twelve centuries later, had some Li Po in him and, given enough time, would have seen the mountain tire first. Many people knew how much he loved and was loved. I am grateful to be one of them.

***American Alpine Journal,* 1983**

How to Kill a Wilderness

Ten Years After I "had not come home, but had just left it" in the High Sierra wilderness, I was in the Alps, but not in wilderness. Our mountain battalion was occupying the little town of Cave del Predil, where we were keeping an eye on Tito's forces just over the Jugoslav border. I had time to write more than the usual letters home. The Alps had been explored and enjoyed to death, and I moved from the battle against Hitler to the battle against despoilers of wild places. The *Sierra Club Bulletin* had already carried some articles about members' war experiences. My lament was added to the list:

Death Isn't a Pleasant Thing to See, but you can get used to it. You may get so that you can just count the bodies; or you may study them academically, to see just how death occurred. The waste of human future is too appalling to ponder upon. Besides, you know that the death of a man is irrevocable. However tragic it may be that he was young and died unnecessarily on a battlefield, you can, because of that irrevocability, learn to accept it.

This is not the only death I have seen. In such parts of the mountains of Italy, Austria, Switzerland, and Jugoslavia as I have been able to observe, are the shattered remains of what must have been beautiful wildernesses. These wild places had their one-time inaccessibility to defend them—their precipices, mountain torrents, their glaciers and forests. But they lost their immunity; they felt the ravages of a conqueror. And now they're dead. Their death isn't irrevocable, as is that of man; but still, in time, you become calloused to it and merely wonder, academically, what caused the demise.

What does a postmortem examination show? Apparently men sought to cure the ills they thought the wilderness suffered from. It was disagreeable, its cliffs too high, its streams too wide; it had no economic value, produced nothing, did no one good save the lucky few who prospered in the oases its streams watered; it wasn't designed for the greatest good to the greatest number; people could not enjoy it; they couldn't even live in it. So they tried their remedies—all sorts of them—and the wilderness died of overdosage.

What were the remedies?

Trails—They now lead everywhere. Some are cowpaths; some are substantial, paved, rock-walled affairs that Italians seem to delight in building; others are perhaps cableways leading to the tops of peaks. Many lead to little cultivated islands among nonproductive slopes; the materials for the cluster of buildings at the heart of each island were carried over these trails by oxcart, even by hand.

Roads—Inevitably some of these trails grew to roads, the roads to highways, with tunnels and bridges matching the increasing elaborateness of the roads. They are everywhere—over the highest passes, into what could have remained the wildest canyons. The Italians' industry, in Yosemite, would by now easily have put a road up by the Leaning Tower, with tunnels for switchbacks, a bridge just over the top of Bridalveil Fall, with a hotel there; then, with a tunnel to the base of Cathedral Spires, the road would continue to the base of Glacier Point. On Half Dome they'd have a small village, complete with church, surrounded by cultivated fields, soil for which had been backpacked from Yosemite Valley by the women. That village would have electric lights, with a powerhouse using part of the drop of Nevada Fall. Colby Meadows—and every meadow in the high Sierra you've ever camped in—would have been enlarged by tree cutting, would be terraced if at all steep, and its center would be a dirty, sooty village, smelling strongly of such of the age-old sewage as they hadn't quite managed to dump into Evolution Creek.

Power—From quaint old mills to lusty powerhouses, fed by anything from tiny rock-lined canals to scarring flumes and penstocks—between these extremes, and including them, the streams are so thoroughly harnessed you can hardly see the water for the leather. Then add to each development the accompanying high-tension lines, towers, and essential roads.

Buildings—Tiny stone farmhouses or refuge huts supplied irritation that proved to have cancerous results. Villages, the villagers just eking a living from their hard-won land, were fatal to some wild places. The huts, built for those who didn't have a tent and wanted shelter, encouraged more people to come—people who didn't have, progressively as the years went by: (1) bedding, (2) equipment of any kind, (3) food, (4) drink, (5) entertainment, and finally who didn't particularly want, in the presence of (4) and (5), any scenery. The final malignant growth that throttled the surrounding wilderness would then be an elaborate hotel. Were Yosemite in Italy, there would be a hotel on the saddle between Mounts Lyell and Maclure, accessible by a very good and prominent tramway.

Mining—The motto: wherever it is, dig it out. Here, however, I am afraid Italy must take a back seat to Colorado, where you may start to admire some cliff for its inaccessibility, and find your reverie shocked by some miner's shack right in the middle of it. No class-six climb ever stopped a Colorado miner. In Italy there is one difference. The country is older, and they have long since dug almost everything out, and increasingly must now look, for their future needs, over borders and over seas. A Kodachrome movie could show this story well. You could make panorama after panorama of a beautiful mountain scene, each ending where some mountainside still festered from the removal, without anesthesia, of large areas of the epidermis of verdure, and even much of the bone. And the surgeon's tools—a tramway, a stamp mill, or a dam to divert a stream—were left lying there and are red with rust.

Fortifications—For every road that made the mountains, and the borders the mountains had held, more attainable, men built fortifications to deny each other that access on call. Forts are everywhere, too—on canyon bottoms, high on the canyon walls, built into commanding peaks—everything from quaint old World War I affairs, dilapidated and all but overgrown, to super downdraft concrete strong points established in the early forties, some so well camouflaged as to have imitation-rock swinging doors over the embrasures. Had they been manned toward the close of the Italian campaign, when the Tenth Mountain Division men, leading others in this theater, were exploiting their Po Valley gains by beating most of the Germans to the Alpine passes, someone else would surely have had to write this piece.

To kill a wilderness, then, the steps are simple:

1. Improve and exploit it. Keep adding the comforts that each preceding addition has brought people to demand. *Procedure*: Build another trail. The users will want a shelter hut. Build that. The guests will want food and drink, hot and cold running water, light. Then they will want room for friends. Or supply the site by plane, and sooner or later you will have a clientele with the same demands. Obviously a road will be needed right to the spot, then beyond it to link with another road of similar origin. The game preserve the road cuts across will shrivel from the wound, but will only be reduced in effective game refuge by about fifty percent. The process may have to be repeated to destroy it utterly. Now you have a newly accessible region that just cries for development. Jobs will be created. The scarlet of the pentstemon, which could only be seen by day, can give way to the day-and-night vermilion of neon. And you can root out the last commercial resource. There is no point in seeking a substitute, nor in saving any of it for a day when the need may be greater.

2. Rely always on the apparently democratic argument that you must produce the greatest good for the greatest number. Chances are no one will call to your attention that irreplaceable treasures are destroyed if they are divided or trampled—that no one would think of cutting into little bits, so that all could enjoy them, Michelangelo's frescoes in the Sistine Chapel. And obviously, you can argue, the wilderness is very big, there still being one place in California where you can be more than a day's travel from a

roadhead, and there isn't much harm that can be done it that will be noticeable in his lifetime.

But don't let people ask you what his children, and theirs, are going to do when they want to see for themselves how wild places used to look before people decided to help God keep them.

***Sierra Club Bulletin*, 1945**

Having mailed my recipe for wilderness destruction off to San Francisco, I signed out of battalion headquarters for the rest leave in Rome that somehow ended up in the Alps. My punishment for being on the Grèpon instead of in Rome was that Colonel Cook named me mess officer for the voyage home. It was painless. I had the good judgment to delegate all responsibilities to the four battalion mess sergeants who knew exactly what to do, which I didn't, and, as the ship rolled, yawed, and skipped across a rough Atlantic, we ate well and tanned well on deck. A day from home we heard about the atomic bomb on Hiroshima and learned about Nagasaki at Camp Patrick Henry, in Virginia. Our mission had been to hit the beaches in Japan. Instead, on V-J Day I was dancing with Anne at the Claremont Hotel in Berkeley and would soon be back at my editorial desk at the University of California Press and deep, once again, into volunteer work at the Sierra Club, with wilderness at the top of my agenda.

Chapter 4
FAMILY

JOHN

IN OCTOBER 1987, to get me to the airport for a flight to Vancouver and a meeting about the Biennial Conference on the Fate and Hope of the Earth being planned for Managua, John has volunteered his Volvo and himself. We don't talk nearly enough. Here is a chance, and we still don't talk enough.

"I'm almost thirty-five," John says. It is hard to believe, because he is our youngest.

"I suppose that since I am seventy-five, that had to happen to you," was my brilliant response. I remember a bit of our joint past, the trips especially, and how much he enjoyed them.

He hasn't taken many trips lately. He doesn't like long drives.

"You need to get some more mountains," I suggested.

"Is this a good time for Yosemite?"

"Yes. The autumn color is just starting. From now into mid-November. You ought to go."

"I'd like to, but in my kind of work they don't give you much time for vacations. And with the rains about to begin, I want to make as much money as I can before the jobs end."

As Ken, his older brother, puts it, John is a kamikaze worker. He cannot stand not getting things done as fast as possible, even if it costs him a hernia. He can take a eucalyptus section apart faster than anyone I have ever watched, and we have a lot of eucalyptus sections in Berkeley he has taken apart. Tiers of split eucalyptus are stored wherever there is space—even where there isn't—in our yard, awaiting his customers.

John remembers trips, to the Sierra, the beaches, to Monument Valley, down Glen Canyon when it was still a canyon, to Europe, twice to Nepal.

"I'd like to be in Kathmandu right now," he tells me. "The weather would be just right."

More important, it would be the take-off place for more walks toward Mount Everest, and he remembers well how good he was there, how competent, no matter what the altitude. And I remember his size-ten Adidas tracks from the 1976 trek he, Barbara, and I made with Mountain Travel. John was going through a tough time then. We wanted him on that trip very much, but we weren't sure he would be on it until the plane door closed, our flight left San Francisco, and he was inside. That trip was so good, and the Himalaya got to him so thoroughly, that he went back, to keep Barbara company for a while as she struggled with her field work in Namche Bazar. But he was soon restless again, waving good-bye to his sister, who was crying, as he headed down the trail toward the Dudh Kosi and the mildly terrifying airport at Lukla.

We are almost at San Francisco airport again now, and back on a familiar subject—recycling. John believes in it, thinks the world is crazy for not taking it seriously, despises our wasteful American ways, and should.

"Why don't we put a bounty on cars, so the wrecks will get to the junkyards, and off the streets?" he asks.

"How much bounty would it take to get your wrecks there?"

John's Volvo wagon is his only operating passenger car. He has another Volvo he got for fifty dollars in Canada, and I helped him drive it to Berkeley from Vancouver. Plus two trucks, one inoperative.

"I want to get parts from them." Some day he may get enough parts to make one of them run, but in this matter mañana doesn't mean "tomorrow," to John, but just "not today."

"They ought to have a better way to recover parts when they wreck cars," he suggests.

"And not just smash them into a lump?" I add. "Mixing up things so badly that they can't be recycled the way they ought to be."

John is more specific. "Just think of the bolts you could recover and sell." We talk about how hard it would be to recover some of them, and how many jobs there would be if cars were taken apart systematically instead of just being gathered into a pile and crunched.

We should be talking about life and times, especially his life and times, but recycling is easier to talk about, and besides, he knows I would like to see him get into it seriously. There are other subjects, such as the variety that the *Manas* journal covered so well, that John liked to read about. Or about photographs. Or the design of a book, about which his judgment is first rate. But back to recycling:

"We've got to recycle the nonrenewables and rebuild the renewables, all around the world," I pontificate, "or we're not going to make it."

When will John put a plan together to get a lot or two, side by side, with space in them to store firewood, get a compost business going, assemble and disassemble old wrecks? What starting capital will it take?

It will be nagging to put these thoughts into spoken words, and John doesn't want things done for him. He would rather do them himself.

Now the airport is just ahead, and my flight into the all-too-well-unregulated, not-all-that-friendly skies. "You're the best father I could have," John says. "I wouldn't want any other. I love you."

He grabs my knee, then my hand, and pulls up, then disembarks me. His is a wonderful face to look into.

"OK, drive carefully. Love you."

He pulls away from the curb as I head for the automatic door, remembering the letters he puts just before his name when he leaves Anne or me a note, telling us how much more than a tongue can tell he loves us: ILYMTATCT, which is unpronounceable but mutual.

BEGINNINGS

HAVING BROUGHT OUR YOUNGEST into the picture, I ought to say something about who, besides his parents, preceded John. I'm not very good at this. I should have paid more attention to John's ancestry, and mine and Anne's, while there were still people around who could check our recollections. One person in every family should assume, or be assigned, this duty. I was not that person.

Vaguely I remember having read the Bible before I hit my teens. Today I can hardly believe I read the whole thing, but I made that claim often enough that I may indeed have done it. What I do remember is that the dullest part was the who-begat-whom department.

Begotten I was. I had two parents and so did they, as did theirs. Anne can make the same claim, which brings us to a total of twenty-eight immediate ancestors, of whom I met only seven. My two grandfathers were born in adjoining counties in New York, one of them being Dutchess County, the other unknown to me, and if I haven't found out by now, I am not likely to. One was Gideon Samuel Brower, the other Solomon Quinby Barlow. My father, Ross J Brower, did not like John as a middle name and settled for the J, minus period. He long ago tried to check out the branches of the tree, how accurately I don't know, though he was not inclined to be careless at any time. Our first Brower to hit the United States, he said, was Jacob, who arrived early in the seventeenth century, having descended from Aneke Jans and before her from William of Orange. I learned early not to take any of this too seriously. One need not go back very many centuries to discover that about twenty-four ancestor-doublings ago there were not enough people in Europe to equal the required number of ancestors, meaning that all people of European descent are related. Go back three-and-a-half billion years and you find

Ross J Brower, Dave's father.

Gideon Brower, Dave's grandfather.

Mary Grace Barlow, Dave's mother, at her 1905 graduation from UC Berkeley.

Dave at age five, in Los Angeles with his cousin, Miriam Caldwell.

David (left) with sister Edith and brother Ralph, 1915.

that we are all related to every other living creature, which, I submit, is more important to understanding the earth than is the structure of a given family tree.

Each of my two grandmothers had four children. My grandfathers went further, having two wives, Solomon's first wife having predeceased him and Gideon's having left him, not to remarry. My parents, Ross Brower and Mary Grace Barlow, had a daughter, Edith Ellen, and sons, Ralph Barlow, David Ross, and Joseph Elmer, the Elmer being my idea, understandably discarded by Joe. It was par for the course to have two parents and four children around the dinner table—for me at least—and Anne produced, with my brief assistance, Kenneth David, Robert Irish, Barbara Anne, and John Stewart. Having learned about the population bomb, we salved our conscience by having but two grandchildren, Anne Kathryn Olsen and David Cornelius Brower. His grandfather Cornelius was an African-American. Grandfather David is a mixture of English (Barlow), Irish (Brandon), Scottish (MacKaye), Dutch (Brouwer), and who knows what else. Grandma Barlow died a year after she suffered a stroke. I was five and have nothing but pleasant memories of her. Grandpa Barlow died seventeen years before I was born. Grandpa Brower was a carpenter, built the first railroad station in El Paso, was a friend of labor leader Samuel Gompers, and ran for governor of California on the Socialist ticket, which was not a route to success. Whenever he came to our house he had little presents for his grandchildren in his overcoat pocket. Grandma Brower had been a beautiful woman, but became quite severely religious. My father was close to her, and neither she nor he had anything to do with alcohol, tobacco, coffee, cards, or dancing. She liked to begin work around the house—which she did often owing to my mother's blindness—at five in the morning and wondered why the rest of us didn't. I had been baptized a Presbyterian, my mother's religion, as early as possible, but that wasn't good enough for Grandma Brower. I had also to be baptized the Baptist way, fully submerged. Grandma Brower also had firm ideas about circumcision, and saw to it, when I went to Alta Bates Hospital for my tonsillectomy at the age of eight, that my parents' intentional oversight was corrected. My father was horrified when he learned of it. Coming out of anesthesia I myself was surprised, frightened, and not at all pleased.

To end this period on a happier note, Grandma Brower, having no use for real coffee, made a brew out of wheat browned in a frying pan in butter and molasses. Some day I'll try to make some myself. Not to drink, but just to see if I can duplicate the heavenly aroma that permeated the kitchen as the brew steeped.

Ross Brower was born in Bath, Michigan. I called him from there on his eightieth birthday, having paused briefly in nearby Lansing to visit the Michigan legislature. I asked him how to find the house he was born in, got the instructions, but the house had left. I remember thinking it would be nice to find someone who remembered him, then realized that the eighty-year interval was prohibitively long. I know little about his travels, except that after El Paso he lived near Fresno and learned how to swim thanks to the abundance of irrigation ditches. He attended the University of California in Berkeley and graduated in mechanical engineering in 1900, married my mother August 27, 1906, and earned a master's degree in engineering at the University of Michigan in 1907. He taught at Oakland Technical High School, became an instructor in mechanical drawing at the University of California, Berkeley, and lost that job through some machinations that I did not understand, remembering only that the *Oakland Tribune* carried a story about them containing the line, " 'Rubbish!' said Brower."

The house my mother was born in, in Two Rock Valley, near Petaluma, California, March 23, 1882, burned down before I could see it, but I can still see the gum grove she watched her father plant on the ranch—back when people thought growing alien eucalyptus would bring quick profits from lumber, but didn't pick the right species. My mother graduated from the University of California, Berkeley, in 1905, majoring in English. She earned her master's at Stanford, in 1906, and married almost immediately thereafter. My sister Edith was born October 10, 1907, while my father was earning his master's in Ann Arbor. They returned to Berkeley, where my brother Ralph was born October 17, 1909, at 2234 Haste Street, just to the rear of 2232, the house our family was to move into in 1916. I was born at 1402 Carleton Street, Berkeley, and the house still stands, looking as good as new. I cannot make the same claim.

One of my first achievements was keeping my father out of combat in the First World War. They called him in for various physical tests, which he passed, but they did not want to draft a father of three.

Joe was born June 26, 1920, in Oakland's Fabiola Hospital, which no longer stands. It was somehow assumed that this pregnancy would correct a problem that had been troubling my mother, but I did not know how or why, being hardly eight when Joe arrived. She was bedridden for some time, and I remember standing at the foot of her bed while she tried to discern me as her vision deteriorated, and finally failed.

As nearly as I can remember it—and I am the only witness left—she lost her sight and my father his university job at about the same time. He was given some part-time work in University Extension, where what was mechanical drawing was renamed descriptive geometry. For this he received twenty dollars a month, not enough to begin to sustain a family. Fortunately we had the two Haste Street houses and their ten income-producing apartments to rely on, the rents ranging from twenty-five to forty dollars a month. I remember one dire time when there were five vacancies, and the threat of mortgage foreclosure alarmed us more than usual. My father tried to augment his income various ways, none successful. He tried to market Eclipse Fire Extinguisher, a pink powder that came in bulk. The children's job was to fill small containers with it in our basement. It did not sell, nor did the "No-Shock" springs, which were demonstrated by a sign hung in front of our 1921 Willys-Knight, which he had equipped with the device. He also tried a real estate venture in the San Joaquin Valley, borrowing money on property my mother had bought in Belmont, California, and losing the money and the property when the venture turned out to be a scam. Farmland in the San Joaquin Valley, near Merced, needs water to be worth much, and what he was persuaded to buy turned out to have no water rights.

There was nothing my father couldn't do with his hands, whether it was carving a missing knight for a chess set, plumbing, wiring, painting, raising the roof to give us dormer windows and sleeping space at 2232 where there had been only an attic before. Earlier in his engineering career, he drafted a plan for a commercial harbor in Berkeley—an idea I shudder to think of. Given an opportunity, he would describe in too great detail how he handled each challenge in apartment-house maintenance. For all his not sparing the rod, I took up smoking at twenty-five. I am sure that this, and my learning how to handle alcohol, distressed him, but he bore with it. He would have been glad to know that when I gave up smoking, a year before his death in 1960, I had given it up for keeps. He would also have been happy to have been fully repaid for the two-thousand-dollar loan he provided to allow Anne and me to buy our Berkeley lot. Perhaps what pleased him most was that I had absorbed enough engineering from him by osmosis to be successful in fighting off the Bureau of Reclamation experts in Dinosaur National Monument. He may well have been more amazed than surprised. I know he was happy about his grandchildren, all nine of them, and pleased that Anne and I had produced three sons who could carry on the Brower name.

About two years after my mother's death in 1939 he married Mae Gabrielson and acquired six stepchildren. I had trouble adjusting, but got over it. I was soon off to war and marriage and, at long last, on my own.

In 1941, before leaving home, I acquired a seedling redwood, some two inches high, in the forest above San Mateo and planted it a foot from our west fence on Haste Street. That redwood is now about eighty feet tall and better than three feet in diameter, breast-high. While I was off to war my father had the foresight to replant it near the center of the front lawn. Had he not done so I am sure our neighbors would have logged the half of the tree which by now would have encroached upon their property. Half a redwood would probably be enough for Ronald Reagan.

Dad kept most of his hair and all of his figure. At seventy he suffered a severe heart attack and we thought we were going to lose him. He fooled us, then gallantly bought a life membership in the Sierra Club and got his money's worth. Shortly after his eighty-first birthday he was high up in a walnut tree at his Clear Lake place, pruning away vigorously. Next day, while weeding the lawn, he felt the chill of a stroke and was sped to a hospital. I rushed up to see how he was doing. I kissed his forehead, something I had never done before, and hoped he recognized me. Next day he was gone.

SISTER

ONE OF MY MOTHER'S GREAT DELIGHTS, as long as she lived, was my sister Edith. Another was Edith's husband, ever-cheerful Ted Grindle. Two more delights were their daughters, Betty and Teddie. My blind mother saw none of her grandchildren with her eyes, but her touch and her hearing told her a great deal about them, and she needed every delight she could get.

Edith was herself delighted in her daughters and their children and, at her eightieth birthday party on October 10, 1987, I saw her look lovingly at her great-grandson. I watched her listen to, and remember, some pieces I tried to play on a little electronic piano. I remembered her playing and singing these pieces more than sixty years ago.

We shared a love of music, and I wish that on that occasion I had played still more that I remembered our sharing, but she was getting tired and I wasn't playing very well on a strange instrument. One of the pieces I remembered well – all the music and most of the words – was in a mixture of French and English – "Bonjour, ma belle, or how you speak, good day." The young man goes on, enraptured, for two verses, the last ending with his sad dismissal by the object of his attentions: "Your words they are si gentil. Alas, what can I say? My hoosband wait outside ze gate. And so, monsieur, good day."

Edith was very fond of that piece, and so was I. She sang beautifully, and might well have gone places with her voice. I was never quite up to accompanying her, but she didn't need me. Her piano playing served very well.

As I remember her life before she married Ted, I don't recall that any of it was easy. She had to stand in for a mother who had the added problem of what we called spells. She would faint and fall, sometimes down our Haste Street stairs. Family finances being what they were, Edith had to go to work, and didn't have a chance to graduate from the university, though she got much farther along than I did. She worked where she could, hard and well. She took to her secretarial work the skill that had made her at a very early age the California State Novice Typing Champion.

We needed more help around the house than Edith or her three brothers could offer, and one of the people who came to help our family was the mother of Alice, Florence, Nadine, Anita, Monroe, and Ted Grindle, with whom Edith fell in love. My mother, my brothers, and I liked Ted very much but my father, for reasons I will never understand, decided to make a barrier of himself.

Edith and I were quite close then. When she worked in Yosemite for a summer, she rented a post-office box so that we could carry on a secret correspondence. Each letter she wrote me was a delight, and occasionally included a small money order, drawn from her tips as a waitress, as a reward to me for the cooking, washing, and ironing I was doing in her absence. While she was in Yosemite, she remembered her commitment to Ted and remained loyal. Her male associates dubbed her P & W – pure and wholesome.

I am sure my father's obstinacy hurt her very much, and the pain was not relieved on her wedding day, at Ted's mother and stepfather's place in Santa Rosa. A daughter should have all her family present on such an occasion, but that didn't happen. And I didn't play "Here Comes the Bride" very well on Ted's mother's piano.

In due course and happily, my father surmounted his problem, and accepted Ted for the extraordinary man he was. Ted and Edith's marriage was already well under way, and was to last beyond their golden anniversary. One of my great regrets was that Edith and Ted never stayed put very long. They were always moving, it seemed to me, from one place to another. I cannot claim that I stayed put very long myself. Although Anne and I, once World War II was over, have lived at one address, our current one, for more than forty years, I never managed to be at home much more than half the time. This got sadly in the way of my keeping up with the Grindles the way I wish I had. I know that on the all-too-few occasions our family dropped by, our children enjoyed Edith and Ted as they enjoyed no one else. They especially loved Ted's spontaneous humor. His daughter Teddie reports that neighboring children would ask, "Can Mr. Grindle come out to play?" I'll always remember that, in the days before Anne picked up the burden of Edith's brother David, whenever I was down it was Edith and Ted who got me back up. What a wonderful world it would be if it were full of couples, and families, like theirs. I thank her for abiding love I can never forget.

BROTHERS

RALPH WAS MY FATHER'S SON, I was my mother's, and Joe, although my brother, was in effect mine. I was eight years older than he and everyone else was busy. Like his father, Ralph earned a degree in engineering, electrical instead of mechanical. His father could play one piece on the piano – "Shepherd Boy" – and I can pick it out by ear still, chords and all. Ralph played no musical instrument. He was fully attentive to Dad's mechanical achievements, even down to the frequent disassembly and reassembly of the ship's-bell clock, which struck beautifully whenever it managed to keep operating, which was seldom.

Ralph approved of my engineering tendencies in rock-climbing. He climbed Mount Dana and Mount Lyell, Yosemite's highest peaks, with Dad and me, and was as uneasy on Dana as any electrical engineer should be when a lightning storm is approaching, everyone's hair stands on end, and the faint bluish light of St. Elmo's fire glows on the summit rocks. Ralph was along on the first ascent of Vasquez Monolith, in Pinnacles National Monument, and was amused by my having typewritten the entry for the register we placed on the summit. The entry included the names of the party and the route we followed to the summit. I had failed on two earlier attempts and if the third attempt had failed I could have torn up the entry and no one would have been the wiser. The first attempt had been on the south face, where the angle was too steep, the holds too scarce and fragile, and pitons could not be placed for protection. The second attempt was via the southeast corner, where a feasible crack led to the summit from a ledge that could be reached only by climbing a tree and trusting a thin branch that extended to the ledge. I climbed high up in the tree, looked at that branch for a long time, tentatively moved along it about halfway, and retreated. I had no wish to take it to the ground with me. Shortly thereafter someone successfully negotiated the branch and reached the ledge, but could go no further.

Next time around, summit entry in my pocket, with Ralph included in the party, and with the knowledge of someone else's previous success, I took on the branch without hesitation, and we had a strong enough party to handle the final crack without difficulty. Pioneering is always easier if someone else has preceded you, and Ralph's pioneering was probably responsible for the little mechanical aptitude I developed. But I never could saw a straight line, as he did, or miss my thumb with a hammer as invariably as he did, or take a car apart and put all the pieces back right as he did, or skate, or fly a kite, or own a bicycle and maintain it properly, or ever understand radios and televisions and phonographs and recorders and computers and airplane manufacture, or be as generous and patient as he was with a brother almost three years younger who stayed single seven years longer. So I went my way, but never so far away that I didn't feel his enduring support. I think he knew how I felt about him and his wife Dorothy Howard—whenever I remembered to keep in touch.

Joe, though younger, was close enough that I could tell, from his brief facial expression and a slight gesture, twenty feet away in a Safeway store, that his first marriage was finished, and could know later that his second was working. Intuition is well honed in the genetic scheme of things and speedily gives us signals about what is safe, dangerous, or deserving of special care, but it was closeness, not intuition, that told me of Joe's bad news. We were close from the day he learned to walk and he was in my care when I wasn't in school. We remain close even now, and my cholesterol count is his concern, if not under his control. Although I was called Ralph by some of the teachers who taught him before they had me, we barely resembled each other. You don't have to look twice to know that Joe and I are brothers, but you can tell us apart because he is handsome, younger, and looks more worried but in better shape.

Though I was a poor mechanic, I could take the coaster brake apart on Ralph's bicycle, grease it, and put it together correctly, even though I occasionally tightened the front-wheel cones too much. But Joe! I despaired of his ever learning how to oil a bicycle. Perhaps he didn't really like bicycles, having put his foot in the spokes of the front wheel once when I was giving him a ride. I did a complete loop in the air and was unhurt, but he received a nasty gash on his forehead. A passerby took us to the emergency hospital where I was treated for shock and he was patched up fairly well. He bears the scar still.

He forgave me at once, and wasn't particularly troubled by my lack of faith in his mechanical ability. He managed to graduate from college, teach, marry earlier than I, climb a little, ski much better, and travel even farther. Perhaps he couldn't oil a bike, but he could navigate an airplane, and did so wherever Pan Am, Flying Tigers, Swissair, Lufthansa, and assorted other airlines wanted to fly until he was replaced by the black box that put navigators out of work.

The son and daughter from Joe's first marriage took their stepfather's name, but Joe kept in touch as well as he could, considering that his navigating had him living, from time to time, in such places as Zurich, Majorca, Guam, San Miguel d'Allende, Squaw Valley, Boston, Oakdale, and Kirkwood Lake. His second marriage was to Gayle Rawls, who had herself been married before—to my successor when my "position was abolished," as publicity manager for the Yosemite Park & Curry Company.

Not intentionally, Joe managed to get even with the brother who scarred him. Early in 1989 he failed to warn me that it was unwise for gringos to be alone on the streets of the Mexican city of Oaxaca after ten o'clock at night, and I was out at ten-thirty, composing a last camcorder shot for the evening at the entrance to the hotel in which Anne and I were visiting Joe and Gayle. With a camcorder on your right shoulder you can easily be blindsided from the right and I was. My assailant thought all he had to do to capture the camcorder was to seize the handle and run. My trigger hand, however, was strapped to the instrument and I went with it. The camcorder hit the street before my forehead (and various other parts of me) did. Twenty minutes later the camcorder and assailant were in custody and three hours later I was patched up. My forehead required three stitches and for a while you could now tell that Joe and I were brothers by our matching scars. But mine disappeared.

ANNE HUS

HYPOCRISY IS BETTER ADMITTED than discovered. I've got it. The evidence? A conservationist with a redwood house, four children, two cars, four color television sets, three video recorders, two video cameras, perhaps a dozen tape recorders (most of them obsolete), two movie cameras (superseded), four still cameras (likewise), one each slide and movie projector, three record players (one operable), three pianos (one electronic), one accordion (poorly played, if ever), two telephone lines, four speaker phones, six that don't speak, computers and printers (three each), about five thousand books (fewer than a thousand of them fully read), thousands and thousands and thousands of black-and-white prints and color slides (uncatalogued). Those are the obvious conspicuous-consumptive sins. There are also thousands of old magazines and a hundred cartons of papers, promised to the Bancroft Library, University of California, an institution unprepared for such a flood. Worse still, in our forty-six years of marriage, I have been an aggregate twenty-four years away from home, with no picture on the piano to remind the children what their father looked like.

Atonement for these sins? None, really, but I can explain away everything when pressed: I need all these things in my work, or will as soon as I can get them fixed up and (or) sorted out. Remember, the Volvo is almost a classic and the company should be proud of it and offer us a free replacement.

The virtues? Very few. No second home. Two grandchildren, one each. One fax machine.

One wife.

Anne Hus prefers my virtues to my sins, and, like a Sierra Club friend mentioned by John McPhee, Anne Brower prefers my sins to others' virtues. She hopes no one will ever find out what I have just revealed.

Anne had persevered through so much before meeting me that she was well prepared to cope when the time came. She was conceived in the south—Oakland is south of Berkeley—just about when I was born in the north. She would have perished a year and a half later had someone not managed to wake a druggist in the middle of the night to get the oxygen she needed to survive her pneumonia.

Her father, François Louis Marinus Hus, was born in Leiden in 1878, came to America when he was seventeen, and at his father's insistence became a dentist. He and his two sisters were musicians, his brother a botanist. Frank mastered four languages. His English, like his handwriting, was beautiful, with only two clues that English wasn't his native language – "Robin Hood" rhymed with "booed," and his "were" was "wear." He was an expert gardener and could repair anything.

He and his wife, Frances Irish, lived with her parents, Colonel John P. Irish and Annie Fletcher. Colonel Irish was a newspaper editor, naval officer of the Port of San Francisco, a member of the Yosemite Commission, and not a friend of John Muir. Anne's mother was Frankie to her daughter and me, and much beloved. Her ebullience could ride out any storm, and had to ride many.

Anne's brother, also a Francis, was seven years older than she but died of a heart attack when he was forty-nine. He was a civilian with the armed forces from which he had retired after serving in the Korean war. I met him as a new lieutenant just leaving Officer Candidate School at Fort Benning when I arrived, a new candidate. His daughter is still another Frances, and Anne keeps thinking of her as her only living relative until I remind her of our four children and their two.

Anne, while she was an undergraduate at UC Berkeley, helped support her family by working in the registrar's office at thirty-five cents an hour. Working for her degree in English, she fared better at the University of California Press, first as secretary to its manager, Samuel T. Farquhar, and later as an editorial assistant to Harold Small. The press, on Barrows Lane, was once a stable for former university president Benjamin Ide Wheeler's horse. Anne, with colleagues, was pleased to move into a new University of California Press building farther from the Hayward Fault and designed to resist earthquakes by Walter Huber, who would later help me try to defeat Glen Canyon Dam.

Anne's years of seniority at the press didn't warm my welcome when I was chosen to share her office at essentially the same salary. Slowly she managed to tolerate me and then, I think, respond to my liking her a lot. Our editing was interrupted by long and longer discussions, not always about editorial subjects or problems. On my thirtieth birthday Anne took me to lunch at Spenger's Fish Grotto. I can show you the table where we sat.

I enjoyed making Anne laugh, and succeed when I avoid puns. She was still attending classes while working as an editor, and that would delay her return from lunch. She had been having problems with a manuscript. Among other things, it was overloaded with footnotes. While she was out I added a page to the manuscript she had left open on her desk. I started out with the author's language, then began to parody it, adding footnotes to suit, the combination becoming increasingly ridiculous. I slipped the page where she would turn to it next, waited for her return, and watched. About halfway down the page she saw what was happening, and her response was one of my early and unforgettable delights. The delight ended when the author asked for the manuscript to make some changes and Anne forgot to take out the page that was spurious. The author was not pleased. He complained to Sam Farquhar, and Sam passed the complaint to Harold. Fortunately they shared Anne's delight in the prank.

Anne invited me once or twice for a sherry with her parents. I remember one particular day when I was not invited. I watched her start to walk home from the press—about a mile's walk—and wanted very much to tear after her. But she was already spoken for, as people used to say, and I didn't think I had a prayer.

On October 12, 1942, I was off to the wars. A few days later, when the train taking me to Camp Carson paused in Berkeley, I telephoned her to say good-bye, and wrote a note or two from Camp Carson. Then one December day at Camp Hale I received a card from her giving me encouragement—her little drawing of a traffic signal with green light on.

So I proposed by mail, sorry, but Anne accepted by mail, we married on May 1, 1943, drove to Denver, she looked for housing, and I went on to Camp Hale to start active duty as a lieutenant. We began a very difficult year.

As it turned out, I was more conscientious than I need have been about my military obligations. I had been oversoaked, perhaps, in mountaineering knowledge, and the army had been undersoaked, certainly. If I did my job right, I reasoned, men's lives would be saved. My job was to do what I could think of, then try to think of what I had not thought of. It was easy, interesting, and glamorous to take myself too seriously and I plunged into it.

I did not get to Denver often enough, or to Glenwood Springs often enough when Anne moved there to be nearer to Camp Hale. Other husbands did better. In October I was sent to West Virginia on detached service and didn't know how to take Anne along. Later she joined me there, but I was not on hand to greet her when she arrived at the train station in Cumberland, or at the bus station in Petersburg. I did not get to the Hermitage, where she was staying, often enough.

When Anne moved to Washington, where she worked with the Historical Division of G-2 in the Pentagon, I didn't visit her often enough. Indeed, I was forbidden by the commanding officer of the West Virginia Mountain Maneuver Area to go to Washington. He thought I had too many friends there and believed I caused problems by telling them too much about what wasn't being done well enough in West Virginia. So I had to sign out for Ardmore, Pennsylvania, giving as my address the home of Corporal Richard Longaker's parents, who would call me at Anne's flat if need be.

There were high points, too, and our spirits were reasonably high when, after the Seneca Assault Climbing School was closed, we rode the

Anne Brower at the Berkeley train station, 1944, leaving for West Virginia. Photograph by Doris Leonard.

train back home and I had a few days' delay in Berkeley en route to my new station in Texas. There I was again without Anne.

In mid-November 1944 I was granted an emergency leave to visit our newborn Ken just before going overseas to who knew what. Our mules had been shipped to Burma, we were told, and we would follow. We were issued summer clothing to cover our track, which was leading instead to Naples. A nice place, no doubt, on many a Christmas Eve, but not this one.

On the way from Italy to Japan eight months later, I was home briefly in August and, since the bombs had fallen in Japan, home for keeps in October. Home, but not quite back in touch.

"Dave, look at him!" Anne pleaded, as a preoccupied father, now back home, failed to return Ken's looking at me. If only I had a grandfather's sense, then, of how important the meeting of eyes is to children, especially one's own.

On July 5, 1946, I was at Carroll Creek, near Lone Pine on the east side of the Sierra, watching the first two weeks of the High Trip get under way. I had planned to spend the night and suffer with the High Trippers as they got up at two in the morning for the long climb to the first camp. Something told me to drive home through the night instead. I arrived home to find it empty. Anne was at Alta Bates Hospital awaiting the arrival of Robert Irish Brower—the Irish for Anne's grandfather.

On the way home from Alta Bates I drove by our recently purchased lot. There were only three houses within two hundred fifty feet of it, and an unobstructed view of San Francisco Bay, a panorama extending from Palo Alto to Point Richmond, with the Golden Gate just to the right of center. The stakes had just been driven showing where the two-bedroom house was to be. It was nice timing.

Children

Ken and Bob did not get their full share of my absences. At the University of California Press I was but a two-mile drive from lunch in Tilden Park. Jim Roof, an expert with plants, was perfecting a High Sierra landscape there, and dubbed our little lunchtime swale in Tilden, there among Sierra aspens, Brower Meadow. The boys, so neatly conditioned just half a mile from home, were prepared to take the Sierra in stride. We had our own Sierra Valhalla for them to stride in—Little Lakes Valley.

At Tom's Place, on Highway 395 at the head of Sherwin Grade, you head into the High Sierra on a road that at one time continued to the head of Rock Creek, in Little Lakes Valley, and turned left into Pine Creek and the vanadium mine that has operated, with few interruptions, since the First World War. Happily, the Forest Service, in a brilliant move, blocked the road at the ten-thousand-foot elevation in Little Lakes Valley, and at the elevation of the mine on Pine Creek. The High Sierra ecosystem has degenerated the road into the trail it once was. At the roadhead, people dependent upon cars camped tentstake to tentstake. There was no wood, no duff for bedsites, and no calm.

These people were wedded to car camping by the weight of their gear. We, however, had been specializing in going light, cutting off pounds and ounces wherever we could in what we carried. We could backpack all our gear, and did. Just a half-mile from the roadhead swarm was a delightful little lone lake, a pebble beach at the lower end. Beyond it, reflected whenever the lake was calm, soared one of the most beautiful Sierra peaks, Bear Creek Spire. It was an easy trail, little used. Anne carried her own sleeping bag and some food and utensils. The boys carried cornflakes. I carried the rest for the half-mile—no problem—and we set up our own private camp with no one in sight. There were so few fish in the lake that fishermen didn't pester it. It was a perfect site, and we returned to it year

Dave, just back from the war, with Anne and Kenneth, 1945.

Dave and Anne's children (from left), Kenneth, John, Bob, and Barbara on Gaylor Peak, Yosemite, 1958.

after year. It was our family's private wilderness threshold—forty years ago.

Ken and Bob had me in my most creative mode. In addition to our games in Tilden, which continued until they could catch a sixty-yard pass, they got the bedtime stories. I carried on, night after night, where Jack and the Beanstalk left off. I gave Jack, whom Ken became, a younger brother Ronnie, and kept them in giantland. They rarely encountered the real giant, and he was sympathetic when he showed up. They explored giant-sized furniture and utensils, took trips in the Hot Sticky Mountains, and made friends with and enjoyed exciting bareback rides on giant eagles Popo and Lele, and rode their growing giant eaglets, Roger, Dodger, Anice, and Janice as soon as they were able to make power dives. When a scene change was needed, we went underground through a mysterious cave to the domain of very little people. Nicodemus was one of the little heroes.

Somehow I managed to dream up episodes that began with excitement, then tapered off in calm, to induce sleep. From time to time, the sleep I induced was my own. I recorded a few episodes, but on equipment that no longer functions. I hope to repair the recorder someday and see if the stories were as good as I remember them.

The alternative to fixing the recorder is to ask Kenneth what he remembers. I would like to think that his remembering of the bedtime stories had something to do with his making up stories himself, and telling them first to his sister and brothers on long boring car trips, then to other children (and the eavesdropping adults) at Sierra Club High Trip campfires, and finally to the wider public reading the several books and score or two of articles he has written, as well as the books he assembled as an editor. There is always tape in Ken's inner camcorder, which has no electronic gremlins in it, and he converts the images and sounds into printed words as well as anyone I have ever read. It would be nice to think that my telling original bedtime stories had something to do with it.

If so, then wouldn't Bob have taken to storytelling and writing, too? Perhaps I unwittingly triggered different impulses by the roles I gave Ken's and Bob's counterparts in the Beanstalk series. Jack (Ken) was not so good at keeping track of directions, and Ronnie (Bob) had to straighten him out. I had somehow felt that Bob, the second son, needed such build-up and the first son could afford the criticism. Little did I know that Ken would respond by making it very clear at all times that he knew exactly where he was and what he was seeing.

If Ken doesn't remember and my obsolete recorder must be fixed, Bob will have to fix it. Both his grandfathers were able to fix anything, an ability that skipped his father but came to Bob. What he has inherited from his father is the determination to collect things to be worked on later, and the ability to fantasize that there will be enough time, later, to start the work. I go further than Bob in fantasizing that he will work on the objects I collect as well as his own.

It is not a misguided faith. Most of the exhibit-format books Ken and I edited for the Sierra Club and Friends of the Earth passed through Bob's hands on the way to press. He produced the mechanicals—took the reproduction proofs from the compositor and cut and pasted them into the final pages from which plates would be made in New York, Kingsport, London, or Verona. He created his own jigs, patterns that enabled him to be extraordinarily precise, meanwhile making sure that his use of space complemented the book's message in word and image. It was a very useful sub-publishing firm we had, Brower & Sons.

Was it all sweetness and light? Not exactly. On April 15, 1979, I wrote Ken and Bob all about my publishing worries—how I was trying desperately to keep the publishing effort alive in Friends of the Earth, how much I had spent of personal funds to help, how dire the scheduling emergencies were, reminding them implicitly of things they had not completed for me, and ending with two sentences I can't believe I wrote, but here they are: "If you are interested in helping get us out of this mess, in helping assiduously, please be assiduous, concentrate on it, stay up nights if need be, to get us out. If not, then please do not let me count on you further."

Ken's undated letter was overdue:

Dad,

Your letter was misaddressed. It was not written to me and Bob, but from Dave to Dave. It was full of awareness of your own thinking and problems, and absolutely no awareness at all of ours. There had been a conflict over our attitudes toward the projects & the deadlines—that you knew. You did not pause to think about it from our point of view, but launched into your two pages of dollars and cents and desperate risks—problems that worry us too, less from concern for Friends of the Earth than for you.

We don't like being treated like cogs, nor with rudeness, as if we were a little bit dumb and lazy.

[He listed the promises I had made but not fulfilled, asking for loyalty, giving none in return, and noted that I could be taken to task, too. His wind-up was properly sobering:]

I know that of late it's mostly your deadline desperation talking. You are in a state of hysteria for good reason. I have three ways to meet the hysteria:

1. I can indulge your unreasonableness, your stop-the-world-for-me tantrums, and meekly do as you demand, though this isn't good for either of us.

2. I can accept your suggestion that I be of no further service—an idea that right now has a lot of appeal for both of us.

3. I can continue to work for you as long as you want—I have no interest in working any longer than that, emotionally or, certainly, financially—by simply ignoring the hysteria, letting it roll off me, smiling & going about my work as I was before, to the best of my ability. I guess I pick No. 3.

Love,
Ken

Children need fathers who tell bedtime stories, and some fathers need children who tell it like it is.

Bob, confronted with a father too full of himself, simply let my thoughtless tirade roll past him. Further, he was more impressed with my concerns about corporate damage to the earth, I think, than our other children were. It certainly made him loath to compound that damage. Lacking training, he often ended up in jobs that unconscionably polluted the people undertaking them. He didn't like the seedy tactics of a sewing machine company he worked for. When another job had him transferring toxic glazes from containers labeled to reveal the toxicity to unlabeled containers destined for school use, he rebelled. He did not like what Lockheed products he was working on would end up doing to people. Above all, Bob wanted and still wants equity, and knows from long, direct experience how little there is of it in the ghetto. Aldo Leopold called dramatically for a land ethic. Bob wants a business ethic and hasn't learned how to call for it. Repeated frustration is a toxin in itself.

Mountains heal his wounds, but do not show up often enough in his life. Ken and Anne have been on a Himalayan trek once; John and I twice; Barbara three times and counting; Bob not at all. There isn't room there for everyone, but equity among Browers requires that he have a look. I keep telling young people to get out of the country. Go before increasing demands preclude it. Go beyond the mountains, beyond the arbitrary boundaries. Go while you can still travel light and cheap. Learn the guitar, take it along, and play for some of your meals. Go quietly, smug-free, look and listen well, and come back with the new understanding the world needs. (Perhaps I should write copy for a travel agency.) Meanwhile, Bob is overdue overseas.

We rather wish Barbara had been overseas less, but are pleased that most of her time there has been in high places. Indeed, I had hoped that Barbara would originate in one of the finest Sierra campsites we ever knew. It was in Nine Lakes Basin, east of the Mineral King Sierra. The site was conveniently remote from the commissary of the High Trip I was leading. We camped on a little island in the stream and had our own exquisite campfire site. Perfection of campsite was not enough, however, and Barbara had to wait a month. This is what probably trained her for a later patience. Anne was drafting letters for UC president Robert Gordon Sproul until five-thirty in the afternoon of May 18, 1950. At ten that evening she telephoned me at a Sierra Club conservation meeting to suggest that I had better take her to Alta Bates Hospital and alert Stewart Kimball, her doctor, who was also attending the meeting, that she would like him to be there, too. Barbara gave her first cry ten minutes before the rest of her body arrived at midnight. Anne's delivery system had attained a remarkable efficiency. Barbara was not quite a year old when she first camped in the Sierra, at the Virginia Lakes trailhead. Although Ken and Bob fared well, tracing circles and figure eights with the ends of long sticks reddened in the campfire, Barbara didn't. It was a cold night, and Anne thinks Barbara suffered a chilblain or two. I was in fine shape.

Twenty-odd years later the situation was reversed. We were climbing from North Lake to Piute Pass, elevation eleven thousand five hundred feet, on our way to a rendezvous in Humphreys Basin. I first camped there with George Rockwood in 1933, and wondered how much it had changed in forty years. What had indeed changed was me. Well before the pass my lack of condition, which had been following me at a respectful distance, caught up. Barbara, who had been well ahead, came back and carried my pack to the summit. At camp I found that Humphreys Basin had not aged a day in those forty years. Its timberline trees were older, but they didn't show it either. The firewood that had abounded beneath them, however, was no longer there. It had fueled many a campfire and cooked many a meal for the travelers of the Rainbow Circle, the trail over Piute Pass, down and around to the Evolution Basin, up to Muir Pass, down into Little Pete Meadow, and out through Dusy Basin to South Lake over Bishop Pass. But in all those wonderful places I had known, the solar energy so cleverly captured and so generously stored in those ancient fragments of lodgepole pine and albicaulis had been spent. I was sorry that Barbara had not shared the joy of spending it.

This was good training for a far more critical firewood situation she would face on the approach to Mount Everest the following year, and even more acutely when, with a Fulbright scholarship, she returned to spend a year at Namche Bazar, elevation eleven thousand feet, with side trips to points seven thousand feet higher, to observe the habits and the environmental and social impact of the yak and yak crossbreeds in Sagarmatha National Park, which includes Mount Everest. Her research led to her becoming an assistant professor of geography about as far away from an Everest environment as she could get—Austin, Texas, where chilblains never bother children.

Two years after Barbara's birth the imminence of John Stewart had me out in front with a shovel, digging up lawn and transplanting our lone birch so that we could start adding enough room to our house to accommodate four children and their parents. The year 1952 was a turbulent one. My Army Reserve work, as director of the Infantry School at the Oakland Army Base, gave me the opportunity to visit Fort Benning once again, this time not for three arduous months as a candidate, but for two relaxed weeks of a quite different experience—as a major in the Infantry Reserve. That was all the good news. Beginning the bad was a sudden illness of Anne's mother. It was probably a stroke, with the added anguish that she was unable to speak. She died in September of that year.

John arrived December 4, 1952, before our two added rooms were habitable and eleven days before the Sierra Club wanted me as executive director for five-sevenths of my time—all the budget would allow. It would be augmented by what I earned as leader of the High Trips and as an Army Reserve officer.

Anne had thought that if I worked for the club instead of volunteering for it, I would have more time at home. It didn't work out that way. One of the first casualties was lunch at Brower Meadow. Next, the bedtime stories became fitful, then silent. Before John was two months old, I was off to Washington to a conference held by Resources for the Future and to testify before Congress for the first time, in defense of Dinosaur National Monument. Life would not be the same again. But then, it never was.

Anne Editor

Anne, However, was always the same, one of the most diligent of working mothers. She lived in that once-upon-a-time era when publishers believed that editors were important, that they could help an author be clear, even if it added to the unit cost of a book.

Anne never had any difficulty in finding editorial work and augmenting our family income, which needed it. She thus was able to help clarify what happened in the battle for Attu when she edited in the Pentagon. When we finally settled down on Stevenson Avenue in Berkeley in January 1947—whenever, that is, the burden of three further pregnancies permitted—she was editing again. She helped with a manuscript I was working on at the UC Press. She almost always looked over my shoulder when I was writing or editing for the Sierra Club, and never stopped at the shoulder.

It would have been much easier for her to stop there, but she couldn't. Words are too important to her. So is her need to see some facility in a writer who is trying to hook words together, especially if that writer happens to be her husband and she has some hopes that he will make sense more often than not.

Together we created a routine. I would work fairly hard on a piece, prepare for a little praise about its lucidity and brilliance, and pass it to Anne for comment. Anne would rarely get past the first line. Her face would cloud. She was too tired right now to read further. I would know I was in trouble and get defensive, perhaps a little abusive, but only orally. That never worked, so I would put on my best sick-cow look and try to persuade her to go on, not stopping for word adjustment but reading through for sense. Reluctantly she would, knowing how impatient I would get that she had not instantly understood the particular nuance I was striving for or, more particularly, the humor I was trying to drag in. I would usually leave the room to spare myself the pain of watching her misery. Ever so lightly, she would pencil suggestions in the margins. I would fuss about them or become otherwise obnoxious. Too often I would stalk away in a mild pout—and quietly make the changes she had suggested. Occasionally I could come up with a better alternative, but not often. The question remains: How often did I express my appreciation properly? Not often enough.

To the best of my recollection, I followed this routine until I was seventy-seven (which happens to be the day I am writing this), when I took every suggestion she made about this very chapter without any fuss at all. We may very well live happily ever after.

Anne's editing was helpful to a host of others. For four years she assisted Mel Webber in his editing of the *Journal of the American Institute of Planners*. We shared her editing problems and the thinking problems of planners as they acceded to the accelerating sprawl of suburbia. We happily disagreed with her editor's conclusion that "soil is old-fashioned." It isn't and never will be. And we agreed with Jane Jacobs's understanding that planners should, in their city planning, provide for the accommodation of humans. I picked up two quotations about planners that I have used ever since: "A planner will accept a catastrophe as long as he has planned it," and "A region is an area safely larger than the one whose problems we last failed to solve." The latter is from Paul Ylvasaker. His name, as well as his remark, is unforgettable.

Then there were Anne's thirteen years as editor for the UC Department of Anthropology. In sharing her interest in this, I learned that anthropologists, like architects and geographers, are really the closest to renaissance people we can find in universities, and to wish that more disciplines would learn to reach out. We were both fascinated with studies of primates, especially since we had our own resident primate, Isabelle, about whom you will hear a great deal in a few moments.

One of the high points of Anne's anthropological editing was our getting to know Theodora Kroeber well, and through her, Ishi, whose story Theodora told so beautifully. We were amazed and pleased at the courage of both parties when she married John Quinn, forty-three years her junior, whom she got to know when he designed her Sierra Club book, *Almost Ancestors*. It was Theodora's conversation with her daughter, Ursula Kroeber Leguin, that produced another memorable comment that I have exploited at every opportunity. They were both in New York, where Theodora was engaged in promoting her UC Press book about Ishi, when the question was raised: "Why do New Yorkers focus on Fifth Avenue and ignore the Hudson River?" The answer: "New Yorkers did not build the Hudson River, and it annoys them."

When Anne retired from anthropology she switched to oral history at the Bancroft Library. Once you have learned to edit, you can never again leave another person's words alone. The Bancroft provided more words to work on. Following the example of Columbia University, the Bancroft developed an excellent regional oral history program and Anne enjoyed being part of it. Her greatest challenge was in gathering together memories of what Walter Gordon's life had been like. He was a pioneer of integration, one of the first African-American greats in football, an officer in the Berkeley Police Department, and governor of the Virgin Islands. Anne interviewed his widow, a general, attorneys, and football players, gathering them into an account of a life about which there were few documents.

Oral history is certainly one of the most neglected areas of what we choose to call history. I have my own prejudices about history; sometimes I wonder whether it really exists. Or is it merely a historian's subjective bias about what he or she believes to be worth writing about objectively? Is our past actually as rife with war as historians would have us believe? Is peace too dull to write about? Were there enough interviews with the principals in history to draw upon, to evaluate and interpret properly? Are too many of the data historians rely upon too raw? Are historians really normal people? I could go on and possibly become serious about all this.

What I prefer to be serious about is the failure to record, now that technology has given us the audio and video equipment, what people who have made major contributions remember about them while their memory is still alive.

Anne's interviewing talent is special. Again and again, I have watched her learn more about a person, by asking good questions, than that person knew before being asked.

Among her other talents are two that you ought to know about. Anne once asked everyone at a party to be quiet, and announced that there was going to be an earthquake. She was right. Further, she can tune in on audio channels I cannot hear. She will have difficulty understanding me when I am at her side, but can pick up a conversation across the room, especially if it is more interesting than what I was saying. Eavesdropping is an art. And no one can out-eavesdrop Anne. Conversation at a party is an art, too. Several people can be talking at once but one's own conversation with a friend will proceed well if both parties select a tone different from that of the neighbors' or the general pitch of the room's cacophony. As for earthquakes—I think she will avoid predicting any more of them, and thus keep her perfect record intact.

Anne's verbal exercises, editorial and other, never took her far from home. That enabled our children to have at least one parent most of the time.

Trips and Adventures

The Best Way I could think of to make up for all my absences was to take the family on trips. As soon as they hit six, they went on Sierra Club trips. We hurried John by taking him when he was three and a half. Too soon, I think. His pulse climbed too high as we approached Bishop Pass, at an elevation of nearly twelve thousand feet, and I had to carry him on my shoulders, which did my pulse no good. Then he was off with us to the North Cascades, tempted from point to point along the trail by the promise of huckleberries, and carried when the berries failed. It was forever raining and his feet were forever wet, but he seems to have forgiven us for that initiation.

Easter vacations meant it was time to head for the Southwest. Monument Valley was a favorite of ours. The children loved the desert—the redder the better. Anyone could drive into the valley from the main road then—anyone who was brave enough. Our 1956 Chevy wagon had enough clearance, and I enough mountain-driving experience, that we could probe deep. The memorable occasion was the night it rained heavily and I decided to get out while the getting was possible. The windshield wipers could not clear the rain fast enough for good visibility, and I misread where the so-called road went and turned up a wash. One does not turn up a wash in a heavy desert rain. I found a place to make a U-turn and was finally on the main road once again and headed for Kayenta and a motel room out of the rain. The dirt road became a muddy road. Traction was disappearing by the minute. Just before Kayenta the road descended to a one-lane railless bridge, which I managed to hit, stay on, and cross. The ten-percent grade up from the bridge was another matter. The rear wheels spun and the car began to slide back. The emergency brake would not stop the sliding, but the foot brake did. I asked Anne to keep her foot on the brake and got out to place a rock behind the wheel. There were no rocks; just clods, dissolving. Finding the biggest, least saturated clod I could, I put it in place and hurried off on foot to Kayenta for help. Anne's braking foot began to shake; the children had long since given up their night's sleep and shared her fear. Fortunately, Kayenta was close, a Navajo had a jeep and tow rope, and we never enjoyed a motel room more.

The children nevertheless continued to love the desert, especially desert canyons with water in them. So we started a series of trips down Glen Canyon, from Hite to the Crossing of the Fathers. Once we flew to Hole-in-the-Rock, the famous Mormon crossing of the Colorado, and followed the amazing route down the canyonside to start our river trip. Construction of Glen Canyon Dam denied us the lower part of Glen Canyon, and finally all its unique beauty was denied us and everyone else. But the children remember it well—too well, perhaps. The Tetons twice,

Kenneth, Dave, and Anne on a Sierra Club High Trip, 1951. Photo by Cedric Wright.

the North Cascades once again, the High Sierra from Yosemite to Army Pass, the Grand Canyon rims, Anasazi ruins, trips to wherever my brother Joe's houses were—these we also remember.

When John McPhee was with Floyd Dominy and me in Glen Canyon, our motorboat entered Cathedral Canyon and took a few turns up its deep meanders. John and I were just behind the windshield and his notebook lay open on the dash. I happened to glance at it for an instant and saw the words, "watching Dave," and quickly looked ahead again lest he watch more closely and see the tears in my eyes.

For I was remembering our earlier family trip, when Anne, all four children, and I were wading up the shallow stream that had carved those meanders in the Navajo sandstone and was still watering the exquisite streamside gardens or, if in a quiet pool, reflecting the tapestries of lichen and precipitated sand that graced the cathedral walls. One pool was too deep to wade and a low waterfall dropped into it. The children swam on ahead, scrambled up beside the waterfall, and rounded the next corner to see what was there. Anne, who doesn't swim, welcomed help from me in navigating and scrambling, and we rounded still more corners, finally catching up with the children.

They were full of an explorer's excitement, eagerly looking for each new wonder where water and wind had been the cathedral's sculptors. One long pool was too deep for John to wade. He floundered, but only briefly before Barbara kept him afloat and Bob hoisted him up the next cascade. The children paused when the canyon walls, leaning back, lost the mystery they had enclosed below, where they rose so high and so steeply that they defined an inner world of their own, with its own magic light ricocheting from cliff to cliff, seeming to be independent of the thin arcs of sky we would occasionally see.

Remembering the joy of those young explorers, and knowing that neither they nor anyone else could ever repeat this experience, I could not stem my grief. My head turned, and John McPhee was spared.

Most of all, we remember Europe. I had dreamed often of going back, but the cost of taking a family to Europe was simply out of the question – until the Sierra Club directors realized that I had not had a regular vacation for years, and decided to allow me three months with pay. We found we could rent our house for those months. We could handle the cost of taking a train across the United States, a student ship across the Atlantic, a train ride to Hannover and the Volkswagen factory, ground and water transportation from Germany to Ireland, and air fare from Shannon to Montreal. All we had to go into debt for was a new Volkswagen bus, which would carry us around Europe for two months and, once shipped across the Atlantic, from Montreal to Berkeley. The trip was on. But a new hazard was introduced. I was urged to obtain an American Express card. It served us well, but led to a plastic addiction that I have not been able to end.

Anne and the children will have to remember their own highlights of the trip. I nevertheless can remember some for them. For John: From the Arc de Triomphe John spied a man selling balloons and insisted that he have one. I risked my life slaloming among the countless cars in the circle to get it and John clung to it with determination – until we reached our high point on the Eiffel Tower. We watched with delight as he released it there and the balloon nodded to Paris until it went out of sight.

Bob's highlight was probably the Palio. I took color slides and movies of the colorful preparations and had started climbing, Bolex in hand, into the bleachers for our family's seats. In a momentary unsteadiness I reached for the arm of one of the seats for balance. It was attached to nothing, came up in my hand, and I fell over backwards, Bolex and all. Our European trip could have ended right there in disaster. But Bob, almost fifteen and already a six-footer, was right behind me. I was then light enough, and he big enough, to end my fall before it could get underway.

Anne's surprise was Italy. She was convinced that I would want to spend endless hours revisiting Monte Belvedere, Monte della Torraccia, Gualandi, the Po, Lake Garda – all these to refight my war. I did, but not endlessly, and the boys, if not Anne and Barbara, liked seeing where the shells had fallen about me. Altogether we spent half of our days on the Continent in Italy, and were glad we did.

As I've mentioned, one of the delightful occupations of Joseph Brower was serving as a navigator for various airlines. He was with Swissair while we were in Europe and had a place in the outskirts of

Zurich. Somehow he and Gayle, with help from the neighbors, were able to handle all six of us graciously on our way to and from Italy.

Our other accommodations were more spartan. Thanks to what the VW bus could carry, we were able to camp for thirty days in Europe, our favorite campsite being at Fiesole, just above Florence. We traveled without reservations, so when we couldn't camp we sought out cheap hotels, exploiting our edition of *Europe on $5 a Day*—when something like that was possible in Europe. The higher the rooms, the lower the cost, so we chose high rooms when we could. Theoretically, the high rooms were more dangerous, diminishing the chances of getting out safely in case of fire. But we were mountain people. I carried a nylon climbing rope, and we all knew how to rappel.

On July 6, we were in a little bed-and-breakfast place in the outskirts of Rome when Maximo, a young man Bob's age, learned that it was Bob's fifteenth birthday. Somehow Maximo rounded up a birthday cake and his parents graciously put the rest of a party together. We were on our way to discovering how many more smiles per person there are in Italy than we had yet encountered elsewhere, probably because Italians don't let their government's eccentricities bother them.

Halfway down the coast toward Naples we found everything a camper could ask for—Sperlonga. A fine old city stood on the cape to the north, there was a little supply store and bath facilities for campers, and a short easy trail led through a truck garden to a perfect lonely beach. We became master sand-castle builders and spent hours in water of as soothing a temperature as we had ever experienced—too soothing for us to realize what the sun was doing to John. Wet feet in the North Cascades, a swarm of mosquito bites in Little Lakes Valley, and now it was blister to blister of Sperlonga sunburn. All this should have cured John of wanting anything more to do with outdoor living, but it hasn't yet.

The grand old Greek columns at Paestum charmed us. We drove as far south as Agropoli, where all I remember is the women selling milk in open-top bottles, assuring us that it was pasteurized. We went without, and headed back to the Amalfi Drive. We were properly scared by it, and I was happy that we were northbound, on the inside of stretches of the road carved into cliffs that sometimes underhung the road. Far more dangerous, actually, was the drive into blinding headlights on the narrow two-lane highway to Venice and our beach cabin at Ponte Sabbione. Mountain people like us should stay away from beaches, we concluded, when our nylon rope was stolen through a partly open window. Henceforth we would have to choose more expensive lower-floor rooms that did not require a rappel in case of fire. A new nylon, had we been able to find one, would have cost more than the low-cost rooms would have saved us.

By the time we were pausing in Cortina while crossing the Alps, John decided that he wanted a butterfly net. My war experience had not taught me the word for butterfly. In a likely little shop I tried using gestures, confident that these would be more easily understood by Italians than by anyone else. During the war Ralph Bromaghin, trying to obtain some wax to repair my accordion, had succeeded with a gesture – twisting a finger in his ear, pointing to the finger, and saying "wax." It worked. So I tried imitating a butterfly's flight with my hands, following by a sweeping arm motion as if I were swinging a net. The clerk caught on. *"Farfalla,"* she said, and reached under the counter and found what we wanted. I say we. John was the one who asked for it, but I wanted it too, for old time's sake. Unfortunately, I was already too old for old time's sake, as I discovered later when trying to overtake a butterfly in a broad meadow in France. The butterfly was not winded.

The summer of sixty-one was simply super, but a little scary on August 13, when we were driving toward Holland and heard the news that the Berlin Wall was going up. Come by some time and I'll show you our movies and slides, including the sad one of a cicada I photographed as it struggled out of its chrysalis and paused, well camouflaged, to dry its wings and take off. Not well enough camouflaged, however. While I watched, a hunting wasp found the cicada, stung it, and converted it to a hearty meal for a wasp-to-be. Nature was not friendly to that cicada, nor to birds as we crossed the Rockies in September, hurrying to get all hands back in school on time. An unseasonal snowfall had hit Loveland Pass, and small birds simply could not handle it and were dying in huge numbers of cold and hunger.

It would be wrong to end the summer of sixty-one on so sad a note, or with the suggestion that only Italy and not the other ten countries we visited had delights. Holland must rank high. Anne was pleased to visit her father's birthplace in Leiden, and her father's sister, once a concert violinist, in The Hague. When I looked at the faces around me, I somehow felt I was home and these people were relatives. Browers (spelled Brouwer) were brewmakers, and I did my best to help support Anne when she owned a little stock in Heineken. For all our heritage, however, we could not avoid the situation I got into. I asked on the telephone for language assistance, and the operator replied, good-naturedly, "You mean your name is Brower and you can't speak Dutch?" We can't even pronounce the name of The Hague's beach – *Scheveningen!*

There was no way Anne and I could have known that twenty-eight years later, on November 10, 1989, we would end a speaking tour in West Germany in Berlin. What goes up must come down, which is what the wall did that day.

If I could go on talking about trips, I could avoid getting into the subject of family education. With a sophomore dropout for a father, and a mother who takes thirteen years to get a B.A., what can you say? Ken's educational resumé reads like his father's. Bob finished high school with a ninety-eight percentile score on his SATs, but is waiting to see what to do with it. John was the fastest college dropout in the West. After two weeks in Berkeley he told Anne, "This isn't for me." Barbara rejected UC Santa Cruz, was rejected by Radcliffe, tried Reed, and came home of her own accord to get her bachelor's, master's, and doctor's at Berkeley and become assistant professor of geography at the University of Texas, in Austin, where she and her husband, Jan Olsen, produced Anne Kathryn, the first Texan in our family. Our women are our educated ones—Anne with her B.A. and an ability to write I only wish I could force her to use, and Professor Barbara about to go back to Nepal with her second Fulbright.

So why should our men worry about education when our women have already done so well with it? What, then, are the prospects? Anne could, ought to, should, must write, and contribute to oral histories while the subjects are still oral. She is good at it.

Ken, possesses a special ability to see the world through the eyes of others, and has already written more books than I have read (a slight exaggeration). My constant delight, and Anne's, is to be known as one of the parents of the author of *The Starship and the Canoe,* which almost everyone seems to have bought, read, or borrowed. They should look up his other works, starting with *A Song for Satawal.*

Bob can fix anything when he wants to, and is the son I call up whenever I have trouble with my electronic equipment, which is often. If somehow a tradition for Honest Maintenance could develop in this country, he would honor it and work at it—if he wanted to. Bob, born with a scientist's mind, is handicapped by his father's disapproval of where Conscienceless Science and Mindless Technology are leading us—toward a reality that is in need of vast improvement.

John annoys people by doing in one hour what they would rather take two or three to do. He is impatient of hour wasters. Impatience is his middle name. Impatience is more understandable in someone who is seventy-seven than in someone who is not quite half that age. If you are seventy-seven, you want people to hurry up so that you can see the results. If you are, as John is now, only thirty-seven, you can wait. John can't.

ISABELLE

OUR HAVING BEEN INTRODUCED to Isabelle was a once-in-a-lifetime opportunity that saved her life and informed ours beautifully. Let me tell you about a most talented member of our family group.

In 1964 Isabelle was attending the University of California but had a serious accident and had to leave. She was refused admittance to

Columbia, her second choice, was soon expelled from the new Athenian School, near Mount Diablo, but was admitted to Reed College. We had hoped that, like two of our friends who had gone there, she would win a Rhodes Scholarship. She was quite bright and an absolutely extraordinary athlete. But that didn't happen. She was asked to leave Reed instead.

Columbia simply hadn't understood who she was or things might well have turned out differently. Berkeley, the Athenian School, and Reed did know, and that was probably the trouble. You see, Isabelle was a blue-bellied, crab-eating iris macaque, easily distinguished from the rest of us, and therefore able to give us a special kind of window through which to look upon the world. Her world began in Malaysia, where the monkeys have no tails—of the prehensile kind. She migrated against her will to Berkeley to have her behavior watched and perhaps be otherwise experimented with. In an altercation in the Strawberry Canyon research center, she panicked, ran, fell, and split her chin so deeply that bone showed. Anthropologist Phyllis Jay took Iz home, where her wound healed. All went well until Phyllis failed to refuse a position at Columbia, or to insist that Iz share it lest she be destroyed in Berkeley. Or be given away.

"I'll take care of her," said Barbara, then twelve. If Anne had not agreed, I would have. Barbara's parents are pushovers. So Iz joined our family for twenty-two years as its smallest member. She was only a foot high but the boldest of the lot. No ordinary macaque, she was in the literature before she was three years old—in the Life Nature Library book, *The Primates*. Whenever we find that volume in someone's library, we refer to pages 132 and 133, where poor Iz, revisiting Strawberry Canyon, goes into panic again.

Although Iz didn't take up much room with her body, it took a lot of room to accommodate where she wanted her body to be from moment to moment. And wherever that small body was, she had command of far more space than you would imagine. She had opposable thumbs on her feet as well as her hands, and her feet could reach farther than her hands if they had to, which was forever catching us and others by surprise. Whatever she could reach she did, and whetted her curiosity with immediately. She must see what was inside it. She could make a ping-pong ball useless instantly. She might well have learned to write, but she preferred to take and crimp pens rather than try to write with them. Strangely, she was good with books. She would turn the pages carefully, but not always leave them dry. If we wanted to be housebroken, that was up to us. She would have none of it. Iz poop was manageable. Unless she was frightened, it was discrete and dry and easily tossed (by us; she never threw it at us). Urine was not so discrete, and a certain warmth would suddenly descend upon us if, for example, she was perched on a shoulder and needed release.

Since she preferred to be unhousebroken we kept her in a cage in the kitchen, initially, which made her miserable. If she felt miserable

Isabelle grooming Barbara. Anne, John, and Dave next. Photo by Arthur Schatz, Life *magazine, ©Time, Inc.*

enough and we had forgotten to anchor the cage, she would put her inertia machine to work and jockey the cage around the kitchen, helping herself to whatever she could reach through the bars. If she could reach the key, she could unlock the padlock—not immediately, but by experimenting and poking around long enough to pop it open.

We finally found a way to move her out. Bob rigged a wire trolley from our chimney to our dying apricot tree and tied one end of a nylon leash to her collar and the other end to a carabiner I was no longer using in climbs, having stopped climbing. That way she had a generous range in the backyard. She didn't care much for climbing the tree, but discovered and used a death-defying route to the roof, where she would sit on the ridge and watch the world go by. That death-defying route included scrambling up a latticework I had built for the purpose, then reaching back to catch the gutter above a two-foot overhang, swing out, and with inimitable dexterity and pederity be on the roof. She made no such move until she determined she had enough slack in the leash not to be caught short.

On the roof she did not limit herself to watching the world. She worked on her leash. She could untie any knot I could tie, and I know a lot of them—but not if I wound some number-14 wire around any available loose ends of the leash. She could undo an ordinary carabiner without a second's thought, so we used a locking carabiner. If we screwed the lock as hard as we could by hand, she could unscrew it. Her fingers were strong, but if not strong enough, she used her teeth, which we well knew were too strong. After bearing a few scars, we had her canines filed down. She didn't need those weapons in our peaceful world.

Naturally, we never discovered each of her new talents of freeing herself until it was too late. In the interim she accomplished wonders:

1. She crossed the street and destroyed our neighbor's hundred-year-old bonsai. Insurance covered it, somehow.

2. Anne came home to discover that she had been loose in the house, but was no longer loose. She had apparently tried to write the novel monkeys can write, given enough time, on my Olivetti portable typewriter, but had been so curious about the ribbon that she had immobilized herself with it.

3. She entered the kitchen window of our next-to-next-door neighbors – three young men who shared the house but were never in when she called. Their door was locked, of course, and Anne could hear Iz disassembling the kitchen, but could only wait until Iz wanted to come back out.

The neighbors took this in stride until she got into their Kodachrome slide collection. She fingerprinted some of them, which wasn't too bad. But she did something they really didn't like: she ate Copenhagen.

She wasn't always in the backyard or the neighbors' house. On good days we'd put her out on the front porch – on leash, of course – where she could watch the passersby. Perhaps she enjoyed their double takes as much as we did, as they passed by but then backed up to say something like, "It's a *monkey!*" Anne occasionally meets full-grown mature women at the supermarket who ask, "How is Isabelle?" They were children when they met her on their way to or from the neighboring school, children who stopped to play with her. She was quite tolerant of children and rarely took advantage of them.

From time to time Iz would get bored with passersby and climb up on the narrow outside windowsill to look in to see what we were up to. If she wanted attention she'd pound on the window. She rattled it with an insistence that stopped conversation. If we still ignored her she would begin a series of her most plaintive cries – and win every time.

Children were usually in free. Not adults. She loved to pick men's pockets but she loved earrings more. If you had pierced ears, she would leave most of the ear but take the ring. Finding that she could not disassemble it, she would tuck it in either of her cheek pouches for later investigation. I somehow learned how to con her out of them. I talked to her in a low, loving, insistent voice, acknowledging that she wasn't going to like it, but I had to get the prize back. She would grimace – more of a wide-mouthed panicky smile – and I would reach gently into whichever cheek pouch I had felt the ring in and retrieve it. I am happy to report that I still have ten fingers—as many as I ever had.

She could and did eat anything we would, including meat. Lest she like it too much, including parts of us, we preferred offering her fruits, nuts, and vegetables. Bananas were a favorite of hers—and ours, since they take no preparation. She could peel them deftly if we didn't. If she wanted one, she would demand it with her own special gesture. She would stand up and pat at the air with her right hand. She did not particularly like artichokes, but if we were eating them, she wanted some, and would make a few scraping passes with her teeth at the right side of a few petals, then give up.

The easiest way to initiate communication with Iz—to cross the species barrier—was to ask her to your lap to groom her or to be groomed. To groom, you imitated her moves—several quick brushes with your finger against the lay of her hair and a quick grasp for whatever your latest stroke may have revealed, whether or not you found anything. Grooming would relax her completely, until you tired of it. She never did, and would be as limp as a damp dishrag, as if fully anesthetized.

She would reciprocate, insistently, and would be very gentle. It could be embarrassing when she pretended she found something interesting and ate it, even though it may only have been dandruff or less. She would groom eyelashes with meticulous care, and her fingers were tiny enough to be exquisitely careful.

She crossed the species barrier with our assorted dogs the same way, except that she never had any trouble finding enough hair on their arms or backs or stomachs or whatever. They would lie quietly and accept her devoted attention. They could not reciprocate. She let it go at that.

The dogs respected her for her kindness, but also for her out-and-out boldness. Her mother never told her to pick on someone her own size. She could cow five dogs ten times her size all at once, her favorite weapon being an eyelid hold. If someone, no matter how small, had hold of your eyelid, you'd probably sit still until the ordeal was over. The dogs did, knowing she could grab that hold faster than they could avoid it.

Our maximum dog count at any one time was twenty-two, most of them from three litters delivered by Bob's dogs, whom he taught nothing about birth control. Iz loved puppies and would take a lot of nonsense from them, quickly turning them upside down if they went too far. When they were nursing, she would lie on the mother and apparently fantasize that she, too, was nursing them. What did we know about her fantasies? Quite a bit. When you have lived with a monkey for a decade or two, and vice versa, body language works. I am sure she knew a lot of our words, and we knew a lot of hers—the tones and intonations that could reveal various kinds of fears, anger, loneliness, and love. She would rarely look you in the eye in daytime, but at dusk she would climb to her bunk spot—some padding we placed on the brick ledge of our outdoor fireplace within our loggia—and look beseechingly, even lovingly, at us. At such times she didn't mind being kissed, preferring that the kisses come from the men in the family. She would place a hand affectionately on your shoulder.

When she was angry or offended or just annoyed she could be fierce—totally, toothfully fierce. She would flash the white areas above her eyes, bare her teeth, and aim them at you in a challenging charge. I found out early how to disarm her. Simply offer her your index finger, knuckle forward. She would proceed with the bite, but it was soft-mouthed and painless. It was her way of saying, "So I win. I'll forget about it."

She had a few real fears. The shadow of a big bird (or a big bird itself) would freak her out, as would the flexible very snakelike fake snake Anne could use to discipline her—well, not exactly discipline her, but just remind her that we had a few tricks, too. And on the dog run in Tilden Regional Park she would be splendidly unconcerned about the approach of an assortment of dogs—unless one of them was a German shepherd. Thereupon she was instantly off the ground and on the nearest human shoulder until the peril was out of sight.

Crab-eating macaque or not, she wanted no part of the Pacific shore and its waves. She liked mountains better, and went to the Sierra with John McPhee and all our family once, apparently enjoying it enormously, riding on a shoulder when her feet got tired of the rocky trail. She learned about snowbanks and how to eat and slide on them. Suddenly she stopped and held her hands to her head, obviously stricken by a high-altitude headache. She had earned it. She had acclimatized to the thousand-foot elevation at our house, and was now at ten thousand feet.

Her trouble with educational institutions began at the Athenian School. I suspect that Barbara, who together with a schoolmate had adopted a small boa constrictor, was not paying Iz enough attention and she misbehaved a little in response.

At Reed College it was different. One time Iz got loose and raided the dormitory, and Barbara had to do a second-story job to get her back. That wasn't too serious. What was too serious happened in the biological laboratory where Iz spent the nights in her cage. One night Barb forgot to anchor the cage. Iz thereupon jockeyed it around the lab and opened the cages of the assorted experimental animals. It was fortunate for Science that she didn't remove the animals' numbers. That, at least, is the way I heard it, and I believe it.

Barbara and Iz hitchhiked home from Portland, to her mother's dismay. "How could you do such a dangerous thing?" Anne asked. "It wasn't dangerous at all," Barb replied, "not with Isabelle to protect me." And on further thought, her parents had to agree that anyone who threatened Barbara in Isabelle's presence would be in for a big, painful, and immediate surprise.

However familiar we may have been with Isabelle's various voices, we heard a cry early one August morning we had not heard before. I got up to check and found her acting strangely. Her tongue began to swell. We rushed her to the only vet we knew who had worked with the Berkeley primates. He was puzzled. We don't quite know what he tried, or might have tried had he known what we later suspected – that a spider she tried to bite had bitten her back on her tongue. At nine o'clock we took her home, and at eleven she died in my arms.

In her time she had made a hole or two in us that healed. This time she left one that hasn't.

FAMILY SUPPLEMENTS

IF ALL LIFE ON THIS PLANET had a common origin – and I accept this – then everything now alive is your cousin and mine, some farther removed than others. I am proud of my relation to our present and former pets, to the redwood, the dolphin, the pelican, the monarch, columbine at timberline, and lichens that are higher still. I tend to regret being related so closely to the sloth.

Next to the members of one's own family come the supplemental members. They may be like the Eskimo children in Chivak, who seem to be at home in anyone's home in town. Our own family has been delightfully augmented by others' children. We have volunteered as supplementary parents for children who have lost their parents and were very close to our own children – the four children, for instance, of Betty and Newell Nelson, who met in 1939 on my first Sierra Club High Trip. Or Justin Curtsinger, whose parents asked that I christen him with a slight sprinkling of Atlantic Ocean, just off Biddeford Pool, Maine. Borrowing liberally from Loren Eiseley, Lawrence Collins, Nancy Newhall, Robinson Jeffers, Terry Russell, and Goethe, I scrawled this bit of litany on the back of an envelope and put it to use on July 19, 1981:

"Under the authority vested in me by virtue of my having been around sixty-nine years longer than you (and by no other authority and little other virtue), I hereby welcome you, Justin Smith, of Mahoney and Curtsinger, like them compounded of dust and the light of a star, to this planet, the living one, third from the sun, and to its tides, already flowing within you and about to touch you gently. It is only a little planet, but it is beautiful, with its lonely flowing waters, it secret-keeping stones, its flowing sky, and the miraculous living things aboard it, which you have joined. Beauty is not on the map and adventure is not in the guidebook, but seek and ye shall find, love and be loved. Whatever you can do or dream you can, begin it; boldness has genius, power, and magic in it. You have already proved this by what you have accomplished in the hardly ten moons since you began, bringing a new kind of love into your household, yours for your parents and theirs for you; you are already living in the hearts of others, as they will live in yours. Congratulations on your arrival, and on your becoming, like the planet, one of a kind. Take it from here!"

It is nice when the initiative comes from outside, as when Terry Hartig, student of wilderness and its healing powers at the University of California, Irvine, adopted Anne and me as alternate parents at the Fourth World Wilderness Congress. It was a case of instant taking to each other. Or when our young Soviet interpreter, Andrei Anatoliovich Surenko, adopted us as grandparents at Lake Baikal.

Most closely related were our neighbors' children, Peter Olson and his older sister, Kristy, who survives his decision that life was too much for him. In May 1983 I was asked to say a few words at his memorial:

"One of the delightful things human beings are blessed with is our built-in color video recorder, complete with sound and instant replay. It enables us to call up beautiful sequences in the lives of people we love. I can't count the number of these on my own inner screen of Peter. Very early ones of a very little Peter Olsen playing on our patio with John, his contemporary; not quite so early, of Little League days; still later, with no picture at all except the wall of our house through which a cascade of trumpet music, played with uncommon skill, poured our way–and every other way, so good to hear; scenes later still, in the Village, in New York, with Peter hurrying along to join a group of us at dinner and to play some of his own compositions later for us on the piano; or on or near our Berkeley driveway, his animated conversations with any of our four children, at various stages of their lives, or with Barbara at a geography department tea.

"It was especially pleasing to me when Peter's interest grew in what was happening at Friends of the Earth–first with books, then with what he might be able to provide to illustrate a book, or a piece in our paper, *Not Man Apart*. Finally, it was right down to earth and we had many good talks about his interest in seeing that intelligent people make intelligent use of the waste products of civilization. When I re-create those scenes–having lunch together, riding BART, going to meetings or hearings, I hear under them the background music of the kind of love you have for a supplementary child, one who has grown up with your children, and who may even have thought of you as a supplementary parent (that useful role, played by a person who has no authority, but can love and, now and then, perhaps even persuade.)

"Peter was important to us, the Browers, and to all of us gathered here. He is important to the wonderful things we remember of him, and of Ozzie, and Judy, and Kristy. As for myself, I just want to get on with the things we were going to do together at Friends of the Earth, things that he thought would be a credit to Berkeley, and to the places far away that find good examples in Berkeley. I think these things would have pleased him, and that is something to cherish, along with all the color and sound of Peter that made it so rewarding to be alive when he was. For his love, and ours of him, I am grateful."

Without his knowing it until five years later, we supplemented our family with a poet, John Daniel. Stanford had me as a guest lecturer in the spring of 1984 and John was in the class. When it was over he sent me a letter and two poems that explain what we feel so much better than we are able to that we thought we had better add him to the group. He wrote on the letterhead of Stanford's Creative Writing Center, through which I found him in Portland, Oregon, and learned that the poems have appeared in his book, *Common Ground*. He wrote in June 1984:

Dear Mr. Brower,

In your first lecture you spoke of the rights of generations to come, and our responsibility for them. Your words stirred up what eventually became "The Unborn," one of the poems enclosed. Please accept it as my thanks for the course and for the cheerful intelligence of your career as an environmentalist. It's been a privilege to have you at Stanford.

Best wishes,
John Daniel

COMMON GROUND

Everywhere on Earth, wet beginnings–

fur, feather, scale, shell, skin, bone, blood

–like an infant discovering sound after sound,
a voice is finding its tongue
in the slop and squall of birth.
It sounds!

And we, in whom Earth chose to light
a clear flame of consciousness,
are only beginning to learn the language–

who are made of the ash of stars,
who carry the sea we were born in,
who spent millions of years learning to breathe,
who shivered in fur at the reptile's feet,
who trained eyes and hands in the trees
and came down slowly straightening
to look over the grasses, to see
that the world not only is
but is beautiful–

we are Earth learning to see itself,
to hear, touch, and taste.

What it wants to be, no one knows. It speaks
in us all: finding a way to starlight and dark,
it begins in beauty,
it asks only time.

THE UNBORN
for David Brower

Whatever they could see
we hold in seed, their faces containing our faces
in the darkness deeper
than anyone can remember,
their voices
that given speech
will speak for us
when we have passed
beyond speech—
whatever it is
we are trying to become
only they can tell,
only in them
can the womb say its name
and only in us
can they speak at all,
they speak
if we speak for them.

The privilege of encountering John Daniel—and two Stanford classes—was mine. It would probably be awkward to adopt them all. But here's to cousins, near and far, and our learning to speak for them!

TRIBAL RIGHTS

THE WORD *family* is too all-encompassing to describe the consortium of Huses, Browers, ancestors, heirs, and unofficially adopted friends that surround us in time and space. *Tribe* sounds pleasantly descriptive until one finds that Webster considers a tribe to be putatively consanguineous, which may or may not be pleasing, and a tribe could become hierarchical very quickly if one is not careful. *Clan* is too exclusive, *extended family* too limited, *overextended family* not limited enough.

What we have and enjoy is an *extensible family*. It includes spouses and significant others; people we can only remember, whose absence makes room for successors; almost-people with whom we share ancestry if we look back far enough; friends who became very close when we were able to be their port when they were caught in a storm, or who became our port; a good twenty people whose names I haven't mentioned yet; and who knows how many who will someday qualify and be unable to extricate themselves. One man's extensible family.

These family members have an advantage over a member of the nuclear family. We have no power to command the members of the wider tribe. That is their right. And it is our right to feel wonderfully free of the obligation to command—not that commanding seems to have overburdened our own children too much. If indeed the commandment to love thy neighbor as thyself is to be revised upward in the interest of world peace, and the new rule is that one love one's neighbor better than oneself, it is a delight to have an extensible family around to practice that love on. This goes for all the people named in this long chapter, and (forgive me for sounding like a disc jockey) it goes as well for Betty, Jane, Susan, Nancy, Tom, Kris, Joe, Phil, Jerry and Jeannie, Dave and Ali, Jim and Margo, Bill and Debbie, George and Ann, Steve and Anne, and still two more Steves, all of whom know who they are. We share a heritage and an advocate's love for it. George will know he is George Dyson, about whom Ken has written so well in *The Starship and the Canoe.* George knows he will always have a special place in our hearts and house, even after his remark that the only thing fit to eat here is the dog food (he was reading about additives on the labels).

Add grandson David Brower, now four, who will probably be climbing things I wouldn't dare, and Anne Kathryn, who at the age of two, and filling that niche brightly, reaches up and says, "Grandma Annie, I want to hold you." Her wish is a command, accepted with joy.

CHAPTER 5

FRIENDS

HAROLD SMALL

ONE OF ANNE'S AND MY CLOSEST FRIENDS, Harold Small, told us that it was wrong to look at a blank piece of paper. "Put a word on it. Any word. Strike it later if you must. The blank piece of paper is a block."

Harold was editor-in-chief of the University of California Press when I met Anne, who was an editor in his outer office. He then generously gave me an opportunity to try to edit for a living. He was H. W. Fowler reincarnated, a living, walking, amusing, irrefutable *Chicago Manual of Style*. If you are going to use adjectives, he would say, get them in order: a round, red, stupendous apple. He would certainly have delighted the Fowler brothers had he and they coexisted. He could have superseded the *Chicago Manual* had he settled down to supersession.

I did not discover this from any long conversations with him in his office. I simply attended the University of Harold Small a little at a time. I acquired bits of wisdom going to and from and during coffee breaks (two blocks each way) and lunch at the Faculty Club (better than a half-mile), augmented by delightful sessions Anne and I enjoyed with Harold and Sally over sherry at his house on the top of the hill.

A couple of hours' conversation per working day for five years allowed me to build a big collection of Small talk.

Oh, if I had only made notes! If he had only written down the words he spoke so easily but with such wit and authority! He would have agreed with the words H. W. Fowler used to appraise his younger brother, Francis G. Fowler. In memory of Francis, H. W. said of *A Dictionary of Modern English Usage:*

"I think of it as it should have been, with its prolixities docked, its dullnesses enlivened, its fads eliminated, its truths multiplied. He had a nimbler wit, a better sense of proportion, and a more open mind than his twelve-year-older partner."

Those who cannot write, edit. Without doubt, this was said by a writer freshly eviscerated by an editor, and all too often I prove that writer correct. Out of my own conviction that no one loves an editor, I thought I would try writing. Following the advice of Harold Small, therefore, I stopped staring, not at a blank piece of paper, but at the blank screen of a laptop computer, and tried the word *friends*. I found immediately what the horns of a dilemma feel like.

On the one horn: an easy way to make an enemy is to make a list of friends and omit one.

On the other horn, if the list must be small, it reveals a grump.

On the third horn (a unicorn just dropped by), if the list is too long, it reveals a name-dropper.

In 1983, as I sped like a glacier toward telling my story, I listed the people I wanted to talk about. There were one hundred seventy-one names dropped on that piece of paper, and I have added at least twenty-nine since then. That does not include the friends I hope I still have in my family and principal next of their kin.

The situation is hopeless. I could add still more—those I hoped would be my friends but who lived too far away, either in time or space. There are those who might not wish to be included as friends, either now or until they are sure I can cause no more trouble. Passing in and out of favor works both ways. I am happy about those who passed out of mine but came back in, or will, when their or my better judgment prevails.

Put the names in a hat? Throw them up into the air and write only about those who land on edge? Only those who have closed their book? Those who adjusted my thinking?

That last one is the proper criterion. But I am afraid they all adjusted it, and may some of them never know how much!

Opportunism has won out. Inasmuch as I have no crystal ball that I can really depend upon, I do not know what I shall be wanting to say when the story thus far is superseded. So it is easy to draw upon the obituaries I have been asked to write, or wrote anyway. I was lucky enough to avoid predeceasing these friends. As for the others, those who have not completed their errand before I complete mine (Fowler would probably prefer "died before I do"), let me assure them that I am not indulging in anticipatory obits the way, for example, the *New York Times* does. One of their reporters, now departed, interviewed me extensively for that purpose in 1970. Is that filed under "David R. Brower; hold for release date"?

I'll confess it. My criteria are wholly assailable. There was a deadline, and I ran with what I had. I fully intend to get to the others before my release date.

But as Harold Small said, write down a word, any word. What better than *friends?*

PAT AND JANE GOLDSWORTHY

ONE'S FAMILY SHOULD CERTAINLY include the alternate parents of one's children, and that is what Anne and I wished Pat and Jane Goldsworthy to be if we disappeared.

Patrick Donovan Goldsworthy was the son of a man who knew me only as someone who displeased him. He was the dean of men at the University of California who called me in to see what I was going to do about my fitful scholarship and attendance. Through no fault of his I should like to forget about him.

But not about Pat. Pat possessed the persevering qualities I did not, or by now I would probably be an entomologist who had retired from selling DDT—because one thing always leads to another. I would never have learned about Pat's addiction to dependability, had it not been for Cedric Wright. I would not have known about Cedric had Hervey Voge and I not encountered the violin Cedric was playing, and we would not have encountered either of them had Virginia Creek, in northern Yosemite's High Sierra, not invited them to accompany its music. This happened on the 1934 Sierra Club High Trip, a club institution initiated in 1901 to get influential—or about-to-be-influential—people into the wilderness (see chapter 7).

Eventually, carrying a violin as well as heavy photographic equipment on Sierra Club High Trips got to be too much for Cedric, so he decided to hire a horse, and that horse was Pat Goldsworthy. He was such a good horse that he soon graduated to a higher echelon in High Trip management, where he excelled owing in no small part to Jane, and especially to an ad hoc reference volume known as "Jane's Brains."

It is not useful to try to describe Jane without being whimsical because that is what Jane was, in the best sense of the word. Perhaps this was true because although she was born in Portland, Oregon, and grew up there, she spent early years as Jane Holmes in a Washington company lumber town called Klickitat, which sounds like horse hooves striking pavement (and, appropriately, is the Indian name for a galloping horse).

"Jane's Brains" was the most important book in the High Trip library. It contained the complete list of all the food requirements she had calculated for the hundred fifty or so people who would walk or pack or lead or feed for from four to six weeks in wilderness. The list was broken down into loads which could be moved to and from each of some ten or fifteen campsites. Jane would make revisions as required by inevitable exigencies, keeping her cool intact by composing parodies of Gilbert and Sullivan for campfire programs that were not recorded but should have been.

I was a leader of these trips for fourteen years, and liked to brag about leading four thousand people over a million person-miles of wilderness trails—with all the people and most of the miles present or accounted for at the end of my last High Trip. I was able to enjoy a good one-third of those person-miles, relaxing and oblivious as always of administrative details, thanks to Pat and Jane.

Those were their easy training days—summers in wilderness, and the rest of the year in the independent progressively liberal nation of Berkeley. In 1952 the Goldsworthys moved to Seattle, where biochemist Dr. Pat did research at the University of Washington Medical School. This did not move them farther from wilderness, but closer to it, the North Cascades being near the city and becoming nearer still to their hearts.

When David Simons got me thoroughly embroiled in the campaign to rescue the North Cascades from clear-cutters and lesser threats, Pat and Jane were ready to be the operating headquarters and leaders of the North Cascades Conservation Council, the N3C in short.

It was in their house, which became a conservation factory, that Jane helped Pat and a whole host of helpers fight the battle against multiple-usemanship (her term). By factory I mean factory. There were indeed some limited spaces in the house where you could eat and sleep or close the bathroom door and find yourself in the dark (in Washington State, the button is always on the outside), but the rest of the house was a meeting room, gallery, library, storage warehouse, and sweatshop for exploiting volunteer slave labor, including Jane's.

First the house had to contain the records of the second non-California chapter of the Sierra Club. The Pacific Northwest Chapter began with an invitation to the eighty-seven members living in its broad expanse to come to dinner. In Jane's watch the membership grew to three thousand. Before that operation had gone very far, the N3C was added, together with the editing and production facilities for its newsletter, *The Wild Cascades*. Without Jane's humor, which must have produced at least a dozen gales of laughter per meeting or work session, this simply would not have had a chance of succeeding for the two decades it did.

The Pacific Northwest would have been left then with nothing more than wilderness on the rocks (David Simons's term for what the Forest Service was determined to reduce the North Cascades wilderness to), a determination that America should eliminate at the earliest possible moment.

Pat, the original president of the N3C and now its chairman, has spent more than three decades trying to rid the world of that threat, and Jane surely would still be trying. But multiple sclerosis hit her and ground her slowly down—but not her humor—until the very last days of 1974. That was a blow for the conservation community as well as Pat, who shortly was hit again by the sudden death of their daughter Katherine Goldsworthy when she was a sophomore in college.

So what the Browers learned about the Goldsworthys on Sierra Club High Trips led us to name them as guardians of our children, the oldest of whom, Ken and Bob, still remember crossing Army Pass in a severe thunderstorm. Their father and Pat were far ahead setting up the next camp, while lightning struck the peaks all around them. Jane was their only security. Who could ask for more?

Ike Livermore

Many Years Ago, the Sierra Club, in cooperation with the Bancroft Library at the University of California, began conducting a series of oral histories of various club principals. Without realizing that it would take four years to complete it, Susan Shrepfer began digging out mine and found two people to write introductions—John B. Oakes of the *New York Times* and Ian Ballantine of Ballantine Books, both of whom agreed with me much of the time. When it came time for Ike Livermore's oral history, an introduction was sought from a man who made a habit of disagreeing with Ike. I was that man. This was the introduction:

Jack Tarr, Before the Name was fixed briefly to a San Francisco hotel, was my roommate in the Tecoyah dormitory in Yosemite Valley, a hostel for male singles who worked for the Yosemite Park & Curry Company. He was a Stanford man, one of the many who gravitated to the company, perhaps because Dr. Don Tresidder was its president. Jack knew another Stanford man. "He doesn't like you," he said, "because of something you wrote for the *Sierra Club Bulletin* that is deprecatory of mules."

The other Stanford man was Ike Livermore, the year was 1936, and the article was "Far from the Madding Mules." Far from being deprecatory of mules, even after editing, it praised one mule, named Jiggs, who helped Hervey Voge and me carry a heavy food cache up to the trailhead beneath the North Palisade, dropping the cache there and leaving us to celebrate the freedom of backpackers for the next several weeks.

Within the next three years, I was able to persuade Ike (whom I suspect had read the title, but not the article) that I really had nothing against mules. By then I was an assistant leader of the Sierra Club High Trip, embarking upon a summertime addiction I would enjoy from 1939 to 1956 (with time out for World War II), throughout most of which I would be pleasantly involved with mules and in argument with Ike.

Among his virtues—and I think there are a great many of them—is the one that enabled him to disagree with me often without ever inciting me to be angry with him, or even more than slightly exasperated at worst.

I remember that he and the packers he led complained quite often about my tendency to choose campsites that were up in inedible rocks rather than down in luscious meadows. We would also disagree, amicably, about how much the Sierra Club should pay for the services of Mount Whitney Pack Trains or the Mineral King Pack Outfit. We usually ended up with an agreement each of us would willingly have accepted either end of.

I think the High Sierra packing business is the one he would have preferred to stay with, but his family brought pressures to bear against his choosing that profession. So there were other disagreements – especially about which redwoods to cut and which to save. He wanted to hear a good many fall that I thought should remain silent. As Governor Reagan's resources secretary, he was quoted as being quite irate with me, to the point of questioning my honesty. This disagreement stemmed from a title I had given a Sierra Club book, *The Last Redwoods*. His brother Putnam entered the breach and things were smoothed over.

Still another disagreement was about my not being militant enough in the battle to prevent trans-Sierra roads. Two proposed roads were an abomination to Ike Livermore – the Porterville-Lone Pine and the Mammoth Pass roads. Both were an abomination to me, too, but it was the diligence of Ike Livermore, not of Dave Brower, that had most to do with their not abominating the Sierra more than they do.

Few introductions to oral histories have celebrated disagreements. Perhaps this is the only one. It may be worthwhile for a moment trying to see what makes it possible for people to exercise their disagreements agreeably. Perhaps the secret is to have them around a High Sierra campfire, preceded by a bit of quiet disarmament.

Ike disarmed people by regaling them. His campfire stories twinkled. It might be a story about the man on the saddle trip who was so fat that the saddle horn wore a blister on his stomach. Or it might be a description of his own travels in the Himalaya astride a mule (or was it a donkey?) that was big enough for a Nepalese, but not big enough to keep Ike's feet from trailing on the ground as he rode. Or it might be my favorite – about the live chickens taken along as part of the larder, chickens hobbled at night with rubber bands, and all of this successfully managed until the Park Service ranger came along, charged the chickens with not being indigenous, required their immediate execution, and stayed for a chicken dinner.

How could you disagree effectively with a man who could tell stories like that? Out of habit, I suppose, and thus it is that I was able to disagree with President Livermore, of the California Fish and Game Commission, about how to rescue the California condor. Captive-breed them, he said. Spare their habitat and them from poisons, hunting pressure, overzealous biologists, and leapfrog subdivisions, I replied; give them a chance to breed by themselves, and wildness to inform them and to make it possible for them to be condors. But even in this disagreement, in which I have given more words to my case than to his, there is an underlying accord that through all the years has let the disagreements be painless, perhaps even creative. I suspect that it is this accord that let him dare ask me to write the introduction to his oral history and that let me be pleased so much to try.

The accord centers on one thing, our mutual devotion to wilderness. Ike Livermore and I are going to agree about that, and know that without wilderness, the world's a cage. Caged people snarl at each other.

***Sierra Club Oral History Project,* 1982**

MARTIN LITTON

BE CAREFUL," Anne admonished me as she dropped me at the Oakland airport to fly to Las Vegas, drive to Boulder City, and there board a small craft that would take a cameraman and me to Marble Gorge Lodge and its unimproved airstrip, with Martin Litton as pilot. Anne remembered all too well Martin's casual reaction to the hostile press coverage when his light plane and a heavy jet flew closer together than the jet pilot thought wise. She also heard my story of how Martin had flown under Navajo Bridge, which spans Marble Gorge of the Grand Canyon with less than five hundred vertical feet between bridge struts and the Colorado River. She knew the story about Martin's setting his alarm, as he commuted from his Grand Canyon Dories headquarters at Hurricane, Utah, to his home near Palo Alto, counting on the alarm to ring when it was time for his small plane to climb high enough to cross over the Sierra Nevada instead of going through it. She had not forgotten my account of Martin's flying Barbara and me over and around the Diablo Canyon nuclear reactor construction activity. When it came time for him to change film, he simply headed his plane up, aimed at some unnamed point in interstellar space, and devoted full attention to the camera and none to the sky. "After all," Martin would say, "there's nothing but room up here, and this plane doesn't fly fast enough to hurt anybody."

We took off from the Boulder City strip, then landed right away to pick up the cameraman, Steve Marts, who had photographed the takeoff and now wanted to shoot over Martin's and my shoulders as we discussed the moments we had shared in battling for the sanctity of the Grand Canyon.

One of Martin's virtues was that he had never wavered in his support of keeping the Colorado River alive in the canyon it had created, whereas I had wavered. In 1949 I had voted with other Sierra Club directors then on the board for damming the Little Colorado at the Coconino site and the main Colorado at Glen Canyon, in Marble Gorge, and at Bridge Canyon. Martin was going to see that I never wavered again.

I had no reason to waver as he flew us over Hoover Dam, above Temple Bar, where I ended my first Grand Canyon river trip with him in 1966, over Pierce's Ferry, its sea of Lake Mead mud now pleasantly covered with only slightly silty water. We flew over various and assorted places where Martin knew that the light and motion would be right for the camera, or that the subject below us would be fit for the casual conversation being recorded for what was to be a documentary on the life and times of an alleged archdruid and friend of the earth.

No, I had no reason to feel like wavering with Martin as the pilot. I was safer with his driving his one-engine plane than I would be driving my own car on the highway—provided I did not upset him by revealing that my car was a Toyota. Martin abhors products from whaling nations, increasingly difficult though it may be to avoid them.

Severe though he may be with whalers, Martin was gentle to me. He learned upon our arrival in Boulder City that I was fighting off a cold, and disappeared briefly to get me some cold medicine—a fifth of Tanqueray gin. The fifth remained intact thanks to the environmental benevolence of the Grand Canyon as we put in at Lee's Ferry and drifted eight miles downstream to Badger Creek rapids. If Norman Cousins can get well on a prescription of laughter, I could and did get well watching the Colorado dig deeper and deeper into the Kaibab formation, looking for climbing routes up the wall I would gladly have tried thirty years earlier. I admired the skill at the oars of a man who knew the Grand Canyon rocks and rapids by their first names. From the rapid's edge I watched Martin demonstrate that skill as he took his dory and passengers through Badger, then I limped upstream (I had put my cold on the shelf, but was now experiencing something quite new to me—a mild onslaught of sciatica) to await the National Park Service ranger who would speed some of us back to Lee's Ferry in his power boat. It wasn't a long wait. I measured it not in time, but in inches, as the increasing releases from Glen Canyon Dam brought the river level up. Looking away from the river briefly, I saw Martin walking toward me through the riverine woods, recognizing him from a distance by his shock of white hair and his gait, marred by a time-wearied knee. There was no need for him to have walked up from the camp his Grand Canyon river-running friends had made just below Badger, but there he was, carrying two plastic cups, one for him and, for me, one with a liberal level of gin in it. Just behind Martin was one of the boatmen, carrying a plastic bottle of tonic. It was happy hour at the camp, and Martin wanted to make sure that I shared it. As the Park Service boat cast off and headed upstream, Martin tried to avoid my parting look of gratitude, but he didn't quite succeed.

I wrote the foreword to the Sierra Club's oral history of Martin Litton:

SOME PEOPLE GET THE KUDOS, and others, out of inequity, don't. Martin Litton is due most of those addressed to me in error: more years than I will ever admit, he has been my conservation conscience. I had to know him before I could accept him as a conscience, and knowing him must have had its beginnings when I saw what the *Los Angeles Times* let him publish when he was in its circulation department. I remember a Martin Litton full-page spread, with his text and his illustrations, on what was going wrong in Kings Canyon National Park. Since the battle for the park had been my first, I was interested. When he came up with a spread on the threat to Dinosaur National Monument, where the Bureau of Reclamation was convinced it must build dams, I got on the telephone to Los Angeles.

We began at once to exploit Martin's ability with lens and words. We didn't have much photographic coverage of Dinosaur at the time. The National Park Service's photographs were for record; Martin's were for interpretation.

That was the beginning, but only the beginning. The proper photohistory of Martin Litton, with accompanying legends, could occupy many volumes. He had begun to photograph intensively pretty much on his own. Then the day came when *Sunset* magazine was looking for a new travel editor, asked me for names, got only one, and took Martin on. *Sunset* was never particularly eager to be activist, and Martin was never eager not to be. Whenever he could add Message to the magazine's front travel section, there it was. If there was a piece of the American environment that had problems, Martin found out about it, wrote about it, and photographed it from the surface or the air. Sometimes he could use his own name. Other times it was Clyde Thomas or Homer Gasquez.

One year, the Sierra Club directors, having voted for Grand Canyon dams and later reversed themselves, were ready to re-reverse. Martin's knowledge and eloquence stopped them. They were ready to go for the wrong Redwood National Park. It was Martin who knew where the best redwoods were, and who had the creativity to propose a comprehensive Redwood National Park that would have been a monument to conservation genius. We didn't get it because organizational jealousies within the movement—one of the major threats to environment—got in the way. It was Martin who knew where the gentle wilderness was on the Kern Plateau—wilderness that should have been added to Sequoia National Park. "Old-boy" conservation trades got in the way. Martin happened to be in Baghdad when the Sierra Club directors voted, without seeing it, to accept Diablo Canyon as an alternative site for the reactor proposed to be built on the Nipomo Dunes. Had he been in San Francisco instead, a different history would have been written.

How do I know? I don't, of course. But I did see how his eloquence brought forth audience applause that reversed what the directors were about to do to the Grand Canyon. I also know how, when the club's board was discussing what to do at Mineral King with respect to Walt Disney's proposed ski development, and when I myself had wobbled and was about to go along, it was Martin who got me to reverse myself right there on the spot, in front of everybody.

In the conservation movement we keep trying to save places, and, often enough to keep our spirits up, we succeed—for the time being. Most of us think the Grand Canyon is safe from dams. It isn't. And if Martin Litton calls you up to save it again, settle down and hear him.

***Sierra Club Oral History Project,* 1982**

Eliot Porter

When Anne and I First Visited Eliot Porter in Tesuque, New Mexico, and she saw him come into his living room, she thought he was his son. None of his sons was anywhere near sixty-one, which Eliot then was. He simply left twenty or so years behind in the wild and there they remained.

Blending with the southwestern architecture of his home is his darkroom next door, part of which is a guest room. Anne and I enjoyed it from time to time as I worked with Eliot on seven exhibit-format volumes, all but one of which, together with a portfolio, were published by the Sierra Club. I never entered the darkroom itself. I was always brought up short by what he had on his work table or desk, or by the hundred or so boxes, as I remember them, filled with his large dye-transfer prints of details he had interpreted, places he had been, and, in boxes of exquisite photographs of clouds, places he had not been. And, of course, birds. No one is likely ever to photograph them better.

People who have made dye-transfer prints assure me that the technique requires great precision. Eliot preceded his darkroom precision with his precise choice of subjects and followed it in the precision he required of those who worked with his photographs. I well remember the first collection he shipped me in Berkeley, all dry-mounted on board and protected by sturdy plywood boxes he had built himself, exactly to fit. As I put a mounted print back into the box, it did not plop to the bottom of the box, but settled gently. The air in the box slowly found a way out past the edges of the print, hissing faintly as it left.

We worked together on books on Thoreau country, Glen Canyon, Baja California, Great Spruce Head Island, the Galapagos Islands, and the forever wild country of the Adirondacks. Eliot was also thinking of books about the Allegheniesn, Grand Canyon, Greece, Iceland, the Brooks

Range, and Lake Baikal, and would add Antarctica and China to the list.

Great Spruce Head Island, in Penobscot Bay, became a family island when Eliot's father bought it and built a retreat there, to which Porters would thereafter repair in summers. A climax in the recollections of the Brower family was the week we spent there as Eliot and Aline's guests. Baseball for the children in the meadow by the house, short sailing ventures in the bay, rough-and-tumble motorboating to Little Spruce Head, probing the trails Eliot's father had built, probing the lobsters trapped that day, distinguishing the songs of the individual whitethroat sparrows, finding all the blueberries you could eat in the wild gardens, checking hurricane damage in the spruce woods, destroying a little of the bourbon in the house of Eliot Porter's brother-in-law, Michael Strauss, former commissioner of the U.S. Bureau of Reclamation and therefore a natural enemy – these were some of the delights. There was a poignant moment, too. Thanks to DDT, osprey had been having a bad time. Eliot pointed to several abandoned nests. On an islet in the channel just south of Great Spruce Head there was still an active nest, where the female had brooded for some time, with the patience one expects of ospreys, hoping her eggs would hatch. As Anne and I rested in the south meadow, her mate flew down and lit beside her for a few moments. Then they both rose, caught an updraft, soared higher and higher, and disappeared to the north, not to return.

Eliot and I worked for some time on the Adirondack book. Ken searched the literature for text to accompany the photographs in a book that would celebrate the foresight that put the words "forever wild" in the New York constitution and the diligence of the people who worked to keep the Adirondacks that way. Harold Hochschild, of American Metals Climax, had generously advanced ten thousand dollars to Eliot for the project, and Eliot had immediately invested this in the expedition to the Galapagos Islands that included his son Stephen and our son Kenneth and led to the Galapagos volumes.

I had spent thirty-five hundred dollars of Sierra Club funds in the Adirondack venture and went to Blue Mountain Lake Museum, of which Mr. Hochschild was the benefactor, to pursue the venture further. I ran into a problem. Mr. Hochschild liked Eliot's Adirondack photographs very much but he wanted some broad Adirondack views – so and so as seen from such and such – more revealing of the countryside. I was already fully aware of Eliot's preference for detail, for strong composition, and for no sky unless the sky had something to say. I wrote Mr. Hochschild in support of the arts and incurred his wrath. He was no longer interested in publishing the book with the Sierra Club. Eliot made the desired photographs and E. P. Dutton became Eliot's publisher through the good offices of Jack Macrae. A long series of successful books ensued and I was glad they did.

Eliot was not pleased with the resistance the club directors and publications committee had built to his Galapagos project and was displeased with my having left his name off the Galapagos jackets – a gaffe I was unaware of at the time. The Sierra Club was displeased with me and by May 1969 I was no longer on the staff. I imagine that Eliot was further displeased when, in Friends of the Earth, I found I must use other photographers for a book on the Brooks Range. I saw him rarely, sharing a platform at a meeting of photographers in Jackson Hole, running into him in the Century Club where he was talking with his New York agent, and after that only by letter or telephone. He graciously agreed to serve on the advisory council of Earth Island Institute, and organized a beautiful exhibition at the Amon Carter Museum in Fort Worth. He spoke at its opening and I spoke on what I knew about him on a later occasion there, learning that he was suffering from Lou Gehrig's disease. He had disposed of his camera equipment, still intended to print, and was leaving his photographic collection to the museum.

Amid all the unhappiness, there was a pleasant note. When I left the staff of the Sierra Club, my friends, in a flurry of activity, saw that my papers went with me. I do not yet know well enough what they contain, but I do know that when Friends of the Earth moved from Spear Street to its terminal address on Sansome Street in San Francisco, something extraordinary was discovered – the original two albums Eliot had sent me to show what his first book could be. That included the dye-transfer prints for *"In Wildness Is the Preservation of the World,"* his typescript of his accompanying anthology of Thoreau, together with assorted fingerprints and diverse markings made by the printers at Barnes Press, where I watched as Eliot approved the work that came off the press. In their own way the albums are a milestone in American publishing. Alan Gussow, artist and then a Friends of the Earth director, thought their sale would bring FOE some helpful revenue. I thought Eliot should know they had been found. Did he want them? He did, and you will find them at the Amon Carter Museum.

It was those albums that led to my initial and continuing appreciation of Eliot Porter, essentially as expressed in my foreword to *"In Wildness Is the Preservation of the World."* The symbiosis in the book is what makes it so great – something he built into that one and I tried to build into the others. Perhaps my principal achievement was to forge ahead and get it published when six major publishers lacked the boldness it took – and the luck. This foreword says what I really believe, as well as I could say it, and Jon Beckmann, Sierra Club publisher, was willing to let it stand for the new edition:

EVEN TO LEAF THROUGH what has been created here is rewarding; but something quite wonderful happens to those who let themselves drift through. This is symbiotic art: Eliot Porter corroborates Thoreau and Thoreau verifies Porter, one never diminishing the other, for reasons Joseph Wood Krutch singles out as he tells how closely these men traveled together a century apart. Just as there is always something new to discover in Thoreau, there is much more than meets the eye in the photographs. A few impressions about the artist—the man who, ten years out of Harvard Medical School, gave up medicine and science for photography—may speed the discovery.

We ourselves discovered—or think we did—that the patience Dr. Porter acquired for bird photography has contributed enormously to the excellence of what he does here with inanimate subjects. He has learned to be alert to what a particular bird is likely to do in the next few minutes and to be ready when the bird meets his expectations. Having mastered the flightiness of such subjects, he could expect little trouble from the dependable peregrinations of sun, wind, and cloud.

The seasons performed just as dependably. Knowing a wild place well, Porter could anticipate what new life and form and color each change in the weather would reveal in that place, even as Thoreau had, and be there at the appointed hour. He would arrive fully sensitized and in sharp focus himself. Lens and image, we can see, responded unfailingly. If need be, abstractions would organize where only reality had been before. None but a very literal person would fail to see that color is his music, that there is melody line, counterpoint, harmony, dynamics, voicing, and phrasing, all there for those who will listen.

There is absolute pitch, too—absolute color pitch. As we looked at the dye-transfer prints in Porter's exhibit, *The Seasons,* which the Smithsonian Institution circulates and from which the book derives, then peered at his four-by-five color transparencies, and finally as we watched him review color proofs, we were quietly amazed about what this man knows about color. He remembers exactly what was where when the shutter let a moment's light in, and he knows what must happen technically if that moment is to be fixed. We have not yet seen all his colors in their natural habitat. But we are confident that if we borrow his acuity and walk out into waldens here and there, we shall find those colors ourselves. If we are very fortunate, once in a while they may perform for us the quiet symphony that responds to his baton.

Others, who are of unquestioned competence in these matters, must pass final judgment on Eliot Porter's greatness as a photographer. Some already have. I myself know only that I never saw color mean more than he makes it mean and that I shall not easily overlook it again. The two

Porter albums—the prints and the selections from Thoreau that were the manuscript for this book—made me vow openly to see it published even if I had to take up a life of crime to get the funds for it. Happily, Belvedere Scientific Fund intervened and provided generous assistance. It took responsible imagination to see as far beyond the mere beauty of the manuscript as needed seeing. Imaginative philanthropy followed.

To me it seems that much of what Henry David Thoreau wrote, more than a century ago, was less timely in his day than it is in ours: we can now prove that the natural and civilized worlds must live together or perish separately. We hope that the attitude of Thoreau and Porter toward unspoiled countryside will be pervasive. For there is no science and no art of greater importance than that which teaches seeing, which builds sensitivity and respect for the natural world, a world that has "visibly been recreated in the night." A natural world thus cherished will bring "morning when men are new-born, men who have the seeds of life in them."

"In Wildness Is the Preservation of the World," **April 1962**

Art Blake

Arthur Ernest Hinman Blake, long-suffering from injuries acquired in France in World War I, was a conservative conservationist whose conservativeness had a major effect on me for years. It was a good thing.

My first winter as a resident of Yosemite Valley excited my enthusiasm for skiing. But Badger Pass, Yosemite's commercialized ski area, raised my enthusiasm not at all. I knew too much about the open grandeur of the High Sierra, and Badger was trapped in a red fir forest. At Ski Top, the Upski (predecessor of the Queen Mary, itself predecessor of the conventional ski lift) allowed skiers no more than a tree-screened peek at the High Sierra's open slopes. Whoever chose Badger Pass was unaware of what ski country should look like and what should be seen from it.

So why not a bold development, a téléphérique that would start at Mirror Lake's four-thousand-foot elevation and carry skiers to the eleven-thousand-foot summit of Mount Hoffmann? Certainly it was technically feasible. It would give winter visitors to Yosemite a fair idea of what real country looked like when the Sierra Nevada lived up to its name—the snowy saw-toothed range. I made the suggestion to Don Tresidder, president of the Yosemite Park & Curry Company. "I'm not sure the directors of the Sierra Club would like the idea," he said. I was not yet aware of what the directors thought. Art Blake was. I forget quite how he quashed the odd idea in my left lobe; it never reappeared.

We shared many trips in the Sierra and many sessions over coffee or over his files at 1505 Holly Street in Berkeley. We also shared concern over the impending battle for Kings Canyon National Park, for blocking ski development on Mount San Gorgonio, for trying to block the tramway on Mount San Jacinto, and for modest recreational development of the Inyo-Mono region on the eastern slope of the Sierra. We were especially fond of Glacier Lodge, on Big Pine Creek, close to our ever-favorite Palisades, and thought that we could develop it better than Bertha Hall had. Bertha let nothing come of that idea.

One of Art Blake's major efforts was his attempt to persuade The Wilderness Society and the National Parks Association not to oppose the creation of Kings Canyon National Park. The grammar and spelling in his letters to Robert Sterling Yard and other doubters needed help, but his ideas didn't. Art knew that the Yosemite-like canyons of the South Fork and Middle Fork of the Kings River ought to be in the proposed national park, but he also knew that the Kings River High Sierra needed prompt protection that the Forest Service could not provide. Water users in the San Joaquin Valley were adamantly opposed to relinquishing the Cedar Grove and Tehipite dam sites at the time. Perhaps they would some day drop their opposition, but we ought not leave the high country unprotected while we waited. The proposed John Muir Wilderness National Park would save the high country, and time was not waiting.

Art's arguments did not prevail in the East but the Sierra Club and its friends did prevail overall. The Forest Service, with well-planned show-me trips and the promise of stronger wilderness regulations, did its best to block the park, even after Franklin Roosevelt had ordered it to cease its opposition. But Irving Brant had done his good work in persuading Roosevelt and Secretary of the Interior Harold Ickes that there should be a national park. Congressman Bertrand Gearhart, in whose district the park would be, was essential to the legislation—and introduced it. The secretary also persuaded doubting Sierra Club directors to give support. Will Colby, a mining lawyer who was John Muir's most loyal disciple and for forty-nine years a director of the club, led the battle for the club. Facing the expected opposition of the California State Chamber of Commerce, the Forest Service, their front organization The California Mountaineers, and the two most powerful park and wilderness organizations in the East, the Sierra Club went to work. Will Colby, by spoken word, letters, and articles, used his influence on key people, club members wrote their members of Congress, and Ansel Adams produced his exquisite book, *The Sierra Nevada: The John Muir Trail*. I helped edit some articles in the *Sierra Club Bulletin,* wrote some in the club's Bay Chapter newsletter, *The Yodeler,* and in the summers of 1939 and 1940 worked with Dick Leonard on a color film.

Art Blake was my coach throughout. He also named the club film—*Sky-Land Trails of the Kings*. It was a silent film, almost an hour long. I had plenty of time those days, and traveled all over California with the projector I talked the Bay Chapter into buying, with the records Charlotte Mauk selected for background music, and with a microphone back at the projector. I loaded and managed the projector, put on the records at the proper time, and talked endlessly about the film and the proposed park.

Art Blake was in the film and in much of its choice of sequences and my choice of words. He was a strong supporter of the group on the club's board that tried to end the approach road in Kings Canyon at the boundary of the park. Will Colby led the other block. He had made a commitment to Chester Warlow that the road would go to Copper Creek. How else, he argued, could President Roosevelt enter the park when he came out to dedicate it?

The road went to Copper Creek, but for all that, no national park in the Lower Forty-Nine has fewer miles of road in it. President Roosevelt never traveled it, nor did he dedicate the park. I don't think Art Blake or his then fellow Republican, Dave Brower, were sorry about the oversight. I was not to abandon party loyalty until I voted for Dewey and, to my wife's surprise and delight, cheered as Harry Truman won. Art Blake never abandoned his—but then, he never had the opportunity to be revised by marriage.

And he always liked to claim that if you climbed up the steps to the front door of the Pacific Union Club, San Francisco's other Republican redoubt, opened its door, and shouted, "Hooray for Eleanor Roosevelt!" the building would fall down.

Art Blake's obituary included these further notes:

IT MUST HAVE BEEN some time in the course of the battle to make a national park in the Kings River High Sierra that Art Blake said it, and I still chuckle whenever I think of it: "She's not afraid to call a spade a steam shovel." He was referring to an evangelical supporter of conservation who was too willing to go overboard too often.

Looking back over the twenty-three years I knew Art Blake, I can think of no occasion when he failed to recognize a spade for what it was and to call it just that.

I knew Art Blake as well as you are likely to know anyone who has taught you for two decades. I was enrolled in his unscheduled conservation class sometime in 1936, in the course of his pointing out to me that precedents are consequences hurrying to happen. . . .

These are still just random notes. The biographical work is yet to be done to let people know what the beginnings were, how the interest was kindled; to tell about the friends enlisted, the defeats suffered, the achievements won by Art Blake, conservationist, whose heart failed him last February, but never failed his mountains.

***Sierra Club Annual*, 1957**

ANSEL ADAMS

ANSEL ADAMS HAD GENEROUSLY AGREED to be honorary chairman of the Second Biennial Conference on the Fate of the Earth, to be held in Washington, D.C., for a week starting September 19, 1984. His doctor did not want him to travel that far, but Ansel would do what he could, and had already started working on a Manifesto for the Earth to save it from Ronald Reagan. With notes and telephone calls we began putting the pieces together. On April 22 the manifesto became but one more essential in the long list of things to do that Ansel could no longer plunge into—a list that it is easy to imagine was about as long as the list of things achieved in Ansel's brief eighty-two years. We were last in touch in early April, thinking ahead to the conference. And now I am thinking back.

I was not quite twenty-one and Ansel was already thirty-one, when we met in the mountains. I had known about him through the *Sierra Club Bulletin.* Two years earlier I had begun dropping by the Sierra Club office in Mills Tower, San Francisco, to buy back issues of the annual magazine. Although the *Bulletin*'s words would get to me later, Ansel's photographs got to me immediately. Editor Francis Farquhar had arranged to highlight Ansel's work in exquisitely executed gravure frontispieces. The first, in 1928, was *Black Kaweah.* In 1929 it was *Mount Robson.* Next, *Banner Peak and Thousand Island Lake.* In 1931 and 1932, two of my all-time favorites—*Half Dome, the Monolith,* now world-famous, and *Mountain Hemlock,* near Yosemite's Volunteer Peak, all but forgotten—one of the negatives lost in the darkroom fire of 1937.

Those frontispieces were exceptionally fine, but so too were Ansel's many contributions to the *Bulletin* over several decades. Three months after I met Ansel, I had joined the Sierra Club—to read the *Bulletin,* climb rocks, and check out the unclimbed peaks in the Sierra Nevada—bearing in mind Ansel's caveat that the Sierra was more than an outdoor gymnasium. I agreed, but did not know how totally I agreed until Ansel had time to work on me. The working over began in Yosemite. By agreement with the Yosemite Park & Curry Company and Don Tresidder, Ansel provided photographs for use by the advertising department so that it could entice more people to come to Yosemite and overcrowd it. There were albums of wonderful Adams prints to pore over and select from. As the company's publicity manager, I had the opportunity to select the prints I liked best—a half-dozen or so each of my favorites, to send out with press releases. That brought me into frequent contact with Ansel, sometimes at his studio in San Francisco, but more often at Best Studio in Yosemite Valley. Better still, we walked along the base of Half Dome looking straight up at the great face he had photographed so stunningly a decade before. I was pleased to show him how to scramble directly down to Mirror Lake. We took a pack trip into the Yosemite High Sierra, complete with Hannes Schroll and yodels. There was a subsequent trip over Tioga Pass, with a pause at Tenaya Lake and Mono Lake. Edward Weston was along, and tried his hand at both lakes. It would be taking sides to say Ansel won.

We walked into a camp near Lake Ediza. With Edward Weston, Virginia Adams, Morgan Harris, and Charis Wilson, we spent happy rainy hours in our tent telling stories and destroying bourbon. Ansel photographed Morgan Harris, clouds, and me on the only Minaret we ever climbed, a small one, that opens Ansel's great book, *Sierra Nevada: The John Muir Trail.* The book was to give major assistance to the creation of Kings Canyon National Park. Secretary of the Interior Harold Ickes thought so, and told Ansel.

The memorable Yosemite days included parties at Best Studio, before it had been remodeled into the Ansel Adams Gallery. The public part was split-level. In the lower level were things to buy, splendidly different from what you'd find in the tourist shops in the valley. Ansel and Virginia saw to that. In the upper level were things to admire – a gallery of Adams prints on the wall, a Steinway concert grand, and plenty of room for people. When Ansel played the Steinway you almost regretted his decision to give up the concert stage for the lens. It was a moving experience to hear how well he got a piano to do his exact bidding. Or it was amusing if he would change pace by playing a cadenza with an orange. For the bump-bump bump-bumps of the Blue Danube, he would half-rise, turn, and play the chords, fulsomely, with his rear. He sat down one day on the sofa in that room, only to realize he had just destroyed one of his finest glass-plate negatives – a horizontal composition of the Half Dome monolith.

The room had further distinctions. As I remember it, the VIPs who dropped in on Yosemite sometimes visited the park superintendent, sometimes visited the company president, but always found the way to Ansel's upper level. It wasn't just for the music or the gallery or the superb bar that Ansel and Virginia ran for their guests, but for the pleasure of being witness to what was going on in the forefront of photography at that moment. The John Muir Trail book was in process, and Ansel delighted in comparing actual contact prints of some of the subjects with same-size halftones, in very fine screen, of the subjects as interpreted by Ansel's then favorite engraver, R.W. Donnelly, in Chicago. It was difficult to tell the original from the copy. If there was a new route to excellence in a photographic technology, Ansel either led the climb or pushed others up it.

The Adamses' camaraderie was epitomized above the fireplace in his San Francisco studio on Twenty-fourth Avenue: O JOY DIVINE OF FRIENDS! That spirit prevailed wherever Virginia was. You somehow knew you were the person she wanted most to see.

Dave (lower peak) and Morgan Harris climbing in The Minarets, Sierra Nevada, California, 1937. Photograph by Ansel Adams, ©Ansel Adams Publishing Rights Trust.

My ability as a photographer inched slowly upward with Ansel's help. My pleasure in photographing visiting celebrities – propping them in front of Half Dome and sending a print and story to the celebrities' hometown papers – diminished. I found myself spending many an hour on many a day in Ansel's darkroom, watching him print, and listening to his advice. I learned about some essentials. What national parks were about. What made them an American first. What stone, space, and sky were doing for us, and the simple growing things. He led me to see what was behind and within a photograph – his, not mine – and what could happen when words and photographs worked their magic together.

Knowing from his own sources that I was not increasing in stature or favor with the company, Ansel proposed a new career for me in 1937 – that I be executive secretary of the Sierra Club. The idea didn't fly – then. Many good things happened between that time and the 1967 afternoon, at a Sierra Club board meeting at Clair Tappaan Lodge, when he was first to suggest that I no longer be executive director of the Sierra Club.

In 1977, when, as Ansel had, I received the club's John Muir Award, he wrote me warm congratulations. His autobiography, written in the interim, included a touch of acid and a bit of honey, not all of either being fully deserved. But that was then. A few years later, Ansel's signature was one of the first on the petition to nominate Brower once again for the club's board. "Will you behave this time?" he asked. I said no, but that didn't bother him.

Let me focus here on some shared years particularly relevant to the Sierra Club. With his help I was elected to the board in 1941. Like Ansel, I served as a High Trip leader and campaigned for Kings Canyon National Park. With his boosts I became the club's first executive director in 1952. Between 1941 and 1952, including my three years with the U.S. Mountain Troops in Colorado, West Virginia, and Italy when only the memory of Ansel was helpful, his generosity with his photographs was constant.

It would be better, about now, if I could edit myself out of all this; but when you have known someone, in good times and other, for five decades plus a year, it helps ease the pain at a great loss to remember things shared. I edit those in.

There could be a lot said here about the Kings Canyon campaign, about the Grand Canyon, Yosemite Valley, and the Tioga Road and its vandalism at Tenaya Lake, about the effort to show that the national-park idea and the wilderness idea were the same, about the happy events on Twenty-fourth Avenue, about the unhappy afternoon there when a club director said, "If Ansel were named president of the Sierra Club, it would destroy the club," about Ansel's bout with infectious mononucleosis (when it was strange and frightening and a bedridden Ansel was thinking about what he'd do with the rest of his life if he survived), about his moving away from San Francisco, center of the art universe, to Carmel, which was hardly just anywhere but was certainly off-center (or so I thought—the Ansel art world was perfectly happy to travel the extra hundred twenty-five miles to its new capital), about Ansel's occasional beating of the great Marco Polo drum above his new and much greater fireplace, about his refusal to become an honorary vice-president of the club because I had been named one, about our recovery from that, about interviews in video Greg Bedayn arranged and in audio that Marc Palmer did, and about a reunion at dinner of three couples, Ansel and Virginia, Edgar and Peggy Wayburn, Anne and Dave Brower, where the very scars of old wounds, long ago healed, vanished before that last meeting ended. But rather than say more I'll say less, and concentrate on a special happening: *This Is the American Earth.*

How did that happening happen? Both collaborators are gone now, Ansel and Nancy Newhall, so I cannot telephone for corroboration. Did it begin on Twenty-fourth Avenue? No. That was just a later blooming of Ansel's perennial creativity. Did it begin in the club's LeConte Lodge, in Yosemite, in 1955? I once thought so. The National Park Service didn't think the club was doing anything important there so Ansel and Nancy, with some financial assistance from Walter Starr, one of the club's illustrious presidents, came up with something important. There could be an exhibit that would reveal wilderness and the national-park idea in a global context.

The exhibit was called "This Is the American Earth," and filled a dozen four-by-eight-foot panels. Half the photographs were Ansel's, the other half drawn from all over, aided by Nancy's experience at George Eastman House and the Museum of Modern Art.

But would the exhibit fit? Anyone who had visited LeConte Lodge knows there is no way to get so many panels in so small a space, but they were installed nevertheless. To see the exhibit, people walked in ever-diminishing circles. Would they ever get out? Certainly they never got out unimpressed. The big photographs had their own dynamic. Other photographs were sized as you would expect in a normal show. Then there were Ansel's "little jewels," as Nancy called them, mostly in Polaroid. A few natural objects were added. All these were the visual and emotional stimulators, and far more beautiful than you might expect. But Nancy, working with Ansel, with my occasional editorial assistance, had added words where they needed to be to assure that voice and image reinforced each other, creating a new dimension that neither could evoke by itself. There is no point in trying to get words alone, on this page, to tell you what the counterpoint was like. It was a symphony.

It moved people. It moved the California Academy of Sciences and Stanford University into showing it. It even moved the U.S. Information Agency. They traveled copies of it around the world.

So it had to be a book. How do you put an exhibit in a book? You come up with a format spacious enough to accommodate images big enough to require that your eyes roam them and to tempt you to dive in and swim. But books had better not be all that big. Coffee tables would have to be reinforced. So we settled on a size, $10^1/_4$ by $13^1/_2$ inches, and a name, *Exhibit Format*. After struggles that would themselves fill a small-format book, the book we wanted appeared in 1960, with major assistance from Max McGraw, of McGraw/Edison. We got the U.S. Register of Copyrights to agree to our moving the title page well into the book, following a several-page prelude. I designed a double-spread-size promotional brochure folded into an envelope that modestly claimed, "The most important announcement the Sierra Club has ever made." I believed it, and so, in due course, did a lot of people–reviewers, editorial writers across the country, and book buyers. Peter Convente's Photogravure and Color Company in New York was most successful in the gravure execution, as with the halftone reproduction in the slightly smaller Ballantine paperback. Alfred Knopf, who helped the club sell it, wanted to put out a smaller book containing Nancy Newhall's text alone. He didn't get around to it. Others, whatever their criticism, were changed by it. I like to think the environmental movement itself was changed, but I have never been accused of going overboard on objectivity. The most beautiful thing about the book is that now, a quarter of a century after it was written, there is nothing in it that has worn out.

But did all this begin in 1955? No, that's not early enough. In Ansel's foreword to a book published by Houghton Mifflin and Virginia Adams in 1950 entitled *My Camera in the National Parks*, the whole idea was set forth. *This Is the American Earth* simply expanded the text and extended the images. You'll have a hard time finding that earlier book. Only five thousand copies were printed, and you probably couldn't afford one, what with the price these days of Ansel's works. You probably couldn't even find the Sierra Club's exhibit-format *These We Inherit: The Parklands of America*, containing the same material and more. But it's worth trying. It's worth seeing what the human mind can conceive and express when it wants to, especially if it is a mind carried around by an Ansel Adams.

What he said, and the way he illustrated it, needs to get around some more. Somehow parts of it must be built into the Ansel Adams Manifesto for the Earth!!! The exclamation points are essential, just as they were in the rubber stamp that for quite a while adorned Ansel's mail: REMEMBER TENAYA!!! As any photographer would know, words are not enough, and require reinforcement. Photographs don't. At the Brower house we have Ansel's *Tenaya Lake* and *Aspens, New Mexico* on our wall. A few hours after Earth Day, 1984, the day Ansel died, Kenneth Brower dropped by our house and paused by our Ansel wall. He saw the beauty that Ansel brought from out there into lives in here, out there where he had found the light eloquent and the moment something that should endure. What he saw still exists out there for the most part, and can itself endure if people want it to and make their own personal commitment to keeping wildness alive because they know intuitively that Thoreau was right.

Ken kept it simple: "Ansel's gone. But his eyes are still here."

Cedric Wright

CEDRIC WRIGHT WORKED ENDLESSLY on his book, *Words of the Earth*. If you caught up with him on a High Sierra trail in the moves High Trips made from camp to camp, you would be read to from out of his latest draft of a chapter. I didn't catch up with him often because I was usually ahead, selecting or organizing the next campsite.

Occasionally I would have done all that the day before, and on moving day could dally and stop for tea. I am afraid I was not so patient as I should have been. I was not ready to understand his hostility toward teachers and toward the hostility of government leaders. He was right, of course. It just took me a while to find out.

It was like trying to find him at High Trip campfires when we wanted an offering from his violin. He was never visible. He felt secure in the prone position, two or three rows back from the fire and in the dark. The violin did not always like his cold fingers.

If Cedric had not stopped you on the trail, he would try to find you in commissary on a layover day, and out would come still another draft of a passage for *Words of the Earth*. There are some that are only run-of-the-mill beautiful and many that I think are quite beautiful. I share Cedric's feeling about trees: "One is aware, lying under trees, of the roots and directions of one's whole being. Perceptions drift in from earth and sky. A vast healing begins."

Actually, Cedric did not work endlessly on his book, and I, therefore, had another opportunity for a publisher's note on the jacket:

ON A PAGE HE WROTE in 1954 to preface one of the many early versions of *Words of the Earth*, Cedric Wright said: "I have been unusually privileged in knowing intimately those wilderness areas where the intangible values sing clearly. It has seemed important to conserve the significance of that singing, to understand its significance not merely in some art form, but rather to try to clarify what it could bring to human life in general. The artist seeks fundamental beauty, the voice of concord, in a world which is presently dominated by opposite types of understanding. Beauty and understanding are the foundations, not only of art, but also of a peaceful human world. It is imperative that in such times as these the artist should use his words and his thought in addition to his art."

With the sensitive aid of Nancy Newhall, Wright has posthumously made an integral whole of words, thought, and art. How all this could happen is a long story that I think will have to be told one day, when people seek out the beginnings of the beauty in this book. But for now I'd like to start merely with my recollection that in the summer of 1953, at a high camp on the Kern, Cedric told me that this was his thirty-third High Trip (the eleventh we had shared.) All too soon after that camp there was a sad task, an obituary to write:

In the High Sierra wilderness country that is the climax of what John Muir liked to call the Range of Light, Wright fell in love with the high world even as Muir had, and each summer brought him closer to its forms, its mood, its tones, its light—and to the thousand textures that unfolded as the trail turned or as a trailless slope opened up on a broad sweep or an intimate glen that no one had seen before.

Oh, others may have stood there, yes. But none could see what he saw, not until with black cloth and box he had worked his magic, had captured and carried away the essence of beauty without harming a hair of it, had printed and fixed its image, had let others see it at last, far from where it was, and had led them, in that way, to look for it and find it next time.

On many of the High Trips, Wright served as the official photographer, meaning that the check he sent in for a reservation on the trip was sent back to him in gratitude for what he had already contributed, worth many times a trip's cost, in exquisite display prints of the previous year's trip. These became the mainstay of the club's permanent photographic collection; they were augmented by Wright's gift to the club of all his Sierra negatives.

People who knew Wright in his mountains—and there are hundreds who did—know that the text of *Words of the Earth* came to him by osmosis as he lay upon some choice piece of the Sierra, in between exposures of film and while he was himself exposed to inaudible words and music. The book contains the best of his poetic expression and of his photographs.

One of the nicest of all memorials to Cedric Wright, however, is the picture so many friends carry in their mind's eye of Cedric before the first of a series of strokes grounded him and impaired his eyesight. For in that picture, he is the Good Samaritan of the trailside, bringing music to a campfire, pouring a warming cup of tea from his billy-can for the weary traveler, brightening the tired end of a day with his good humor and his good heart. Above all, we, his friends, are grateful that because he saw clearly, we can begin to see clearly, or at least be less unseeing.

As a postscript, I should share with you two of the notes, written on odd-sized pieces of paper, that turned up in the vast collection of splendid negatives. One says:

"Explanation of my filing system. All the best negatives from over three or four years past are in this box. Recent years' negatives have been left in the straw basket—each High Trip, 1949 on—in packings by themselves. It might be well to give all my negatives to the Sierra Club."

And the other: "It's been beyond me to figure out how to file all my negatives intelligently. Most all my portrait negatives are in the cellar in fruit boxes."

***Sierra Club Bulletin,* September 1960**

I simply couldn't resist including Cedric's notes about his filing system. It is so much like my own, but better. The book itself is indeed beautiful. Too few people have discovered it, and too little has been done with the Sierra Club's collection of his negatives. It is not yet too late to help identify them, or to drop by and suggest to the club that you would like to write some further words of the earth to accompany what he saw.

BESTOR ROBINSON

GREEK STENTORS COULD HAVE LEARNED a lot from Bestor Robinson, and it wasn't until I was asked to say a few words about him, just before he failed to reach his ninetieth birthday, that I finally realized what he had taught me.

His full name had a James Merritt in front of it. He unloaded the excess baggage and settled for the unusual third name, Bestor. I should long ago have learned when it was time to jettison extraneous things, he once tried to tell me at a Sierra Club board meeting. I might have listened better had he not been the almost constant antagonist for whatever I was protagonizing. At that particular meeting I was lecturing the board about what its role ought to be concerning the Columbia Basin and its river, which year after year carried ten times as much water from mountains to sea as the Colorado River did. I had learned more than I ever expected to about the Colorado and now was becoming enchanted by the Columbia. I had done a lot of homework, talking with then Congressman Lee Metcalf, with dam-builder and Sierra Club leader Walter Huber, with Richard Perle of the Senate Interior Committee staff, with Ottis Peterson of the Bureau of Reclamation, with Ira Gabrielson and others who were trying to help Senator Wayne Morse stop the proposed Hells Canyon Dam—I had done my homework and I wanted to let the board know all about it.

"But Dave," Bestor admonished, holding his cigarette (a relief from his pipe) at a jaunty angle (at what other angle does one hold a cigarette?), "you have the votes. You don't have to tell us anymore."

Since he was the one director I thought I needed to persuade, I subsided. Perhaps the Columbia Basin policy thus established still holds. I am not sure how many of the club's more than five hundred thousand members know whether it does. Having held some club office or other for fifty-three years out of my fifty-six in the club, I ought to know how to find out, but I don't. The procedure of making policy requires a process for letting people know what the policy is.

Bestor was very good at citing policies he agreed with. On British Columbia's highest summit, Mount Waddington, I learned to like most of Bestor's mountain-climbing policy. Carry no excess weight. Drill holes in your toothbrush and save milligrams wherever you can. Step over logs; don't climb up and down their prostrate bodies. On a glacier, travel where the underlying strata are concave and compress the glacier's surface. When the opposite happens, travel the snow troughs alongside the lateral moraines. If you are holed up too many hours or days at a time by bad weather, recite poetry to each other.

One of his mountain policies was no good at all, but Dick Leonard and I could not talk him out of it. Bestor saw no reason for moving our final assault camp up to the Epaulette Glacier, high on Waddington's west shoulder. Instead, he argued, we should spare ourselves the arduous task of moving all our camp equipment so high. We should attempt the summit from our base camp on the Dais Glacier, three thousand vertical feet below the Epaulette and six thousand feet below the summit. Dick and I remain convinced that it was this strategy of Bestor's that denied us a fair shot at the peak. Since we failed, we should be happy to have something to blame the failure on.

Bestor's strategy for the first winter ascent, in 1936, of Yosemite's highest peak, Mount Lyell, was flawless, so we had better blame our success on him. The same goes for the victory on New Mexico's Shiprock in 1939. And it is unlikely that the many years of hard work that went into the construction of Sierra Club ski-touring huts, and more particularly of the club's Clair Tappaan Lodge at Donner Summit, could ever have succeeded without attorney Bestor Robinson's engineering genius and prestidigitatorial art in placing skyhooks where they never were before, without which massive logs would never again have known the heights they achieved to hold the building up.

Bestor was at his best when he could pore over maps and photographs that could help him find ways to get where he and we wanted to go, or over plans for building something, whether a ski lodge or, within his home on Bridgeview Drive in Oakland, an indoor waterfall or a subbasement air-raid shelter.

If the maps, photographs, and plans called for an encroachment on wild places, we had problems with him—not just with the idea itself, but the power of Bestor's clear, deliberate, confident, well-intoned, matter-of-fact genius as a persuader of judges, juries, and Sierra Club directors.

Develop Mount San Gorgonio's wilderness for skiing? Build a tramway from Palm Springs to the wild summit of Mount San Jacinto? Log the great redwoods along the Avenue of the Giants because they were "killer trees" that struck innocent highway travelers? Complete the trans-Sierra highway through the wilderness of Mammoth Pass? Compromise by building just one dam, not two, within Dinosaur National Monument? Go along with the Forest Service plan to lace the gentle wilderness of the Kern Plateau with logging roads? Build the Glen Canyon Dam so as to trap silt and make downstream dams feasible? Build the Coconino Dam on the Little Colorado River for the same reason? Settle for the Marble Gorge and Bridge Canyon dams within the Grand Canyon as long as the Bureau of Reclamation promises good recreational development on the reservoirs? Forge ahead with the devastating overengineering of the new Tioga Road past Tenaya Lake? Put a nuclear reactor within the proposed state park at Bodega Head? Make sure we have a good definition of wilderness before we set about saving it? Clip Dave Brower's wings?

Yes, said Bestor, to each of these. He prevailed on five—Glen Canyon Dam, the Kern Plateau logging roads, the desecration of Tenaya, the San Jacinto tram, and the wing-clipping. Let no one underestimate the energy it took to keep him from prevailing on the others and to try to bypass him on the last one.

What did I learn from all this? All those years of confrontation must have taught me something. Voice control, for example. I am glad there was no one at hand to hear me, time after time as I drove over the Bay Bridge to Sierra Club meetings in San Francisco. I practiced at the stentor's knee but in his absence. I would speak aloud, to no one (not counting myself), presenting an argument in my own voice, then again in Bestor's voice, trying hard to be clear, deliberate in pace, confident in manner, well-toned in voice, speaking as if my conclusions were inevitable—and altogether being a persuasive genius. But I never could get it all together. And when I tried mixing any of these attributes into my conversations with Anne, I got nowhere at all. I would simply revert to trying to be me, and was occasionally successful.

However mischievously Bestor may have accepted my presentation on the Columbia Basin, he was outright laudatory when I came up with the proposal for the Scenic Resources Review—the idea that we plan for intangible resources the way the Forest Service planned to log the national forests.

"That's the best idea you ever had," Bestor said in front of the board, God, and everybody. If anyone else had said that I would have been damned pleased. To hear it from Bestor was an honor.

David Ralph Simons

For David Simons, it did not pay to be a conservationist. The Cascades of Washington and Oregon consumed all his spare time and big chunks of time he would otherwise have spent on his studies at the University of California at Berkeley. His grades suffered, he lost his student deferment, and the army got him. A good fifty years before anyone should have had to, I wrote his obituary:

This Note Must Bear the sad news of the death of David Simons after a two-day illness at Fort Bragg, North Carolina, where he was stationed.

I never before saw so much talent cut off so short. I don't know how the Cascades of Oregon and Washington could have had a better friend.

Dave was completing a second report on the North Cascades and was printing up some of his beautiful photographs of the Oregon country when he contracted hepatitis and died in the army hospital on December 21. His family in Springfield, Oregon, has graciously concurred with the suggestion that the Sierra Club establish a fund in Dave's memory, to be used to further the Cascades conservation objectives to which he contributed so much. His mother thinks that his "These Are the Shining Mountains" in the 1959 annual was one of the finest things written in his twenty-four short years. But there was so much more he wanted to write!

We find ourselves now surrounded with the parts of things he was putting together—drafts of letters, a chapter for a book, photographs, motion pictures, reports, field notes, layouts for brochures, original maps, and other ephemera that show an incisive and abundant wit—all evidence of a young man of exceeding insight, of real genius.

In odd hours of off-duty time this past year, in a barrack a continent away, he tried to bring into focus the vitally needed conservation material he had gathered. Odd hours were not enough but he tried anyway. He rode a bus across the continent and back—at his own expense—to attend an organizational meeting of the Oregon Cascades Conservation Council (he was also a director of the North Cascades Conservation Council in Washington), and by his letters he invigorated it. He would travel up to Washington, D.C., on weekend passes to talk to conservationists there and it was there that I last saw him—and felt from him the need for still more action on behalf of the scenic resources of the Pacific Northwest.

One of the sad things is that so few people know how very much David did—including the stirring of people at least twice his age into action, and well-advised action, too. Few will know how great a loss his death means to conservation. It means that much history which should have been written now cannot be—not in the absence of the unique combination of talents David was. But perhaps we can improvise, put most of the pieces together in some semblance of the order he would have worked out. We can try, and Dave would like that.

***Sierra Club Bulletin*, December 1960**

The Reverend D. Hugh Peniston, at the Simons service in Springfield, added words I wish I had said:

"Often people say, 'No one is indispensable,' but it is not true. Every human being is unique, but when a person discovers the real purpose of his life, the unique purpose for which it seems he was created, he is irreplaceable, and there is no one else who can fill the gap which he leaves when he dies. I suppose only a few people discover this real purpose, but to do so is the richest satisfaction of life. David Simons discovered it in a few short years, thus going beyond many who have not discovered it in a lifetime."

Twenty-nine years after David's death I visited Springfield by mistake, having turned too early for Eugene, and discovered one of the ugliest and smelliest of communities in Oregon, victim of an industry determined to make Oregon's mountains the mangiest of all with unalleviated clear-cutting. I told friends at a conference in Eugene why David had become such a good conservationist: in Springfield there was no alternative.

I cannot prove it, but no one can persuade me to conclude otherwise: if David Simons had put just a little more effort into his studies and less into helping me at the time, his grades would have been adequate, his talents would not have been diverted to the army and his life lost there, and we would have an Oregon Volcanic Cascades National Park and a reformed U.S. Forest Service by now. There can still be a park, but never the superlative one that could have been established before the Forest Service allowed vindictive cuts to be made—cuts made far within the proposed park—in an attempt, I must infer, to make the park idea moot.

With a reforestation effort conducted by people who understand the forest mechanism rather than timber mechanics, there is still a chance for a national park that will be beautiful enough after a century of recovery.

It will not be easy now to campaign for this, and it would not have been easy then, but that would not have bothered Dave.

A Roomful of Bradleys

DON'T CONDEMN MY OLD HOUSE, BOB. Let me finish using it and I'll give it to you." Bob was Robert Gordon Sproul, president of the University of California. The house was 2639 Durant Avenue, in Berkeley, the residence of Harold C. Bradley, professor emeritus of chemistry,

University of Wisconsin. I am not sure that when he retired to Berkeley he was prescient enough to foresee many of the consequences, much less do anything to thwart them. That house was to become an alternate Sierra Club headquarters. The living room was large enough to accommodate well-attended meetings of the Sierra Club Conservation Committee. The kitchen and dining room kept the attendees refreshed, and somewhere in the nether regions there was a busy darkroom and space to accommodate a large number of Bradleys.

Originally the house accommodated Cornelius Beach Bradley, charter member of the club and editor of the *Sierra Club Bulletin,* 1895–97. He was Harold's father. I never met him, nor did I ever meet Harold, Jr., but I did know and love Harold's wife, Josephine, and her other six sons—Charles, David, Steve, Joe, Ric, and Bill—and enough of *their* children to lose count.

With some urging from me, Harold served as president of the club from 1957 to 1959. He was reluctant to take the job on. At seventy-eight, he knew his ears were losing the high notes and feared that other faculties, such as judgment, would become impaired and people would be too kind to tell him. He was also disappointed that the club directors had not been supportive of his effort to spare Yosemite National Park from an over-engineered Tioga Road. Despite a few misgivings, he agreed to serve, and served well.

My father and Harold were born the same year but Harold outlived my father by sixteen years and became my father figure. It was good to have one among the Sierra Club presidents, all of whom I have known except the first—John Muir.

We were close allies on the question of national park roads, and we studied many a mile of them in Harold's old Cadillac. With his clinometer we would measure grades. We measured the amplitude of curves by mentally calibrating the steering wheel. He liked mountain driving, as I do, and we were both disturbed by the amount of national park terrain and beauty the National Park Service was willing to give up in order to spare park visitors from the delights of mountain roads. The last twenty-one miles of the Tioga Road to be superseded were the best in Yosemite. It was a little like driving a trail. Trees had been spared, not considered an obstacle. The steep grade out of the Yosemite Creek basin was a place to relax. You just shifted into low, leaned back, let the car do the work, and enjoyed the view at your leisure. At Tenaya Lake the glacier polish still lay alongside the road, and at a few places on the shoulder you could drive on it with one wheel. You could touch trees by reaching out the car window.

The Park Service acceded to only one of Harold's suggestions for the Tioga Road. While that twenty-one miles existed, the service placed signs on both ends, calling attention to the history of the road and the reward of meeting its challenge as you drove it. Harold wrote the words. There is a photograph of them in the 1958 *Sierra Club Bulletin.*

"TIOGA MINE ROAD–TWENTY-ONE MILES. This is the last remaining section of the old Tioga Mine Road, completed in 1883. Over it machinery and supplies were freighted in horse-drawn wagons to the Tioga Mine, located at the crest of the range near Tioga Pass.

"It is a typical mountain road–narrow, winding, sometimes steep, and little changed today."

In its stead we have a high-speed highway. The trees have been cleared far out of reach–farther still to spare the highway from windfalls caused by the clearing. The highway will get you over Yosemite's Sierra faster. You do not have to waste time drinking in the scene. And the National Park Service gets to count more people faster as they pass on through.

Harold and I did not concern ourselves, unfortunately, with what happened to the Tioga Road on the far side of Tioga Pass–in Mono National Forest. There the California Division of Highways took charge with no one in our business having time to object. Lee Vining Canyon was butchered, needlessly sacrificed to the eternal combustion engine. I should have said internal, but we seem to be up against something more lasting.

There should be a biography of Harold, and his sons should collaborate on it–his real sons who could legitimately call him Pop.

First there is Charlie–geologist, musician, well endowed with wit–whom I met when I arrived at Camp Hale as a new second lieutenant. He was one of the keepers of the mountain troop songs, having composed some himself in close association with Ralph Bromaghin. Our association was interrupted by higher headquarters, who dispatched us to whatever part of the country suited their convenience and the furthering of mountain training.

I met his likeness after the war in Wheeler Auditorium, UC Berkeley. Against the far wall was a man whom I approached to say: "You have to be a Bradley. Charlie's brother." That was brother Dave, M.D., still living in the outskirts of Dartmouth, through which all Bradleys passed at one time or another. Dave is the husband of Lil McLane, whose brother Charles had briefly been my roommate at Camp Hale. Lil's sister Mary graces many of my audiotapes with her exquisite songs, which you must hear sometime. But that is another story. David Bradley spent some time at Bikini Atoll, about which he wrote *No Place To Hide* in 1948.

Before meeting David I met Bill, who came to the Seneca Assault Climbing School in West Virginia to help us teach special detachments from several infantry divisions how to climb rocks. Bill later fell victim to polio, just before people stopped falling victim thanks to Jonas Salk, but he finished his education in spite of this problem, teaches geology, and skis with more imaginative use of ski poles than is usually required.

Joe was in a hospital in Madison, quite fortunately it turned out, when a strange thing happened to him. Something like a birthmark on his brain, for some reason, started bleeding. Perhaps nowhere else in the country could the symptoms have been recognized and corrective surgery initiated. But not before great damage had been done. Joe's efforts to restore faculties he had possessed just before that event included his having to learn again how to swallow. Imagine trying to learn how to do something that has always been automatic! He also relearned typing. But getting a given finger to accept, reluctantly, his attempts to control it – this became a major chore. Joe cut the chore in half by omitting vowels from what he typed. Ths ws stll ndrstndbl ngh tht h cntnd hs schlng nd wn hs PhD.

Ric, now professor emeritus of physics at Colorado College in Colorado Springs, is also a musician and composer, and has found that it takes several days to compose five minutes of music. It is time well spent. I did not know of his musical ability until he recorded my mountain troop song, "Moving Out," when I played it on his piano in Colorado Springs. Ric then transcribed that recording into written music. I am certain that he did it correctly because I know from listening to his composition that he knows my chords. But I can't really tell for sure, because my ability to read music never got out of the Eocene epoch. I'd like to do for his compositions what he did for mine.

Steve Bradley is a painter and skier, and I knew about both these talents before I met him. He testified before Congress in opposition to the proposed dams in Dinosaur National Monument. He had learned what was at stake on the river trip Harold organized and filmed that awakened the Sierra Club to the importance of Dinosaur to the National Park System and of Echo Park and the living Yampa and Green rivers to Dinosaur. Steve described that trip in the *Sierra Club Bulletin*. I should like very much to have met Hal, Harold's namesake, but our trails never crossed and his premature death denies me the chance. I'll have to depend upon some Bradley son, and I suppose it should be David, the writer, to come forth with the real Bradley story.

A remarkable pride of sons and a remarkable father! But the mother is the most remarkable part of the story. At the age of eighteen months, Josephine Crane, of the plumbing Cranes, contracted a virulent form of measles and lost her hearing. Not hearing her own voice, she found it difficult to communicate with outsiders. Her family could understand her, which was the most important factor. I had great difficulty. Anne had little difficulty, and enjoyed long conversations with Josephine, whose lipreading was superb. One story that Anne learned was that Josephine was often offended by silent movies, where what the actors were saying with their lips was not what the titles reported, occasionally including obscenities the

Hays Office, which provided moral control for the movies but could not read lips, did not cope with.

At mealtime, the children got Josephine's attention by tapping on the table. I imagine that each child's tap had its own individuality and she knew which way to look. I know what my own mother could sense when touch had to substitute for seeing. The substitute faculty acquires almost unimaginable brilliance.

In the congressional hearings on Dinosaur National Monument and the Colorado River Storage Project, Josephine did not testify. But I think just about every other Bradley did. There was more than testimony. Ric exchanged letters with the Bureau of Reclamation, including Commissioner W. A. Dexheimer, who had not yet discovered that the Bradleys were Sierra Club members. In an unguarded moment, Mr. Dexheimer revealed Reclamation's concern about the foundation rock for Glen Canyon Dam. On October 26, 1954, he wrote: "At present our design specialists are quite concerned as to whether or not the foundation characteristics of the Glen Canyon and Gray Canyon sites are capable of safely supporting high dams seven hundred feet and five hundred seventy-five, respectively." All Bradleys would be delighted if his apprehensions proved to be correct, and the scenic masterpieces of Glen Canyon when the dam collapses, could again see the sun and begin to recover.

One of Ric's greatest achievements in the Grand Canyon battle that followed Dinosaur was the article he wrote for *Reader's Digest*. The *Digest* people were impressed enough that they arranged for a Grand Canyon conference at the South Rim. Conservationists from all over were invited and came.

Reclamationists, not invited, crashed. The Bureau of Reclamation brought its huge relief map, showing how insignificantly little of the canyon would be occupied by the reservoirs behind the proposed Marble Gorge and Bridge Canyon dams. That insignificant little just happens to be the heart of the canyon. Senator Barry Goldwater and Congressman Morris Udall came as the bureau's heavies. They did not prevail.

For one thing, they had been outmaneuvered by the Bradley clan. Somewhere there exists what must be a trunkful of negatives and prints that Harold and family started producing after their river trip through Dinosaur. Harold's photographs were priceless counterpoint, in my favorite Sierra Club brochure, for the words we borrowed from Secretary of the Interior Douglas McKay: "What we have done at Lake Mead is what we have in mind for Dinosaur." The photographs? Vast expanses of Lake Mead at drawdown—acres upon acres of drying, cracking mud.

I don't want to leave the Bradleys in the mud. Far better to leave them in the High Sierra in winter. They took many winter trips to Tuolumne Meadows, and Harold participated until, at seventy-five, he thought better of it. Perhaps he shared the attitude of Benton MacKaye,

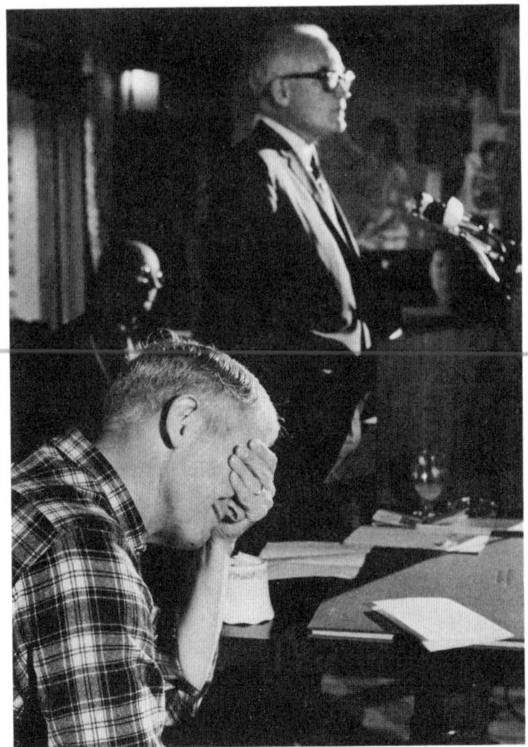

Barry Goldwater arguing for Grand Canyon dams; Brower disagreeing on the South Rim of the Grand Canyon, 1966. Photo by Arthur Schatz, Life *magazine, ©Time, Inc.*

pioneer eastern conservationist, who at a similar age said he did not have to climb Katahdin any more.

After all, Harold started his ski trips in the Sierra early—January 1, 1921, when he did what no one, or at most but a few, other than Snowshoe Thompson had accomplished—skiing across the whole thing. He wrote about his pioneering in the 1922 *Sierra Club Bulletin,* and I like the way he ended that article:

"It will not be long, I think, before the Sierra Club will route its winter trips, from cabin to cabin through the snows, as it now does its summer excursions, making possible, for a few enthusiasts at least, that return to the untouched primitive world which in summer grows each year more difficult to find."

Indeed, one of the cabins that now contributes to that opportunity is, most appropriately, the Bradley Hut. I should get back in shape and go!

A Roomful of Leopolds

ALDO LEOPOLD WAS A FRIEND I never met. Harold Bradley introduced me to him by writing Aldo's obituary for the *Sierra Club Bulletin*. Shortly thereafter Harold presented me with a copy of his greatest book—*A Sand County Almanac and Sketches Here and There*. If anyone else in the Sierra Club knew about Aldo's genius, they didn't tell me, and I determined to tell them. I called up Oxford University Press and asked for permission to quote little gems from *Sand County* in the *Sierra Club Bulletin* ever after. Three favorites from Leopold's *Round River* went into the first edition of the *Sierra Club Handbook* that followed Leopold's death:

Conservation—and Tinkering

CONSERVATION IS A STATE of harmony between men and land. By land is meant all of the things on, over, or in the earth. Harmony with the land is like harmony with a friend; you cannot cherish his right hand and chop off his left. . . . The outstanding scientific discovery of the twentieth century is not television, or radio, but rather the complexity of the land organism. Only those who know most about it can appreciate how little we know about it. The last word in ignorance is the man who says of an animal or plant: "What good is it?" If the land mechanism as a whole is good, then every part is good, whether we understand it or not. If the biota, in the course of eons, has built something we like but do not understand, then who but a fool would discard seemingly useless parts? To keep every cog and wheel is the first precaution of intelligent tinkering.

How Much for Their Signature?

Is it profitable for the individual to build a beautiful home? To give his children a higher education? No, it is seldom profitable, yet we do both. These are, in fact, ethical and aesthetic premises which underlie the economic system. Once accepted, economic forces tend to align the smaller details of social organization into harmony with them.

No such ethical premise yet exists for the condition of the land these children must live on. Our children are our signature to the roster of history; our land is merely the place our money was made. There is as yet no social stigma in the possession of a gullied farm, a wrecked forest, or a polluted stream, provided the dividends suffice to send the youngsters to college. Whatever ails the land, the government will fix it.

I think we have here the root of the problem. What conservation education must build is an ethical underpinning for land economics and a universal curiosity to understand the land mechanism. Conservation may then follow.

Holograph

I have congenital hunting fever and three sons. As little tots, they spent their time playing with my decoys and scouring vacant lots with wooden guns. I hope to leave them good health, an education, and possibly even a competence. But what are they going to do with these things if there is no more deer in the hills, and no more quail in the coverts? No more snipe whistling in the meadow, no more piping of widgeons and chattering of teal as darkness covers the marshes; no more whistling of swift wings when the morning star pales in the east? And when the dawn wind stirs through the ancient cottonwoods, and the gray light steals down from the hills over the old river sliding softly past its wide brown sandbars—what if there is to be no more goose music?

When Aldo Starker Leopold came into the Sierra Club's life we began to learn what Leopolds were all about. Starker was not happy about being introduced as the son of Aldo; with his own good works, he just about turned things around to where Aldo might be spoken of as Starker's father. He had his facts straight, a wonderful sense of humor, and he could sing.

Next I learned of Luna Leopold, and was grateful for his having gone through his father's journals to produce *Round River,* published posthumously. I spoke so often of this book that Anne Crowe, wife of Harold Crowe, club president in whose regime I became executive director, asked that I get her a copy of the book. But would I please staple together, so she couldn't read them, the pages that described Aldo's hunting exploits? I had not enjoyed those pages, and she didn't want to take a chance.

Years later, when Ian Ballantine was deeply involved in environmental publishing, I suggested that he include in his survival series a mass-market paperback of *Sand County,* combined with the non-hunting essays in *Round River*. He did, and my copy of the 1972 edition is the seventeenth printing.

Aldo's, Starker's, and Luna's love of hunting kept my mind partly open to an attempt to understand the drive behind the sport of killing, not for food, but for pleasure. Reluctantly, I became willing to soften my objections to an activity that had contributed in any way to Aldo's conceiving and developing the conservation ethic as he did. That rationalizing let me relax a little. It helped very much to learn that Aldo eventually gave up hunting.

Perhaps if I had become a hunter myself, things would have been different. I tried, but I didn't like it when the cost of my first success with a BB gun was a dead tiny innocent bird. I did not think that my wiping out its life for no good reason had contributed much to my own joy of living.

My first success with a shotgun killed a jackrabbit, whose last act, perhaps some desperate gesture toward perpetuating the species, was to ejaculate. That did it for me. From then I could settle for trying to hit the glass insulators on telephone poles with a .22 along Fish Ranch Road in the Berkeley Hills. The poles shouldn't have been there anyway.

World War II, where I was taught to kill or be killed, was different. As an intelligence officer, I was fortunately not required to shoot anybody. I had occasion to call for concentrations of artillery on the enemy, but I did not have to see the killing I had requested of people who didn't like the war any more than I did.

Starker and Luna never gave up hunting, and so far as I know, Estella and Nina, the two Leopold daughters I met, never took it up. I never met the third son. So with Starker and Luna I just avoided the subject. There were plenty of other subjects to talk about.

Starker and Sir Frank Fraser Darling were my nominees for the title, the "Einstein of Biology." Starker also acquired great acumen in political science, an unusual combination. He described for me a biological tragedy that I relate often to illustrate the harm that can result from monoculture in forestry. Foresters in Germany opted for a pure spruce forest. The first generation rewarded them. The second was a so-so affair. The third simply didn't make it. The nutrient base had been so impoverished by monoculture that steps had to be taken to rebuild the soil, including the reintroduction of ants. I should have asked for references and be able now to turn to my own library and back this up. It is simply filed in my memory, where the retrieval system is not anything I would want to franchise. In any event, I like that story, and don't want to be disillusioned. After all, I heard it from Starker.

Luna taught me all I know about aggradation. I first met Luna by mail, when he told me that I should stick to my bird-watching instead of trying to outguess the engineers of the Bureau of Reclamation. He later gave me permission to go on with my second-guessing. My first lesson in aggradation came when I finally met him in person in a laboratory in Pasadena, where he arranged to have a small stream of water flow down a table some fifty feet long and filled with sand. The slope was so gradual that the stream could form meanders. By varying the flow he could assess the meander-building process, the rate of erosion, and the erosive capability of water according to its sediment load. Where the slope flattened out, he could observe the rate of aggradation, which occurs when the stream slows down, whereupon it must deposit part of its load. Thus a stream entering a reservoir will begin to build back its original gradient up to a slope, Luna said, of one and a half feet per mile on the Colorado.

I recently plugged this into my Colorado River calculations and conclude that when the reservoir behind Glen Canyon Dam is completely silted in, about three centuries from now, the depth of sediment at the reservoir's present head, one hundred eighty-six miles upstream, will be about two hundred eighty feet above the present maximum water level. This means that the deposit of sediment will extend upstream until the one-and-a-half-foot slope of aggradation intersects the natural grade of the river.

Using Bureau of Reclamation data from 1954 House hearings on the Colorado River Storage Project, one gets into problems. On facing pages the elevations of Flaming Gorge reservoir vary by twenty feet. A table says the Moab dam site is 69.6 miles above the Green River junction and the accompanying diagram puts it at more than a hundred. Rough calculations are all you dare try, but they are informing, and I'll bet the Bureau of Reclamation didn't get around to them.

For example, using Luna's figure, Hoover Dam's eventual sedimentation, uninterrupted, would bury the proposed Bridge Canyon power house, in the Grand Canyon, about one hundred thirty feet deep. Glen Canyon's sediment will extend one hundred thirty miles above the present head of Lake Powell and bury the Moab dam site and the lower forty miles of the Green River. Glen Canyon Dam will hold about sixty percent more mud than it does water. Flaming Gorge Dam's sediment will extend one hundred miles beyond the present head of Flaming Gorge Reservoir and the Union Pacific Railroad bridge will be sixty-five feet under at Green River, Wyoming, if there is still a railroad or a Green River, Wyoming, then. The Union Pacific is gone already.

When will this happen? Again, I have only the old Bureau of Reclamation figures, which I doubt. But if you use them, you can start with the one hundred fifty thousand acre-feet of sediment the Colorado could deposit every year in Lake Mead if sediment were not shortstopped upstream. One third of that comes in below Glen Canyon Dam with no shortstops. Visualize one hundred fifty thousand acre-feet—a column the area of a football field and thirty miles high. No, that's too hard to visualize. Try thirty football fields one mile high. Or cover all Rhode Island with a fifth of a foot of mud, probably a bit more, every year, or more than forty feet since it became a state. But why does everyone always pick on Rhode Island? Pity Green River, Wyoming, covered that deep a mere century from now.

Think of the fun I would have missed if Aldo had not fathered Luna and I never got to take my sedimental journey!

By the way, I also calculated the slope extending up the Colorado tributary of Aztec Creek and up its tributary of Bridge Creek, which flows under Rainbow Bridge. By this projection, the sediment deposition caused by Glen Canyon Dam will be high above the present Bridge Creek channel, extending well above the abutments of Rainbow Bridge. Flash floods and the meander-building mechanism will combine to erode the supports and bring down Rainbow Bridge—much too high a cost for hydroelectricity.

When I was in the Grand Canyon with Reclamation Commissioner Floyd Dominy and John McPhee, I pointed out that the sediment slope created by the proposed Bridge Canyon dam would extend into Grand Canyon National Park and well up Havasu Creek. Mr. Dominy rejected the reality of aggradation. He liked flat water, and sediment had damned well better stay as flat as the water. I think that this rejection was the result of the Bureau of Reclamation's possessing such power within the Department of the Interior that it does not have to listen to the U.S. Geological Survey, and indeed can force it to shut up. Luna was with the Geological Survey. I was fortunate to have a direct channel to him, without having the message intercepted and buried in Reclamation sediment. We were delighted to have Luna's good judgment on the Sierra Club board of directors.

Starker, in addition to having served, earlier than Luna, but also with good judgment, on the Sierra Club board, was director of the University of California Museum of Vertebrate Zoology and privy to, or victim of, university politics. In spite of the power struggle with the UC School of Forestry, he accomplished wonders. His was a major role in establishing Sierra Club wildlife policy, in the club's effort toward setting aside the Arctic National Wildlife Range, in creating, at the request of Secretary of the Interior Stewart Udall, a comprehensive wildlife policy for the national parks. Knowing Spanish well, he was also able to persuade the Mexican government to protect the California gray whale's breeding waters in Scammon's Lagoon, off Baja California.

One day he telephoned to see if I could find out what was happening at Bodega Head. The California Division of Beaches and Parks wanted to set aside a state park there, and the University of California wished to establish a marine biology research station. Suddenly both institutions were told to forget their plans. Why?

The why turned out to be that the Pacific Gas & Electric Company planned to build a nuclear reactor on Bodega Head. The utility knew that the reactor needed a big buffer of open space in case of trouble, and that state parks and research stations were not likely to be unoccupied. Therefore, no park or research station at Bodega Head. It would be helpful, also, to keep the Point Reyes Peninsula unoccupied, or at least not committed to condominiums. National Seashore status could at least block residential development. This did no harm to the effort to establish the Point Reyes National Seashore.

University politics being what they were, and Pacific Gas & Electric being a major donor to the university, Starker was unable to help us defend Bodega Head on behalf of the park and the university. Fortunately, the San Andreas Fault came to the rescue. It passes right through the six-million-dollar hole that was to have been part of the nuclear facility. The fault did not bother the utility until environmental activist David Pesonen lent his modest weight to the fault's ability to lift mountains. He was forced by my

David Brower (right) looks on as President Kennedy signs the bill making Point Reyes a National Seashore. Congressmen and senators (left to right) are: Wayne Aspinall, Colorado; John Rutherford, Texas; Hubert Humphrey; Secretary of the Interior Stewart Udall; John P. Saylor, Pennsylvania; Dana Bible, Nevada; Clair Engle, California; Clem Miller, California; Jeffrey Cohelan, California; Hilary Tolson, Associate Director of the National Park Service.

superiors to leave the Sierra Club staff in order to do so. Thanks to him, and not to the club, the Reactor Safety Board of the Atomic Energy Commission told PG&E to forget Bodega Head. The utility stubbornly refused, however, to learn to respect the San Andreas Fault at Cape Mendocino until David went to work again, and scoffed at the Hosgri Fault, near Diablo Canyon, leading an officer of Gulf Atomic to comment, at a public hearing: "I refuse to be held responsible for the stupidity of the Pacific Gas & Electric Company." That disclaimer led me to comment later that a nuclear reactor is a sophisticated device that enables utilities to locate earthquake faults. The utility, its stockholders, and its ratepayers would have saved five billion dollars had they been less stubborn. Conventional wisdom can be extremely costly. Southern California Edison Company installed that sophisticated device at San Onofre. Its destruction could render Southern California uninhabitable.

I can only guess what Aldo might have done if caught between a rock and a hard place. He certainly must have been in that situation often in the Forest Service, in its insistence on discarding seemingly useless parts of the biota. To close the circle, Charles Bradley married Nina Leopold and they live near Aldo's old shack on the Baribou River.

LOREN EISELEY

ONE OF THE THINGS that can strain a marriage is to have your wife talk to you about a book she has just been moved by, not quite listen to her, then tell her excitedly about the book when a stranger has told you about it and you have listened. That is exactly what I did with Loren Eiseley's *The Immense Journey*. Anne may forgive me. We'll see.

It was David Hales who got my attention. He was not exactly a stranger, for he represented both the Sierra Club and the University of California Press in New York City. It was through him, after I had read *The Immense Journey* (which I found on the shelves labeled "Travel" in Scribner's big Fifth Avenue bookstore) and a few other Eiseley books, that I first met Loren.

In the course of several meetings I persuaded him to write an introduction to the club's anthology of Robinson Jeffers (*Not Man Apart*) and an article for the *Sierra Club Bulletin*. I tried also to persuade him to join the expedition to the Galapagos Islands that Eliot Porter instigated. Loren's wife, who was to survive him, was ill at the time and he did not wish to be that far away from her for so long, but he did contribute a superb chapter to the first of the two-volume work, *Galapagos: The Flow of Wildness*.

We met from time to time Under the Clock at the Biltmore in New York (before it was so ruthlessly destroyed by conversion into a meaningless high-rise), for that is where everybody met. On one occasion I walked right by him, a little impatient that he was late. When I started to walk by the second time he called my name, and with a little difficulty I recognized not the big portly man who looked like a railroad executive, but a man who was now indeed trim. Between meetings he had gone on a weight-losing orgy and enjoyed it so much, as he put it, that he didn't know when to stop.

A joint plot that never worked out was a series of Sierra Club books on the great naturalists, which Loren would introduce and annotate—an idea suggested to him by his success with *Darwin's Century*. I'm sorry we missed.

If you thumb through the books I helped the Sierra Club and Friends of the Earth publish, you will find that I reached for Eiseley often. There is power in what an anthropologist who is also a poet can evoke with words. I drew on my favorites in remembering him for FOE's journal:

WE ARE COMPOUNDED OF DUST and the light of a star, Loren Eiseley wrote. His many books, his poetry, his anthropologist's curiosity about the fields of human endeavor around his own, show how important one man's light can be.

Perhaps his greatest book is *The Immense Journey*, and in it one of the most moving passages is "The Judgment of the Birds." We drew upon it in the Sierra Club's *The Place No One Knew* and again in the club's next to last annual magazine number of its *Bulletin*, in 1965. A sermon based on this passage was given in Grace Cathedral, San Francisco, in 1969. "If there is magic on this planet," he wrote, "it is contained in water." It was also contained in Loren Eiseley and endures in his work.

THE JUDGMENT OF THE BIRDS

It was a late hour on a cold, wind-bitten day when I climbed a great hill
spined like a dinosaur's back and tried to take my bearings.
The tumbled waste fell away like waves in all directions.
Blue air was darkening into purple along the bases of the hills.
I shifted my knapsack, heavy with the petrified bones
of long-vanished creatures, and studied my compass.
I wanted to be out there by nightfall,
and already the sun was going down sullenly in the west.

It was then that I saw the flight coming on.
It was moving like a little close-knit body
of black specks that danced and darted and closed again.
It was pouring from the north and heading toward me
with the undeviating relentlessness of a compass needle.
It streamed through the shadows rising out of monstrous gorges.
It rushed out over towering pinnacles in the red light of the sun,
or momentarily sank from sight within their shade.
Across that desert of eroding clay and wind-worn stone
they came with a faint wild twittering that filled all the air about me
as those tiny living bullets hurtled past into the night.

It may not strike you as a marvel. It would not, perhaps,
unless you stood in the middle of a dead world at sunset,
but that is where I stood.
Fifty million years lay under my feet, fifty million years of monsters
bellowing in a green world now gone so utterly
that its very light was traveling on the farther edge of space.
The chemicals of all that vanished age lay about me on the ground.
Around me still lay the shearing molars of dead titanotheres,
the delicate sabers of soft-stepping cats, the hollow sockets
that held the eyes of many a strange, outmoded beast.
Those eyes had looked out upon a world as real as ours;
dark savage brains had roamed and roared
their challenges into the steaming night.

Now they were still here, or put it as you will the chemicals
that made them were here about me on the ground.
The carbon that had driven them ran blackly into the eroding stone.
The stain of iron was in the clays.
The iron did not remember the blood it had once moved within,
the phosphorus had forgot the savage brain.
The little individual moment had ebbed
from all those strange combinations of chemicals
as it would ebb from our living bodies
into the sinks and runnels of oncoming time.

I had lifted up a fistful of that ground. I held it while that wild flight
of southbound warblers hurtled over me into the oncoming dark.
There went phosphorus, there went iron, there went carbon,
there beat the calcium in those hurrying wings.
Alone on a dead planet I watched that incredible miracle speeding past.
It ran by some true compass over field and waste land.
It cried its individual ecstasies into the air until the gullies rang.
It swerved like a single body; it knew itself
and lonely, it bunched close in the racing darkness,
its individual entities feeling about them the rising night.
And so, crying to each other their identity,
they passed away out of my view.

I dropped my fistful of earth. I heard it roll inanimate
back into the gully at the base of the hill:
iron, carbon, the chemicals of life.
Like men from those wild tribes who had haunted these hills
before me seeking visions, I made my sign to the great darkness.
It was not a mocking sign, and I was not mocked. . . .

When I gave the sermon at Grace Cathedral in San Francisco I must have said something of my own, but I have forgotten it. I knew, from various attempts to read "The Judgment of the Birds" aloud, that I was going to have trouble, and had to scrunch my toes so hard they hurt in order to keep my voice from breaking. That wasn't the only time.

Rachel Carson

There may be a Better Editor, some day, than William Shawn, but I don't think so. What he did for *The New Yorker* is what all editors should be trained to do for whatever they edit. What other editor would publish Rachel Carson's first book in one issue, or Jonathan Schell's *The Fate of the Earth,* or give an entire issue to John Hersey's *Hiroshima* (or three consecutive issues to an archdruid)? Five thousand words is as much as the usual editor can handle. It was thanks to his judgment that I was able to start reading "Silent Spring" in *The New Yorker.* I could not put it down until I had finished it–in the Salt Lake City airport.

She removed a veil that had concealed from me, before that, what the life force consists of, and how interrelated are all of us who share in it. For the first time I began to understand that some of the essential building blocks of life were the same in people as they were in the lesser creatures people decided to kill with poison. It was amazing that so simple a truth had escaped so many–until Rachel Carson caught it.

The vigor of the chemical industry's defense mechanisms, mixed with the vitriol of apologists, was something to watch. It was easy to distinguish self-interest from public interest. Two of my mountaineer friends became early partakers of the photo-op and ate DDT on television in attempts to demonstrate its innocuousness. My faith in science–rather, my faith in some scientists–began to fade, even as my faith in government faded when President Eisenhower denied that U-2 overflights of the Soviet Union were spy missions.

One does not delight in seeing one's idols smashed, but I was grateful to Rachel Carson for her role, perhaps not in smashing idols, but in baring the clay feet of such scientists.

It took quite a while for the Sierra Club directors to share my gratitude. One of my early defeats as the club's executive director took place in Tuolumne Meadows. The club directors voted down my attempt to have them protest the spraying of DDT on the lodgepole needle miners that were defoliating the lodgepoles on the club's property at Soda Springs. The needle miner, I argued, was indigenous, did not endanger the lodgepole, and could help keep lodgepoles in balance with the rest of their ecosystem. I learned that lodgepoles could withstand seven defoliations. I broke off a twig at random to show that new needles were on the way to refurbish the defoliated tree. Moreover, the Sierra Club could set a good example by protecting its own property from the National Park Service, whose spraying orgy was ignoring its own expert regional biologist.

The winning counterargument was that the directors did not want unfiltered sunlight and needle miner poop falling on their picnic tables.

I don't know whether Rachel Carson heard about that. She did know, by 1960, that a chemist from Lederle Laboratories had vigorously protested Nancy Newhall's mentioning of "killer chemicals" in her text for *This Is the American Earth*. He still more vigorously protested my refusal to change the language in the next edition. The club's board supported dosing Yosemite needle miners with DDT by a margin of one vote, as I remember it, and I was forced to infer that my Lederle friend's nomination of another chemist for the board at the next election boded ill. There were no other Atlantic Chapter nominees and his chance of being elected was, I thought, too good. The board would too easily stay swung the wrong way on spraying. I had no difficulty in persuading members to petition that another candidate from the Atlantic be offered the voters—Rachel Carson's publisher, Paul Brooks. He was easily elected, and nature won out.

I had few chances to meet Rachel Carson. One of them was a black-tie affair in New York City where she was awarded the Audubon Medal. She did not look well. Shortly thereafter she came west to attend a conference at San Francisco and telephoned to see if I could help her see Muir Woods. With Anne and Barbara I joined her and a National Park Service guide at the entrance to Muir Woods. They had a wheelchair for her, and we made our way slowly through the great trees. It was too late in the year for salmon to be spawning there, a sight I know she would have enjoyed. The stream isn't really deep enough for spawning salmon, but they charge upstream anyway with their backs awash.

But the word must have been abroad among wild creatures that Rachel Carson was here and that it would be her last trip. We drove out of Muir Woods and off for the beach at Fort Cronkhite, where I gathered for her a few of the many-colored shiny pebbles that the Pacific creates from the Franciscan formation of the shore. Those were nice, but what counted most was in the Rodeo Lagoon. It was the first time I had seen them there. Not surprising, given what DDT had previously done to their eggs. But there they were, thanks to Miss Carson and her book—a whole gaggle of Brown pelicans, some two hundred of them, jubilant.

So was she.

However it may have happened, Rachel Carson learned to like the Sierra Club well enough to change her will. There was a prescribed waiting period, whereupon the club learned she had left it more than three hundred thousand dollars.

I proposed a way in which the largesse could be invested in something more important than a bank account and that would also more than return the investment. I proposed a dedication to a new edition of the long-absent *Sierra Club Handbook:*

AN OPENING LINE in Rachel Carson's book, *Silent Spring,* was from the poet, Keats: "The sedge has withered by the lake, and no birds sing." This was the book that warned of a silence no one wished to hear, but toward which civilization–in particular the chemical industry's contribution to it–was moving all too rapidly. *Silent Spring* evoked protest from the right enemies and admiration from the right friends.

The Sierra Club was among the latter, but that friendship came by a difficult route. It was not easy for some of us to give up willingly our enjoyment of the short-term advantages of the poisons we had invented to wipe out what we have chosen to call "pests." We did not quite realize how closely related the building blocks of life are, whether in the worm the robin eats, within the robin itself, also within whatever eats the robin, or whatever decomposes the robin's predator. Not many of us are given to eating robins, but we are blessed with the same well-tested building blocks, and we are not yet sure, when we fire at a pest, that we have not cast a boomerang, the avenging flight of which may be delayed long enough to fool us.

We know now, for example, that we cheered too soon about our victory over malaria. Yes, DDT killed the mosquito that served as malaria's vector, but it also killed natural enemies of the mosquito. The malaria organism's timetable for creating a new generation was so much faster than its enemy's that it could evolve around the DDT obstacle, and the enemy's schedule for replicating itself was too slow to be that lucky. As mosquitoes evolved around pesticide after pesticide, we began to conclude that the only satisfactory weapon against mosquitoes was slapping them. While others were celebrating pesticides, Rachel Carson was warning about their side effects. The chemical industry developed a consuming fury and fought her with some of its finest sophists. They were not unsuccessful, and many on the Sierra Club's board were taken in. After a crucial board election the Sierra Club stopped wavering about pesticides, and has adhered to a sound policy ever since. Learning of this, Rachel Carson was most generous to the club in her last will and testament.

It is out of the belief that Rachel Carson would approve of the strength this book can add to the continuing effectiveness of the Sierra Club that the board of directors determined that it was appropriate for her final generosity to be the vehicle that made possible the

> re-emergence of this book. It carries on where *The Sierra Club Handbook* left off two decades earlier.
>
> We would like Rachel Carson to be remembered by this book, and by the editions that follow, as the Sierra Club approaches its first centennial and prepares for the next. But the Sierra Club does not wish to have these editions as sole reminders of the Rachel Carson legacy. The Rachel Carson Fund will be replenished regularly from the benefits that will inure to generations—and, we hope, to forthcoming generations all over.
>
> It is our hope that, thanks to this book and its successors, more people than ever before will understand what the Sierra Club, and the host of organizations playing in the orchestra of which the club is a part, are all about, and will come to us in increasing numbers, inform us about what we can do better together, and stay with us in a lifetime commitment to one idea—that the earth when we leave it will be at least as beautiful as the earth was when we saw it the first time.

The directors rejected this idea, which was not a surprise. A new handbook, and a fine one, appeared early in 1989, without using these words or this idea. The Rachel Carson Fund remains intact, earning interest. The opportunity to honor her and replenish the funds may knock again. I hope so.

IRA GABRIELSON

GIVE THE BOOK A SHORT TITLE, *GABE*. It probably will be a long book. But get it written! Year after year I made this plea that someone get going on a biography of Ira N. Gabrielson, then president of the Wildlife Management Institute. I did my pleading at the North American Wildlife and Conservation Conference, convened annually by the institute. The conferees assemble in March every other year in Washington, D.C., and every other other year in whatever city needs it most.

My plea failed, perhaps because I made it at the reception following the annual banquet, where what was stimulated was not always the memory. His biography was certainly deserved, and he was not getting any younger, nor were the people who knew the stories about him that he might have forgotten or been too modest to reveal. So far as I knew then or know now, there was no oral history, which is sad in itself. It is unfortunate that few if any foundations are deeply enough interested in history to correct such oversights as the failure to track down Gabe's. But why worry about oral history?

Children will always have trouble remembering their parents' early years. Employers will have forgotten or have departed. Spouses, other contemporaries, and colleagues are mortal. Employees may suffer from damaged objectivity. Neighbors are likely to be unreliable. News stories will probably have been overedited by people more concerned about space than about facts. How else could there be so many errors in any story you yourself know the facts about? Television and radio interviews will have disappeared into outer space or from archives. FBI and CIA files are probably just piles of undocumented, unevaluated, uninterpreted data. Minutes of meetings omit what was off the record and remember only what the secretary chooses to remember, and hardly more accurately. There are no attics full of trunks containing old letters anymore. Telephone calls are not supposed to be recorded. Hardly anyone makes good notes of casual meetings and conversations. You are not supposed to have pencil and paper in evidence at mealtimes at, for example, the Cosmos Club in Washington, the Century Club in New York, or the Bohemian Club in San Francisco. And the biographer who shows up late may be more interested in taking subjects apart posthumously than in putting them together. The best you have is what close friends or associates remember before Mr. Alzheimer intervenes.

Carefully planned oral histories are in order, and all too rare. We will not know, therefore, what we ought to know about Gabe. He left before John McPhee or Kenneth Brower could talk to him, or at least talk to Pink Gutermuth, his closest associate in the Wildlife Management Institute.

If only I remembered more about Gabe! He was Mr. Conservation for decades and we need far more than my pitiful fragments.

Not too mindful of calories, Gabe occupied quite a bit of space. So did his smile, even if he were telling you off (the smile made it easier to take). He was a major cohesive force when it came to keeping the game and nongame people from each others' throats. He did not hesitate to lecture hunters about the danger of trying to hunt in the national parks. Try that, he would say, and you will have all the women's and garden clubs on your back and they'll win.

The WMI banquets, as long as I attended them—twenty-five years or so—had a head table two or three miles long, two tiers deep. Gabe loved to introduce the leaders of the scores of conservation organizations represented there. After that there would be one speech, the introduction of the annual recipient of the Aldo Leopold Medal, the institute's highest award. Secrecy preceded the award, and the introducer would begin with the least known clues and contrive to keep up the suspense as long as possible. Following the standing ovation and a few words of thanks by the medalist, there would be nothing but entertainment. Nothing, that is, but a further reception, for a few dozen of the quietly invited, in Gabe's command post. As executive director of the Sierra Club, and later as president of Friends of the Earth, I enjoyed those receptions, always renewing my plea that the institute get someone on Gabe's biography. We would try, some of us, to get some other business done. On one occasion I thought I had interested some visiting Chinese in forming Friends of the Earth in China. They didn't. One of my brighter moves was to ask Bruce Kilgore to accompany me when he and I were both working for the Sierra Club. He stayed on the soft stuff and made better mental notes than I did. After all, I rationalized, I had no real responsibilities on the following Wednesday's closing sessions and camaraderie was absolutely essential. I gave it second place, however, in 1954, when Gabe gave me the opportunity in New York City to give the closing talk at the conference.

I visited Gabe's home in Virginia only once, seeing not much of his house but a great deal of his garden, of which he was very proud. He enjoyed experimenting with ways to control interlopers in his garden. He may have called them weeds, but I wouldn't call them that. Thinking teleologically, I prefer to call them the soil's device for overcoming abuse by humans as rapidly as possible.

What I prefer to remember is Gabe in his command post, high atop whatever hotel was housing the wildlife conference. It was always a roomy suite with a well-stocked bar that would open not too soon before lunch. Gabe was there, as far as I could determine, whenever he did not have to appear somewhere else, and not just for the days of the wildlife conference, but also during the preceding annual meeting of the National Wildlife Federation, which for many years was back-to-back with the wildlife conference.

The protocol, as far as I could determine it, was for various leaders to be invited, or ask to be invited, to meet with Gabe a few at a time. The sessions were carefully scheduled, and one group knew, as a new group arrived, that it was time to depart.

For several years, my special mission was to gather Alaska leaders together for a session with Gabe on that year's strategy for Alaska. There would be a dozen or so, and I'd spot them as they showed up at the conference and tell them that year's day and hour for meeting Gabe in the CP. Alaska is a lot better off than it would have been thanks to the cohesiveness he built there. So are a lot of other places and species.

When a session's departure time came, there was no feeling of a bum's rush to make room for the new group. Gabe had a way of making you feel he didn't want you to go. I didn't want him to, either.

Newton B. Drury

Grown Men Don't Cry, but in 1940 I was not all that grown and could be excused. The occasion for a sudden burst, quickly controlled, was a very brief notice in The *San Francisco Chronicle*. Newton B. Drury had been appointed as director of the National Park Service. I was overwhelmed that something so good for the national parks could actually have happened.

I had not been very close to him, but for several years I had been close enough to believe that this was the beginning of a new era. We would not always agree, which is just as well. A world in which everyone agrees would be monotonous indeed. Disagreements or not, my feelings about what Newton did for us welled up in still another obituary I wrote for *Not Man Apart*. To all older people is given, I fear, the obligation to remember what they can of their slightly older friends:

SPEAKING PRIVATELY, as director of the National Park Service, to a group of eight Sierra Club directors, Newton Drury once said: "We have no money; we can do no harm."

That would seem to be a strange remark, coming from a man who, as one of the founders of the Save-the-Redwoods League in 1919, was key to the league's raising twenty-six million dollars to save the redwoods. But his remark epitomized his attitude toward what perceptive people ought to find unharmed in the primeval national parks, as opposed to what could be bought and brought in.

Newton Drury understood what parks were all about as Gifford Pinchot did not and John Muir did. Pinchot was the utilizationist, Muir the preservationist, and Drury the preservationist's preservationist before the word was muddied.

"If we are going to succeed in preserving the greatness of the national parks," Drury once wrote, "they must be held inviolate. They represent the last stand of primitive America. If we are going to whittle away at them, we should recognize, at the very beginning, that all such whittlings are cumulative and that the end result will be mediocrity. Greatness will be gone."

Drury's thinking paralleled that of Frederick Law Olmsted, dean of America's landscape architects, in his succinct statement of the national-park idea before there was a national park. Recuperating from his work in establishing Central Park, Olmsted was in Yosemite just after Lincoln signed the legislation setting it aside as a park to be administered for the nation by California. In 1865, Olmsted said that the first requirement was to protect the scenery and restrict within the narrowest limits the necessary accommodation of visitors. Structures could not detract from the dignity of the scenery. "In permitting the sacrifice of anything that would be of the slightest value to future visitors," he wrote, "to the convenience, bad taste, playfulness, carelessness, or wanton destructiveness of present visitors we probably yield in each case the interest of uncounted millions to the selfishness of a few."

I got my first glimmer of what this philosophy meant in the Save-the-Redwoods League's first year. My father joined and photographs of redwoods the league wished to save were all over the house. It may well have been their beauty that bent this twig. It was almost two decades later before I knew how important Newton and Aubrey Drury's work was toward saving redwoods and strengthening California's state parks. Perhaps Newton's clearest imprint is that lack of imprint in the Point Lobos State Reserve, one of the best preserved pieces of land that ever survived in a tourist mecca. I remember arranging an evening meeting where he could talk to Sierra Club members about all this—an evening with small attendance, but at which the audience attended every word.

By 1951 his philosophy had got him into trouble. The Bureau of Reclamation, then the power broker in the Department of the Interior, had ideas about Dinosaur National Monument that were as repugnant to Newton as they would have been to Olmsted. Director Drury objected and Secretary of the Interior Oscar Chapman backed the bureau and sought another head for the National Park Service. The bureau budgeted twenty-one million dollars for its recreational development of its planned Dinosaur reservoirs and the Park Service subsided into silence. "Dinosaur is a dead duck," Newton said and went on to other opportunities. Dinosaur was saved by people outside the Park Service whose understanding of parks he had nurtured. Governor Earl Warren of California quickly appointed him head of California's Division of Beaches and Parks. When mandatory retirement ended his splendid work in that office, he returned to the Save-the-Redwoods League, preserving things as vigorously as ever.

In February 1977, Richard Kauffman and Friends of the Earth presented a copy of *Headlands* to Newton, and I was pleased to be the bearer of the book that paid tribute to his work in saving those Point Lobos headlands. His wife Elizabeth had died within four months of what would have been their fifty-ninth anniversary, and the loss was overwhelming. But he continued to do all he could for his redwoods, until a fall and its consequences were more than he could recover from, and the career ended of a preservationist whose achievements are not likely to be equaled.

The tribute to Newton Drury that may serve best is all those redwoods that still fill the sky, thanks to him, and may go on doing that for millennia.

Not Man Apart, February 1979

As I look back on it all, and on the several things Newton Drury did that I do not approve of, I come back to the old questions: Where was he coming from? That I felt good about. What was driving him? That I didn't. I am a little more careful, as I work my way through my seventies, about assessing blame. Why, for example, was Newton Drury willing to concede too much of the primeval forests on the Olympic Peninsula to timber interests? In all likelihood, because enough public support had not developed for their preservation. Why had he not helped that support develop? I don't know. But I can imagine that it is easier, on the outside, to say the ball was in his court than to admit that the ball may very likely have been in ours.

I'll remember him for what he did for preservation–intently enough that Horace Albright said of Newton: he was so pure that he insisted tourists leave their contraceptives at the gate when they entered a national park. I never told this story to Newton, nor did I ask whether he had made up a similar one about Horace. What they did for the national-park idea in their own way and time is not what I would have done in mine were I to have had the opportunity. I do remember that Stewart Udall, when he was Secretary of the Interior and I was pressuring him about national-park problems, said in jest that he would like to hire me and shut me up.

"I'm running down," Newton told me when he was eighty-eight–the last time we saw each other. He knew how much, overall, I admired his lifetime achievements. For the first time and last time we hugged.

John P. Saylor

Some People, I suppose, learn to feel relaxed in and around the corridors of Capitol Hill. I never did and never will, and feel a bit suspicious about people who relax there easily. They either have too big a lobbying budget, meaning that they are not environmentalists or, if they are, they're too prone to trading or too fond of trade-offs. In my view, we elect people to compromise because the legislative process requires that they seek the best balance they can among conflicting views and demands. We don't hire nongovernmental people to compromise, but to stand firm and thus enable the legislator, if compromise is necessary, to get the best possible deal.

I am not saying this in a vacuum. I am protesting what I see too much of–premature compromising that is passed off as professionalism.

Congressman John P. Saylor made his compromises when he felt he had to and would not tolerate our going the least bit soft, thus making where he wanted to go a harder place to get to.

Perhaps it was this attitude of his that made his office the place on the Hill I felt easiest in. It was a little like dropping in for confession. It was also, strangely enough, a little like coming by as a representative of the casting director. You can infer why from the obituary I wrote for *Not Man Apart*. Before his trip down the rivers of Dinosaur National Monument, I think he was a pretty conservative Republican. When the rivers converted him to a liberal Republican, we did our best to thank, praise, and honor him for his role and thus encourage him never to leave it.

SOME PEOPLE HAVE GREAT TREES and cities named in their memory, or build pyramids or other monuments to mark where they have been. John Saylor didn't build a monument; he saved one. And if something is to be named in his honor, it should not be a tree but a system. The monument is Dinosaur National Monument, still damless and intact, thanks to his leadership in Congress. The system is the National Wilderness Preservation System. Without his dynamic leadership, in combination with the devoted, inspired work of the late Howard Zahniser of The Wilderness Society, the Wilderness Act of 1964 would surely never have become law.

In the battle to save Dinosaur National Monument from the Bureau of Reclamation's proposed Echo Park and Split Mountain dams, one of the favorite arguments of the bureau and its Upper Colorado Basin supporters was that river travel through the monument on the Yampa and Green rivers was only for people with a strong death wish. Two people who led the way in unhooking this kind of argument were Harold Bradley and John Saylor. In 1952, when Harold Bradley was a mere seventy-four, he took a large assortment of his children and grandchildren on a Dinosaur boat trip. Their trip inspired a series of Sierra Club river trips. These trips built a powerful constituency of people who knew what they were talking about because they had been there.

Almost all of them got a glimpse of the late Bus Hatch, veteran riverman. Hatch had many perceptions that were important to all who love wild rivers. Notable among those perceptions was one about a man he got to know briefly on the river in 1952. He wrote, "I think Congressman Saylor is going to help us out." Never did the word "help" have so much territory to cover.

Who knows what started John Saylor's driving force for a substantial preservation quotient in the conservation movement? Perhaps the late Joseph W. Penfold, staunch leader for decades of Izaak Walton League conservation, put a finger on it. Joe and one of his young sons were along, as was Bus Hatch, when John Saylor took John Phillips II down the Yampa. What the Dinosaur canyons did to those two boys, Joe said later, really got to John, and he never got over it.

Joe, Howard Zahniser, and I found during the decade between our first leaning heavily on John Saylor and Zahnie's untimely death, that our paths shared the same right-of-way repeatedly. Again and again, we would have councils of conservation war in the Cosmos Club, a principal way station in that right-of-way. Again and again, we would meet by chance or intent in the other principal way station—John Saylor's office.

There is nothing uncommon about this relationship, I suppose, but it becomes extraordinary when it goes on for two decades and when you count up the conservation victories that simply would not have happened without John Saylor's counsel, encouragement, and lovingkindness.

Our efforts to coordinate things didn't always work. We would be planning on Saylor's questions at critical hearings, upon his rescuing us from being overbadgered by the various members of the House Committee on Interior and Insular Affairs who never understood how anything could ever take precedence over the orderly eradication of wilderness. Mr. Saylor would be delayed in Johnstown or somewhere, and we would feel very alone in a withering crossfire. When we next met, and he saw the anxiety in our eyes, he explained how he handled the problem his way, if not ours. We remember the times when we wanted to rest weary feet or heads in his office and he would say, "We're not going to save anything sitting here talking about it. Get out and do your missionary work!"

You expect the most from those who have failed you least. Usually they are the busiest people. Busy because they know how to get things done and thus have unceasing demands on their help. John Saylor could become deeply occupied, and not just busy, in an Interior Committee hearing. He was big in scope, in presence, and in a full six-foot-three stature. When John Saylor bore down on a witness who required the searching questions—such as a U.S. Commissioner of Reclamation or his secretaries, undersecretaries, and assistant secretaries and the platoons of technicians determined to dam something—the voice rose, stentorian vibrations set in, the bemused face became stern, and John Saylor was adducing evidence the agencies had not really intended ever to let out. When you don't want the truth out, you have to invent substitutes for the truth. John Saylor could spot a truth substitute a mile away.

***Not Man Apart,* 1973**

One of my special pleasures, on election eves from 1954 to 1972, was to call John's Johnstown home from our house in Berkeley to see how well he had done. He never missed, and the joyous background sound of revelry confirmed his success. One of the reasons, he once explained to us, was what he told his conservative supporters: "If you want to be represented by a Democrat, that's what you'll have if I go conservative."

The moral of this story? Never forget to thank John Saylor, or whoever it may be, for good things done for the Earth.

LEE METCALF

IN NEPAL, IT IS SAID, there are two sins—embarrassing someone and making a child cry. Thanks to Lee Metcalf, I came very close to committing sin. I made a member of Congress cry. It was Gracie Pfost, of Idaho, and because her office was close to Lee Metcalf's, she was invited over to see my film. I wasn't there. Howard Zahniser was showing it. He had arranged somehow to rent a continuous 16-mm projector, and a film I had made for the campaign to save Dinosaur National Monument was in the projector's loop. Somehow, when you showed the eleven minutes of *Two Yosemites* it was ready to show again, without rewinding. I still haven't figured out how it worked, and it was equally puzzling to the members of Congress Zahnie was showing it to.

He would not ask whether he could show the member a film. That would surely bring a "no." He just asked for an appointment and, with typical Zahniser self-effacing boldness, would wheel the projector in and so fascinate his audience with its simple complexity that he could have the film under way before anyone could say, "I object!"

The film was intended to sadden the viewer about the unnecessary loss of the second yosemite in Yosemite National Park—Hetch Hetchy Valley. Its loss grieved John Muir, perhaps fatally. We didn't want the same thing to happen to Echo Park. It shouldn't ever and it hasn't yet.

Attending a wilderness conference in Great Falls in December 1989, I found that Lee Metcalf was the senator the loss of whom Montanans grieve most. *Not Man Apart* carried the obituary I wrote about him:

TESTIFYING BEFORE COMMITTEES of Congress can be harrowing, especially if there is no friend among the members seated high above you and there is inquisition in the wind, as for example, when only the reclamationists are on hand and you are speaking in opposition to a favorite dam proposal. If, however, there is a friend up there—just one—things are different. Your voice steadies, your manner eases, and your hopes rise. There will be good questions to emphasize the points you did not stress well enough.

That is the way things were if you were a conservationist—or, subsequently, an environmentalist—testifying before any committee on which Lee Metcalf served, as a congressman from 1952 to 1960, and as a senator from that year's election until his untimely death, just a few weeks short of his sixty-seventh birthday.

Lee Metcalf was born in Montana, spent his undergraduate days out of the state at Stanford, his military days in a tank destroyer unit, was admitted to the bar in 1936, lobbied the Montana legislature briefly, served as assistant attorney general for four years and as associate justice of the Montana Supreme Court for six, before he went to Congress.

It was in the House of Representatives, testifying against the proposed dams in Dinosaur National Monument, that I first encountered him. He was the friend on the Democratic side of the Committee on Interior and Insular Affairs, an ally every bit as helpful as was John Saylor on the Republican side. And not just in the committee room. There were long sessions in his office and with his friendly staff, in which I began to learn about the habits of the Columbia River and what ought, and ought not, be done to it by the Corps of Engineers and the Bureau of Reclamation. Persuasive sessions, both ways. I found myself writing an article in favor of a dam–the proposed Paradise Dam on the Clark Fork, to save it from underdevelopment at the hands of the Montana Power Company that could lead to a revival of plans to build Glacier View Dam in Glacier National Park.

In his first term as congressman, he was cited for distinguished service to conservation by five national conservation organizations. He became a powerful supporter of the Wilderness Bill, from its introduction June 7, 1956, by Hubert Humphrey, until it was signed into law by Lyndon Johnson on September 3, 1964.

Lee Metcalf did not live to see the completion–to add his own great strength to assure maximum success in attempts to save the greatest wilderness under this nation's jurisdiction–Alaska. His unfinished agenda is a long one in many fields of government. He had no time to rest on his oars. He had planned on some rest but missed out, and joined the lengthening list of wilderness heroes whose joy concerning the efforts for wilderness was in knowing it would survive them.

May some part of that wilderness, commemorating what Lee Metcalf has done, bear his name!

***Not Man Apart,* 1978**

HOWARD ZAHNISER

CRASHING BASKETBALL GAMES was never my forte, but Howard Zahniser wanted me to watch his son Matthias play one night in Washington and neither of us had tickets. When we reached the gym's ticket-taker, Zahnie said, "Wait here." In no time at all, by some unknown route, he was inside, behind the ticket-taker, and inviting me in. He never explained how he did it. Nor did he explain how, when he was in some minor financial difficulty, he solved his problem by buying a Buick convertible. Although I never learned how to crash games, some people who know me will allege that I managed to pick up some of his financial acumen. Certainly, I did pick up some far more important tips. Zahnie was my principal coach in the conservation business.

One thing I learned early was that it costs a lot less to telephone than to write letters. Penny-pinchers were forever telling me how cheap postage stamps were. Zahnie and I knew exactly what you had to pay for them, but we also knew what they cost. Although letters arrived far more promptly than they do now, throughout the fourteen years we worked together they never arrived soon enough for what we needed. Letters have a purpose, of course. You can read them over as often as you need to. They make a paper trail and you can use them in court, enter them in hearings, carry on a romance, blackmail people, or be reminded of the wonderful days of long ago.

But they are worthless if you need instant response, or assurance right now that you have not been misunderstood, perhaps by typing "not" instead of "now." Or realization that you have not been agreed with, and need to revector your presentation. Or confirmation that the person upstairs who is "not in today" really is in but is avoiding you. The list of things a telephone will let you know quickly and a letter may never let you know is a long list. End the list with some more things a postage stamp will never tell you, whatever its cost: the sound of a familiar human voice, or the sound of silence while a friend seeks words, or the anguish or laughter in a voice. Besides, by the time this book gets to your eyes, who knows how much more they will be asking for postage?

So Zahnie and I talked on the telephone, in the aggregate, for a good month of minutes when he was in his Washington office or Bethesda home and I was in San Francisco or Berkeley. We would never have kept dams out of Dinosaur National Monument without the telephone, and certainly it would have been far more difficult to establish the National Wilderness Preservation System.

Some day I will find a way to transfer the various kinds of recording of our telephone conversations to modern audiocassettes and see which of them ought to be transcribed—for the book about Zahnie that must be written but which, so far as I know, is on no one's agenda. The environmental movement needs that book badly.

Naturally, there will be far more than excerpts of telephone calls in it. One essential category of information would be what the walls of the Cosmos Club heard Zahnie say. I was one of the privileged many who were able to stay there not as a member, which I never got around to trying to be, but as Zahnie's guest. Between 1954 and 1964 I probably stayed there a total of six months. The club was founded in 1869 by John Wesley Powell to accommodate visiting scientists he thought should play a major role in what the federal government was up to. By the time I arrived, not as a scientist but as a sciolist with full portfolio, the Cosmos Club had long since been moved to the old Sumner Welles mansion, to which spare but multitudinous sleeping quarters had been added.

It was in the far corner of the mansion's high-ceilinged grand ballroom that we fortified ourselves for lunch and devised and revised strategies and tactics. Zahnie traditionally ordered a Rob Roy. He never explained why he preferred scotch to bourbon. Heeding the advice of my doctor, Stewart Kimball, I sought the relaxation afforded by bourbon and soda, and will claim, without fear of contradiction, that I drowned the ulcer Stewart had diagnosed with bourbon. He did not diagnose it with bourbon, much preferring varietal wines of his own making. I drowned it with bourbon, this being my pre-Tanqueray period.

We were seldom alone in our far corner. Zahnie knew well which people to include in our plotting. We would prepare for our sessions as well as we could in Zahnie's office on the second floor at 2144 P Street, downstairs from Fred Packard's National Parks Association office. I was always happy to walk the block and a half to the Cosmos Club so that our sessions would not be so often interrupted by Zahnie's prolonged sessions on the telephone. I couldn't object, considering how much of his telephone time I usurped. I did, however, relish the club's respite from the telephone.

What Zahnie supplied skillfully and generously, and no one since has provided nearly so well, is glue in the conservation movement. He was naturally eager to have The Wilderness Society grow and prosper, but he was determined that it was wilderness he was there to save, not the society. So it was that his ideas for a national wilderness system, derived from Benton MacKaye's earlier suggestions, were ideas to share, not to keep close to his chest. One of the essential steps toward informing the public about wilderness preservation was a series of biennial wilderness conferences. The usual conservation executive would make sure that it was his own organization that would undertake the series and reap the public relations benefits. Not Zahnie. He talked the Sierra Club into undertaking the task, and gave the club every assistance he could in making the conferences successful. As a result of this gesture, he engaged the growing energy of the Sierra Club in carrying out the task John Muir had founded it to carry out, but which it was almost forgetting. The series of Sierra Club biennial conferences, and the books born of their proceedings, reached out to the fields of medicine, engineering, planning, forestry, religion, politics, law, and ecology, to name a few.

If the Sierra Club could help that much, who else? With Zahnie's gentle persuasion, the Federation of Western Outdoor Clubs undertook its own biennial wilderness conferences in alternate years. It was at the first of the FWOC conferences that Zahnie presented his first draft of the Wilderness Bill to the public. But not until he had, with typical deliberateness and attention to detail, told the audience of his, Joe Penfold's, and my encounter with a dead horse. The three of us were walking from his office to the Cosmos Club for dinner and, to our surprise, came upon a dead horse halfway through the block from P Street to Massachusetts Avenue. A distraught man beside the horse begged for our assistance. He wanted us to help him get the dead horse upstairs into his house, right there on Twenty-second Street, in front of which the horse had died.

It was no easy task. It wasn't a huge workhorse, but it was very heavy. Zahnie, with a heart condition, couldn't apply as much energy as he would have liked to, so he was at the upstairs end of the portage.

You can imagine how hard it was to get a horse up to the front door and through it. But that wasn't enough. He wanted us to take the horse into the house–indeed, into the bathroom, and put it in the bathtub.

Once you get involved in a situation like this, it is difficult to back out. We didn't, and after some extremely difficult maneuvering, we succeeded. It was a tight fit, but the horse was in the tub.

We felt, by now, that we were owed an explanation.

"Why, for the love of the Lord, did you ask us to do this?" Of course, anyone with due intelligence would have asked the question sooner. We hadn't, but by now couldn't let the matter rest without asking.

"Well," he answered, looking a bit abashed, "it's this way:

"I share this house with a good friend. He is out of town now, but he will be home tonight. He's a good man, and for the most part we get along well. But he is constantly doing something that at first only bothered me, but as time went by it really got to me, and I knew I must do something to break this terrible habit of his."

"What was this horrible habit?" you might ask, and we did.

"Well, it's a simple one, but it has reached a point where I can't take it anymore. Almost invariably, when I try to make conversation and tell him something that I've run into and think might interest him, he deflates me by saying, 'I know.' No matter what I say, there is always this damned 'I know.' 'Yeah, I know.'

"So he is coming home tonight. And I am going to be sitting in the living room, reading. And because it has been a long trip, the first thing he is going to do is go to the bathroom. And he is going to come charging out of the bathroom to tell me, 'There's a dead horse in the bathtub!'

"And I'm going to smile and say, 'I know.' "

The Wilderness Bill that Zahnie then revealed, once the audience had got the shaggy dog out of the auditorium and had settled back, was a long way from being enacted into law. Although Zahnie didn't tell his audience about it, he had learned right at the start how arduous the task would be. He had wanted–indeed, expected–help from the Forest Service in moving the proposal forward. After all, the founder of The Wilderness Society, Robert Marshall, had been the strongest of advocates of wilderness preservation. At the time of his death in 1939, he served as chief of recreation and lands in the service. The Wilderness Society itself, through Marshall and through Aldo Leopold, had intentionally tied itself closely to the Forest Service, to be its nongovernmental supporter and watchdog, even as the National Parks Association had tied itself to the National Park Service.

Therefore, the first government agency that Zahnie showed his Wilderness Bill draft to was the Forest Service, through its then chief of recreation and lands, John Sieker. Zahnie expected friendly suggestions. The next day, before Zahnie heard a word from Mr. Sieker, mimeographed copies of the draft were in the hands of the principal opponents of wilderness the Forest Service dealt with.

This was the first of many shocks, and they wore on Zahnie's health if not on his patience. Next time around I am going to remember that, and his friendly diligence, and copy him as best I can, with full attribution. I will especially try to remember his quiet reply to the anti-wilderness executive secretary of the American Forestry Association, who had accused him of being emotional: "I am impressed by the passion with which you accuse me of emotionalism."

Two hurdles Zahnie would rather not have had to encounter were the attempts to establish a North Cascades National Park and the Outdoor Recreation Resources Review Commission. He thought that they diluted the effort needed for success with the Wilderness Bill. Both attempts added to the Park Service/Forest Service rivalry he was trying to cool, which cooled our relationship; I was, and stubbornly remained, a staunch advocate of all three. Fortunately, all three efforts succeeded. And we both survived the unhappiness of the disagreement.

Zahnie's patience had two major trials that diligence could not overcome. Before Congressman Wayne Aspinall of Colorado would let the Wilderness Bill out of his House Interior Committee, some drastic compromises had to be accepted. One was the twenty-year extension, to 1984, of the time miners would be allowed to make claims in wilderness. The other, more painful, was the elimination of the Wilderness Council Zahnie had very much wanted to see created by the legislation. That council would have had the authority to observe and report regularly to the public on what was happening in the wilderness in all the various federal jurisdictions—National Park Service, U.S. Forest Service, Fish and Wildlife Service, and Bureau of Land Management. From his own governmental experience, Zahnie knew how important that function of the council would be. The forces—private and public—that still had hopes of invading wilderness knew what a barrier to their schemes such a council would be, and they had the financial strength and friends in Congress to kill it.

Zahnie's heart frightened him once, slowing him down. He was still able, however, to get into the wilderness itself, and one of the scenes I am fond of in the Sierra Club film, *Wilderness Alps of Stehekin,* is of Zahnie and his family. They are plodding, at Zahnie's pace, up the trail at White Pass for a look at Glacier Peak. I never learned what his pace was before he had his heart problem, and was not curious enough to ask about the trips he took when he worked as an editor for the old U.S. Biological Survey. But from my fourteen years of knowing Zahnie, I know one trip he never took. An ego trip. I keep hoping his example will some day rub off on me.

The National Wilderness Preservation System became law in September 1964, when President Lyndon Johnson put his signature on it in the Rose Garden. Mardie Murie, widow of Olaus Murie, one of the act's chief advocates, was there. So was Alice Zahniser, who was widowed five months before when Zahnie died suddenly of a massive heart attack.

The Wilderness System itself will always be a most fitting memorial to its principal architect. We should remember his admonition that its passage constitutes a job description for all of us, the job being to make sure that the system exists not just in the law, but on the land. The sooner the rest of us resurrect the Wilderness Council idea and get a president's signature on it, creating the body that will help people accomplish that ultimate goal, the better Zahnie's memory will be served.

William O. Douglas

It Was Thanks to Howard Zahniser that I met William O. Douglas – one hero of mine introducing me to another. I wrote about my dealings with him in *NMA:*

From All Who Knew William Orville Douglas, who served the United States on its Supreme Court longer than anyone else, must come the story that he almost told. Some months before his death I was asked by the Regional Oral History Office of the Bancroft Library, Berkeley, to persuade Bill Douglas to consent to a series of interviews on his conservation experiences. Through the good offices of his wife, Cathleen, I succeeded and, with delight, passed the word on. The effort began, but it was too much. The ravages of the stroke he had suffered were too severe. It was too hard for words to tell what his brain knew.

So the question now is, who remembers? And what can we do so that the quality of this man's love for the earth will not be forgotten?

Perhaps it will help if I tell a little of what I remember, and start the flow in the minds of those who knew Justice Douglas far better. Let us gather together what we know and let it be known. And let us go beyond that and establish the William O. Douglas Prize. Remember how the Nobel Prize began, and all the wide-ranging stimulation that has emanated from that idea; a green-ribbon committee could award William O. Douglas Prizes for the finest achievements in many fields toward the renaissance of a conservation conscience.

What Justice Douglas did in the field of law probably warrants his receiving the prize posthumously. He would also have been a serious contender in several other fields.

Entering the hallowed halls and offices of the Supreme Court building was almost as sobering as stepping inside St. Peter's, but Bill's mountain memorabilia and warmth relaxed you right away. Talk flowed easily, too easily perhaps, for me, but it was a start. Much more was to follow.

There were the walks. One when Bill was at the head of the column of some five hundred people making an anniversary walk along the C&O Canal. Helicopters with photographers made noise overhead. Other photographers appeared now and then at the head of the column, walking backwards at some peril. There was almost as crowded a walk along New York City's Croton Aqueduct. Then a quiet one along the C&O, with Bill Douglas, Grant McConnell, Charles Reich, and David Brinkley's dog, all of us trying to think of how to get the Forest Service to be less interested in logging and more interested in forests.

Topping it all was a walk in the Sierra, a pack trip starting on Reversed Creek and visiting Thousand Island Lake, Garnet Shadow, the Devil's Postpile, and the Purple Lake country. That was 1959, and he wasn't supposed to walk too far at that altitude. He tried and his second wife, Mercedes, threatened that if he didn't stop walking and board his horse, she would walk out. Dutifully he rode. I remember her letter, soon after that, warning that if we wanted to have Bill do too much, we wouldn't have him long.

We didn't listen too well and I was as guilty as any. Somehow, I was able to persuade him to serve on the Sierra Club board of directors. On one occasion I contrived, by the simple expedient of calling the airline, to find out where he was sitting on his return trip to Washington and to reserve the seat alongside. What security! I was not as chagrined as I ought to have been when he told me on the telephone that the club's director's meetings were "a cross between a mourner's bench and a ladies' sewing circle." I had a little trouble with them myself from time to time. His impatience could extend far beyond that—to Forest Service leadership and on to the broadest field of all, stewardship of the ocean.

We shared a Malta Conference, the first one on *Pacem in Maribus*. He held a small birthday party on July 1 for Lord Ritchie Calder. My wife and I were invited because it was my birthday, too. The entrée was Mediterranean whitefish from a dying sea. He observed that the entire conference seemed to be devoted to deciding who was to Balkanize and overexploit the seas, not whether anyone should.

Bill Douglas responded to countless calls. He could make a few, too. One of my greatest pleasures was to receive a brief letter describing his having attended a Ford Foundation banquet where, seated next to the foundation's director, he learned that the conservation program was about to be thoroughly reviewed and they wanted his recommendations. One could not expect a higher honor than his closing line to me: "What shall I say?"

With Robert Golden, the best ecologist on the Sierra Club staff, I set about suggesting five projects that then seemed to be taboo in foundation circles: (1) a blueprint for the economics of peaceful stability, (2) a center for the advanced study of ecosystems, (3) a plan for a reinterpretation of nature, (4) a crash program for reserving the irreplaceables, and (5) building careers in preservation. Justice Douglas presented most of the ideas in his own words, and later let me lobby the Ford Foundation with our original wording, without appreciable success. The opportunity remains to persuade current foundation members to follow through. Top achievements in each of these areas could be awarded the William O. Douglas Prize, once it is funded.

At the 1961 Wilderness Conference banquet, Bill Douglas introduced Stewart Udall, whose principal address, "Conservation in the 1960s: Action or Stalemate?" could well be repeated now, as a new decade starts with retreat. His speech included Wallace Stegner's unmatched letter on the Wilderness Idea, read in full by a Secretary of the Interior whose ecological conscience has not been matched in that office. Justice Douglas's introduction also appears in full in the Sierra Club book, *Wilderness: America's Living Heritage*. I borrowed one particular paragraph, with attribution, when speaking to a Minnesota audience recently, and Minneapolis's laughter came where San Francisco's had:

"So many of the things which are advertised as conservation are indeed destructive of it! With your permission, I will read you a little book review that I picked up that reminds me of some of these confusing things that we hear about conservation. This is a review of a book called *Lady Chatterley's Lover* that maybe you have heard about. And the book review says: 'Although written many years ago, *Lady Chatterley's Lover* has just been reissued by Grove Press, and this fictional account of the day-by-day life of an English gamekeeper is still of considerable interest to outdoor-minded readers, as it contains many passages on pheasant raising, the apprehending of poachers, ways to control vermin, and other chores and duties of the professional gamekeeper. Unfortunately, one is obliged to wade through many pages of extraneous material in order to discover and savor these sidelights on the management of a Midlands shooting estate, and in this reviewer's opinion this book cannot take the place of J.R. Miller's *Practical Gamekeeping*.' Conservation also passes under many false labels."

The false labels are around us still, especially in corporate-image advertisements serving brainwashed readers who don't have time to think. Even ubiquitous attacks on regulation masquerade as conservation. They capitalize on the ease with which people who do not like being poisoned can be led to say they hate regulating poisons. A book on corporate advertisements in this vein might be put together. Jerry Mander would be the one to edit it and the best foreword of all would have come from Bill Douglas.

But it can't now, of course, and for that loss, and a thousand others, we are all the poorer.

His sense was fully as keen on other roles in government that too often get short shrift. Just before he gave Stewart Udall the floor, and adding kindly that the lines would not apply to the secretary, he said: "I was five years in the executive branch and though I never had more than eighteen hundred people under me and only five laws to administer, I barely kept my head above water. For everyone, there are only twenty-four hours in a day. Six o'clock comes and the outgoing mail piles high. The letters are ready for signature, each prepared by somebody down in the hierarchy. There are people still in the anteroom. And one suddenly remembers that he has a seven-thirty dinner, black tie. Are those letters to be signed without being read? If they are, the faceless bureaucracy remains supreme."

In his own speech to the same wilderness conference, Justice Douglas closed with these lines:

Man's greatest mission is to preserve life, not destroy it. When the land becomes the symbol of poverty and sterility, when the wonders of creation have been destroyed, youth has no place to go but the alleys, and a blight lies across the land. . . .

We stand on the new frontier where Science and its machines threaten man. Our industrial plants and our modern conveniences have ruined many of our rivers and lakes. The roar of motors penetrates deeper and deeper into the remaining wilderness areas. Man has a constantly diminishing chance to find any retreat. . . .

Man was designed neither to be a cog *in the machine as the communists conceive him, a* statistic *as Science conceives him, nor a* consumer *as Madison Avenue views him.*

Man's pursuit of happiness, which Jefferson made a concern of government in our Declaration of Independence, must be our concern. While man needs a full rice bowl, he also needs more. His chief destiny is not to satisfy his physical needs. Man is a spiritual being. By our Bill of Rights, we have placed many of his civil rights beyond the reach of government. We need to expand our conception of liberty, enlarge his individual rights, and give them priority over Science.

Those Human Rights include the right to put one's face in clear, pure water, to discover the wonders of sphagnum moss, and to hear the song of whippoorwills at dawn in a forest where the wilderness bowl is unbroken.

For this understanding, and so much more, we are all the richer.

***Not Man Apart,* March 1980**

DICK AND DORIS LEONARD

RICHARD MANNING LEONARD was born October 22, 1908, in the Philippines. Doris Corcoran, his secretary and soon-to-be wife, was born in the United States November 11 of that year. Theirs is one of the abiding friendships of my life, and for many years theirs was my second home.

I am reminded of that closeness at the moment. It is October 12, 1989. We have just left Shiprock behind us. As our flight from Oakland to Dallas passed over the remarkable and still unspoiled canyons of the upper Escalante River, then proceeded north of Monument Valley, I knew that Shiprock—to the Navajo a great bird, its basalt wings outspread—would soon be under us, and there it was, conveniently to starboard, right below my window seat. I had mentioned its imminence to the cabin attendant and she told the captain. As we were passing over it, he spoke on the public address system, pointed Shiprock out, told of its geological past, and added: "By coincidence, we have David Brower on board. He was the first person to climb Shiprock, and did it just fifty years ago today." Passengers clapped and I was awarded two glasses of wine.

Dick Leonard found our route up Shiprock but was not on the climb. He was attending a meeting, just out of reach, of National Park Service officials. He had hoped to climb with us, and had gathered photographs, ground and air, over which we pored in his apartment facing Oakland's Lake Merritt. I say he found the route; I think he did. Maybe it was I. My mind, like his, has minor lapses. As I have already revealed, he was uncertain in 1934 about what phase of the moon was required for an eclipse. In 1935 he thought I suffered from snow blindness on Mount Waddington because I wasn't wearing sunglasses. We were both wearing them, and we both went snow-blind—but not seriously. We played chess in our tent for the day it took us to recover.

Dick won the chess games, I am sure. I dabbled at chess. He never dabbles at anything. Things would have been vastly different for me had he dabbled just a little. He didn't when he sponsored my application to join the Sierra Club in 1933, or when, 1967–69, he wrote the pink slip making it no longer necessary for me to be executive director of the club. Had he dabbled, where would I be now?

Soon after I joined the club, Dick was coaching my first attempt to rappel. I was atop a cliff I didn't like at all, hanging onto a rope I didn't believe in, and he had to urge me to be bold and go over the brink. We were at Grizzly Caves, one of the Berkeley rocks used for climbing practice. Since 1932 people have been learning there how to apply techniques exported from the Appalachian Mountain Club to the Sierra Club through the efforts of Robert Lindley Murray Underhill. His mountaineering knowledge came from the Alps via Boston. Francis Farquhar, interested in informing the heathen westerners of Bostonian craft, persuaded Bob Underhill to go on a Sierra Club High Trip and explain the use and management of the rope to us. Dick Leonard took it from there. His genius improved upon Underhill's, and thenceforth we were explaining things to Boston.

Dick started the Cragmont Climbing Club in 1932, and just before I joined the club in 1933, the San Francisco Bay Chapter accepted rock-climbing as an authorized activity. In 1989 the insurance industry, in its abiding ignorance and with its exorbitant rates, squelched the effort to teach people to climb safely. Had the insurance industry been at work two millennia ago, there would be no Good Samaritans. Liability coverage would not have been available and damaged people would have had to suffer on their own. In a typical surge of energy, Dick catalogued the unclimbed peaks of the Sierra. I joined the effort and did my best to shorten the list. He had already shortened it by making the first ascent, along with Bestor Robinson and Jules Eichorn, of Yosemite's Higher Cathedral Spire, and shortly thereafter the Lower Cathedral Spire. Dick and I climbed together often on the Berkeley and nearby rocks, and with Raffi Bedayn, also of Shiprock, made the first ascent of the east face of Glacier Point in Yosemite, surely one of our happiest climbs. Unlike Dick, I did not squeeze tennis balls between classes to strengthen my climbing fingers. I wasn't that involved in classes. Nor did I ever use a piton for a spoon or open a can of tomato juice, and do it joyously, with the ball end of a ball-peen hammer. (Fortunately, we were outdoors at the time.) I could, however, imitate precisely his attempt to yodel, a harmless manifestation of hysteria. He called it his coyote call, never quite realizing how demeaning it was to coyotes.

We shared much more than snow blindness on Mount Waddington. Both of us opposed Bestor Robinson's strategy for the attempt on the higher summit, and both of us were unsuccessful. Both of us managed to gain weight on the expedition, an unprecedented feat. When the Waddington expedition was over and Dick sent me the album of his photographs, asking which I wanted, I wanted the whole album, and am delighted to have it still. When he read my Waddington story, he objected to my criticism of the lumber industry, with its "rafts of plunder in tow." I left it out, having no idea at the time how much more disastrous plundering of British Columbia's forests lay ahead.

It took Dick a while to make up his own mind about a career. He had and still has a deep interest in chemistry and botany. But Boalt Hall, at the University of California, Berkeley, won out, and by Shiprock time, the bar he had been admitted to was earning him ten thousand dollars a year, an amount I thought was fabulous. I don't think he thought so. I am sure there have been many high points in his legal career. I know of two.

First, there was the Echo Lake avalanche. Summer homes were wiped out. The owners' insurance policies said nothing about avalanches but provided protection against wind damage. Dick, with his mountaineering knowledge, pointed out that in avalanches of dry powder snow it is not the snow that hurts, but the tremendous wind that precedes it. The insurance companies paid up, complaining that Dick had all the experts on his side.

Second was a large farm on the San Francisco Peninsula, inhabited by a university—Stanford. I suppose there were some legal specifications requiring that the farmlike setting be maintained in perpetuity. Perpetuity is such a long period of time that ninety-nine years is a hardly significant part of it, so ninety-nine-year leases were created to provide the handsome revenue Stanford needed and to allow, on the farm, the planting of the seeds of the industries, including Varian Associates, of Silicon Valley.

Dick helped me get on committees as well as climbs and High Trips. Following their marriage in 1934, Dick and Doris were staunch supporters of this sophomore dropout. When I was jobless after being fired in Yosemite, Dick found odd jobs for me to do, as did Francis Farquhar. It was Dick who wrote, when I was not enthusiastic enough about some of the jobs, that I shunned whatever was not easy, interesting, or glamorous, a talent of mine that Anne frequently reminds me of.

Nevertheless, when the threat of the draft was two weeks away, Dick arranged for the telegram to be sent by the adjutant general assigning me to mountain training as an enlisted man and as an officer, should I ever become one. It was on Dick (and on Bestor Robinson and Einar Nilsson, frequent ski-mountaineering companion and one-time treasurer of the club) that I unloaded my mountain-training ideas and complaints on frequent weekend leaves I took in Washington. We did not complain about our nylon ropes; but for Dick, we would not have had them.

In 1952 Dick carried the ball when, had he not, I would not have become the club's first executive director. Surely that was enough. Not for Dick. When he was club president and I the new executive director, the duty of defending Dinosaur National Monument sent me on protracted trips to Washington. Dick, in addition to his professional duties as a busy practicing attorney, happily took on the club duties I was not on hand to cover.

So whether I was looking for new peaks to climb, needing a job as an assistant leader on the club's High Trips, co-filming and then producing the club's first film, *Sky-Land Trails of the Kings,* or was needing someone to praise my cinematography or support the efforts to keep all roads out of the new Kings Canyon National Park, or to laud my Dinosaur testimony—if these were my needs, it was Dick Leonard who filled them, effusively.

The Leonards moved to Berkeley, first living on Miller Avenue and then settling forever a block away at 980 Keeler, and I was beyond reasonable doubt their most frequent visitor. I would like to think I was the favorite visitor of their daughters, Frances and Betty, and certainly their Boston terriers, Susie and Bonnie. The finest early photographs we have of our own growing family were taken by Doris in her spare-time devotion to portraiture.

Then came a board meeting when club finances were at issue (they rarely weren't), the budget was more than tight, the opportunities—indeed the requirements—exceeded the budget, and I was vociferously arguing, as I always will, that a green earth deserves precedence over a black bottom line. Trying to reason with me, Dick said, "Dave, we are only trying to help you." I responded, "You are helping me with the back of your hand." It was one of my better displays of insensitivity. I would rather forget what it did immediately to Dick's face, reflecting as it did a crash of his spirit. This gaffe preceded my telling the club board, in the presence of Ansel Adams and Eliot Porter, that Eliot was the club's most valuable property.

Some gaffes require more talent than others. I am gifted. Even sophomore-dropout philosophers know that human relations soar and plunge. One challenge is to find out what triggers either the up or the down and to be ready with amelioration, either way. I was poor at meeting that challenge and would love learning how to some day. I had little to do with Dick and Doris's recovery from the blow I struck, but they did recover. Dick continued to support the executive director. He did question in 1961, with good reason, what kind of commitment my rapidly rising fascination with book publishing would do to the club's net worth. He foresaw what I did not. The publishing of books requires substantial investment in inventory and in accounts receivable. You can be floating with respect to budget but sink if cash flow fails. Real success can be really disastrous unless new financial support can be found. I found some and was comfortable with investment of the club's Permanent Fund in a renewable resource, an earth scarred less because we were willing to spend a hoped-for permanent fund for a more likely permanent earth, thanks to the book program. I didn't express it quite that way, but would have, given a chance. Nice expressions, however, do not make cash flow.

Dick's patience abided. For all Bestor Robinson's eloquence, it was Dick's grasp of conservation that prevailed in Sierra Club counsels. And I was grateful.

Enter the Pacific Gas & Electric Company, on whose board Doris Leonard would later serve. She, Dorothy Varian, and George Collins had formed a new organization, Conservation Associates. The law offices of Leonard and Dole, which had been on the tenth floor of the Mills Building, a minute's walk from the Sierra Club's office at 1050 Mills Tower, moved to the fifteenth floor of the tower in association with Francis Farquhar and his accounting partner, Cliff Heimbucher. The team of four had been enormously helpful to the innovative electronics firm, Varian Associates. Russell Varian was deeply concerned with conservation, as was his wife, Dorothy Hill Varian, who had once gone with John Dyer, one of our Shiprock four.

With help from the Mills Tower's fifteenth floor, Varian Associates prospered. Upon the death of Sigurd Varian, then of Russell, Dorothy used her Varian income skillfully. She was the angel of Conservation Associates. They all knew Ansel Adams well and were enchanted by his photographic interpretation of a splendid stretch of the California coast, the Nipomo Dunes, which they wanted spared.

Pacific Gas & Electric Company wanted to build a nuclear reactor there. Ansel, Doris, Dorothy, and George, with the assistance of Dick Leonard and Will Siri, then president of the Sierra Club, combined their individual powers to persuade PG&E to build its reactor somewhere else.

I heard about this at a Sierra Club board meeting in 1967. The "else" was to be Diablo Canyon, a place none of the attending directors had seen. Having helped give away Glen Canyon unseen, as a later chapter on the Colorado River will disclose, I was not anxious to repeat. The people who had persuaded the largest investor-owned public utility in all the world to pull up stakes and put its reactor somewhere else were not anxious to undo an unprecedented agreement. I thought it quite important that PG&E, not yet having invested substantially in the new site, should look a little further. I was not yet mature enough to be against reactors. I was, however, against misplacing a reactor and was thus opposed to selecting for obliteration or otherwise cluttering an undeveloped piece of the California coast. Little enough was still wild or likely to remain so. Why not build where there was already development, including access roads, housing for employees, a transmission-line corridor that could handle more lines—all this with the same Pacific Ocean for cooling water? Above all, why not wait until the directors had an opportunity to look at the new sacrifice area, to see whether it was indeed "a treeless slot," as it was described for them by the head of the local chapter. At the very least, the board should wait for some directors to have a look and let the board's executive committee make the decision after someone had seen what they were deciding about.

It was not to be. On that day the contest began that would require my walking the plank two years later. If a contest can be orchestrated, this one was, and Dick, determined to prevail, did not dabble. He orchestrated and prevailed.

The first year the Diablo supporters thought they had me. Will Siri told me the board had the votes to ship me off to New York City, where I would be assigned to publishing and remain relatively harmless. But what they were planning to do hit the press, especially the readers of Herb

Caen—that is, all the readers of the *San Francisco Chronicle.* The public responded. Instead of winning a place on the plank, I received a unanimous vote of confidence.

Confidence had a short life. A young director who had won election, at least in part, on the basis of supporting the executive director and who for several years had been almost a supplementary member of the Brower family, switched his position upon being elected and took every convenient opportunity—some not so convenient—to do just the opposite. In the heat of battle a lot of people do what I don't think they would care to repeat. That includes me and the Pacific Gas & Electric Company, which in its heart of hearts (doesn't a corporation surely have a heart somewhere?) must now regret its mistake. Without knowing it at the time, I had done my best to save the company the five billion dollars more they were going to have to spend on Diablo than they had estimated—with about that much more to spend and pass on to ratepayers when it comes time to decommission the two reactors now at Diablo Canyon. Provided, of course, that when decommissioning time comes, they will have learned, with the specter of Three Mile Island and Chernobyl hovering ever closer, how the hell to do it.

If they could be a bit grateful to me now, they certainly were not then. One of the Bay Area's biggest corporations could exert influence on the Bay Area's most effective conservation organization, and did. Every incompetence I had exhibited as executive director—and I could list the plethora of them but would rather not—was brought to the surface and heralded. I might as well list some of my finer shortcomings: unanswered calls and correspondence, book-production delays, underendowment of tact, inability to find time to keep the directors posted, underapplied discretion. These were not new. I had spent years perfecting them. They had been tolerated in the past. No longer.

As the battle intensified, it occurred to me that I, as executive director, should run for election to the board myself, with four other candidates who were committed to changing the club's position on the Diablo reactors. Stewart Ogilvy thought this a brilliant idea. It was assumed that if I ran while I was serving as executive director I would have an inordinate advantage. I was granted leave without pay. If there was any inordinate advantage, and indeed there was, it inhered to the Diablo supporters. It's a long story. Our view simply didn't get out except for one mailing at our side's expense, and which cost an unexpected thirty-five hundred dollars in added postage because the printer shifted to heavier paper than we had planned on. Chapter newsletters and phone trees went to work. The chance to get a fair presentation of both sides in the *Sierra Club Bulletin* was torpedoed. I still thought that name recognition (I had more than my share) would at least get me elected.

I was wrong. We all lost. It wasn't even close. Habituated to being executive director, I tried to think of some way I could continue with well-clipped wings. It wasn't to be. My farewell speech was touching. It is somewhere in our house, because I never throw anything away—nor do I hardly ever find anything. There were tears, even in the eyes of grown men.

I was gone from the staff, out in the hall, and talking to the *New York Times* about the imminent founding of Friends of the Earth and the League of Conservation Voters. The hard news in the story was the proposed League of Conservation Voters. My 1957 suggestion that there be one interested no one in the Sierra Club but Phil Berry. But Friends of the Earth would need to include much more than that. It should be free to lobby and to be international. Dick Leonard had not approved of my putting the Sierra Club's tax-deductible status in jeopardy with the Grand Canyon ads, and he argued that it was *ultra vires* for the club to have a London office and try to be international. He certainly disagreed with my views on nuclear power and my enthusiasm for the club's book publishing. So Friends of the Earth had its charge in draft form already: be politically and legislatively active internationally; suspect nuclear power and its undisclosed impacts; charge ahead with publishing; and damn the torpedoes.

I was not gone from the club. I had been a member for thirty-six years and was not about to stop adding to the count. It takes a unanimous vote to be named an honorary vice-president of the club. As I understand it, Larry Moss would not vote for any other nominees, however deserving, unless the board voted such an honor to me. In December 1972, two and a half years after my departure from staff, I was so honored.

In 1983, as revealed a few pages ago, Ansel Adams was first to sign the petition nominating me for a return to the Sierra Club board, on which I had last served in 1952. The petition worked.

The second signature on the petition was Dick Leonard's.

STEWART M. OGILVY

THAT'S A BRILLIANT IDEA," Stewart Ogilvy told me. I had just explained over the telephone how I, as Sierra Club executive director, intended to run for the club's board of directors with a slate of four others who were interested in changing the club's position with respect to the nuclear reactors that the Pacific Gas & Electric Company proposed for the mouth of Diablo Canyon on the Pacific coast just south of Morro Bay.

The idea may have been brilliant, but it didn't turn out the way either of us expected it to. In no time at all I found that I did not know how to fight city hall. The pro-Diablo wing of the club board became that city hall. I had no choice but to become the club's first former executive director.

In all this hassle Stewart was on and at my side, so encouragingly that PG&E questioned his value to his employer, *Fortune* magazine. He was my most valuable counsel as I prepared for a meeting of the new board on May 3, 1969. In New York City he, David Sive, Alfred Forsyth, Max Linn, and others met to discuss what to do after I left the plank's far end.

Tom Turner suggested that the new organization we talked about forming ought to be called the Muir League, but we settled on Anne Brower's alternative. She knew of Friends of the Bancroft Library at the University of California at Berkeley, and Friends of the Earth seemed to be appropriate for what we were up to. The acronym, FOE, was in conflict with the name, but we could point out that we were foe of the earth's enemies and let it go at that.

Twelve years earlier I had proposed that the Sierra Club form a league of conservation voters but nothing had come of it. Now was the time to get LCV started. As a result, the nugget of news in the *New York Times* story covering my demise was of the imminent birth of Friends of the Earth, with the League of Conservation Voters as part of it.

Stewart Ogilvy was the man I leaned on because he was so good at tying ideas and details together. He got a small group together in the New York office of David Sive and incorporated Friends of the Earth.

That was but a point in time in the flow of our relationship. Without looking up my sometime daily journal now in storage at the Bancroft Library, I would say that most of my long distance calls from San Francisco were to Howard Zahniser in Washington. Next most were the calls to Stewart in New York or in Yonkers, depending upon the time of day. Before Yonkers, if the *Fortune* office had closed, the calls were to his apartment in the Upper West Side of Manhattan.

It was that West Side apartment that Stewart moved out of temporarily so that my entire family, in the course of our departure for our once-in-a-lifetime ten-week European trip, could move in for our stay in New York City. It's one thing to allow someone to occupy a guest room. But to move out entirely in order to let a family of six move in was an act putting the Good Samaritan to shame. Stewart Ogilvy made a habit of doing that, and not just for Dave Brower. That generosity, fortunately, was not all. Stewart and his wife Avis were also good analysts, ever ready to offer a needed critique, even when I didn't want to hear it. As a congenital editor, always ready to criticize the work of others, I should have welcomed Ogilvy analyses more graciously than I usually did.

For an example, Stewart told me exactly what I ought to hear after he and Avis had listened to my presentation before the New School, in Manhattan:

May 10, 1972

Dear Dave:

It was good last night to have the opportunity again after a long lapse to hear Brower address an audience. As always, a stirring speech, well paced, filled with interesting ideas, fascinating illustrations, much important new information—and, into the bargain, witty and inspiring.

Having said that, I wonder if you and I are good enough friends for me to offer some advice as well. I do so only because I think so highly of what Dave Brower is doing for conservation that I want him to do it in the perfection of which I know he is capable—and indeed realizes in so many ways and so often,

First, I think you overrate your audience's alertness—at least last night's audience and also the Brooklyn College audience I last heard you speak to (about a year ago). Your hearers have to be attentive every second, and many are not. A word missed may lose them the thread of a major section of your exposition. Might not just a little repetition be useful—an "in other words" injected here and there where the going is a trifle dense.

Last night several people, though generally commendatory, commented in my hearing that they couldn't quite follow you. Your week-of-creation illustration, I think, may be a case in point. Unless the hearer has completely understood your concept of telescoping all the earth's history into a single week, all the subsequent references—"now we're at 11 o'clock Saturday," "now it's 11:59"—are lost and puzzling. The mike last night may have aggravated this, but I think you'd do well to repeat the basic concept at least once in different words, so the audience surely has the idea in mind before you apply specifics.

I expect your college audiences are very quick on the uptake, but last night's was not. For such as it, I think you have to be more explicit, less elliptical, than you were in places. For instance, you spoke of "the China effect" of a reactor meltdown, but you failed to explain it (though I've heard you do so in the past). Thus that grim joke was lost on most of your hearers.

Another niggle: Several times you made remarks such as, "Here I usually explain . . ." or "Now, I tell audiences . . ." I wonder if some newcomers' reaction to this isn't likely to be: "So, he's just giving us the old boiler plate. I came to hear something new, thoughtful, and important; instead I'm getting the broken-record hysteria of a professional doom-crier."

Finally, about answering questions: Mostly, you were great. But you failed to answer the woman who inquired about the likelihood of a Nixon executive order protecting de facto wilderness. I sure couldn't have answered her, but I thought you might better have said "I don't know" than to have talked all around her question and then dodged it. Maybe, of course, you didn't really hear it, but it seemed like dodging.

Well, please forgive the gratuitous lecture. I hope you'll believe that it's intended only to help perfect something that is already very good indeed.

Sincerely,
Stew

It is reasonable to assume, and I do, that I listened to what Stewart had to say well enough that he engineered the honorary degree I received from the New School a few years later. I do not know this. I do know, however, that it was he who persuaded Hobart College to give me my first honorary degree, and was there to photograph my being hooded.

Stewart's critiques, at board meetings of Friends of the Earth or of Friends of the Earth Foundation, which he also helped found, were gentle but insistent. Avis's were insistent and I think intended to be gentle. Together, they gave us, in both organizations, the grades we needed to strive for and sometimes earned in our running of the two organizations. Meanwhile, they both analyzed the work of the Atlantic Chapter of the Sierra Club, which profited from their diligence even as Friends of the Earth did.

Quite appropriately, when Stewart no longer wished to serve on the FOE and FEF boards, he was named honorary president of Friends of the Earth, and fully deserved the honor.

Stewart loved the English language, and was able to use it with an economy I shall always envy. I learned about that early. To my surprise, I found that he could also use numbers with—and for—an economy, to wit, the economy of Friends of the Earth. In one of our first financial dilemmas—and there were more than one—he and I sat together one long evening and his contribution was a FOE budget that rescued us from despair.

If you needed to know someone, Stewart would either know that person or be close to someone who did. His closest competitor was Perry Knowlton, head of the international literary agency of Curtis Brown and an early member of the FOE board. Between them, they came up with a panoply of illustrious names for the Advisory Council of FOE and FEF. It isn't easy to get such names as Candace Bergen, Alexander Calder, Lord Caradon, Barry Commoner, Jacques Cousteau, Norman Cousins, John Denver, Paul Ehrlich, Duke Ellington, James Farmer, Milton Glaser, Hazel Henderson, Konrad Lorenz, Karl Menninger, Paul Newman, John B. Oakes, Linus Pauling, Aurelio Peccei, George Plimpton, Robert Redford, Pete Seeger, Noel Simon, C. P. Snow, Gary Snyder, Maurice Strong, Mark Van Doren, Harriet Van Horne, George Wald, and Joanne Woodward. Altogether, it was an incredible list of people who liked FOE's goal well enough to lend their names. It was Stewart who stressed the importance of seeking them out. As one of Stewart's friends' achievements, Time-Life suites at Essex House, in New York City, were made available for FEF board meetings. The friend was Charles Bear, a group vice-president of Time, Inc., whom Stewart persuaded to serve on the FEF board. The better of the two suites, and the one we used more often, was on the twenty-fifth floor and looked out upon Central Park. We met there almost every other month, the only stipulation being that Time-Life people had precedence if they wished to use the room.

There was a big entry hall, a large living room complete with a big television set, a large table, enough chairs for a small meeting, with more available on request, a bedroom and bath (in which, lacking other things to do, I would watch the effect of wind on a high-rise by observing the waves it created in the toilet bowl), but far more important, a kitchen with a cupboard full of stimulants and a refrigerator full of what needed to go with them.

The stimulants I am missing most are the words that Stewart Ogilvy, as honorary president of Friends of the Earth, would have spoken or written to me about how to handle the problems besetting the organization that led to my being voted off its board (in an action nullified by the court), and a year later being voted out of the chairs of FOE and the Friends of the Earth Foundation. I was, nevertheless, allowed to remain as founder of both organizations.

If anyone is interested in the details, they will be found in a vast accumulation of papers I am labeling "FOE Flak" as I pass them on to the University of California's Bancroft Library to join the still vaster lifetime accumulation of papers already there. In the second part of my autobiography *(Work in Progress),* I will try to approach this and similar problems in a positive way, talking about valuable lessons to be learned, which is not nearly as much fun as assigning hero and villain roles for battle scenes.

In short, FOE went into a three-hundred-seventy-thousand-dollar debt in order to initiate programs, build staff, and recruit members. Some two hundred fifty thousand dollars of the total initial cost was covered by revenue from FOE's publishing program. That program was FOE's principal outreach. It included an extraordinarily good journal, *Not Man Apart* (which won a prestigious award and became a semimonthly), and a library of books, including ten exhibit-format volumes in The Earth's Wild Places series, three in the Celebrating the Earth series, twelve mass-market Ballantine paperbacks, as well as milestone books about energy conservation by Amory Lovins. The several other books included two editions of *Progress As If Survival Mattered.* In addition, for almost a decade, Mead Paper produced Friends of the Earth school supplies with Brower quotations and paid FOE a royalty. In summary, some thirty million people spent about forty million dollars to read FOE's message, and seventeen thousand people joined FOE in its first two years.

FOE's directors were almost all easterners and Stewart was the most active. I was executive director of the John Muir Institute, which I had co-founded in 1968 with Max Linn, an unpaid president of FOE. Beginning in 1972, I switched to the FOE payroll for half my time and obtained enough honoraria for the other half that I could begin contributing to FOE many times my cost. By 1978, FOE was essentially out of debt and FEF was handsomely in the black. This was, in part, due to the formation of Friends of the Earth Foundation and to major assistance from Stewart Ogilvy and Administrative Director Mark Horlings, taking full advantage of what Harvard Law School had taught him.

Affiliate FOE organizations were founded in thirty-six countries altogether. Three have dropped out. In 1972, six FOE groups initiated an international newspaper, the *Stockholm Conference Eco.* Since then its reporters have traveled to and reported on a score of international conferences of environmental importance.

Working together in 1974, FOE Australia, France, U.K., and U.S. catalyzed the formation of the Environmental Liaison Center in Nairobi to augment the work of the new United Nations Environment Program. For several years FOE groups put on spectacular exhibits at the Frankfurt Book Fair. Altogether, Friends of the Earth International became a multinational, beautifully decentralized activist environmental organization on which the sun was always rising somewhere, with an aggregate membership approaching two hundred thousand.

Stewart Ogilvy's longtime interest in population control and in world government (as a World Federalist) influenced our global agenda. Edwin Spencer Matthews, Jr., applying his considerable knowledge of international law from his office home and his home office in Paris, contributed to the entire effort indispensably, far beyond what could be expected from one human being. I believed Edwin ought to become FOE's president, and in 1979 he was elected to that office and I became chairman of the boards of FOE and its foundation. Edwin served for a year at enormous personal sacrifice and not too happily. He was succeeded by Rafe Pomerance, who had been FOE's legislative director in Washington, D.C.

FOE's U.S. membership peaked at thirty-nine thousand but its fortune flagged. The debt began rising, people and programs were cut, and the debt rose further, exceeding half a million dollars. The publishing program was remaindered at a heavy loss and further and more severe cuts were proposed, including the cutting of the frequency of *Not Man Apart,* closing offices, and continual deferring of the attempt to recruit new members.

I led the opposition and lost. The main office, in San Francisco, was closed and the most experienced staff members were dropped. With a few hours' notice and a cashier's check, I was able to buy the library for Earth Island Institute, which also picked up some of the programs and people FOE had dropped.

In 1989, FOE and FEF merged with the Oceanic Society and the Environmental Policy Institute, which had splintered from FOE many years before as the Environmental Policy Center, taking with it all of FOE's Washington staff but George Alderson, who had led the battle to defeat the SST. Before the merger the four organizations kept about sixty-five directors busy. Mergers invariably result in staff cuts and board cuts, too. Some fifty directors became available as volunteers for other organizations.

The merged organization hosted the meeting of FOE International in Washington, D.C., in 1989, FOE's twentieth anniversary. As founder of FOE, FEF, and FOE International, I was invited to a dinner "to be honored." I asked to attend the meeting itself to seek FOE International help in the ensuing Fate and Hope of the Earth Congress and FOE participation in the environmental restoration movement. I also hoped to see what cooperation could develop between FOE International and Earth Island Institute. The London office of FOE U.K. told me the dates of the meeting. I told the Washington office a few weeks ahead of time of my wish to attend and arranged low-cost nonrefundable air transportation. On the morning of departure, I telephoned to find where the meeting would be and was told, "You are not invited to the meeting and if you show up you will not be admitted." Unavoidably late, I arrived for the dinner to find no one expecting me. I had dinner with a friend at my favorite Mexican restaurant.

I hear from FOE through *Not Man Apart,* now appearing ten times a year and still being an exceedingly good journal. FOE's peak U.S. membership dropped to about a fourth of its number in 1989. FOE U.K., in a country with a fifth of the U.S. population, has a membership a dozen times bigger than that of FOE U.S., which now has a splendid opportunity to catch up, and I hope it does. If Stewart Ogilvy and his cool counsel had remained with us, I don't think the gap would ever have developed.

There is a new salesman helping FOE International. On Thanksgiving Day 1989, a Beatle came back. Paul McCartney began his first U.S. tour in thirteen years before the sold-out Forum in Inglewood. Robert Hilburn reported in the *Los Angeles Times:*

"A sense of basic values extends beyond McCartney's music and manner. He is using the tour—which continues its first North American swing with concerts in Chicago, Toronto, Montreal and New York—to promote environmental concerns.

"In both the 100-page program distributed free to the audience and in his brief remarks from the stage Thursday he urged fans to look into Friends of the Earth, an environmental advocacy organization, and to 'vote for a clean world.' "

Stewart Ogilvy would promptly have found out who persuaded Paul McCartney to extend his values and would have written a letter thanking them both. "The Educated Heart" is a chapter in a long out-of-print book by Gelett Burgess, *The Bromide and Other Theories*. Stewart's heart earned a Ph.D.

* * *

Stewart's well-educated heart served him and us well as he participated in our complex family of organizations—Friends of the Earth, the League of Conservation Voters, and Friends of the Earth Foundation (which succeeded the John Muir Institute for Environmental Studies as our tax-deductible ally). We were covering three important environmental fields: legislative, political, and educational. We added litigation when FOE joined the suits to block the trans-Alaska pipeline and to reverse the position of the Federal Communications Commission on the Fairness Doctrine—two temporary successes.

At Stewart's suggestion we tried to add a profit-making corporate channel, Environmental Alternatives, Inc., to manufacture and distribute goods that were environmentally benign, profits from which could accrue to the environmental cause, including further legislative activity. We couldn't get over the hurdles, not even with a specific effort at environmental publishing under the aegis of Earth Island, Inc.

An Earth Island Limited was, indeed, formed to be the publishing arm of FOE in the U.K. Our limited capital there disappeared after the publication of seven books—good ones, but not profitable enough to keep the corporation afloat. Earth Island, Inc., with even less capital, lent funds to FOE U.S. to help it acquire some books. The loan was never repaid.

It was Margaret Mead's allusion to "the island earth"—two beautiful words—that led me to choose the name Earth Island, much too good a name to let go dormant. In 1982, always ready to have a new organization in the wings for contingencies, I incorporated a tax-deductible Earth Island Institute. Its goal would be to instill ecological conscience into as many spheres of human society as we could enter. *Time* magazine had not yet published its cover story, "Whatever Happened to Ethics?," but we knew something had happened and we might as well join the search for the missing human attribute. Aldo Leopold had long ago urged a conservation ethic, and we would be working for the same objective with a different adjective.

We also wanted Earth Island to have a harbor for people with ideas about ships that might not meet the Conventional Wisdom port requirements of existing organizations. In all this I hoped we would accommodate the philosophy in one of my favorite quotations: "A ship in harbor is safe, but that is not what ships are built for."

Stewart Ogilvy would have been the perfect honorary president for Earth Island Institute. I could certainly have used his advice when, in 1984, we saw that we were about to offer harbor to Friends of the Earth boat people. I need his advice as we get Earth Island Action Group underway and prepare for an Earth Island Restoration Defense Council, Earth Island Voters, and Earth Island Biosphere Conservancy. In one hundred words or less of succinct prose, Stewart would have provided us with the *raison d'être* for each of these, suggesting possible sources of funds, directors, and advisors for all of them.

I will always remember Essex House fondly, even though Stewart, Avis, and I were not always in total agreement about what happened in our meetings there toward the end. And I remember Stewart's voice on the telephone: he had but to say my name, Dave, in an elongated syllable, ending about five notes below where it started, and I knew immediately that it was he and that I was going to need very much to hear what he was about to say. I hoped for more at the earliest opportunity. I was waiting to hear from him upon his return from a long overdue cruise, but he didn't come home. He deserved—and why wasn't it awarded to him?—the twenty-year extension I have asked for and could never use so well.

CHAPTER 6

WHY WILDERNESS?

INTRODUCTION: JOHN MCPHEE

JOHN MCPHEE EXPLAINED, when I couldn't, what it was that kept me from being the totally scattered person that I suspected I was. He was working on a piece for *The New Yorker* and was about halfway through his year-long, self-appointed task of arranging and chronicling various encounters with a man he was to call an archdruid. John had been listening to a series of my speeches, looking over my shoulder at notes and clippings, wondering about the arguments I was forever setting forth, getting well acquainted with my widow and orphaned children, and now was driving me from New York City to Poughkeepsie to listen to yet another speech. In his own gentle way he asked what kept me from spreading myself too thin.

Not thinking of myself as anything but, I hesitated to admit it and was quiet so long that he came to my rescue. Not being the good reporter he is, I remember only the gist of what he said. I was probably too tired, he put it, to respond, but he thought he knew the answer anyway: whatever I took on had to be related to wilderness—exploring it, enjoying it, and doing whatever I could to protect it.

To spare me any further penetrating questions or answers, John told me the life story of oranges, and how he came to write an entire book about the golden apples of the Hesperides. The miles went by quickly. It was fun to listen and to not talk.

John McPhee was manifestly charitable, and is probably right. I am reminded of John Muir, when he first hit Oakland and was asked where he wanted to go. He replied, "Anywhere that's wild." I'll buy that, especially if it is wild in the Sierra Nevada.

From time to time I remind others of John Muir, perhaps because I keep writing or talking about wild places, as he did. He spoke and wrote books. I spoke and wrote forewords to the books of others. I never missed an opportunity to preach. More and more I felt the sermons to be necessary to slow the loss of more and more wilderness. I wrote the brief piece

David Brower in the Earth Island library, 1988. He founded Friends of the Earth, League of Conservation Voters, and Earth Island Institute.

"How to Kill a Wilderness" before returning from combat in Italy. Two years later I was at it again, and kept at it in building support for the proposed National Wilderness Preservation System with more forewords, more speeches, and testimony before Congress. As the years passed, I found new arguments to present, new ways to present old arguments, and ended with maxims that I thought bore repetition. I have tried to eliminate most of that repetition in what follows. Please practice speed reading where I failed:

Sierra Club Handbook

Shortly before the Army promoted me to captain and put me in the Infantry Reserve, Francis Farquhar took me out of reserve and designated me as his successor as editor of the *Sierra Club Bulletin,* and that included the editing of its November 1947 special issue, *A Member's Handbook,* and the onslaught of my addiction to writing forewords began. The focus was on California features (redwoods and mountains) which the club would soon move beyond. Strangely enough, the word "wilderness" appeared only once. I had already become addicted to wilderness, but the word was not entrenched in my vocabulary. It soon would be.

America's Resources of Scenery that we explore and enjoy today are not set aside through accident. National parks and forests, state and county redwood groves and beaches, wilderness areas and primeval regions—these are not now open to free public enjoyment just through happenstance, just because the country is so big and its resources so limitless that no one has yet got around to fencing them in.

These areas, to which millions go each year for escape, exercise, or rest, are available only because people have fought for them. We who enjoy the mountains today owe a debt to generations now gone, or now no longer able to be fully active, who have thought of long-range public use and enjoyment rather than immediate development and exploitation. The people of America owe to these people of vision much of what we most enjoy—the national parks; the preservation of some of the forests; the recreational areas of the national forests, whether set aside as wilderness or opened to controlled roadside development; the unfenced beaches; the national monuments; the county and city parks.

Opposed to the people of vision there have always been some too-enterprising people of commerce, who have been slow to comprehend that the retention of outstanding scenic and recreational areas as public land is good business in the long run, who are forever seeking the lever with which to move the earth, and who in their commercial role hear only today's ring of the cash register.

The campaign between people of vision and the cash-register people has been long. Where the people of vision have lost battles, we see unpleasant things when the dust of battle settles. We see the flood where there used to be the scenic masterpiece of Hetch Hetchy Valley, drowned for a purpose which other valleys, not scenic masterpieces, would have served better. We see many a sylvan dell in the mountains, and many an acre of rich agricultural land dredged inside out, with heaps of debris left as monuments to false economy—the saving of the few cents a ton which would have leveled off the piles of boulders and given nature a chance to build soil again. We see inadequate metropolitan zoning, sewage dumped into waters the shore of which could otherwise rival the Riviera. We see all-but-ageless Big Tree stands blasted down for fenceposts and grape stakes (the fragments being hardly good for anything else). We have seen wasteful logging methods that have given too little thought to a recurrent yield, and we're still seeing them. We've seen a bonanzalike salmon run reduced to insignificance, herds of sea otters stoned and skinned, mountain meadows irreparably damaged to produce a few extra pounds of meat. We've seen a race to pump up oil—a resource that will not be replaced in this civilization's time or that of many civilizations to come—by halfway methods for extravagant use. To look at the scene in its most terrible implication, we can see that people of one generation's time—the generation that saw two world wars—have "developed" (that is, have used up) more of the earth's resources than all preceding generations of all known civilizations.

It is far too late now to advocate, even if we would, a return to the teepee—to the Indian's custom of living on the income of natural resources, the replenishable deer, acorns, pine nuts, and grasshoppers. It's too late to urge that we quit our present-day habit of squandering large portions of a bountiful natural endowment of resources (thinking ourselves incomparably clever and enterprising as we admire the gain of the moment).

No, we won't return voluntarily to the tepee. Our descendants can live there later, when the inevitable eviction notice is served.

But we can be cognizant of the conflagration to which we are contributing our small part, and think hard before we stoke the flames now consuming the resources of a land which those resources have made great.

In thinking twice, we can look more carefully at our own chosen field, conservation as it applies to the natural scene. We can thank the people who have handed down to us such mountain recreation lands as we now enjoy. We can realize that our debt can never be paid to them. We can be reasonably sure that they would thank us, and consider the debt well paid, if we took care of the unspoiled places they saved for us, if we didn't overgraze, overlumber, overmechanize, overski them, but passed them on with as few scars as possible to their grandchildren.

Each day, whether in Congress, in state legislatures, or in a park or a forest, some new challenge presents itself, and someone must take the conservative role of the conservationist in accepting that challenge. In this handbook the member who seeks it can discover his own role, a chance to apply the initiative required for checking those who would squander resources that should be saved for tomorrow.

Yes, a debt to the past becomes a debt to the future. In our own field, each pleasant day in mountains should perhaps be charged against us;

our account should then be credited for each day on which we extend our vision and give a nod to posterity, on which we act for the unnumbered people who will have to be less prodigal than we and who are entitled to explore and enjoy mountains as pleasant as ours. The challenge to conserve is best met by those who know and love that which they are called upon to save. To this end, the Sierra Club has always sponsored appropriate activities. These pages, then, give the form and function of the Sierra Club. They tell what it is—what the principal activities of its members are and how they have developed. They tell what the club has done, relying upon members who may have entered the club primarily to participate in physical activities, but whose interest far outlasted any mere physical participation. Finally, these pages will imply what the Sierra Club can do in the years to come. It is hoped that all members, in knowing more fully what the club is, can thereupon increase its value to them and theirs to it and to its cause.

A Member's Handbook,
***Sierra Club Bulletin,* November 1947**

The same ideas were still applicable forty-one years later, when after twenty years' absence the *Sierra Club Handbook* appeared, renamed but with the same preface, only slightly modified. For example, in eight places where it now says *people,* as presented here and in the new handbook, it formerly said *man* or *men*. In 1947, the Sierra Club had four thousand members. Now, approaching its centennial in 1992, it has more than a half million.

Neither the club nor the scores of kindred organizations have reason to feel smug. What is happening to the earth in spite of their numbers means that instead of feeling satisfied, they can be proud of what they are going to do with the opportunities they are about to seize, just in time. That is a prediction, and it had better be right.

Wilderness and Self-Interest

In the Sierra Club Book, *Wildlands in Our Civilization* (1957), Bruce Kilgore, who edited the *Sierra Club Bulletin,* signed a piece I'd written for him for the most part. We had speech writers even then, but spoke no others' words we didn't believe.

It Seems to Me that if a democracy is to work, we must assume that effective citizens are informed citizens willing to act. They may need to act before all the data are in, if—in their own good judgment—there will be nothing to act about if they wait until all the data are in and all the comprehensive studies are completed and evaluated and there is coordination at all levels of government.

It is up to us—as conservationists—to inform the citizen. Our toughest job is to overcome the insulation citizens have to build around themselves if they are to remain sane in an adman's world of perpetual bombardment. There is so much information flowing, and crises are so constant, that specialists can't even keep up with specialists. A chemist would have a hard time even reading the index to chemical abstracts—about ten pages of fine print per day! But we must try, and we must also keep ourselves informed, and not succumb too often to the cliché that we spend too much time talking to ourselves. We don't spend enough because there isn't enough time.

What will motivate a citizen to act? In the last analysis, people act to preserve themselves. They must and they will. It is a built-in instinct. We need to capitalize upon it and we can. We can show that it is in our self-interest to protect wilderness. We had better show it, because it relates to our preserving ourselves.

In the first place, we can and we must show that wilderness can only survive in a society designed for peaceful stability. It requires getting rid of a pet delusion, and a dangerous one. We have developed the habit of exhorting ourselves to produce more to aid the "vigorous, growing economy." Yet continuation of such growing production is not possible on an earth of fixed size—and continuing attempts to produce it are the basic threat not only to wilderness, but also to peace.

The U.N. is now studying the question, "Can the economy withstand peace?" The related question, which we have indirectly been asking, is: Can limited resources withstand a constantly increasing expenditure? The answers to these two questions are obvious—and carefully avoided by almost everyone. It is in no one's self-interest to avoid them much longer.

In a second broad area, we must lend all the support we can muster to a program which will permit our biologists and ecologists—our natural scientists—to continue their study of life in all its aspects. We need a center to further the advanced study of environment—more specifically, of ecosystems. Such a center would seek out the best minds in the field of biology and give them a chance to get on record. It would provide the opportunity to find or to develop some Einsteins of biology.

They have an important gap to fill. For there is tragically little known about the speed with which technology is wiping out the world's organic wealth—and the variety of living organisms built up through the eons since life began. In all likelihood, these interrelated living plants and animals are essential to the continuation of life as we know it. Yet we continue to tear up the last remnants of habitat, on earth and even beneath the sea, much as a ne'er-do-well spends his inheritance.

One practical example: At our wilderness conference last spring, Professor Robert Stebbins brought to his panel table a small shrub, a plant he had known as a boy in the Mojave Desert. No one realized it amounted to anything, and had there been a proposal to run a freeway through the last remaining habitat of this plant, no one would have thought much about it. But now it is high on the Department of Agriculture's research program—for it has been discovered that the seed has a liquid wax with a very high melting point and that the wax may be useful in hardening oils used in heavy machinery. It has value as a forage plant, and the wax can be used to make smokeless candles.

But where are we to keep this type of plant and all the other as yet undiscovered species—where are we going to allow the organic diversity the future may need for its very existence? As more and more organisms are displaced and as population pressures eliminate wild species, we are simplifying our genetic pool. It may be very important to have these wild organisms around; we don't know when we may need some of their traits. We don't even know that they are not already a vital but undiscovered link in a chain we now depend on.

Other examples are legion of our continually needing to fall back on nature for solutions to problems technology creates. We have a unique talent for getting out on a limb and then trying to saw it off behind us.

What worth wilderness? How much wilderness is needed? Must every wilderness be a "working wilderness" in an economic sense?

Can the American public afford to be satisfied with occasional "wilderness on the rocks" plus a few so-called landscape management areas where "timber will be managed to produce a thrifty, healthy forest cover that is aesthetically pleasing"? Will such a philosophy save the goat-nut plants, the countless other as yet undiscovered keys to life which remain in the natural plant and animal associations found in wilderness and perhaps nowhere else?

What then can the citizen do to further the philosophy of peaceful stability and to help provide a climate in which the sound ecological thinking of our biologists can be applied in so many critical areas of public thought and decision?

We have to tell our story, as widely as we can, and we must make it the vital, living, dynamic story it is.

With all the accomplishments of man in the space age, with manned spacecraft circling the earth and all our accomplishments in subduing the earth to our needs, we need to retain full respect for the life force, the genetic reservoir that made each of us possible, and all our parts—for the force that brought about all we live with on earth. We must keep that respect—and we must communicate the urgency of keeping it. With that reverence for life will come a respect for wilderness and assurance that enough of it will be preserved to prevent the genetic reservoir from being silted in and destroyed.

As I said at the outset, in the last analysis people act to preserve themselves. They act in their own self-interest. It's our job, therefore, to show our friends, our leaders of thought and of action, that all humanity is involved in these islands of wilderness. We are tinkering with our environment; and the absolute requirement of intelligent tinkering, as Aldo Leopold pointed out, is to save all the parts. Wilderness is the place for their safekeeping—the essential place—the necessity.

Our concern for wilderness is not just a quixotic concern. More and more we're learning the truth of what Thoreau said more than a century ago: "In wildness is the preservation of the world."

Wildlands in Our Civilization,
***Sierra Club Bulletin,* June 1957**

I would find good reason to use these excerpts incessantly ever after. The quotation from Thoreau was not the result of digging by Bruce Kilgore or me. Howard Zahniser had already singled it out for everyone to see by using it on the letterhead of The Wilderness Society.

WILDERNESS—CONFLICT AND CONSCIENCE

THE SIERRA CLUB Wilderness Conference reported on in the book, *Wildlands in Our Civilization,* was building support for the wilderness-protecting legislation initially conceived by Benton MacKaye and given substance and a growing constituency through the work of Howard Zahniser. I was picking up steam—his steam—when I wrote this in 1957:

YOU LIKE WILDERNESS, let's suppose, and want to see some of it saved. Not just a thin strip of roadside with a "Don't pick the flowers" sign. Not just a wild garden behind the hotel or a pleasant woods within shouting distance of the highway. But *real* wilderness, big wilderness—country big enough to have a beyond to it and an inside. With space enough to separate you from the buzz, bang, screech, ring, yammer, and roar of the twenty-four-hour commercial you wish hard your life wouldn't be. Wilderness that is a beautiful piece of world. Where as you start up a trail and your nine-year-old Bob asks, "Is there civilization behind that ridge?" you can say no and share his "That's good!" feeling.

Yes, a place where you can rescue your *self* from what Ortega calls the *other*—all the extraneities that pile on you too deep. So deep, to quote my wife Anne's *bon mot,* that "the life you lead is not your own."

So you want a place where you can be serene, that will let you contemplate and connect two consecutive thoughts, or that if need be can stir you up as you were made to be stirred up, until you blend with the wind and water and earth you almost forgot you came from. You like wilderness, then, and need it. And suddenly you encounter practical people who never learned that they need it, too, or don't remember. It doesn't take you long to encounter them, because there are a lot of them, many in places of influence, all adding up to a political force that can jeopardize wilderness if it chooses to, and choose it seems to.

You can malign them, and insure that the conflict will continue over the need for wilderness. But let's assume you'd rather align them, get straight to his conscience, end the conflict, and save the wilderness. Then what?

At the Fifth Biennial Wilderness Conference, on March 15 in San Francisco, I tried to develop one approach and I have drawn upon it fully in what follows, adapted from my remarks there. Let's call it a starting point, and let us hope that it will suggest to you a different and better approach to a goal that happily still remains and should persist.

To start with, let's address ourselves to a very important question. How much right does one generation have to another generation's freedom? Can we of this generation, in conscience, pay for our freedom by mortgaging the freedom of our children? Is it our ethic that we are privileged to write the rules to which all the subsequent generations of our civilization must be committed, and by which they must abide, irrespective of their own wishes?

Thomas Jefferson, long ago, said that one generation could not bind another; each had the right to set its own course. Go out across this land and try to find someone to argue that he was wrong. You won't find a taker. It is the national consensus.

But deeds are not matching words. This generation is speedily using up, beyond recall, a very important right that belongs to future generations—the right to have wilderness in their civilization, even as we have it in ours; the right to find solitude somewhere; the right to see, and enjoy, and be inspired and renewed, somewhere, by those places where the hand of God has not been obscured by the industry of man.

Our decisions today will determine the fate of that right, so far as people of our time can pass opportunity along to our children. Apathy here can mean that we pass them a dead torch. Or we can keep it aflame, knowing that this is a very special torch that we cannot light again.

Belatedly we are becoming generally concerned about our scenic resources and about resolving conflicts that must be resolved if we are to retain islands of open space in the sea of tomorrow's civilization. The early history of civilization dealt with the problem of finding enough enclosed spaces—caves in the beginning, then crude shelters, then walled cities, followed by the early beginnings of suburbia when there was no longer room enough within the walls for all the people of the cities. Only recently have we begun to change our concern. The problem seems no longer to be one of enclosing space, but of leaving enough of it open to meet our needs for greenery and for everyone's "slice of sky" Wallace Stegner speaks of. We know we need some of this in our own garden for the edges of our daily existence—something to look out upon at breakfast, or before dinner. We need more space nearby for our weekends, where on a March day a child may fly a kite, or a family may picnic and stroll. For our holidays we need accessible open space within range of our faster transportation, and better roads [please forgive me], bearing in mind that we shall soon have more three-day weekends than we have now. For our lengthening vacations we'll need the big spaces of national parks and wilderness.

These outdoor spaces—daylight-saving *plots,* weekend and holiday *areas,* and vacation *regions*—won't set themselves aside. We have to plan for them as the population avalanche flows over the land, and plan generously if civilization is not only to improve living standards, but also to sustain our standards for life.

The Sierra Club has been concerned with the use of wildlife, wilderness, and national parks ever since John Muir founded the club in 1892 with the general purpose of exploring, enjoying, and protecting our scenic resources. In none of its sixty-five years has the club been free of the controversy that results when one seeks to protect what another would exploit. That has meant sixty-five years' experience in trying to resolve a crescendo of conflicts—experience that we can draw upon as we consider today's major controversies and the still more critical contests that tomorrow will inevitably bring.

These conflicts will underline the need for conservation education; more than that, they will require the education of conservationists. There's quite a difference.

On the one hand, *conservation* alludes to management of the commodity resources, to using them wisely that they may last longer. We all approve of conservation, even as we approve of motherhood—even while we go on expending our nonrenewable resources at a constantly accelerating rate (more in this century than in all previous history). We intend to do better. In the end, however, we know that no matter how well we manage our commodity resources and our raw materials, time will catch up with us. Conservation means spreading a given resource over a given period of time. Time finally runs out and the resource is gone, or at best, is a rarity.

On the other hand, the *conservationist,* and I stress the *-ist,* has come to be known as the person who is concerned with preserving for all our time certain important scenic resources—our resources of wilderness, parks, wildlife, and the recreation and inspiration we may always derive from them. Always, that is, if each generation, including ours, takes care of the few places we have left where those resources still survive.

To use a figure, there are two sides to conservation just as there are two sides to a coin. On one side, tangible quantities; on the other, intangible qualities. Each side is presently oriented to look in opposite directions. Yet each must live with the other. We may need a coin of transparent material, so that each side can look in both directions.

Conservationists, then, are people *more* concerned about what certain natural resources do for their soul than for their bank balance. Each of us is a conservationist part of the time in our thinking, if not in our action.

There are a great number of people who are conservationists in their action also – more than eleven thousand in the Sierra Club, and about two million who are loosely organized in the Natural Resources Council of America. The numbers are growing more rapidly than is our population. Every time a scenic hill is bulldozed for a new tract of houses, or a new freeway blots out more acres of green quietude, or a new dam inundates a trout stream, or there's a vacant space where a great tree was, or another whooping crane turns up missing – every time one of these things happens, the conservationist force grows stronger as more people realize the need to protect a rarity from extinction. Theirs is not a force of blind opposition to progress, but of opposition to blind progress. Theirs is a force determined to see that progress does not take away important things from humanity, forever, in order to benefit a few people.

The conservationist force, I submit, is not a pressure group. It merely demonstrates the pressure of conscience, of innate knowledge that there are certain things we may not ethically do to the only world we will ever have, and to the strictly rationed resource of natural beauty which still exists in that world. The conservationist force does not need to be pressed into action. It needs only be made to realize what is happening, and its voice of conscience speaks.

That sounds simple. It isn't. I need not go into any detail to convince you of the difficulty of making people realize something – of their making it real to themselves – not imaginary – but actual. You know how hard it is to be heard in the clamor around us. And we all know how hard it is to get the voice of conscience to speak audibly enough to have effect. For example, how many times a week do you feel something needs to be done for the public good – and how many of those times can you find the few minutes to do something about it yourself?

So the conservationist force, for all its conscience, still needs to realize more, and to speak more. Conservation controversies, like prefabricated telephone booths, are ubiquitous. All of them are conflicts for space. The resolution of these conflicts should depend upon the answer to the question: Who needs the space most? Unfortunately, many of the decisions are being made now, and irrevocably, not on the basis of who needs the space most, but on who got there first with the most dramatic plan of development and the biggest earth-moving equipment.

It would be helpful, in resolving the coming conflicts for space, to have on hand a battalion with the wisdom of Solomon. Not having even one Solomon, let us nevertheless see what we can do to: consider a few of the conflict types in some detail; list the tools we have for resolving conflicts; try to arrive at the criteria for decision; and suggest some courses of immediate action. This is a big order. If in the course of this I make noises like an oracle, please forgive me. To be brief, I'll stick to direct sentences. In your own mind please add "it seems to me" to each sentence.

What Are Some of the Conflicts?

People against Numbers—People have demonstrated, as clearly as they have demonstrated anything, that they are prolific enough to explode across the land—not with the rapidity of an epidemic, of course, but more thoroughly and with far more lasting devastation of the natural resources of the only world we have yet contrived to live upon. We can label this statement "neo-Malthusian," but the labeling solves no resource problem. The members of what we could label "the Science-Will-Save-Us-Society" will have quite a burden to prove that science really can save us. Science can do wonderful things, but our scientists can only begin to gather data on the new problems civilization presents every year, and in turn can only begin to publish and interpret their data.

A serious problem confronting scientists, and one upon which no conservation organization I know of has adopted a policy, is the population problem—an especially touchy cat to put a bell on.

Natural scientists know full well what happens when there is an explosion of population in deer; the deer themselves lose vitality and starve by the thousands because they have overloaded their range. Mankind has a range, too, and it has a maximum carrying capacity consistent with a good life—a life with enough resources on hand for all to spare us the final quarrel over them. We may argue about how many people the range can withstand, but we can hardly argue that there is no limit. We have strong intimations, as we watch the sea of smog rise around us, that the limit is approaching faster than we thought, and from a different quarter. It may well be shortage of clean air, not of water, that brings us to a sudden halt in California.

Whatever the limiting factor, and, though our engineers cover the earth with a mezzanine floor, we know that we shall come to a day when we can no longer double our population, or even add to it, without lasting regret. We could continue to worship Growth until midnight of that last day. But there is a brighter possibility and it is worth working hard for. When the light turns red, you stop before you hit the car ahead. If you don't, you're in trouble. The margin between us and trouble is our scenic open space and our wilderness. We vaguely sense the shape of this need; later and wiser people will know it surely, in the crowded world we are letting their heritage become. For them, we could choose to skimp a little on gadgets, even our most elaborate gadgets, even as they shall one day be forced to skimp, and with so much less wild world to repair to.

The brighter possibility, then, is to look for substitutes before we have completely used up a given resource. Perhaps we, as present stewards for the natural resources of all generations, could revive the practice of tithing – saving ten percent for the future. Not ten percent of what this generation received from the last, but a tithe of what was here, in our best estimate, when white man began to spread over this continent. If that sounds overgenerous, remember how few the generations who have used up the ninety percent, and how many generations will need what's left, to leaven their otherwise ersatz world.

Water Development – Where water development and wilderness preservation are in conflict, we can remember that gravity will take water through parks and wilderness and out to places where people want to use it or store it. Optimum development downstream can preclude irrevocable damage to wilderness values upstream. Quite often it will cost less; but even if it were to cost more in dollars, it would save what dollars cannot put together again.

The conflict with hydroelectric development is more direct, for people want to get energy from the water that gravity brings down. Alternate sources of energy are coming fast, however, and we can afford to wait for their perfection rather than sacrifice scenically important streams and valleys. [If only I had thought then about energy conservation!] We need to remember that our choice to preserve is a temporary determination at best. Our choice to sacrifice, however, requires all future people to live by our choice. We will have written the rules for them, and indelibly.

Wood Products – The Timber Resources Review recently completed by the Forest Service has demonstrated that our principal opportunity to meet the future's need for timber lies elsewhere than in the virgin forests of our best wilderness and park lands. The National Lumbermen's Association has gone even further. Its recent releases have stressed the need for expanding the timber market and have stated that we are growing one-third more timber than we are harvesting; they therefore opposed the timber-reserve part of the Soil Bank. Plywood people want much less plywood imported. Moreover, in the immediate future we can see a minor revolution in the wood-products industry in the promise of the chipper, particle board, and alternate sources of cellulose that will have to substitute for virgin-forest timber sooner or later. In the absence of a policy which provides specific criteria for determining how much wilderness we shall need to preserve, and in the presence of abundant promise of substitutes for wilderness timber, and considering also the many values for mankind the wilderness forest affords—multiple use of the highest, most diverse order—we should not be hard put to decide the course to vote for in the timber-versus-wilderness conflict.

Highways—These had better go around our scenic gems, not through them, unless we want the face of our land crisscrossed by high-speed routes to beautiful places that might have been. We have the potential of drowning ourselves with automobiles, of so overloading our hardened arterials that first the pleasure of driving will disappear—and then the motion.

Our children shall need parklike places where they can have a change of pace and mood—where they can spend a good chunk of time and become part of the scene for a while. It will not be enough for them to screech to a stop because of a traffic light or traffic jam, then roll down the window for a quick sniff of the great outdoors before the person behind blows a horn. Many people fear that our engineers are more skillful at moving vehicles than at moving people, and that a lot of space is being too freely used up in the process.

We are enamoured of horsepower, of highways and freeways, of covering more ground more quickly and with greater safety. In our ardor, however, we may well consider that it is very hard to undo a freeway and impossible to redo a wilderness.

Other Conflicts—There are other conflicting demands for our present scenic open spaces—conflicts brought on by our needs for flood control, industry, mining, food and forage and fiber, by urbanization, and by recreation, too. There is no need to go into detail about them now. They all come from real needs for things we want and believe in. But with reasonable restraint we can eat cake and have some too—have conveniences *and* wilderness, so long as we remember that there are some areas where convenience costs too much.

What Tools for Resolving Conflicts?

What tools have we already fashioned, or what can we invent, to resolve these conflicts?

Facts—First, we need facts about resources. Many organizations are assembling them, and more help is needed. For scenic resources, the organizations prepared to do the best job nationally are the National Park Service, which has a program based upon a 1936 law and Mission 66; the Forest Service, which has now come up with its Operation Outdoors; and the Fish and Wildlife Service, now developing its own Operation Waterfowl. California is off to a good, if late start with its imminent recreation plan now before the legislature. Many other agencies are involved, and coordination is essential.

Interpretation—But facts are not enough. One of our unheralded national surpluses is the surplus of undigested data which, if laid end to end, would reach too far. A fact has meaning only when it gets from producer to market, only when it is published and interpreted well. We are badly in need of equitable interpretation of the facts we are gathering about our natural resources.

Most important, we must to the best of our ability project all future needs on the same screen with the same projection distance and same focal length of lens for each scene, and also, to the best of our ability, with the same illumination. Let the light be a cool one.

So far we have had quite a disparity in distances, lenses, and light. In California, for example, we know that water development is going to make heavy demands upon what land we have for other purposes. To project that scene, we have elaborate equipment that has been derived from an eight-year effort at a cost of better than one million dollars per year. But water isn't all we'll be needing in the year 2000; it is only one of many things.

What kind of equipment do we have, whether in California or in the country as a whole, to project our other needs? By comparison, we can project our needs for scenic resources with little more than a nineteenth-century magic lantern, lit by a lone flame. Unless we can demonstrate the need for equity, we stand a good chance, so far as this particular conflict goes in California, of having the best-watered, most crowded, biggest-grossing state in the Union—and the least beautiful one. Our white-water streams will be so fully harnessed for use that you can't see running water; each pleasant little valley in the hills and mountains will be replaced by a fluctuating reservoir, its watershed cropped and gravely impaired; and suburbia will spread almost everywhere else. Bear in mind that our state director of water resources, in opposing the wilderness bill, listed in his reasons for doing so that the bill would hamper California Water Plan hopes for dams or water structures in Lava Beds and Joshua Tree National Monuments and Yosemite National Park, as well as the plan's hopes to use the Marble Mountains Wilderness as a dumping place for spoil. We don't need water that badly. And no bill would stop these things if the people should ever really need them.

Public Information—The public needs information, too. All our facts and interpretation will mean little if the public isn't taken into confidence. After all, the public must consent to whatever proposal we come up with. "The engineering of consent" is the concise definition of public relations. Meetings such as the Wilderness Conferences are a starting point. What we do after we leave the meetings will determine how far the cause moves.

Legislation—An informed public will want a clear statement of policy, which is a statement in law, and will want continuing legislative interest in what happens under the policy. Congress, for example, is the nation's board of directors. It should reserve the power to review irreversible staff decisions which lead to the extinction of a given resource. Right now the federal staff can extinguish wilderness with a pen stroke—and the pen is striking.

Administration—The executive branch, armed with administrative regulations based upon law, will supply the preponderance of protection, for only this branch of government has staff enough to do the job full-time. Loosely worded regulations, which were adequate for a loosely populated land largely free of conflict, will have to become specific—and must in turn be based upon more specific law if we are to avoid a dangerous overconcentration of discretion. For instance, there will need to be a clearer understanding of the full meaning of multiple use and of the limitations of multiple use. This has never meant a great number of cooks working over the same pot of broth, although many people think so.

Education—The legislative and executive branches, with help from lay organizations, will then need to continue the effort of public education—the engineering of support. The need for this is stressed whenever any two people discuss the subject of conservation, and sometimes even when the discussion is only a monologue. We have a long way to go—or to say it another way, we have a great opportunity.

These are the tools. They are all necessary. Those named last will be of little use if we don't have equitably interpreted facts to start with.

What Criteria for Making Decisions?

Let us go back briefly to that matter of correctly interpreting facts, for it is from this interpretation that we shall have to derive our criteria for decision.

We must make one decision before we shall know how to sort out our facts. Shall we on the one hand resurrect the rejected philosophy of *après moi le déluge,* or on the other hand shall we seek the exact opposite for those who follow us—for them a world as beautiful as ours? I don't think this will be a hard decision to make but we shall need to keep reminding ourselves that we made it.

Since wilderness is our primary concern here, let us list the points we need to consider in weighing wilderness preservation against a potential conflicting use. This weighing will set a pattern for the scenic resources which are less fragile than wilderness. And wilderness conflicts are hardest to solve and most critical.

1. The wilderness we have now is all that we, and all people, will ever have.

2. Much of our wild land which is presently used for wilderness will be lost to wilderness use. It has not been dedicated, and remains only by accident or oversight, or because of the slight value of its raw materials.

When it goes, its human load must be added to that placed upon dedicated wilderness, wherever it is left.

3. We don't know what the carrying capacity in people is now, either for accidental or dedicated wilderness—carrying capacity that should be expressed in two ways: (a) What human use will a place withstand and still recover naturally, and (b) how many people will it withstand at a given time without their eliminating its aesthetic value at the time?

With respect to recoverability: We must not be fooled by vastness of a total area. The key terrain, or the heartland, or the living space, or the camping base—whatever you may call it—is that rare, scarce oasis that has real scenic appeal, that has water and shade, wood and forage, that is gentle enough in slope to camp on, and that possesses a wild setting (without which one might as well camp in Central Park). There is precious little key terrain, even in the vastest reserves. And what key terrain there *is* is likely also to be a good reservoir site.

With respect to aesthetic capacity: Wilderness cannot be false-front wilderness and fulfill what we need in it—no green-belt fringe obscuring a periodic sea of stumps. There must be assurance that a person's wild slice of sky won't have too many elbows in it, or administrative conveniences either. There must be room enough for time—where the sun can calibrate the day, not the wristwatch, for days or weeks of unordered time—time enough to forget the feel of the pavement and to get the feel of the earth, and of what is natural, and right.

4. Whatever the carrying capacity may be, we can predict that it will be limited—so limited that wilderness can probably never again be abundant enough for all people to walk in it. But after all, only the small child must handle a thing to know it; adults need only look. Those in between need a little of both. So some people will be able to walk in wilderness and most of them will be the better for it. Some may wish to but never make it. Some may not think they care to at all, nor expect their children to care. But wilderness must be there, or the world's a cage.

5. It follows that our expanding population will need more wilderness than exists, and far more than has yet been set aside for preservation.

6. Therefore, we can conclude that any step to discard our vestige of dedicated American wilderness, or to reduce its protection, is premature at this time. And knowing this, we are obligated to insure its protection the best way we know how: by law, regulation, and understanding.

To those who for materialistic convenience want to extinguish just part of that dedicated wilderness, we can cite Solomon's precedent. We all remember his most famous decision, when one mother wanted the child divided and the other wanted the child spared, even if she herself were not to have it. Let the judgment favor those who want the wilderness to remain whole. A decision adverse to that whole can never be rescinded.

Suggestions for Immediate Action

It will take time to seek out facts and reach decisions in the long-range public interest—three years at the very least. In the interim an immediate holding action is needed, and I have a brief suggestion. Let federal and state executives appoint task forces who can set about promptly to put up three kinds of signs in places where it is the consensus of conservationists that they belong:

"Sample, Don't Sell" should be posted for each of our crown jewels—our parks, dedicated wilderness, or their equivalent in scenic caliber.

"Closed During Inventory" ought to be posted on certain areas in controversy in which the scenic, recreational, and scientific values are probably high, lest we find that the forthcoming inventory of our scenic resources consists of checking off our choicest treasures as they vanish.

"Business As Usual" signs can be posted everywhere else. [No. Look what business as usual has achieved in a mere thirty-two years!]

In any event, some kind of moratorium is essential. A three-year wait on some of our development projects is not long compared to the eternity our descendants shall otherwise have to live by any mistakes we make out of premature commitment. For example, consider the tragically premature decision at Hetch Hetchy, in Yosemite National Park, a controversy that is all water behind the dam—the dam in Hetch Hetchy Valley from which San Francisco gets the same water it could have diverted outside the park. There was one unclouded crystal ball four decades ago, and William E. Colby, now honorary president of the Sierra Club, was looking into it when he wrote the membership on the last day of 1909:

"I predict that long before Hetch Hetchy could possibly be needed for a water supply for San Francisco, the travel thither will have become so great and its needs as a campground, particularly in relation to the surrounding park, so urgent, as to preclude the possibility of its use as a reservoir. What I am opposed to is the determination right now that the Hetch Hetchy shall be flooded fifty years from now. I feel that the decision ought properly to be reserved for those who live fifty years hence. We surely can trust that their decision will be a wiser one than any we can make for them." The decision, we know, would have been entirely different in 1959. But how many wrong decisions are we rushing to make now that will erase other Hetch Hetchys for all time? Our children deserve better.

We could sum it all up this way:

Our civilized world is the house that Jack built. We like most of it.

Our living wilderness is the garden that Jack hasn't built on, the open space and the wildland beauty that graces his house. It is his only garden, and we know that there is no more where it came from.

Jack is very capable; he can doggedly expand his house, build a three-car garage, and pave the remaining space except for an outcrop or two of rock in the northwest forty. And we can see that he's on the verge.

If only Jack would pause a moment, to look up and to see! He isn't going to like the end result himself, and his children surely will prefer to inherit a balanced estate, for they will have no place else to go.

Wildlands in Our Civilization,
***Sierra Club Bulletin,* June 1957**

THE MEANING OF WILDERNESS TO SCIENCE

RESTORATION WOULD HAVE BEEN a great subject for a conference in 1959, but we had not yet foreseen its importance. We were more concerned with preserving a resource that is not restorable – wilderness. It is simply not possible to restore elements of an ecosystem that have not yet been discovered and named, much less understood. Wilderness is full of just such elements. How full? We do not know, and may never know. Which adds to the fascination of wilderness.

We were ready, however, to look into the meaning of wilderness to science. We had seen how important this aspect was in public hearings on the Wilderness Bill conducted by Oregon's Senator Richard Neuberger. He thought it important, and if he did, we had better build science's case in more detail.

The Sierra Club book, *The Meaning of Wilderness to Science,* is still, in my mind, the best of the series of volumes the biennial conferences made possible, and this is not to demean the others. There were so few printed of any of them that a responsible reprint publisher should get to work and get them back in print.

The 1959 book has forty-eight pages of black-and-white photographic illustrations. They were reproduced well by letterpress – even varnished – and the originals are probably scattered beyond recall. So the few copies of the original edition should be treasured, if only for the illustrations – by Ansel Adams and Lowell Sumner (who liked to photograph and pilot simultaneously), with a superb series of photographs of wildlife and Alaska by Warren Steenbergh, Charles Ott, and Herb and Lois Crisler.

Then, of course, there is the text, with contributions that should be available in all natural resources libraries, by Daniel Beard, Stanley Cain, Luna Leopold, Robert Rausch, Ian McTaggert Cowan, Raymond B. Cowles, Frank Fraser Darling, and a piece by G. M. Trevelyan, "The Call and Claims of Natural Beauty," which added the poetry the scientists may not have had time to include. Inevitably, there was another foreword:

SIX BIENNIAL WILDERNESS CONFERENCES have been held in the San Francisco Bay region since 1949, sponsored by the Sierra Club. They began with the idea of hearing out the views of various users and administrators of wilderness in the Sierra Nevada on the question of how to enjoy wilderness without wearing it out, or, stated another way, how not to love it to death. It all could be summarized as the threat from the *inside,* a threat not to be minimized.

But the first conference had hardly got under way before people realized that the inside threat, important though it was, paled before the *outside* threat, the threat to exploit wilderness to extinction. The vanguard of wilderness preservers saw that it would do little good to argue about whether to bury litter in wilderness or to carry it out if, meanwhile, mop-up crews of exploiters were busy rolling up the boundaries of wilderness and getting rid of it.

It was noted that each exploitative group was fond of wilderness, and wanted only its own special kind of concession in it—just roads to take out the bug trees and improve the forest so that it would not be a biological desert, or to enable sportsmen to harvest the surplus game because it was a biological Eden, or to make it accessible to the lame and the halt, or to harvest the tree crop to avoid waste; just water development to maintain streamflow or improve forage for deer or to render it more accessible for outboard motors or to enhance the scenery; just a chance to try out man's new experiment, wildlands management. Each concession was admirable in itself. Each necessary in its place. But was wilderness the place? Or was wilderness something that needed guarding more than managing, careful respect for the forces that had built it and kept it, that were still building it and could still keep it, without benefit of technology? Was it possible that the chief managerial task in wilderness was to manage management lest wilderness, by definition, be managed to death? There was growing conviction that wilderness could enhance the American standard of living—if the American standard of *having* did not extinguish wilderness first. It was postulated that if America were to ignore, for utilitarian purposes, that small part of its land area which is still wilderness, if America were to consider it there just to be enjoyed for what it is and not for what it could be remodeled into, then the nation would still survive handsomely—perhaps even more so. Just pretend it isn't there, the theory runs, and carry on business as usual *around* it; you won't regret it. There isn't too much heresy in the concept. Successful corporations call it a reserve. A successfully civilized nation ought to be able to set aside a reserve, not of money for a rainy day, but of wilderness for a rainy century—and enjoy it *as wilderness* until the rains come or even beyond that.

Early conferences cast about for some way to achieve this. Surely there must be a role for at least two branches of the government of a nation if something as irreplaceable as wilderness was at stake on the nation's land. The executive branch could designate and guard it, but the legislative branch should at least recognize it and grant wilderness an automatic stay of execution, whoever might wish to cancel it out. Out of all this the Wilderness Bill emerged. And out of the extended consideration the various versions of the bill received, the meaning of wilderness in the whole context of national resources became clearer. Perhaps what follows is a fair sketch of the relationship that has been seen to exist.

It has been the custom to look at natural resources as of two kinds: renewable, such as foods and fibers; and nonrenewable, such as metals, minerals, and fossil fuels. It is now of major importance to look anew, to consider not how renewable a resource is, but whether we have prospects of finding a substitute for it.

This is so for two reasons:

1. Our rate of depleting the nonrenewables is accelerating in spite of our knowledge of the following fact, succinctly put by Sir Charles Darwin: "During the whole of man's history there has been a great deal of mineral extracted from the earth, gold, copper, iron, coal, and so on. *More than half the grand total* of these metals and minerals has been taken out of the ground since 1920" (from the Rede Lecture, 1958, Cambridge).

2. Our renewables depend entirely upon the earth's thin skin of soil, and we are wasting these, at a rapidly increasing rate, through erosion by water and bulldozer; through burial, inundation, and poisoning; and through eradication of species of unknown value to our own future.

We know from the U.S. Geological Survey that the prospects are good of finding substitutes for the nonrenewables, through vastly improved technology in the processing of sea water and common rocks, aided by the almost unlimited store of energy from the atom [bite my tongue!] and the sun that we are learning to control.

We have no assurance that we can find substitutes for the myriad, and for all we know, indispensable forms of life—in the soil, on the land, and in the air—upon which the entire chain of life depends.

Wilderness. The most important source of the vital organic forms constituting the chain of life is the gene bank that exists in wilderness, where the life force has gone on since the beginning uninterrupted by man and his technology. For this reason alone, it is important that the remnants of wilderness which we still have on our public lands be preserved by the best methods our form of government can find. The proposed National Wilderness Preservation System (now before the Congress) provides an excellent route to that goal, and especially dynamic leadership in the Congress and the administration will be required during the next decade to achieve the goal of wilderness preservation which the system would make possible. There will be important subsidiary benefits to recreation, to watershed protection, and to the beauty of the land.

A growing economy will have availed us nothing if it extinguishes our all-important wilderness. A gross misunderstanding of wilderness, in which it is evaluated according to the number of hikers who get into it, has been fostered for the past several years, to the great detriment of all the future. There must be no more needless, careless losses. There is no substitute for wilderness. What we now have is all that we shall ever have.

Other resource problems are of secondary importance, but still far more important than one would assume from a regular perusal of the nation's financial pages, or from most public speeches.

Forestry. The government badly needs a program that will bring to forestry a full realization that forests mean far more than timber and pulp. On many forests other uses should be given precedence, but rarely are. The overwhelming emphasis in the training of forest-land managers, and in the decisions they make, is on timber production. Reforestation, watershed protection, recreation, wildlife restoration, and wilderness preservation are suffering severely as a result.

Water. Reliance upon the reimbursable dollar as the primary criterion for water development can bring about bad projects and prevent good ones as long as there is no satisfactory means of assessing the perpetual dollar value of natural land and streams. The nation needs to proceed without delay to a classification of streams that will present to future generations a countryside with optimum water development and wild-stream preservation. Some of the streams should be primitive, some semi-primitive, some partly developed, and some fully developed. We have waited too long already to develop a national water plan based upon this simple and clearly necessary foundation. The interim delay in the effort to clean up open sewers cannot be continued.

Parks—Little time remains in which to rough out the undedicated areas having high scenic, wilderness, and wildlife values which should be added to the National Park System. The only error we can make now is to preserve too little. It has been much too long since a major scenic reservation was made in the United States proper, either by creation of new national parks by Congress or national monuments by proclamation. There has been too much "Let Roosevelt do it"—Teddy or Franklin. There is far too much parochialism evident now that the effort to round out the parks is getting belatedly into motion. Some one hundred eighty million acres were set aside as national forests in a bold, sweeping motion more than half a century ago. Within these areas are some of the finest potential parks, and a transfer of a small fraction of the national forest total could greatly enrich the National Park System without appreciable impoverishment of our national forests—especially when the nation has some fifty million acres of forest land that was allowed to become impoverished and is critically in need of reforestation.

Wildlife—We need an expanded program of habitat improvement on developed lands and a fuller understanding of the importance, to many species, of preserving a natural regimen, in wildlife refuges and game ranges as well as in wilderness. Of primary importance is a still more intensive program of research in methods of control of herbicides and pesticides so as to reduce peril to wildlife and to people.

Roads and highways—Construction of roads has proceeded so rapidly that there has not been time to evaluate properly their cost to the nation in impairment of the economic feasibility of efficient mass transportation, or in the cholesterol laid down in the cities' arteries, or in soil, beauty, and wilderness lost. It is now time to reappraise the high priority given to roads in the expenditure of public funds in view of the lagging programs in many critical fields, such as education, world health, redevelopment, and preservation.

We have lately been playing a game of strip poker with the American earth. A relatively few people have been winning the early hands—people interested in quick profits from the sale of conveniences—and all but guaranteeing that our children will lose as the game goes on, not just conveniences, but necessities as well.

We need wider realization that milk does not come from a bottle, nor water from a tap, nor gasoline from a throttle. These are all part of our natural resources, wealth put by nature on the only world we are ever likely to live on comfortably. The nation needs men who can match its mountain depleters, who will realize that we must never again deplete, at the rate we have been depleting since World War I, resources of the earth for which there are no known substitutes, including the tiny vestige which constitutes all the remaining wilderness on the earth.

Perhaps this would have been thought an extreme appraisal and not a fair one, a few years ago. But not any longer. For there is a rapidly growing readiness to scrutinize these issues, and not to dismiss them merely because they may not accord with the Conventional Wisdom. These are issues to be faced honestly in our own interest, if survival interests us. Other species—and wilderness too—will then also survive as a happy coincidence.

***The Meaning of Wilderness to Science,* 1959**

What leads to what, somehow? If everything is interconnected, what happens at the intersections? These are good questions warranting a MacArthur grant and a chair at a university. So my foreword somehow pleased Kenneth Bechtel, thanks in no small part to his new wife, Nancy Foote Slusser. She had been on Sierra Club High Trips with me and was fascinated with photography, enough that she persuaded her husband, who had been hesitant, to be magnanimously supportive. The book publishing program received a fifty-thousand-dollar boost in grant and loan. *"In Wildness Is the Preservation of the World"* might otherwise never have been published.

What did *The Meaning of Wilderness to Science* lead to? Among other things, the Arctic National Wildlife Range, inasmuch as its principal advocates attended the Wilderness Conference from which the book was derived. Probably more far reaching was Professor Raymond Cowles's presentation, "Population Pressure and Natural Resources." Professor Cowles was a prominent ecologist born in South Africa, concerned about the impact of humanity on the African wilderness. He wrote *Zulu Journal,* published by the University of California Press, which led to his being invited to the conference. Population was a subject environmental organizations, including the Sierra Club, had not wished to tangle with. He involved the club and a host of other listeners. Otherwise the club would not have been ready to publish Dr. Daniel Luten's article, "How Dense Can People Be?" and refuse to be dismayed by the handful of resignations the article stimulated. Nor would the club have been ready, nine years later, to co-publish Paul Ehrlich's *The Population Bomb* with Ballantine Books, thereby creating a major global wave of grave concern about the rising and preemptive tide of humanity.

Professor Cowles said in his opening, "Behind everything I am going to say is the Malthusian principle, expressed one hundred fifty to two hundred years ago, that man has the capacity to outgrow his resources by continued multiplication until some limiting factor stops reproduction, and he comes into equilibrium with his environment."

Malthus's picture was gloomy, Cowles thought, and did not come true, and has been discredited because his timing was wrong. I have argued since then that Malthus was not wrong, nor was his timing; he erred only in failing to foresee that humanity would be perfectly willing to mine its renewable resources as well as those that were not renewable in order to feed itself.

Professor Cowles's words were followed by stimulating discussion, and only the few hundred people who listened or those who bother to read the book if they can find it, have any idea of the importance of what was said. I am simply happy to recommend it to people who would rather learn from history than suffer the alternative.

SKIS TO THE WINTER WILDERNESS

JUST BEFORE WORLD WAR II caught up with me I was given the First Class Skier award by the California Ski Association and also by the Sierra Club. The award customarily went to top competitors, and one had to be very good to get it. Mine came as a result of my various efforts in ski-mountaineering, where the competition was negligible. My philosophy was stated succinctly—an adverb rarely appropriate to what I have to say—in the legend for a photograph in the 1962 edition of the *Manual of Ski Mountaineering*. I still like it:

"The main thing is to take off. We have nothing against the practice slopes and the standard runs; but if that's all you know, you have missed something special, something lost behind the ranges, a sparkling new white world, with its hard edges covered over for the winter, and you its discoverer."

Before World War II, I edited the manual for the University of California Press to help the war effort, and the war effort in turn helped subsequent editions. The book was in print for twenty-seven years. If you can find a copy of the later editions—some sixty thousand were printed—you will find the illustrations that accompany the following introduction:

THE WIND HAD A MEAN EDGE on it as it curved to cross the crest of the Sierra Nevada and found us there, two thousand feet above the site of the Donner Party tragedy, trying to find out how to camp in deep snow. It was deep snow that caught the Donner's immigrants back in 1846. Thirty-six people died from cold and starvation, and more would have starved, probably, but for cannibalism.

Our exposed spot on the crest was not where you would expect to find a father pushing fifty, much less being pushed by his two teenage sons. But there we were anyway, and by plan.

We knew that California has come (or gone) quite a distance since the Donner Party's ordeal. Skiing technique has progressed quite a bit, too, since Snowshoe Thompson carried the trans-Sierra mails in the late fifties (the *eighteen*-fifties, that is) on his eleven-foot skis and since his contemporaries set eighty-five-mile-per-hour speed records in the earliest American ski races on record.

More relevantly, we also knew that California has gone a fair distance in making a sport of the best of what the Donners and Thompson learned—how to survive in snow and how to ski safely through rugged, untracked terrain. The ice-edged wind found us looking at the very peaks upon which that new sport, ski-mountaineering, had been adapted to California terrain by the Sierra Club and then exported to help the armed forces in World War II. I was exported, too, and saw how our ski-mountaineering technique and equipment aided the troops, myself included, giving them combat mobility and *esprit* that should be recorded better than it has been before it is forgotten.

Now, after too long a lapse, I was back in old Sierra haunts. I brought my sons to this crest, not to expose them to danger but to try to show them how to avoid it. I wanted very much to see them feel at home on the snow, far back in the winter wilderness, all around the clock and all around the compass.

Moreover, I also had a suspicion that every generation needs to invent contests which it can be first to win. This certainly seems to be true of people who look to mountains for their contests. The two generations before mine won their contests – most of them – on the great peaks of the Alps and the major summits of the United States. My generation finished off the Himalayan giants. I mean, that's what climbers did who could afford such expeditions; the less affluent of us settled for little-known peaks or for switching seasons or routes on climbs of the well-known summits.

To pioneer, my father never had it so rough; he had only to find a peak. I could still pioneer merely by finding hard ways up easy peaks – and going back down to spend the night in comfort. Today's mountaineers, however, must look for the hardest way up the hardest peaks, and be willing to spend several successive nights trying to sleep partly inside a sack partly suspended from a cliff. The suspense is tremendous!

What next? As a parent of children who may momentarily join the ranks of today's mountaineers, I care. I dread their feeling they must outdo the Eiger and Yosemite men. I hope their pioneering can have more fun in it, no less challenge, and fewer of the spices of danger.

Not too subtly, then, I was trying to expose my delegates to the new generation to the good things that could happen if they were to turn their skis to the wilderness for a few winter weekends at least. I hope the exposure will take. For one thing, it will really stretch their skiing budget – four ski weekends for the price of one! – and will simultaneously shorten the ski-lift lines. More important, they'll have new frontiers to explore every time there is a new fall of snow. They'll find country – especially the western uplands – measured in millions of acres where skis have never penetrated. And they'll learn that there is need for all their new skill in inventing ways to achieve more mobility and safety with less weight. In the course of all this they'll also find out that in winter one of the finest methods of transportation ever invented is a man's own two feet – plus seven-foot skis. [I then believed in a long wheelbase.]

I'm not just dreaming. I'm lucky enough to have children who walk. They simply take it for granted – so far – that walking is the only way to get to the best places, those wild places where cars can't go and shouldn't.

My sons, Ken, who is seventeen, and Bob, who is sixteen, like the look of snow where the only ski tracks are those behind them and where, ahead, the tracks of wildlife are mysteries to try to unravel. They like to top a rise and start down into the far valley knowing that there's no one there, that it is just as wild as if creation had been yesterday. They may even like the sense of relief, of getting away from the compulsion to perfect skiing form—and forget its substance—in succession after frenetic succession of turns down the beat, nicked slopes above the long chair-lift lines.

I'm not trying to paint my boys as antisocial, nor myself as averse to resort skiing. We are all, however, prone to like change of scene. Fending off the chiselers in the lift lines, relaxing briefly while we ride the chairs, and fighting our way back down the slopes, running over the tails of the slow skis ahead of us or trying not to be run over by the faster skis behind—all this is good fun for a certain number of weekends. Then we're ready to get back to fundamentals.

Out our way spring is the best time for those fundamentals. The days are long enough to light a several-mile ski tour and the sun is usually mature enough to warm a lunchtime bask. The snowpack is at its deepest, smoothing out the high country. The Sierra Club's touring huts are especially inviting then, each an easy day's travel sandwiched between snug nights. Well, not *too* easy a sandwich. They are a good warm-up for ski-mountaineering.

Borrowing what I could remember of my early ski-mountaineering days, I appointed myself coach. In accepting me in that role, Ken and Bob tacitly accepted (for the moment, at least) my pronouncements drawn from early editions of the *Manual of Ski Mountaineering.*

For example, those of us who compiled the book like a ski boot with a sole that will bend—not easily, but that will at least *bend.* We want bindings that will allow the heel free play in level gliding and in uphill travel; otherwise blisters are guaranteed. We'll settle for ordinary downhill skis. If there's likely to be much soft snow, our poles must have a big enough snow ring to give some thrust when we push back. A ski-mountaineer must really *use* his poles, not just wave them.

Clothing need be no problem. Over the far hill there are no people to impress and to look pretty for. This is a chance to squeeze the last wear out of older ski clothes, to scrape the last thread bare. Stretch pants will get by, but impede circulation, ventilation, and insulation. The baggier the parka, the better—for the same reason. The main requirement of clothing is that it be adjustable; layers will need to be subtracted or added easily to avoid over- or underheating.

A few of the prewar axioms still hold: (1) Two light layers trap more air and insulate better than one heavy layer. (2) It is easier to *keep* warm than to *get* warm. (3) If you don't want a chill, don't work up a sweat.

"If your hands or feet get cold," I admonished the boys, "put on an extra sweater." They looked unbelieving, but I meant it and tried to explain about the body's thermostats which, when they must choose, will always shut down on circulation to the skin and the extremities if this is necessary to conserve heat for the vital organs. I wasn't too lucid, for we had shouldered our GI rucksacks and I found it discreet to conserve words as we started up the grade.

For a fairly long uphill stint we ordinarily would tie climbers on our skis. Plush will do but sealskins are better—they slide forward but not back, even on a thirty-percent slope. I let the boys know that going uphill is nothing but honest toil. They would discover toil's own good reward for themselves, and I needed to concentrate, between puffs, on hoping that I would *re*discover it.

We didn't pick the warmest place for lunch. We stayed out where the view was sweeping, and the wind too. To help save weight, we carried concentrated foodstuffs—pumpernickel, cheese, bologna, nuts, dried fruit, chocolate—but took the curse off our dehydration with a can of fruit juice, brought along purely and forgivably for luxury—"instead of a canteen," I said, getting soft, knowing full well the *Manual* would not tolerate such weakness. Theoretically, we should have melted snow instead, and would indeed have done so had we really been out to make progress in all our technique of going light. Instead I chose the modified spartanism of an old friend of mine who insisted on a cold shower every morning, but explained, "I always add enough warm water to make it comfortable." We weren't going to make this trip an ordeal by hunger or by thirst.

Nor by miles. We traveled only a short distance after lunch and allowed plenty of time to make camp. Bob asked, when he saw me looking uphill for a site, "Why not camp down there in the trees?" This showed good sense but I had another purpose in mind. There must be a demonstration that our camping equipment could make us cozy in an exposed position. So I chose a spot just under the crest, well above any trees.

"Remember to keep well back of the edge," I cautioned. "It's a snow cornice with a big overhang, and all set to collapse." Indeed, we had seen a cornice collapse on our way up, and how swiftly an avalanche could start.

Safely back from the edge we set about excavating a snow platform in pseudo-Himalayan style—but without a lightweight snow shovel. The snow was wind-packed, and of just the right consistency for sawing into blocks.

"Use your ski tails as a saw and a shovel," I said, but warned, "Don't pry; just slice."

I learned this the hard way myself—harder for a friend than for me. I pried, ever so gently, and cracked a ski tail—his.

The excavating went rapidly. You push the tail straight down a foot or so in a series of stabs outlining a snow block, then diagonally slide the tail under the block and slice it out. The snow was perfect for an igloo, but Eskimo engineering and snow-cave digging could come on a later trip. We cut into the slope about three feet on the uphill side and piled our blocks below, ending up with a platform about eight feet square. Using a ski's edge as bulldozer, we leveled it. By now the platform was compacted to ice.

Our Logan-type tent—a twelve-pound wonder—came out of the pack next. Ken volunteered to put up the sectional center pole—an inside job. "I know a good thing when I see it," he told Bob, and got in out of the wind. With the center pole, Ken gave the tent height; Bob and I staked it with ski poles and tied it to skis to give it semblance of shape. The inside man set to work inflating the air mattress (half length was enough for a multiple hip pad), unrolled the down-and-processed-feather sleeping bags (army surplus), and got the Primus stove set up.

Bob passed in a small foam-rubber pad to experiment with. Maybe it would be better than a shared air mattress—he who shares his neighbor's air mattress also shares his neighbor's every bounce. We should find something better. Searches for improvement, big and little, have been one of my own major ski-mountaineering pleasures and could be theirs, too.

I marveled as I climbed into the Logan tent. It must have been designed by a recluse who abhorred proximity. You can even stand up in it! They call it a three-man tent but it could have held our whole family (all six of us) and left room for a friendly guest.

Lying in the luxurious open space of this mansion-on-the-snow, I regaled Ken and Bob with the sad story of the "Home-on-the-Snow" tent I designed just before World War II. Until I die I shall insist this should have been the army's official mountain tent instead of the dank, impractical, inhospitable cul-de-sac the army ended up with. The Home-on-the-Snow was theoretically a two-man tent but we never had fewer than three in it and seldom fewer than four. With four, it would have an extra sag on top caused by the bulge on the sides. It was as snug and revealing as a sweater. Only one person could sit up at a time. No one could stand in it, nor need try.

All in all, this design had antifreeze advantages. It also had a built-in rest inhibitor: when it was full, you could turn over only by mutual consent.

Its minor disadvantages, I still insist, are far outweighed by its virtues, among them its lightness in weight—less than a pound per man. Another, its streamlining and low silhouette, important in high winds. Its worst feature was that it could be snowed in because it was so low. Its best feature was by all odds its cooking space, a vented floorless area in the sloping front. Here your snow mine, which is to say your water supply, is right at hand. You scoop up snow as needed for melting on the stove. If someone tips the stove over—and someone always will—you don't have to rely upon the sleeping bags' blotting up the soup. The snow in the open floor space soaks it up instead, and if you happen to scoop up a little frozen soup when melting snow for your coffee, who's the poorer?

My point isn't to argue the merit of tents, but to suggest that tent building can be fun. I experimented with paper models, then a cloth miniature, and finally the pilot project. It went on many trips before I built its successor, with different material and (let's face it) slightly larger dimensions.

"The perfect tent is yet to be invented," I told Bob, our mechanical son, "and a lot of people are going to have fun trying to invent it." Then I remembered my clincher: "Besides, that first tent only cost me $4.60 for materials." Someone else had all the fun making the Logan—and it cost us eighty-eight dollars.

As with tents, so with packs and stoves. Plenty of room for progress. Whatever the item, the search for a lighter, better, affordable design can be fun. I threw the boys the epitomizing challenge as we sat there luxuriating and I remembered earlier, harder days.

"Beat our twenty-one-pound record if you can," I said. "In my heyday we could take off on a three-day trip and spend two nights out with only twenty-one pounds per man. That included the food, tents, sleeping bags, stoves, utensils, first aid for us and for our skis, and our extra clothing—for seven of us." But it didn't include what we wore, such as our skis and poles.

A pack as light as that, I could add, doesn't play hob with one's downhill ski technique. More important, it doesn't put too great a strain on the swivel muscles that are the hallmark of the chairborne.

Lightness of pack can also make ski-mountaineering co-educational, as we proved during one Easter week in Little Lakes Valley in the High Sierra. Our party of twenty-two included four women. A little more distaff over the hot kitchen Primus could do a world of good. *Anything* would help. Ski-mountaineering menus are wide open for pioneering and whatever I would like to say about the blending of foodstuffs that were never intended to be mixed in the light of day, and the resulting mayhem-in-the-pantry, is privileged information. I swiftly change the subject and claim merely that no ski-mountaineer has ever starved or even gone hungry, and that no man who has done an honest day's toil *need* be a gourmet.

Continuing our honest toil, we struggled to keep the kerosene out of such food as we did have—a struggle that is always very much worth the effort—and we didn't quite succeed. The aftertaste is unforgettable—almost immortal.

I wanted to tell the boys more, but remembered in time that the less a father says to his own sons, the more they are likely to remember. Advice comes best from those who cannot command. I will just disclose to you a few of the things I should like to have told them. They will never know what is said here for they long ago made it a point never to read anything I write if there is the slightest possibility that I'd like them to.

First, I would have cautioned them, if you should ever decide to take up ski-mountaineering on your own, don't go alone or with a weak party or underequipped or anywhere beyond reasonable expectation of safe retreat. Secretly not wanting them to dash too far ahead of me, I would have warned them that if they were *over*burdened with energy, they should save it, thus keeping the party strong if someone else's *under*burden of energy should show up—mine, for instance.

Sounding even more fatherlike, I would have warned them in capital italics about *AVALANCHE HAZARD,* and would have illustrated it with a very hairy story about how four friends of mine would now be dead, their death having been brought about by a very simple-minded avalanche, had a fifth friend not had a cold that day. There I would have ended the story abruptly until they pounded me for details, which I would spoon out with liberal accompaniment of vital avalanche lore.

Finally I would have tried to explain to them what ski-mountaineering had meant to me; about the peaks I had made first ascents of, for the most part on skis; of the high snow camps I had known and what it was like to be up on top in early winter morning and evening, when the world is painted with a very special light; of the kind of competence and even braveness, maybe, that one picks up from good friends and challenging peaks, up there when the storms hit and the snow pelts the fabric all through the night; of the kind of exhilaration we got when, after two winter struggles, the third put us on top of a fourteen-thousander and we were first to be there in winter and see how magnificently winter treats a high land we already knew well in summer but in a lesser beauty; of the long vibrant moments when we were back on our skis, skimming down the uncrevassed glacier on just the right depth of new powder, letting our skis go, finding that every turn worked, hearing the vigorous flapping of our ski pants even though the wind was singing in our ears and stinging our faces, sensing how rapidly the peaks climbed above us, those peaks that had dropped so reluctantly to our level in all the slow day's climb; of the care we had to take after night found us out and we sideslipped and sidestepped down into the tortuous little basins and then into the hummocky forest floor that lay in darkness between us and camp; I would have described that hot cup of soup I cuddled in my hand in exhaustion, sipping slowly to absorb its warmth and its energy at a retainable rate; and I would speak of the morning after and, not its hangover, but its glow as I looked back up to the rocky palisade above the glacier and was just pleased as hell to have got there at last—pleased with the weather, the companions, and the luck—and also forgivably pleased a little that I could do it.

But I didn't tell them all that. This is the sort of thing you find out for yourself, that comes when you escape into the reality of the wilderness and discover how amazingly well man has been designed to cope with just such reality. This is the sort of thing I would want them to find out for themselves. Maybe then, after that, we could compare notes. That would be the best reward of all!

Our Logan was really cozy now. We were in that especially blissful camping situation only the ski-mountaineer or the expeditioner finds himself in. You tie the wind and the chill outside. To insulate yourself doubly against the cold, you climb into the sack, taking off only your boots. Propped on your elbows, you arrange to have dinner served to you in bed – friendly self-service – even as your breakfast will be. The Primus has a friendly roar that can outshout all but the most hostile winds and you listen to your friend. It warms your tent while it roars, but not too much, for you need to keep a circulation of fresh air coming in the tunnel entrance, and the stove exhaust going out the vent near the tent's peak.

We had the entrance tied back and were watching the shadows develop among the turrets of Castle Peak when two skiers christied to a stop at the edge of the brink below them and us.

One of them called over: "Now that really looks comfortable! When do you serve the martinis?"

"They'll be ready for your next run," I said, lying.

"Are you going to spend the night up here?" "We're all set up to, and the boys would like to," I replied; and the boys had indeed said they wished they could. "But we're just trying this business a step at a time. We'll try for an overnight stop next trip."

They took the steep pitch below us in style, like the ski-patrol pros they were. But they never did get back for the martinis, for the lift had stopped running to the top of Signal Hill, a hundred yards above us, and there was no easy way for them to get back up. In less than half an hour we ourselves had struck camp and made our way back to the car, just as the sun left it, and were home four hours later.

On the drive home I had some more fatherly advice for my sons. "When you're old enough for martinis," I counseled, "if you do decide to take up ski-mountaineering and really get back into the wilderness, remember you've got to watch your weight. 'When in doubt, leave it out,' is what we always taught them in the mountain troops.

"Now the way to save weight on martinis," I said, "is to take no vermouth at all."

Perhaps I should have suggested better things not to take.

***Manual of Ski Mountaineering,* 1962**

One of the things I did not take on a ski trip after this experience was myself. Somehow, winter after winter, the snow was gone before I took time to realize it had been there, and three important factors in my skiing became obsolete: my equipment, my technique, and my body.

Gentle Wilderness

Except for the *Ski Mountaineering* introduction, the forewords assembled here had limited distribution. The edition size of the Wilderness Conference proceedings was usually two thousand copies or fewer, and they are very hard to find. The 1964 foreword to *Gentle Wilderness* was another matter. The exhibit-format edition has been available now for twenty-five years and there are hundreds of thousands of Ballantine paperbacks of the book, in two sizes. The first copy did not appear until three months after President Johnson had signed the National Wilderness Preservation Act. The book therefore had nothing to do with that legislation. John Muir's text, which was originally published before I was born, instilled the love of wilderness that motivated a whole constituency for wilderness and still motivates me.

The book and the foreword will both remain useful, I hope, in the task Howard Zahniser foresaw – that the Wilderness Act would be our job description until the National Wilderness System is complete:

What John Muir had to say in *My First Summer in the Sierra* led me, forty years ago, to feel I had already been in the Yosemite High Sierra he was discovering for the first time. Nearly a century after John Muir's first summer, Richard Kauffman has come along with camera instead of notebook to recapture the sense of discovery, and the vividness of what Muir called the Range of Light. Here is the Sierra the way Muir saw it, the way others have seen their first summers confirmed, when they read of Muir's. A cool Sierra wind blows through the photographs, a gentle wind. It is a Sierra illumined by the light of the gentle hours, warm light on a friendly, inviting land.

Is it really gentle wilderness? There is room for argument. Certainly the gentleness of this Sierra wilderness is never soft enough to be cloying. Fear can be mixed with your exhilaration. The passes come impressively high, your breath short, and your pulse rapid. Some of the deepest snows in North America fall there and nothing is gentle about the avalanches when the slopes unload, or about winter temperatures that may drop to fifty-five below. You don't feel very pampered when you are on a half-inch ledge halfway up one of the half-mile-high sheer Yosemite cliffs, or when the March wind finds you and, even though you brace against it with ski poles, flattens you on Mount Lyell's icy shoulder, or when a driving spray drenches you if you venture within a hundred yards of the foot of Vernal Fall in flood, or when a desert sun bakes you at the foot of the Sierra's eastern escarpment, two vertical miles below the summit of Mount Whitney.

Still there is always enough gentleness in the Sierra, or soon will be, when the storm clears or the rough climb ends. No other of the world's great ranges that Mr. Kauffman knows, or that I know, or that so far as we know Muir knew, is as gentle as the Sierra.

If there is to be objection, it is that the Sierra is too gentle—too gentle to counter our assaults against it. John Muir saw this in his first summer and in the later summers and winters when the Sierra was his address. He dedicated his life to a counterassault on the misuse of wilderness and wildlife. He helped establish national parks, enlisted support of national leaders in a preservation movement, battled Gifford Pinchot's predominantly utilitarian interest in conservation, wrote and talked and led with exuberant energy—with the same energy that took him through his favorite forests, among the alpine gardens he loved, and on up so many of the Sierra peaks. He also founded the Sierra Club "to explore, enjoy, and render accessible" the mountain range it was named after. In 1911 he dedicated *First Summer* to the members of the club for their good work.

One of his ideas for rendering the Sierra accessible was a program of summer wilderness outings which he and William E. Colby initiated in 1901. Too many of the places he loved were being lost because too few people knew about them. There would be no hope of sparing Sierra meadows from being overgrazed and devastated by domestic sheep, for instance, unless people saw the damage firsthand and also saw unspoiled meadows so as to evaluate the loss. The giant sequoias were being logged for grape stakes. Hetch Hetchy Valley itself was to be dammed—in the last analysis to produce hydroelectric power for San Francisco. It was not enough to write about the beauty of these places and the tragedy of losing them. People must see for themselves, appraise the danger to the spot on the spot. Informed, devoted defense would ensue.

For sixty-three years since then the concept has worked, modified only slightly. Early in the game Muir had felt that accessibility should include a fairly formidable road net through the High Sierra. Late in the twenties the Sierra Club directors were still advocating several trans-Sierra roads they would shudder to think about today. The words "render accessible" were being misunderstood as an argument for mechanized access and were amended out of the bylaws. The emphasis shifted to getting people to know wilderness as wilderness, to travel there by foot, to leave the fewest possible marks, to spare for another generation the opportunity to discover that which they themselves had loved.

There was not yet much concern about what the foot—a man's or a mule's—might do to wilderness. The high country was still fairly empty. Today a thousand people may walk up the east-side trail to the summit of Mount Whitney over the Labor Day weekend; forty thousand may hit Yosemite Valley over a Memorial Day weekend. There is a new dimension in mountain use—"visitation," the National Park Service calls it. Park

Service ecologists have now identified a few hot spots in the high country above Kings Canyon and Sequoia national parks, places where recreational erosion exceeds a given camping area's capability of recovering. Human erosion itself is not too noticeable, but the associated grazing, trampling, and littering by packstock is severe. What Muir had objected to in the impact of commercial sheep is now being accomplished by animals hired for pleasure. A Forest Service ranger spent a year studying what sheer numbers were doing along Bear Creek, south of Yosemite, and concluded that large groups of wilderness travelers should be eliminated: don't concentrate use in a few places, but disperse it and build primitive toilets and fireplaces in many parts of the wilderness to encourage the dispersal. Not a hundred people in one spot, but ten people in ten spots, or five in twenty.

Meanwhile, in Washington the Forest Service was arguing before Congress that there was probably already too much wilderness set aside; considering the little use it was getting, it was far more important to expedite the construction of timber-access roads and logging operations into undedicated wilderness and to make sure that dedicated wilderness was as free as possible of commercial trees. Too little use, yet so much use the land suffered; log it and end the debate! The confusion continues. The big-trip use that Muir had advocated was the easiest target to hit, or to encourage others to hit. It also happens to be the trip that could serve the widest range of physical and financial abilities. The man too old to carry much of a pack, or the child too young to, can still walk a wilderness trail. Packstock can carry the duffel, the food, the camp equipment. Crew members (usually students who can travel fast enough to break one camp late and make the next one early) allow the wilderness visitor maximum time to enjoy the country with minimum housekeeping. If the moves aren't too far, the stock can relay loads, and half the number of stock can serve the same number of people. Four or more wilderness travelers can thus be served per head of packstock on a moving trip, the kind that gives the visitor the feel of big, continuous wilderness.

Could wilderness be experienced in such a crowd? Could you see the mountains for the people? As a knapsacker I thought not, but changed my mind in the course of spending a year of summer days on Sierra Club High Trips, making careful notes of what happened, checking with Forest Service and National Park Service observers and ecologists, joining with trip leaders and packers in taking the dozens of steps that minimized the impact of people, whether on the wilderness itself or on other people. I was partial then, and still am eight years later, to the moving trip that can give the visitor the feel of a big, continuous wilderness—one in which you can cross pass after pass and know that on the other side you don't drop into civilization, but stay in wilderness instead. In big wilderness you learn how important size itself is to the viability of wilderness. It needs enough buffer to keep its heartland essentially free from the pervasive influences of technology. Such big wilderness is scarce, and is vanishing at the rate of about a million acres a year, chiefly to the chainsaw. People who know it can save it. No one else.

Were Muir alive today he would see the issue clearly and would keep it clear of all the conscious and unconscious confusion. He would know that the choice was not between pristine wilderness and wilderness overused in spots, but between some overuse and no wilderness at all. He would not forget irreplaceable Glen Canyon, hard-hit at some camps along the river, but still not known by enough people to be saved. The Bureau of Reclamation solved the problem of slightly overused campsites by drowning the entire length of the canyon, permanently, with an unnecessary reservoir.

Muir would see what was happening in the Sierra, and would not be fooled by the forces hostile to preservation who now point a diversionary finger at wilderness footprints. He would point out the marks far more damaging than footprints—logging roads, stumps, and trash-clogged streams—that forever killed gentle wilderness on the Kern Plateau because of too little conservationist use. He would note how the real, unbroken wilderness of the High Sierra climax, extending from the Tioga Road in Yosemite down to the Kern, is still vulnerable: a corridor for a needless trans-Sierra road is relentlessly being kept open at Mammoth Pass, and another south of Whitney Meadows. Because there had been too little use, Muir would observe, the wilderness of Vermilion Valley and of a beautiful basin in the North Fork of the Kings had been drowned by power reservoirs—in a day when hydroelectric power means less and less and unspoiled recreation places mean more and more. Muir would not have been impressed by tears about footprints in eyes that winked at mechanized scooters snorting over wilderness trails.

I am sure that John Muir would still believe that firsthand knowledge of places is vital to their survival and that their survival is vital to us. We need places where we can be reminded that civilization is only a thin veneer over the deep evolutionary flow of things that built us. Let wilderness live, and it would always tell us truth.

For all the losses since John Muir's time, an invaluable resource still lives. Much of the Sierra wilderness is essentially what it was half a century ago, altered only by natural succession. The favorite, untouched high places are a constant that can reassure us. So is the roll of familiar things you pass on your way up the heights—the oak savannah, the digger pines, the orderly succession of ponderosa, incense cedar, sugar pine, the firs, then the denizens of timberline. One trouble these days is that you have to call the roll of friends too fast. Speed and the wide highway have brought a deprivation, for the right reason perhaps, but in the wrong places. Speed shrinks wilderness, and there wasn't really enough in Muir's day to serve all those who followed him to California or who will one day be here to look or to live.

Even as in Muir's time, the Sierra Club's purpose is still to gather together people from all over who know how important it is that there should always be some land wild and free. They are needed to counter the rationalizations of the highway builders, and dam and logging-road builders, who would slice through and dismember the wilderness. The purpose of this book is to remind everyone (to paraphrase Newton Drury) that neither California nor the rest of America is rich enough to lose any more of the Gentle Wilderness or poor enough to need to.

We are mindful of all who have encouraged the club's publishing program, especially the exhibit-format series and who with their support and suggestions have helped the Sierra Club broaden the understanding of what wildness means to civilized people.

More than anything, we hope the series will do something lasting for wilderness. We need to save enough of it, what we know viscerally is enough without waiting for all the statistics. We can safely assume that, for all our shortcomings, we are bright enough to carry on our civilization on the ninety-five percent or so of the land we have already disrupted. We are wise enough to recognize that we will not have a bright land, nor really serve ourselves well, if we hurry to disrupt that last five percent on the pretext that progress will otherwise cease. It won't. It will cease, however, if we cannot be kind enough to tomorrow's people to leave for them, in big wilderness, a chance to seek answers to questions we have not yet learned how to ask.

***Gentle Wilderness,* 1964**

The very last line lacks attribution to Nancy Newhall, who put it this way: "The wilderness holds answers to more questions than we yet know how to ask"–the most important statement yet made about wilderness.

WILDLANDS IN OUR CIVILIZATION

FOR BIBLIOGRAPHERS WHO MAY BE PUZZLED, the first five Wilderness Conferences didn't get a book of their own, but were highlighted in the 1964 book, *Wildlands in Our Civilization.* The 1957 annual *Sierra Club Bulletin,* with the same title, was devoted primarily to the fifth conference.

One of the chapters, "De Facto Wilderness: What Is Its Place?" was signed by me but written primarily by David Pesonen. Before he became famous by blocking the construction of nuclear reactors on the San Andreas Fault he made a major contribution to wilderness preservation when working with the Wildlands Research Center at the University of California on a contract with the Outdoor Recreation Resources Review Commission. His greatest accomplishment there was to persuade Wallace Stegner to write his memorable letter about wilderness and the geography of hope, a letter that should be referred to in any book that speaks of wilderness.

In David Pesonen's piece, I did manage to write the two introductory paragraphs myself, about frequent flights, of enjoying the view, and a growing concern:

"One of my pet games is looking for fairly big pieces of handsome terrain that have no roads or developments in them. Big sweeps of country in the Rockies, for example, where thanks to the spruce budworm or to wildfire, we have slopes that are the glory of the Rockies, especially in mountain springtime and autumn–aspen mixed with evergreen instead of an unmitigated monotonous spruce desert. This diversity is the result of land management by the Creator. The very best management.

"There are still a few unspoiled, unroaded places. I have seen them become fewer. Some of them are duly designated as Forest Service Primitive, Wild, or Wilderness Areas. Some are not so designated but are given even greater protection by being in national parks. Others aren't legally wilderness at all. They're just plain wild. They are de facto wilderness. In my favorite definition, they are simply 'wilderness areas which have been set aside by God but which have not yet been created by the Forest Service.' "

In the 1957 *Bulletin* an article by William Bridge Cook, "Wilderness Fungi–The Silent Scavengers," was about mycorrhizae and drove me into another foreword:

"When we evaluate wilderness and its meaning to man [sic], it is easy and natural to think first about the broad vistas of forest and mountain, or the beauty of stream and flowers, or the vitality of birds and mammals, for it is the impression of these things that is most pervasive if we have little time for the little things. We may not notice at all the smallest of little things, the silent scavengers of the wilderness forest–fungi.

"Few people would think of a fungus as beautiful. It is apt to connote unpleasant things–parasitism, disease, decay. It may even be a little frightening, as strange objects often are. Fear, however, often breeds curiosity, which is a fortunate thing. For curiosity about the enemy, mold, has discovered the friend, penicillin. This discovery alone opens up a broad and promising prospect, and suggests that fungi and their tiny relatives may be more beneficial than ever dreamed. Some of them may continue to be very troublesome, but who is to say which? Who knows what seed of blessing may be encased in what husk of trouble? Mindful of these things, let us look anew at our wilderness, wherein undiscovered seeds surely live still. Let us contemplate what beauty of function we may discover in them, function which we consider to be beautiful in form, too, once we know it better."

It seems all too clear that I felt I had some explaining to do to an audience that might not otherwise want to read about rot and slimy things. I myself had a lot to learn about the miracle of soil, and still do.

That was a short fungal foreword. The book *Wildlands* itself, I thought, needed a long one, and I resurrected the one speech I was ever asked to make at a North American Wildlife Conference. I was selling the Wilderness Bill for all I was worth. On March 4, 1959, in New York City, I tried to describe some of the broader meanings of wilderness in the search for broader support for it. Those remarks are included here, thirty years later, to serve the same purpose:

THE NEWS HAS PROBABLY been kept from you but the story is being given credence out on the Coast that New York is about to make way, within the next decade, for California: the land of sunshine, oranges, and Forest Lawn is about to become the nation's most populous state. So I have been sent back here on a search for space, for land on which California can resettle its surplus citizens.

I wish that this pretense were as humorous as it is ridiculous. But it isn't. Since I left San Francisco three days ago some four thousand people have added themselves to the California population permanently—and the number is permanent even if the people are mortally not so. This sort of addition has been going on all year, ever since the war for that matter, and isn't expected to slow down. This is what causes our earthquakes, such as the one the papers just reported, although no scientist has yet made the announcement. You see, the land is merely adjusting itself to the weight of the new people! So now suburban sprawl has spread the full thirty miles south of San Francisco along both sides of the San Francisco Bay. For each new house there is at least one new automobile, in keeping with the current conviction that every person needs two tons of steel to get from bed to desk and some three hundred square feet of pavement to park the steel on at both ends of the run.

Mass transportation is withering, but we are solving this little annoyance with vision and vigor. We solve our problem with what you call throughways and turnpikes and what we call, by strange semantic twist, *free*ways. Why free? I don't know. Not in money, for they cost millions. Not in land, for they cost us thousands of acres of our most productive soil. They aren't free in movement, either. Our engineers boast that we can travel half the length of the Bay without meeting a stoplight. (Our Spanish predecessors could make the same claim!) But they're talking in pleasant theories, not of actual fact. All too often rush hours find a given freeway jammed bumper to bumper, and the array of stoplights stretched out before you is something to behold. Our most popular disk-jockey program at rush hour spends less time on music than on news of the latest jam, and what route you should try to take to get around it, if you're not caught in it yet. Some of our freeways become obsolete before the ribbon is cut in our standard opening ceremony.

That, in a slightly distorted view, is how we are solving our problem. And if Northern California thinks it has a problem, you can pardon Southern California for laughing. Their growth is three times as fast as ours. No need to worry, of course. After all, the universe is an expanding universe.

So we'd like to expand your way. What can you offer? How many half-acre lots, with space for a three- or four-bedroom ranch house plus garden? With plenty of good schooling nearby. Not far from where we want to work. Smog-free. A small park close by—where the children can find playground apparatus, the youths can enjoy big-muscle play, where the parents can stroll and unwind the week's tension, and where elders can sit and watch and remember when the days weren't so tense.

And by the way, can you add to these things, what with the shorter work week and longer vacation we're counting on—can you also add some untrammeled seashore and mountains?

I suspect that I've pushed a troubling point far enough, but let me add Ossa on Pelion—two cheering statistics. In this century the world has used up, and has lost forever, more natural resources than has all previous history.

And there are now alive, with an unprecedented appetite for resources, ten percent of all the people who ever lived on this earth. Twenty-five billion people in the long million years since the dawn of man. [Make it five percent of one hundred billion if you prefer—new numbers but the same problem.] Two and a half billion since Yellowstone National Park was created, people using up more resources, including space, than all the rest, and at greater speed. Yes, using up all the resources available to mankind except the resource of restraint.

While the ushers pass out the sackcloth and ashes, contemplate these figures. But please don't take time to check my arithmetic. It comes from a good source, but the accuracy of the source doesn't really matter. Time is running out. Whatever the time left, we can do better with it than we are doing. I agree with Allen Morgan, who says about wild open spaces that "what we save in the next few years is all that will ever be saved."

The important opportunity is to accept the fact that we are confronted with a problem the likes of which our predecessors hardly dreamed of, that it is a problem that we created and that we can solve, but not by reaching for a tranquilizer and curling up with the slick magazine that reassures us, with charts and diagrams in three colors, that science will save us; science, unaided by people.

* * *

If you feel the need, about now, for a draft of fresh air, be assured that I do, too, and that is what I'm here to talk about. About wildness – and wilderness, where the best of wildness lives. Wilderness is fairly close to the best place of all in which to find a draft of fresh air, in which to take stock, in which to find yourself, discover the *you* that so many distractions have kept you away from so long.

What about wilderness? What is it? Where is how much of it? For whom and why? How can we keep some for a still more crowded world than ours, a world that will probably need the raw materials of wilderness more than we think we do, and that will need the spiritual resources ever so much more than we do?

We could easily devote an hour's discussion to each of these questions. But let me assure any of you who is tempted to rush for the exit that I shall limit myself instead to no more than a few minutes' musing on all the questions put together.

But first, a definition of wilderness is in order.

The prophet Isaiah seems to have had it in mind when he wrote what was translated as "Woe unto them that join house to house, that lay field to field, till there be no place, that they may be placed alone in the midst of the earth!" Moses found opportunity for his people in wilderness – wilderness much of which was turned to desert before the Sermon on the Mount admonished man to consider the lilies of the field – (the natural field, I assume) – and how they were arrayed. That particular wilderness was subsequently utterly stripped of its verdure by man, including the exploitation of the Cedars of Lebanon, which went down to the sea as ships.

To compress the history of the wilderness idea into a few lines: The Middle Ages, and nothing. Then the Renaissance, and Conrad Gesner finding reason for the admiration of mountains. Very little more until William Blake worried about those dark Satanic mills. More recently Olmsted, Emerson, Thoreau, and Muir. Finally the explosion of people across the earth, and here, in the United States, wilderness vanishing with such velocity that we knew, inescapably, that we alone were responsible for the loss. The 1920s and the Forest Service trying hard, under the leadership of Aldo Leopold and Robert Marshall, to define what should *not* happen in wilderness. In 1930 Robert Marshall defining what we *should* find in wilderness, ought to find, had to find if the spirit that stood us upright was not to perish in an overcivilized lukewarm world.

Marshall used the word wilderness "to denote a region which contains no permanent inhabitants, possesses no possibility of conveyance by mechanical means, and is sufficiently spacious that a person crossing it must have the experience of sleeping out." Survival in it, he said, is up to you. Find environment *in* it; don't bring one with you.

This idea of wilderness, new though it is, is now quite widely accepted. It isn't yet underwritten by federal law, but it does appear, strangely, in an international treaty on nature protection and wildlife preservation in the Western Hemisphere which was signed by the United States eighteen years ago. In this treaty wilderness is defined as "a region under public control characterized by primitive conditions of flora, fauna, transportation, and habitation wherein there is no provision for the passage of motorized transportation and all commercial developments are excluded."

Let me add one more definition and then move on. This one comes from the Wilderness Bill: "A wilderness, in contrast with those areas where man and his own works dominate the landscape, is hereby recognized as an area where the earth and its community of life are untrammeled by man, where man himself is a visitor who does not remain."

This is a lot of detail about definition. Why? Because when people are about to be tempted to cash in on a priceless heirloom rather than work a little harder for the money instead, it is high time to look hard at that heirloom, find out what it means to them, and decide whether they should let it slip away or pass it on to their children instead, as it was passed on to them.

My analogy isn't very good, for wilderness goes far beyond being a mere heirloom. There is no sentimentality about wilderness.

As Howard Zahniser, of The Wilderness Society, has put it: "We work for wilderness preservation not primarily for the right of a minority to have the kind of fun it prefers, but rather to ensure for everyone the perpetuation of areas where human enjoyment and the apprehension of the interrelations of the whole community of life are possible, and to preserve for all the freedom of choosing to know the primeval if they so wish."

And we work hard, with a sense of urgency. The wilderness we now have is all the wilderness we shall ever have in America. There is little left—less than one-third acre per person in the United States if you count all the wilderness that has any administrative protection in our national parks and forests and wildlife refuges and on Indian lands. One-third acre per person today; less per person as our population expands still further; all of it subject to being struck out by an administrator's pen.

I say all this about wilderness because it is the essence of the wilds we need around us. Since it lives but once, there should be ample opportunity to review the death sentence that so many people in the chambers of commercialism would like to inflict upon wilderness.

Many of us feel that wilderness should have an automatic stay of execution, and that Congress should provide it.

Hence the Wilderness Bill—the proposal to establish a National Wilderness Preservation System.

There has already been a decade of careful study leading up to the present Wilderness Bill. There is immediate need for what William H. Whyte, Jr., calls "retroactive planning"—for protecting *now* the land we think is needed, rather than rationalizing later how right we were all along not to have done it. If too much wilderness is protected this way, we can always correct the situation later. If too little is protected, if too much has been turned over to exploitation, then we cannot unfry the egg.

Wilderness protection must not be delayed. If you will remember your first aid course, you will remember these priorities: breathing, bleeding, shock. It does little good, if a breathless patient is bleeding to death, to sit down and study objectively what kind of bandage will be needed on the wound. You restore breathing and stop the bleeding. Otherwise you'll have nothing to bandage but a corpse.

Support for the Wilderness Bill comes from no hastily organized battalion of rugged hikers, no "wilderness lobby"; it reflects broad public concern about direction. It reflects growing conviction that, as Dr. Daniel B. Luten puts it, "the nation does not exist to serve its economy"; that there must be more public participation in the treatment of the single heritage of land that must serve all the generations, and that to "leave these things to the experts" is to resort to absentee citizenship.

It also reflects the dawning realization that Growth without end is soon monstrous, then malignant, and finally, lethal.

I was trying to make this point in Berkeley a short time ago and a question came up from the floor: Could we afford to do anything less than keep growing inasmuch as that was what the Russians were doing? While I struggled ineptly with a reply, Dr. Luten came to my rescue. "You've heard of the game of 'chicken,' haven't you?" he asked. "It's sort of a Russian roulette on wheels. Two juveniles head directly toward each other at high speed on the highway, and the first one who turns to avert the crash is chicken. We frown on such behavior in adolescents, but we seem to accept it as national policy."

Supporters of wilderness—and of the restraint that is inherent in preserving it—are fond of civilization. They like it well enough not to want it to take too many steps, with "the bland leading the bland" (Galbraith), down the road paved with good inventions, on which there may be no turning.

Whoever should look for the words, "Wilderness Lobby," on the door of some office near Capitol Hill would be looking in the wrong direction. He should look instead at the land—all the land the country is ever going to have for all the U.S. citizens ever to be born—and the rapidity with which many of its nonrenewable resources have been used up for so few. He should resist escape into the "Science will save us" club until he has counted the ever-more-perplexing problems the saving is bringing us. And he should look at a few recent books that cannot be isolated from a common concern about an uncommon threat to civilization: Brown's *The Challenge of Man's Future;* Galbraith's *The Affluent Society;* Packard's *Hidden Persuaders;* Whyte's *The Organization Man* and *The Exploding Metropolis;* Keats's *The Insolent Chariots;* Huxley's *Brave New World Revisited;* Gary's *The Roots of Heaven;* Callison's *American Natural Resources;* and Leopold's *A Sand County Almanac.* The list ends too soon and is almost humorously disparate. Yet it has a common denominator of substantial uneasiness about what we are letting happen to us, about things that are forcing us into a corner where we must choose to live with less or not at all, witnessing instead, in that last blinding flash, the final glimpse of struggle between economies seeking to out-exploit one another.

The connection between the ability of civilization to protect wildness and the ability for civilization to survive is not so tenuous as we might wish. It is worth energetic scrutiny, and at length. For the kind of thinking that motivates the grab for what's left on the bottom of the barrel—the pitiful fragment of resources in the remaining wilderness—is the kind of thinking that has lost this country friends it cannot afford to lose. The ultimate in selfishness is evidenced in those opponents of wilderness preservation who have demanded an open door for exploiting wilderness while they slam another door in the face of friends needed overseas and north of the border. Don't import oil, wood, plywood, lead, zinc, the opponents say, whatever such restriction may do to the economy of our friends. Don't import them because we have more than enough of our own. And concurrently opponents urge that nothing interfere with their looking for still more of their own—anywhere in the public's dedicated wilderness!

The international economic and political difficulties the wilderness opponents would thus aggravate are serious. The difficulties may not stem from their opposition to wilderness, but there is certainly guilt by association. They stem from what could be called a philosophy of last things first.

It has remained for a physicist to single out the biological peril. As Dr. J. A. Rush put it: "When man obliterates wilderness, he repudiates the evolutionary force that put him on this planet. In a deeply terrifying sense, man is on his own."

As a handy example, I have beside me in my hand a small object, about the size of the letter *o,* which the evolutionary force has built. Within it is embodied a direct living connection all the way back through all the eons to the very first appearance of life on this planet. Against that space of time man's life span is insignificant, his ken is barely significant, the entire duration of mankind is hardly noticeable. The object, of course, is a seed. Packed in a fragment of its space is all the know-how needed to perpetuate redwoods on earth, even if every other seed and existing redwood were to be wiped out. Included in that know-how is the ability, should a once-in-a-century flood bury the base of the mature tree in silt, to activate the pushing of new roots—out through bark two feet thick, and out at just the right level below the new surface of soil in which the tree now stands.

I know of no research to determine in just what gene area this particular know-how exists, or what its biochemical formula is. Fortunately, no scientist has to know this. But the tree that otherwise could not survive *does* know it. Man did not have to steady the Teacher's hand when it found out, or when all the other forms of life found out how to perpetuate themselves, through good times and bad, in the wilderness they are designed to live in together, in dynamic equilibrium.

Do we dare be so arrogant as to assume that we must take it upon ourselves to steady the omnipotent force throughout the land, even to the last two percent of wilderness? Perhaps Dr. Rush had some question like this in mind when he spoke of wilderness, the evolutionary force, and the terrifying prospect if we try to stay on this planet without it. The Wilderness Bill is a needed step toward the recognition of this truth. Not just any bill, but a strong one, recognizing as national policy that wilderness is where you find it and keep it. There is little left to find, and scant little time remaining in which to resolve to keep some of that little—to rescue it from the raw materialism which threatens not only wilderness, but survival, too.

My protracted foreword, like the Wilderness Conferences, began in 1959. Before the book could appear, two major events took place. We may now celebrate the fact that the Wilderness Act was signed September 3, 1964, by President Lyndon B. Johnson. Before that could happen, conservationists were shocked by the death of Howard Zahniser, who made the act (and this book) possible. I would like to dedicate this book to his memory, and in his memory, to all who strive to equal his public service. Long may Howard Zahniser's example endure in our thoughts about wilderness, and in what those thoughts lead us to do for it!

***Wildlands in Our Civilization*, 1964**

The 1959 speech was the last one at the New York conference and worked well. But we still had a long way to go.

INDIVIDUAL FREEDOM IN PUBLIC WILDERNESS

RESTIVE IS EXACTLY the right word for describing the young users of wilderness attending a conference at Timberline Lodge, on Mount Hood, in 1976. They did not like being regulated. This time I was asked to give a speech, not write a foreword, and it was fortunate that I wrote it instead of referring to a few key words on the back of a boarding pass and winging it. I arrived at Timberline in good health and failed to notice that

Montezuma, seeking revenge, registered right after I did. In the next twenty-four hours I lost eleven pounds as a result. I still had vocal chords, but there was nobody inside to make them work.

If you wanted someone else to read your speech for you, whom above all would you ask for? I asked, and got him, and what I wrote was read for me by Edward Abbey. Montezuma lost after all.

ELEVEN YEARS AND ONE MONTH AGO a man just a little younger than most of you brought to my house in Berkeley a hand-hewn book that is before me now. It is bound in leather, and inside are color photographs (from the drugstore) and a text in fine calligraphy on heavy art paper, all handsomely bound in leather. Terry Russell's February 1965 foreword ends:

Terry and Renny Russell, planet Earth, twentieth century after Christ. We live in a house that God built but that the former tenants remodelled—blew up, it looks like—before we arrived. Poking through the rubble in our odd hours, we've found the corners that were spared and have hidden in them as much as we could. Not to escape from but to escape to: not to forget but to remember. We've been learning to take care of ourselves in places where it really matters. The next step is to take care of the places *that really matter. Crazy kids on the loose; but on the loose in the wilderness. That makes all the difference.*

One of the quotations in the book—a rare mixture of the old wisdom of others and the young wisdom of Terry and Renny (especially of Terry)—is from Thoreau, and whether you know it by heart or not, I think most of you practice it:

Remember thy creator in the days of thy youth. Rise free from care before the dawn, and seek adventures. Let the noon find thee by other lakes, and the night overtake thee everywhere at home. . . . Grow wild according to thy nature, like these sedges and brakes, which will never become English hay. . . . Let not to get a living be thy trade, but thy sport. Enjoy the land, but own it not. Through want of enterprize and faith men are where they are, buying and selling, and spending their lives like serfs.

In June Terry and Renny, no serfs, were rafting down the Green River. They had invited my daughter to go along but by telephone from the East a father exercised his veto, believing that although the brothers knew how to handle a raft in Glen Canyon's gentle waters, they were not yet experienced enough in rough water. A newly formed rapid surprised them, with life jackets off, as they rounded a bend. The raft upset. "Grab something that's floating!" Terry yelled to Renny. Renny did. Terry didn't, and was lost.

If you know the book, *On the Loose,* you know how great the loss was. It hit our family very hard. We had spent a lot of time in Glen with Terry, and he was at our house often. I was very pleased that he wanted to know what I thought of the book, and was grateful when the Sierra Club's publications committee, somewhat reluctantly, approved the club's publication of the book. It is still selling extremely well.

Its spirit is so much like your spirit, I think, that it has helped me understand what is going on here in you—an undercurrent that might otherwise have disturbed me a lot. I come here battle-scarred. The mountains I contend with these days are mountains of paper, most of the paper bearing warnings and records of struggle in the battle to save wilderness wherever it still lives, a battle that preempts the time I'd really rather spend in wilderness rather than worrying over it. Recently, most of the paper is about nuclear matters (if we don't end nuclear proliferation, it will no longer be necessary to worry about wilderness). So it is annoying not to get into wilderness enough, and a little annoying also to keep noticing that more and more people are younger. I get bothered by the "me and wilderness" syndrome, as if *me* should come first and let wilderness come last. So I wonder: Why are you so all-fired concerned about freedom in wilderness that you seem to be giving last priority to the task of saving wilderness to be free in?

Then I remember Terry and Renny, and my own four children, now ranging from twenty-three to thirty-one, all of them having ranged in wilderness a lot themselves. There is my own wilderness to remember, too, and what it was like the first time, back in the summer of 1930. There were earlier pseudo-wilderness experiences, of course: car camping in 1918, when it took three days by dirt road to get from Berkeley to Donner Summit in a 1916 Maxwell.

I remember especially my own insistence on wilderness freedom in 1933, when climbing on The Thumb, above one of the small Palisade glaciers in the Sierra Nevada. Rules were for someone else, even the rules for climbing safely, so I was reckless enough to deserve a terminal seventy-foot fall. That I didn't fall was sheer luck.

The other freedoms, however, I still kept to myself, including the freedom, reminiscent of cut-and-get-out loggers, of grabbing all the first ascents of Sierra peaks one could easily lay hands on, as if no one else would ever like one.

So by now my freedoms to be reckless and to brag had been encroached upon. Another freedom fell by the wayside soon after. In that summer of thirty-four, my friend and I saw no one but each other for an entire month along the John Muir trail and laterals to it. Nothing like that has happened since, nor is it likely to. For the next four years, first winter ascents of Sierra peaks and summer ascents of Yosemite walls were free for the asking. Wipe a lot of that freedom away, too!

Freedom Fades

Then, for sixteen summers, not counting the three summers during which the army had other plans for me, I watched the fading out of other wilderness freedoms—the freedom to go in large parties (never more than two hundred) with as many as fifteen or twenty strings of packstock (up to one hundred twenty head) into various western wildernesses. The big need then was to demonstrate use—that this was country needed by people of various ages and decision-making or -influencing powers more than by loggers, dammers, roadbuilders, miners, and subdividers.

The constituency of savers of wilderness was absolutely necessary to overcome the political power of the exploiters of wilderness and to bring about the passage of the Wilderness Act. The legislation had been opposed by every private interest you could think of. But it passed by almost unanimous vote.

But a big crowd, even in big mountains, still hits hard on the country, as well as on the small independent party of two or three that was out to discover wilderness for itself—then, upon rounding a turn, discovered a hundred or so spaced-out Sierra Club High Trippers—and passed through their scattered numbers for half a day. Being invited to a sumptuous dinner that night was some compensating reward, but only if you were headed in the opposite direction.

What Kind of Lemonade?

The freedom to travel in so large a group, congenial though it was to most of us, is gone, or to camp freely, or to take splendidly weathered wood home by the bundle, or to make bough beds, or to improvise field-expedient camp furniture, or hack away with a scout ax, or even to drink water from a sparkling wilderness stream that coliform bacteria didn't get to first, or to be alone more than an hour or so.

The freedom isn't gone everywhere, of course. Alaska's Brooks Range is as big, in itself, as the entire state of California. If you stay away from the pipeline crossing and from subsistence hunters who would rather you were somewhere else, your wilderness freedom will be encroached upon only by the weather and the spectacular abundance of squish and insects. The freedom is still fairly intact in the Lower Forty-Nine in winter, too. But we'll have to face the fact that a lot of freedom has slipped away from the wilderness, formally dedicated or not, that we used to count on, because of the rapid increase of human pressure. Total freedom of the wilderness probably vanished when humanity left its hunter-gatherer phase. There were only twenty-five million or so people on earth then, getting by nicely on twenty-five hours a week of hunting and gathering.

Civilization has spared us this leisure and this wild, free space.

If the best we have left is a poor compromise, a world made smaller and tighter by speed and numbers, with very little of the essential information in the Creator's great encyclopedia left to be passed on to us on untorn, unsmeared pages, the question remains: what kind of lemonade must we make if all we have left is lemons, or a reasonable facsimile?

First, I think we can renew our admiration of the excellence that remains. We can sign up for a course in Humility 1A and realize that nature still has all the rights, even though our attorneys are slow to understand this. Nature's rights come from Natural Law, a most complex mechanism only the smallest part of which we have yet perceived. Let anyone who thinks differently explain how photosynthesis works and how chlorophyll does it—that commonest and most essential of photochemical reactions, whose mysteries still escape us. Remember that all the essential creative capability of DNA was shaped in wilderness, not in civilization, for all but the last few centuries of the billions of years life has been present on the planet.

Let us then fit our imagined rights in with nature's real rights, and enjoy the most important freedom—the boundless scope of the human mind to contemplate wonders, and to begin to understand their meaning. Let us, in our anxiety about freedom and wilderness, remember that we cannot make more wilderness; that is strictly God's business, and not even the Forest Service can claim to be co-creator. We have proved, of course, that we can make deserts; but the market for them is drying up.

What we can do, then, is to take the common bond that unites us here—a real thirst for what wilderness, and only wilderness, can quench—and make the most of it. We can resist the pleasant temptation to splinter ourselves into young, middle, and old, into private and public, into gymnasts and mediators, into whatever isn't elite after we have charged all our adversaries with being elitist. We can remember that the only chance to experience a fair simulation of the old freedom of the wilderness is to see that we lose no more of what little is left. Tie the reciprocating engine, the wheel, even the rickshaw outside. Earn our chance to know what wilderness has to teach us. Earn it by walking there, or leaving it untouched so our children can walk there if we ourselves haven't perfected the urge to enjoy what happens when you put one foot after another for a generous piece of time.

You can remember to join with others to achieve, for yourself and others, what you will never achieve by yourself alone, genius though you really are. You are individual, and upright, and unique. You are different from every person who was ever here before. You are full of promise that is not to be denied idly, intentionally, selfishly, or through wanton carelessness. You, too, can see that these places are cared for just the way

Frederick Law Olmsted, Jr., paraphrasing his illustrious father, said they should be: used in such a manner that their God-given naturalness can be enjoyed in perpetuity.

There is an old, senior-citizen sound to my didacticism. Let Terry Russell end this piece:

God secure me from security, now and forever, Amen.
Who's afraid of the universe?
It's midnight on the desert or the coast or high
above timberline, the Milky Way is close
and the stars are singing.
I am not small, I fill the sphere.
I tremble before the cosmos no more than a
fish trembles before the tides.

We fear what we don't know;
I know what the hills are there for and they
know me.
Cut the root and the plant dies.
City life is the scary life, inane, tiny
and alone.
Learn wildness and you don't fear anything.
Except people afraid.

Terry Russell should have the last words, my favorite selection from *On the Loose*:

Adventure is not in the Guidebook,
Beauty is not on the map.
Seek and ye shall find.

Terry Russell. Photograph from the dust jacket of the original edition of On the Loose.

CHAPTER 7

OUTINGS

SIERRA CLUB HIGH TRIPS

SENIOR AMONG SIERRA CLUB OUTINGS, the High Trip was invented by John Muir and William E. Colby for a political purpose: to introduce large numbers of people to big wilderness and let them fall in love with it, whereupon they would join forces to see that the experience and the wilderness would be passed down the generations intact. If, as Thoreau said, "In Wildness is the Preservation of the World," the High Trip would be a device for saving both.

With fellow knapsackers George Rockwood and Hervey Voge I had sampled the 1933 and 1934 High Trips and failed to understand how anyone would want so little solitude in the mountains. By spending the next four summers and intervening seasons in Yosemite, I found that a mere two hundred people were no crowd at all. So when in 1938, with Virginia Adams, I drove over Tioga Pass and we traveled on horseback from Agnew Meadow to Shadow Lake, where the High Trip was camped amid record snows, and when at campfire that night they asked Virginia to sing and I saw the pleasure it brought them, I was ready for 1939 and the motley mob of twenty packers, eighteen commissary crew, and roughly one hundred seventy guests who would comprise that summer's High Trip.

Dick Leonard, knowing my need for some remunerative work and my love of the Sierra, added me to the commissary group to help in the kitchen (I was experienced enough to handle coffee, chocolate, oatmeal, and soup), to lead some climbs, to talk occasionally at campfire, and to film the party's experience in what we hoped would become Kings Canyon National Park. I learned, among other things, that at the high altitude of our campsites—High Trips, in their four Sierra weeks, would set up some ten camps a day's walk apart, most of them nearly two miles high—garbanzos needed more than four weeks' cooking to tenderize them in the soup. I also learned to play the accordion but not to persuade Anne ever to like it. Worst of all, I learned to like talking at campfire, and have never been able not to talk when I detect the presence of an audience.

Dave playing a borrowed accordion at a Sierra High Trip camp, 1940. Photograph by Cedric Wright.

I talked myself onto the next two High Trips, on which Dick Leonard named me assistant leader. And in 1942 Ike Livermore talked me into leading his Sierra Club saddle trip in the Mineral King country, inasmuch as the United States Navy had other plans for his next few summers.

Not willing to abandon the idea that the mountains deserved some solitude, I had proposed in 1938 that the Sierra Club also conduct knapsack trips, but ease the load by having food supplies packed in and cached at strategic points—cache and carry trips, we called them. W. Kenneth Davis, later to be a vice-president of the Bechtel Corporation and a Deputy Secretary of Energy and, later, of Defense, led the trip in 1938. I led it in 1939, carrying the movie camera I had been using on the High Trip into still

Four well-known High Trip leaders seated by the dunnage-bag pile: (left to right) Oliver Kehrlein, William E. Colby, Richard M. Leonard, David R. Brower, 1939. Photograph by Cedric Wright.

Sierra Club High Trip campfire, Benson Lake, Yosemite, 1941. Brower at the accordion. Photograph by Cedric Wright.

other parts of the proposed Kings Canyon National Park. Quite a bit of what the camera saw was also seen by members of Congress as part of the club's park campaign. It was a silent film, and I traveled widely with it to give it a voice, once I got it out of the camera.

What Muir and Colby had done for the Sierra wilderness needed to be done for the wild canyons of Dinosaur National Monument. Dam-building engineers loved them too much, and too few people knew what was there. The course of the Yampa and Green rivers through the canyons was alleged to be too dangerous to warrant sparing them. So we were forced to invent Sierra Club river trips. The two hundred people who rode Dinosaur's rivers in 1953 proved that it was not all that dangerous an adventure. Charles Eggert made the club's first sound and color film, *Wilderness River Trail,* which the Bureau of Reclamation said was the preservationists' most effective weapon against them. Those who thus experienced Dinosaur, and helped save it, proved Muir and Colby right, and the film helped them prove it. The combination of the two, and the Sierra Club's success in the Dinosaur campaign, did something else. For years the telling insignia of High Trippers was the Sierra Club cup, now universally imitated (the Sierra Club imitated the Appalachian Mountain Club's cup, but that is a secret), the bottom of which was embossed "Sierra Club of California." The "of California" was lost in Dinosaur National Monument. The club had fought many earlier battles for places outside California, but never with so much press.

Mountain experiences with our own children led me to lower the age requirements on the High Trip to six, Ken's age when we were sure he could make the trip if coaxed along the trail, by Anne's judicious release of Lifesavers. Our family had earlier found how enjoyable a wilderness experience could be near a roadhead of the small lake in Little Lakes Valley. This was a threshold to wilderness, and that is what I suggested the club add to its outing program—the Wilderness Threshold Trip. I had no further inventions to offer.

ARE MULES NECESSARY?

IN 1956 I LED HIGH TRIPS to Glacier National Park and the Tetons, and this, my seventeenth participation in High Trips, was my last. The trips themselves weren't to last much longer, either. The elements that led to their demise—unfortunate, I think—are implicit in my account of the 1947 High Trips, "Are Mules Necessary?" This appeared in the 1948 annual magazine number of the *Sierra Club Bulletin.* Articles on the annual outing—for years the alternate name for the High Trip—were a tradition in the *Bulletin* since the trip's inception. I managed to have two of mine published in the *Bulletin,* perhaps because I was editor. One of my writing habits then was to use the word "man" and its sexist derivatives ubiquitously. What follows has been purged:

THE 1947 HIGH TRIP was over. The last mule string was in, and with a minimum of skittishness, mules were letting the last slingful of dunnage bags be dropped to the dust of the Pine Creek roadhead, to be all but lost among the slings, box and canvas kyacks, pack ropes, stoves and other kitchen paraphernalia, surplus food, fishing rods, trucks, cars, milling hoofs, and boots. Somewhere from the midst of the thinning group someone would emerge, dressed half for the mountains and half for dinner in Bishop, to claim the last dunnage and to lash it to a fender, to a ski rack, or to stow it in a bulging trunk. Soon the last farewells would have been exchanged, Pete Garner and Ike Livermore would lead the last mules down canyon to the corral, the last car would crunch off in the gravel to disappear down around the turn, and the roadhead dust would settle.

The last of the one hundred sixty persons who had just spent from two to four weeks traveling the High Sierra wilderness trails through Sierra and Inyo national forests would be safely on their way home. Everyone would be accounted for, and the management could relax for the three-hundred-mile drive home—after a nonwilderness steak in Bishop.

It was dusk as we headed north. A short time earlier the sun had set behind Mount Humphreys—in about the same way it had set a month before, when we started the trip. There was no ordered procession of happy recollections, but just a vague feeling that something good had ended too soon.

We knew, without a doubt, that the mountains—the wilderness—had done something for us, something to us. But another question had been in the minds of many of us throughout the trip—and for some years before the trip. What were we doing to the mountains? The trip was over, yes. But how completely over was it? When would the duff we had ground into dust at the roadhead be replenished? When would the boggy bits of meadow that served, in places, as trail for the mules, none of whom wanted to step in the other's fresh-churned mud—when would these green bits recover from the seventy-five sets of hoofs that had ground them into a wet black ooze? Had the meadows provided more forage than they could afford? Had serving lines, stove and tea-fire and campfire sites, garbage pits, and boudoirs beaten too many gardens beyond recognition? Would hoof-cut waterbreaks on the steep stretches of trail be repaired before erosion set in? Had this same sort of wear and tear on the mountains, repeated year after year by large pack trips, caused an irreparable damage? If so, was the wear inordinate in reference to the number of people who had enjoyed the mountains that were worn because they had enjoyed them? Or, to end the forensic recapitulation with one gloriously ambiguous question, when and where should the mountains be used how and by whom?

That such a series of questions should ever be asked would probably astound John Muir and his contemporaries who, with him, sought to entice more and more people to the Sierra, to make it more accessible, in order that there would be a strong, well-informed group ever ready to protect the best of the Sierra from use that would mar its beauty and its wildness. Muir could hardly have anticipated the day when people—practical people at that—got together and agreed that we should stop building roads into California's high mountains, much less the day when they should begin to worry about traffic on the trails. Yet that day has come. And the Sierra Club's High Trip, being the largest single contribution to wilderness travel today, is the one which many people worry most about.

They worry in part about the large number of people—that has troubled them for years. They'll ask, How can you see the mountain for the people? Most likely, because most of the worriers are anglers, they'll fear that the thundering horde will clean out all the lakes and streams, as did the fisherman with whom Dick Leonard passed the time of day as he was descending south from Glen Pass. "The Sierra Club's been through," the man said, pointing his rod in the general direction of Bullfrog Lake, "and they've cleaned it out." Leonard explained that he was leading the Sierra Club High Trip, was looking for the next campsite, that the members hadn't even seen Bullfrog yet, not to mention fished in it. He could have added later that High Trip fishermen that year were no better than usual, and that the trip as a whole averaged one-half trout per person day—hardly enough to clean out any lake in a day's time.

Observers who are more cautious than the fisherman in their conclusions are less concerned about trout—which can be planted in proportion to the number of effective fishermen—than they are about the meadows, critical as the grasslands are in the ecology of the High Sierra traveler. They point out that those meadows along the main trails that are within a day's travel from roadheads are called upon for more grass than they can grow, either from trip to trip or from year to year. They compare the deterioration of overgrazed or overtrampled meadows with the luxuriance of High Sierra gardens that have never felt a mule's tooth or hoof. They recall that knapsackers eat no grass, that the burros eat little more, that the stock used by spot campers enjoy no more than a snack from an overburdened meadow before the animals are turned around and headed back to the hay of their roadhead corral. Some of the observers see no harm in a series of huts or camps an easy day's walk apart, such as those in the Yosemite High Sierra, supplied by stock that round-trip it in a day from road to camp to road. Others have no objection to stock as long as the strings are few and their visits to a given meadow are infrequent. Still others like neither to see mules in meadows nor to be reminded that mules have been along their trail. Finally, there has been a cry for a ceiling on a given trip's mule count and person count.

Where, then, does the big trip, inaugurated by the Sierra Club in 1901 and carried on today, in approximate ascending order of size by the Contra Costa Hills Club, the California Alpine Club, the Trail Riders of the Wilderness, and the Sierra Club—where does the big traveling trip stand? Should it go on, or should it just go?

I am not sure that a person who has participated in the management of six big trips, with a seventh coming up, can be considered disinterested enough to attempt to answer objectively such multi-ramified questions. True, I did learn how the other half lives by knapsacking quite a bit, but that was a few years back. The problem trees of High Trip details are very clearly framing, if not obscuring, my vista of the mountain-use forest. Nevertheless, it seems important that a person who has been in the midst of management problems of a big trip, and at the same time has been able to see what the trip has meant to those who have taken it, should at least submit his conclusions for whatever they are worth, and then perhaps abstain from voting.

Herewith, then, on behalf of those who since 1901 have enjoyed High Trips, as well as for those who in years to come should perhaps be permitted similar enjoyment, there are presented forty-three exhibits. The first forty-two High Trips, from 1901 to 1946, almost all of them duly recorded in the pages of the *Sierra Club Bulletin*. The forty-third exhibit, the 1947 trip, is described in some detail. Perhaps a few of the foregoing questions raised will find their answers in the descriptions. That, at least, is my intention. . . .

Agnew Meadows—rather more forest than meadow—served as the High Trip rendezvous point, and from midmorning until after dark the members assembled at the end of one of the poorest roads in the Sierra—a road almost too narrow to permit the driver of a modern low-slung car to maneuver enough to avoid the alarming crunch of oil pan against rock.

The packstock had already been trucked in from Lone Pine and was now happily dispersed in the meadows, except for those being shod or otherwise worked over in the corral improvised with rope in a small, out-of-the-way opening in the lodgepole forest. There were some seventy-five head in all, watched over by Ike Livermore and his contingent, as pleasant a group as ever gave a string of mules a bad time or a good time, depending upon the need of the moment. Pete Garner, whose ancestors were in this country when the *Mayflower* arrived, was second in command to Ike, and a veteran packer who handled with equal ease and serenity the heaviest loads—the stoves—and the mules that carried them. Bud Steele, another veteran, was one of the men—if you would believe him—who helped the devil pack in and set up the Devil's Postpile. If he didn't look old enough for that role, at least he was talented enough. Tommy Jefferson, a full-blooded Mono, had a tireless smile that let you know you were welcome to the land of his fathers. During the day he charmed one of the strings of mules that carried commissary impedimenta; and in the evening, we knew from last year, he could charm both a guitar and those who listened to his repertoire of songs. Among the others who handled a horse and a string of five mules per man were old-time packers from Owens Valley and college students who wanted to learn something about livestock in its least prosaic environment. Ed Thistlethwaite, Owens Valley artist with a broad accent that was anything but indigenous, was our night hawk. It was his job, when the camp was heavy with sleep on a moving morning—and that is earlier than would sound reasonable in print—to get up and watch the dawn in the high and relatively inaccessible pasture lands to which the stock had been pushed, then to round them up and bring them down to work. A lad from Yale watched over the saddle horses, a few of which had been brought along for people who either already knew they weren't in condition for a hard day on the trail or who would find out before the day ended. Ike Livermore thought that his wife, who came along to take care of the man who was taking care of the packing operation, should have some title; so Dina Livermore was Assistant Saddle Horse Boy.

The commissary group was less glamorous, but hardly less important. Ted Grubb, the assistant leader, and now chairman of the San Francisco Bay Chapter, had been on many High Trips, and was so industrious, we knew, that he would several times have to be driven out of camp to relax and look at the mountains. He was to be last man out of camp, and principal landscape architect. Jim Harkins, chef, and member-at-large of the club membership committee, was the only man in High Trip history to combine the talents that would enable him to cook breakfast, lead a party up Mount Ritter, and return fast enough and fresh enough to cook dinner. His name was on more Sierra peaks than he could count without sitting down with a map for a long time. Charlotte Mauk, co-cook and a director of the club, was planner-in-chief of menus, and had spent many a winter and spring evening computing the relative amounts of each item that should be on hand in order to turn the daily quarter-ton of food into three well-balanced meals—and she was versatile enough as well to know how those meals could best be balanced on a mule and which course should be on which mule in order to reach the next camp in time to be ready for dinner. These were the veteran veterans; but several others—Bill Blair, Bob Breckenfeld, Toni Bristow, Eleonore Ginno, Pat Goldsworthy, Jack Heyneman, Howard Parker, Helen Smith, Nance Wale, Joe Wampler—had been on High Trips before and well knew the traditions of the trip; the rest of the group, new to the game, were Clark Aaronson, Anne Brower, Joan Clark, Jane Goldsworthy, and Stephen Jory. Their collective effort was in the main a labor of love—a love for the type of trip and a high regard for the mountains it took them into. The leader's main job was to see that the traditions were kept alive and the mechanism kept rolling that had been so extraordinarily well built up through the decades by William E. Colby, Francis Tappaan, and Dick Leonard. The machine had merely to be adapted to the situation and the terrain.

All but inseparable from commissary proper were those old-time High Trippers who had paid to go on the trip year after year, for whom no really good designation has yet been coined. Take Bob Lipman, for example. Years ago he himself was in commissary and never has forgotten how welcome was the helping hand. Always one of the first into camp, he was also one of the first to grab an ax and start splitting wood for the stoves. Cedric Wright, who has probably been on more High Trips than anyone, always manages to arrive just ahead of the first raindrop if there is a tarpaulin to be pitched, and he is as versatile a tarp hanger—and no two can ever be hung the same way—as he is a photographer. Then there are the main body of High Trippers, the guests who are not guests because, although they are the people for whom the trip is run, still it is their trip, and they all lend a hand.

The important thing about the guests is their diversity. There is some significance in the variety of physical ability, taste, and temperament that this trip successfully brings together for enjoyment of the Sierra. In 1947 we had no octogenarians along, but some have made the trip in the past; we had to be satisfied with an age range that included several in their sixties and one who had just hit ten. Grandparents to grandchildren, professional people and wage slaves, teachers and the taught or the learning—these were the main categories. They had in common, aside from a liking for mountains, a certain affluence, for the trip did cost nearly five dollars a day for three meals, for half a mule per person to transport everything, and for a chance to sleep on pine needles (that's what inflation has done to the original cost of less than a dollar a day!). But here they were happily together, exploring and enjoying mountains in their own individual way. Some took to the peaks; others took to the streams or the high lake basins or the meadows or the sunny granite benches. Most of the younger members had the physical condition to take off on their own cross-country knapsack trips, and with a little more experience could probably do this on their own, quite independent of the High Trip. Others, not necessarily older, might be forever incapable of penetrating wild country on their own. Perhaps they preferred their solitude diluted a little; or they might have neither the physique to forsake the mule and shoulder all their own loads, nor the knack of getting along with mule or burro should they not wish to forsake them; they might have an equal horror of depending either upon their own cooking or upon their ability to tell one mountain from another and keep on a trail.

I myself, having in 1939 conquered my fear of so large a crowd, learned that same year that it was pleasant indeed to travel with a group the variety of which could match the variety of the mountains. It strikes me that in the presence of both varieties, one is less apt to be bored with either. Ordinarily a High Trip can't accommodate young children, but I'd say that it is most desirable to have youngsters along on a trip, so long as they have enough family along to get them washed behind their ears once every week or so. For through a child's eyes you rekindle your interest in the commonplace; watch them, and you awake each morning to a strange and wonderful world of streams and rocks and of living things that have no names and that you have to find out all about before the day gets too old—perhaps even before breakfast. In 1947 I watched ten-year-old Dave Armstrong, a tiny figure in blue jeans and a broad straw hat, far out in a broad green meadow with the shine of glacier-polished granite above it, now running along the stream, now bending over with his legs apart and hands on his knees in deep study—of a frog, no doubt—then off again to look for a log crossing, with no one near him and no helping hand to be tolerated—the Minarets that already towered above him gaining in stature a thousand feet for every foot he had not yet grown. And I'd find myself much more philosophical about the problem of the missing climbing ropes that someone at my right elbow had broken into my reverie with.

We camped under the Minarets in a scattered grove of graceful hemlocks above Lake Ediza, an easy day from Agnew, camped up on a bench closer to the peaks—and as Ike Livermore looked at it, nearer the rocks and farther from grass—than a High Trip had camped before. The standing operating procedure for High Trips had governed the setting up of camp, and its consideration of the terrain bears a little looking into. First we considered the mules. Could they reach the site in an easy day and make a backtracking round trip next day for the balance of the supplies? Was feed for them near enough? Where in the general area were there enough bed sites for the five categories of sleepers: men, women, married, commissary, packers (not in order of importance; to this I refuse to commit myself); and was there room enough between sleepers for the mules to run to and fro when they tired of eating and sought amusement? Then commissary. Was there water, a level spot for the stoves, trees about it for tarps if needed, disintegrated granite or duff for main lines of traffic that would otherwise wear down the meadows, shade for the perishable foods and a pool or snowbank for the frailest perishables, nearby bed sites for the early-rising commissary people, diggable ground for fire and garbage pits and—preferably not too awfully far away—for the sanitary facilities? Were there two or three dead lodgepoles handy for Joe Wampler and his volunteers to fell and split? Could the mules reach this site to unload and was there room for the unloading of several strings at once? Where could the women's mules unload, and the men's? And not too near the exact center of women's camp, could packers set up their rope corral in which to feed grain and saddle up? My principal challenge was that of sprinting along the trail fast enough to reach camp and make all the decisions before those who had been breathing hot on my neck wanted the answers. Then I'd collapse and worry about details—and catch glimpses of little Dave out there in the meadow.

In the end it is always the mules who determine the itinerary of a High Trip. Once the optimum requirements of a campsite have been determined, it is then necessary only to find a series of optimum campsites that are so spaced as to allow the strings to move the balance of supplies to them on the next one or two days, with an occasional day's rest for mules and packer. If the campsites are the most scenic in the area, that's fortunate. If the most scenic of the sites are those where the trip must lay over longest while the mules shuttle, that's amazing. And if one of those scenic spots should be hit at the same time by the High Trip and by any other large party, that's impossible—and is now precluded in pre-trip discussions.

As usual, the mules determined the 1947 itinerary, which connected a series of place names meaningful to those who know the places and meaningless to those who either haven't been to them or don't distinguish one name from another place or vice versa. From Lake Ediza we moved to Reds Meadow and its unavoidable road, then hurried on in a long, warm, dry day to Purple Lake for a layover. A spot near Lake of the Lone Indian—but not nearly so near as advertised—came next, followed by a long, cool, refreshing day that saw us over Silver Pass and partway up Mono Creek, opposite Second Recess. Mono Pass served as the trade route for two-weekers, who went out and came in via the Little Lakes Valley road. For the mules who made the round trip over the pass from Second Recess, the sight of the meadow expanses of upper Mono Creek proved too much. At their first unfettered opportunity they returned to their greener pastures, not to be rounded up in time the next moving day for dinner to be punctual at Bear Creek camp. For some ninety of the High Trippers, that wait for dinner was especially long, for they had allowed themselves to be talked into a cross-country deviation from the John Muir Trail that took them from Second Recess camp on a beeline (if the ups and downs be disregarded) right through First Recess to the Bear Creek site. The Hilgard Branch of Bear Creek, close under Lake Italy and untouched by previous High Trips, came next. Then it was over Selden Pass to Sally Keyes Lake, where Ollo Baldauf discovered two mountaineering rattlesnakes far beyond their recorded altitudinal range. One more move remained before we should leave the mountains, and this was to be Contour Day.

We were camped, on Sally Keyes Lake, at an elevation of ten thousand one hundred feet. Our next camp, in French Canyon, was to be at the same elevation. The trail was most thoughtlessly laid out to drop into a hole—the Piute Creek Canyon—about three thousand feet, and then climb back out. What, then, could be more logical, for persons who didn't fancy so much drop and climb, than that they should follow the ten-thousand-one-hundred-foot contour to the next camp with as few compromises as possible? This, in gist, was the proposal I made at campfire, quickly following it with additional remarks that were indeed more logical. The trail was better for those who had doubts of their cross-country technique and was a beautiful if arduous trip for those who hadn't seen it already. The "contour" route would involve only slightly less ascending and descending, and although it would be some six miles shorter and would afford splendid vistas that would be lost to the canyon plodders, those six miles would cost in difficulty of steps every bit of what they saved in number. Routes that seemed good on the map were actually seldom what they seemed. We ended up in four major groups. The trail travelers took off early in groups of two or three at their own good pace. Dr. Stewart Kimball led a second group of slightly-less-than-trail travelers, who explored a trail that was still shown on the map, but rarely appeared on the ground. Lewis Clark took a small party back over Selden Pass, up under Seven Gables to the headwaters of the East Fork of Bear Creek, and crossed a knapsack pass into the French Canyon watershed. The route that struck my fancy, and apparently that of nineteen others, traded the three-thousand-foot drop for three knapsack passes, only one of which I had ever previously seen both sides of. One I had never before seen either side of turned out to be badly mapped: a broad, almost-gentle, nivated (unglaciated; affected only by rain, frost, snow pressure, and gravity) slope that showed on the map became a chute that afforded a bit of rock scrambling. But the entire party, right on down to Dave Armstrong, were game and made the whole trip well. Dave did, it should be recorded, consent to be expedited for the last mile, trading tired horses for fresh ones every few hundred yards. He arrived in camp fully as pert as his piggyback steeds.

Already we were in our last camp. For days on end—but never enough—we had enjoyed the High Sierra wilderness just as the members of previous High Trips had. There were close-ups of sand and granite, grass and wildflowers, distant vistas of peaks and, at long last, of clouds; there were strange and familiar friendly sounds and smells, by day and by night; there were stops, long and short, to talk about things that were important and things that needn't be; there was a growing sense of being fully alive, fit, vital, of being a collection of cells acting as one surging, directed, homogenous entity. We were awake, fully awake to our world. And what was a blister or two or a pine needle in the soup?

It would be overenthusiastic to maintain that the vitality we found in the wilderness could be found nowhere else. Skiers' spirits may soar when they descend a crowded slope, composers' when they stumble upon and try to hold a series of chords whose relation is all too evanescent, editors' when from nowhere they pick up the word their author just missed—to all their own heady drink, one's stimulus no doubt being the other's sedative. Here in the Sierra wildland, people found or renewed vitality that didn't come to them in any other context, whether in 1947 or in 1901.

Then came the first final campfire for some, the final final campfire, perhaps, for others. The auld-lang-syne feeling ran high—who would object?—and the embers burned themselves out.

That last Saturday morning Ted Grubb, chief landscaper, laid the embers to rest, just as they had been laid to rest in the other camps. Cans were smashed—cans that preceded us to the camp as well as our own. Papers, cans, bottles, and those indestructible embers were gathered by willing hands and tossed into the garbage pit. Old cartons were consigned to the top and burned, a little lime was sprinkled on top to complete the deodorizing so that later fur-bearing passersby would not undispose of our disposals. Disinterred rocks, sand, soil, and the carefully saved sod were in turn placed over the pit. The leftover firewood from split-up trees was piled where it could serve later travelers who would not be equipped to use full-sized dead trees. The most prominent tracks—they were almost trails—around commissary were given a scattering of needles. The stoves and pots and the small surplus of food were loaded on the mules to follow the outgoing High Trippers and dunnage strings over Pine Creek Pass. Then French Canyon was quiet again. For a few days there it hadn't been what you could call pure wilderness. After all, pure wilderness can't exist so long as there's a yodel in the air, not to mention an early-morning wake-up call and several dozen discordant, off-key echoes. Pure unadulterated wilderness could hardly survive human contamination of any sort; we need criteria that will allow people who feel the need for inspiration—to overwork the word—to take as much of it as they need from the wilderness with as little damage as possible to its source.

The criterion of use realized in the High Trip turns out to be this: the people who come, and the things they need, come by trail and leave the way they came. . . .

Maybe a few of the answers to our questions—questions that were intended to be complicated and searching—are implicit in these notes on a High Trip. Perhaps more of the answers are missing. I would not presume that they aren't. But a few simple conclusions are indicated. Although some damage to the mountains occurred, it would seem to be less per person day of enjoyment than it is in other trips. Compared to other pack trips, the High Trip uses far fewer head of stock per person, and these are grazed for the most part in meadows not ordinarily accessible to smaller parties, that cannot easily detour too far from their planned route. Compared to unorganized trips of any kind, the High Trip leaves the mountains cleaner; signs of human activity and metabolism are so concentrated that they may be properly disposed of instead of being scattered from sagebrush to timberline.

So it would seem that the big traveling trips through the wilderness, such as those initiated by the Sierra Club in that first annual outing, should be continued, by whatever organizations may be qualified to conduct them. The argument that John Muir presented remains essentially valid. If we want mountain wilderness—the spacious scenic wilderness that means something—we must make it known to the people who, knowing it, will protect it. An overemphasis on spot camps, which can be successfully conducted within a few hundred yards of chalet development, may well leave us only those protectors of mountains who feel that a Yosemite Valley is wild enough. Doubtless there are few who would not wish to maintain the present, nearly ideal zoning of mountain recreational areas, which now properly or improperly accommodate all manner of tastes, whether in the clubs and motor courts at Tahoe, in the hotels, campgrounds, and High Sierra camps in Yosemite and Sequoia, in the packers' and anglers' spot camps one day in from roadheads on the east and west slopes of the Sierra, or in the wide undeveloped spaces of the High Sierra Wilderness Area and the back country of Yosemite, Kings Canyon, and Sequoia national parks. All but the last of these tastes—the taste for wilderness—can be expected to fare well without our being concerned. To hold the wilderness, however, we need defenders of all ages who have at some time in their lives traveled the wilderness trails. We need so many of them that we must, as the pressure for all types of mountain recreation grows, get as many of these defenders out on those trails as we can with the least possible damage per person per visit.

Accomplish this and we can be certain, when the embers of another final campfire in French Canyon burn themselves out, that they have not gone out forever. We shall know that another year will bring new faces into the campfire circle. Whether ours are there or not is of no great matter. But there must be faces, there must be firewood to be gathered, and all around the trees that flickeringly hold the night back from the campfire there must be wilderness.

***Sierra Club Bulletin*, 1948 Annual**

Perhaps there will be one more High Trip reunion, organized by the youngest of the young people who were once in commissary. Attendees will be the old ones, or their children, themselves graying. Reunions help people remember the good times and the bad, the latter usually being more clearly recorded. Old pictures will emerge and nostalgia will flow deep. That's all right.

I went back to the Sierra in 1983 to look for some of it, crossing Piute Pass into Humphreys Basin and to a campsite near where George

Rockwood and I had settled in at Golden Trout Lake forty years before. The thing that had changed most was me. Barbara offered to carry my pack when I faltered near the pass. I envied Mount Humphreys, which hadn't aged an iota, from where I stood. Perhaps a rock or two had fallen from its fractured summit. Certainly the talus slopes beneath the chutes had grown, but the growth didn't show. The denizens of tree line (don't call it timberline and tempt the loggers there) were essentially the same. A whitebark pine can put on forty years without showing a trace of wear and tear. I have a piece of root from an upturned whitebark pine that had withstood nine hundred winters and summers before it fell. The carpet of flowers, unpretentious, clinging close to the golden granite sand for security, was subtly miraculous in its unmanaged perfection. If you needed wood for cooking or campfire, you had but to scavenge under the trees in the dry duff, or reach for the readily accessible dead branches and pop some off. But where were they? They weren't. The firewood shortage of the Third World had reached the High Sierra world. In both you must walk and search far and long to get enough fuel for a tea fire.

There is also a water problem. In the high country streams are never far apart. You can drink from any of them? Not unless you like giardia, which now pervades the high country everywhere.

And you can camp anywhere you want to? Yes, if the area is designated as a campsite and you can get a permit for a limited stay.

Gridlock has not yet come to the John Muir Trail that connects Yosemite Valley with Mount Whitney, but you do not have to be too good at fantasy to imagine it.

So I wonder if the High Trip wasn't ended too soon, if other regulatory steps should have been taken first, steps that might have precluded its loss.

The High Trip used wood small parties were not equipped to handle. There was enough experienced leadership and followership to keep the impact low, to cover tracks, even to cover spoor and keep it away from streams. Packstock impact had been heavy, but careful studies of high-meadow ecology and meticulous management had controlled and reduced the impact. High Trip participants were indeed welded into an effective force for protecting big wilderness, whereas a host of people traveling widely separated in twos and threes are usually more concerned about themselves than about organizing into groups that can be legislatively and politically effective.

The impact of present overcrowding by many small groups is much heavier, I submit, than that of the few large groups, especially large groups that travel far in a given season in a given wilderness.

Whatever the cause, the result has been that travelers are less careful, less resistant to the constant encroachment of access roads, less forceful in requiring that the millions of acres of de facto wilderness we had be set aside in perpetuity for use as wilderness. Millions of acres have been set aside, all right, but set aside as clear-cut areas, havens for mining debris, for overgrazing, for roadside recreation as long as it fits with other uses. The less de facto wilderness there is, the more crowded the dedicated areas become. So the Forest Service and other government agencies scrutinized the footprints, too often looking the other way when bulldozers, chainsaws, dam builders, condominiumizers, and their innovative friends dismantled wilderness that could not be replaced. It need not have been so.

Forty years ago! I can't think of the number without remembering an article in the 1933 *Sierra Club Bulletin* annual magazine. It was by Theodore Seixas Solomons, who had explored the High Sierra for a high-mountain route in the early nineties. He gave the Sierra some of its finest place names. The Evolution region bears most of them – Evolution Lake itself, and Mounts Darwin, Haeckel, Huxley, Wallace, Fiske, Spencer, Lamarck (added by the U.S.G.S. in about 1908), and Mendel (added by D.R.B. in 1942), Scylla and Charybdis, Disappearing Creek, and the Enchanted Gorge.

In "After Forty Years," Solomons tells of his return to the Sierra after a long absence. He could still climb almost as well but not descend nearly so well. Thanks to the ups and downs, he lost thirty-five pounds temporarily. For the young and girthless he had two suggestions. First, spend less time thinking about the peaks. "More revealing, more enthralling often, are these miniature books in the running brooks, these sermons in the smallest stones – these microcosms in the great Sierran macrocosm."

And second? "The other suggestion is, it's a good thing – I speak from experience – to go into the High Sierra at least every forty years. Get the habit!"

KALA PATTAR

THE YEAR 1956 was the last for my leading High Trips and for thinking of leading a major climb, and in 1960 dust began to gather on my skis and never left them. I could still walk. But how high? The year 1976 would tell. Kala Pattar, elevation eighteen thousand feet, was where everyone wanted to go, but I didn't expect to join them there. Originally our trek had planned to peak at the Everest Base Camp, but the 1976 American expedition had left the place so dirty, we were told, that we would rather not see it. Besides, Kala Pattar was just as high, and provided a better perspective on what everyone wanted to see, the north and west bastions of the great mountain itself, its summit eleven thousand feet higher still.

Our daughter, Barbara, and our youngest son, John, were along, their self-appointed task being to see that their sixty-four-year-old father, in his twilight years, not overdo. They were well ahead and, for all I knew, nearing the top of Kala Pattar itself, far beyond my reach. My altitudinal limit, I was sure, had already been tested and set the day before, when I could barely poke around the massive moraine boulders above our camp at Lobuje, sixteen thousand feet above a faraway sea. I kept my pace slow enough by photographing the splendid displays of lichen. I recommend to the aging mountaineer the leisurely one-step-at-a-time study and photography of lichens; their pace makes that of moss look reckless. Imitating lichens, I survived the afternoon.

A vigorous chill arrived before twilight, and I was delighted to put a tent and sleeping bag between me and it as soon as possible after dinner, hoping that a good night's sleep would restore me enough that I could at least approach Kala Pattar. I might even reach Gorak Shep, to see if I could find the place where Dick Emerson had photographed the grazing yaks immortalized in the Sierra Club book, *Everest: The West Ridge,* which I was now reliving the lower part of. There may have been many good nights' sleep at camp that night; three Mountain Travel treks had somehow got their calendars confused and were all camped there at once. That night's population of a little summer herder's outpost was close to one hundred trekkers and Sherpas. Our tent was directly downwind of a warming fire that a higher trekking party kept going all night – a fire fueled with yak dung. Airborne particulates of recycled yak pasture drifted down to us and into me all too much of the night. John seemed to be sleeping the sleep of the young and the innocent. Lacking both virtues, I awoke exhausted.

By the time I was walking everyone had long left camp and was far ahead – everyone but the Sherpa who had been assigned to follow me, no matter how slow I might be. With hand gestures and other suitable body language I tried to persuade him to give up on me; I would just poke along and return to camp when I felt the need. But when I moved, he moved, and when I sat, so did he, a good fifteen paces behind, smiling understandingly, but determined.

Even if he had not been there, I would not have been alone. I was accompanied by a twisted but sturdy staff, handed me two days before by a Frenchman several years younger who was returning from Kala Pattar and was disturbed to see that I was trying to go anywhere at all without a walking stick. This was his trophy, but he generously gave it to me. It was this staff that kept me going, taking one step beside me for every two steps I took.

It had taken much more than a walking stick to get me to that day in late November. The preceding January 1 had caught me weighing two hundred seventeen pounds between shower and breakfast. In other words, that was as low as I could get the scales to read, and it was perfectly clear that unless I got lower I would never get higher.

Getting a lot higher was something I had dreamed about from the early thirties, when I first got avaricious about reading, then collecting books about mountains, then dreaming about mountains. John Muir and Clarence King let me see the Sierra Nevada, my hills of home, in a new light. Geoffrey Winthrop Young and Guido Rey told of adventure in the Alps, and Mummery added humor to the adventure. And as I read them and many others I saw that no one had caught mountaineers and tourists more lovingly than Samivel, with his books of cartoons and paintings and his sly way of reminding mountaineers not to take themselves too seriously.

By 1936 none of my shelf of Himalayan books had impressed me more with the range's grandeur than *Nanga Parbat Adventure,* thanks to its superb reproduction of mountain photographs. I wanted to be on a river that had helped make it possible for a mountain to rise twenty-three thousand feet above it. I wanted to be, myself, where Erwin Schneider stood when he made his photograph of Fairy Meadow, with its counterpoint of one of the world's highest meadows and one of the world's highest peaks. But I never expected to get there, of course. There was half a world between my shelf-full of Himalaya and the real thing.

When Charles Houston, in 1935, invited me to join the expedition to K–2 that produced Bob Bates's book, *Five Miles High,* I had nowhere near enough money. Seventeen years later, when I was asked to be of some assistance on an expedition to Dhaulagiri, I still had nowhere near enough money—and too much family to leave at home anyway.

One book on the Himalayan shelf made the difference. It was William H. Murray's *The Scottish Himalayan Expedition.* It was published in London in 1951 and a copy was given me by Howard Zahniser to review for *The Living Wilderness.* I enjoyed the book immensely. In it four Scottish mountaineers somehow got themselves organized, got to the Himalaya, circled Nanda Devi, climbed a few lower peaks, kept within budget, and had a very good time. Though I have yet to review the book, Howard Zahniser forgave me my dilatoriness long before he died. I quoted liberally from it in *Everest: The West Ridge* and *Return to the Alps.* I even got Bill Murray's forgiveness as well as his promise to write a book on the Scottish Highlands and to help organize Friends of the Earth in the United Kingdom when Anne and I met him in Glasgow in 1970. Best of all, I got to thank him for having written what had proved to be the epitome of my religion.

Murray's pages six and seven tell how they limited themselves to four climbers and never more than twenty porters. Still, they faced formidable challenges. Theirs was the first Scottish expedition, lacking Himalayan experience, language, adequate maps, or planning time. And in post-war Britain the food they would require was strictly rationed. Murray sat back and relaxed, waited a week for a friend's initiative. The friend asked Murray to issue orders—but "from beginning to end my own constant endeavor was never to issue orders." Near the top of page six he said, "Nothing had yet been done." A few lines later he retracts: "I erred in one important matter . . . We had put down our passage money." And he ends the paragraph with a passage that has affected me ever since, perhaps because it describes something that is within me:

Until one is committed there is hesitancy, the chance to draw back, always ineffectiveness. Concerning all acts of initiative (and creation), there is one elementary truth, the ignorance of which kills countless ideas and splendid plans; that the moment one definitely commits oneself, then Providence moves too. All sorts of things occur to help one that would never otherwise have occurred. A whole stream of events issues from the decision, raising in one's favour all manner of unforeseen incidents and meetings and material assistance, which no man could have dreamt would have come his way. I have learned a deep respect for one of Goethe's couplets:

> *"Whatever you can do, or dream you can, begin it.*
> *Boldness has genius, power, and magic in it."*

Following this, Murray lists the battalion orders he thereupon drew up—what Tom Weir was to do about food and transport, Douglas Scott about plans and equipment, Tom MacKinnon about medicine, and Murray about everything else. They were committed.

Having helped get me to several places before the Himalaya, Messrs. Murray and Goethe now moved me closer to Kala Pattar itself. Somehow the walking cleared my lungs, though the air was still too thin, and I found myself resting again, this time at Gorak Shep, at the far edge of an old sandy lake bed. I learned that John had got into a foot race across it with the Sherpas and had won. Though the length of his legs may have made the race unfair, his stamina encouraged me to see what my portion of the family gene pool might do for me.

Kala Pattar is a slight pause, just a thousand feet above Gorak Shep, in the west ridge of Pumori, near the top of which a climber had been caught by a stiff wind a few years before and blown away into Tibet. John, having just sampled this wind, met me on his return from the top of Kala Pattar and warned, "When you get up there, Dave, hang onto something."

He said "when," not "if," I noted, as the air and my thinking thinned. He'd been watching me for three weeks, and if he thought I could do it, I determined to press on. So I called for staff support and got it more and more frequently, with the staff taking a step every time either of my feet stepped. I inhaled and exhaled completely between moves. I relished the ounces of effort that staff spared me by making unnecessary the ordinarily automatic exertion of keeping in balance. Just a simple stout stick of just the right length and feel. How fond I grew of it! The top of Mount Whitney, my previous high point, was now three thousand feet below me. No mountaineering skills were needed here. I was not going anywhere yaks had not already been. This is not to demean yaks. The yaks had packed our gear once we reached altitude too cold for the Sherpas' bare feet. I had come to marvel at their footwork. In difficult terrain – on talus, for example – a horse or a mule will put the left rear foot exactly where the left front foot has stepped, and thus need find but one good spot for those two feet to use – consecutively, of course. The yak has independent four-wheel suspension. Even in roughest terrain the yak selects and memorizes separate footholds for all four feet and moves confidently on.

Yaks had preceded me, and I was still up to going where they had been, since I had only to find support for two feet and a stick. I remembered Yosemite Valley climbs, Sierra peaks, the ice summit in the Waddington region, a Dolomite, the Matterhorn, the Grèpon, and, in an entirely different mountain family, Shiprock, where old fears of height and exposure had been overcome, and there was hardly a question of the body's willingness to follow where the eye had led and to follow with some agility, even now and then a feeling of grace. But that was then and this was now. Hang on, Brower. One foot forward, brace, breathe, breathe again, the other foot, and it certainly is no effort to get your lungs to hit bottom, is it? And thank you, walking stick, for supporting a lot more weight than you had ever dreamed of. The people ahead had stopped now. Why? Because they were there. In a few moments more I was too, to be congratulated by those who, like me, had thought I might very well wave good-bye to them back at Thyangboche, at a comfortable thirteen thousand feet, and there await their return.

I had now thoroughly unjustified the trip doctor's worry about the sixty-four-year-old. My eyes had already withstood a doctor's peering into them at Periche, four thousand feet lower, where the retinal blood seemed to be staying properly within the banks of its channels. That meant that I had acclimatized well up to that altitude. And so help me, after I had sat a few minutes and checked it, my pulse was running at eighty at Kala Pattar. Just like home.

Although I thought my acuity was fine, my camera knew better. I got fuzzy on what counteradjustment I was to make to compensate for an electric eye unaccustomed to altitude, and badly underexposed the Kala Pattar roll. I did have an eye for lichens, however, and found one that would not burden me, since it weighed only about an ounce and a half. I walked down with Barbara, breathing easily, and remembering what Bill Murray had done for me without even including me in his battalion orders.

For I had made a commitment. If I were ever to see the Himalaya, there were limits to how long I could put it off. There would be no way to get two hundred seventeen pounds up where I wanted to be. So put away the car keys, put away far less food, push away Tanqueray martinis and all the lesser ones as well, walk down to mass transit every day and walk the

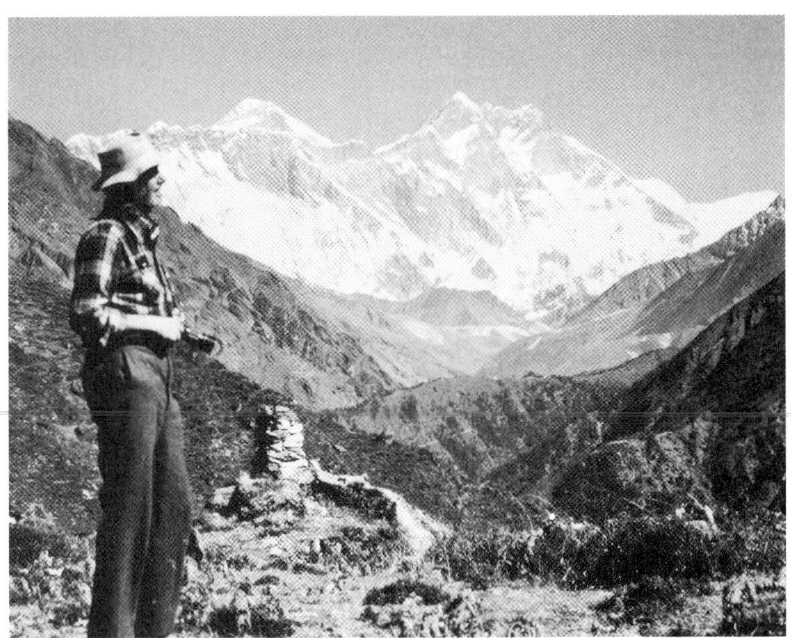

Dave at sixty-four on the way to eighteen-thousand-foot Kala Pattar, from just above Namche Bazar. Mount Everest directly behind the cairn.

vertical eight hundred feet back up, put five hundred miles on your boots and five thousand fewer on the Volvo, discard twenty-five unnecessary pounds, save travel and parking expense of three thousand dollars in ten months, join Barbara and John and twenty others on a five-week trek, leave another twenty-two pounds behind in Nepal, and arrive home weighing what you did when your wife agreed to marry you, and see, rumpled and bearded and wrinkled though you now are, if that disposal of waist helps any.

It did, and the rewards of an easily arranged change in what I was doing to my body, doing something for it instead, led me to threaten anyone who would listen that although I had planned on retiring at sixty-four, I was now going to wait until I was one hundred twenty-eight.

CHAPTER 8

ALONG THE COLORADO

PRESERVING DINOSAUR

When the Weather is Good on flights between Salt Lake City and Denver there are fine views of the Uintas, which must have been formed by a tectonic plate that was traveling off course. Why else would the range follow a parallel, not a meridian, as American mountains are supposed to do?

At the eastern end the Uintas become Dinosaur National Monument and I am at a window seat looking hard at the places I remember floating by in 1953 with sons Ken and Bob, from Lily Park down the Yampa to its junction with the Green River just below Echo Park, then down the Green through Island Park and the rapids of Split Mountain Gorge. I like the look of things because Echo Park and Split Mountain dams and reservoirs aren't there. They aren't because the Sierra Club led the battle against them and won, and I worked hard—for the club but mostly for Dinosaur—in that battle.

Trouble began on the Colorado, without our quite knowing it, in the legislation establishing Grand Canyon National Park in 1919. It included a time bomb: "The Secretary of the Interior is authorized to permit the utilization of areas therein which may be necessary for the development and maintenance of government reclamation projects." Fortunately the act also provided a defusing device, the clause immediately preceding the authorization: "Whenever consistent with the primary purpose of said park, . . ."

A 1944 treaty promised Mexico one and a half million acre-feet of Colorado River water per year. The Colorado River Compact of 1922 had already promised seven and a half million acre-feet each to the Upper Basin (Wyoming, Colorado, Utah, New Mexico, and a little bit of Arizona) and the Lower Basin (California, Nevada, and the rest of Arizona). The problem? There wasn't that much water in the river.

In the Upper Colorado River Compact of 1948, the respective states allocated their share among themselves. In 1952, Arizona took California to the U.S. Supreme Court to prevent California from continuing to take as much as it was getting, and in 1963 the court sided with Arizona. In the late nineteen forties, before this litigation, the Sierra Club dabbled with the Colorado, approved an invasion of Grand Canyon proposed by reclamationists, then reversed itself.

The club's serious concern began in 1950 and it became my principal concern at the close of 1952, when I became the club's first executive director and was swallowed by Dinosaur. It was an exhilarating experience, becoming a gastrolith that way, and was probably the only polishing I would ever have. It led to a lot of travel, writing, photographing, publishing, organizing, and testimony, the latter peaking in 1954 when Senators Anderson of New Mexico, Millikan of Colorado, and Watkins of Utah alternated in keeping me testifying for two hours and fifty-seven minutes. I had testified briefly before the House Committee on Interior and Insular Affairs in early 1953 and, later, in 1955 at great length, but it was on January 26, 1954, that I began my most challenging experience testifying. I was new at the game of appearing in the House and had carefully prepared my testimony in advance and made copies available to the committee the day before. Representatives Aspinall, Dawson, and Miller, allied with Mr. Jacobson from the Bureau of Reclamation, were on hand to try to tear it apart and hear what I had to say:

I AM EXECUTIVE DIRECTOR of the Sierra Club, a national conservation organization of eight thousand members founded in 1892 by John Muir, Warren Olney, and colleagues to explore, enjoy, and protect the nation's scenic assets. The club's headquarters are in San Francisco; its members live in forty-six states, the District of Columbia, the territories, and fifteen foreign countries.

I have also been asked to speak on behalf of the Federation of Western Outdoor Clubs, a group of thirty-one organizations in the states of Washington, Oregon, California, and Utah whose total membership exceeds twenty-one thousand.

As a citizen and taxpayer, I have been very much interested in the testimony here, technical though much of it has been. I have been impressed by the mass of detail that has been compiled and made available by the Department of the Interior. I hope the 1946 survey of recreational resources of the Colorado River Basin is in your file. I must say that I wish, in my capacity as a citizen bystander here, that I could have heard more from objective experts, government and private, on engineering, agriculture, and economics, for it has occurred to me that the first two and one-half days' testimony has consisted in large part of a single bureau's looking upon its own work and pronouncing it good. But I feel sure that this committee, before it makes up its own mind on this tremendous project, will have received and considered such testimony.

As a citizen of a state which contributes eight percent of the federal government's income (that would be about one hundred twenty-five million dollars of the federal expenditure envisioned for the total Upper Colorado River Project as estimated a year ago), I have no objection to seeing the federal government find some means for authorizing such a project, but I do hope that ample time will be allowed for the very thorough scrutiny such a proposal needs before the nation as a whole commits itself to the very complicated and necessarily costly project which is before you. I am sure there is time for the thorough review we need. In spite of all the study to date, the project is not yet shaken down.

I should like to address myself to some matters that concern ideals and principles and their relation to America the beautiful – the America we are all very happy to step outside into after such sessions as these. We all have an interest in America's beauty. The Congress itself, beginning back in Lincoln's administration and continuing to this moment, has diligently sought means of assuring that the best of our scenery is not to be sold, or given, or destroyed, or altered. It is to be preserved unimpaired for the enjoyment of this and future generations – one of the finest steps in land-use administration ever devised in the history of the world.

Congress set Yosemite Valley aside for the nation ninety years ago, Yellowstone eight years later. The number of scenic reservations increased, and their use, too. About three hundred people visited Yosemite in the year 1893. Last year there were just a few less than a million – probably thirty million in all the parks. Many people have not seen any parks, and possibly never will; but they are happy to have them there to take care of those people who like that sort of thing.

Who are those people? Perhaps not everyone here. There are probably quite a few, for example, who would not care to rough it to see any of the parks' back country, who wouldn't care to climb into a rubber boat and float down the rapid and calm stretches of Dinosaur's beautiful canyons. But to some people this very trip has been the finest scenic experience they ever had. Two of my kids and I feel that way. We were there.

Many of you won't feel that way, but will still defend the right of others to have a chance to. Even if we did not like opera, we should hesitate to close the best opera house – or to alter it so that you still had some of the house, but couldn't hear the music.

Who are the people who fight for this right – the present-day Thoreaus and Leopolds and Marshalls?

Look at the Sierra Club, for instance, which wants to persuade you to protect Dinosaur and the parks, just as other Congresses have done for so long. What kind of people are in it? Teenage kids, out to climb, hike, and ski; office workers, teachers, professional men – we even have a mailman who comes on our Sierra outings to walk ninety or a hundred miles during two weeks in the wilderness. Strange people, slightly odd? Some, perhaps. But also the past president of the American Society of Civil Engineers, the current president of the American Society of Radio Engineers, the next president of the American Chemical Society, the president of a major pharmaceutical house, of a major railroad, of a major mining firm, an assistant U.S. attorney general. We have these, too. All of them, whether kids getting away from too much homework or executives getting away from too many telephones ringing on one desk, all have this in common: a love for the beautiful, unspoiled places—places they work hard (at no pay) to preserve, and long after they themselves can no longer enjoy them.

It is a noble human endeavor that leads them to do this. It is this type of endeavor I am hoping I can communicate to you as something every bit as important as the type of enterprise so earnestly supported here—and entirely laudable in its place—the urge to produce, to grow, to develop, to profit, and to spend. This Sierra Club is a good organization, devoted to idealism, and I am proud of it. It is but one of many, all just as good. I wish you were all members. It would cost you only $3.50 per year.

Here are three questions which we feel have not been answered properly yet.

1. What are the important park values in Dinosaur?
2. Would they be destroyed by Echo Park and Split Mountain dams?
3. Can Dinosaur's scenery be made accessible without dams?

As you may have guessed, our answer is that this area has superlative park values. They would indeed be destroyed by the proposed dams. And the dams are not needed to make this area accessible. Briefly, this is why:

What about the park values?

I am tempted to set myself up as an expert on this. I have seen a lot of outstanding scenery in the last thirty-five years, in this and other countries. In Dinosaur I have been out to the Quarry, on Harper's Corner, and up on Round Top, and with two of my boys, nine and seven years old, I have floated eighty-six miles across the monument, from Lily Park through Split Mountain Gorge, camping at Anderson Hole, Bull Park, Mantle's Ranch, Echo Park, and Jones Hole. *I have never had a scenic experience to equal that one*—and as a native Californian I fully expect to be hanged from a yardarm in San Francisco Bay for saying so. To me, and to the two hundred other Sierra Club members who took the same trip last summer, it is a magnificent place.

If you haven't been all the way through the canyons or haven't seen one of the four color movies now available that show the trip, you cannot begin to appreciate why we are so determined in wanting to preserve it.

I should like to try to give you a quick account of what the trip is like and how it makes you feel about the place. I will if you ask me to. But to spare your time, I'll ask you just to take my word for it that this is a totally wonderful place, certainly the equal of any canyon park except Grand Canyon—and it beats Grand Canyon all hollow in the ease with which you can effortlessly see the best of it from the bottom looking up, riding those rainbow rivers.

Would the dams destroy the park values? My own opinion is that the values which now give this area its great natural significance would indeed be destroyed and that if you should be led into the mistake of authorizing those dams, you should at the same time throw the area out of the park system. We should, if that tragedy came about, let the states develop the recreation area, chiefly of local value, that would be left. And that should be the rule, we submit, for reservoir recreation throughout the upper basin project and elsewhere. Develop and administer it at state expense.

I have seen in the Utah papers the claim that the dams would improve the canyons, which seem to these writers (if they have seen the canyons) to be a collection of ugly snags and quicksand. They are entitled to their opinion, but we do not accept that as a disinterested opinion. When I am sick I go to a doctor, not an engineer, and when I want studied opinion on park values, I go to people who have made the study of those values a career (reserving the right to disagree). I think we do well here to quote the Park Service, which has said in writing that the effects of these dams upon irreplaceable values of national significance would be deplorable. This statement is quoted in House Document 419. Deplorable is a mild word to describe what would happen to the scenery in Dinosaur were we to permit these dams to be built there. The Echo Park project alone calls for a dam five hundred twenty-five feet high, backing up one hundred seven miles of reservoir, inundating the intimate, close-up scenes and living space with nearly six and a half million acre-feet of water. There would be construction roads in the canyon and above it, tunnels, the whole power installation and transmission lines, the rapid build-up of silt at the upper end of the reservoirs, and the periodic drawdowns of the reservoir to enable it to fulfill its function—a fluctuation that would play hob with fish and wildlife. The piñon pines, the Douglas firs, the maples and cottonwoods, the grasses and other flora that line the banks, the green living things that shine in the sun against the rich colors of the cliffs—these would all go. The river, its surge and its sound, the living sculptor of this place, would be silent forever, and all the fascination of its movement and the fun of riding it, quietly gliding through these cathedral corridors of stone—all done in for good. The tops of the cliffs you could still see, of course. As reservoirs go, it would be a handsome one—but remember the two hundred fifty-one other reservoir sites in the upper basin and the hundreds of reservoir sites elsewhere in the country. We don't want Dinosaur to be just another reservoir. We want it to remain the *only* Dinosaur, which it is now.

If we should accept the amazing statement that Echo Park dam would not destroy Dinosaur, but would only alter Dinosaur, we should also accept such statements as these:

1. A dam from El Capitan to Bridalveil Fall would not destroy Yosemite, but just alter it.

2. Other dams would only alter Yellowstone, Glacier National Park, Mammoth Caves National Park, Kings Canyon National Park.

3. Removal of the rain forest would only alter Olympic National Park.

4. Cutting the three-thousand-year-old Big Trees and making them into grape stakes would only alter Sequoia National Park. After all, the ground would still be there, and the sky, and the distant views. All you would have done is alter it, that is, take away its reason for being.

Maybe "alter" isn't the word. Just say "cut the heart out."

Those who have been working to help save the parks for future generations for all these years can understand how people who have not yet had the privilege of enjoying the great scenic parks would think that a dam might improve Dinosaur. We can understand it, but we *completely* disagree. We cannot, however, hide our grave apprehension at finding that federal department officials charged by law with protecting our parks show such poor appreciation of them as to call this destruction "altering."

It certainly argues that those of us who appreciate the national-park idea – the members of Congress who through the decades have steadfastly supported the park idea, and the others who selflessly volunteer their services on behalf of people not yet born – all of us need to do a better job of helping to explain to those who do not know, how important a spiritual and inspirational asset we do have in our national park system.

Perhaps Undersecretary of the Interior Ralph Tudor would have felt differently about the impact of the dams upon this irreplaceable asset of Dinosaur had he been able to devote more time to looking at it. You will recall his telling you that he flew over some of the proposed alternate dam sites and was in the monument three days. But I gather that he was able to see little of the canyons themselves on the ground – or rather, on the river.

Echo Park, which he did see, is a magnificent place, alone worthy of being preserved inviolate. However, the Dinosaur canyons reach their scenic climax, not at Echo, but above and below it. The best of the Yampa is the stretch from Bull Park down to Echo, which our party took two days to float through, and where I should like to spend a week, exploring for Indian signs and little things under those great, noble cliffs. The Canyon of Lodore – from the Gates of Lodore down to Echo – is the best of the best. But you can't just fly over it and have the foggiest idea of its beauty. You need to ride the river and camp along the way. Two or three days ought to be allowed, although you can race through if you feel you must.

Arrangements could easily be made for a smooth, quiet glide around the charming winding canyon from Mantle's Ranch to Echo. You could leave U.S. Highway 40, take this ride, and be back on the highway the same day, much richer for this superb wilderness experience. You could, that is, if they would fix the roads just a little and if the people of Vernal did not warn you, "Don't waste your time there; there's nothing to see and it's treacherous"—an unbelievable lack of understanding of the facts.

A climax of its own special kind is the ride through the spire-walled Split Mountain Gorge—a roller-coaster ride that takes only two or three hours and leaves you wanting more right now. And you can do it for the price of a couple of tickets to a football game. But wear your Levis; you may get splashed a little. And try to be there before too late in October, for the river may get too low then.

That upper Yampa corridor has one of the most awesome spectacles in all the world. I call it the "Grand Overhang" (it's in the *Sierra Club Bulletin* you have before you; it should have a much better name, and you can only appreciate it if you see it yourself or get Cinerama to photograph it in color). The Yampa River really did a job here, in the course of some ninety million years, entrenching itself in a giant meander right in the heart of the Uinta Mountains.

I am afraid Mr. Tudor, in addition to missing the entire corridor, Lodore, and Split Mountain Gorge, could not have seen this beetling overhang from above. Once you get close enough to the edge to look down, it's too late. It's a terrific drop. It would take you about twelve slow seconds to complete the fall, and you'd land on the opposite bank of the Yampa River.

You just can't go down that river—all of it—and come out with a statement that a dam would only alter it. You come off that trip convinced that a dam would be the tragedy of our generation.

And Mr. Tudor would have you trade all this for what he has been told might be 100,000 to 200,000 acre-feet of water! Very recently they were saying 350,000 acre-feet officially. It makes a friend of mine wonder how much lower they can go—and *still be wrong.*

I have some statements that I think we ought to start the rest of this discussion with. We have been quite concerned with the reliability, although we want to rely on them, of the Bureau's figures, the Interior figures. I think I can demonstrate, if you will follow the arithmetic, what folly it is to follow those figures. Mr. Tudor in his testimony on Monday said, for one thing, "The most important single factor in favor of the recommended plan, as contrasted to suggested alternates, is its comparatively smaller water wastage through evaporation." Then he said on page 23 [of the transcript]: "The fourth alternative [one that he rejected] would be the high Glen Canyon Dam, which is considerably more elevation, 3,750 feet. It would then have a gross storage capacity of 31,700,000 acre-feet. The exposed reservoir surface is 186,000 acres and the evaporation is 691,000 acre-feet per year. Again, that figure must not be compared with the evaporation from Echo Park but with the combined evaporation of Echo Park and lower Glen Canyon." He concluded that paragraph saying, "So the net difference is 165,000 acre-feet."

Then he made a statement later, on page 26: "In the final analysis, the increased losses of water by evaporation from the alternate sites is the fundamental issue upon which the Department has felt it necessary to give any consideration to the Echo Park dam and reservoir."

On page 33, just as a footnote for what I am going to carry on with, he said, "The difference between Echo Park and the other most favorable dam site is about 108,000 acre-feet."

From Mr. Tudor's own figures – or the figures someone worked out for him – it can be shown that one of the alternates he investigated does not evaporate 165,000 acre-feet more than Echo Park dam, as he testified, but 2,610 acre-feet *less*, while storing some 700,000 acre-feet more. It is hard to believe, I know, but if I am wrong, it must surely be because *he* is wrong, and he is not supposed to be wrong in engineering matters or figures.

But I submit that he made three big errors and one little one in this one matter alone. I refer to the comparison between Echo and Little Glen and Big Glen, as I call it. All the evidence you need is on pages 12, 13, and 14 of his opening testimony, which I did not check carefully during his reading of it. I should have checked sooner, because editors are trained to check, even if they do not know engineering. They are supposed to know ninth-grade arithmetic. I shall be glad to do the arithmetic, if you wish, but for now will just mention the four errors that might have cost us our park.

[Adjournment for the day, on January 27, interrupted the demonstration of the errors, which was resumed the following morning, a blackboard being provided upon request. It had also been arranged to have Mr. C. B. Jacobson, engineer in charge of Colorado River Storage Project Studies, Bureau of Reclamation (Salt Lake office), on hand to comment upon the demonstration of errors, which, together with the question period, occupies eleven pages of the published hearings, excerpts from which appear below.]

Before I worry about the "serious difficulty of protecting Rainbow Bridge" that Mr. Tudor worried about, I should like to sit back to see what happens if they go over their pages of figures with a well-oiled slide rule to see if there are as many critical errors on the other pages.

It would be nice to think that whoever it is who audits the arithmetic will change his approach to one of protecting, and not altering, the Park System, which we all want to preserve for future generations for the beautiful thing it is, and Dinosaur along with it. I know, and I'll bet Reclamation knows, that if the river disappeared in its course through Dinosaur, or was somehow unavailable, a sound Upper Colorado Storage Project could be developed elsewhere. The axiom for protecting the Park System is to consider that it is dedicated country, hallowed ground to leave as beautiful as we have found it, and not country in which man should be so impressed with himself that he tries to improve God's handiwork.

As it is, so it can be enjoyed. Mr. Dawson [committee member William A. Dawson, of Utah], in a letter to all the members of the House, you used the word "treacherous" to describe the rivers. I think that the two hundred Sierra Club members who went down them over the course of a single month last summer would like me to disagree with your application of the word. It could be used far better to describe Highway 40. We were all delighted to get off that treacherous highway and to settle back and relax in those safe boats on a thrilling but not treacherous river, to watch the trees, the wildlife, and the cliffs go by as we trailed our hands in the water, and now and then jumped out to float quietly along with the boats into the middle of the most amazing river wilderness I know.

Take that ride with us next summer and I'll bet that you'll agree with me. Between now and next June, if somehow you can persuade your colleagues to persuade the Department of the Interior to spend ten percent of the twenty-one million dollars Mr. McKay has proposed to spend on helping Dinosaur, after it's been spoiled, it will be easier, a whole lot easier, to get from U.S. 40 to the river's edge, where life really becomes simple and fun, and you can feel your nerves relaxing one by one—so long as you don't mind a few nights out in a sleeping bag on an air mattress.

Right now, as you probably know, it is pretty hard to get to Mantle's Ranch or to Echo Park. For those of the committee who do not know, let me say that last summer, when we hit Echo Park on our fourth afternoon down the river from Lily Park, we had planned to have a truck take us up for that view from Harper's Corner, back at where we had been and down to where we were headed. But there had been a heavy rain five days before and Bus Hatch, our boatman, said we couldn't take the truck up. "I checked with Doug Chew, about the road," Bus said (Doug owns the ranch at Echo), "and he said it was pretty rough. And when he says it's rough, I'd hesitate to fly a kite over it."

Gentlemen, I hope you all meet Bus—and I especially hope you leave him the chance to make the thousands of people happy who have just begun to learn about those wonderful wilderness river trails of Dinosaur, and the bobbing rubber boats that should still be riding those trails—perhaps with a patch or two—when the next century rolls around.

***Sierra Club Bulletin,* June 1954**

The Dinosaur battle was a big first for the club and for me. Preparing and presenting testimony is one thing, almost routine. Encountering hostile questions from a congressional committee and rebuttal from a Bureau of Reclamation expert is another. Call it harrowing. The volume published on the hearings held in January 1954 reminds me vividly of the excitement of the day and reveals what the questioning uncovered. I remember how nervous I got. I didn't take my pulse, but I knew it was there. These excerpts include the questions fired at me:

MR. BROWER: My point is to demonstrate to this committee that they would be making a great mistake to rely upon the figures presented by the Bureau of Reclamation when they cannot add, subtract, multiply, or divide. I am not trying to sound smart, but it is an important thing.

MR. ASPINALL. And you are a layman and you are making that charge against the engineers of the Bureau of Reclamation?

MR. BROWER. I am a man who has gone through ninth grade and learned his arithmetic. I do not know engineering. I have only taken Mr. Tudor's own figures which he used and calculated in error to justify invading Dinosaur National Monument.

MR. ASPINALL. Of course, the conclusion which mr. Tudor tried to leave with this committee was to the effect that there would be a shortage of almost three hundred thousand kilowatts if the big reservoir at Glen Canyon was constructed rather than the reservoir contemplated at Echo Park. That was the conclusion which he really left, was it not?

MR. BROWER. I do not believe so, Mr. Aspinall. I think that was an incidental part put in his statement: "In conclusion, in the final analysis, the increased loss of water by evaporation for the ultimate site is the fundamental issue upon which the department has felt it necessary to give any consideration to the Echo Park Dam and the reservoir."

Now the other point, I grant you, was in his testimony, and I can talk about that too, if you wish, just giving a few figures that they do not give.

MR. ASPINALL. No.

MR. BROWER. But this table gives the Low Glen that is in the present plan as illustrated on your map; gives Mr. Tudor's figures for High Glen and the figures for Echo Park and Split Mountain. . . . [Here I demonstrated how useful it is to have a mind full of numbers. It would be unkind to repeat them.]. . . I do not think Mr. Tudor can find any mistakes in what I have done with his figures. If you would like to submit those to Mr. Tudor, I certainly would be happy to.

MR. ASPINALL. Mr. Chairman, I would suggest the witness try to contact Mr. Tudor or whoever works for him in the bureau because most certainly it is a direct criticism of Mr. Tudor's ability which has been challenged here.

MR. BROWER. It has been.

MR. ASPINALL. And we would like to have that resolved before this committee, and I would like to have the witness state that he will get in touch with the bureau and give us the results of the bureau's reaction as well as his.

MR. DAWSON. Will you yield to me?

MR. ASPINALL. Certainly.

MR. DAWSON. I made this suggestion yesterday, I believe it was, and one I intend to follow up at the appropriate time. I think we should have these people who profess to be engineers come in here and meet with us in executive session with the Bureau of Reclamation engineers and go over these figures for the benefit of the committee. If Mr. Brower is willing to do that, I think he certainly should be invited.

MR. BROWER. Thank you very much for that suggestion. I point out again, Mr. Dawson and members of the committee, I do not profess to be an engineer. All I am doing is using arithmetic and Mr. Tudor's figures, using the same method he did.

MR. DAWSON. That is the point I am making—it is arithmetic that is concerned, and I think for the benefit of the committee that should be thrashed out. My colleague from Colorado is perfectly right, we should have these people in here to go over these figures.

MR. BROWER. I certainly could offer to do this: I could leave these figures with somebody who lives nearer than I live. . . .

MR. HARRISON. May I interrupt? I understand Mr. Jacobson from the bureau is here. Would you come up? When Mr. Brower finishes there, give us your reaction and we will get this settled now.

MR. JACOBSON. I believe I can.

MR. HARRISON. Proceed, Mr. Brower.

MR. BROWER. Now the point I want to make and Mr. Dawson brings it up when he says "Those who profess to be engineers," please do not lump me with those. I come here, I am very interested in seeing this place preserved, and there is a reason for doing it if we can find alternatives which will do it with no substantial loss. If we can, I think we certainly should want to, and I think most of the committee here would agree if there is a feasible alternative we should not then sacrifice a national monument.

Here I only provide what my arithmetic has shown me, and I think the arithmetic is reasonably accurate.

I would close this little interlude with this statement, which represents our policy. Right now the last impression I am leaving with you is one of figures. I did not come here to do arithmetic. I came here to try to advocate the principle. I would suggest as a closing statement here:

Before we sell out our parks, shouldn't we attack real waste first? Wasteful irrigation methods, for one thing. Wasteful pollution for another. Wasteful soil erosion due to small-watershed mismanagement. The list of wasteful things we do is nothing to be proud of.

When we've whittled that list down, then—and not until then—let's see where else to pare. When the pinch comes, then see if we must sacrifice the delights we have clung to, in our civilization, for the good of our soul, even if those delights don't affect the Dow-Jones average, and produce nothing but a little relief from tension, maybe.

In that dark day, if our children should find that religion and symphony, gardens and parks, trout streams and golf courses, don't pay off at the cash register, and if cash is all we have taught them to think about, then let's leave to them the choice of selling their birthright.

They won't even have a chance to choose unless we leave them that birthright, unless we bring about an enlightened approach to the parks in this, their darkest hour.

I don't know whether you want to question me at this time.

MR. HARRISON. Mr. Jacobson, will you proceed to explain?

MR. JACOBSON. If I may, Mr. Chairman, inasmuch as I was the man who accompanied Mr. Tudor around this basin during his inspection of alternatives, I would like to make this brief statement.

MR. HARRISON. It will be received, and this, of course, will not be chargeable to the opponents so far as time is concerned.

MR. JACOBSON. It is charged that Mr. Tudor did not look at all these items. He did spend considerable time in the monument. For instance, at the overhang point that the gentleman refers to, Mr. Tudor actually laid on his stomach and viewed the river fourteen hundred feet below. He got into a boat in the river almost an equal distance from the point around the bend, but the river was too low for navigation. He did view a good number of the areas in the monument itself. He actually flew over the areas that he did not otherwise view. And you can get a good view of Lodore Canyon from the air, a view you cannot get any other way.

You do not go down Lodore Canyon for two football tickets. I know because the trips I have made on the river have been financed by my own resources—I have not had a dime from the government to travel the river—and I know what it costs. I can also testify it is a treacherous trip because I swam part of it on one occasion.

So I think we ought to—when we (the Bureau of Reclamation) are accused of making misstatements in figures—have the opportunity to defend them.

MR. MILLER. I believe people who go down the river now, even in so-called low water, have to wear life preservers and have some protection so if they do get dumped they will be safe.

MR. JACOBSON. There are no insurance companies that will insure you for that trip.

MR. MILLER. Then the old and aged and invalid do not very often make that trip. I would be ruled out, I suppose. [Laughter.]

MR. JACOBSON. Now as to the figures.

Engineering is not just ninth-grade arithmetic, I assure you gentlemen. After you have taken your ninth-grade arithmetic, you have to start out with a course in algebra, plane geometry, solid geometry, trigonometry, spherical trigonometry, college algebra, and calculus. And these matters enter into such a complicated matter as computing evaporation from reservoirs.

We have a slight error in the figures that are in Mr. Tudor's statement. You will notice that Glen Canyon was an afterthought, or has been added to Mr. Tudor's explanation of these other alternatives. He did that because that is one of the suggestions that has come up since we made our detailed investigations. However, we have studied a great number of combinations involving the High Glen Canyon. In using the elevation of 3,750 feet, this figure was misprinted in Mr. Tudor's statement. I checked his statement. I am responsible that that figure was not printed as 3,735 feet.

This 3,750 figure refers to the height of the dam, the top of the dam. This column [indicating] refers to the water surface. Thus the 3,750 figure is in error. But regardless, the 186,000 acres involved and the 691,000 acre-feet of evaporation are correct and correspond to the 3,735 figure. So it is merely a misprint in the record and not an actual error.

MR. BROWER. Could I ask what happened there to the relationship in solving X? [X =calculated volume of water lost to evaporation.]

MR. HARRISON. Let him explain.

MR. JACOBSON. My mathematics do not arrive at this figure. [Again, a few numbers are omitted.] But the annual evaporation from a reservoir is arrived at from the operation of that reservoir over a wide fluctuation. I think you gentlemen realize that. It is not related to the maximum surface of the reservoir. The same applies to the little Glen as to the large Glen.

Here is where your higher mathematics comes in. The gentleman fails to express them when he takes straight-line ratios. Had he compared the areas at the centroids of the respective volumes, he would be more nearly correct. But when you superimpose capacity on top of one water surface it spreads out over a larger area. The reservoir is not a cube. It is more like a cone. The area of the cone at this point [indicating] is not a direct relationship of the depth of the reservoir. In this case it varies with the square root of the radius, which is a direct relationship to the depth of the reservoir.

And how does the volume vary? The volume varies as the cube power. So you just cannot use ratios and run the old slide stick and get any answer you want. In fact, on the slide rule, you have two or three scales: one deals with cube and another the square root. So the proposition the gentleman puts before you lacks engineering practicability.

MR. BROWER. May I make a comment or two?

MR. HARRISON. Yes.

MR. BROWER. Mr. Jacobson has explained some things of which I would like to have seen in the testimony since this evaporation is the thing Mr. Tudor wants to base Echo Park on. That is the most important thing according to Mr. Tudor. All I could do was–

MR. HARRISON. The Chair will have to insist that you limit yourself to some explanation of the figures and not to any statement upon Mr. Tudor because we are just involved in this one question: Whose figures are right?

MR. BROWER. I would point out that when we start using the cone we are talking about relationships which are already reflected and brought into a straight-line relationship when you talk about area, because the area of one is to the area of the other as a different level in the cone.

Now if this evaporation is figured at a lower level, the evaporating level of the lake, then this one should be, too [indicating]. I do not think we have got worked out in complete detail what the operating level of the lake must be if we put in additional Echo storage down there. And there are lots of figures we need then. I still have this little joker here about the comparative, the subtraction. We can argue for quite a while, and I will stand by my arithmetic, on the straight-line method of solving for X, and we can have a duel with chalk whenever the committee has the time.

I do not know any relationship here except one of straight subtraction, which if you do nothing else, takes it down to 70,000 feet, which is quite below the 100,000 or 200,000 that Mr. Tudor gave us.

This [indicating] was an error and a misprint. I am glad that is corrected now. Would it have been corrected had I not raised the question? And would it not be well to get competent engineers to raise the question about a lot of these other facts?

MR. HARRISON. The Chair might say I do not think it is proper for the witness to impugn the ability of the engineers.

MR. BROWER. You are quite correct. May I withdraw that last one? I think it is good to have further checks made because certainly we can vary in results, and if we do not check why, we can let some errors stay in.

I apologize for that "competent engineers." But I am still wondering where we get this now. We have this 3,735. In the bureau's own testimony on pages 146 and 147 it says that you will get forty-seven million acre-feet storage if you go up just twenty-five feet. Now why do we have to go up thirty-seven? I do not know.

MR. HARRISON. Thank you very much, Mr. Brower.

MR. DAWSON. I would just like to make one comment. If Mr. Tudor is such a poor engineer as you seem to claim he is I am surprised he ever got that Golden Gate Bridge down in your town to meet at the center.

MR. BROWER. Mr. Tudor made a great contribution on the San Francisco Bridge.

MR. DAWSON. The Bay Bridge or the Golden Gate Bridge?

MR. BROWER. The Bay Bridge, I think.

MR. DAWSON. I think that was quite an engineering feat, and I think he has done quite a job. So it would surprise me if he does not know figures any better than you say he does.

MR. HARRISON. Thank you very much. Are there any further questions? If not, we will proceed to the next witness.

MR. ASPINALL. Wait just a minute. This witness has not been questioned.

MR. HARRISON. Pardon me. The Chair is in error. Mr. Miller?

MR. MILLER. Are you an engineer?

MR. BROWER. No, sir, I am an editor.

MR. MILLER. You do not propose to know the engineering techniques that go into the building of a dam or the estimate of storage?

MR. BROWER. All I can apply, Dr. Miller, is just an editor's natural suspicion when he is working over a manuscript. I have worked for the University Press for many years, and I have had a lot of scientific monographs to go over. I know nothing about some subjects, but you can be suspicious, and it is amazing what you can turn up.

In my own bulletin, which I turned over to you, for example, which I edited this issue of, I have a pretty bad error there myself on page 7.

MR. HARRISON. I think the witness has answered the question.

MR. ASPINALL. Mr. Brower, I am very much interested in the fine publicity you have given Dinosaur Monument, and I am in favor of as many people as possible getting to the area. How many times have you been in Dinosaur National Park?

MR. BROWER. I have been there over a period of eight days, and that was in the course of last summer. I guess it was nine days altogether.

MR. ASPINALL. Why did you go not to Dinosaur Monument before this last year?

MR. BROWER. I can tell you that very briefly, and it is sort of a confession.

MR. ASPINALL. Just briefly.

MR. BROWER. The first I saw of Dinosaur was when the controversy came up around 1950. I saw a lot of black-and-white photographs, which is all we were able to afford to put in our little sheet. I thought, "Well now, in black and white maybe it is fine," but I did not get the impression. A winter ago I saw a color movie of it and it knocked my hat off, and I knew I had to get there. I am planning to go again next summer. I might add that the Sierra Club planned a trip last summer and has already reserved space for two hundred forty people to go down next summer.

MR. ASPINALL. Do you know anything about the canyons of the Dolores River?

MR. BROWER. No, Mr. Aspinall, in spite of the fact that Colorado will be my second adopted state, and I have seen a lot of it because I trained as a mountain trooper, I have not seen that. I have seen a lot of Colorado.

MR. ASPINALL. Have you seen Black Canyon?

MR. BROWER. I have not see Black Canyon.

MR. ASPINALL. Have you seen Glenwood Springs Canyon?

MR. BROWER. Yes.

MR. ASPINALL. Gore Canyon?

MR. BROWER. Yes.

MR. ASPINALL. Have you ever been to Maroon Bells?

MR. BROWER. Yes.

MR. ASPINALL. Crystal Canyon at Marble?

MR. BROWER. I have not been to Crystal Canyon.

MR. ASPINALL. Hells Gate on the headwaters of the Fryingpan?

MR. BROWER. Pretty close to there.

MR. ASPINALL. Hesperus Canyon?

MR. BROWER. That I do not know.

MR. ASPINALL. You like to run rivers, as I understand it?

MR. BROWER. I never ran a river before last summer. I do know I would like to take as many river trips as I can before the places are flooded out with the reservoirs which are planned.

MR. ASPINALL. All I can say is that if you give these other places in my district, where we have forty-two of the sixty-seven mountains in the United States which are over fourteen thousand feet high, the same publicity, you are not going to find people falling all over themselves to get down into this Dinosaur National Monument to get its beauty, because this place has no corner on it. It is very beautiful, but it has no corner on it.

MR. BROWER. Mr. Aspinall, correct me if I am wrong, but it has the best wilderness quality and primitive quality of these canyons.

MR. ASPINALL. I am not an expert on that matter, but I can take you into areas of the same extent which to my opinion are just as much wilderness and farther away from man than this one is.

MR. BROWER. I want to get to see them. I hope I live long enough.

***Congressional Hearing Record,* January 28, 1954**

Mr. Aspinall did not ask whether I had seen Glen Canyon. I wish he had asked, but infinitely more than that I wish I had seen it. The Salt Lake papers scorned my "ninth-grade arithmetic" (the year I learned about algebra) and my attempts to second-guess engineers.

Before the Dinosaur battle was over I was calling Mr. Jacobson, of the Bureau of Reclamation, "Jake," just as his colleagues did. It was he who made my day when John Oakes was at Dinosaur National Monument for the *New York Times*. Jake did not have an answer to John's question about a detail of the project. Jake asked me for the answer, and I had it. That felt good. What felt better was the subsequent photograph in one of the Salt Lake papers of the bureau's regional director being awarded the rubber slide rule "for stretching the truth" about evaporation figures. I don't think Anne, who had pled with me by telephone not to try to tackle the bureau's numbers, really felt comfortable until that story appeared.

LOSING GLEN CANYON

IF I HAD A HAND in keeping Dinosaur unimpaired—and generous people credit me for that—I also had a hand in what I don't like to see when flying south of Dinosaur. The reservoir behind Glen Canyon Dam. They call it Lake Powell, but this is blasphemous. Books and maps with that name on it should be removed from the shelves and the former commissioner of the Bureau of Reclamation should be required to dismantle the dam with hammer and star drill. John Wesley Powell admired, perhaps even revered what he saw in Glen Canyon. Floyd Dominy rejoiced in destroying it.

The Sierra Club was the keystone in the fight against the Colorado River Storage Project, which included Flaming Gorge, Echo Park, Split Mountain, and Glen Canyon dams. We built an alliance strong enough to defeat the entire project. When the project was coming to a final vote in the House, I was in Washington, as usual at the Cosmos Club, when I received a telegram from the Sierra Club's executive committee stating that if Echo Park and Split Mountain dams were removed from the project, the club would withdraw its opposition. With that withdrawal the opposition would surely collapse.

The Dinosaur dams would have violated the National Park System and Sierra Club policy. Glen Canyon Dam also violated Sierra Club policy providing that no major scenic resource should be sacrificed for power generation. I had considerable influence with the club board at that time, and had I immediately flown to San Francisco and asked for an emergency meeting of the board, the club's opposition to the entire project would have remained intact.

I sat there in the House gallery instead and watched the vote go through. Congressman Craig Hosmer, of Southern California, couldn't believe that the club had dropped its opposition. Congressman Wayne Aspinall of Colorado, leading the floor fight, spotted me in the gallery and came up to ask me what the situation was and I replied that the club had indeed withdrawn its opposition. The bloc of some two hundred votes that were with us was thus released. The bill passed the House and had no trouble in the Senate. In October 1956 President Dwight Eisenhower put his finger on a button, initiating a blast in the west wall of Glen Canyon at the dam site. The destruction of what was certainly one of the most magnificent scenic resources on the planet had begun.

Shortly thereafter Senator Paul Douglas of Illinois asked why the club had pulled out and let this happen. Senator Anderson said that if the project had not been passed by that Congress, it would never have passed. I asked Dave Brower why he just sat there and have continued to ask him. He has no answer. It is not because he mistakenly urged an even higher Glen Canyon Dam to increase storage capacity and thus substantially reduce loss of water through evaporation. It was not that he had not heard, from those who knew, how beautiful Glen Canyon was. It was not that he thought Glen Canyon Dam was necessary, because he knew it was not. It was not that he was afraid of flying or of the Sierra Club board. It was because, as he often tells audiences, he just for some inexplicable reason sat on his duff instead of acting, and now takes refuge in the third person singular.

What I finally realize is that in 1956 I had not yet gone through Glen Canyon the several times I was to go, with family and friends. It would have been a different story if I had known Glen Canyon in 1956 the way I was to know it just a year later.

As I remember it, the first person to protest my proposed higher Glen Canyon Dam was Dr. William R. Halliday, who, unlike me, knew what he was talking about. Wallace Stegner confirmed Bill Halliday's appraisal of what we would be losing in Glen Canyon. With the die cast, Charles Eggert, now sold on what rivers meant to Dinosaur National Monument, undertook the last trip that was to be made down the Green from Green River, Wyoming, all the way to its junction with the lesser Colorado, and on through to Lake Mead. *Canyon Voyage* is his documentary of the voyage.

One of the many trips I subsequently made to Glen was high-tech. We flew in big helicopters from Page, Arizona, to a spacious mesa above Aztec Creek, then transferred to little ones, about the size of a fully gorged mosquito, to take us down into Aztec Creek itself and to Rainbow Bridge. Secretary of the Interior Stewart Udall was there, National Park Service Director Conrad Wirth, Reclamation Commissioner Floyd Dominy, and a bunch of us civilian conservationists who were to be shown how difficult and damaging it would be to protect Rainbow Bridge National Monument as required by law.

The best of several methods of protecting Rainbow was a cutoff dam at so-called Site C, which would keep the rising waters of the Glen Canyon reservoir out of the monument. The flow down Aztec Creek would need to be pumped up into the reservoir. With the secretary and the commissioner, I walked to the site, which the commissioner disqualified by kicking at the sand in the stream bottom nearby and stating that it could not serve as dam-building material. Prior to that, the Bureau of Reclamation had alarmed Fred Packard, of the National Parks Association, by warning of the huge amount of local scenery that would be maimed in excavating rocks and gravel for the dam. I pointed out that it was a little late to reveal now what damage was implied by a project that Reclamation had claimed was feasible at authorization time. I added that the necessary material could be barged up the reservoir when the water was high enough, and if worst came to worst, they could build the dam under water—a feat I was informed had been accomplished elsewhere with no great problem.

The only success of the trip was that I climbed Rainbow Bridge with Stewart Udall and taught him how to rappel on the way down. I wrote about my disappointment in "Wilderness River Betrayal":

WILDERNESS RIVER BETRAYAL

IT WAS JUST THREE YEARS AGO that Charles Eggert's "Forbidden Passage" appeared, illustrated with Philip Hyde's photographs. "A butte rises from the Colorado River's edge," Eggert said, "a great sentinel marking the entrance to Glen Canyon. Here some Indian god must have stood, pointing the way to paradise. If anywhere, that place was below—through the one hundred forty-seven miles of Glen Canyon. What exquisite and wondrous beauty was there!"

What beauty *is* there, he might have said, but the *was* had a purpose. Most of the beauty would go under once the gates closed in the diversion tunnels at Glen Canyon Dam. We now know that the life expectancy of one of America's greatest scenic resources, including the pristine approach to Rainbow Bridge, is reduced to fourteen months. The exact time is not important here. What needs to be chronicled is a flagrant betrayal, unequaled in the conservation history that sixty-eight years of *Sierra Club Bulletin*s have recorded.

"If there is weeping to be done," Eggert wrote, "cry over the destruction of this place."

Anyone who knows Glen Canyon unspoiled, or who discovers it in its final year, is to be allowed whatever relief tears may bring. If they are derived from nostalgia, we will be the last to underestimate what may be a deep-down, absolutely essential role in survival itself that is played by nostalgic attraction to the natural world.

If the tears stem from anger, we will know exactly why.

The United States Bureau of Reclamation is destroying Glen Canyon needlessly, and in doing so is violating the promise it gave with a straight face and without which it would never have been permitted to proceed with its superfluous, destructive program. The strangely ingenious way with which the agreement is being broken is in the record. It will anger anyone who has time to read the facts.

But there's the rub. Who has time? A huge dam-building bureau, bent on self-perpetuation, can emit plausible-looking statistics and diagrams, can plant articles, and can hold press interviews faster than a true interpretation can overtake them. That is how Glen Canyon Dam got through in the first place, in spite of geologists' doubts about design, hydrologists' assurance that the water storage was wasteful, and power engineers' prediction that kilowatts could come cheaper from a longer-lasting resource—the depressed coal industry—than from a short-lived public-power dam on the overengineered, silt-laden, uniquely beautiful Colorado. The citizens—and the Congress—were very lenient. Too busy to check the facts, and hardly knowing where to go to get people to check who did not fear reprisals were any criticism to be publicly attributed to them, they let Glen Canyon Dam start. They trusted the Bureau of Reclamation's word, solemnly given and written into law, that the National Park System, including Rainbow Bridge and Echo Park, would not be invaded.

The high price of being naïve is now clear to all, including the cosigners of the Bureau of Reclamation's promissory note: former President Eisenhower, upon advice and assurance of the late Douglas McKay, his first secretary of the interior; the United States Senate and House of Representatives, and especially their cognizant committees on interior and insular affairs, who authorized the project and the promise; former Secretary of the Interior Fred A. Seaton, who was honored for saving Rainbow Bridge but was undercut by his own Bureau of Reclamation; and now, Secretary Udall. As a congressman, Stewart Udall was momentarily persuaded by the bureau that protection of Rainbow was not feasible; but he subsequently perceived the validity of the conservationist position and argued for funds for protection, only to receive the same treatment accorded Fred Seaton—a powerful bureau lobbying and inspiring public reaction against its own secretary.

A bureau out of hand is now openly espousing a Bridge Canyon dam and Kanab diversion that would put Grand Canyon National Park in a pincers. An attempt has been made to amend the Wilderness Bill to open the way for Echo Park Dam. And that's the way the old park system crumbles.

An earlier reclamation commissioner was once taken severely to task in a national magazine as "Our Most Arrogant Bureaucrat." The citizen may now well wonder if bureaus themselves have developed too much momentum, if even their long-term chiefs cannot control them, much less the short-term secretaries.

Reconsidering Glen Canyon, citizens need to "remember these things lost"; they are to be forgiven if they look back in anger at a shoddy record; and they are to be understood if they ask whether the Bureau of Reclamation has forfeited the right to be trusted further if it can honor neither the law nor its own word.

But the future may not forgive or understand the citizen who, not being able to care less, is silent.

Charlie Eggert modified a chapter of *Forbidden Passage,* a book he was writing, to tell readers of the *Sierra Club Bulletin* about his experience. By 1957 both Philip Hyde and my family, piloted by Dick Norgaard, had been fascinated by our first look at Glen. Charlie's article preceded fourteen photographs by Phil, a beautiful interpretation in black and white of high cliffs, tapestries, antiquities, side canyons, people, boats, a bank beaver, and especially moving images of Hidden Passage and Music Temple. I wrote some accompanying text, trying to outdo Nancy Newhall by speaking in two voices, or shall I say, in large roman and small italic. Nancy wasn't sure it worked, but I liked it so well that I ran it in the November 1958 *Bulletin* and again in the October 1961 *Bulletin* for the many new members who had not yet seen it:

The last days of Glen Canyon . . .

Drifting here, you learned to perceive, not to preconceive, what makes a land beautiful. Beauty is where you see it and you saw it often where the big river, thin-edged with green, slid along under the pastel tapestries. An old river had built the stone grain by grain, and the new river was shaping it – imperceptibly aided by artists who left long ago. You didn't quite catch the river in the act of sculpturing, but the color of the Colorado assured you that creation was still going on.

. . . the last of surprises in the side canyons . . .

Down in the main gorge the vista was fine enough, but what really counted was what you could seek out in a hundred tributary clefts. Georgie White knew when the big boats should be tied up and people should start walking, and you learned to know Warm Springs, the silence of Moki Canyon, and the strangeness of Hole-in-the-Rock.

There were the antiquities that you discovered, and some that would never be.

. . . of somber color in places the desert sun never knew . . .

High above the noonday twilight of Hidden Passage you might have looked small but you felt big. For all the massiveness and height, your own good feet could put you there and had. There was time to rest in shady silence, to wonder how, to begin to understand why, once again, to know yourself.

. . . and of the flood-scoured avenue to the Rainbow–

You forgot how far away from the river the great bridge was, once that last turn revealed it to you; and as you walked back down what the flash floods had carved, you were amazed that they had spared so delicate an arch.

Bridge Creek joined Aztec Creek, and Aztec the Colorado, where bank beavers had a home but their progeny will not. For the flood will come that does not recede and the natural world will miss what the ages built here, and here alone. Just a few miles below the junction the great dam is building. Not to put water on land. Not to control the river. Not to save water in an arid land. But to divert the force that created beauty, to generate kilowatt-hours of electricity instead, while other sources of energy lie idle. For a replaceable commodity we spent this irreplaceable grandeur. Your children may pass close to it. But neither they nor anyone yet to be born will ever again know it, nor will the intimate things that gave this place its magic ever again know the sun.

–remember these things lost;
and under the vaulting roof of Music Temple
burn a candle to the memory.

***Sierra Club Bulletin*, October 1961**

THE PLACE NO ONE KNEW

ENTER ELIOT PORTER. The book he did for the Sierra Club, *"In Wildness Is the Preservation of the World,"* was an instant success and an excuse for my visiting his home and darkroom in Tusuque, New Mexico. Eliot had been in Glen Canyon before I had and also joined one of our family trips, and followed with more of his own. What he saw there and took back on color film was exactly what we needed, if only as a requiem for Glen Canyon. He and I both thought the exhibit-format (10¼ by 13½ inches) the Sierra Club was using for its new series was not large enough–nor dynamic enough–for our purpose. We were ready for what we would call gallery-format (12½ by 17 inches). Barnes Press, in New York, calmed us down with the simple fact that the cost of a larger format would be prohibitive unless there were far fewer photographs. We had a good format going, they said; stick with it. We did.

On March 13, 1963, the day I sent final corrections to the compositor, and just fifty days after the battle was lost–when I failed to reach Secretary of the Interior Stewart Udall and persuade him to order that the river valves not be closed until everyone had looked harder at all the consequences. I think now that he wishes he had let me try and that I had persuaded him. To look at what Eliot Porter captured of the magic of Glen Canyon, and to realize, upon closing the book, that the book had indeed been closed forever in Glen Canyon itself, is a blow to the soul, the heart, or wherever a person stores any sense of reverence for the Earth. Wayne Aspinall, then chairman of the House Interior Committee, was as staunch a supporter of Glen Canyon Dam as anyone. The book made him cry. The foreword explains why many people should:

GLEN CANYON DIED in 1963 and I was partly responsible for its needless death. So were you. Neither you nor I, nor anyone else, knew it well enough to insist that at all costs it should endure. When we began to find out, it was too late. On January 21, 1963, the last day on which the execution of one of the planet's greatest scenic antiquities could yet have been stayed, the man who theoretically had the power to save this place did not find a way to pick up a telephone and give the necessary order. I was within a few feet of his desk in Washington that day and witnessed how the forces long at work finally had their way. So a steel gate dropped, choking off the flow in the canyon's carotid artery, and from that moment the canyon's life force ebbed quickly. A huge reservoir, absolutely not needed in this century, almost certainly not needed in the next, and conceivably never to be needed at all, began to fill. At this writing the rising waters are destined to blot out everything of beauty which this book records.

It is Eliot Porter's gift to be able to reveal this beauty as no other photographer has done. Color is indeed his music, as all will believe who in due course follow him and have any wish to listen to light. I was fortunate enough to do this myself on three trips to Glen Canyon. I learned that you can no more impose preconceptions of color on this place than you can impose patterns of alpine structure on Colorado River canyon forms.

The inner world of the side canyons, walled in shadows, will never know the sun but may catch reflected hues from a high opposite wall. The thin crescent of blue is the inner world's only fragment of sky, and any shiny place in the depths will mirror but distort it. The reflected light cannot be conventional when the incident light is not, but thinking can almost make it so. The camera, however, must come closer to the truth, especially when it is in the hands of a colorist. Eliot Porter's name will be inseparable from the spirit of Glen Canyon, just as John Wesley Powell's is from the discovery of the canyon, because of what Eliot's perceptive camera has recorded there.

The best of the canyon is going or gone. Some second-best beauty remains along the Colorado, of course, but much of its meaning vanished when Glen Canyon died. The rest will go the way Glen Canyon did unless enough people begin to feel uneasy about the current interpretation of what progress consists of—unless they are willing to ask if progress has really served good purpose if it wipes out so many of the things that make life worthwhile.

Evolution demonstrates the value of learning from mistakes; so perhaps we can evolve a subservient technology—one that follows us instead of leading us. The closing of Glen Canyon Dam in our time was a major mistake to learn from, and our purpose here is to help the world remember these things lost.

There could be long and acrimonious debate over the accusation of mistake. Good men, who have plans for the Colorado River whereby "a natural menace becomes a natural resource," would argue tirelessly that the Colorado must be controlled, that its energy should be tapped and sold to finance agricultural development in the arid West. But our point here is that for all their good intentions these men had too insular a notion of what our relation to our environment should be, and it is tragic that their insularity was heeded. The natural Colorado—what is left of it—is a miracle, not a menace. The menace is more likely the notion that growth and progress are the same, and that the gross national product is the measure of the good life.

It is a well-documented fact that the Colorado River is being overdeveloped. A bookkeeping transaction could have served the ostensible purpose of Glen Canyon Dam, which without that transaction emerges as a costly device to make sure water will flow downhill. What water this reservoir holds back for credit above the arbitrary division point of Lee's Ferry could be credited in Lake Mead much more economically and far less wastefully. The dam irrigates nothing. Instead, it evaporates an enormous quantity of water that could otherwise have irrigated land or supplied cities in an arid region that is short of water. To the extent reservoir storage adds to the already high mineral content of the water, the water's quality is diminished for all downstream use, including Mexico's. The transcendent purpose of the dam is to produce hydroelectric power, and the revenues incident thereto, which could finance irrigation of new and costly agriculture—as if there were no way to finance development of a region other than to sacrifice irretrievably its most important scenic assets—assets equaled nowhere else on earth.

Hoover, Parker, and Davis dams already exist and control the river adequately; they could probably continue to do so until Lake Mead is silted in completely, perhaps two hundred years from now. The Colorado-Big Thompson diversion project and developments like it which are already under way or planned will exploit the Colorado's waters upstream, where nearly half the flow has been allocated. Glen Canyon Dam is a monument to man's lack of flexibility—to his having concluded that the only way to finance reclamation is to sell the hydroelectric power produced by falling water of the streams he proposes to irrigate with. Revenue by other routes, including that from other sources of power which are already, or will soon be, less expensive to develop, was not politically attainable at the moment. This public failure—the inability to finance reasonable development of the West by means that financed it elsewhere – has cost all people, for all time, the miracle of an unspoiled Glen Canyon.

Other miracles will vanish by the same route unless we can learn from this mistake. The plans are well under way to eradicate the finest of those miracles left on the Colorado, as well as on other major rivers. A similar mistake was made early in the century at Hetch Hetchy in the Sierra Nevada, where a second yosemite, now much needed for its natural beauty, was flooded to provide power for San Francisco. Alternative sources of water and power that could have saved Hetch Hetchy are still unused. Out of that mistake grew the National Park Act of 1916. If the destruction of Glen Canyon leads indirectly to a diminishing of such forces of rapacity, or can somehow correct the belief that man's only road to salvation is a paved one, then there will be some amelioration. The alternatives that could have saved Glen Canyon are still unused. Fossil fuels, for one. The states of the upper basin of the Colorado contain a major part of the earth's coal reserves. The development of these resources is in the doldrums – and they are a much longer-lived source of energy than the short-lived reservoirs planned for the silty Colorado. Atomic and solar sources of energy will beyond doubt, generations before Lake Mead is silted in, make the destruction of Glen Canyon appear to have been the most naïve of choices in the search for electricity. Nothing our technology will have taught us, in this century or any other, will be able to put Glen Canyon back together again.

The Place No One Knew has a moral – which is why the Sierra Club publishes it – and the moral is simple: Progress need not deny to the people their inalienable right to be informed and to choose. In Glen Canyon the people never knew what the choices were. Next time, in other stretches of the Colorado, on other rivers that are still free, and wherever there is wildness that can be part of our civilization instead of victim to it, the people need to know before a bureau's elite decide to wipe out what no one can replace. The Sierra Club has no better purpose than to try to let people know in time. In Glen Canyon we failed. There could hardly be a costlier peacetime mistake. With support from people who care, we hope in the years to come to help deter similar ravages of blind progress.

***The Place No One Knew*, 1963**

The Last Days of the Best

CLOSING OF THE RIVER VALVES at Glen Canyon Dam did not end trips in the canyon, but they became progressively shorter as the Colorado River began to drown in itself, farther and farther upstream from the dam. Trips had previously been limited to the take-out point at Crossing of the Fathers. Below there the water backed up by the cofferdam, built at the

Glen Canyon site to permit construction of the dam itself, would allow no escape. Now we had the sad trips, last looks, final farewells to a friend.

THE APPROACH TO MUSIC TEMPLE was so beautiful that people arrived there hushed. Photographers never quite captured what you saw. It was only a short walk from the easiest of float trips down a living river in Glen Canyon, and thousands had seen it. Millions, in the generations to come, should have had a chance to stand by the quiet pool, to look up at the flutings where the waterfall entered, to look out at the cliffs that echoed the music this place was named for when Powell first found it. But the rising waters of Lake Powell have already inundated everything that mattered in the temple and have obliterated the matchless approach to its serenity.

In mid-June 1964 the approach to the Cathedral in the Desert was still above the rising Lake Powell, but not far above it. There were still twenty minutes to walk and fifty feet to climb. It was not easy to travel the distance without reverence, or without being grateful that an already-beautiful world could here exceed itself. Mysterious seepings patterned the tapestries and living green tinged the sandstone's red. The trail was Clear Creek itself–a stream that could make you look twice at the country it flowed through, at the colors it watered and revealed. Everywhere you looked you knew what a setting meant to a place. And in the Cathedral, whether you looked up at evening or in the morning at this miracle of color and design, or whether you looked at the gardens by the altar or the stream that flowed from the nave, you knew what this place meant to its setting. There would never be anything like it again.

The bureau operating Glen Canyon Dam will destroy this place, too, and all that it meant or could mean throughout this civilization's time. It will begin to go under just as soon as the reservoir is allowed to rise a mere twenty-five feet above the minimum level needed to produce power. A full reservoir would wipe out all trace of the great room. At low water its bleached remnants would be exhumed. All this will produce electricity at a reasonably competitive cost–electricity that could have come from coal for centuries, and from the atom after that, but is coming instead from the destruction of places like the Cathedral, which man could neither build nor restore. The engineers call this deprivation progress and speak of making accessible that which they put forever beyond our reach.

Only a miracle could save Glen Canyon's Cathedral. Clear thinking, compounded with devotion to the things that make America beautiful–and applied with conviction–can still save in Grand Canyon the only near equivalent to the Glen Canyon excellence that still exists on earth. Or apathy can let the Bureau of Reclamation win by default–and permanently deprive humanity of a piece of environment that need not and should not be sacrificed. People–you, you and the people you confront from day to day who hear you–need to know. They will somehow need to act from

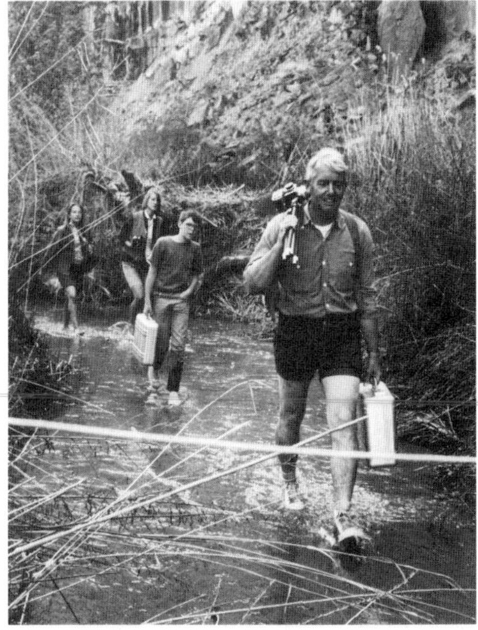

Dave, filmmaker, on one of his many trips to Glen Canyon after it was dammed. Accompanied by (left to right) daughter Barbara, her friend Nancy Eberle, and son John (1966). (Photo by Arthur Schatz, Life *magazine,* ©*Time, Inc.*

their knowledge that it takes a living river to keep a canyon alive, including the Grand Canyon of the Colorado. Kept alive, this canyon is still more; it can remain a symbol of our remembering not to be too arrogant about the natural forces that built us and that built the only earth we are equipped to survive on.

***Time and the River Flowing: Grand Canyon,* 1964**

Added to my overwhelming everlasting regret at missing the opportunity to save Glen Canyon are some minor regrets. I was ready to sacrifice part of the Clark Fork of the Columbia River to dams at either the Knowles or Paradise sites because I wanted very much to appear reasonable, if only once, to the dambuilders. I had seen neither site. I now feel that sacrificing a place may be a sin, but it certainly is if you have not seen the place. I reasoned, in the attempt to appear reasonable, that dams at either of those sites would discourage the Montana Power Company from trying to build the Glacier View Dam, affecting Glacier National Park, in

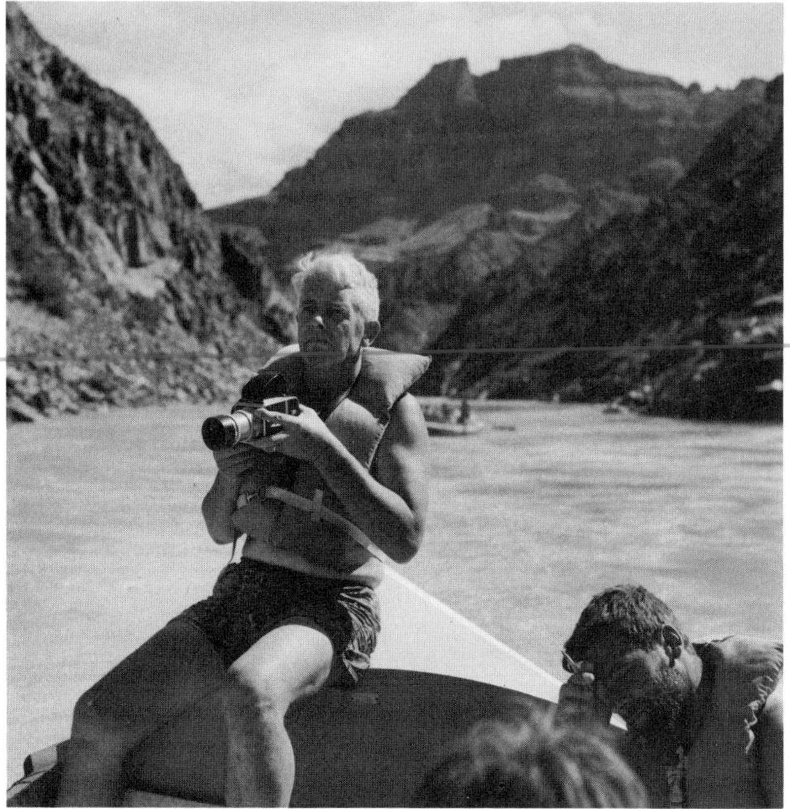

On the Colorado River in the Grand Canyon with Jeff Ingram. Photo by Martin Litton.

order to produce maximum revenue at its Buffalo Rapids dams and power houses.

In my enthusiasm for alternatives to dams and hydroelectric power, I even urged the substitution of power from coal-burning or nuclear power-generating plants. All these sins were directly due to my not having considered the limits to growth and to my not having met Amory Lovins and what he was to teach the world about energy conservation and efficiency.

The completion of the dam did more than destroy Glen Canyon. It created a perpetual threat to the Grand Canyon by containing the sediment that would make dams in the Marble Gorge, or at Bridge Canyon (within one of the world's wonders) engineeringly unfeasible. As long as those dam sites remain unused, developers will covet them. And as far as I am concerned, they can have them, as long as they first build a separate but equal Grand Canyon somewhere else.

THE GRAND CANYON

THE GLEN CANYON BOOK locked the barn after the horse was stolen. The book and the Glen Canyon film the Sierra Club produced from Phil Pennington's and Charles Washburn's slide show told graphically how beautiful the horse was and how sad the loss. It was time now to concentrate on the barn downstream, and all the hydroelectric horses in it. It was time for another book.

François Leydet, a writer with the *San Francisco Chronicle,* had edited the proceedings of a Sierra Club Wilderness Conference and was ready for another assignment. So was Philip Hyde, the all-but-staff-photographer for the club. Martin Litton probably already knew the Grand Canyon better than the back of his hand and knew how to take them down it. He added to his already broad photographic coverage of the canyon but we were required to credit his photographs to a nonexistent Clyde Thomas. Ansel Adams had made some color photographs on the canyon's rims and let us use them. For wildlife photographs we drew upon the collection of Joseph Hall, who had made himself unforgettable with his quip when he felt ill on the way to Rainbow Bridge, "I look down and see myself but there's nobody inside pushing." Clyde Childress, who on a later trip almost lost his life in Lava Falls trying to pursue his camera after his boat overturned, added beautifully to the illustrations. Richard Norgaard did the same. I added a few of my Hasselblad shots.

Leydet wrote a well-structured and moving text, augmented by quotations from all over. I wrote the title, *Time and the River Flowing: Grand Canyon,* borrowing five of the words from Edith Warner and the other two from the map. Wanting to contribute something more original, I wrote the foreword, longer than usual, for good reason, I thought:

The canyon is at least two things besides spectacle. It is a biological unit and the most revealing single page of earth's history anywhere open on the face of the globe.

JOSEPH WOOD KRUTCH

TIME, TWO BILLION YEARS OF IT, laid down the stone of what Powell called the Plateau Province. Within that plateau would be some of the most colorful and dramatic natural sculpture anyone ever saw.

Time and the river flowing—the Colorado River through the millenniums—carved deep, created the great canyon, and is still shaping it.

Standing on its rim in 1903, Theodore Roosevelt said: "In the Grand Canyon, Arizona has a natural wonder which, so far as I know, is in kind absolutely unparalleled. . . . I want to ask you to do one thing in connection with it in your own interest and in the interest of the country. . . . Leave it as it is. You cannot improve on it. The ages have been at work on it, and man can only mar it."

Upstream and unmarred was the exquisite beauty of Glen Canyon. Most of it was destroyed early in 1963 when the U.S. Bureau of Reclamation closed a dam that was not necessary for this century and perhaps would never have been necessary. Now the same bureau has proposed to build dams in Grand Canyon itself as part of its Pacific Southwest Water Plan—to end the living river's flowing for all this civilization's time.

The dams the bureau plans to build in Marble Gorge and at Bridge Canyon, within the Grand Canyon proper, would destroy not only the living river but also the unique life forms that through the ages have come to depend upon the river's life. The major part of the canyon walls would still be there, but the pulsing heart of the place would be stopped. A chain of destructive forces would be begun in what by law was set apart as part of the National Park System, to be preserved unimpaired for all America's future.

And needlessly. Looked at hard, these dams are nothing more than hydroelectric power devices to produce electricity and dollars from its sale to pay for projects that ought to be financed by less costly means. The dams would make no water available that is not available already. Indeed they would waste enough to supply a major city and impair the quality of the too little that is left: water already too saline is made more so by evaporation, to the peril of downstream users, especially of neighbors in Mexico. All this on a river that already has more dams than it has water to fill them.

Grand Canyon will go the way Glen Canyon did, as *The Place No One Knew* pointed out, unless enough people begin to feel uneasy about the current interpretation of what progress consists of. *Time and the River Flowing* has a moral: True progress does not deny to the people their inalienable right to be informed and to choose.

When the Sierra Club undertook the book on Glen Canyon, there was almost no literature on the subject. John Wesley Powell treated it briefly in his accounts of his Colorado River exploration, and we used much of what he said. We borrowed heavily from writing about the Colorado in general, using excerpts that worked well with Eliot Porter's color photographs and augmented his own splendid chapter, "The Living Canyon." And we drew upon what Wallace Stegner described as "a chorus of voices *for* the wilderness." That book was too late to help save Glen Canyon.

With Grand Canyon it is different. The world knows it already. Millions of people have seen it and photographed it from the rims. Thousands have taken the trails into it and have learned about the canyon's depth at the quarter-way point—when they reach the bottom and must climb the vertical mile back out. Hundreds have followed Powell's example and, profiting from his mistakes, have run the Colorado down through its grandest canyon. A handful have run up it. At least one man has walked it, although not at river level.

The literature is impressive—about the place itself, about the meaning of the park, about the meaning of the Colorado to an arid land, about the life which that land supports. None of the literature, however, seemed sufficient in itself to combine with photographs and get to the heart of the crucial issue: what is important, in Grand Canyon, about the living river? We knew it was important for a number of vital reasons, but saw no easy way to demonstrate it. After all, wasn't the river running clear now and then, thanks to Glen Canyon Dam? In a canyon more than a mile deep, what difference would a blue lake make, so small in those depths? Wouldn't it let tourists go up and down the canyon in power boats? And wasn't the Colorado River already dead, killed by Glen Canyon Dam? Would modest releases of water from that dam ever revive it? As Wallace Stegner pointed out, every side canyon whose flood debris used to be swept away by the spring flood would now dump boulders and snags into the reduced river. Wouldn't this create permanent barriers and turn the river into a series of pools? In summation, what harm would it do to change the blue pools of an already-dead river to a continuous blue pool, or even to divert the dead river into a dark tunnel between its fluctuating reservoirs, then squeeze the power out of it with one more hydropower installation, and by this device put more water on a thirsty land? There must be a book to help people understand, to involve them. What should it say? Some inkling came to me in two significantly different trips up the head of Lake Mead. The first of these was in spring 1962. The river was still free in Glen Canyon, but Lake Mead was nevertheless heavily drawn down. For all that, a man who really knew how to navigate through mud could get into the canyon beyond the Pierce Ferry silt dump, where the river drowns and inters itself at its contact with the reservoir.

Bill Belknap, of Boulder City, knew the regimen of Lake Mead mud extremely well. Sensing where the channel was and scraping bottom only once, he took the Sierra Club's editor, Bruce Kilgore, and me some thirty miles above Pierce Ferry to Spencer Canyon. We spent the night at Spencer's Bar. Not far from the reservoir's high-water mark in Spencer Canyon—beyond the jungle in which tamarisks and sand bars had alternately lived and died in their impenetrable symbiosis—we discovered that there could still persist in that remote side canyon most of the elements needed for a renewing wilderness experience. The next day we had pushed up still farther, past Separation Canyon, past Bridge Canyon dam site, into an inner sanctum revealed when the Colorado cut into the Vishnu schist, the oldest rock yet exposed on earth. There was something almost sacred about what the river, with grain upon grain in its turbid load, had relentlessly chiseled and rounded and polished in that old obdurate stone. We went just a little bit farther up the river, up into the middle of the lowest of the Colorado's remaining rapids, which were still safely above the waters of Lake Mead that had long since drowned Separation Rapid. Bill Belknap could have taken us on up into the canyon, but we didn't have the time. So he found a convenient standing wave, turned around it, and headed back downriver. Not, however, until we had felt the river's pulse. There it was, the big river, the sum of its thousand tributaries, boiling, whirling, and above all, alive.

Two Easters later my wife and two of my children were at Spencer Canyon, lucky to make it: perhaps no one but Mack Miller, of Temple Bar, could have found a way through the massive silt barrier now denying lower Grand Canyon to all lesser river people than he. Lake Mead was really down now. The effort to fill Lake Powell left far too little water for Mead. Twice Mr. Miller told us he couldn't make it. Then he tried once more. He took us up to the edge of the silt dump, eased his jet boat into it here and there, looked hard at the water, then backed far enough away to charge full speed across the murky reservoir surface. He aimed at where he thought the channel was and guessed right.

We were now speeding up through a strange, sad world in which the Colorado was running again, the first time since the closing of Hoover Dam obliterated its channel. The world was mud, its surface cracking, oozing, and tottering into the opaque river, which had resumed its interrupted assignment and was seeking but not finding the sculptured shores the river had taken a lifetime to create. There wasn't much flow. Very little water was being released from Glen Canyon's gates and not much was being added from the Paria or the Little Colorado. Yet we saw no blue pools. The water totally lacked the clarity a new Bureau of Reclamation film, *Clear Water on the Colorado,* had tried bravely to sell the public. The water was just about as muddy as it had ever been. We knew that four thousand cubic feet of Colorado per second, or even the eight thousand to twelve thousand which the releases might one day average out, was much less than the one hundred thousand or more an uncontrolled flood might bring were there no Glen Canyon Dam. Separation Canyon and Spencer Canyon showed us what would happen. Flash floods would still come down the side canyons and had. The old bars were gone – the pleasant reservoir beaches where you could nose your boat in, plop ashore, camp in the tamarisks, and explore upstream. Only an untamed Colorado could build those bars back. A tamed Colorado could not do it.

Mack Miller took us up to the lowest now-exposed rapid. In spite of the extremely low flow, the river was still working; it still had its tools and its pulse. Living things came as close to the river banks as the floods had ever let them. The river swirled and murmured and sang, whirlpooled in the sucks and exhaled bubbles in the boils, foamed over the rocks and ground at them along the edges, deposited a cool softness alongside where herons could track it, floated the ducks that had paced us upstream, watered willows, continued to chisel for what might lie below the schist, stood in throbbing waves alongside our boat, splashed us, excited us – and was vital throughout. While it lived, so would the canyon.

If we could see how alive the river was from that brief experience, François Leydet and his river-expert friends and photographers were learning far more. They were two hundred miles upstream at the time, riding the river down. We are grateful for what they saw and for what the book can therefore reveal. We are grateful, too, to those who weren't there but whose wisdom we have borrowed and have used as counterpoint – especially to authors Loren Eiseley, Joseph Wood Krutch, and Wallace Stegner.

We could testify that the river was now injured, but different from the dead stream Wallace Stegner once feared it might be. He would have seen that even a vestige of the Colorado is a force to be reckoned with. All along he has understood the river as few men are likely to. One of his finest contributions has been his book, *Beyond the Hundredth Meridian*. In it he has important things to say about two conflicting forces in the arid lands. One was represented by the vision of Powell, who wanted science to serve government; a government so served could have preserved the best of this country. The other force came from the pervasive illusions of the overoptimistic arid-lands promoter, William Gilpin – illusions such as seem now to inspire the Bureau of Reclamation's attempts to destroy the river by overextending man's dependence upon it. Mr. Stegner's book and Bernard DeVoto's introduction to it are essential to an understanding of the conflict over the Colorado.

In a sense, *Time and the River Flowing* is a continuation of *The Place No One Knew*. Each book tells about the same extraordinary river and its greatest canyons, both fully deserving national-park protection, even though there was not yet vision enough to provide it. Each book draws heavily upon perceptive interpretation by many of America's best writers of what these canyons mean to the world – what Glen Canyon could have meant and what Grand Canyon can always mean. Both books tell of the massive inflexibility and compulsive engineering that lost one canyon forever and seem determined to lose the other. Both books make the plea that this generation do better for all other generations than to let the Bureau of Reclamation carry out its present plans to destroy what is most important in Grand Canyon. The two books reinforce each other, this one reiterating just enough of the Glen Canyon story to underline the tragedy it would be to let the Bureau of Reclamation repeat its mistake – not out of evil intent or incompetence, but from adamantly following a course of action that reveres engineering values and technology and ignores the human soul and sense of wonder.

Let me illustrate. Last summer I was speaking with Mike Strauss, a former United States Commissioner of Reclamation who had promoted Colorado River development with zeal for many years, who had claimed in public that his bureau liked "to push rivers around," who had spoken disdainfully of opposition by "conservationists in their air-conditioned caves," and who in retirement was trying to help other countries get on with their dam building. He was talking enthusiastically of one especially massive project in China. "What kind of country would the reservoir inundate?" I asked him. "Nothing but a mess of mountains," he replied.

The Sierra Club has consistently tried to oppose blind progress and to support the kind of values this reclamation commissioner was unable to perceive in a particular mess of mountains. The club is rarely qualified to support a particular engineering solution in river development but does favor what Edward Higbee calls "preventive engineering." Accordingly, in the Columbia River Basin the club has supported a major dam on the Clark Fork at either the Paradise or Knowles sites because adequate development there could end the threat of upstream dams that would encroach on a national park, on a wilderness area, and on lands of high scenic-resource values that should be dedicated.

The club takes no part in the controversy over allocation of waters of the Colorado River. The club opposed water development that would serve San Francisco, the city of its birth, at the cost of destroying an important part of Yosemite National Park; the club opposes dams threatening parklands on the Colorado just as intensely—except that there are more and more people concerned about the less and less there is to preserve. The club avoids the struggle between private and public power. (There is probably virtue in having both, each to watch the other.)

Neither in this struggle nor in any other does the club feel omniscient. The club leadership went through painful confusion in the Hetch Hetchy Dam struggle at the turn of the century, a battle which John Muir and the club lost, as did national park visitors from there on out. The confusion was renewed in the late forties when the then club president persuaded the club's directors and the leaders of many major conservation organizations to approve construction of a high Bridge Canyon dam in Grand Canyon providing several conditions were first met: "prior action on construction of Glen Canyon and Coconino dams for silt control; prior amendment of the Grand Canyon National Park Act eliminating secretarial authority to permit reclamation projects within the park; prior legislative action disapproving the Kanab project; prior incorporation of Grand Canyon National Monument into Grand Canyon National Park together with certain boundary adjustments; limitation of the high-water level below the junction of Tapeats Creek; and prior commitment to maintain the reservoir at a stable level."

By the following year it was seen that the proponents of Bridge Canyon dam were unwilling to accept the proposed restrictions, so the club directors voted unanimously to oppose construction of any dam within Grand Canyon National Monument.

There was momentary confusion again in the battle for Dinosaur National Monument when one club officer suggested that construction of Echo Park Dam within the monument could be blocked best by permitting the construction of Split Mountain Dam, also within the same monument but downstream. None of the other directors concurred, and opposition to the entire Colorado River Storage Project continued until the Bureau of Reclamation had made an agreement that was written into law: no project dam or reservoir would lie within any national park or monument and Rainbow Bridge National Monument would be protected from the reservoir behind Glen Canyon Dam. At that time too few club leaders knew what was at stake in Glen Canyon. The conservationist force in America could have blocked the dam.

The confusion is not over yet. There are still a few conservationists who think that the only way to keep the Bureau of Reclamation from building an unnecessary dam in Bridge Canyon, violating the national park and monument, is to permit the bureau to build an unnecessary dam at Marble Gorge, which is technically outside the park but would violate it nonetheless. This book demonstrates the magnitude of the violation.

It is uncomfortable to talk about one's own confusion, but it is honest, and perhaps it can help others escape similar confusion. It is my own feeling that if we are still confused, it is only in underestimating the determination of an informed public to prevent any more Glen Canyon tragedies. As things stand now, the club seeks the widest possible support for the kind of policy expressed in resolutions evolving out of the years of study, struggle, and debate.

The club recognizes the value of water power, but notes also that it is not indispensable. Substitute power is available now and in the foreseeable future from oil, gas, coal, or atomic reactors. In fact, a very large proportion of the nation's power economy will always be provided by sources other than water. Scenic resources, on the other hand, have no substitutes that can be bought at a slightly higher price—or at any price. Furthermore, the enjoyment of scenery, wildlife, and wilderness recreation is a part of the American way of life, and the human need for scenic resources continually increases as the pressures of civilization and the availability of leisure time increase. The club therefore opposes in principle the sacrifice for water-power purposes of any area that has been dedicated for scenic-resource preservation. The club also opposes in principle the sacrifice for water power of any high-quality scenic-resource area which has not been dedicated, but whose need as a dedicated area has not yet been thoroughly considered. Scenic resources are understood to include areas suitable for scenic state parks; national parks and monuments; national-forest wild, wilderness, natural, scenic, and recreational areas; wildlife refuges; and similar dedications.

The club urges, with respect to dams and reservoirs having significant values for flood control and irrigation, but involving destruction of significant scenic or wildlife values, that no decision be made on any such project by the proposing agency until (a) the proposing agency has developed and made available to the public a so-called white paper fully analyzing the engineering and economic factors involved in the proposal and in the better alternatives, such white paper to be made available before approval of the project feasibility report by the proposing agency; and (b) reasonable opportunity has been afforded for presentation by interested persons or organizations of analyses weighing loss of scenic recreational and wildlife values against potential economic gain. [Note: the "white paper" proposal was precursor to the National Environmental Policy Act of 1969.]

Time and the River Flowing combs the literature about the canyon's meaning, and the meaning of the river to the canyon, both to the world and to the future. The book works best if the reader and everybody else who has a stake in Grand Canyon becomes a participant, not just a spectator. What is in the book will stand on its own; but standing will not be enough. We hope it will move readers to constitute themselves members of the committee determined to save Grand Canyon. There is evidence here, in photographs and text. There is beauty that ought to be lasting. There is reinforcement in what the people say whose thinking and perception we have gratefully borrowed. There is a chance for readers to clarify for themselves the relationship between all these elements, and then to clarify it for others.

Above all, there is still a canyon to battle for, to explore, to photograph, to interpret, to share with other living things that are more and more being crowded off the planet. It will remain a living canyon if enough people realize the urgency, take this book as a starting point, and carry on in each of its several aspects the work the book seeks to get going.

People must disrupt a great part of the planet in order to sustain themselves in their present numbers and, reserving judgment about when enough population is enough, the club is in favor of people. It is also in favor of our being intelligent enough to do better with the ninety-five percent of the American earth we have already disrupted before we covet the unmanipulated five percent. The club believes that Grand Canyon National Park and Grand Canyon National Monument should be extended to protect the integrity of the Grand Canyon between Lee's Ferry and the Grand Wash Cliffs, or that this area should be protected by other suitable means that would preserve unimpaired this outstanding scenic part of the river. The club opposes any further dams or diversions in this stretch.

In the course of seeking out the kind of conservationist support that saved Dinosaur National Monument and could, if continued, have saved Glen Canyon, I asked several leading conservationists how we could get around a most troublesome obstacle, the Reclamation Bureau's technique of drafting and (or) signing replies to protests about its activities, no matter to whom in the administration they were addressed.

Dr. Ira Gabrielson, president of the Wildlife Management Institute and certainly one of America's foremost conservationists, responded:

"The only answer . . . that might work would be to have a board of review composed of eminent scientists who should not be connected with any government bureau either directly or indirectly.

"The big problem with Reclamation as with the Army Engineers and to a lesser extent also with other agencies is that they are the ones who do the planning, who carry out the plan, and who are the final judges as to whether it is a good plan. I am and always have been against this type of setup, but it is a very popular one with Congress. It makes it easier for pork-barrel projects when there is enough political pressure behind them.

"I have no illusions but that we are in for a hell of a scrap on this southwest water project. If we lose in the effort to protect the Grand Canyon National Park, I would begin to wonder if we could ever protect any park from blatant commercialism of any kind."

This kind of battle is in the history of every great place that has been preserved. Not just the ancient history, either. In Grand Canyon, as in the other park and wilderness reserves, the battle must be renewed each time someone of great enterprise conspires to reduce wilderness to something else and something less. The Sierra Club seeks help in persuading such people to conspire somewhere else, and this book is part of that search.

It is one thing to know that you have a book, and another to know how to finance its publication when you are a nonprofit organization and the work to be done exceeds the funds available to do it. We asked several of the people who have been especially interested in the Sierra Club for help and are grateful to the following, who generously responded. [There were one hundred fifty-one donors.]

The most reassuring part of the whole effort to publish the book was the wealth of material we found about the wilderness idea—the *national-park* idea, if we go back to the concept that underlay the first great parks and that has been a unique American contribution toward harmony between man and the natural world. We hope that the testimony of the text, combined with the photographers' powers of observation, will serve lasting purpose by in some way stepping up the pace with which humanity preserves what is left of the world's irreplaceables.

***Time and the River Flowing: Grand Canyon,* 1964**

ADVERTISING FOR A CAUSE

BOOKS AND FILMS REACH OUT. So does word of mouth. Interviews help when you can get them, especially if you are able to review what the interviewer thinks you said and fix it before it gets into print, in newspapers, magazines, or books. I have been luckier than most, but could fill a book with corrections of errors, such as the time I was interviewed by a *New York Times* reporter at seven o'clock in the evening. There was no time to check the story—the Sierra Club and the IRS—with me. When it appeared the next morning there were thirteen errors in it.

Howard Gossage, head of one of the most innovative advertising agencies in San Francisco, told me: "Most people know this," he said, "and that's why they don't believe newspapers. But they do believe ads."

That was news to me then, but not now. Following the Redwood National Park and Grand Canyon ads, I had a hand in many others in the Sierra Club, Friends of the Earth, and Earth Island Institute—and have a lot more in mind. They are written more carefully than the Bible, I will say, perhaps exaggerating to make the point.

Jerry Mander wrote most of the ads I have signed or advised about and I hope to collaborate with him in some way for the next twenty years or so. His ads have a lot of copy. Others would say far too much copy. But Jerry's get read. I have watched people, when riding mass transit, flip through a paper, hit upon one of his ads, and read it all the way through. His secret? The ad must have a sky head you cannot pass by. It cannot have a dull sentence in it, or even a sentence so complicated that the reader has to pause to reread it. The reader will turn the page instead. And as Howard Gossage points out in my section on "Grand Canyon Battle Ads" in the book *Grand Canyon of the Living Colorado,* it is important that the ad be good enough to be talked about, which his were.

Our ads were, shall we say, misread by the Grand Canyon dam proponents. They accused us, for example, of claiming the dams would "flood out" the Grand Canyon. The canyon is a mile deep, and a mile-high dam, attempting to flood it out, would reroute the river long before the canyon was "flooded out." We said it would be flooded. We gave the maximum reservoir depth as five hundred feet—in a mile-deep canyon—and used Bureau of Reclamation photographs to show how much would be flooded. In *Encounters with the Archdruid,* John McPhee quotes Reclamation Commissioner Floyd Dominy as saying: "I can't talk to Brower, because he's so God-damned ridiculous. I can't even reason with the man. I once debated with him in Chicago, and he was shaking with fear. Once, after a hearing on the Hill, I accused him of garbling facts, and he said, 'Anything is fair in love and war.' For Christ's sake."

I don't remember such debate. I could not have been shaking with fear. And the "anything is fair" remark could not have come from anyone's conversation with me. I am in love and have been in war, and "anything" is definitely not fair in either. "After another hearing one time," Dominy told McPhee, "I told him he didn't know what he was talking about, and said I wished I could show him, I wished he would come with me to the Grand Canyon someday, and he said, 'Well, save some of it, and maybe I will.' "

I remember that. He didn't save any of it, but I did go, and a few of us did save all of it, so far. Our ads helped that happen. They were read.

One Sierra Club ad that wasn't read was the North Cascades ad with a sky head reading, "An Open Pit Mine Big Enough To Be Seen From the Moon." McPhee commented: "The fact that this was not true did not slow up Brower or the Sierra Club. In the war strategy of the conservation movement, exaggeration is a standard weapon and is used consciously on broad fronts." I would have to quarrel with John McPhee's conclusion here, but almost nowhere else. The Sierra Club didn't run it and I didn't sign it. The conservation movement even now hardly has the budget to do all the research necessary. It must use the figures of others, and try to add them up correctly. To exaggerate would be to shoot ourselves in the foot, and we like trails too much for that.

Actually, the club had tried for a year to run an ad for the North Cascades National Park but I couldn't get it through the club's bureaucracy. That is why the North Cascades Conservation Council took it on. It was written in San Francisco by Freeman, Mander, and Gossage. I remember debates on what one could discern from how far away. One of our scientists, Dr. Dan Luten, thought he could discern vertical cables three inches in diameter from his house, fifteen miles away from the Golden Gate Bridge. Perhaps his acuity is that good. Mine isn't. At that ratio, the open pit on the moon would need to be about ten miles across. I have not yet been on the moon looking back, but a very good authority told the Sierra Club that the open pit at Bingham, Utah, could be seen from the moon. The authority is a former president of the American Association for the Advancement of Science and the publisher of *Scientific American*, Gerard Piel.

Whether or not it could be seen from the moon, the point is that there ought to be no open pit whatever in the North Cascades. That is no exaggeration. John McPhee spoke of the ads as being written in "Early Paul Revere." Whatever the style, it, like John McPhee's book, was read then and is now.

THE FIRST FULL-PAGE ADVERTISEMENT on behalf of the American wilderness came to the aid of the Colorado River system on October 31, 1955, when, through the philanthropy of the late Edward H. Mallinckrodt, Jr., and the public relations genius of Frederick M. Smith, an unusual page appeared in the *Denver Post*. Signed by the Council of Conservationists, it warned sponsors of the Colorado River Storage Project, who were meeting in Denver at the time, that they should abandon plans to build Echo Park and Split Mountain dams in Dinosaur National Monument. The ad made clear that unless these dams were irrevocably deleted from their plans, the wilderness lobby would use every legal means to block passage of the rest of the project. Aware of the power of organized conservationists, and wanting above all to obtain water and power for the Southwest, the sponsors agreed to take the controversial dams out of the bill.

Not until December 1965 was a full-page ad used for a similar conservation end. Representatives of various conservation organizations and foundations were to meet with Secretary of the Interior Stewart L. Udall to discuss the boundaries of a potential Redwood National Park—a long-dormant proposal brought back to life through the leadership of Martin Litton, Edgar Wayburn, François Leydet, and Philip Hyde, whose work helped create the Sierra Club's book, *The Last Redwoods*.

I urged the advertisement as a means of bringing forcibly to the secretary's and the nation's attention the urgency of protecting as much as possible of the Redwood Creek watershed in that park—an urgency the secretary's meeting was about to overlook. The ad was run concurrently in five newspapers—the *New York Times, Washington Post, San Francisco Chronicle, Los Angeles Times,* and *Sacramento Bee*. The ad, and almost three years of successful work following it, helped measurably in rescuing part of the superlative forests of Redwood Creek. The Internal Revenue Service demonstrated no concern about the form or vigor of the club's action. The administration favored a Redwood National Park.

By the following June, however, another battle raged in which the administration favored the building of two dams in the Grand Canyon. A series of ads that was to make conservation history was begun. Between June 9, 1966, and April 16, 1967, the Sierra Club placed four full-page ads in the *New York Times* (some of them were repeated in many other newspapers and magazines) to carry forward the battle to keep dams out of the Grand Canyon.

The first of the series was extraordinary in two ways. It was a split run—something the *Times* had never undertaken before in its daily paper. Half of the June 9 copies of the *Times* contained my relatively quiet open letter to Secretary Udall, asking him to help save Grand Canyon and asking the public to speak up, too. It contained one coupon, addressed to the Sierra Club.

The other version was professionally written, for the most part by Jerry Mander, and it outpulled the amateur ad by about three to two. It contained seven coupons, to be filled in and mailed if the reader could not find time to write individual letters. The coupons were addressed to the president, Secretary Udall, Congressman Wayne Aspinall of the House Interior Committee, to the reader's individual representative and senators, and to the Sierra Club. (On this last coupon readers were given the options of contributing money to help the fight, buying a Grand Canyon book, or joining the club.)

The Mander ad brought, in due course, a notable response in coupons sent to Washington and in money sent to the club (enough to cover the cost of the ads). The ad also brought an immediate response from the Internal Revenue Service – a letter, hand-delivered to Sierra Club headquarters in San Francisco the next day, clouding the club's tax-deductible status in such a way as to cut off major contributions to the club at once, an unprecedented application of administrative penalty in advance of investigation. The club submitted a painstaking defense of its position, but the Internal Revenue Service's cursory reply – not delivered until almost two years later – officially affirmed the club's loss of its valuable tax-deductible standing. The IRS action cost the club some half a million dollars in major contributions.

But there was a concurrent spectacular gain. Small nondeductible contributions multiplied. In three years the membership of the club doubled (from thirty-nine thousand in June 1966 to seventy-eight thousand in June 1969). And sympathy for the club exploded nationally, in editorials, newspapers and magazine articles, and in the still more convincing route of communication – word of mouth. People who had never heard of the Sierra Club began asking Sierra Club members how the club was getting along with the IRS. And people who had always known about the Grand Canyon but who had been quite unaware of any threat to it were now very much aware of the threat. The further advertisements, in the face of the IRS action, kept the public aware.

The Sierra Club realized it was far more concerned about a canyon than about tax status. And backlash from the IRS intervention was probably one of the important factors in staving off the dams. The American public, it turned out, did not wish the tax man to jeopardize the world's only Grand Canyon.

***Grand Canyon of the Living Colorado,* 1970**

THE NEW YORK TIMES, THURSDAY, JUNE 9, 1966. L 35

ADVERTISEMENT ADVERTISEMENT ADVERTISEMENT ADVERTISEMENT

(If they can turn Grand Canyon into a "cash register" is any national park safe? You know the answer.)

Now Only You Can Save Grand Canyon From Being Flooded...For Profit

Yes, that's right, *Grand Canyon!* The facts are these:

1. Bill H.R. 4671 is now before Rep. Wayne Aspinall's (Colo.) House Committee on Interior and Insular Affairs. This bill provides for two dams—Bridge Canyon and Marble Gorge—which would stop the Colorado River and flood water back into the canyon.

2. Should the bill pass, two standing lakes will fill what is presently 130 miles of canyon gorge. As for the wild, running Colorado River, the canyon's sculptor for 25,000,000 years, it will become dead water.

3. In some places the canyon will be submerged five hundred feet deep. "The most revealing single page of the earth's history," as Joseph Wood Krutch has described the fantastic canyon walls, will be drowned.

The new artificial shoreline will fluctuate on hydroelectric demand. Some days there will only be acres of mud where the flowing river and living canyon now are.

4. Why are these dams being built, then? For commercial power. They are dams of the sort which their sponsor, the Bureau of Reclamation of the Department of the Interior, calls "cash registers."

In other words, these dams aren't even to store water for people and farms, but to provide *auxiliary* power for industry. Arizona power politics in your Grand Canyon.

Moreover, Arizona doesn't need the dams to carry out its water development. Actually, it would have more water without the dams.

5. For, the most remarkable fact is that, as Congressional hearings have confirmed, seepage and evaporation at these remote damsites would annually *lose* enough water to supply both Phoenix and Tucson.

As for the remainder, far more efficient power sources are available right now, and at lower net cost. For the truth is, that the Grand Canyon dams will cost far more than they can earn.

6. Recognizing the threat to Grand Canyon, the Bureau of the Budget (which speaks for the President on such matters) has already suggested a moratorium on one of the dams and proposed a commission consider alternatives.

This suggestion has been steadily resisted by Mr. Aspinall's House Committee, which continues to proceed with H. R. 4671. It has been actively fought by the Bureau of Reclamation.

7. At the same time, interestingly, other Bureaus within Secretary Udall's domain (notably National Parks, Fish and Wildlife, Indian Affairs, Mines, Outdoor Recreation, Geological Survey) have been discouraged from presenting their findings, obtained at public expense. Only the Reclamation Bureau has been heard.

8. Meanwhile, in a matter of days the bill will be on the floor of Congress and—let us make the shocking fact completely clear—it will probably pass.

The only thing that can stop it is your prompt action.

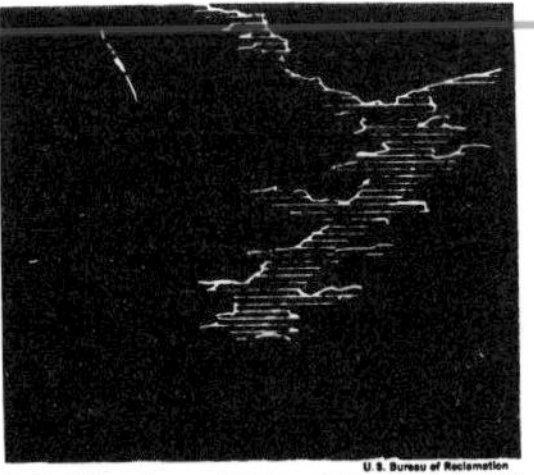

U. S. Bureau of Reclamation

The Grand Canyon: How man plans to improve it. *(Newsweek, May 30, 1966)*

9. What to do? Letters and wires are effective, and so are the forms at right once you have signed them and mailed them. (You will notice that there is also one in the box below to the Sierra Club; that's us.)

10. Remember, with all the complexities of Washington politics and Arizona politics, and the ins and outs of committees and procedures, there is only one simple, incredible issue here: This time it's the Grand Canyon they want to flood. *The Grand Canyon.*

WHAT THE SIERRA CLUB IS FOR

The Sierra Club, founded in 1892 by John Muir, is nonprofit, supported by people who sense what Thoreau sensed when he wrote, "In wildness is the preservation of the world." The club's program is nationwide, includes wilderness trips, books, and films—and a major effort to protect the remnant of wilderness in the Americas.

There are now twenty chapters, branch offices in New York, Washington, Albuquerque, Seattle, and Los Angeles, and a main office in San Francisco.

This advertisement has been made possible by individual contributions, particularly from our Atlantic, Rocky Mountain, Rio Grande, Southern California and Grand Canyon chapter members, and by buyers of Sierra Club books everywhere, especially the twelve in the highly praised Exhibit Format Series, which includes books on Grand Canyon, Glen Canyon, the Redwoods, the Northern Cascades, Mount Everest, and the Sierra.

David Brower, Executive Director,
Sierra Club
Mills Tower, San Francisco, California

- ☐ Please send me more of the details of the battle to save Grand Canyon.
- ☐ I know how much this sort of constructive protest costs. Here is my donation of $________ to help you continue your work.
- ☐ Please send me a copy of "Time and the River Flowing," the famous four-color book by Philip Hyde and François Leydet which tells the whole story of Grand Canyon and the battle to save it. I am enclosing $25.00
- ☐ I would like to be a member of the Sierra Club. Enclosed is $14.00 for entrance fee and first year's dues.

Name__________
Address__________
City______ State______ Zip______

Note: All contributions and membership dues are deductible.

PLEASE CLIP THESE AND MAIL THEM

No. 1

THE PRESIDENT
THE WHITE HOUSE
WASHINGTON 25, D.C.

THANK YOU FOR YOUR STAND, THROUGH THE BUREAU OF THE BUDGET, PROTECTING GRAND CANYON. WOULD YOU PLEASE ASK CONGRESS TO DEFER BOTH GRAND CANYON DAMS PENDING INVESTIGATION OF THE ALTERNATE POWER SOURCES. THANK YOU AGAIN.

Name__________
Address__________
City______ State______ Zip______

No. 2

SECRETARY OF THE INTERIOR STEWART UDALL
WASHINGTON 25, D.C.

ALL YOUR SPLENDID CONSERVATION WORK OF THE PAST WILL BE BLIGHTED IF YOU ALLOW THE LIVING GRAND CANYON TO DIE AT THE HANDS OF YOUR BUREAU OF RECLAMATION. WOULD YOU PLEASE ALLOW THE FINDINGS OF YOUR OTHER BUREAUS TO BE REPORTED FULLY TO CONGRESS BEFORE THE VOTE ON H.R. 4671? THANK YOU.

Name__________
Address__________
City______ State______ Zip______

No. 3

REPRESENTATIVE WAYNE ASPINALL
HOUSE OF REPRESENTATIVES
WASHINGTON 25, D.C.

I URGE YOU TO HALT PROCEEDINGS ON H.R. 4671, NOW IN YOUR COMMITTEE, AND TO SEEK EXPERT TESTIMONY FROM THE MANY INTERIOR DEPARTMENT AGENCIES THAT HAVE NOT YET APPEARED BEFORE YOU. THANK YOU.

Name__________
Address__________
City______ State______ Zip______

No. 4 (To your Congressman)

REPRESENTATIVE __________
HOUSE OF REPRESENTATIVES
WASHINGTON 25, D.C.

PLEASE JOIN IN THE FIGHT TO SAVE GRAND CANYON BY URGING DELETION OF BOTH DAMS PROPOSED IN H. R. 4671. THANK YOU.

Name__________
Address__________
City______ State______ Zip______

No. 5 (To one of your U. S. Senators)

SENATOR __________
UNITED STATES SENATE
WASHINGTON 25, D.C.

PLEASE JOIN IN THE FIGHT TO SAVE GRAND CANYON BY URGING DELETION OF BOTH DAMS PROPOSED IN H. R. 4671. THANK YOU.

Name__________
Address__________
City______ State______ Zip______

No. 6 (To your state's other Senator)

SENATOR __________
UNITED STATES SENATE
WASHINGTON 25, D.C.

PLEASE JOIN IN THE FIGHT TO SAVE GRAND CANYON BY URGING DELETION OF BOTH DAMS PROPOSED IN H. R. 4671. THANK YOU.

Name__________
Address__________
City______ State______ Zip______

SR THE NEW YORK TIMES, THURSDAY, JUNE 9, 1966. C 35

ADVERTISEMENT ADVERTISEMENT ADVERTISEMENT ADVERTISEMENT

Who Can Save Grand Canyon?

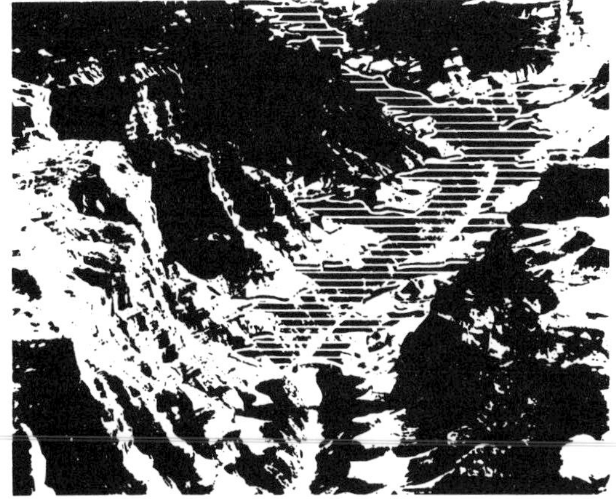

The Grand Canyon: How man plans to improve it (*Newsweek, May 30, 1966*) Photograph by U. S. Bureau of Reclamation

You Can *. . . and Secretary Udall can too, if he will.*

You can help convince him. Here is why he should:

[*An Open Letter*]

The Honorable Stewart L. Udall
Secretary of the Interior

Dear Mr. Udall:

If Congress lets your Reclamation Bureau ruin Grand Canyon with two dams, can any national park be safe?

Your Reclamation engineers, if you give them a chance, will kill the river that created Grand Canyon and is still creating it. They will flood out 130 miles of the living Colorado (they have already done this to 600 miles of it), shunt more of it through a tunnel, drown or shrivel the oases along the river's edge – vital to wildlife, important to America's natural beauty, and essential to people who like what Grand Canyon is.

The Bureau wants to build these dams to make money. The same Bureau has threatened the National Park System whenever its Secretary let it. The Bureau people talk about water for Arizona. But they waste water. Their obsolete methods already evaporate enough of the Colorado River to supply two or three Denvers, and now they want to waste enough more for Phoenix and your Tucson.

1902 Bureau methods don't add up in 1966

You remember our proving how bad their arithmetic about reservoir evaporation was a few years ago – how in the Echo Park battle they were awarded a rubber slide rule for stretching the truth.

They are still at it. Now they claim they need two cash-register dams (their term) in Grand Canyon. They don't. This is their way to finance pumping water to Arizona from an existing reservoir and to take water from the Columbia River, much of it for southern California.

But accurate arithmetic has proved before the House Interior Committee (in spite of an attempt to block conservation testimony) that the dams really aren't the way to help the Southwest. They are simply the Bureau way, the 1902 way in an atomic age the Bureau can't quite face.

Who really pays? A good question

To build their dams, the Bureau people want to borrow a billion-odd dollars from the Treasury, pay enormously less interest than the Treasury itself pays to get the money, and promise to repay most of their debt out of revenues from Hoover and Parker and Davis dams after paying what they still owe on them. They probably wouldn't want Price-Waterhouse or Dun & Bradstreet to check them out. We would. For the Bureau's own figures, added up correctly, show that ***they don't need the dams to carry out their water development, and they would have more water without the dams***

After Reclamation ruins Grand Canyon, then what?

Mr. Secretary, suppose you let your Bureau ruin Grand Canyon with dams. What would the Bureau do for an encore?

Projections show that the dams would satisfy the Southwest's growing appetite for power for only three years, if that. Let's imagine Grand Canyon dammed and its river dead; your fellow Arizonans would have to look right away for new sources of power, and would find them.

Too late. The Bureau's kind of blind planning has now destroyed Glen Canyon, just upstream from Grand Canyon to produce electricity – power that will be available cheaper from alternate sources before Glen Canyon reservoir is half full.

So why not skip Grand Canyon dams and start with the encore? Why not start with the alternatives and strike a useful blow for sound planning, not a low blow at Grand Canyon?

You will remember what Theodore Roosevelt said about the Canyon in 1903: "Leave it as it is. You cannot improve on it. The ages have been at work on it and man can only mar it." We, and Arizonans (some of them secretly), know he was right.

The living river still counts

Time and the river flowing – these created the Grand Canyon. The exquisite sculpture of stone two billion years old is now being revealed in the inner gorges as the river turns the pages it has been turning for twenty-five million years. The artificial lakes your Reclamation Bureau would back up behind the dams, in their own compulsion to invade the National Park System and to kill wild rivers, will cover the finest Grand Canyon pages with mud. A living river – nothing else – can keep the Canyon alive to tell its ageless story.

In five years your Reclamation engineers can close the Grand Canyon show – the essence and excellence of it – end it for all our civilization's time.

Won't you please find them something better to do?

Sincerely,

David Brower,
Executive Director, Sierra Club

Grand Canyon's destiny:
an aging Bureau's cash register, or
an ageless National Park?

You can help save Grand Canyon. You are unique, possessed of your own brand of genius and of the power to do what counts.

You remember what Rachel Carson did to prevent pesticides from ushering in a silent spring, what Ralph Nader is doing to make cars safe, what people you know have achieved who do their homework, who care, and **who stand up to be counted.**

Your letters—especially your follow-up—
will make the difference.

The prediction is that Mr. Aspinall's House Interior Committee will soon act to bring the Lower Colorado River development legislation (H.R. 4671) to the House floor for vote. Now is the time to express your wish—if it is your wish—by asking your own Congressman to insist that the Grand Canyon dams be deleted from this legislation and that alternatives be found to save money and, above all, to spare Grand Canyon. Don't be satisfied with the all-too-frequent reply—the Bureau's self-serving statement.

If you care enough, you can do something no one else can do—write in your own way, soon, to the men listed below.

The President, The White House

The Honorable Stewart L. Udall

Your two Senators, Senate Office Building

Your Representative, House Office Building

(All are in Washington, D. C.; your postmaster can supply missing names and zip codes.)

If you will, write us too and let us know how you made out.

What the Sierra Club is for

The Sierra Club, founded in 1892 by John Muir, is nonprofit, supported by people who sense what Thoreau sensed when he wrote, "In wildness is the preservation of the world." The club's program is nationwide, includes wilderness trips, books, and films—and a major effort to protect the remnant of wilderness in the Americas.

There are now twenty chapters, branch offices in New York, Washington, Albuquerque, Seattle, and Los Angeles, and a main office in San Francisco. Annual dues, $9; admission fee, $5; further generosity is all right.

This advertisement has been made possible by individual contributions, particularly from our Atlantic, Rocky Mountain, Rio Grande, and Grand Canyon chapter members, and by buyers of Sierra Club books everywhere, especially the twelve in the highly praised Exhibit Format Series, which includes books on Grand Canyon, Glen Canyon, the Redwoods, the Northern Cascades, Mount Everest, and even the Sierra.

Sierra Club, Mills Tower, San Francisco 94104

☐ Please tell me more about saving Grand Canyon.

☐ To help save it, here is ($)

☐ Please tell me how to support your work and that of organizations like yours.

Name__________

Address__________

City__________ State__________ Zip__________

(dues and contributions are deductible)

After all, it's the Grand Canyon. That's enough for us. We hope it's enough for you.

SHOULD WE ALSO FLOOD THE SISTINE CHAPEL SO TOURISTS CAN GET NEARER THE CEILING?

EARTH began four billion years ago and Man two million. The Age of Technology, on the other hand, is hardly a hundred years old, and on our time chart we have been generous to give it even the little line we have.

It seems to us hasty, therefore, during this blip of time, for Man to think of directing his fascinating new tools toward altering irrevocably the forces which made him. Nonetheless, in these few brief years among four billion, wilderness has all but disappeared. And now these:

1) There are proposals before Congress to "improve" Grand Canyon. Two dams would back up artificial lakes into 148 miles of canyon gorge. This would benefit tourists in power boats, it is argued, who would enjoy viewing the canyon wall more closely. (See headline). Submerged underneath the tourists would be part of the most revealing single page of earth's history. The lakes would be as deep as 600 feet (deeper for example, than all but a handful of New York buildings are high) but in a century, silting would have replaced the water with that much mud, wall to wall.

There is no part of the wild Colorado River, the Grand Canyon's sculptor, that would not be maimed.

Tourist recreation, as a reason for the dams, is in fact an afterthought. The Bureau of Reclamation, which has backed them, has called the dams "cash registers." It expects the dams would make money by sale of commercial power.

They will not provide anyone with water.

2) In Northern California, four lumber companies have nearly completed logging the private virgin redwood forests, an operation which to give you an idea of its size, has taken fifty years.

Where nature's tallest living things have stood silently since the age of the dinosaurs, much further cutting could make creation of a redwood national park absurd.

The companies have said tourists want only enough roadside trees for the snapping of photos. They offered to spare trees for this purpose, and not much more. The result would remind you of the places on your face you missed while you were shaving.

3) And up the Hudson, there are plans for a power complex —a plant, transmission lines, and a reservoir near and on Storm King Mountain—effectively destroying one of the last wild and high and beautiful spots near New York City.

4) A proposal to flood a region in Alaska as large as Lake Erie would eliminate at once the breeding grounds of more wildlife than conservationists have preserved in history.

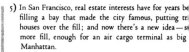

AGE OF TECHNOLOGY
FIRST MAN 2 MILLION YRS AGO
FIRST ELEPHANTS 60 MILLION YRS AGO
FIRST REDWOODS 130 MILLION YRS AGO
FIRST MAMMALS 160 MILLION YRS AGO
FIRST DINOSAURS 180 MILLION YRS AGO
FIRST TREES 250 MILLION YRS AGO
FIRST REPTILES 275 MILLION YRS AGO
FIRST FISHES 400 MILLION YRS AGO
GRAND CANYON 550 MILLION YRS AGO
FIRST CORALS 575 MILLION YRS AGO
FIRST SPONGES 650 MILLION YRS AGO

5) In San Francisco, real estate interests have for years be filling a bay that made the city famous, putting tr houses over the fill; and now there's a new idea—s more fill, enough for an air cargo terminal as big Manhattan.

There exists today a mentality which can conceive su destruction, giving commerce as ample reason. For 74 yea the Sierra Club (now with 46,000 members) has opposed t mentality. But now, when even Grand Canyon is endanger we are at a critical moment in time.

This generation will decide if something untrammelled a free remains, as testimony we had love for those who follo

We have been taking ads, therefore, asking people write their Congressmen and Senators; Secretary of the terior Stewart Udall; The President; and to send us funds continue the battle. Thousands *have* written, but meanwh Grand Canyon legislation still stands a chance of passa More letters are needed and much more money, to help fig the notion that Man no longer needs nature.*

David Brower, Executive Director
Sierra Club
Mills Tower, San Francisco

☐ Please send me more details on how I may help.

☐ Here is a donation of $________ to continue your effort to keep the public informed.

☐ Send me "Time and the River Flowing," famous four color book which tells the complete story of Grand Canyon, and why T. Roosevelt said, "leave it as it is." ($25.00)

☐ Send me "The Last Redwoods" which tells the complete story of the opportunity as well as the destruction in the redwoods. ($17.50)

☐ I would like to be a member of the Sierra Club. Enclosed is $14.00 for entrance and first year's dues.

Name____________________

Address____________________

City__________ State________ Zip_____

*The previous ads, urging that readers exercise a constitutional righ petition, to save Grand Canyon, produced an unprecedented reaction by Internal Revenue Service threatening our tax deductible status. IRS the ads may be a "substantial" effort to "influence legislation." Undefi these terms leave organizations like ours at the mercy of administra whim. (The question has not been raised with any organizations that f Grand Canyon dams.) So we cannot now promise that contributions send us are deductible—pending results of what may be a long legal ba

The Sierra Club, founded in 1892 by John Muir, is nonprofit, suppo by people who, like Thoreau, believe "In wildness is the preservatio the world." The club's program is nationwide, includes wilderness tr books and films—as well as such efforts as this to protect the remnan wilderness in the Americas. There are now twenty chapters, branch off in New York (Biltmore Hotel), Washington (Dupont Circle Building), Angeles (Auditorium Building), Albuquerque, Seattle, and main offic San Francisco.

SUPPOSE WE SIMPLY DIDN'T FILL IT?

WE HAD SAVED THE GRAND CANYON, at least for the time being. And we almost had a chance to save much of what was left of Glen Canyon. We had already failed in the legislative and administrative branches of government. There was still the court, and we came close, but not close enough. In May 1973 I marshalled arguments for filling "Lake" Powell to a much lower level than its planned elevation.

These arguments may be helpful again if Glen Canyon Dam ever falls apart, as it almost did in 1983. That was a year of heavy snowfall in the Colorado River Basin. Probably for economic reasons, that is, to keep the reservoir as full as possible for maximum power head and revenue, the operators did not leave an adequate flood reserve for the imminent snowmelt. The reservoir quickly filled, overtaxed the penstocks to the generators within the dam, shaking it, then overtaxed and began tearing concrete out of the spillway tunnels. River travelers downstream were warned that releases would hit ninety thousand cubic feet per second – the maximum that could be released – and that they should camp high. A plywood wall eleven feet high was built at the dam, adding two million acre-feet to the reservoir's capacity.

So the dam is still there. But those who do not like the dam can always remember the concern of the Bureau of Reclamation about the adequacy of the Navajo sandstone that supports the dam – and hope. That could lead to a story entitled "Suppose It Empties." And if God happened to listen to Edward Abbey and favor Earth First!, Hoover, Parker, and Davis dams would in all probability be overwhelmed and lost as well. Mexico would then receive almost as much water as it did when I was in my teens.

The arguments were described in *Not Man Apart:*

FEDERAL JUDGE WILLIS RITTER recently ruled (in a suit by Friends of the Earth, Kenneth Sleight, and the Wasatch Mountain Club) that the Interior Department must take steps to prevent Lake Powell (which is actually the reservoir backed up behind Glen Canyon Dam) from invading Rainbow Bridge National Monument. Unless the monument can be protected by some other means, Lake Powell will have to be kept no higher than it is now – at about thirty-six hundred feet above sea level – rather than be allowed to fill to capacity at about thirty-seven hundred feet.

Subsequently, Senator Frank Moss (D-Utah) introduced legislation that would have the effect of nullifying FOE's suit and Judge Ritter's decision. In addition, the Interior Department asked Judge Ritter to stay his decision until the case can be heard by a higher court. At press time, the judge had not ruled on Interior's request.

As FOE president, I draw on twenty-five years' experience in Colorado River controversies. I have been frequently credited with (or damned for) administering the coup de grace to a proposed Bureau of Reclamation dam that would have violated Dinosaur National Monument. I think Judge Ritter's decision is in the regional as well as the national interest.

It was clear to congressional leaders in 1955–56 that the bill to authorize the Colorado River Storage Project (CRSP) would go down to defeat unless conservationists' objections were met. Provisions requiring the protection of national parks and monuments in the CRSP area in general—and of Rainbow Bridge National Monument in particular—were written into the bill before it could be passed.

But when the CRSP Act had been enacted, the Bureau of Reclamation promptly began lobbying against fulfillment of the promise to protect Rainbow Bridge. The most promising site for a cutoff dam to protect the monument from the rising waters of Lake Powell, known as Site C, was allowed to go under.

Judge Willis Ritter's decision affirming that the CRSP Act must be complied with now makes possible unexpected advantages to the states of the Colorado River Basin, the most important of these being:

a. the fulfillment of a commitment without which there would have been no CRSP;

b. avoidance of unnecessary damage to scenic resources of great importance, economic as well as spiritual, to the region and the nation;

c. conservation of water, crucial to the states of the Colorado River Basin, that would otherwise be lost; and

d. generation of power at other sites, which would, in large part, compensate for losses resulting from lowering the power head at Glen Canyon Dam.

The economic advantage to the Colorado River Basin states would probably exceed one and a half billion dollars by the year 2059 as a result of strict adherence to the Ritter decision and the immediate drawdown that would make adherence possible.

***Not Man Apart*, May 1973**

Judge Ritter's decision was overturned and the world lost.

CHAPTER 9

NATIONAL PARKS

THE WHITE MOUNTAINS

NEW ENGLAND'S WHITE MOUNTAINS are the hills of home; they are lived in and shape the lives that live in them. Backyard mountains with backcountry in them, they are a little wildness close to home, to look at, to walk into, or simply to enjoy because it is there taking care of itself in its own delightful way. Stuart Little had a fair idea of what the White Mountains mean thanks to the good investigative reporting of E. B. White, who wrote about "the loveliest town of all, where the houses were white and high and the elm trees were green and higher than the houses, where the front yards were wide and pleasant and the backyards were bushy and worth finding out about, where the streets sloped down to the stream and the stream flowed quietly under the bridge, where the lawns ended in orchards and the orchards ended in fields and the fields ended in pastures and the pastures climbed the hill and disappeared over the top toward the wonderful wide sky. . . ." Towns can be lovelier still if the wide sky has White Mountains in it.

Less lovely towns are hard by. Two-thirds of the Americans who live in the United States live in the East, and about half of them live within a day's drive of the tiny wild backcountry of the White Mountain National Forest. It is to the eastern megalopolis what Central Park is to Manhattan. The ways lovers of the White Mountains use them could condemn this old range's backcountry to a slow death beneath encircling camps, ski courses cut through the forests, and millions of tramping or sliding feet.

The bearers of these feet can speak and vote; the bearers of forests cannot. Mountains can use a voice, and Frederick Law Olmsted was one of the first to try to speak for them. Recuperating in Yosemite from the strain of establishing Central Park, he proposed the rights for landscape implicit in the national-park idea. The first requirement, he said, is to preserve the natural scenery and restrict within the narrowest limits the necessary accommodation of visitors. Structures should not detract from the dignity of the scene. "In permitting the sacrifice of anything that would be of the slightest value to future visitors," he wrote, "to the convenience, bad taste, playfulness, carelessness, or wanton destructiveness of present visitors, we probably yield in each case the interest of uncounted millions to the selfishness of a few."

Thus, in 1864, did an idea born on one coast reach another. Both coasts would contribute to its flowering. In 1868, just four years later, John Muir was in Oakland, having seen Central Park and fled west, telling the first person who asked where he wanted to go, "anywhere that's wild." He found what he wanted in the Sierra—wildness, more than scenery, wild creatures that belonged there and domestic creatures that did not. Urged by an eastern editor to gather some friends together to save the Sierra from sheep, he founded the Sierra Club in 1892. The editor, Robert Underwood Johnson of *Century* magazine, for which Muir had written, camped with Muir in Yosemite in 1889. Muir was persuasive; in 1890 Johnson had the bill introduced in Congress which established Yosemite National Park.

Perhaps Johnson suggested a mountain club because of what had happened in 1876 in Boston, when ninety-two men and eighteen women founded the Appalachian Mountain Club. The AMC had a once-known wilderness to restore. The Sierra Club had a little-known wilderness to rescue. Starting life a little bigger than the AMC (one hundred eighty-two charter members to one hundred ten), it almost immediately plunged into vigorous legislative activity and has not let up.

At first both organizations gave most of their attention to the mountains they were born near. They grew slowly, the AMC comfortably in the lead. As the fifties began, the Sierra Club, nudged by The Wilderness Society, forty-three years its junior, decided to go national and to relearn what John Muir had taught it about the importance of wildness, extending its concern, as Muir had his, to the last great wilderness—Alaska's. The Sierra Club found itself contending with all the federal land agencies, getting deeper into legislative activity (and thereby losing its tax-deductible status), and carrying the battle for wilderness into the courts and overseas. It broadened its scope as it saw that cities and farms and commercial forests should be run better, and population be controlled, or the wilderness that civilization needed around it would be lost. The Sierra Club's rapid outreach did not arrive without inner conflict. One conflict led to the founding of Friends of the Earth in 1969. Muir's goals were now sought globally, and the combined membership of the Sierra Club and FOE grew to a quarter of a million. Like kindred organizations, with hundreds of millions of acres of wide-open spaces to be concerned about, they believed that they must persuade the federal government to spend the necessary money and the effort to manage and protect these places, with help now and then from the states.

In the White Mountains something quite else was happening, and the AMC was key to it. Antedating the Forest Service and the National Park Service—antedating even the Forest Reserve, most of the national parks, and the mapmaking functions of the Geological Survey—the AMC in its first quarter century concentrated on the exploration and mapping of the New England highlands, still uncharted. For two more quarter centuries the AMC strove to make the White Mountain region accessible through trails, a hut system, guidebooks, generous financial assistance, timely impatience, and well-placed influence. Senior to agencies and endowed with remarkable continuity, the AMC developed a kind of governance of its own. It could guide, interpret, oversee, and help house and rescue the throngs that visited one of the loveliest, and most heavily used, recreation areas of all.

Agencies may come and go. The AMC, we pray, is staying. Government bureaus should indeed go at the age of ten, Justice William O. Douglas once advised President Franklin D. Roosevelt, lest they think too much about themselves and too little about their mission. Career-management plans help this happen: high-echelon bureau people wanting to get ahead must travel widely through the bureau's bailiwick, learning the politics of an agency's holding its own, and discovering the Parkinson's Laws that make the world safe for bureaucracy. This may be great for careers. If the career is one in land management, it bodes ill for the land. The rising careerist has too little time to travel widely at Concord, as Thoreau did, or to understand what Aldo Leopold considered the outstanding scientific discovery of the twentieth century—the complexity of the land organism. "If the land mechanism as a whole is good," he said, "then every part is good, whether we understand it or not. . . . To keep every cog and wheel is the first precaution of intelligent tinkering."

For its first whole century, the AMC made a career of learning about the cogs and wheels of the White Mountains. For a slightly shorter span, an individual did the same thing, and never underestimate Individual Power. Drawing upon his experience as a planner and AMC climber (1908–10), Benton MacKaye became a legend in his own time, in the appraisal of Paul Oehser of the Smithsonian. Benton "was forever young in heart, and eternally grateful for the privilege of living so long in the best world that he knew of, imperfect though it was." He was old enough to vote at the turn of the century, but just before voting conceived of an Appalachian Trail, presenting the idea comprehensively in 1921. The trail was to be much more than a long path through wild mountains. He saw it as "the backbone of a primeval environment, a sort of refuge from civilization which was becoming too mechanized." He wanted clusters of parks around this backbone, and a network of trails planned to intersect at strategic points with railroads. He liked the idea of triangle vacations: train to trail to train to home.

What Benton MacKaye called the crassitudes of civilization—billboard, pavement, or auto horn—were negations of the wilderness, itself "the perfect norm, wild and untouched land as distinguished from domesticated cornfield, pasture, or farm woodlot." Wilderness was the product of paleontology, a reservoir of stored experience in the ways of life before man. He urged: "We must win back our wilderness because we are losing it. We have upset the balance of the . . . 'Big Three' states of living (primeval, agrarian, industrial) . . . there should be room enough for all—both for the gregariously minded folks who like parks and playgrounds, and for the solitary-minded who seek the lonely shores."

Like Johnson and Muir, he wanted to organize to defend wilderness, and became one of the founders of The Wilderness Society, advocating at the time that "any body of people coming together for a purpose (whatever it may be) should consist of persons wholly wedded to that purpose and should consist of nobody else. If the purpose be cannibalism . . . then nobody but a cannibal should be admitted. There should be plenty of discussion and disagreement as to how and the means, but none whatever as to the ends."

He wanted each member of the society, in each locality, to find some local job to do—a variation of his Appalachian Trail program of local groups' voluntarily building and taking care of their own sections of the trail, bringing many into enjoyable and useful activity. He also proposed a series of ecological study areas throughout the continent to represent the several natural communities in each of them, and in 1935 proposed that there be a national wilderness system. In December 1975, a few days before he died, Benton MacKaye thanked Stuart Chase for an article calling attention to the worldwide devastation of forest lands, and added, "It is the same old story which led me into forestry under Gifford Pinchot seventy years ago last June."

The hills of home had found their match, and tributes to him fill half of the March 1976 *The Living Wilderness*. One of the most moving is Lewis Mumford's about a man, an idea, and the difference they made together.

Mumford first visited Benton's home in Shirley Center in the spring of 1929. "What surprised me there," he wrote, "is what surprised me in Thoreau's Concord: that such a passionate love for the natural landscape in its most rugged moments could have been nourished in an environment so mild and gentle, with rolling meadows and patches of woodland and marshland . . . and a distant glimpse of the far-from-overpowering heights of Wachusett. The whole countryside seemed but one step away from complete cultivation and domestication." Perhaps that very fact, Mumford thought, may have encouraged young MacKaye to deeper exploration.

Like Thoreau, MacKaye appreciated the communal values of New England villages, and even better than Thoreau, the culture of cities. Mumford continued: "So far from believing that man's three major environments, the primeval, the rural, and the communal or urban, were mutually exclusive, MacKaye held rather that they were complementary, and all three were necessary for man's full development. . . . If one part of MacKaye was attached to the rehabilitation of indigenous American values, he was equally concerned to develop a global strategy favorable to the maintenance of similar values in other habitats and cultures."

One indigenous value his Appalachian Trail awaits is the rehabilitation of its railroads. The White Mountain section of the trail itself was completed in 1932, when railroads still went to little places, with the marking of the existing trails then managed by the AMC and the Dartmouth Outing Club, the Maine Appalachian Trail Club agreeing to continue the trail to Mount Katahdin. In 1938 the National Park Service and Forest Service established the Appalachian Trailway, a zone two miles wide along the trail to be free of motor transport or any development incompatible with recreational uses of the trail. Myron Avery, with Arthur Perkins, inherited MacKaye's idea and led in the task of connecting it with the earth. In 1952 Avery declared at a meeting of the Appalachian Trail Conference that the Maine-to-Georgia trail was complete. Congress, in 1968, passed the National Trail System legislation introduced in 1964 by Senator Gaylord Nelson, and the Appalachian Trail was recognized in federal law. We now suggest that the Army Corps of Engineers, who are very effective in these matters, be persuaded to leave wild rivers in their courses and get tired railroads back on the track, thus rescuing Benton MacKaye's original idea.

Whatever the origins of protection, the White Mountains continue to fare well thanks to several groups whose combined energies insure that good management does not stop at artificial boundaries, whether of national parks, national forests, state lands, or private lands. Many conservation groups not already engaged in management are partly equipped to do so, and, as the AMC's Tom Deans and Ken Olson suggest, may well extend their capability as they realize that the survival of wilderness depends on husbandry as well as advocacy. It also depends upon the generosity of its beneficiaries. Institutions that put the public weal before private gain are customarily endowed well. Wilderness deserves such support, too, and the opportunity to endow the open university of wilderness is impressive. To help realize it, funds need to be channeled into organizations like the Appalachian Trail Conference, the Nature Conservancy, the Sierra Club, the Trust for Public Land, The Wilderness Society, and of course the Appalachian Mountain Club, and Friends of the Earth. Such funds can most appropriately come from the people who now enjoy wild places, or have enjoyed them, or would like Frederick Law Olmsted's uncounted millions to enjoy them. Current contributions and last gifts can mean a lasting wilderness.

Wilderness is what the White Mountains had, but lost. The once-vast area in which the web of life perfected itself with no assistance from bureaus or technology has been severed and severed again. The species that were lost in that severing are ended. We shall never know what they might have meant to their surroundings or to us. Beautiful pockets of wildness nonetheless remain and some might almost grow back together again. Tomorrow's White Mountain restoration, to all but the most discerning, could be indistinguishable from the original. For this to happen, however, the mountains cannot be periodically disrupted by dam and road building, mining and quarrying, logging and clearing, and by recreational excesses and the pervasive effects of pollution of the surrounding air. Glaciers, of course, could unpave the way toward recovery, especially if they were once again to be two thousand feet deeper than Mount Washington is high; but no one is urging so drastic a remedial step.

Various courses lie open to public and private organizations in managing people so as to hasten the healing in wild places. These places can be hurt by those who love them. It will ease the damage, when it threatens to be severe, to push access points back a bit so that the wheel does less work and the foot does more. If wilderness must be rationed, those who are willing to earn it should be favored. This is Garrett Hardin's point, and he makes it knowing that it rules him out. Paul Brooks perceives another kind of rationing: "If you are in a canoe traveling at three miles an hour, the lake on which you are paddling is ten times as long and ten times as broad as it is to the man in a speedboat going thirty. . . . More people can use the same space with the same results." So speed limits are in order. Other limits may be in time, such as those river travelers observe in the Grand Canyon; they are required to take out everything they bring in except urine. The successive steps needed to reduce human impact on wilderness surely increase the impact upon the freedom that wilderness was able to grant when the world was less crowded. Those limits do mean, however, that when the visitor has gone, the wilderness is still there, not smothered in an embrace, but essentially intact.

Impact that might otherwise be ubiquitous is concentrated by the judicious placing of huts, as the AMC has demonstrated. But a hut has a basic drawback. Move a hut in, and wildness pulls back, in fact and in spirit. The hut user shares the problem of the man in Samivel's cartoon who could enjoy solitude more if it were only less lonely.

The impact most serious of all comes from there being too few people—too few who know a given place, who have learned to understand and love it, and thus are prepared to protect it. Glen Canyon was the place no one knew, and it is gone. No visitor impact can compete with a dam, a chainsaw, or a bulldozer—or, for that matter, the impact of acid rain or radioactive fallout. The AMC huts, like Sierra Club wilderness outings, have built battalions of people who care. Without those people, there might have been no solitude at all. Be grateful, if you will, for their own special love for the mountain or shore of their home country, for their speaking in behalf of high-rimmed valleys and of views from summits, of whole forests and free streams, of nonhuman denizens and of human visitors, too, and human needs far into the future. They are in the tradition of the Olmsteds, Thoreaus, Muirs, MacKayes, Leopolds—a tradition to keep alive if wildness is to remain the preservation of the world Thoreau believed it to be.

Otherwise progress as presently misconstrued will erase the last vestige of original America. How fast it has gone! A mere one hundred thirty years ago, when oil was first discovered in Pennsylvania and John Muir was nine years old, Thoreau wrote: "I am reminded by my journey how exceedingly new this country still is. . . . We live only on the shores of a continent even yet, and hardly know where the rivers come from which float our navy. The very timber and boards and shingles of which our houses are made, grew but yesterday in a wilderness where the Indian still hunts and the moose runs wild."

Thirty years later, the AMC was born. Three more, Benton MacKaye. Add thirteen, the Sierra Club. Twice as many more, and World War I was over; an epidemic of Spanish influenza was followed by one of automobiles. Another eleven, and a world half as populous as today's entered the Great Depression. A second world war came within a decade, and its end marked the beginning of the atomic age and the race for ever-grosser national products. The earth grew no larger.

For fifty years big wilderness has been disappearing at the rate of a million acres a year in the national forests, and still more has disappeared outside the forests. Other wildness may go, too—the most remarkable wild heritage of all, DNA. In the last five years the urge was born to second-guess a force that has been created, honed, and perfected in wilderness for three and a half thousand million years. A trace of its first day on earth is still alive in today's wilderness, and in each of us.

Given another decade or two, humanity could quite handily erase the last of the earth's wilderness. Or it could heed Aldo Leopold's warning: "When the last corner lot is covered with tenements we can still make a playground by tearing them down, but when the last antelope goes by the board, not all the playground associations in Christendom can do aught to replace the loss." For as Wallace Stegner has said, "It is not given to man to create wilderness." We could pledge never to tell tomorrow's children what they missed, or we could take a new look at progress and continue only that kind that avoids the mindless growth that destroys its feedstock. Surely we can let the wildness that still is still be. We can go back where we ravaged, and restore, if we try soon enough. We can, upright people that we are, rediscover the foot; we can save a place to walk in, and an antelope, too. Every child who is there on the first day of our tercentenary still has a chance, through us, to wake up in an America that is still spacious, still beautiful, still wild enough in places. Wilder, perhaps, than it now is in New England's oldest climax, these, the White Mountains of home.

***New England's White Mountains: At Home in the Wild,* 1978**

MOUNT ANSEL ADAMS

THERE ARE NO NATIONAL PARKS in the White Mountains, and glaciers will probably carve deep U-shaped valleys in hell before the Thirteen Colonies will permit one to be established. It should be noted in passing that glaciers were once very effective in that part of the world. And it is not up to me, a Californian, to observe that the place is looking more and more like hell. That is becoming conventional wisdom, and I know all about what the kettle should not retort to the pot.

None of this was in my mind in Tuolumne Meadows in August 1984. Some five hundred people had gathered there at the invitation of Jeanne Adams for a dual celebration—the official naming of Mount Ansel Adams, in the Yosemite High Sierra, and the naming of Yosemite National Park as a World Heritage site.

It is possible that I had known Ansel longer than anyone there except his widow Virginia, and was therefore invited to speak. Then there were the luminaries—among them Secretary of the Interior Don Hodel, Senator Alan Cranston, Wallace Stegner, and Robert Redford.

One of the projects Ansel and I were working on at the time of his death was a Manifesto for the Earth, and I managed to work some of our joint ideas into my talk, and my hopes as well, after Jeanne's husband Michael, whose parents I had known longer than he had, introduced me:

THANK YOU, MICHAEL. Thank you, Virginia and Ansel, for Michael. Thank you, Michael, for Jeanne. And thank you, Jeanne, for the party.

I think that for a long time I have considered Yosemite, Ansel, and Virginia synonymous, but they didn't begin quite soon enough.

Back in the National Aquarium there is something carved in stone that says, "We do not inherit the Earth from our fathers; we borrow it from our children." What we need to do to take care of that requirement, it seems to me, is to comprehend that that idea and the national-park idea are the nearest things we have so far to remind us not to borrow from our children but to leave things for them. The national-park idea was born in Yosemite. I'm going to be chauvinistic enough to tell all you Yellowstone fans that you came late. In 1863 Frederick Law Olmsted, *père,* was having trouble with his board of directors in Central Park, came out to the Fremont Estate near Mariposa to manage it, and got acquainted with

Yosemite Valley. He was "the right man in the right place at the right time." He was one who could inform other people, including Senator Conness—a mountain is named after him here—that there should be a park. I'll read you a little of the language about the park that he was suggesting:

"That cleft or gorge in the granite peak of the Sierra Nevada Mountains, situated in the county of Mariposa, on the headwaters of the Merced River and known as Yosemite Valley, with its branches and spurs, in length fifteen miles and a good one mile back from the main edge of the precipices, should be set aside for the nation.

"I pick this length and width to secure the approaches from any annoyance. The southwest end is narrow and filled by the Merced River. The northeast end leads to Mono, is narrow and filled with rocks and impassable to a mule."

Olmsted worked for a year for the creation of a Yosemite Park, after this letter, which was of February 6, 1863. It took another three months before there was a park. The park bill passed Congress and was signed by President Lincoln in June 1864. The park was turned over to the State of California for administration because there was no Park Service or any other agency to handle it.

Mr. Olmsted wrote a report to the state legislature in which he gave the national-park idea its most important embodiment, as far as I am concerned.

What Ansel Adams called "the noble gestures of the natural world" have no better protection than the national-park idea, which recognizes that the park is for people, but especially for people who love what the park is, who are content to wonder at what has always been beautiful, and leave it that way.

The national-park idea started here, and there are ripples that are still going on. That is what I want to talk about most, but briefly.

The ripple soon brought Yellowstone, eight years after Yosemite. They decided that Yellowstone ought to be a park to save those strange features—the geysers and that sort of thing. The park was created, and since there was not a state, but only a territory to delegate its administration to, the feds kept it.

A few years later it was realized that Yosemite Valley was not enough to save. If you wanted to save Yosemite Valley, you needed to save the surroundings of the valley that fed the streams into it. So we had Yosemite National Park in 1890.

But it was only a million acres. Now we have to have a broader idea to think about, and that's what I think we should think about. Because if Ansel were here, he would not want us just to sit here and celebrate. He would want us to have an agenda about what we can do next that is going to be important, catch the public fancy, and help us match our mountains.

Yosemite itself is not well enough protected. I'll pause here to say that the Yosemite idea, the national-park idea, has spread around the world. The constituency for national parks is global. We have people from all over the world coming here and we have people from this audience going all over the world to see what things have been saved by virtue of the national-park idea. The World Heritage idea, which preserves natural and cultural places of global importance, is itself an outgrowth of the national-park idea. The idea spread. It needs to spread further.

How did the idea happen to spread in the first place—how did Yosemite become the first, and Number One? Largely through artists, and in part through landscape architects such as the Olmsteds. Of them it was said that their landscapes were painted with forests, with hills, with sky, with water—that's the way they painted.

Then there were the photographers, starting with C. L. Weed and C. E. Watkins, and proceeding to Ansel Adams, who took the photography of natural beauty a step beyond what had ever been achieved before.

There were other artists—T. A. Ayres and his pencil sketches, Albert Bierstadt, Charles Robinson, Thomas Hill, William Keith, and Virginia's father, Harry Cassie Best. Just a partial list. There were the writers, too—Thomas Hutchings, John Muir of course, and the current writers, including Wallace Stegner, from whom you are going to hear soon.

Let us thank the artists who helped get the word and picture out. And let us look for the artists we shall need to call upon to spread the word further.

Right now there is a scheme afoot to protect the ecological environment of Yellowstone National Park, a plan that would encompass a vast area, that would include the Tetons, the forests surrounding Yellowstone, private land, public land, national forests, and state lands, protecting them under a blanket that would save the setting and the jewel within it, Yellowstone itself.

The same thing needs to be done for Yosemite. The present boundaries cannot be enlarged a great deal. But we can do something that has been done before, and do it better here. In the Adirondack Mountains, long ago, they drew a green line. It was to be the Green Line Park. Within that line, whatever the ownership, whether it was private or public, there was a very important goal: that place was to stay beautiful, under whatever management. We need a green-line addition to Yosemite. As far as I am concerned, it should start at the far end of Mono Lake, where its highest shorelines were, include the Mono Basin country, extend through Yosemite, and go on down the Merced, all the way down the Merced to where it stops in McClure reservoir. We don't need any new development between that and where the Merced River begins.

That gets me to Mount Ansel Adams, because that's where the Merced River begins. Actually it begins just a little bit behind Mount Ansel Adams, which has the humility to be not quite so high as some of the peaks around it, like Mount Lyell or Electra or Foerster.

From Ansel's mountain you look down on one of the places I have wanted to go to more than any other place in the Sierra. I haven't been there yet. I had planned to go right after this speech and start over the hill and go to the Lyell Fork of the Merced. But I found that it was twenty miles, and I didn't get into shape for that. Next year we'll all go.

You get a sense of what the Merced River has done, what the Tuolumne River has done, to create one of the great natural gestures of the Earth. And you don't need to be timid about protecting all the Merced River that's still unspoiled. From the approach on the east side, this is all one unit. We do want a greater national park here that is a transect of the great Sierra uplift. We don't want to throw out private owners; we don't want to throw out the Forest Service or the state. But we want to put a protective blanket over what they do and require the highest performance standards in their deeds.

And that blanket, that goal, will be essentially what Frederick Law Olmsted was saying: the important thing to remember is the natural scenery, keeping whatever structures there are to a minimum, keeping them harmonious, and remembering that everything we do for anyone's convenience ought not to be at too great a cost for all the millions of people yet to come. They will need to enjoy this place, and may need it more than we do.

It would be very convenient if we had a road up the Lyell Fork and a téléphérique up Mount Ansel Adams. But it would be very inconvenient to anyone who would prefer to see Mount Ansel Adams *au naturel*. It might be a lift for us, but it would be a downer for them.

So that's the goal that I would talk about, remembering Ansel and all the things I worked with him on—especially what we were working on but didn't quite finish when he died, his idea of a Manifesto for the Earth. I think he would like something like a Greater Yosemite National Park.

I learned more about conservation from Ansel than from anyone else, and I'd just like to think that were he here he'd be just pushing on, pushing on. There are things to be done for the Big Sur Coast, for the Columbia Gorge, for the Greater Yosemite, for the Greater Yellowstone, that we can still do, and there isn't a great deal of time to do them. But we can do them, and Ansel would be honored if we did. So I think.

Let us remember not to borrow from our children something that they will then be deprived of forever because we used it up. That's the opportunity I think we should commit ourselves to.

Rachel Carson did her homework, minded her English, and cared. That's something all of us can do. There is no one here who cannot make an important contribution to the Greater Yosemite, from the farther shorelines of ancient Mono Lake down to the reservoir where the Merced River goes to sleep.

That's the goal. We can do it, if we make a commitment to it, if we lobby our senators, we lobby our members of Congress, and help them let it happen. Let's do it!

Let us set aside something that will transcend the dedicating of Mount Ansel Adams, beautiful peak though it is. Let's try for the big plan that will carry the national-park idea forward.

"These we inherit," he wrote. We inherit the parks. We can pass them on bigger than we found them. How's that for a call to action?

If you make the commitment, that will make the difference. A mountaineer friend of mine wrote about commitment. He said, "Until one is committed, there is hesitation, the chance to draw back, always ineffectiveness. But the moment one fully commits oneself, then Providence moves too"—and all sorts of things happen that would never otherwise have happened. He liked the couplet from Goethe that I end my speech with.

Whatever you can do,
or dream you can, begin it.
Boldness has genius,
power, and magic in it.

There is magic in everyone here, and that can bring out the ultimate memorial to Ansel Adams—the Greater Yosemite National Park, and the things that achievement will set going around the Earth.

Let your magic out!

***Mount Ansel Adams Ceremony,* 1984**

Mountaineer William H. Murray's offhand remark about commitment, complete with his couplet from Goethe, became an essential part of my religion in 1951, before I had delved more than seven pages into *The Scottish Himalayan Expedition* (J. M. Dent & Sons, London, 1915). Anyone who has heard me speak more than once in the past twenty-five years has heard me cite Messrs. Murray and Goethe at least twice, and that may very well happen in this book. Their lines have served me well, and were appropriately displayed in two exhibit-format books about mountains that I edited—*Everest: The West Ridge* (with Kenneth Brower's expert and predominant help) and *Return to the Alps*. Those lines should be in all books on mountains, and ought to be memorized by anyone who works in or for an environment.

On Burning the Furniture

One of the First Words anyone who is working for the environment and therefore opposing any kind of development for whatever reason encounters is *jobs*. How can you possibly think of protecting endangered species by sparing an ancient forest, or controlling lung damage and global warming by opposing freeways and offshore oil drilling, or saving wildlife and water recreation by opposing dams, or saving the ozone barrier by cooling it on styrofoam and refrigeration – the list can go on, but won't – when all your do-goodery costs jobs?

In April 1975, I tackled this one – people in my business must do so perpetually – in a little piece, "Shall We Burn the Furniture in the Oval Office?" I wrote for *Not Man Apart:*

Latter-day Timber Barons are apparently unwilling to be as responsible for the environment and society in which they live as the rest of us must be, under the National Environmental Policy Act. They are putting their employees up to some rather ugly demonstrations, which seem aimed at frightening the new governor, his officers, the legislature, the courts, and the public.

The company officials are like people described by Dr. Dan Luten, "who would rather die than change their habits." It is all too easy to infer that they will not change their habit of cutting down virgin redwood stands, unique to California, until they have cut the last of them, or have severely impaired what they cannot reach yet.

Since they are going to have to change their habits eventually, it makes sense to have them change those habits now, while we still have some chance to save the vestige they left us of what should have been a great Redwood National Park.

We are in sympathy with the straits of the unemployed loggers, but before we let sympathy be an easy route to expedience, let us consider who else needs some sympathy.

Not, for one, former Governor Reagan, famous for his "Once you've seen one redwood you've seen them all." That was long ago appropriately countered with "Once you've seen one redwood *stump*, you've seen them all." Neither statement is true, of course, as anyone would know who has recently flown over the thousands of unnecessary redwood stumps that mark the boundary of the pitifully thin line of Redwood Creek giants finally included in Redwood National Park. You can be excused for the rage you feel at the vindictive logging, or call it the preemptive logging, that put those great trees down and out, precluding forever, for us and all who follow us, the chance to see what that park should have been.

You can be excused for feeling that the people who let this happen should be locked up for the grand larceny against the future they took part in. You wonder what would have happened if a lot of people had not sat on their hands, or been defensive–if they had paid attention and had been bold enough. You could wonder, too, what might have happened if former Governor Reagan had appointed Claire Dedrick as his resource secretary instead of Norman B. ("Ike") Livermore, Jr., whose feeling toward redwoods (if not toward Sierra wilderness, which he worked courageously to save) was conditioned so long by his having been an officer of Pacific Lumber Company. You wonder what might have happened had Martin Litton been appointed–the man who more than anyone else was trying to get the National Park Service, the Save-the-Redwoods League, and the Sierra Club to listen to what he knew about where the finest redwoods were for a national park. The Sierra Club listened.

How much sympathy should go to an industry that won't change its ways, or workers who won't change theirs, until something has been destroyed that belongs to all the future, and not really to them?

In environmental controversies, industry invariably brings up the question of jobs. So did Dick Cavett. When *Encounters with the Archdruid* was published, he asked the author to appear on his show. John McPhee, with perhaps more modesty than was necessary, declined. As one might expect, the archdruid leapt at the opportunity and was joined there by Arthur Godfrey. Mr. Cavett asked if I was alarmed by what was happening to the environment. Trying hard to sound reasonable, I gave a nondescript answer. Arthur Godfrey intervened to say, "It scares the hell out of me!"

Dick Cavett happened to look down at Mr. Godfrey's shoes and could not forego a comment about their being made of alligator leather, then went after me. "What," he asked, "do you tell those who say environmentalists are putting people out of work?"

I was about to come up with a nonconfrontational answer, but he didn't wait.

"I think I can answer that one," he said. "I suppose a lot of people lost their jobs when they closed the furnaces at Dachau."

Shocked by his own extemporaneity, he quickly changed the subject. When I told Daniel Ellsberg about the occasion, his comment was chilling: "We took the furnaces to the people."

Indeed we did, at Hiroshima, Nagasaki, and wherever we fired white phosphorous in World War II or, in the Vietnam War, dropped napalm. As the decades flow by, we still keep these furnaces, now burning far hotter, in our arsenal.

For security? Good question.

War makes brutal jobs, and we have ended unemployment that way more than once. Pollution makes jobs. Napalm-making makes jobs and, as a friend has observed, takes the furnace to the people. Dumping asbestos into Lake Superior makes jobs. Making teratogenic herbicides like 2,4,5–T makes jobs. Making reactors makes jobs, and the proposal to make still more reactors and plant them in various and sundry countries we seek favors from would make jobs. Putting a multi-billion-dollar Trident base in the Hood Canal would make jobs. Making bigger, faster, fuel-gulping cars and airplanes makes jobs. Anything else?

Yes. Trying to put a tiny fragment of ecosystem back together can make jobs, and is doing just that in a tiny national park in Australia. Trouble is, they aren't succeeding. They are finding out that just as you can't put Humpty Dumpty together again, or unscramble an egg, or make pancakes in a toaster, you cannot put a whole web of life back together once you have taken it apart. It takes God to do that and, we understand, a generous allowance of time.

Closer at hand, there are nevertheless many jobs in trying as best we can to put a forest back together, in letting people do carefully what machines do recklessly, as if they were all thumbs, or bulldozers in a china shop. There are tiny good examples, such as what people can do in a commune when they set about healing a piece of earth instead of ripping it up. And there are big examples, such as in Boeing's learning how to survive nicely, even better, without an SST business, and in what this nation did in getting some twelve million men and women out of wartime work and into peaceful jobs in a few months of assiduous retraining.

You yourself can suggest jobs that need doing, that are indeed needed so much that there should be federal and state financial support for retraining and re-equipping unemployed loggers and logging industries to accomplish them. There are substitutes for overmechanized, over-energy-intensive timber operations. There are substitutes for the hundreds of thousands of unrestocked or poorly restocked forest lands that earlier cut-and-get-out loggers bequeathed their descendants—loggers as well as all the rest of us. Indeed, there are substitutes for wasteful use of lumber, as any Italian stonemason will tell you. And those Italian substitutes, travelers to Rome note, last a great deal longer than wood.

There are no substitutes for the last intact virgin redwood stands, and there are no substitutes, in this crowded world, for acting responsibly toward the society and the environment in which we live, and in which we hope thousands of future generations of people and other live things will be living. Enjoyably, we hope. With a chance to see more than one two-thousand-year-old redwood, and to see it in the right setting.

We would not expect the president, in a fuel shortage, to burn the furniture in the Oval Office to keep the fireplace going in some other part of the house that is lent him. Logging company presidents, please copy.

***Not Man Apart,* April 1975**

WILDERNESS AND PEOPLE

CLEARLY, LUMBER BARONS AND LOGGERS should stay out of the last wild places and concentrate on the tree farms that look so handsome in their advertisements. But should people—except for visitors like us—also be kept out?

This question was slow in coming. The national-park idea did not need to contend with it. Places selected for America's first national parks were too remote and hostile to entice people, or the natives had already been killed off or put on reservations by the early developers. In other lands the International Union for the Conservation of Nature and Natural Resources (IUCN) soon found that three words needed to be added if lands were to be protected—"national parks *or equivalent reserves*."

There simply weren't that many empty places in the Old World, developed or developing.

The most recent concept is one that I had hoped my mountaineer friends, Dick Emerson and his wife, Pat, would write a book about: The Inhabited Wilderness. Our own Wilderness Act language, "where man is a visitor who does not remain," fits fewer and fewer places around the world in which wildness, if not wilderness by our definition, desperately needs protection. These are places that people like Chief Seattle, who knew what should not be done to land as he watched us do it, were removed from to make way for the Industrial Age.

The Biosphere Reserve concept was initiated by Michel Batisse, of UNESCO, as part of the Man in the Biosphere Program in the late sixties—a different kind of preservation of nature that could accommodate people who were not visitors but could remain and find their well-being enhanced by the preservation, and vice versa.

My scripture in these matters is in the writings of Raymond Fredric Dasmann, one of the world's top ecologists, now at the University of California, Santa Cruz. In February 1975, Ray gave a paper in Wellington, New Zealand, just as Kenneth Brower, as author, and Robert Wenkam, as photographer, were completing the eighth book in the Friends of the Earth series, *The Earth's Wild Places*. Ray's paper, "Parks, Nature Conservation, and 'Future Primitive,' " contained just what our book, *Micronesia: Island Wilderness*, needed up front.

"I recently postulated," Ray wrote, "that there are two types of people in the world, *ecosystem people* and *biosphere people*. In the former category are all the members of indigenous traditional cultures and some who have seceded from, or have been pushed out of, technological society; in the latter are those who are tied in with the global technological civilization. Ecosystem people live within a single ecosystem, or at most two or three adjacent and closely related ecosystems. They are dependent upon them for their survival. If they persistently violate their ecological rules, they must necessarily perish." If they kill more wild game than can be produced, or if they overfish, or fail to keep soil in place and restore its fertility, they are in trouble.

"Island people," he continues, "have lived under particularly strong restraints, and could not tolerate any great increase in their own numbers." They know where the shore of their island is. "Only continental people," Ray adds, "can develop myths of unlimited resources."

Have you seen any continental people lately? They—we—are the biosphere people, who "draw their support not from the resources of any one ecosystem, but from the entire biosphere." Any corner of the earth that now escapes their tentacles will not automatically escape them long. "Consequently, biosphere people can exert incredible pressure upon an ecosystem that they wish to exploit, and can create great devastation"—unthinkable for ecosystem people.

Even if the intentions of the biosphere people are the best, and they seldom are, their efforts break down the local constraints, the traditional practices that have held the delicate balance between humanity and nature, and thus allow ecosystem destruction to take place.

Ray's rules for new parks do not suggest turning back the clock. Rather, he urges that we think harder about what the clock will be seeing if we biospherists go on as usual. He wants us to respect the rights of indigenous cultures, to recognize the balances they have established between themselves and nature, to coordinate the protection of the parks with the people in surrounding lands, and to negotiate to keep the outside land use compatible with that inside the park.

Ray proposes that the answer for nature conservation will be found to lie in the direction of "Future Primitive." This does not mean the rejection of the best of modern technology, but it does mean the avoidance of the worst. It does mean using the tools and energy that are still available to create something permanent, to create a way of life that can be *sustained.* In such a way of life, nature conservation would necessarily be taken for granted, since people will recognize that their future depends on the health and diversity of the natural world.

RESTORING HETCH HETCHY

BIOSPHERE PEOPLE, in order to take it easier on the ecosystems of others, might well try to get some of their own natural world back. They should have welcomed, rather than been suspicious of, the Reagan administration proposal to restore Yosemite National Park's Hetch Hetchy Valley. The proposal came from Secretary of the Interior Don Hodel. In

Rocky Mountain National Park he had seen what damage the failure of a small dam within the park had caused. Noting that there were two other dams there that could cause similar damage, he wanted them taken down by man, not nature. At the party to dedicate Mount Ansel Adams in Tuolumne Meadows, he came down from some rock-climbing on Lembert Dome, where no mob was in sight, to tell an unbelieving audience that Yosemite was not overcrowded. Somewhere between that observation and his recommendation that two little dams be disassembled in Rocky Mountain, he saw the photograph of O'Shaughnessy Dam, at Hetch Hetchy, with an Earth First! plastic crack draped over it and a sign reading, "Free the river—John Muir."

If two little dams could go for good purpose, how about a big one? Imagine the benefit of returning Yosemite National Park's second yosemite valley back to the people!

I loved the idea, and went to Sacramento to support it at a meeting called by Secretary Hodel. The Sierra Club had supplied him with large blow-ups of Hetch Hetchy scenes, mostly the work of the club's long-time honorary president, Little Joe LeConte. One of the scenes was of John Muir standing in front of handsome cliffs. I started my brief presentation with a correction.

"I'm sorry, Mr. Secretary, but John Muir is not standing in Hetch Hetchy. He is standing in Yosemite Valley."

"Are you sure?"

"Very sure. I lived in the valley three years. That's Washington Column, and those are the Royal Arches. My office was in the Ahwahnee Hotel, right under the Arches."

"The Sierra Club assured me," he said, "that this is a picture of Hetch Hetchy."

"I'll speak to the Sierra Club. They are forgetting what their own Sierra looks like. In last year's calendar they gave Yosemite Falls to Colorado!"

The secretary had the picture turn its head to the wall, and I went on to support his idea, but announced that I would take the afternoon plane to Washington to testify against the oil development he was proposing for the Arctic National Wildlife Range. He was not surprised.

I urged the Sierra Club to do an instant book about restoring Hetch Hetchy, but was not persuasive enough. I did, however, write something for the *Earth Island Journal,* published in its summer 1987 issue. The journal was originally weekly, produced by a Stanford University class I taught in the spring quarter of 1982. I hope it will become a weekly again. It is now produced quarterly, and my article had to be shortened. This is all of it:

WHETHER OR NOT he meant it that way, when Secretary of the Interior Hodel suggested draining Hetch Hetchy reservoir in Yosemite National Park, he advanced a superb idea for environmental restoration.

From John Muir's writing and Joseph LeConte's photographs, I had learned of the splendor of the Hetch Hetchy Valley that was and had now become a candidate for restoration. It was more like the Merced River Yosemite that everybody knows than like the Kings River yosemite that forms the western entrance to Kings Canyon National Park. I knew it best from May 15, 1955, the day I took the color-film footage that was to become the Sierra Club's film, *Two Yosemites*—an eleven-minute film cut out of the five hundred feet of Kodachrome that my original budget allowed.

Philip Hyde accompanied me, making black-and-white photographs we were to use in our campaign to keep Dinosaur National Monument from suffering Hetch Hetchy's fate. We were able to take a boat to the head of the reservoir, at that time drawn down to accommodate the late May and June heavy flow of the Tuolumne River. The drawdown meant an extensive area of exhumed stumps and silty reservoir shore. It also provided a dustbowl, as the wind whirled clouds of silt and sediment into the Sierra sky—a fitting background for the narrative quoting various experts saying that the reservoir would create a beautiful lake, reflecting all about it. The narration went on to lament the loss of the valley. "The walls are still there, and the waterfalls, gleaming in the sunshine. But where is the setting, the heartland of this place. It is gone, lost irretrievably to all men, thanks to the dam, where plaques praise the men who took so much from so many for all our time. How much we lost we'll never know. . . ."

Although Secretary Hodel's proposal to tear down the O'Shaughnessy Dam was not the first suggestion that this be done, it came from higher authority than any other. And it provides a splendid opportunity to prove my narration wrong. We can indeed take the dam down in our time, and we can rediscover what we have lost. The rediscovery can be spectacular, and warrants careful documentation of the natural forces of renewal, which can begin centuries before they would have were we to wait for nature to take the dam down after the reservoir has been filled with sediment and the Tuolumne River begins wearing away the top of the dam and, eventually, the whole damn thing.

The Hodel proposal produced the expected panic in San Francisco. Mayor Diane Feinstein wanted it shredded. Alarmists (and I can tell one when I see one) warned that the alternative to Hetch Hetchy would be the proposed and despised Auburn Dam and Peripheral Canal and other adjustments, the cost of which would probably total six billion dollars. The media reported all this with but a halfhearted attempt to check. A forester told them how long it would take the trees to grow, and a reclamation writer told how long it would take for the lake bed to dry out and be usable. The mayor understandably did not want San Francisco to lose the thirty million dollars a year from the sale of Hetch Hetchy project electricity.

At the time I had been advocating that the Sierra Club initiate a second Remove Secretary Watt petition campaign, this time aimed at his successor. And now I was confronted with the need to praise Secretary Hodel for his brilliant suggestion. Here at last, I could assume, he had realized that because he had been wrong he didn't have to stay wrong.

The secretary, perhaps a bit stunned by San Francisco's abuse, said that what he wanted was a study of the proposal. We all know how long studies can take, and I would suggest that it is important to get on with the restoration of Hetch Hetchy Valley right away. Secretary Hodel and the Reagan administration could take credit for a major environmental achievement.

Let's do a cost-benefit analysis of the restoration ourselves, right here.

First, we have to take the dam down and we have no cost history of dam disassembly. We know that nature took down the Teton Dam, or the San Francisquito Dam, for example, and sent no bill at all (although the consequences were quite costly). Mountaineer George Bell, when he was working at Los Alamos and heard people joking about taking down Glen Canyon Dam, said, "Oh, I think we have something on the shelf at Los Alamos that could do that." His solution, alas, would result in excessive radioactivity. What else? I would suggest that we turn it over to the freeway builders. They make a practice of moving, or rather, removing mountains whenever the mountains are in the way of automobiles. A concrete mountain should present no insuperable problems. Failing that, try the Army Corps of Engineers, who among their strategies for causing the enemy difficulty would need to know how to produce a great deal of it by destroying a dam. Charge the cost to the Department of Defense, Maneuver Budget.

But don't forget, first, to get the reservoir level down to its minimum. We want no unnecessarily high water downstream.

Second, where will San Francisco get substitute water? The city will not need it. More water will be available every year at the present diversion point, below the Moccasin Creek Power Station. San Francisco has no wish to divert it earlier, because that would reduce hydroelectric revenue. And the city has bought and paid for, but does not use, five hundred thousand acre-feet of water storage space at the Don Pedro Reservoir—half again as much as was stored in Hetch Hetchy Valley. More water will be available because it can no longer be wasted through evaporation from a reservoir that no longer exists. There will be some added evaporation when the Hetch Hetchy water increases the evaporative area at Don Pedro, but there will still be a net gain in water available.

Third, how about the power revenue? There is no question but that less power will be generated. Although the potential energy of Hetch Hetchy Valley water is a constant (an acre-foot of water can create a kilowatt-hour of electricity for every foot it falls), present facilities are not adequate to divert the entire flow of the Tuolumne in the peak-flow months and to turn that entire potential into hydroelectric power, nor is the market presently scheduled to absorb all that electricity during the peak flow of the river. Moreover, there is nothing quite so nice as a reservoir full of water, with a valve below it to produce electricity in a hurry during the peak times of energy use.

Energy utilities have learned, however, how to survive without the delight of hydroelectricity for peaking power. They call it load management, and they can get customer cooperation by charging more for peak power and less for base power. They also know how to wheel power to each other's market areas, which can have different peak hours.

So when the Tuolumne River is flowing at its peak, San Francisco can hold all possible water in storage at the Lloyd and Eleanor reservoirs, divert as much as possible of flow through the lower tunnels, penstocks, and generators, and put the excess into the grid at dump-power rates. The city can raise the rates somewhat to its existing customers. And to make up for the difference, San Francisco can become a leader in energy conservation. It is hardly even a follower now. Invite Amory Lovins to town for advice on how to get in step and save money doing it.

This reform will not be free of hardship for city customers. But San Francisco has a debt to the nation. The city's total revenue from power from its Hetch Hetchy project's origin until now has far exceeded the cost of the facilities to produce it, and that excess has in effect been a free ride for San Francisco at a substantial cost to the people who have been denied the intangible benefits of Hetch Hetchy Valley for all those years. We are not talking about just "a campground," as Mayor Feinstein is reported to have described Hetch Hetchy. We are talking about an integral part of a national park that belongs not to San Francisco, not to California, not to the United States, but to the world as part of the World Heritage.

San Francisco owes us this one. It took Hetch Hetchy under false pretenses in the first place. The city claimed that no other site would do, and that was false. It claimed that a beautiful lake would be produced. That, too, was false. Don Pedro Dam could have been built in the first place, and a major scenic resource could have been retained, lakeless and beautiful. The proponents claimed that the dam would be easily covered with grasses and vines. To date, not a vine or a blade. The city agreed not to sell its electricity to a private utility, and violated that promise. It agreed to build roads and trails to provide recreational use elsewhere, and indeed built a few and contributes to their maintenance. They are no substitute for a restored Hetch Hetchy.

In summary, Auburn Dam and the Peripheral Canal are not needed to substitute for Hetch Hetchy Valley's storage. That is pure smokescreen.

Power generation will be reduced, but compensatory steps are feasible, and national parks do not exist to produce hydroelectric revenue for San Francisco. It will cost something to take the dam down, but not any six billion or anything within three orders of magnitude of that.

And it would cost San Francisco an infinite amount to build a separate-but-equal Hetch Hetchy Valley somewhere else and give it to whom it belongs.

What about the valley itself? What would it cost to restore it?

First, if whoever thought it would take the valley two years to dry out would go to the head of the reservoir next May, he or she would find that it had dried out too much already. The problem will not be to dry it out, but to keep it from blowing away.

Bear in mind that the lake became usable as a valley once before. Like Yosemite Valley, Hetch Hetchy Valley was a lake when the Tuolumne Glacier left the valley. The Merced Glacier left a spectacular Lake Yosemite when it retreated. The lake was half a mile deep beneath Glacier Point, at its head, and only one hundred feet or so deep beneath El Capitan. Slowly the Merced River filled the lake with sediment, but the lower twenty-five hundred feet of the lake could not be dried out. Ten thousand years later there is still a vast store of water in the interstices of the sediment, but that does not make Yosemite unusable. One excessive bit of drying out resulted when the El Capitan moraine–the glacier's farthest reach in its Wisconsin stage–was blasted and lowered a few feet. One theory has it that this lowering also lowered the water table in the valley and permitted an excessive encroachment of forest species that do not like wet feet. And once a forest gets started, its ever-deepening root system and its transpiration can accelerate the drying out.

Hetch Hetchy Valley has a similar history. So it will probably be necessary to expedite the growth of grass for the first year. Ask the Park Service people in Yosemite which grasses to use. They are experts in growing it where hotels and highways used to be. The California Native Plant Society could give advice about what to sow first to control the dust.

Leave the rest to nature, and enjoy the spectacle of recovery. The jay and squirrel are experts at planting oaks. The wind can find the seeds that know how to grow wings rather than use a bird's. The wind also carries a whole inventory of spores, so there come the ferns, mosses, and lichens. Pines and other conifers know how to roll seeds downhill, and Hetch Hetchy Valley owes its existence to hills. Happily, Hetch Hetchy Valley is narrow, and the forces of renewal can creep across it.

Watch the process. Record it with word and sketch, as John Muir would have done, or with your video camera, so that you can report nature's progress to others before the day is over.

I lived in Yosemite Valley for three years and have been visiting it for seventy. I have a rough idea of what might be brought to Hetch Hetchy Valley if people are too impatient to wait for nature.

Here is my list. Reintroduce oaks, maples, dogwood, mistletoe of course, azaleas, Douglas fir, ponderosa pine, incense cedar, yew, a lodgepole or two, and plant them in random order, not in regimented rows. Add frogs, crickets, and coyotes for night music. Daytime birds are welcome, especially canyon wrens. Squirrels too, gray squirrels preferred, because Muir liked them best. Foxes, raccoons, and bears, but a limited visa for bears that have become addicted to human dietary habits. Add an eager throng of tourists, and all the wise owls you can get.

To all of them, WELCOME BACK HOME!

Urge the National Park Service to begin work on a master plan for the restored Hetch Hetchy Valley right away, asking the public for ideas.

Above all, feel blessed that you are able to watch all this happen, and that your children may even have a hard time finding the bathtub ring the reservoir left on the valley walls, the dead zone that was caused by the ever-rising and falling reservoir. Lichens will come back, though slowly. Trees and shrubs will plant themselves on the ledges, with no fear of being drowned next June. Exfoliation of the granite walls will continue, and resume where it was interrupted. Rocks will fall, and the rockfall scars will soften the edges of the old bathtub rings, and lichens will soften the scars. Just don't let MCA paint the rocks the way they once did in Yosemite Valley to improve the background for a film they were shooting. The signs at the Yosemite entrances will no longer say "All campgrounds full" quite so soon. You will have a fair chance of getting a reservation without waiting a year or so at Hetch Hetchy Lodge or in the tent cabins at Camp Muir. From the Park Service visitor center there will be daily tours, led by rangers or docents, explaining each new achievement in Hetch Hetchy Valley's recovery. Wildlife will reoccupy each restored habitat. For a while, there won't be much campfire smoke because wood will not have grown long enough to die and become fuel. So you'll have a good shot at the stars each clear night. Wapama Falls will make sound again, because there will be people around to hear it. (Of course, it has been making noise all the time, but what good does it do?) Kolano Rock will be admired again in its splendor. The Tuolumne River will remember the score it used to play and you will hear its music again. Wary trout will lurk in it (the unwary having made some angler happy).

Creation will resume, and the annual deadly flooding will cease. Hetch Hetchy Valley will return to its original owner.

Earth Island Journal, **Summer 1987**

A LETTER TO A NEW DIRECTOR OF THE NATIONAL PARK SERVICE

IN MAY 1989, I was in my Mecca, Yosemite Valley, visiting Garrett DeBell, author of environmental handbooks—three so far—about his work as ecological consultant to the Yosemite concessionaire. He handed me a most encouraging document, the likes of which I had never expected to see or to respond to so soon, and with such delight. My missive to James M. Ridenour, newly appointed director of the National Park Service, was on its way June 23, rather presumptuous, but hardly more so than one would expect from a septuagenarian bearing battle scars—how many of them self-inflicted?—from a half-century of attempts to protect and augment the national parks. The letter is a distillation, I insist, without really expecting to be believed. Hang on!

Dear Mr. Ridenour:

Herewith I am taking advantage of your remarkable paper, "Philosophical Thoughts on National Park Service," written upon your being named director of the National Park Service, succeeding William Penn Mott. Your paper, dated April 17, 1989, provides an unexpected opportunity for me to discuss your philosophy without your having to reply.

I'll start with your numbered remarks, and freewheel it from there. In my own comment, I'll present what I think are my complementary thoughts. In a letter of May 10 I presented, with pleasure, my complimentary remarks. You may not have seen it. This is what it said:

"For an uncounted number of times since my first visit to Yosemite National Park in 1918—seventy-one years ago—I have made my pilgrimage to Yosemite Valley to see Yosemite Falls at their peak. The falls are beautiful, as expected. The unexpected delight of this trip was my chance to see your 'Philosophical Thoughts on National Park Service, April 17, 1989.' I hasten to thank you for what you have written and, more than that, to congratulate you for its clarity of expression and nobility of purpose. Your statement, by coincidence, has reached me just as I was undertaking, in Yosemite Valley, to write the chapter on the national-park idea for my autobiography. If you have no objection, I should like to take your thirty-two points as my basic outline, adding a few of my thoughts—consonant ones—to what you have said.

"I had intended to write a separate chapter on national parks of the future. You seem to have anticipated me. I shall nevertheless try to think of something to add.

"Just today I happened to meet Yosemite Superintendent (now Associate Director) John Morehead and Yosemite Park & Curry Company President Ed Hardy. I spoke to them briefly of my delight with what you have written, and am sharing this letter with them.

"At an early opportunity I should like to meet with you and discuss my own feelings about what the National Park Service can contribute to the era of environmental restoration now being entered. I should like to add my encouragement that it include the restoration to Yosemite National Park of the second yosemite it contains, Hetch Hetchy Valley. We strongly supported Secretary Hodel's bold proposal and believe it can inhere to San Francisco's advantage, not to mention that of the rest of the world.

"Thank you again. You made my year! More exactly you made my fifty-first year of campaigns in behalf of the national-park idea.

"DRB"

The June 23 letter is a philosophical discussion about the national parks and the park idea that Mr. Ridenour's letter led me to.

Mr. James M. Ridenour [henceforth JMR]: 1. Additional units of the National Park System should truly be places of national significance.

DRB: National significance, in its practical application, is evolving. The original national parks were spectacular, as in Yosemite, or curious, as in Yellowstone's thermal phenomena, combined with its spectacular display of wild animals. They were areas for which there was little if any competitive use in view. There are still spectacular places to save, but there are also ecosystems that are not spectacular but contain biological diversity of national or international importance. When they are understood, they will merit page-one attention as well as books and television specials. They probably harbor endangered species that we have not yet identified—samples of the millions of species of plants and animals that are in that category. The danger to them is that they will be destroyed by development before we learn that they exist and what we are destroying. In short, the national-park idea, as it develops, needs to encompass wildness that we cannot replace but can only spare and celebrate. This does not mean that the National Park Service must administer these places, but that it should take the lead in discovering them and seeing that they are afforded protection.

JMR: 2. We must continue to pursue a course of stewardship that allows us to conserve and protect these national treasures.

DRB: It is important that stewards undertake their task as if they were children, open to learning, able to listen eloquently to the message wildness has to teach, realizing that the message is indeed not fully understood. We have barely begun to understand it.

We will begin to understand even better if we add "restore" to "conserve and protect." The National Park Service is perhaps without peer in what it has learned about healing areas that people have bruised or severely wounded. There is much much more to learn, particularly where the wounds have been mortal, and the task of restoring what was there is like piecing together a jigsaw puzzle after a hurricane. Success is unlikely, but the effort itself will be at once rewarding and salutary. The National Park Service should take the lead in building a national ethic for restoration and a curriculum for its practice.

JMR: 3. Our first responsibility is to make sure that we are properly safeguarding the treasures we now possess.

DRB: What we have learned through bitter experience is that proper safeguarding requires more than a castle wall or moat. It also requires peripheral zoning. The national-park gem needs a handsome setting, even as a beautiful home needs a garden. More about this later.

Safeguarding requires something else that has been too long overlooked. It needs protection from overprotection. The great sequoia parks of the Sierra Nevada provide the immediate example. Overprotection has threatened their survival. Natural fires caused by lightning, or fires lit by Indians once they had arrived on the scene, kept competitive species under control and permitted regeneration of sequoias. For example, the Mariposa Grove of Big Trees, set aside by President Lincoln in 1864, was totally protected from fire and thereby made vulnerable to a greater hazard—the blocking of regeneration of sequoias and the unchecked growth of such competing species as white fir to an extent that threatens the old trees with crown fires to which they had previously been almost immune. Had prescribed burning (Indian-like fires) been practiced from the beginning, all would have been well. The underbudgeted attempt to correct the overprotection too rapidly has caused unnecessary damage to an irreplaceable scenic resource. The Calaveras Grove State Park provides an example of how properly to carry out a program of prescribed burning. The Sequoia National Park example is outrageous.

JMR: 4. Operating within the bounds of fiscal reality and common sense, we should add appropriate acreage to the National Park System.

DRB: Fiscal reality and common sense lead inevitably to one conclusion: if the acreage is appropriate, it should be purchased while the price is within reach, and in this matter time is even more of the essence than usual. A pay-as-you-go plan for acquisition can mean pay-through-the-nose acquisition because you didn't go sooner. We know enough about the escalation of prices for land to know that we must act swiftly. We also know how impossible it is to fund the restoration of land that has been paved with condominiums (greedlocked, shall we say?). That land will cost us an arm and a leg.

Therefore, park and wildland bond issues are in order at all levels of government, and major foundations need to invest part of their capital in protecting critical areas while governments get their plans in order. This is one expenditure future generations will be grateful for, and willing to pick up the tab for—especially if we don't delay so long that it becomes an astronomical tab.

Incidentally, if the major foundations invest in such land, they themselves are likely to exert the pressure needed to get the government to play its own proper role before Lake Bonneville fills again [and icebergs return to Mono Lake].

JMR: 5. We should continue to explore innovative ways to preserve and protect lands other than by fee-simple purchase. Leases and easements are examples of areas to explore. There are many others.

DRB: The National Park Service should hold periodic conferences to explore the examples listed and to initiate many other routes to preservation and protection. One other way would be to improve upon the greenline park idea in New York's Adirondack Forest Preserve. Ownership may be varied so long as certain protective performance standards are established and adhered to.

For example, a Greater Yosemite Biosphere Reserve could be established, providing that existing ownership could continue or, considering the several federal and state agencies involved, that existing management could continue so long as performance standards are adhered to. One, for example, could be that existing wildlands would not be encroached upon and areas now developed would be enhanced and other areas now derelict would be restored. Private owners and their heirs would receive tax incentives or other subsidies for meeting the standards, their holdings to be transferred to government ownership, at appropriate level, and with due compensation, should they fail to perform well.

What is proposed above is merely a guideline for guidelines.

It is important to remember what happened to the south end of Lake Tahoe owing to a lack of performance standards, and what did not happen at nearby Echo Lakes, where performance standards have been set and adhered to by the Forest Service and cabin owners on land leased from the Forest Service.

I believe there is an important and appropriate role for another federal agency in putting such national biosphere reserves together—the Bureau of Land Management, renamed the Public Land Service to express its more progressive and exciting role.

JMR: 6. As a nation, we should be moving toward the goal of acquiring parklands close to the people. It is essential that all levels of government work together in a spirit of cooperation in this objective.

DRB: This is a noble idea, but it requires new performance standards for interagency committees – the goal is to serve the public, not to tend agency turf. In 1956 I proposed a national Scenic Resources Review, which was not well named, the purpose of which was lost sight of when the name was changed to Outdoor Recreation Resources Review. This led to the short-lived Bureau of Outdoor Recreation. Much more than recreation is at stake. What is needed is a broad public understanding of the meaning of wildness to civilization.

We should try again. This time, forget turf-tending. Whoever's turf it may end up being, the National Park Service should revive its effort to bring parks to the people. Let it become the nation's park clearinghouse.

JMR: Each opportunity will be unique and should be evaluated on its merit. There are times when federal ownership is warranted; there are times when state or local ownership makes more sense. There may be times when combinations, including the private sector or foundations, make sense. Outright fee-simple federal ownership is not the automatic "correct" answer to our nation's need for more parklands.

DRB: My comments above are in agreement with what you state here – and with what I stated at Tuolumne Meadows in 1984 when I spoke at the dedication of Mount Ansel Adams and Yosemite's being added to the World Heritage. At that time I advocated the Greater Yosemite National Park, to be extended eastward to the farthest shore of ancient Mono Lake, westward to Lake McClure, and north and south into National Forest land as appropriate. I was advocating multiple ownership roles at the time, and Mono County Supervisor Andrea Lawrence gave me the term I was looking for: performance standards.

The automatic correct answer is to get more wildlands, not necessarily parklands, set aside while they are set-aside-able.

JMR: 7. We have an obligation to be a global leader in our environmental ethic and in resource management in its broadest sense. We must continue to expand our efforts to gather baseline scientific data for use in making the best possible resource management decisions.

DRB: One National Park Service role in global leadership that needs fuller augmentation is the NPS role with respect to the World Heritage System. New initiative is badly needed. The system needs a new, bold approach.

The natural areas included as of early 1989 consist largely of places already protected by national-park status or set aside as equivalent reserves. One hundred two nations have signed the World Heritage Convention of 1972, but only sixty natural areas have been included. In the United States they include Yosemite, Yellowstone, Mesa Verde, the Redwoods, Grand Canyon – all great places, fully worthy of being included, and a splendid foundation for what still needs to be added. Before the convention was proposed by President Nixon (and it was Russell Train's idea) a group of us, including Russ, John Milton, Ray Dasmann, Noel Simon, and Frank Fraser Darling, came up with a list of one hundred areas that ought to be included but only a few of these have yet been included.

We had conceived of large exhibit-format volumes, similar to the twenty-five produced by the Sierra Club and the ten by Friends of the Earth, for each of the hundred candidates. Two volumes on the Galapagos Islands and one on Mount Everest helped in protecting these places in the World Heritage. Those on Kauai, the Brooks Range, the Golden Coast of Georgia, and Baja California have not succeeded yet. The missing areas and missing volumes are still on my agenda.

A World Heritage Trust Fund exists, but is not widely enough known. It needs the kind of attention given the World Wildlife Fund. The U.S. budget for the World Heritage is miniscule, in no way adequate to get the job done in time, and now is the time for all private foundations and individuals to get to work. What we save in the next few years, as Allen Morgan said in the mid-sixties, is all that will ever be saved. Places did not disappear as fast as he expected then. They are disappearing faster now.

JMR: 8. Just as the world has become a global economy, we are increasingly bound together in our environmental world. It is in our own self-interest that we show, by leadership and example, our strong commitment to environmental protection. We have the ability to influence global thinking on many important environmental issues.

DRB: It may be helpful in assuming this role for the NPS to downplay self-interest; our self-interest is not always pleasing to other nations. It is possible that we have much to learn from cultures that are senior to our own, and that have lived with their land ten times longer than we have lived with ours. It may be well for us to remember that the success of American culture is based in large part on oil, which is near exhaustion, and on a resource of soil the fertility of which is already badly depleted. Perhaps our hubris grew too well in our soil and exhausted it.

Considering the ephemeral quality of the resources that fueled our rise to power, and noting from history how rises have been followed by falls, and noting also that humanity has yet to produce a sustainable society, we may be wise to go forth to learn others' good habits, and not to teach our bad ones.

While we consider the wisdom of being a little humble, we can be proud of what I think has been our finest export—the national-park idea. I'll go along with Jerry Mander, who wrote the most innovative of Sierra Club ads, one urging that we treat the earth as a conservation district in the universe, a sort of Earth National Park.

Let our National Park Service spread the word!

JMR: 9. We should explore creative ways to work with private groups and individuals to further our goals and objectives in protecting valuable land. As an example, the Indiana Heritage Protection Campaign has raised $5 million in private funds to be matched by an equal amount of money by the state legislature for the purpose of purchasing and maintaining areas of critical concern to the state. Other states have passed similar legislation.

I encourage you to identify opportunities to work with foundations, private sources of revenue, both corporations and individuals, that would help us in furthering the goals and objectives of the National Park Service.

DRB: Being a Californian, I must counter with some examples from California. The Save-the-Redwoods League, in its seventy-three-year history, has raised sixty million dollars to save 150,000 acres of redwoods in thirty-two California state parks. That investment is now worth $2 billion—but is not for sale. Since the California State Park System was founded in 1928, the people of California have voted many more millions in bonds for the purchase of state parklands. The Nature Conservancy has raised millions for preservation of endangered California ecosystems. One of their big contributions was the raising of $4.5 million to acquire Santa Cruz Island for the National Park Service. The Trust for Public Land has protected 53,890 acres, worth $123,600,000, for urban and rural conservation purposes. There are many county land trusts in California striving to protect open space and amenity.

The federal government picked up a huge tab for Redwood National Park and Point Reyes National Seashore. The California state government protects 1,250,000 acres in its State Park System, most of it in fee ownership. Of the total, 154,000 acres have been acquired through arrangements with the Bureau of Land Management, the Forest Service, the Bureau of Reclamation, the Coast Guard, the State Land Commission, the Department of Water Resources, and city and county resources.

For all this progress, we have not been able to keep ahead of developers. One issue of the *New York Times* (May 16, 1989, which I picked up to read just before writing this comment on national parks) announced a $2-billion plan to build ten thousand condominium apartments on beachfront land in Queens, a $9-billion plan to build a new city of thirty-five thousand on the Southern California desert in Antelope Valley, and a $274-million highway extension to be bulldozed through one of Atlanta's most affluent neighborhoods in order to accommodate a $10-billion development. My own rule of thumb is that one should budget about fifteen percent for promotion, which would mean that the proposals reported in that one day's *Times* would budget $3 billion for promotion, ample for buying all the legislative influence that would be needed. State after state seems determined to develop another Los Angeles in a nation that deserves only one. That is why park acquisition must be expedited.

It is for this reason that I have come to believe our only salvation lies in the control, perhaps the reversal, of the addiction to growth. We need the courage to face, and accept blame for, the cost of addictive growth to the Earth and to the future of humanity.

It occurred to me on the day I read of those multi-billion-dollar developments and had just been driven past acres of derelict land within the New York metropolitan area, that it would be salutary to restore Manhattan to its pristine state and get the beads back from the Indians.

JMR: 10. The Park Service is well known for its efforts to work effectively with volunteers. Efforts to increase and expand volunteerism should become even more important in our agenda than ever before. People want to help; it is up to us to figure out the best way to utilize the spirit and interest of volunteers.

DRB: One of the best ways to reach volunteers is through the host of conservation organizations. For example, the Sierra Club has been concerned about national parks twenty-four years longer than the National Park Service has, enlisting public and Congressional support for their establishment and protection and for the creation of the National Park Service itself. The National Parks and Conservation Association was founded for this purpose with the support of the first NPS director, Stephen T. Mather. The Wilderness Society, though initially more concerned with national forests than with national parks, now remains deeply concerned with the most important resource within national parks—their wilderness.

The three organizations listed are but a sample of the potential human resource ready to help complete, protect, restore, and inform the public about the National Park System. Philanthropists and enlightened corporations have made major contributions. Some individuals have given their time, if not their money. My own participation began in 1938 in the campaign to establish Kings Canyon National Park. I am credited with contributing to the establishment of five other national-park areas. I hope to work for many more and for good protection for them all. Almost all my own contribution came through the Sierra Club, and the club's through the influence of John Muir, father of the national parks.

All this is just to suggest what enormous organizational resources are available to the National Park Service in citizen organizations.

JMR: 11. Education, both internal and external, has always been a mainstay in Park Service programs. Our interpretation program enjoys a worldwide reputation of excellence. With President Bush and Secretary Lujan strongly supporting efforts in this area, I urge you to examine our programs with the goal of further strengthening our education commitment.

DRB: From my own experience, I would say that the interpretive program has been stronger in the past than it is now. Horace Albright recommended to President Eisenhower, as I understand it, that the program be de-emphasized and that rangers get back to being rangers, not interpreters. The Yosemite School of Field Natural History suffered a severe setback as a result. This had been a major educational effort strongly supported by philanthropist C. M. Goethe. It brought many volunteers into fieldwork important to the understanding of Yosemite's landforms, biota, and management—all under the guidance of the park naturalist and his interpretive team.

The educational programs themselves could give more attention than they presently do to the national-park idea, how it developed, and how it is spreading. The battle between John Muir and Gifford Pinchot still continues on the land, and the National Park Service and the national parks would benefit if the interpreters would explain why Muir was right.

JMR: 12. We must strengthen and expand our efforts to recruit and promote women and minorities. This effort should be reflected in our internal education and training programs, and we should encourage external institutions from which we traditionally recruit to strengthen their efforts to recruit, train, and provide educational opportunities for women and minorities.

DRB: Here is an extraordinary opportunity to broaden support for protecting and restoring the earth's life-support system. Have these women and minorities, once trained, accompany roadshows that can revive the program of bringing national parks to the people. The diverse hues of the park interpreters—hues of the human rainbow—could build a new kind of support for parks and for the environment as a whole.

The building of new parks in restored urban areas—restored in large part through volunteer effort—has proved to be of great social value. The Trust for Public Land can provide data on this. So can landscape architect Karl Linn, who is now working for the Earth Island Institute.

JMR: 13. Our work force and the facilities and lands we supervise must be drug free. We must commit to this goal servicewide and do everything in our power to help battle this scourge that threatens us as a people and as a nation.

DRB: Assuming that caffeine, alcohol, nicotine, and gasoline are not included in the drug category, my comment here can best begin with a statement by Phil Frank through *Farley,* his cartoon appearing daily in the *San Francisco Chronicle.*

The drug problem does not originate in the lack of police, judges, jails, and border guards. It originates in the lack of hope, in frustration, in boredom, in the feeling of powerlessness, and in the need to escape from the resulting melancholy. If people can't get there any other way, they travel by the drug route.

Like Thoreau, these people can learn, with National Park Service help, to "travel widely in Concord"—to find a new and rewarding kind of excitement in the ever-changing, always mysterious way that nature works. If these people, through National Park Service instigation of

Reprinted by permission of Phil Frank, San Francisco Chronicle.

imaginative programs, can be put to work restoring the place in which they live, in building their sense of place, in teaching and guiding others, they will have made a major step toward changing the grim reality they have known to the bright one they deserve a chance to know. There is a green movement building around the world, not a moment too soon. Let its goal be Farley's – Improve Reality!

JMR: *User fees*

1. User fees are an appropriate method of providing support to the National Park System; however, fees should be appropriate to the services provided and should not prohibit the use of our parks by anyone on the basis of economic status.

2. Those who prefer more costly service should expect to pay for the level of service provided. For example, a campsite that has electricity, water, and a sanitary sewer hookup, should cost an appropriate amount when compared to a primitive campsite with few amenities.

3. Prices for the use of national park facilities should be kept as reasonable as possible and should not be significantly out of line with comparable services provided in the public sector.

4. The philosophy should be that all are welcome to the park at a minimal cost where entrance fees are charged. Once inside the park, the individual or family may, by choice, opt for services provided at an appropriate cost or may tour and recreate on the lands with little or minor additional financial commitment.

DRB: The public attitude toward user fees, once hostile, now seems one of understanding – recognition that the parks the public owns are a great bargain and well worth contributing to. In a way it is unfortunate that the most heavily used national park area, the Golden Gate National Recreation Area, collects no user fee.

You appropriately use the word *appropriate* four times and *reasonable* only once. Would it be appropriate and reasonable to extend the method of collecting the user fees that are used to pay, for example, for the free shuttle buses that have been such a boon to Yosemite Valley? The concessioner picks up the cost of the buses. To pick up the revenue, the concessioner adds an appropriate amount to what the visitor pays for food, lodging, and other services.

If this proves workable (or if it indeed has already worked elsewhere as it has for Yosemite shuttle buses), I am ready to propose a restoration fee, to be collected at the point of sale for everything we buy, to finance the essential task of keeping the life-support system in working order everywhere. In other words, replacement pricing. You pay enough to provide means for replacing what you just bought. This is a device to avoid our taking the best for ourselves and leaving the dregs for the children.

JMR: *Role of the concessioner*

1. Concessioner operations play a vital role in Park Service delivery systems. It is doubtful that the Park Service could deliver the level of service that the public demands without the assistance of concession-run operations within the park.

2. I support and encourage the concept of joint government/private arrangements of providing needed service to the public as long as the public is well served and the government receives an appropriate proportion of the revenue stream. It is my philosophy that where appropriate the Park Service should enter into businesslike arrangements with the private sector where the public can expect that its government is adequately protected and compensated for the use of public lands by private concessioners.

DRB: If there is anything to suggest here, it is that concern should not be limited to appropriate distribution of the revenue stream. I have been influenced by Ansel Adams enough to think there should be more attention to what flows in the gift-shop stream and its appropriateness to the national park. If, for example, the public visiting the national park in Nairobi were to demand ivory products, the public should accept being disappointed. What is presented for purchase in a national park ought to be related to enjoyment and understanding of the park and why the park is there, not to its contribution to the revenue stream.

I would gladly see national park gift shops everywhere sell souvenir fragments of the dam at Hetch Hetchy in Yosemite, the fragment accompanied by a congratulatory note thanking the purchasers for their role in carrying away the garbage, thus helping restore Hetch Hetchy Valley to what it was before San Francisco dammed it for its hydroelectric potential.

JMR: *Land and water conservation fund*

1. I have been and remain a supporter of the concept of this fund. It has a proved track record of being one of the best "tools in the bag" to help preserve, conserve, and protect our public lands. President Bush has

indicated his support of this program to the extent our financial situation will allow, and I believe we will continue to see some form of this program in the future.

2. The concept of comprehensive planning for our recreation and resource needs at all levels of government is as valid today as it has been for many years. I support these planning efforts at all levels of government and would urge continuation of this program.

DRB: Having had a hand in the fund's creation, I support it, too, and regret that its use has been placed on hold too long. It is related to the replacement-pricing concept. If we are giving up something permanently for our own present benefit, such as the oil we find and burn up, we should invest comparably in something we preserve permanently, such as wilderness. When we so invest, we are accommodating more than recreation and resource needs in the ordinary sense of the words. We are preserving the ultimate encyclopedia of nature, the irreplaceable source of information about how the world works. The land and water fund can continue to contribute to this, but needs to be augmented by further investment while the price is right. Meanwhile, the land and water fund should be considered a trust fund, independent of the federal budget. What comes from severance should go to restoration. This has worked especially well in California in the Investing for Prosperity Program invented by Huey Johnson when he was California's secretary of resources.

JMR: *Historic preservation*

1. I am in firm support of the basic philosophy behind our historic preservation efforts. As a country, we need to be mindful of our past, its inherent natural features, and the beauty and culture we have created.

2. I believe the tax incentive program has done more for historic preservation than almost any mechanism I can think of—and it has done it in a way that has created economic momentum in our communities. Much of our country's history and culture would have met the wrecking ball had it not been for this innovative program.

3. I do have a concern that there has been a trend to exclude those not of the "professional historic community" from this program. During my years as state historic preservation officer of Indiana, I witnessed an ever tightening of the maze that complicates the submittal of an application to have a property considered for the National Register of Historic Places.

Those who hire architects, historians, and good lawyers who know the buzzwords that state and federal officials want to hear often get properties on the National Register with few problems. Those without the means to hire consultants sometimes give up in frustration while trying to figure out the tangle of the system.

I do not want to see these people and the places of historic significance they represent left out of the system and will work to see that it does not happen.

DRB: That the National Park Service has developed and continues to play a role in historic preservation is of great political importance to the service. This role gives the service a voice in many communities in which it would otherwise hardly be heard of or from. The Army Corps of Engineers learned this long ago, when they came up with the idea that a dam or work project in every congressional district was good politics.

This gain needs to be used to strengthen the major purpose of the National Park Service—protecting the primeval national parks and the wilderness the national-park idea protects better than has any other concept.

Older nations have their antiquities—the pyramids, the temples, the forums, the coliseums. We cannot compete with these. The American antiquities are the great wilderness reaches we have saved. Other nations have lost theirs without thinking about what the loss would mean to their future. I still want to publish a book entitled *These Are the American Antiquities,* demonstrating among other things how important our National Antiquities Act of 1906 has been to their being preserved.

JMR: 4. Our archaeological history cries for survey. Realistically, there is not enough money in our entire budget to survey properly all the lands under public ownership, let alone the lands in private hands. Within the bounds of available funds and common sense, I ask that we add to our base of knowledge whenever and wherever possible and that we preserve and protect those areas and artifacts of value that we find. The sanctity of burial grounds must be respected, and I ask that you work with state and local governments to see that we do our part.

DRB: It would seem appropriate for the National Park Service to deepen its historic-site preservation role and thus accommodate and protect national archaeological sites. The next National Park Service budget should be increased to cover this role. [I should know but do not: Is new legislation necessary to give the NPS this function?] Although the NPS has present budget constraints, can the NPS lean on archaeological budgets and expertise at universities and museums, they in turn leaning on the National Science Foundation? I am not aware of the existence of an archaeological action group having a tax status that allows it to be fully active in the legislative, hence political, arena. There should be, and perhaps the NPS can encourage its being formed. We are already having too much trouble protecting burial sites and other sacred grounds, and I remember all too well the shortcomings of salvage archaeology in such places as Glen Canyon, where there wasn't enough time or budget to permit the collection of essential data before Lake Powell was allowed to inundate the sites.

To reverse your comment a little, I should like to see the NPS work with state and local governments to persuade *them* to do *their* part.

JMR: *Management style*

1. I am not nor do I intend to become a micro manager. I expect to work with you as Park Service employees to set the tone and direction, but I fully expect you to carry out the objective once it has been set.

2. I expect short, concise summaries of documents you want to call to my attention.

3. When decisions are to be made, I will expect that alternatives will be researched and presented. I will also ask that you have a recommendation for my consideration.

4. Once I am familiar with our operation and people you may find that I call directly on people in the field for answers to questions from time to time. This is not done to undermine the chain of command, but it is my way of getting at information I need immediately. You may want to ask employees who report to you and whom I call or visit to inform you of all that takes place. This is fine with me; my goal is to speed up the process and not set up animosity within your areas.

5. When the public makes inquiries of us, I expect to be as responsive as possible and in a timely fashion. In order to be as consistent as possible in our responses, I ask that we strengthen the communications links between those responsible for public information in our offices. As soon as I get a feel for the paperwork load, I expect to set a reasonable turnaround time for the answering of inquiries. Even if the answer is going to take considerable time to prepare I find that a short note to the sender indicating we are working on an answer engenders much good will.

6. Once I get settled in, I will increase my travel schedule as much as can be reasonably expected. I fully intend to get out in the field; I know from experience that it is difficult to imagine the full consequences of a problem or opportunity from behind a desk at headquarters.

7. I hope to meet and talk with as many employees as possible in order to get a broad feel for our situation. Let's be serious, but not take ourselves too seriously, and let's enjoy ourselves.

DRB: This sounds a little more military than park people have been accustomed to ever since the U.S. Army was succeeded by the U.S. National Park Service in park protection and operation. What is not intended to undermine the chain of command may nevertheless undermine it. This is just an observation from outside, but is based on fifty years of management experience, including army schools and combat operations. I have had quite a bit of experience with Park Service and concessioner leaders and employees. I think most of them are where they are because of their love of national parks, and would like to be assured that the director loves them, too, and wants Park Service people to persuade the public to love the parks for what is there, not for the artifacts that are added.

Your statement is delightful appreciation of the great poems the parks are, in their context of everyday national prose.

If we lose the wildness that exists in the National Park System, we cannot restore it. We can reassemble some parts, but we will be running on retreads and, in a way, on empty. There is still an opportunity to extend the protection afforded by the national-park idea to still other superlative areas. There is the opportunity to add to their protection by building better buffers around them. There is still the opportunity to spread around the earth Thoreau's message that "in wildness is the preservation of the world" and to help the world understand why.

This is the mission of the National Park Service as I see it.

A few other bits of evidence concerning my various national-park biases are contained in my foreword to *At Home in the Wild: New England's White Mountains,* with its bit of history; in my narration for the film *Wilderness Alps of Stehekin,* one of our tools for establishing the North Cascades National Park; and in my narration for the film *Two Yosemites,* made to help save Dinosaur National Monument from dams and now, I hope, useful in saving Hetch Hetchy Valley from the dam that is already there. I could send these to you if I have not exhausted you already.

Here's to a new and dynamic role for the National Park Service in the Restoration Movement!

Mr. Ridenour responded a week later:

"Just a quick note to let you know I have received your thoughts of June 23, and forgive you for the length of your writing. I am a relatively young pup, though aging fast – I have known of you for all my adult years and I am flattered that you took the time to respond to my rather random thoughts.

"I have a long plane trip this weekend where I will find the time to read your thoughts more carefully but I must say I was delighted with my first, rather hurried, quick reading. Of course, you may use my thoughts in any way you see appropriate.

"I got a kick out of your comments on management style and would agree that they are a little forced. I did that on purpose as former directors and others cautioned me not to allow the day-to-day crush of the bureaucracy to keep me from accomplishing things on a larger scale. That is why I am trying to force brushfires to be fought at the level of the organization closest to the fires and not to clog up my office. So far I haven't been successful, but I am still trying.

"I am in complete agreement with your thoughts on fire. We routinely used it in Indiana to preserve our few remaining prairie remnants. First appointments are here – must run – more later.

"Thanks."

A Park Experience

There Is One Especially Good Place to be to discuss the national-park idea—Yosemite Valley, where the idea began. Yellowstone precedes Yosemite alphabetically, but not historically, and the National Park Service has great difficulty getting this straight. Almost a decade before the campfire where people wondered how to preserve Yellowstone's strange natural curiosities, the idea of protecting nature for itself was mature enough to be put into legislative form.

In 1864 President Abraham Lincoln signed the bill setting aside Yosemite Valley and the Mariposa Grove of Big Trees for the nation and the future. There was no National Park Service or equivalent national agency to administer and protect Yosemite, so this task was delegated to the State of California. Hot Springs National Reserve was senior to it, but was a curiosity, like Yellowstone. California accepted the assignment and handled it well, but not well enough.

Yellowstone was set aside to protect its geysers and surrounding terrain in 1882. Wyoming did not yet exist as a state so the federal government retained control. Thus, in a literal sense, it became the second national park, preceded by Hot Springs National Reserve. But neither was preceded by an inquiry into what the national-park concept was or could become. Hot Springs was too early, and Yellowstone too late. Yosemite was the place, the first park set aside by the U.S. Congress to be preserved for the nation's benefit.

Yosemite, then, was the first national park worthy of the name. Yellowstone was the first National Park for those who think capitalizing the N and the P should determine precedence.

I do not. But then, I am prejudiced, at this writing celebrating the seventy-first anniversary of my first visit to Yosemite. When I lived here from 1935 to 1938, the number of visitors hit one-half million, and they made more impact on the valley than three million visitors are making fifty years later.

I have seen two kinds of impact from increased visitors. In 1952 I observed, in the foreword to the Sierra Club book, *Going Light—With Backpack or Burro,* that people who worried about the crowd on the valley floor should bear in mind that the density of visitors drops according to the square of the distance from the highway and the cube of the elevation above it on the valley walls. But now there seem to be waiting lists for the people who want to climb the walls, whereas the automobile traffic has been substantially reduced thanks to the shuttle-bus system run by the concessionaire and financed, wisely and to everyone's advantage, by a slight addition to the cost of food and pillow space.

John Muir wanted more people to visit Yosemite Valley. They are there. He wanted automobiles admitted, too. My guess is that he would gladly head a move to get them out. So would I.

Although John Muir would hardly recognize the Sierra Club of today, he would have no trouble recognizing Yosemite Valley. For all the things that have gone wrong with its management, the principal resource, the valley itself, has been kept essentially intact, in spite of the three million people. Moreover, some of the old scars—caused by the racetrack, the sewage-treatment plant, and some old roads no longer needed—have been remarkably restored. Try to find the old Ahwahnee golf course, the highway across the Ahwahnee Meadow, the Old Sentinel Hotel and Cedar Cottage, the Indian Canyon trail, the old Oak Flat Road.

When I lived in Yosemite I worked for the Yosemite Park & Curry Company and, even though fired by the company, was impressed by its managers' concern for the valley. So, as I say, I am prejudiced. Even more so now, as I marvel at the genius with which the impact of six million human feet is kept to a minimum.

Anne, Ken, and I are now in full view of Upper Yosemite Fall. A huge cumulus is moving toward the notch from which the great fall drops, reminding us how its water got there in the first place. The warmth of the sun tells where the energy came from that put the cloud there. Yosemite Point rises an abrupt three thousand feet above us. To its left is the Lost Arrow, the summit of which I had predicted would never be climbed, possibly because I had absolutely no interest in ever being there myself. My prediction was rendered invalid the next year.

Peaking through the ponderosa foliage to the right is something less appalling, the Arrowhead, and Morgan Harris and I felt quite comfortable there in 1937, when we made the first ascent with two movie cameras recording our good fortune.

Between the Lost Arrow and the Arrowhead is the Yosemite Point Couloir. Morg, Torcom Bedayan, and I were first to find a way up this shortcut to the north rim. I remember just one place where I felt uneasy. That was back in the days when exposure to anything more than twenty feet of uninterrupted air beneath my feet could make me uneasy. It looks to me as if present-day climbers require two thousand feet to achieve the same unease.

Behind me is Sentinel Rock, where Morg and I fried in the sun in our first attempt on the west face but found a route up it easy enough for us. To its right, Taft Arête reminds me of Morg's and my first ascent of that alternate route from the valley floor, when Clyde Nelson and Bill Rice accompanied us, shortly before Bill lost his life climbing in the Tetons.

The arête was fun, but for sheer pleasure, my favorite Yosemite climb was with Bruce Meyer on the Lost Brother, just beyond Taft Arête and across the valley from the Three Brothers everybody knows. Morg and I traversed them. On the Middle Brother I almost fell, but somehow kept a foot and hand in place and swung out like a rusty gate, fully alarmed, until I somehow swung back and spared Morg the job of holding a fall. My swinging took some of the fun out of the climb.

The Lost Brother was all fun, with a spectacular long chimney to look out of as we climbed within it, deliciously secure. Best of all was the summit, spacious enough to relax on and to launch yodels from. There was freedom then that has been lost now. I could camp where I wished, build fires where I wished, drink giardia-free water almost everywhere, and yodel at will.

John McPhee didn't think I yodeled very well, but he simply didn't know what I was trying to do. You cannot expect a man who likes symphony, for example, to understand the intricacies of a thumb piano, or vice versa. There was a symphonic, thumb-piano quality to my yodeling, something I was able to get few others to understand. I almost mastered the European kind thanks to Hannes Schroll, whom I distressed only in my poor response to his ski teaching, not to his yodel teaching or to my yodeling in counterpoint with him in Yosemite's High Sierra.

What John McPhee didn't understand was my chords, of up to thirteen notes, my modulation, and the need for my incredible volume. All the yodel itself did was carry all this other baggage. What is essential is that there be a series of chords, free of dissonance, of good barber-shop variety but voiced better than average, in modulations that are exciting and beautiful (the progression in Liszt's "Liebestraum" will do), properly spaced, and very loud. The real ultimately religious requirement of yodeling is that you find a place where you can yodel in counterpoint with yourself. Echoes must come from a respectable, varying distance so that you can be silent and prepare to enjoy them. That means you have to start out with full volume. Each chord should come to you independently, one not crowding the other, all of them ignoring what a metronome might expect in mechanical timing. If you want a pretty progression, the chord notes must return to you separate and free. If, on the other hand, you want them to sound like magnificently voiced pipe-organ chords, another technique is required. That will be covered in Lesson Two. As I said, John McPhee could not be expected to know all this, and I'm glad he didn't ask.

If you want the best progression on earth, you must climb the Lost Brother, and hope that the people who would be bothered by your yodeling are somewhere else. There are no echoes like these anywhere else.

And that's why I have asked Bill Travers, who is helping me make sense of my autobiography, to check out the Lost Brother. His rock-climbing reminds me, as he tells of it, of my own earlier days. What I need to know is whether the kind of climb Bruce and I enjoyed so much forty-

Yodel music in Brower's hand.

eight years ago is something mountaineers are capable of enjoying now. And do well-placed, imaginatively modulated yodel chords still come back as superbly as they did? I ask, with a footnote here, if he would help future generations of climbers know that a climb does not have to be 5.11 to be fun and beautiful.

The thunderhead above Yosemite Falls is dwarfed by its overpowering rival above Glacier Point. For the moment, Anne, Ken, and I sit in sun that has driven us to shade. Only a few drops of rain have fallen so far. Rain or shine, I don't care. I'm home. Or will be as soon as I hear those echoes again.

You can't hear anything like them in Yellowstone. If for no other reason, that's why Yosemite is first.

But let's not argue. It is the idea that counts. Thoreau and Muir were right. Anywhere that's wild.

CHAPTER 10

NATIONAL FORESTS

A RUNNING BATTLE

DEAN MCCULLOUGH, when he headed the Forestry School at Oregon State (then) College, was not fond of conservation types who got in the way of logging, and at one point referred to them as the daffodil wing of the flower lovers, or of the birdwatchers. Whichever, it didn't go over very well with those of us who preferred forests to sawlog merchants. Dr. Karl Onthank, at the University of Oregon, asked for equal time at the next meeting of supervisors of Region VI of the U.S. Forest Service. Among other duties, Karl was dean of Oregon conservationists, faithfully supported in this work by his wife Ruth. They were instrumental in bringing Michael McCloskey and David Simons into conservation work.

Karl was granted the equal time he requested, and asked me to use it. I was more than delighted.

One of the few courses I had taken at Berkeley was Forestry 1, generally considered a pipe course. I was already fond of forests for what they were, and was distressed to see the primeval forests I had known from my first trips along the Lincoln Highway reduced to stump fields. In my Echo Lake days I was distressed by the trees killed by the Pacific Gas & Electric Company when it turned Desolation Valley into Lake Aloha. I didn't like the way the Forest Service played dirty in its opposition to Kings Canyon National Park. The service gave wilderness short shrift in its support of developing Mount San Gorgonio for skiing. It was urging a forest access road across the narrow waist of Sierra wilderness at Mammoth Pass. It performed despicably in its eagerness to log the finest Jeffrey pine forest of all along Highway 395 at Deadman Summit, near Mammoth Lakes. Having heard from a Mammoth Lakes resident, John Haddaway, how miserable the logging practices were at Deadman, I crossed the Sierra for his guided tour a day before Sierra Club directors were to get a Forest Service guided tour. The Forest Service showed us areas they had carefully tidied up, carefully skirting the areas that had been devastated.

Following this the regional forester told my directors that my trouble was that I didn't want any trees cut.

The Washington office of the Forest Service double-crossed Howard Zahniser in order, I am forced to infer, to build opposition to the Wilderness Bill. The service fought against the North Cascades National Park and Redwood National Park proposals, even as it had fought against the National Park Act in 1916 and the Antiquities Act, providing for presidential proclamation of national monuments, in 1906. It had fought against the proclamation of Olympic National Monument, and against the inclusion of adequate primeval forest in Olympic National Park. The service blocked the preservation of wilderness on the Sierra's Kern Plateau, which should be preserved in Sequoia National Park, and against the major Interior-Agriculture exchange I had proposed to save places of national-park caliber from timber interests. It would be against my proposal for a Scenic Resources Review, which even Bestor Robinson, my traditional opponent on the Sierra Club board, thought was a good idea.

Yes, I was more than delighted. It seemed appropriate to play a little trick on the foresters gathered in Portland. Through the efforts of Robert Wolf, a forester who would later move to the General Accounting Office, my talk was placed in the *Congressional Record* of May 17, 1957, by Senator Wayne Morse of Oregon. Both Oregon senators, especially Richard Neuberger, had good relations with the Sierra Club and me, and it was rewarding to see Senator Morse's introductory comments and to see my speech, trick and all, in print:

TODAY, WITH A VAST STORE of scientific knowledge and what we prefer to regard as a high level of intelligence, we look with tolerance on the superstitions and folklore of our ancestors. We appreciate the ingenuity often displayed in arriving at a wrong answer. We try to understand the mental inertia and the fear of the unfamiliar that caused backward peoples to resist the encroachments of scientific thinking.

But are we equally appreciative of some of the ready-made answers that today take the place of rational thinking and scientific investigation? Do we realize that our actions have been guided for many years by pronouncements made by the medicine men of forestry? Are we fully conscious of the extent to which we accept without question the traditional and sometimes fallacious beliefs that have established and continue to establish our attitudes toward forest economics? Are not many of us still planting our seeds of thought in the dark of the moon, and grinding up unicorns' horns to ward off the things we fear in the future?

This is not to imply that there is no constructive thinking being done in the field of forest economics today. Both in public service and in private industry a healthy scientific attitude can be found, and many sincere attempts are being made to understand and straighten out tangled relations.

But because studies in forest economics have been slow to develop, we have accepted doctrines and beliefs that have never been tested adequately. So firmly established is this body of bromide and folklore that it is almost heresy to question it, just as it was once heresy to question the movement of the sun around the earth or the displeasure of the gods that caused crops to fail and animals to die.

The dominance of the silviculturists in forestry has been a major factor retarding the development of a sound body of economic doctrine. The belief that silvicultural perfection is the ultimate goal of forestry, and the preemptive assumption that what is silviculturally good is economically sound, often threaten to relegate forest economics to a minor role or to complete extinction.

But our actions are still influenced by the traditional emphasis on silviculture. From habit rather than as the result of rational processes we are inclined to conceive the most desirable forest to be one with fully stocked stands of a preferred species, rather than one that will provide the maximum returns in the form of watershed protection, game refuges, community support, useful products, and direct financial return. We fight what often seems to be a losing battle to protect a favored but disappearing species against insects, disease, fire, and cutting. We fail to consider the fact that protection from fire often encourages the less desirable species, or that the forest of useful species is often actually the product of long periods of uncontrolled natural fires. Only after years of fighting blister rust and fire, with expenditures running into millions of dollars, do we finally begin to question the economic justification of these efforts. Perhaps we should be devoting more effort to making the most of the so-called inferior species that seem destined to replace some of our old favorites.

The silvicultural bias leads us not only to an advocacy of cultural practices that may be uneconomic, but to a belief that it is wasteful to leave any land idle if forests would grow on it. Nature's opinion of a vacuum is nothing more than a mild dislike compared to an ardent forester's abhorrence of an idle acre. . . .

Part of the doctrine that has guided the thinking of many forestry protagonists is the belief that there will be profitable markets for all the timber that can be produced. If we err in our attempt to produce the correct quantity of timber for the future an excess would probably be more desirable than a deficit as a matter of public policy. But public policy should be justified on the basis of possible emergency or public security rather than by unsupported assumptions of future demand. The statement that future markets will take all the timber that can be produced may be true. Or it may only be wishful thinking. It is not true simply because it has been stated by some of our high priests and repeated over and over again. Nor can all the reasons advanced in support of this doctrine be accepted without question. . . .

The doctrine of unlimited demand is also supported by the belief in the indispensability of wood. It is true that wood is now necessary for railway ties, for newsprint, for bobbins and shuttles, and for crates. There is a preference for wood over other materials for many other uses. But the indispensability of wood has been challenged many times. New materials and new methods are constantly threatening markets for forest products. The idea of indispensability, much as we may like it, is another that is subject to question. . . .

The idea of sustained yield has been glorified by those who condemn forest destruction. But failure to define sustained yield precisely has encouraged its loose usage by forest owners and operators. Without complete and clear definition, sustained yield is almost meaningless. The forester may mean a high level of intensive cultural management, but the owner can use the term to describe a liquidation operation if he is holding and protecting his cutover lands. The public is taught that sustained yield is necessary to preserve our forest economy, and is lulled into a sense of security when it is told that millions of acres in private ownership are on a sustained-yield basis. (*Bromides and Folklore in Forest Economics,* Ralph W. Marquis, forest economist, United States Forest Service, Washington, D.C.)

As a group, foresters have done little to promote intelligent, productive use of the forest for recreation, or even to manifest much interest in it. It has been largely forced upon them by public demand. They have not been leaders but followers in respect to this resource. In this position, they are finding themselves faced with the necessity of solving problems for which they are not too well prepared with answers. Whether they will play a constructive part in future development and administration of this rapidly growing forest resource remains to be seen.

The reluctance of foresters in the early days to encourage recreational use of forest lands is understandable. The influx of people increased the difficulty of protecting and utilizing timber, forage, and water. In the early days the only justification for recreational expenditures was either from the standpoint of fire protection or sanitation. These were negative approaches. Summer homes were originally permitted on public lands since it was thought the additional occupants would assist in fire suppression. Some foresters have been unsympathetic, either by temperament or education, because they dislike to deal with intangible values like recreation.

Professionally, many foresters assign and accept only materialistic objectives and returns. The results of their professional activity that they can accept are those which can be measured in terms of board, cubic, or linear feet, cords, pieces, or tons. Watershed protection became respectable only as it began to be expressed in second- or acre-feet of waterflow, height of flood crest, or plus or minus cubic yards, or acre-feet of sedimentation. There is much more to a forest than material goods. Even an undisturbed forest is not necessarily an unmanaged forest, for it may have an economic value as well as an aesthetic attraction that no cut-over land has.

. . . Some foresters no doubt believe that before forest recreation can attain respectability commensurate with timber production, forage, and other uses, formulas must be devised with which to measure precisely the number or the worth of the happy hearts of children or the contented hours of adults eased of the tensions of modern existence, and thus made more productive or at least saved from deterioration. They believe that to bring forest recreation into its own, methods must be devised through which human enjoyment can be measured in standard units and assigned a cash value. However, less materialistic and more realistic foresters already appreciate that there are human values which transcend the dollar values of ordinary business.

. . . The forest profession has gone a long way from the days in which the forester thought of himself primarily, if not only, as a producer of cellulose. The term "multiple use" is now an accepted description of the attitude of the forestry profession toward the forest. There is probably no one element of forest use which touches a greater number of people than the recreation element. I am not certain, but I am inclined to believe that if trustworthy statistics were available it would be found that, from a commercial standpoint, the forest in its service of recreation runs into figures that would compare favorably with the timber production and other commercial aspects of the forestry business. It is for this reason that my feeling is very strong that in training men for forestry work real emphasis should be put on the value of the forest from the recreation standpoint.

Regardless of the soundness of the multiple-use principle in the sense of the unified administration of several or all uses of wildland by a given agency or single management, the optimum combination of uses on a single area or site is subject to constant change due largely to the constant change in economic and social conditions. Optimum use on a given area might require a single use or possibly the exclusion of several subordinate uses in favor of the dominant use or uses. There are, however, strong forces at work in the direction of making recreation a more dominant use on wildlands, and the trend of public thinking is definitely in that direction. Therefore, in the long-range planning of public wildlands in particular, recreation should be given the benefit of the doubt where there is a question as to which are the present and prospective dominant, codominant and subordinate uses.

The forestry profession should reexamine its views and standards regarding the economic and social utility and significance of forests.

Technology now serves, or promises to serve, with other forms or things many material needs hitherto served best or exclusively by the products of forests. But it offers no such promise for those recreational or spiritual needs of the American people hitherto and now served best or only by forests. As population and urbanization increase, and as forests decrease, these spiritual needs will become greater and more acute. It may well develop that the professional forester of the future will depend for his place in the sun upon his contributions in this field to an equal or even greater degree than upon the requirements for the time-honored and traditional material products of the forest. . . .

There is the belief that if we could have forest recreation, wildlife activities, and other similar forms of nature programs in the hands of professional foresters, we should be ahead in promoting the general purposes of forest conservation. In the few instances where we have technical foresters who have also specialized in some of these other uses of the forest, results indicate a much better balance in our recreation program. . . .

Here is a challenge to the schools of forestry and conservation as well as to the foresters themselves. Recognizing the present trend in public use of the forests, adequate adjustments and expansion in the training program for forestry students must be made so that when graduated they will have a more comprehensive grasp of these newer trends of forest management in order to meet the demands placed upon them as forest administrators. It follows that adjustments will also have to be made in the examinations given to foresters in order to get qualified persons for positions in the broader field of management.

It is only when the intangibles of forestry are added to the wholly material values that professional permanency and security become well established. The professional forester would be unwise were he to fail or refuse to recognize the part and place of these intangibles in this professional field. The continuity and adequacy of a forest policy rest wholly on the attitude of mind of the American people and the thinking of those people is not influenced so much by fear of a shortage of inch boards or two-by-fours as it is by the hope or desire to spend a happy vacation in a scene of unimpaired forest beauty. Up to a certain point, emphasis upon an impending deficiency of timber supply may be wholly justified but it is only partially effective. Emphasis, from here on, on the dual value of the forest as the scene and opportunity for wholesome forms of outdoor recreation, and on the formulation of plans of management and development which fully feature and provide for such dual use in optimum measure, is a more potent argument and one with tremendously popular appeal. If foresters are to furnish the talent for good land management, they should know something about all the multiple uses of that land, how each use affects the others, and how they can be coordinated in a related program for the greatest good to the greatest number in the long run. The I. Q. rating of professional foresters will be determined by the way in which they respond to this situation. (*Recreational Forest Management as a Part of the Forestry Profession,* Ray E. Bassett, Chief, Section of Forest Recreation, U.S. Forest Service, Milwaukee, Wisconsin)

The continuous maintenance of a forest cover may involve periods of anywhere from forty to two hundred years to complete the cycle from seedling to harvest. This means that the working plans made today may contemplate a future where the authors and original administrators may be dead and buried for a century or more before their plans come into fruition. This further means that the management of the public forests is not determined solely by the exigencies of the moment nor the needs of one decade. Public forest management, unlike that of individuals or corporations, is not limited to the benefit of an immediate generation, but is projected far into a future where people yet unborn may enjoy a full measure of the things we guard today. . . .

On the part of Americans, since the beginnings of the nation, there has been an inherent feeling of common ownership of the great waters, mountains, and forests of the country, and all that is in them. Psychological it is, perhaps, but the attitude is a persistent force, that the high and wide places, the sea, and the wild forested areas are nature's solitudes and belong to all the people. The fish, the game, the wildlife of the forests, and man's right to wander obscure paths into the wildernesses of the woods are common rights—not to be seriously abrogated, and then only in the public interest.

The degree of emphasis to be given recreation in the management of public forest properties cannot be safely based on a dollars-and-cents comparison of recreation with other resources. In the first place, no satisfactory basis of evaluating recreational features has ever been worked out. One cannot place a cash value on a sermon or an immortal musical composition in cataloging man's achievements. Neither can we put a dollar value on a thrush's song or an autumn sunset. Even fishing and hunting, whose end results so many people erroneously appraise only in pounds of meat, cannot be appraised in terms of the inner satisfaction which animates a genuine sportsman.

The amount of time and money which people will spend to enjoy the forests is, after all, only a partial and unsatisfactory yardstick, which does not reflect accurately the circumstances in life of an individual or of a human generation. Of one thing only we may be sure, and that is that, as time goes on, the recreational desires and the recreational needs of the American people will most definitely increase. Consequently, it will become more important but probably not too difficult to strike a satisfactory balance between recreation and the other values existing in the forests.

No one can forecast what changes will be forced by the population pressures of the future. We do know that human needs and human nature will be essentially the same when we have two hundred million people in this country as they are right now.

This means that forest recreation is not only here to stay, but will take on greater and greater intensity as time goes on. Out of this certain prospect come two major conclusions:

First. We must maintain our present national forests in public ownership and continue to handle all their combined multiple uses and values for the permanent benefits of all the people.

Second. The Forest Service must evaluate the spiritual and physical recreation needs of the nation, not simply on the basis of the present, but also with vision and purpose so that we may adequately meet future needs as fast as they develop.

Foresters sometimes have to look ahead two hundred years in charting a working plan for a forest stand. We also have the infinitely more difficult task of charting a form of management that will recognize and protect all of the recreation values which will be so sorely needed much earlier than two hundred years.

We cannot afford to make any serious mistakes. If we err at all it must be on the conservative side of overestimating recreational needs of the people. We dare not and we must not shortchange the future. (*The Place of Recreation in the Multiple-Use Management of the National Forests,* John W. Spencer, Regional Forester, Denver, Colorado)

[The foregoing are excerpts from excerpts that read in full about five times as many words. Then I shifted to my own words.]

I don't know how much of what I have said you will agree with. Chief Forester McArdle recently wrote to a conservationist friend of mine that he did not expect that you people would agree with everything I have to say here. I don't even imagine that all foresters in the Forest Service agree with each other. Let me pause now to point out that every word I have read so far has been unmercifully plagiarized—from foresters, foresters with whose quoted remarks I myself agree. A professor of forestry helped me round up the quotations for this occasion, and they all come from the proceedings of the Society of American Foresters' meeting in Minneapolis in 1947. All material quoted was from men who were in the Forest Service at the time.

This has been a trick, I'll grant you, and I apologize for it. But perhaps it will help to dramatize in your own minds what changes, if any, have come about in the past nine and a half years. You will know far better than I. From here on I'll proceed under my own steam. Any similarity between what follows and what others have written is purely coincidental.

As a preface to the rest of my remarks, let me start with a subject I know firsthand, and then branch out into your subject, about which I shall try to propound questions rather than attempt to carry coals to Newcastle in a knapsack. At present I am chairman of the Natural Resources Council of America, an organization founded in 1946 to help forty national conservation organizations keep each other informed about mutual needs and problems. Their total membership exceeds two million, and includes the Sierra Club, second oldest of the group and the oldest of them devoted to conservation of scenic resources. The Sierra Club was founded in 1892, now has more than eleven thousand members, and I am its executive director.

For sixteen years before the word "conservation" became popular, the Sierra Club was practicing it, just as John Muir had before the club was founded. Conservation has meant many things, and through the years members of the club have individually been interested in all of them, including the conservation of soil, water, forests, and materials in general—conservation in the sense of wise use, with minimum waste, of the resources the earth affords for our economy. The club itself, however, has never been more than indirectly concerned with the economics of resource conservation. From the beginning its specialty has been the preservation of natural scenery, in national parks and monuments, in national-forest recreation areas, in wilderness under whatever jurisdiction, in state and local parks, together with a deep interest in the wildlife that makes these places complete. Whether justifiably or not, those who work for conservation of natural scenery and wildlife have come to be known as conservationists, a term which excludes the people who have a role in managing a resource for profit, even though they may conserve it in doing so.

Thus the Sierra Club is a group of conservationists, active and potentially active, whose interest in the cause of conservation has received its impetus from direct knowledge of scenic America which the members have acquired in the club's program of outings and other outdoor activities. This, at least, was the principal stimulus of conservation interest in the early decades of the club. More recently there has been a pronounced rise in the number who support the club solely to further its public-service program, only rarely to enjoy its activities.

In all its program, the club has carefully avoided taking action that would benefit itself or its members any more than it would benefit the public as a whole. This does not mean that the club has not been misunderstood at times. For example, it has always been easy for people who have not known the whole story to assume that because the club advocates the preservation of wilderness and also conducts wilderness outings, the club therefore strives to protect wilderness for its own selfish purposes. While it is true that the club's wilderness outings would cease if there were no wilderness, so would all wilderness outings, whatever their sponsorship—

and the club's contribution to wilderness travel in toto is very minute. Moreover, the club outings are nonprofit.

The club, in its conservationist role, has placed special emphasis on wilderness preservation in the last quarter century (which saw the dropping of the words "to render accessible" from the club's purposes because too many people thought this meant "accessible by road or tramway") because wilderness, after all, is the most precious of our scenic possessions. It is least likely to get support from the branch of conservation devoted to resource management. And it can never be replaced if the resource managers covet it successfully.

Which brings us, as conservationists, full circle – back to where we collectively need to keep our conservation interest broad enough to be aware enough of resource-management needs to preserve wilderness from management. For instance, wilderness will be safest from exploitation by lumbermen if the extensive tree-bearing areas that need not be wild are managed with maximum long-range efficiency. It behooves us, then, to know enough about the technique of forestry to know when it is not efficient – to be able to point out to the lumbermen who covet the wilderness rain forest of Olympic National Park that there are other ways, if they operate efficiently, to get the lumber Olympic's dedicated forests could produce but should not.

Now, what can a mere urban conservationist who has mastered no forestry and managed no resources contribute to a broad-gauge look at conservation in its whole context? He can think about the problems and he can seek out the ways in which utilization and preservation may both be accommodated, each in its own place. On the one hand, he is in a good position. His lack of familiarity with a resource subject may also mean a lack of bias and can insure a good perspective, so long as he keeps an open, inquiring mind and minds his logic. On the other hand, of course, the conservationist is in peril – all the peril that awaits the sciolist and his little knowledge that can be a dangerous thing.

Such is the layman's dilemma; and with this explanation of my position here I'll embark upon my own question period, hoping to learn some answers after I have yielded the floor. The questions derive from what I think is an absolute truth: If Nature does something, there's a good reason for it, and it is ecologically right. A noted forester told a group of us last year, "Nature never does anything right." However, I'll stick by my assumption, realizing that one of the things Nature did, alas, was to allow man to be arrogant – as overendowed with self-esteem, perhaps, as the dinosaurs were overendowed with self-armament. But on to the questions:

1. Is *multiple use* a shibboleth? At our Biennial Wilderness Conference which convened in San Francisco last month one conservationist stated that multiple use was a concept that lip service was paid to, and

no more. He serves on the advisory board of the California region and is also chairman of the Secretary of the Interior's Advisory Committee on Conservation. I think he meant what he said. Just two weeks ago in Portland, Regional Forester Stone said that he didn't like the term *multiple use,* but preferred *coordinate use.*

Does multiple use mean a multiplicity of uses on each acre of a forest? Of course not, but many people think so. Does it mean the whole galaxy of uses in each ranger district, or on each forest, or in each region, or in the system as a whole? Is it a system of zones, or of priorities? Is it clearly defined by law or in the Forest Service Manual? I have yet to hear a forester explain the difference between national forests and national parks without saying that national forests are for multiple use and national parks are for single use. Do you think this is true? If so, you must have a clear definition of multiple use in mind. I don't happen to think it is true at all.

2. Do you say that multiple use consists of timber production plus something else? I have heard this definition suggested more than once. I think everyone here would reject it, without giving it a second thought. But let's give it a second thought. First, how many hours of a forester's training are directly and indirectly devoted to timber–to the art of getting soil, water, and sunlight to market in the form of wood products? And how many hours to all other forest uses? We have the periodic, multi-million-dollar Timber Resource Review, but how well along are we in producing equivalent reviews for other forest uses? In the management plan for any forest, how many man-hours go into problems of producing board-feet compared to problems relating to all other uses? What, then, is the meaning of multiple use?

3. Is the drive to provide the greatest good for the greatest number in the long run a noble objective, but not a route to it? I think we are badly in need of clear definition of greatest good now that the crowded world is upon us. And hasn't that phrase "in the long run" been omitted from quite a few publications lately? It's a serious omission, many conservationists feel, not only of words but also in thinking.

4. How important is that phrase "in the long run"? One of the most impressive papers given at our Wilderness Conference was by an ecologist who had just completed a study in all the Easts–Near, Middle, and Far. Some of his most dramatic photographs were of deserts which resulted from forestry practice that forgot the long run; instead, it was forestry for the short-term gain that sent the Cedars of Lebanon–most of them–out to sea. The greatest good for the greatest number at the time–and desert thenceforth. No, it wasn't a change in climate that created those deserts, the ecologist assured us. He showed slides taken nearby and in the same climatic zone, of handsome mixed forest abounding with wildlife, which still exist because they were protected from exploitation by accident–pitifully

small islands of an Eden, too small to ward off enduring poverty. The Promised Land that Moses led his people into was a beautiful wilderness; but the cardinal rule of good stewardship, thinking of the long run, was forgotten. And now there's a desert, the barren stone skeleton of the greater Eden.

But to move from biblical times to our own, I have also been impressed by the grave difficulty recently encountered in Germany with fourth-generation forest that had been managed so as to produce pure spruce. Do we begin to know enough about what happens to watershed protection and to timber production itself when we shift from the so-called climax forest that we find on a piece of land, and try to grow there instead, without rotation of the crop, a single species for several generations? I am confident that we don't know enough. As of last year the Forest Service did not yet have a single research project underway on that subject. I asked Oregon State's Dean McCullough about that last May, and he wrote: "The Forest Service is only fifty years old. We will have to wait two hundred fifty or three hundred fifty years to appraise the results of several generations of the same species on the same site."

Must we wait that long? I myself have an appointment to keep before the returns are in, and several subsequent generations will be in the same fix.

I don't think we need to wait that long, nor do I think that we may ethically do nothing because it is such a long wait. We can take a cue from the geneticist, who has devised very effective experiments with Drosophila, those fruit-flies who go from generation to generation so fast that centuries, by our standards, can be telescoped into a single student's course. The botanical equivalent, from which valuable extrapolations could be made, would be the annuals—plants and grasses. Or take a cue from the medical researchers, and extrapolate from short-lived, guinea-pig tree species. These methods won't provide the clearest of crystal balls for forestry, but they should help, and the results can be correlated with what history tells us and what paleobotanists have uncovered. Our own generation will not reap many of the benefits of such research, but will anyone here argue that we should therefore skip it? I think not.

5. What studies does the Forest Service contemplate of the changing trends in forest uses? And of the long-range compatibility of uses, each with the others? This is an especially leading question, and heads me back toward my own primary concern about how the Forest Service can revive the intensity of interest in wilderness preservation which was so evident in the work of Aldo Leopold and Robert Marshall and the chiefs and secretaries who backed them up.

6. What is happening to wilderness protection? Seven years' study and four Wilderness Conferences in which hundreds of resource managers and conservationists participated, led to legislation reflecting their

consensus as nearly as possible. In Washington, D.C., a year ago, three of us submitted to the Forest and Park Services the first draft of that bill to establish a National Wilderness Preservation System. We asked for further advice and counsel. Within a few hours—and long before advice or counsel were received—copies of this draft were in the hands of the American Mining Congress, the stockmen, and the United States Chamber of Commerce. The chamber very quickly claimed, in its "Natural Resources Notes," that this proposal was a threat to multiple use of the forest, and this same fear was subsequently expressed by the American Forestry Association and by various other chambers of commerce. All these groups favored wilderness, but they didn't want it frozen or, one could presume, otherwise preserved. In the California chamber's committee discussion, one forester put it this way: Wilderness is fine in the rocky, untimbered country of national forests so long as there are enough roads to make it easily accessible. This was the forester who had said that nature never did anything right.

7. What about wilderness and multiple use? I submit that wilderness dedication is multiple use in perpetuity. Does any evidence back this up? First, let's try this definition of multiple use: In national forest management the term relates to management of the forest as a whole, and not of a particular acre. Some plots may be zoned for an exclusive use; on others, a paramount use is designated, with which a few others may be coordinated.

What are the various uses? I count eleven, some already recognized by tradition, and some likely to be:

Timber: This was once the most important use of national forests.

Watershed (and soil) conservation: This is now the most important use of most national forest lands.

Mining.

Grazing.

Fish and game habitat protection: For recreation and for the fish and game per se.

Science: A control area for research, and a genetic reservoir of unmanaged species and strains of incalculable value to the future.

Education: A natural museum for public information about resource values.

Roadside recreation of all kinds, including some in which the natural beauty of the whole scenic setting is preserved.

Reservoirs and other water-development structures.

Conservation reserve of commodity resources for future generations if they must choose to use them.

Wilderness recreation.

All these uses could be accommodated on a big national forest. But how many of these are fully compatible within a particular area? There's room for a wide spread of opinion here. Conceivably some people would think timber production was fully compatible with all the other uses. I don't think it fully compatible with any, but I would say it was partly compatible with grazing, fish and wildlife, roadside recreation, and reservoirs.

I won't take the time to list all the various intercompatibilities, full and partial, and doubt that any two people would agree anyway. A committee, however, might come up with some interesting results. I will say, however, that wilderness preservation is almost fully compatible with five other uses—watershed protection, fish and game habitat, science, education, and conservation reserve—almost all of which are mutually compatible.

However we rate them now, the relative importance of the uses has changed and will change. For example, watershed management is assuming enormous importance; forest recreation, hardly thought of thirty years ago, is now the dominant use on many forests. We are only beginning to realize the irreplaceable value of the genetic strains and microbiota to be found only in the natural complex of wildlands. (For example, what pest-resistant genes may we lose, or what new wonder drugs, if we lose wilderness? We don't know.) Forest lands will become increasingly important for outdoor wild museums as suburbia spreads over the land. And it was hardly three decades ago that we began to realize that wilderness was vanishing so rapidly as to have a scarcity value. More and more people will have more and more time for multiple-use enjoyment of wilderness—whatever wilderness, that is, that we save for them.

Would it not be helpful to attempt a monetary estimate of the worth of each combination of uses? This could be developed in several ways: (a) totals, in terms of a constant dollar, for each decade of national-forest history; (b) totals, per decade, from now until the year 2000 according to our best estimates; and (c) variations of the estimates as they would be effected by various combinations of preference uses.

For example, according to studies on the Roosevelt National Forest, Colorado, returns per acre of forest per year were as follows:

Grazing (federal receipts from permits)	$0.50
Timber (federal receipts)	1.00
Water (at headgate)	5.50
Recreation (spent by users)	25.00

It must be borne in mind, of course, that the grazing and timber receipts are gross receipts. Legitimate offsetting costs, not shown, are the increased costs of personnel to manage the timber as well as federal costs of access roads and watershed restoration that would not be necessary if the area were left as wilderness. The receipts for water probably reflect only the amortization of development works and the cost of labor, and so forth, and nothing for the water itself. So our analysis would require our finding an honest yardstick for measuring values.

Such an analysis of the various uses would, I think, demonstrate that wilderness preservation fits in nicely with the most valuable blend of uses, in the long run, that can be found on the national forests.

The traditional national-forest crops—wood products, minerals, forage—will more and more come from alternative sources: wood products from gentle-sloped woodlots and private forests in the humid regions, minerals from seawater reduction, forage from irrigated pasture. Water and wilderness, I think, can get along fine together; wilderness will insure good protection of the quantity and quality of water, and gravity will bring it down to civilization. I am aware, of course, of work on the Frazer Experimental Forest seeking to increase water yield by cutting windows in the forest. I am also aware of the pressure to initiate an Operation Tin Roof in the Salt River watershed in Arizona. But I think we will do well to have our wilderness standing by, untinkered with. It can reveal how we may stop the chain reactions we invariably unleash, for all our scientific skill, when we upset nature's balance. For example, thanks to wildlands near that German experiment with spruce forests, scientists were able to observe the important ecological role of the lowly ant, and thus to reintroduce ants where monoculture had wiped them out—and the timber crop along with them.

Let me close with a plea, a statistic, and a try at philosophy.

The plea: That you all assume a role in making sure that we look ahead to all the needs our forests must fulfill as thoroughly as we have been looking ahead to timber-resource needs.

The statistic: In the past four decades and their two world wars, this world has used up more of its resources than have all previous generations of people.

And philosophy: This generation is speedily using up, beyond recall, a very important right that belongs to future generations—the right to have wilderness in their civilization, even as we have it in ours; the right to find solitude somewhere; the right to find themselves there; the right to see, and enjoy, and be inspired and renewed, somewhere, by those places where the hand of God has not been obscured by the industry of man.

As of the year 1957, the United States Forest Service has a key role in the preservation of this right, as it pertains to many of the most beautiful samples of original America. Your leadership will go far to determine the fate of that right, so far as people of our time can pass opportunity along to their children. Apathy can mean that we pass them a dead torch. Or, knowing that this is a very special kind of torch that we cannot light again, we can keep it aflame. I am convinced that we shall, for that is the emerging American temper.

Statement to forest supervisors,
***Portland, Oregon,* April 5, 1957**

How To Excoriate Foresters

My Portland Audience consisting of foresters, I had to summon all my tact (always in short supply), cool my ardor, and quench my ire. By the time the Sierra Club's 1961 Biennial Wilderness Conference had ended, my ire had intensified, and a three-month family trip to Europe did not ameliorate matters.

Bruce Kilgore, then editing the *Sierra Club Bulletin,* had covered for me in my long absence, but had been too swamped to expedite publication of the Wilderness Conference proceedings. I put the finishing touches on the book, *Wilderness: America's Living Heritage.* The reviewer in *American Forests* commented that if any foresters wished to be driven up the wall, they should read the foreword:

Wilderness Was the Frontier and Progress celebrated its retreat. As we destroyed wilderness, it built us. If the warp of our national fabric was traced in the threads of our move westward, the weft was the wilderness we moved over and under and through. Without it our fabric would have been a flimsy thing, transparent, too easily tattered to meet the tests that came. But we had wild grandeur, and its ruggedness was reflected in what our fathers did.

They forged on to submerge the old culture along the Pacific so rapidly that they passed through the wilderness without destroying it all. The easy tendency now is for us to turn around, rearm, and clean out the last few strongholds for the iota their resources can add to our national growth, for the few minutes an utter exploitation can postpone our day of reckoning.

The iota is there. The few areas of unbroken forest, for example, could indeed add to the timber economy, and most of them are being extinguished to do just that. They are but a vestige, however, of our inheritance; the rest has already been converted into the capital necessary for a nation to grow. We are now in the late autumn of the era which could exploit the virgin forests, and if we have learned anything from the Pilgrim fathers, we know it is time to hold out the reserves that will see us through the winter or serve a transcending purpose.

Today we realize the hazard of using up the last of any resource and are learning to protect the remnants, especially of wilderness. In meeting the revised needs of man, we are saving some unrevised works of God. As Newton Drury has said well, this nation is not so poor that it must expend its beauty, nor so rich in beauty that it can afford to. We are becoming poor in wilderness faster than most of us know. The speed of loss is great, there are few remote places, and they will not multiply or fuse or become a frontier again.

Facing today's kind of frontier, we see a challenge that will engage the best research, education, human creativity, and drive we can produce. The new challenge is to retrace steps through mistreated land, learn to heal, to rebuild, to reinvigorate it—and pay whatever extra this new attitude costs us. We must increasingly substitute resourcefulness for resources in order not to overdraw an account our children would have to cover for us.

All that I have said so far could be said aloud before mining, damming, grazing, paving, subdividing, and logging conventions without causing much ripple. Everybody loves children, conservation, and wilderness—and America, the beautiful.

But just try to save some of it—really save it! Unanimity vanishes.

For a starter, try to save clean air. There is no more vital resource. Without it we die. Yet almost everyone shrugs—that is, everyone is very busy with something else—while it deteriorates. In autopsies nowadays the color of lung tissue tells at once whether the victim lived in country or city. The subject is disagreeable; the fact is worse. There is but one pair of lungs per customer and our children are starting out life in miserably poorer air than we did. The breath of life should be sweeter, and not with mock-sweetness from a spray bottle. If you agree, then you have an obligation—to make clear to the people or agency trying to improve your air that you like what they are doing. You will help fight the opposing coalition of smog spewers who allege they cannot stop because it would add excessively to the unit cost of producing a pound of steel or mile of travel. You know you want an end to the befouling of your air to achieve someone else's economies. You want your child to breathe freely even if it costs you more. Do you say so?

Or try to keep water pure. Presumably you approve of water and are concerned lest multiple-use developments accommodate every requirement except one: that your water retain some natural purity and not display a race between a good chemical and a bad one to see which can assault your nostrils before you taste it. You believe that water will be better with comprehensive planning of river basins—a balance between the uses that will control floods, generate power, abate pollution, stabilize soil, improve forestry, reserve wild streams, and keep big unscarred watersheds for their time-proved guarantee of pure water—and for their oasis of unspoiled scenery that anyone wants who can see beyond the next meal or our last dollar.

Some such reasoning may coincide with yours. But you live in a city that wants to invade wilderness for water or power when there is ample (if polluted) water running right by the city and an alternative (if more expensive) source of power. Do you insist that the alternatives be exhausted; do you let your city know, from top to bottom, that you will pay another mill or two per hundred gallons or per kilowatt-hour if you must, that you want to spare your children the impossible cost of replacing a wilderness?

As a third example of the difficulty of saving things for your children, consider the war between the wilderness forest and the sawlog forester.

The sawlog forester, you find after painful study, is the man who somehow thought that the College of Forestry was a trade school. He majored in Machinery Against the Land and learned almost nothing about the mechanism of land. Speaking about foresters and the land mechanism, an eminent biologist has said, "An ecological conscience [a concept of the late Aldo Leopold, for many years a Forest Service leader in wilderness preservation] is a constant and trying burden on the owner, leaving him unable to communicate with most of his fellows, tormenting him with a constant awareness of grave wounds on the landscape–wounds neither seen nor tended by most others." The man we here call "sawlog forester" feels no such burden or, feeling it, is unmoved. There are very many of him and he does not see the forest for the sawlogs.

He constitutes, collectively, the greatest single threat to wilderness today. He covets the forest preserved in dedicated areas, even though it would meet but a year's demand for saw timber. Perhaps another year's cut, if *not* cut, would *half*-meet the additional outdoor needs of the more crowded, more leisurely future we keep hearing about. But you don't know how much is eligible or needed for dedication because we don't have studies except for a few that foresters made. It doesn't matter, for if you ask the sawlog forester not to cut this conservation reserve–or even call it anything but an old-growth, decadent, diseased, and overmature stand–he is apt to consider you an extreme, shrill, single-use wilderness zealot who strikes at the heart of his multiple-use policy, to list a partial glossary of sawlog slogans.

Then you look further and find that we are badly behind in repairing the damaged land the loggers have been leaving in their wake in past centuries and have churned up more violently in the last decade. You learn also of the progress in finding substitutes that are far better than wood for some uses and safer, too, as the fire insurance companies insist. Study, you find out, also reveals that the sawlog forester is well financed and often hits the slicks with expensive four-color displays (paid for in your lumber bill) extolling multiple use and banishing wilderness lovers to the tree-free realm of mountain goats.

The principal locality in the sawlog novel, you discover, is the Tree Farm. One uncharitably perceptive critic has defined a tree farm as a place where you cut down one thousand trees and put up one sign. You begin to wonder how many real tree farms there are. The sawlog forester usually applies the sign to areas where he has yet to reap a crop his clan has sown.

His profession is too new for him to know what degeneration his practices will produce if continued over several forest generations—particularly his practice of depriving the soil of the complex organic diversity which was there until he came. As a tree farmer he expects sustained yield without initial investment, implicit in his repeated cutting of the same species without fertilizing—a practice that would ruin a real farmer.

This kind of forester, you finally perceive, exploits a confusion left over from the days of old when Predators were Evil. Biologists know they aren't; that instead, predators are essential to the improvement of species, including forest species; but the sawlog forester won't allow himself to know this. The evil beetle and its allies are an excuse to rush in with chainsaws to save the forest from itself, to interrupt the essential play of the force of succession that alone, through the ages, has made the forest possible and durable.

Then there is always "roadside recreation" to develop by logging.

If this land belonged to this forester and not to the ages, it wouldn't be so bad. If there were an automatic replacement in kind so that the next generation of sawlog foresters could repeat the same errors on the same land, it wouldn't be so bad. If the quality of water and soil were not severely impaired, it wouldn't be so bad. If the ravages were committed on lesser, gentler lands that *have* to go commercial instead of being rushed up to the high dedicated borders to preclude good wilderness dedication for the future, it wouldn't be so bad. But none of the *ifs* work and it *is* bad, tragically bad—for soil, which is mined, and for wilderness, which is killed.

A man who hates trees cannot be all bad, W. C. Fields might have interpolated. Right! Let it be said again that commercial logging operations are going to have to continue on ninety percent of the forest land—while it lasts. Research, if heeded, will make the land last longer; the better it produces, the safer wilderness forest will be. But wilderness forest is what is in planned peril right now. The peril grows plainer each day.

With these findings at hand, you have an obligation: to let others know how shallow the sawlog forester's love for wilderness is; to insist that he be relieved of the responsibility of guarding it unless he changes his ways. And certainly you let it be known that you yourself would gladly use second-growth-timber products, or substitutes for wood, even at higher cost, rather than see outstanding primeval forests given over to logging, even "selective logging" (and maybe you remember the Les Pengelly definition: "You select a forest and you log it").

The foregoing conclusions, if not the phrasing, have expert support outside the working circle of foresters, and some silent support within. At the very least, the remarks underline the need for first-rate conservation journalists to look hard at and report forcibly about what is happening to the forests. They must dig for themselves, beware the conducted tour, not fear reprisals, and fear what will happen if there is no reform.

Conservation journalism will not be enough. Special study committees and symposiums will help. They won't be enough either. Only *you,* to paraphrase Smokey, can prevent fires—the slow fires, fed by myth, which still continue, in our land, the ruin that history records so chillingly in faraway places.

This is controversy, and controversy is non-U and exhausting. The Sierra Club, in concert with the Federation of Western Outdoor Clubs, has tried to reduce the cause of controversy—chiefly, a refusal to let the nonlogging public be heard when virgin forests are sought by loggers—but we have yet to succeed. We have become unpopular among loggers of primeval forests, who hurry to cut deep while the public is asleep.

In frustrated moments, we fall into wistful thinking: Perhaps government in America has reached the point where the citizen organization or advisory board has outlived its usefulness, except to help a given agency get around red tape or opposition. Perhaps we should no longer call shots as we see them; we should blandly accept what the agency predetermines to be best for us. Perhaps the old school try has cost too much—more than can be afforded by an organization that seeks no glory and has nothing to sell for a profit. If we succeed, who but posterity would reward our effort, and how would *we* spend the reward?

We put this all down because we believe it needs to be considered. A book on wilderness, our most fragile living resource, cannot responsibly be soft on the most serious threat to that resource.

The threat exists because truth is locked up behind the bars of jargon. There is a subliminal attack on fact. Clarity is lost in a sea of shibboleth, cliché, and misty concept; prejudice is exploited, the easy slogan used instead of hard thought; public relations outranks public interest; primeval resources are committed without fair trial, irrevocably, to the highest bidder, not the highest use. The threat is one of the worst: a serious overconcentration of power.

America has known overconcentrations of power before. Such men as Theodore Roosevelt, assuming a mandate, summoning great courage, and deciding that he would rather wear out than rust out, came to grips with the graspers of power. He won that round. But graspers don't stay down, are not self-limiting, and are usually too insensitive to perceive the damage they do. The people have to speak.

What can they, *you,* say? We have no blueprint. We offer no substitute here for citizenship and its requirement that all citizens who are concerned about their society and their world should contribute a tithe of their own sweat. We offer no easy way to sweat. The only way out is *through* and you have to involve yourself. Either that or plead guilty when your children ask what happened to the beautiful world you inherited.

Which brings us right back to this book and what it can do to keep you in the clear in your children's memory. For one thing, you can act for wilderness reassured by the support expressed here by so many eminent people. Wilderness, you will know, is not "for the rugged, wealthy few" but for the intelligent many.

In the present controversy, the spotlight should probably be on the portions by Justice Douglas and Professor McConnell, who perceive why the Constitution wanted Congress to protect the public from public bureaus, and the need for Congress to remember always the great handicap under which the citizen operates. On the one hand, the citizens must pay their public servants, write their own letters, buy their transportation to hearings, and dig into their limited resources to help some underfinanced citizen organization speak for them when their work keeps them home. On the other hand is the bureau, numbering thousands of well-disciplined employees who will go where they are sent and bring to bear all the pressure they are told to exert in the bureau's behalf. At public expense. We need our bureaus badly. But they and Congress should remember the tremendous power and advantage possessed by the bureaus and the titan dependent industries; they should give the citizen who supports wilderness the benefit of any doubt. After all, unlike us, those who would exploit wilderness can afford to lose the battle again and again. Once they win, wilderness and the future lose forever. For wilderness goes down a one-way road. A little that is wild may creep back alongside, but not the wholeness, and we lose living links in the chain of life that humanity requires for survival.

The conservationist, in this decade of the Last Chance to Decide, has got to insist upon fair treatment. When a living heritage is being put to death—perpetual, eternal, permanent death—there is no fairness in giving the attacker and the savior equal time. There is no impartiality in dividing the heritage in two and letting the attackers spend their half for their immediate personal benefit while requiring the defenders of the other half to stave off the attackers again next year, and to protect this fragment for all the future. There is no use pretending equity exists in a law that makes it as hard to add wilderness as to subtract it, or makes additions harder. This is unfair advantage to the attackers—a heads-they-win, tails-let's-flip-again game with America's living heritage—putting wilderness on a short-term, half-life basis. Yet the Rough Riders complain because the Bird-Watchers have it that good!

There is survival to work for. We dare not repudiate the evolutionary force; we should keep better watch on how our own society evolves. Its increasing complexity and growth can overcome us, or we can channel and control it. We still have the choice. To keep the choice, we can sharpen our understanding of the irreplaceables and our laws preserving them. Without suffering, we can be generous to the future by extending the systems of national parks and other wilderness. We can rescue rural land from the rampaging highwaymen, and, to sustain our sanity, hold out for the open greenness around the emerging supercities. Noting the growth in our economy and anxiety, we can strive for a more rapid growth in our own competence and honesty.

Competent, honest people will learn to live in peace, and by so living will avoid a squandering of our one ration of natural resources. With the race to squander called off, they may even drop the compulsion to keep up with the Joneses, over the fence and over the sea. We will relax a little, lower our pitch, our stress, our coveting, and our wear and tear on the only environment we had better count on, and must share well or no longer know.

***Wilderness: America's Living Heritage*, 1962**

MYCORRHIZAE

IN 1952 OREGON STATE COLLEGE published a list of U.S. forestry school dissertations and theses, revealing an overwhelming preponderance of concern for timber production and negligible concern for recreation, wilderness, or forest influences, a term covering what trees need for a sustainable habitat. I was already appalled at the lack of U.S. research into the dangers of forest monoculture, and in 1987, quite belatedly, would begin to learn about what is now known about mycorrhizae and the general ignorance on the part of industry, forestry schools, and Forest Service of all-important forest soils. This led me to suggest in 1987, in lumber towns of Corvallis and Bremerton, and in 1989 in the non-lumber town of New Haven, that the present Forest Service should be transferred from Agriculture to Commerce, and a new agency created to save the national forests from logging. The suggestion brought applause in the lumber towns, and approval at a Yale Forestry School seminar and subsequent happy hour.

That may sound like a far-out recommendation, but let me tell you what new problems have led to it.

Someone writing for *Earth First!* put the word *mycorrhiza,* which I had forgotten for thirty years, back into my vocabulary: *the association, usually symbiotic, of the mycelium of various fungi and the roots of seed plants*. Mycelium? *The mass of interwoven threadlike filaments forming the vegetative portion of the thallus in fungi*. Earth First! was concerned about the relation of this intricacy to the well-being of old growth forest and the threat to this well-being posed by the timber industry and its devotees in forestry schools and the Forest Service. This led me to the workshop on mycorrhizae (the plural) held at the Restoring the Earth Conference in Berkeley in January 1988, where the panelists revealed how little was known about the mycorrhizal content of soil. It was simply "the right stuff."

A congenital questioner, schooled in making statements disguised as questions, I asked:

Some forty years ago, when Bernie Frank was chief of forest influences in the U.S. Forest Service office in Washington, D.C., he told me, "We know next to nothing about forest soils." In view of what you have been telling us about mycorrhizae, what would you say the knowledge of forest soils now is in the industry, in forestry schools, and in the Forest Service?

The answer? "We know even less."

If I wanted to know more, I should check with Chris Maser, in Corvallis. I did, and read the manuscript for his first book. In his opinion, which corroborated my own intuitive conclusion, there is no sustainable forestry being practiced anywhere on earth except by nature. My own conclusions had been that the industry and its subservient forestry schools and Forest Service were not practicing silviculture but were mining forests. The evidence of their misdeeds would not appear until they were dead and gone, unpunished for what they were stealing from the future. The ravages of the spores of infectious monoculture they were inflicting would not appear for decades, perhaps a dozen or so. They are leaving the future, in the words of Professor Daniel Janzen, "living biotic debris," too scattered to reassemble, violating Aldo Leopold's observation that the first rule of intelligent tinkering is to save all the parts. Thus my conclusion, consonant with that of *Earth First!* The practice of clear-cutting is an ecologically illiterate exercise in economic opportunism, a form of slow-motion terrorism committed against those who need forest beauty now and forest products in the future. Comments like this, of course, are labeled "extremist" by those who haven't heard of my definition of extremist: someone who disagrees with you too effectively.

So I don't like clear-cutting. Nor do I believe there should be any further destruction of old growth (I prefer "primeval") forests. It will take the present breed of sawlog foresters no time at all to get rid of them, and it is futile to speculate on whether they could accomplish this within a decade or within two. If permitted to accomplish this destruction, they will then be forced to depend upon second-growth forests to stay in business and will find poorer than secondhand information, having wiped out the encyclopedia of silviculture perfected by nature in eons past.

Which is bad news for the eons to come, need not be allowed, and must not be tolerated any longer.

It is healing time on Earth.

LETTER TO A CONSERVATION DIRECTOR

EVERYTHING BEING CONNECTED to everything else in the universe, as John Muir said, I found the connection between mycorrhizae, ancient forests, and the urgent need for prompt application of healing remedies was leading to a rapid deterioration of my patience, which my advancing years are somehow using up faster and faster. This in turn led to a venting of my anxiety that pervades the letter I wrote in midyear 1989 to the conservation director of the Sierra Club, concerning the club's action regarding national forests:

AT THE SIERRA CLUB INTERNATIONAL ASSEMBLY in Ann Arbor you heard my "rhetoric" and I heard your advice about the real world of decision making. Perhaps we're even. We are not, however, in agreement. Neither of us has yet been persuaded by the other, especially on the Sierra Club's role in compromise. So under my new philosophy I need to try to find out where you are coming from and what drives you. Or what drove you away from where you seemed to be coming from when I first knew you. Answers to both these questions may emerge better from long discussions than from an exchange of letters. I think answers are needed. Perhaps what follows will stimulate some.

My thesis is that compromise is often necessary but that it ought not originate with the Sierra Club. We are to hold fast to what we believe is right, fight for it, and find allies and adduce all possible arguments for our cause. If we cannot find enough vigor in us or them to win, then let someone else propose the compromise. We thereupon work hard to coax it our way. We become a nucleus around which the strongest force can build and function.

For a specific example, take the proposed Grand Canyon dams. You alluded to them but missed the point in doing so. We said we'd accept no dams. People knew what we stood for and gathered around. If we had said (or thought) we'd accept one, but not two, clarity would have vanished from our deeds and faces. People would have seen that we were just arguing about how much rape, not opposing it. They would have gathered elsewhere if at all.

In 1938 the Sierra Club would have given in to Forest Service decision makers about the Kings Canyon High Sierra had Secretary Harold Ickes not come out to stiffen the board's resolve. With a film (mine), a book (Ansel's), a brochure (Colby's), and a lot of *Bulletin* articles (many authors), we got a national park—in spite of opposition by the National Parks Association, The Wilderness Society, Forest Service, and California State Chamber of Commerce. We then had only three thousand members and World War II was under way. (I was working half-time for the club at seventy-five dollars per month.)

The Sierra Club wanted to compromise on the Colorado in 1949. First, Dinosaur was just "sagebrush country" not worth fighting for. Then Bestor Robinson proposed that we go for one dam (Split Mountain), not two, a suggestion happily abandoned. The club wanted two dams in the Grand provided Reclamation first build silt-retaining dams in Glen Canyon and on the Little Colorado, construct nice tourist facilities for flat-water boating on the reservoirs, and slightly enlarge Grand Canyon National Park. Bestor again. He had the directors trying to please the decision makers in the Bureau of Reclamation. I fell for it for a year, then climbed back up, as did the board. I didn't fall at all in Dinosaur. I stayed out of the compromise business and persuaded the club to stay out.

There are no dams in Dinosaur or in the Grand Canyon. If I had followed what is now your advice there would be two dams in each.

So I was pretty good, right? No. Because I became a wimp, somehow, and let the board compromise on Glen Canyon. The decision makers put the dam there, and we could have stopped them had we refused to compromise and simply stood up for our own club policy. Instead we pleased the decision makers.

The board compromised on Diablo. There are two reactors there. It compromised again at Bodega Head—a compromise violating club policy. Dick Leonard said, "That's our policy but we're not going to do anything about it," and we didn't. There's a hole in Bodega Head, but not a reactor on it—thanks to Dave Pesonen, who would not compromise, and had to leave club employ because he wouldn't.

There is massive scenic vandalism along the Tioga Road, perpetrated by the decision makers of the National Park Service, because the club compromised. We could have stopped that destruction. There is a highway to Copper Creek in Kings Canyon for the same reason. It could have remained entirely a wilderness national park if the board had stood firm. The board had good reason to, but didn't.

The Alaska pipeline, bad though it is, is not so bad as it would have been. Four organizations joined and won a lawsuit but lost in Congress by one vote—Spiro Agnew's tie breaker—a law that authorized the pipeline and denied opponents the NEPA remedy. The pipe might not be there at all, and the Valdez spill avoided, had the Sierra Club not backed out of the suit in order to play Alaska state politics. If the club had lent its preponderant weight, we might well have got the Canadian railroad alternative—or a program of energy conservation—under way much sooner, a big enough program to remove financial feasibility from the pipeline.

The second Rancho Seco reactor does not exist, nor does the pair proposed for Sun Desert. Somehow the club was nowhere on this. Friends of the Earth, refusing to compromise, came up with the numbers that blocked the three reactors. And now, in part thanks to those numbers, and the bold predictions by Jim Harding, the first Rancho Seco has been voted out of action.

The Sierra Club favored the Peripheral Canal, a potential disaster for San Francisco Bay and the Delta. FOE opposed the club's proposed compromise and rescued Northern California. Happily, the next time around, the club's Bay Chapter joined Earth Island in successful opposition to the "son of the Peripheral Canal." In the early years Brock Evans thought we had to accept a nuclear alternative to the proposed high Hells Canyon Dam. We didn't. Mike McCloskey thought it impossible to block the decision makers' determination to build the proposed Rampart Dam on the Yukon. I didn't compromise. Neither dam is there. We stuck to our guns and found lots of help. The board scolded me for sending Phil Hyde and Paul Brooks to the Yukon, and they were key to saving it. The board scolded me for spending thirty-five hundred dollars from my discretionary fund to get them there. The board disapproved of my having helped David Sive stay on the milestone Storm King battle, which I think would otherwise have been dropped. The help cost fifteen hundred dollars.

The club folded on the proposed Mammoth Pass highway. Ike Livermore didn't, and the road isn't there. The club folded on the superb Jeffrey pine forest at Deadman Summit, and on the preservation of the Kern Plateau, and we lost both because of that folding. The club was about to accede to the decision makers of the Forest Service and ski business in the battle for the San Gorgonio wilderness. I did a Paul Revere act most of one winter night, the board stiffened, and the wilderness is still there. We forced different decisions. The board was ready to fold on the Disney proposal for Mineral King. So was I. Martin Litton wasn't, and saved the day. I forgot how to play Paul Revere and Glen Canyon isn't there.

The Sierra Club compromised enough to lose its best antinuclear group. The club has compromised enough to be of little force or effect in slowing the arms race. The club was asked to act four years ago about environmental concerns in Nicaragua, but has remained silent. The club backed away from saving the California condor in the wild. The club did not join in the fight to block the new San Onofre reactors (a failure of which, quite possibly, could make Southern California uninhabitable). The club so misjudges the arms race that it discourages the San Diego Chapter from protesting in Nevada, as if such a global problem must be left exclusively to the Toiyabe Chapter. The national club, and Sierra Club California, seem to think that the inexcusable charring of giant sequoias in Sequoia National Park and the terminal isolation of giant sequoias of Sequoia National Forest, and the monocultural new plantations being planted around them, is the province of the Kern-Kaweah chapter and severe damage continues. The club thinks that stopping the charring of sequoias in Yosemite is the business of the Tehipite Chapter, and the damage

Brower (left) taking part in an antinuclear press conference with John Gofman, Ralph Nader, and Paul Ehrlich, 1973. Photograph by Peter Vilms.

continues. The club has not recognized that prescribed burning can be conducted properly, as in the Calaveras Grove, where the state has protected giant sequoias without defacing them.

I do not propose that the foregoing, nor what follows, go into the next edition of the Sierra Club Guide, but I do fear that it will be in someone else's guide, "How the Sierra Club Misuses Power and Talent, or How to Avoid the Four-Letter B-Word (BOLD)."

The club is so eager to appear reasonable that it goes soft, undercuts the strong grassroots efforts of chapters, groups, and other organizations – as if the new professionalization and prioritization requires rampant tenderization. I go along with Ray Dasmann, when he speaks of those who want to appear reasonable to the Fortune 500 and allies, and who therefore go to lunches, or to other lengths, to demonstrate their credibility, access, insiderness, and reasonable strategy. Ray says it is a meeting of Bambi and Godzilla.

Then I get to the crisis of the ancient forests and the club's role that is so faltering that SCLDF [Sierra Club Legal Defense Fund] had to come to the rescue of the trees by hiring a lobbyist. And I think of the rude treatment of Dave Foreman, a club-invited speaker whom the assembly audience had admired for his courage, courage which gives the club a field to be bolder in, which the club should be grateful for.

Yes, the club has saved millions of acres of wilderness, thousands of acres of ancient forests, thousands (or millions?) of acres of desert, and other very self-satisfying numbers. The club saved them, that is, long enough to let later generations keep saving them if they can–unless they opt for compromise.

So the glass is half full.

It is also more than half empty, and there's a pluggable hole that will remain open unless the club gets its courage up. Dave Foreman's question is the one we cannot dodge. The club didn't create that wilderness. It helped, more than most, I am sure, to draw a line around part of it. So we added sixty-nine million to the number of acres within that line, most of them in Alaska, where all we had to overcome was one congressman and two senators (someone else's judgment, spoken to me). Meanwhile, twice that number of acres, land that might have been preserved as real wilderness, wildness that did exist, have been lost permanently. They slipped through the cracks in the Forest Service and BLM floors. The club had other major campaigns to contend with. No books, no film, little in *Sierra*. No video.

I don't know which number to accept about how much ancient forest we have left, or how long it will last at the present accelerating rate of ecologically illiterate clear-cutting. What I think is the best argument is being ignored by those who think compromise is the essential in the real world of decision makers. This argument could reach even Senator Hatfield and still leave him a friend in other critical matters if the club really tried.

That argument, simply stated, is that whatever ancient forest is left, and however long it will last, the end is imminent. Responsible leaders–of the U.S. Timber Service, of logging corporations, of forestry schools, and of the Sierra Club–must demand that these people move to their fallback position now.

What will they do by 1995 or 2000 when the ancient forests are gone and the successors of James Watt covet what is left in the national parks? Then it is too late. There is still time to preserve and restore.

The fallback position should be:

1. Stop the export of any but maximum-value-added wood products.
2. Raise prices as necessary to supply wood products from lesser forests and to fund massive recycling.
3. At public expense, train displaced people dependent upon ancient-forest jobs for careers with a future.
4. At public expense, restore derelict forest land, but not with monocultures.
5. Establish Oregon Volcanic Cascades National Park; let the National Park Service protect what the Forest Service refuses to.
6. Add Glacier Peak Wilderness to the North Cascades National Park.

7. Place all other ancient forests, including all giant sequoias in national forests, in a biosphere reserve, with a moratorium on any impairment pending a five-year study, modeled on the Outdoor Recreation Resources Review, on how best to protect what would take from five to thirty centuries to replace.

Sierra Club must stiffen, organize, and fight to require that this program begin now. We need the equivalent of the club's and FOE's oust-Watt petitions, publicized with full-page ads, major segments in "60 Minutes," "20-20," Charles Kuralt, Bill Moyers, Dave Foreman on "The Tonight Show," and feature videos for VCR owners to buy, copy, and disseminate, all with the help of other organizations, with *Sierra* holding off on auto and Chevron ads and giving major space to the effort, plus a mass-market paperback and Sierra Club Save-the-Ancient-Forests traveling vans. This needs to be a major campaign, and if the club's addiction to priorities gets in the way, send such an addiction out to whoever can treat it.

What seems to have been happening is that the club has heard and rejected arguments for comprehensive action on ancient forests for far too long.

We need another David Simons, but Springfield, Oregon, cannot be expected to produce another. The Sierra Club must find one, discard its hubris, learn anew how to listen, abandon its obsolete conventional wisdom (a redundant term), and get a move on. As I said while leaving the staff on May 3, 1969, Nice Nelly won't get the job done.

David Simons came up with the bold idea of an Oregon Volcanic Cascades National Park, an idea that died with him. Where is the innovative courage he had? Imagine, if you will, how reformed the Forest Service would have become had the club picked up that ball. It didn't. The kind of people who had been Muir's opponents, the proliferating Disciples of Pinchot, can now perceive that the club is willing to compromise, and thus propose a scheme that hardly delays the rate of cutting and eviscerates our hard-won ability to litigate when the government becomes irresponsible.

That, at least, is the way I read it, as do many people in other organizations undercut by the Sierra Club. Yes, the club can thus preserve access, remain an insider, be credible, and appear reasonable in the world of decisions. But what has the club lost for the world? Thousands, perhaps millions, of endangered species. Those are the plants and animals not yet identified, but up for sacrifice if the club lets those priceless ancient forests vanish the way they have been vanishing, vanishing while the board and staff deliberate, so often behind closed doors, about priorities and black bottom lines.

Then there's the matter of SCCOPE's backing away from its most important function—exerting the major influence it should in all conscience have found means to exert in the presidential election. Certainly the club could have found a way to do so without troubling funders, and diehard Republicans need to be troubled—about their party's environmental record. I hope you remember the reaction of the audience to my remark, "Thank George Bush for saying he is an environmentalist, and thank him again when he becomes one." You liked it well enough to repeat it. The Sierra Club members liked it both times. But where was the club leadership when it had a chance to give the country someone better to thank? Think how lonely Bill Reilly must now feel!

Perhaps you can understand why some people are contemplating full-page ads wondering what has become of John Muir's Sierra Club, and asking me about it. I fully expect another computer message from John Muir (via his hacker), threatening once again to resign as founder of the Sierra Club. [When I was at the Meadow Creek Project in Arkansas and the club board was in Deep Hesitation Mode about Hetch Hetchy, a pained message from Muir showed up on my computer screen and I telephoned it to the board. Can anyone imagine how the message got there?]

In my mountaineering days I learned that when one is lost, one must stay calm, retrace steps to the last known landmark, and proceed from there on a different course.

Has the club leadership lost its way? Remember the members' response to the two Daves. Standing ovations. Again and again members have asked me to "tell it like it is to the club," based on what I have learned in fifty-one years of fighting what Muir fought for. You can see from this letter how much I held back in my Ann Arbor talk.

You, too, received a standing ovation. How much did that applause come from your telling it like you thought they'd like to hear it? You told them how good they are, and what they ought to do first thing next week to empower themselves. But you told only five hundred listeners out of the five hundred thousand members. Isn't this something *Sierra* should long since have provided the background on, monthly, not bimonthly, if the club is to exert its strength on issues so important? How much applause was linked to your talk's being the final one in a great conference?

Do you feel as confident as you sounded that you are doing everything right and need no new ideas? Can you tell this alleged what's-his-name-reincarnate, what has driven you from the damn-the-torpedoes man you were for the Alaska Coalition? Did you like the splendid idea of the Chico Mendes award, or Mike McCloskey's bold move to get people to vote environmentally, better than they ever have before, with their dollars? You didn't say so. At a time like this, before the club's international assembly, should you appear to believe that existing strategies are adequate? Perhaps I wasn't listening carefully enough.

In any event, I am troubled for you and the club—troubled enough to write a letter like this, with copies to people I think care and may want to let you know. Incidentally, I'd like to see our exchange in my autobiography if you think it can help. People might understand several current problems better, instead of having to rely on what the book on the club history has muddied so badly, as opposed to what you reported in *The Sierra Club: A Guide*.

I know we agree on many things—especially that the Earth's present brief tenants are indeed the last who will have the opportunity to know wildness as we have known it, unless we pass it on. Perhaps you will also agree with the Alwyn Rhys quote Amory Lovins dug up, with a new twist: When you have reached the edge of an abyss, the only progressive move you can make is to turn around and step forward.

You have made great contributions, and I know there are greater to come.

Sincerely,
Dave Brower
Personal correspondence, **July 1989**

Yes, it is healing time on Earth. Aspirin and Band-Aids won't be enough. Surgery, prosthesis, and therapy will be required. And a generous application of TLC, which is always in short supply.

CHAPTER 11

WILDLIFE

FARMER BROWN'S BOY

How Do You Cross the Species Barrier? Talk to creatures who have no way of understanding your words? Devise body language that will communicate with someone in a different phylum? Extend a vulnerable hand as a gesture of friendship? Stroke or hug? Or just look with love?

It's hard enough to achieve a real connection within our own species. But how rewarding it is to have one of these offerings accepted, understood, and returned by someone built and endowed quite differently! What would you give to be able to sit beside a gorilla in the wild, offer the gorilla a pen, watch her give the pen a once-over and hand it back? Or to be able to let a fantasy soar and imagine yourself in the place of a cricket trying very hard not to be eaten tonight?

How does one even get interested in thinking this way? Or, to put the question more challengingly, how did we ever forget how to think this way? Who created the barrier between the wildness and intuition, the ancient knowing within us—and the corresponding miracle everywhere outside us? Not who, perhaps, but what? What took the wholeness we were part of and separated us out? And why did it take me seven decades or so to start asking these questions?

I had a good start. It is very helpful to have a parent or a grandparent, especially a grandparent with time to spare, invite you to think about these things. And it certainly was helpful to me to have my mother read bedtime stories to me from Thornton W. Burgess and suggest that I read more of them myself. If Bambi had been around then, something else might have happened, because Bambi always was a bit much. Bobby Coon, however, although ridiculously dressed by Harrison Cady, who illustrated the Burgess books, and although he spoke very good English for his age, was believable. A raccoon would very probably think just what he thought, but in raccoon language, not in mine.

How do I know this? I have a copy of the *Adventures of Bobby Coon.* It was published in 1919, and my mother read it to me that year or, at the latest, in early 1920. I probably read it for myself a year or two later, but that copy has been long lost. Sixty-eight years later Anne bought a copy for me for thirty-five cents, and a year after that I read the first half again. It blew me away. I discovered, after all these years, that I am Farmer Brown's Boy. Farmer Brown cut down the old dead hollow chestnut tree that was Bobby's home, and Bobby's foreleg was broken in the fall. Farmer Brown's Boy saw his predicament, gently threw his coat over Bobby, carried him home, splinted his leg, helped Old Mother Nature nurse him back to health, loved him and was loved back, then read in Bobby's eyes that he wanted to go back home to the Green Forest. Farmer Brown's Boy was forever talking gently to Bobby, feeding him goodies, petting him, as fond of him as he could be. Finally, warning Bobby about hunters, he took him back to the forest and set him free. That's all I have wanted to do ever since. You will find evidence of this in all that follows, though I will be using more sophisticated language part of the time than Farmer Brown's Boy spoke to Bobby Coon.

HUNTING

SO THERE IS FARMER BROWN'S BOY on the one hand, and there are the hunters on the other, and I have made my bias clear. I have also tried to be reasonable, and tried hard in correspondence that was published in the Friends of the Earth journal, *Not Man Apart*, in 1973. *NMA* had printed David Gancher's review of Cleveland Amory's book, *Man Kind?*, and it must have been a favorable review, because it brought automatic response from people who do not agree with Cleveland Amory on anything. This is how it went, followed by my response:

DEAR MR. BROWER:

I can only assume that David Gancher's review of *Man Kind?* reflects the policy of FOE.

I regard anti-hunting vegetarians as a sort of "weird cult." I can't really understand them, and indeed don't even know any, but they have my respect. At least they live according to the standards and morals they have set for themselves.

But any anti-hunting advocate who is not a strict vegetarian possesses one of the most despicable traits the human race has acquired: he is a hypocrite. He considers hunting wrong, so he pays someone else—his butcher—to do a job that his morals won't allow him to do. Is there a difference between shooting an animal and "slaughtering" it? Is there a difference between shooting a man and hanging him? Is it immoral to shoot a man, but acceptable to pay someone else to shoot that man?

I won't go into the need for hunting in the practice of good game management; books have been written on the subject and I don't have the time right now to add another.

I consider myself an outspoken conservationist. I also consider my friends who hunt as conservationists. You are only hurting your own conservation movement by taking an anti-hunting position. I won't join a group that opposes hunting; I won't suggest FOE to my friends; it won't be hard to urge my brother to let his membership expire.

I wouldn't have bothered to write this letter if I wasn't concerned about conservation and FOE's place in the conservation movement. I hope I am able to join FOE someday.

H. Martin Altepeter III
St. Louis, Missouri

Some wise old person counseled that it is folly to argue religion or politics. Add hunting. Friends of the Earth has issued no pronouncement on hunting and our policy will gradually evolve from contests we get into and what we think is right. If we are wrong, we'll try not to stay wrong.

When a given policy does arrive, we would hope that our members who don't agree with our views, say, on hunting, will still like what we are doing for them on nuclear, supersonic, clean-air, and wilderness matters (and *Not Man Apart,* too). Diversity is the strength of ecosystems—and other kinds of organization.

On hunting, right now FOE is for not hunting whales and for an end of the overhunting of fish and the drowning of porpoises for the convenience of certain tuna hunters. We don't like hunting with cruel traps or broad-spectrum poisons.

On other aspects of hunting, we probably have varying prejudices. My own (and "you can't reason prejudice out of a person, because it doesn't get in that way"—Les Pengelly) is that there is a one-hundred-eighty-degree difference between killing for essential food and killing for non-essential fun. I like to see a bit of sky filled with geese, and goose music; I do not at all like the empty space a shotgun leaves there for no reason except "sport."

I like the essential cooperation between hunters and nonhunters that has brought most of our conservation gains, despite all the arms-manufacturer and chemical-industry support that goes to some wildlife groups who are in business to maintain targets. The cooperation has kept land open and saved ranges that would otherwise be built on or paved. But I don't like the growing opposition hunters too often express to setting aside places where those who don't hunt can be safe.

I don't like the hunter who boasts of his conservation dedication and talks wildlife-management rationalizations, but who in real life rarely if ever gets back to where problems are. He hunts instead from the berm of some road, between swigs of strong drink and episodes of armed bullying of people who have posted their land because they like wild things wild, not served, garnished, to titillate jaded appetites.

I like the hunters who have changed their ways because they have perceived that what was once great sport is now hazardous—and getting more so in each passing hunting season—with fewer and fewer places that are sanctuaries from those who feel more manly when they see an animal die of their skill with a long-range technical advantage. And while waiting for more hunters to change their ways, I will thank those who, though hunting for sport, do not lobby against handgun control and the people who die for the lack of it. I wish these hunting friends would write the National Rifle Association (with whom we cooperate when we can) and ask it to change its ways.

For all the prejudice thus confessed, remember that it is not a consensus in Friends of the Earth. Perhaps it can be someday, and those FOE members who disagree will still support us for what they agree with—and the NRA et al. for a hunting stance they like better than ours. Perhaps we can all agree, right now, that conservation would be years behind where it is now had Aldo Leopold not loved to hunt, and had that pursuit not told him so well how the land mechanism works. The question remains, would he have loved hunting in a full land as much as he loved it in an empty one? There's no way to get his answer. We can only seek our own, without dividing and being conquered.

***Not Man Apart,* October 1973**

CARIBOU AND THE PHILLIPS ZOO

HOW, INDEED, do we avoid being divided and conquered, or to play it the other way—divide and conquer our opponents? Major in political science, I suppose, and I didn't. Without such formal training we should at least improve our ability to disagree with our friends less violently than we tend to, or even try to make new ones. Sigurd Olson, naturalist, writer, and conservation leader, was always willing to try:

"Let's go down to Interior and talk with Fred Seaton," Sig Olson suggested, and I agreed, although not quite realizing that Fred Seaton was the new secretary of the interior appointed by Dwight Eisenhower to replace Douglas McKay, whom many in my field of work were to conclude was much better at selling Chevrolets in Oregon than in serving as the chief conservation officer of the United States.

Sig Olson was bard of the Boundary Waters, very active in the Izaak Walton League and National Parks Association, conversant with Great Slave Lake, loons, and the Porcupine herd of some one hundred eighty thousand caribou who did not recognize the border between Canada and Alaska and needed protection whichever side they were on. Sig knew who Fred Seaton was, and I found out that day. There was good reason for renewed hope in the conservation movement and for the caribou.

To this day I have yet to meet a caribou in the wild. I want to live until I do and want the herds to live as long as the planet is habitable. I never want to see one in a zoo unless it is a Phillips Zoo. You will know what you need to know about a Phillips Zoo when David Phillips, Executive Director of Earth Island Institute, writes his book about his as-yet-unrealized invention. There will be no unwillingly incarcerated, formerly wild animals in it, living out ersatz lives behind bars or in fenced fields or in dioramas beyond moats or lying in their own dung on concrete alongside putrid pools. They never did anything to deserve that, nor have we done anything to justify our ogling them, with misguided curiosity, in their misery.

You don't see real animals in a zoo. You see only a shape they cannot escape in a place they would escape if they could. I remember the poignant last words of the Scott expedition, marooned in Antarctica: "Had we but lived." That surely must have been what the gorilla was thinking I once saw in the Central Park Zoo—or menagerie, as Fairfield Osborn called it. This sad great creature just sat there, with nothing to look at but its captors, caged, barred from a life that would count, remembering freedom, and that word again, being ogled. What kind of creatures are we, who would do this to creatures like that, for amusement?

For education? Only in an ethical vacuum, teaching children to find freedom by taking it from someone else. Some*one?* Well, not quite, according to Henry Beston:

For the animal shall not be measured by man. In a world older and more complete than ours they move finished and complete, gifted with extensions of the senses we have lost or never attained, living by voices we shall never hear. They are not brethren, they are not underlings; they are other nations, caught with ourselves in the net of life and time, fellow prisoners of the splendour and travail of the earth.

The Phillips Zoo respects these "other nations." It uses technology not to cage them as conventional zoos do, but to keep them free, to make perfectly clear how good they really are, when they are where they really belong.

The technology is extremely complicated and sophisticated, but it is available everywhere that is civilized enough to have uncivil zoos. Film.

Videotape. All-around projection. Environments on a screen, in three dimensions if you must, with no need to feed or clean up after the wild creatures because photographers have been intrepid and ingenious enough to bring them to us on film, unharmed.

Imagine what David Phillips has in mind—and let your imagination add to his. Remember what "Nova" has revealed to you on your small TV screen. Perhaps it was penguins falling or sliding down a slope and diving into the one place they can fly—underwater. Imagine what photomicrography has revealed of the wildness within other creatures and the parallel wildness within you. Imagine one of the microrooms in the Phillips Zoo, where children wander from one little exhibit to another and push a button to start each brief story. Imagine the macroroom. Here your seat can tilt back in a giant screen environment that can flood your entire field of vision with a Grand Canyon, a Niagara, a rain forest viewed from above or better still from below, its canopy and mysterious population almost overwhelming you. Imagine how overwhelming an all-encompassing caribou migration might be.

So I am not able to tolerate having caribou behind a fence to pet, tease, or offer peanuts to. If that's what young people desire, let them have a live cow or pony or burro or pig or domesticated goose, chicken, duck, or turkey. We have already helped reduce them to what they are, and they probably expect us to act the way we do.

Caribou don't, and never ought to.

I wasn't this angry when I wrote a foreword for a great book about caribou, but I am now. The people who have it in for caribou and their kin must also have it in for us. We, too, are kin.

IF YOU HAVE NEVER SEEN CARIBOU, even from the air, you ought to apologize before attempting to write about them. I do. You can make up for it by being suitably vicarious in the most ordinary sense—by experiencing or realizing, through imagination or sympathetic participation, the experience of another person. In *Caribou and the barren-lands,* George Calef makes that task an easy one. Through his photographs and his writing, he evokes the beauty of these animals and the majesty of the vast landscape over which they roam.

The beauty of the caribou and its homeland have long been celebrated by the Eskimo people:

Glorious it is to see
The caribou flocking down
From the forests
And beginning
Their wandering to the north.
Timidly they watch
For the pitfalls of man.
Glorious it is to see
The great herds from the forests
Spreading out over plains of white.
Glorious to see
Yayai–ya–yiya.

Glorious it is
To see long-haired
winter caribou
Returning to the forests.
Fearfully they watch
For the little people,
While the herd follows the
Ebb-mark of the sea
With a storm of clattering hooves.
Glorious it is
When wandering time is come.
Yayai–ya–yiya.

The poem is by Netsit, and appears in *Earth and the Great Weather: The Brooks Range*, by Kenneth Brower (Friends of the Earth, 1971).

The world of the caribou is not inviolate. The threats facing it were apparent long ago to Olaus and Mardie Murie, Robert Marshall, Sir Frank Fraser Darling, A. Starker Leopold, Lowell Sumner, George Collins, Ian McTaggart Cowan, Sigurd Olson, Ira N. Gabrielson, and Clinton Raymond ("Pink") Gutermuth. Throughout the 1950s they and many others worked to secure the designation of the Arctic National Wildlife Range in Alaska. Its nine million acres were set aside by U.S. Secretary of the Interior Fred Seaton in December 1960. When Secretary Seaton's successor, Stewart Udall, sought to reverse the decision, the forces of conservation were once again mobilized to dissuade him.

For decades attempts were made to seek Canada's help in a major expansion of key caribou habitat into an international Arctic Wildlife Range. The joint effort led, in October 1970, to the Arctic International Wildlife Range Conference, held in Whitehorse and chaired by Andrew Thompson. The opening paragraphs of the address by James Smith, then commissioner of the Yukon Territory, bear repeating here:

"The wildlife resources of the Arctic symbolize our common heritage. Their preservation, being a matter of deep concern to both nations, provides a challenge and hopefully an opportunity for cooperation. . . .

"There are compelling reasons which call for a global initiative to save the animals from extinction. One thing we have all learned recently is that in birth, in life and in death each species of animal and each species of plant performs innumerable functions that are crucial to the other species of life including man, and to the environment that supports all species. This complexity in the natural environment is a delicate web of relationships so that the slightest tampering with one part of the environment can have a disastrous effect on the whole. Every time we eliminate a species . . . we reduce the complexity of the systems upon which our very existence depends. Our emotional concern to save the animals from extinction is therefore a reflection of man's desire to extend his own survival on this planet."

One of the most effective efforts on behalf of the Far North was achieved by Justice Thomas Berger's Mackenzie Valley Pipeline Inquiry, the report of which came out in 1977. Justice Berger advocated a wilderness park-wildlife area, to cover approximately the same area as the Canadian part of the proposed Arctic International Wildlife Range, and to adjoin the Arctic National Wildlife Range in Alaska. The impetus given by Berger led the Canadian government in July 1978 to freeze all the lands north of the Porcupine River in the Yukon and to begin a process aimed at establishing a management regime for the area. Following logically from this was the need for an international treaty to protect the Porcupine caribou herd. Negotiations over such a treaty began in earnest in 1979, but have since floundered and now appear to be stalled indefinitely. The brave intentions of government to guarantee the preservation of this magnificent herd and this wilderness area are quickly being dissipated.

Defenders of the natural world cannot rest, for wilderness can be changed irrevocably. At the 1970 conference James Smith spoke of man's long and intimate association with the animal world, reminding us of the animal kingdom's rich complexities and urging us to take action to save our inheritance from extinction. He counseled our generation to recognize its international responsibility for "the wonderful, mysterious, furred and feathered creatures who share our destiny and our doom."

If it were just our own doom, that would be bad enough. But to insist on taking along with us so many of the life forms that preceded us on earth by so many eons—that insistence ought to be immensely troubling. The recently published *Global 2000 Report to the President* gives us the frightening number of species of plants and animals—from five hundred thousand to two million—that will be removed from the earth by the year 2000 *by us,* if humanity refuses to change its present habit of attacking the natural world as if there were no end to it. Looking to the Arctic and the industrial development plans for it, we can foresee that our present habit of searching for and exhausting energy resources at an increasing rate can quickly destroy the North. We face a choice. Caribou or ever more kilowatts? Whales or oil spills on troubled waters? Wilderness or wantonness with the throttle?

There are few who would suggest that arctic oil ought never to be used; many believe that the oil under the northern seas should be the last to be exploited, and that the exploitation should await improvements in technology and in our understanding of, and commitment to, arctic ecosystems. A great deal more needs to be learned about what arctic oil will do in arctic waters—under the ice, over the ice, on the water's surface, and, decade after decade of slow decomposition, on the sea's floor.

Dynamic energy conservation and major strides in the efficiency with which we use energy can allow time for a deliberate approach to the use of the nonrenewable resource of oil. And if slowing the gush of the black blood of energy should slow the speed with which we extinguish resources that will never be renewed, I hear no future generation complaining. If certain habits of growth are going to have to end sometime, why not while the earth, humanity, and caribou are still intact? One way of life does not have to die so that another can live.

Caribou and the barren-lands tells us of one of the splendid ways of life that must not die. It tells us beautifully. It reminds us that people can still take the time to seek truth from the natural world, to learn about a small but magnificent part of this planet. To have a chance to learn this truth, we had better save all the vestiges we can of the way the world was before the Industrial Revolution let us tear so much of the planet's surface apart. We ought to be brilliant enough to make do with where we've been already, trying harder to heal and less to harm.

***Caribou and the barren-lands*, 1981**

The California Condor

In 1984, When I Was Seventy-two, I saw my first California condors, and I would have happily never seen them if that could make their life in the wild any easier or surer. But it was becoming clear that I had better try to see one or two and thus get moved into battling on their behalf. I am glad I did, and am sorry for the California condor that the battle was lost. I am sorry to know that at Mount Pinos, at the southern end of the California coast ranges, I saw creatures that for a hundred thousand years had known freedom there and would probably never know it again.

That there would be a battle was certain. The condor population was dropping. The U.S. Fish and Wildlife Service Condor Recovery Program, (*Federal Register,* volume 46, number 106) proposed:

"Purpose: Recovery of the species through captive propagation, radio telemetry, and other scientified research techniques.

"Long Range Objective: To establish a secure and self-sustaining wild population of California condors."

The duration of the study would be through the year 2015.

Let this condor story begin with an exchange with Russell Peterson, with whom I suspect I agreed on almost everything but the condor, when he was president of the National Audubon Society. Largest of the California chapters of the National Audubon Society, the Golden Gate Audubon Society opposed the national society's approach to a condor recovery program, opposition expressed in a letter to the national president, Russell

Peterson, from Jerry Emory, the Golden Gate Society's young executive director. On August 15 Dr. Peterson replied. The reply was apparently given wide circulation and was presented in full in the Friends of the Earth book, *The Condor Question,* as was my reply of September 11, 1980:

DEAR RUSS:

Several of our members have seen and forwarded copies of your letter of August 15 to Jerry Emory (of the Golden Gate Audubon Society to which I have long belonged) about the condor and your deep concern.

My own concern goes back a long way and quite a bit of it is relevant. In 1941, when John Baker was organizing the National Audubon Society, I applied to him for a job but lost out to Bert Harwell, whose work with birds I had known well from my years in Yosemite. Instead I became an editor at the University of California Press, which enabled me to work on many monographs from the Life Sciences Building, most of them from the Museum of Vertebrate Zoology. Some of my work was with Loye Miller, but much more was with his son Alden, then director of MVZ and for some time chairman of the university's editorial committee. I also worked with Frank Pitelka and Robert C. Stebbins.

It was this UC connection that enabled me to publish condor material in the *Sierra Club Bulletin,* the editing of which I was deeply involved in from 1935 to 1969. I was also deeply involved in the Sierra Club Conservation Committee, which I helped organize in 1940. I rarely missed a meeting, stimulated as I was by the success of the club's effort in the battle to establish Kings Canyon National Park. Carl Koford used to attend those meetings. My interest in the condor began at about the same time he began his Audubon/University of California study.

Carl's work still informs me, and I wish it informed all who are concerned with saving the condor. The hapless chick [a condor chick died while being measured and photographed in the nest] would still be alive. On page 1 of the book he did for Audubon—*The California Condor*—Carl warned, "Because of the danger of injury, it is inadvisable to trap and mark condors." On the next-to-last page: "Therefore, the only way of completely protecting condors from molestation is through the cooperation of people throughout the range of the condors. Sensational publicity is harmful in that it causes persons who otherwise would have no direct influence upon condors to seek the birds and to disturb them." Such an admonition led me long ago to decide that I would rather hear about condors than see them, if the seeing might in any way disturb and endanger them.

My other concerns with wildlife grew as I worked with Lowell Sumner, George Collins, and Victor Cahalane of the National Park Service, with E. Raymond Hall, with Starker Leopold and his students, including Lee Talbot, and with Olaus and Mardie Murie. I first began to like birds a great deal in 1937, when my most frequent climbing companion was Morgan Harris, an amateur birder who would become chairman of the Department of Zoology at Berkeley and is still active. He, along with many others, is not at all happy about the hands-on part of the Condor Recovery Plan. Some of us are beginning to call it the Condor Disposal Program. It worried Dave Phillips, Ray Dasmann, and me when we first had a chance to discuss it together in the course of Ray's receiving the Aldo Leopold Medal in Toronto.

This long prelude was stimulated by your writing of "personally reviewing all the facts in this matter." Your subsequent remarks show that you have missed a substantial body of vital information, including, we think, that which we have been quite assiduous in digging up. I think it worthwhile to go point by point over the matters where we think you are wrong.

You imply that those who disagree with you wish to abandon the three-part program. They don't. They merely want the dangerous part that calls for captive propagation dropped – its danger is something we predicted and the recovery team has proved. By all means more research, but research on the natural behavior of the condor, not the behavior of a molested one. By all means expanded habitat protection – the kind advocated by Alden Miller, Carl Koford, and a long list of people who know a great deal about the bird's natural habitat, as much as is left of it. I have been close enough to behaviorists to know the importance of the observer's melting into the natural background. That melting does not accommodate harassment, capture, marking, surgery, or captive breeding.

An essential point you speak of is "to ensure the perpetuation of a wild, free-flying population of the condor." We wish you would carefully read Carl Koford's and Dick Smith's books so that you would no longer misconstrue what "wild and free-flying" consists of. San Diego is not wild, and whatever its virtues, it cannot inform a condor the way its wild range can, or its free-flying parents. Condor competence did not evolve by virtue of human help, nor can that competence be expected to survive an obsession with management. That is not the way genes get to know what they must if they are to keep a creature alive in the wild.

To miss that essential point is to miss one of the most important warnings in *The Global 2000 Report to the President:* If people go on doing what they are doing, then by the year 2000 between five hundred thousand and two million species of plants and animals that are now here won't be here anymore. No species has the right to do that to other species and to expect or deserve to survive them. What leads to this dire projection is humanity's messing up habitat and wildness. The present Condor "Recovery" Plan exacerbates the problem instead of providing the best possible example of ways in which humanity can reform, and spare the extinctions that Joseph Wood Krutch said would make our voyage on this planet a lonely one. The present plan's research stresses gadgetry instead of wildness, its contribution to habitat protection has lamentably been negligible, and *captive* by definition is the opposite of *free*. I cannot see how to consider a panel of ornithologists to have been either objective or expert if they have not seriously addressed the problem *The Global 2000 Report* presents. They ought to have participated in the three-year study the report required; indeed, they should have anticipated its relation to the condor. Surely the world needs a better idea than spending twenty or thirty million dollars each to take species off the endangered species list. The better idea, we think, is to save the ecosystem that enables an endangered species to remain natural, not to become an artifact.

You state, in short, that the death of the chick does not change anything. We hope that it will lead to some contrition, to the admission of possible fallibility, to a willingness to re-examine the most controversial step National Audubon has taken on in all its years. I do not see how you can remain confident that you are right when so many good people believe Carl Koford was right. His recommendations remain the sound ones. The program National Audubon supports, moreover, ignored the warnings of many members of the public and the scientific community, and deceived the Fish and Game Commission and the director of the Department of Fish and Game in California.

There are times when it is wise to return to Square One. I think the condors would like you to. Technology assessment has had its inning. I think it is time for behaviorists' biological assessment to have its time at bat. A thirty-to-forty-year program for the condor is an excellent idea. But it ought to be for the condor, not for a managed facsimile of the original—provided captive breeding succeeds.

You speak of perceiving mistakes in hindsight. It troubles us that people around the recovery team were foreseeing these mistakes, but warnings were lost in the deafness that overconfidence brings. What the condor needs now is not a modification of equipment or procedures involved in trapping, but a reformation of human concept and performance.

Your reference to the Cape Canaveral tragedy has bothered a lot of people. If there were only twenty-nine humans left, and through bad luck or stupidity the technology for sending them off the planet incinerated three of them, then surely the remedy would not be merely to improve the technology, but to reassess the goal. Will a distant, untried environment be safer? Or, instead of seeking escape, should we concentrate on fixing the place we are in, and have been adapted to and shaped by? Incidentally, Wes Jackson observes that we did not place men on the moon. They did not even touch it. What did touch it was the sophisticated bit of earth environment that they were encapsulated with. That's not the way for condors to go!

Your comment about filming the episode so as not to hide anything misses several critical points. First, though the handling of condors' chicks was acknowledged to have risks, the action was never brought before the Fish and Game Commission or the public. John Ogden, National Audubon Society's condor research biologist, subsequently commented that he could not conduct his research in the "public arena." Earlier in 1967, there had been severe criticism of the National Wildlife Federation's disturbing condors by the very act of filming them for a special issue of *National Wildlife*. Koford, the McMillans, and others repeatedly warned of the immediate and delayed threat to condors resulting from disturbance, and that ought to be seen to include disturbance caused by photographers. Dick Smith, in *Condor Journal,* told of some of the disturbance caused by photographers who were well concealed in blinds. Jeff Foott and Tupper Blake were not concealed at all—certainly not from the chicks being photographed, and conceivably not from the parents. The condor's ability to discern disturbance from afar ought to be assumed. Observers assigned to give radio warning of the parents' return should not presume they could see distant condors as well as distant condors could observe what was going on in their most critical environment of all—their nests.

As a further point, please look carefully at the footage taken by Jeff Foott, and estimate how much the fatally traumatized chick was handled in order to get close-ups as well as medium shots of the various actions—capture, pulling, stuffing into the horse-feed bag, stuffing into the knapsack, weighing, measuring wing length, straddling, and measuring beak length. After all that, Jeff Foott reportedly became alarmed, put the camera down, and tried to help, thus missing the final death throes.

We are not happy that photographers were permitted to accompany the team, but not the promised veterinarian or the independent observers we had urged to be present. It is easy to conclude that the photography related more to public relations than to an effort to document good and bad moves. Except in an Andy Warhol film that omits nothing, the camera will get only what the photographer is ready to shoot—provided it comes out. Photography helps, but the expert observer's eye is what counts. When the chick was killed, no experts were watching, either to advise or to remember, and the shots dwelling on the Audubon arm patch are a bit embarrassing. Without the film, for all the other errors, there might well now be two chicks, not one, both less traumatized. Far from its being a safeguard, the filming added a hazard. We are forced to infer that the USFWS and National Audubon Society researchers knew that if they had brought their plan for close-range photography and handling before the commission, it would not have been allowed. With condor-recovery priorities where we urged that they should be, there would have been no trauma. New initiatives for habitat protection would be under way, not stalled.

While you regret the unfortunate death, in the Cronkite segment on the tragedy your field crew said the handling of the chick was normal. That should have alarmed the society as it does us. Nor should there be comfort in the hope that the death might persuade the parents to breed again sooner. If "normal handling" loses one chick out of two, the condors won't gain appreciably.

Late in your letter you restate your earlier misconception. Despite your repeated concern, we have heard no one, including Jerry Emory, argue that the entire California condor program be abandoned. Your many opponents argue that the program should be strengthened by placing a moratorium on trapping, handling, capture, marking, surgery, and caged breeding until, after a major effort in habitat protection, such captive breeding is proved necessary and has been proved successful on surrogate species. We are still duly concerned that even if captive breeding were to "succeed," it would more likely ensure a dependent population than one able to survive on its own.

Conscientious human intervention on many fronts, such as you call for, should begin with intervention against the human intervenors. If, given a chance because we all work to assure that chance, the condor begins to recover by virtue of its own proved fecundity on its own ground, then we will have some of the information essential for recovering for the condor some of the former breeding range you speak of. For now, we need to hang on hard to the known nest areas, present and recent.

You discuss the amount of range a condor needs. Carl Koford, in 1952, narrowed the nesting sites essentially to the terrain between fifteen hundred and forty-five hundred feet within a gross area of some two million acres. Condors ranged beyond that, of course, but ranged back. Nesting, roosting, and watering sites, suitably isolated, seem to have been the critical requirement then, and must still be now. We need to know much more, and Carl Koford, Dick Smith, the McMillans, and others have shown us how to find out. Eyes on! Surely much of the essential range must be wild. Thus we would like very much to see Audubon's strong support for the proposed Sespe-Frazier Wilderness, but it has by no means materialized. Our check, and the Sierra Club's, has turned up only the one letter from John Borneman to Congressman Lagomarsino and a brief one to the California Fish and Game Commission, both of which are welcome, but much more is needed. Faint heart will not win fair maiden. And Mr. Borneman, after the chick's death, reverted to his old argument against wilderness: it is a "people magnet." It is true that more people use wilderness now than when Aldo Leopold got us the Gila Wilderness. It is also true that California's population has quintupled since then. We believe that the most dangerous magnet now is the resource magnet. Without wilderness protection this area will attract the people who care least about condors, the people who want to bring in all the encumbrances of resource exploitation. Their marks would be of far more lasting impact on condors than trail-walkers' footprints.

We grant that there is excitement, challenge, and romance in the enthusiasm for captive breeding. There have manifestly been some short-term successes, and there may well be more. But beware how one manipulative step leads to another: intervene, protect, mollycoddle, spoil, and destroy.

It is worth thinking hard about Carl Koford's warning to the Fish and Wildlife Service on November 27, 1967. Concerning Topa Topa, presumably before the bird was captured, he wrote: "I recommend feeding it on the spot without capturing it and later, if necessary, moving it to a higher point away from human habitation. In addition, I specifically recommend keeping it out of the zoo, especially the Los Angeles one." He then noted that after the bird had been captive for more than a month, it had been exposed to zoo diseases and was otherwise "spoiled for potential release to the wild." There was then a consensus that "the captive was not to be used for public display or zoo publicity, but apparently it is now being used for both." It still is used for both and so, we fear, is the ill-fated Condor Recovery Plan National Audubon so ardently espouses. We could wish Topa Topa better luck, considering its narrow escape from death when John Borneman tried to release it, with a leash still attached, in the vicinity of wild birds that were now hostile to it.

For all the people expert in wildlife matters that I have worked with and learned from, Robinson Jeffers (whom I never met) taught me most with the fewest words:

What but the wolf's tooth whittled so fine
The fleet limbs of the antelope?
What but fear winged the birds, and hunger
Jewelled with such eyes the great goshawk's head?

This truth has escaped the captive breeders, and should escape them no longer. They must learn what the force of creation consists of, how long it has been successful, and how little they know about it. While wilderness, to John Borneman, and to others who support it timidly, may be a people magnet, it was understood far better by Nancy Newhall: "Wilderness holds answers," she wrote, "to more questions than we have yet learned how to ask." The captive-breeding approach speeds and excuses its demise.

We dare not let the last wilderness on earth go by our own hand, and hope that technology will somehow get us to a new wilderness on some remote planet. Or that somehow we can save little samples of genes in bottles or on ice, isolated and manageable, or reduce the great vistas to long-lasting videotape, destroying the originals to sustain the balance of trade and of egos.

Back to Jeffers again, and his powerful poem, "The Answer":

. . . however ugly the parts appear
the whole remains beautiful. A severed hand
Is an ugly thing, and man dissevered from the earth and stars
and his history . . . for contemplation or in fact . . .
Often appears atrociously ugly. Integrity is wholeness,
the greatest beauty is
Organic wholeness, the wholeness of life and things, the divine beauty
of the universe. Love that, not man
Apart from that, or else you will share man's pitiful confusions,
or drown in despair when his days darken.

The Global 2000 Report to the President has certainly projected dark days on the screen. I think we must surely agree that the prospect, for the year 2000, of five billion new acres of desert, and of two million missing species of plants and animals, is an entirely unacceptable prospect. It will not do to settle for dioramas of tropical forest—or of the Sespe-Frazier and environs—in some hall of the American Museum of Natural History. It will not do to be so presumptuous as to think we can quick-freeze the flow of wildness through two million species, to dispose of if it loses its integrity, or to release when convenient into a habitat that neither knows these species nor is known by them. It will not do to continue the illusion that a condor and zoo are compatible. A condor severed from the wild is an ugly thing; the whole is beautiful, and William Dawson knew it. In *Birds of California,* he wrote: "But for me the heart of California lies in the condor country. And for me the heart of mystery, of wonder, and of desire lies with the California condor, that majestic and almost legendary figure, which still haunts the fastnesses of our lessening wilderness."

A condor in a zoo, however elaborate the enclosure, is to be pitied. The National Audubon Society should play no further role in such sad incarceration. We pray that the society and you, in the words of Maurice Strong, can adjust your thinking. There is vital work to be done to save the condor. The present condor recovery plan is not doing it. Let us join forces and get about it!

***The Condor Question,* 1981**

Perhaps David Phillips would never have developed his distaste for zoos had he not become deeply involved in the California condor controversy. That involvement led to his catalyzing and editing Friends of the Earth's book, *The Condor Question: Captive or Forever Free?* The condor, soaring on its nine-foot wingspan, unperturbed by gusts that would send lesser birds to shelter, had a splendor all its own. Ancient, magnificent, and controversial, it was forced into a vestige of wilderness that is itself on the verge of extinction. Biologists specializing in hands-on technology, as my letter shows, were determined to capture the condor to save it.

The Condor Question presented a better idea, selected from the writings of friends of the condor whose work had essentially been ignored. The book listed twenty-four steps to assure, without cannon-netting, radio-tagging, sex-probing, or cage-breeding, that the condors and their sanctuary could be kept intact. These steps called for land acquisition, improved management of federal lands, law enforcement, research, comprehensive habitat protection, and the preparation of an environmental impact statement before judging the permit request of the U.S. Fish and Wildlife Service. The twenty-four steps were milestones on the road not taken.

I wrote the concluding chapter of the book:

USE IT TOO OFTEN and the word *habitat* begins to shed its meaning. The word *environment* already suffers, and but feebly connotes the entity that makes it possible for us to be. *Ecosystem* and *ecosphere* vaunt themselves too much. *Niche* has a good ecological spot in the book but is too small for a condor. So how about *place?*

In 1971 Alan Gussow, in his book, *A Sense of Place: The Artist and the American Land,* wrote about "the qualities in certain natural places which certain men and women have responded to with love. . . . For all of us have our loved places; all of us have laid claim to parts of the earth; and all of us, whether we know it or not, are in some measure the products of our sense of place."

Like most of us, Mr. Gussow was conscious of man as a violator of the earth's lovely places. "There is a great deal of talk these days," he said, "about saving the environment. We must, for the environment sustains our bodies. But as humans we also require support for our spirits, and this is what certain kinds of places provide." He saw the earth as a collection of places that sustain our humanity. "We are homesick for places, we are reminded of places, and it is the sounds and smells and sights of places which haunt us." Against them we measure our past and present. My own prefatorial remark in the book agreed with John Muir about places: Throughout the course of life on earth, wildness has flowed from form to form, each more beautiful than what went before. But, I added, "suddenly, with a speed of attack there is no precedent for, man undertook to simplify that wildness, foreclose on diversity, dry up springs, and praise himself."

What condors need most right now is our sense of their place. To attain that insight, according to former Audubon screen-tour lecturer John Taft, we might try to think like a condor, and realize how superior to ours is a condor's visual grasp of its place. Roland Ross goes further. Recently he was demonstrating condor aerodynamics before the California Fish and Game Commission, and was so realistic in his gestures that he might well have become airborne had the room been bigger. A room is no place to be a condor in.

It should help us to wonder what kinds of places are necessary to let condors' spirits fly. What sustains their condorness? What sounds, smells, and sights, what flow of wildness? What tradition or social custom? It must surely be tradition, for example, that persuades condors to use the same roosting tree on the Tejon Ranch for thirty-five years. They find that ranch part of their social custom, a keystone, more aptly, in the mountain arc they range, and they could collapse without it. A huge keystone it is, a ranch occupying nearly two hundred eighty thousand acres where the San Joaquin Valley yields to the Tehachapis. It harbors a large roosting and foraging area for the condors. How important is it to them?

"The Tejon Ranch is absolutely vital to the population for its winter survival," said the Advisory Panel on the California Condor in its report of May 28, 1978, to the National Audubon Society and the American Ornithologists' Union. "The loss of the ranch to development or to a marked change in ranching practices would be disastrous."

Thirty months later they were saying, "There is presently no way to know what constitutes critical habitat for the condor." In that interim there had arisen a need to rationalize radio tagging of condors. They were right in May. What could have caused the switch?

The Rancho El Tejon Draft Environmental Impact Report of May 21, 1981, suggests an answer. It proposes a monumental development and quite substantial change in ranching practices. For a ranch on which as much as two-thirds of the condor population spends half the year, the proposal calls for "2,500 permanent dwelling units, 7,554 second homes ranging from cabins to rural estates, and 2,460 campsites that would convert approximately 17,143 acres of extensive agricultural lands to a variety of residential, recreational, and agricultural uses." Contemplating the general proposal in October 1980, Kern County officials said that a preliminary analysis indicated that "existing water supplies would not be adequate and that only the Peripheral Canal or a comparable water-importation system would make the project feasible." Thus the canal would become a major threat to the condors by leading to incompatible development of their favorite ranch.

El Tejon, incidentally, means *the badger.* It is an unhappy coincidence that the Badger Ranch seems destined to be the place where condors may be most effectively badgered. Permission to trap condors there has apparently been arranged with the ranch management, and it is not difficult to infer that conversion of the 17,143 acres would be easier if the condors were frightened away, trapped, or shipped away to pens in Los Angeles and San Diego. The pen or the zoo thus becomes the easy way out, captive breeding the "safety net" for disappearing species. The combination provides a guilt-assuaging way of saving the gorilla, for example, from destruction of its habitat by primitive people. Or the wild condors from sophisticated developers. Thus could good civilized intentions come to threaten a wild creature as thoroughly as primitive hunger. One wonders how much good intentions should be influenced by bad schemes.

One of the hard questions confronting people who care about the condor or other endangered species is the question of growth in California. The proposed Tejon development is but a step, although a major one, toward a California future in which a traveler would have to contend with freeway signs reading: LOS ANGELES—NEXT 250 EXITS.

Must Paul Bunyan move to California, go into real estate, and ride a giant leaping frog, racing north from Los Angeles in twenty-mile leapfrog hops, leaving colossal subdivision plans at each landing? If so, the destruction of California that Raymond Dasmann wrote a book about in 1965 will remain on schedule. No one in leadership dares to say *STOP!* So count on Japan's present population as the model for California's year 2080, and China's for the United States as a whole; after all, we are talking about roughly the same respective areas. Such a grim future, with its coalescing cities and suburbs, will have far too little room for people and no room at all for condors.

We believe that there is a better future for people and condors. It is implicit in the long-range objective of the California Condor Recovery Plan—"to establish a secure and self-sustaining wild population of the California condor." A secure condor would symbolize a new maturity in our thinking: we would be back in reasonable balance, thanks to self-restraint, willingness to live and let live, and living better for it.

That noble long-range objective, however, is immediately aborted in the very program thereupon presented to achieve it. A wild population requires wildness, and the program speeds the demise of wildness for condors and everyone else as well. It has already cost the life of one condor chick, possibly another, and the lives of various living things in the hundred acres a program-initiated forest fire burned over. Such losses, and the concomitant disturbing of adults, will not speed condor recovery.

A disturbing event that took place some forty years ago was related to me by Roland Ross. A naturalist, then like Ross, a Cooper Club member and avid condor student, set up a blind under a cliff in which condors were nesting. He came out for exercise only after dark, and in various ways kept himself out of the condors' ken well enough that the pair was not upset by his presence. One day one of the condors became extraordinarily agitated, moved up and down the cliff, then into the nest and broke the egg. The nest was thereupon deserted. The naturalist had looked at his watch and later noted that the agitation coincided with the arrival, ten miles away, of a steer carcass brought in by horse and sled as supplementary food for the condors, a supplement the naturalist had arranged for. Carl Koford told David Phillips in a 1979 interview of the same incident or a similar one when Dr. Koford was there with the naturalist—who later denied the happening to Dr. Koford, refused ten years ago to discuss it with Professor Ross, and recently said it was someone else.

Forty years can blur details, of course, but some events are etched clearly and don't blur easily. The egg might well have been destroyed for another reason. There remains the chance, however, that its breaking was more than coincident with the arrival of the carcass. And had the nest not been discovered and the food not brought in, a condor might have been spared to be a parent for ten or fifteen more condors. One can further wonder what condors caught in cannon nets, variously explored, radio-tagged, and released, might do upon return to their nests.

In any event, the 1980 condor chick died of shock caused by the trauma of handling. The death of the 1981 chick could be due to overzealousness of the Condor Research Center observers. Details are hard to uncover, but from what we have been able to piece together, the parents of the first chick killed were soon nesting again about a mile away. Perhaps because of the apprehension about the research-center observers nearby, they next moved five miles away from their first disaster and there produced and incubated an egg. Observers moved close. Unprecedented condor behavior resulted. The male was disturbed enough to destroy the egg or the newly hatched chick—the observers were not quite close enough to be sure. Chances are, however, they were close enough to cause aberrant behavior. This account may be wrong, too. It is nevertheless a fair indication of what could reasonably be expected. We do know the research-center members, in trying out their cannon nets, created a new problem, described in identical editorials. The *Ventura County Star-Free Press* headed its editorial of August 14, 1981: "Strike two on the condor-savers."

A *Tulare Advance-Register* editorial five days later was headlined: "Protecting the California condors—even if it kills all of them." It continued:

"It's starting to sound like the scenario for an old-time movie script: 'Laurel and Hardy Save the Condor.' But so far, the scenes aren't very funny.

"First, the condor-savers killed a baby condor. Then they started a brush fire that burned 100 acres and nearly burned some homes. . . . As part of the condor-saving program, a baby condor chick died while being handled in the wilds by an Audubon Society biologist last year. One official explanation was that the condor chick may have been 'predisposed to die,' which would make it mere coincidence that the chick happened to die while it was being handled.

"Obviously, the only reason to believe that is to want to believe it. The only impartial conclusion is, the condor-savers killed a baby condor.

"That put the condor-saving program on 'hold' for months, while the wisdom of trapping was debated some more. But those who pushed trapping were undeterred by the death of the condor chick.

"Grown condors are harder to trap than chicks, since they know how to fly, so grabbing them by hand doesn't work. (Lucky for them.) The technique to be used to trap adult condors is a net shot from a cannon. (How's that for preserving their natural habitat?)

"Some members of the Audubon Society were practicing with the cannon last Wednesday in Southern California, trying to trap buzzards as a tune-up for trapping condors. The cannon started a brush fire that quickly burned more than 100 acres before firemen got it under control. It took 150 firefighters, 18 engines, 3 water tenders, 3 helicopters, 2 planes and 2 bulldozers to knock down the fire and save half a dozen homes.

"Nobody doubts the sincerity of the naturalists who believe that aggressive tactics are needed to save the condor, such as trapping and handling and measuring and tagging those released, and trying to breed others in captivity. Neither should anyone doubt the sincerity of the naturalists who believe the way to save the condor is naturally—by keeping people away from the condor refuge and keeping hands off the condors.

"It's not a debate that's easily resolved, but one thing is clear at this point: The 'hands-off' naturalists haven't killed any condors or started any fires.

"There was a report that some buzzards escaped and some were burned. This was denied, and the denial is probably correct. But birds could easily have been burned and were certainly traumatized."

The hands-on people seem clearly to lack the sensitivity epitomized by Carl Koford in his last interview. In the fall of 1979, just a week before he died, he was asked a last question by David Phillips: "Do you think it's possible to protect the habitat in a way that would let condors increase their population to a sustainable level?" Koford replied:

"Yes, I think so. The question is, how do you do it? The Eb McMillan way, I think—which is, the best thing that can happen to a condor nest is that nobody finds it. Because once people find it, they're going to be observing it. And they don't realize . . . the damage you can do to condor nesting even by standing up and looking at it from half a mile away. . . . If you just add up the statistics, and separate nests which were visited from those that weren't visited, you'll see that even one visit to the nest decreases by about ten percent the chances of fledging a bird. Any disturbance is too much, and you can't tell by looking at the bird. You're sitting there, and the condor is sitting there, but the condor isn't going in and feeding the young, which is what it would be doing if you weren't there. There's no way you can judge how disturbed a bird is."

There will surely be less disturbance if one recognizes, as Les Reid of the Sierra Club does, that condors have rights. That includes the right to their own dignity. We can grant them their rights, or we can preempt them all. One particular right the condor once had was freedom of the sky. From the coast ranges, eastward along the Tehachapis, and north to the old sequoias of the Sierra Nevada, an array of thermals and condors' knowing the wind kept the huge birds aloft and made that vast mountain arc their home. Then the different flood came, as humanity reached its second billion in the late twenties and its most recent billion since the assassination of John F. Kennedy. This new flood, as it surges ever higher, extinguishes old freedoms. What replaces them is not new freedom but license, an arrogant assumption that no title to a place is valid unless we write it in our newly invented language and insist, as one of the most recent arrivals on the planet, that we must second-guess the Creator and manage it all.

If we remove condors from the wild and, with convenient rationalization, move ourselves in, we lose. As Professor Starker Leopold has pointed out, "Unless the causes of reproductive failure are understood *and corrected* there is nothing to be gained by pen-raising birds and putting them back in an unreceptive environment."

If we cannot save a receptive environment for the condor, symbol of the global threat to endangered species, what can we save? California and the condor deserve better than the present high-technology condor-disaster plan. It is high time for the federal government to obey its own requirements in the National Environmental Protection Act. By providing the essential environmental impact statement conservationists have been asking for, the NEPA approach can search out alternatives and find the dynamic one. Our choice would be a spacious international condor reserve with congenial development on the edges, not in dead center.

Americans can save the condor's place from ourselves. There are twenty-four steps that ought to precede any further molestation of the condor, and will probably preclude molestation. Steps like these can be followed elsewhere for other species, to slow the reckless attack on the earth's diversity and save its organic wholeness.

"What's the use of a house," Thoreau asked, "if you haven't got a tolerable planet to put it on?" He knew what losses in his time had made the place less and less tolerable. In his journal for March 23, 1856, he regretted that "the nobler animals have been exterminated here—the cougar, panther, lynx, wolverine, wolf, bear, moose, deer, the beaver, the turkey," leaving him a tamed and emasculated country, a maimed and imperfect nature like "a tribe of Indians that had lost all its warriors."

What he wanted instead was not attainable then, much less now, but can still give us pause:

I seek acquaintance with Nature, to know her moods and manners. I take infinite pains to know all the phenomena of the spring, for instance, thinking that I have here the entire poem, and then, to my chagrin, I hear that it is but an imperfect copy that I possess and have read, that my ancestors have torn out many of the first leaves and grandest passages, and mutilated it in many places. I should not like to think that some demigod had come before me and picked out some of the best of the stars. I wish to know an entire heaven and an entire earth.

Thoreau's ancestors were novices at mutilation. We can mutilate at breakneck speed. We seem determined in our own time to elbow two million species of plants and animals into oblivion in the next two decades, and will succeed if we insist on flooding the earth with our own numbers and draining it of unreplenishable resources. Sparing us from this latter-day flood will require a good many more Noahs than are now at work. They can succeed where today's few institutions for the future have faltered. There can be a new ark, and it is not too late for the splendid creature the condor is—and for many lesser ones we have yet to learn about. The miraculous flow of information in their wild genes, their unique chemistries, and their love of life can be passed on. We need not be wanton and banish them. They can survive and hold onto their freedom.

The Condor Question, we hope, will enhance the opportunity for the rest of us to keep intact the wildness and wild living things that remain in the sea, on the land, and in the air, to prevent a wake for them and their not-so-distant relatives, ourselves. We and they need our places, our islands of sanctuary.

Let it speed the California condor's recovery to measure the bird arbitrarily about like this: A condor is five percent feathers, flesh, blood, and bone. All the rest is *place.* Condors are soaring manifestations of the place that built them and coded their genes. That place requires space to nest in, to teach fledglings, to roost in unmolested, to bathe and drink in, to find other condors in and not too many biologists, and to fly over wild and free. If it is to be worthy at all, our sense of ethics about other living things requires our being able to grant that their place transcends our urge to satisfy our curiosity, to probe, to draw blood, to insult, to incarcerate. We can respect the dignity of a creature that has done our species no wrong—except, perhaps, to prefer us at a distance.

***The Condor Question,* 1981**

In 1990 we are no longer at a distance. All the condors were captured and placed in zoos in Los Angeles and San Diego. What we can still do is rescue from development and other abuses the areas that condors require in order to be condors, then release them, praying that they haven't forgotten what to do there. The rescue will be expensive, but not cost as much as our guilt will if we don't try.

What alarms me about captive breeding is its use as an excuse for raiding the critical habitat of some other species; what is supposed to help the condor is fatal to the others. Removing the condor from its key range has opened that range to development beyond mitigation. Fair compensation for the condor would include restoring the Los Angeles Basin to its pristine state, which once accommodated condors. There may be other good reasons for such restoration, but it is, shall we say, highly unlikely.

If we could be assured that development of the Tejon Ranch biome and its neighborhood will be blocked, at public expense, until the new population of captive-bred condors has reached a satisfactory level, that would spare us from considering the captive breeding of condors with untempered cynicism. We are not likely to be thus assured.

But suppose we are. Will the breeders dare to release the condors to the wild? I think not. I am afraid that they are breeding condors imprinted to humans, not to the wild. It frightens me to see what I think is a misguided effort to help condor chicks out of their shells. My sad experience with swallowtail butterfly chrysalids warns me that these chicks have thus been denied a form of exertion essential to their development. I simply cannot forget the essay I read in my brief time in college, "The Harm That Good Men Do." I share the growing regret that Smokey the Bear led us to overprotect forests, and that we are now paying for that overprotection. Or that well-intentioned foreign aid has produced ecological disasters around the world. Overprotection is a disaster to the condor.

Since worrying is my business, I'll add one more worry. Captive breeding cannot be considered a successful procedure until captive-bred birds, when released to the wild, produce a generation capable, in the wild, of producing a generation that is at home in the wild. That will not work if there is not the right kind of wild to go home to, or the right kind of wildness within the bird.

The test will need to be species specific: you can't grow apples on a saguaro. In other words, it would be folly to think that success with the peregrine falcon means success with the California condor. You have to know what is in the gene package. The Arctic tern, for example, has a sky map in its genes. The young leave the Arctic nesting site ahead of their parents and reach the Southern Hemisphere on their own. That is almost as remarkable as the monarch butterfly. The egg laid in Canada produces a caterpillar that transforms into a monarch as expected; but unexpectedly, and without a mother to guide it, junior can fly to a prearranged wintering spot in Mexico and back to Canada in the spring for the laying of the next season's eggs.

Your child would need a little more help, and so does a condor chick. The chick spends a year at the nest and the juvenile five years in the air learning from its parents, in due course, what *they* learned from *theirs* about how condors survive. The bigger it is, the longer the learning curve.

Think like a condor! Would you want to be helped out of your egg, fed by a puppet, and left to learn where food, water, roosts, nest sites, and thermals are in San Diego or Los Angeles, within very narrow confines?

I will never again see the miracle of a condor in flight, headed where the great bird wishes to go, knowing the sky, finding the thermals that can lift it to nine thousand feet and let it glide west in freedom.

The good news is that I witnessed that miracle. The bad is that you cannot.

WHALES

IF IT IS EASY TO GET INTO TROUBLE by opposing hunters, or still more trouble by opposing the National Rifle Association, or deep trouble by opposing the National Audubon Society, the deepest trouble of all comes from supporting the hunting of whales. If the species of whale is thought to be endangered and you accede to their being hunted, it is time to get into another business.

When controversy arose over hunting the bowhead whale, my mind was made up: Bowhead whales had my vote. Joan McIntyre's love of whales had affected me. But one woman's influence would be overcome, in five years, by the influence of two other women, and Joan would probably not object.

In 1970 Joan organized Friends of the Earth's campaign to protect furbearers from fur wearers ("Fur looks better on the original owner"). She next made it clear that mammals need not be furry and cuddly to deserve protection. She helped persuade the 1972 Stockholm Conference on Human Environment to pass a resolution protecting whales and, in Malta a month later, persuaded the *Pacem in Maribus* Conference to do likewise.

Joan wanted Friends of the Earth to publish an exhibit-format book on whales. I wondered how we would illustrate a big book about the biggest mammals. Photographers had not yet shared the depths with whales. My only ideas were to illustrate the book with views of coasts as seen by spy-hopping cetaceans, and underwater scenes of dolphins in marine parks, punctuated here and there with flukes about to disappear as whales dove for the depths. FOE never got that book together but would follow years later with a much grander book, *Wake of the Whale*. Joan took her ideas to the Sierra Club, and *Mind in the Waters* became a most successful book.

The International Whaling Commission (IWC) needed attention next. It consisted of members from whaling nations, of which the United States was one, and was solely concerned with such regulation of whaling as would attain the maximum sustainable yield. The United States was not interested in whale meat for human consumption, but was very interested in sperm-whale oil, for example, as an excellent ingredient for automatic transmissions, cosmetics, and pet food. Joan wanted no whales hunted, and neither did I.

Five years passed.

It was a hot day in Washington. I was glad to be in walking shorts on my way to a FOE staff dinner party, expecting no trouble and less heat. There I revealed my considered judgment about the plight of the bowhead whale. Since whales cannot vote, it is up to people, who can vote, to think like a whale. Thinking like a bowhead, I knew I would not like to be hunted by Eskimos. It was obviously correct to be as right as a right whale (the bowhead *is* a right whale) and to grant the endangered bowhead the right to live instead of sacrificing it to an Eskimo hunting rite.

"Oh, Dave," Pam Rich said, much grieved. She was from Fairbanks, Alaska, and was one of the key FOE staff members who initiated the Alaska Coalition, which the Sierra Club later successfully operated out of its Washington office. Her grief was echoed by Anne Wickham, another of the key initiators. I was in trouble.

Patiently they worked me over, point by point, and changed my mind—a mind, by the way, that vigorously resists being changed. Pam helped me understand the Eskimo's ancient culture in which whales and Eskimos coexisted peacefully. I was ready to present the correct view thereafter, whether as a member of the U.S. delegation to the International Whaling Commission meeting in Tokyo, or making speeches, or arguing with misguided members of the FOE board, or trying to persuade Martin Litton (who ordinarily is my conservation conscience) to agree with my reformed attitude about whales.

Martin was outraged by my backing away from boycotting Japanese products until Japan stopped commercial whaling. The FOE board members who were furious with my waffling in favor of subsistence hunting of the bowhead by indigenous people included Marion Edey and Charles Warren, who also served on the Council on Environmental Quality while it was alive and well, and Dan Luten, my neighbor and principal coach in matters pertaining to controlling population, growth, and economists.

It was with help from Anne and Pam that I became a delegate to the IWC meeting in Tokyo. I could talk with easy conscience to an Eskimo, Arnold Brower, who may well be a very distant cousin by way of Charles Brower, author of *Fifty Years below Zero*. Arnold's brother shares my name. You can tell us apart; first I was never postmaster at Point Barrow. Arnold and I talked comfortably in Tokyo and later in Washington, D.C., where he and other Eskimos illustrated how little the people from southern climes understand northern dietary needs. Southerners, with the best of balanced-diet intentions, shipped dried milk north in flour sacks—which the Eskimos found useful after dumping the contents.

The battle for the bowhead was intense, ugly at times. The bowhead count, it was argued, was down to fifteen hundred and dropping rapidly, and warranted a total ban on the subsistence hunt. The mid-October *Not Man Apart* picked up the complicated story:

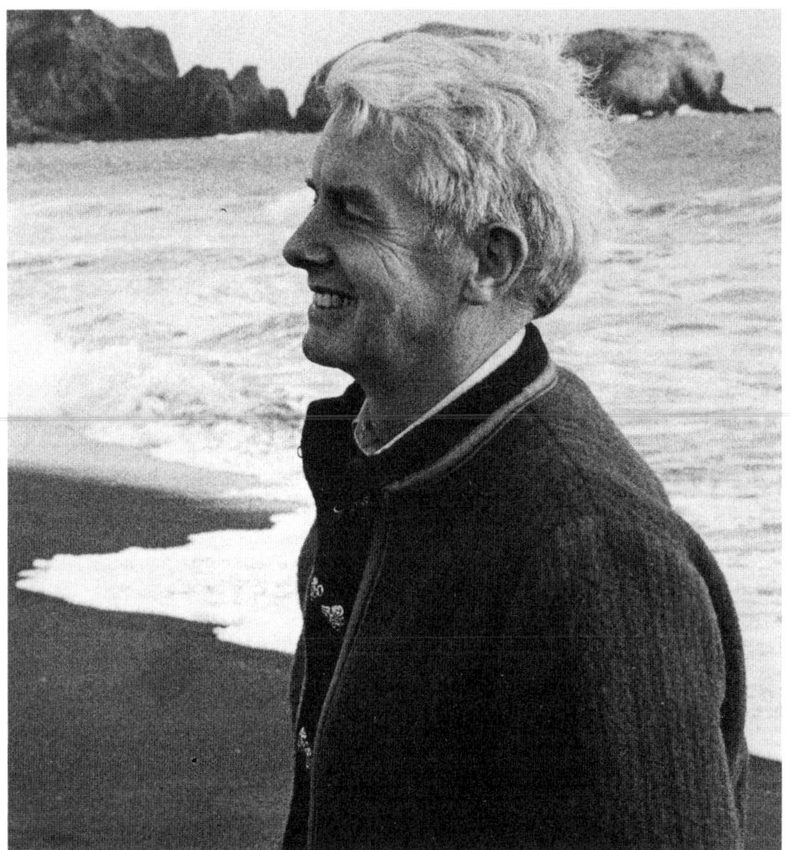

Brower's dedication to the Earth includes all its natural land and water forms and the creatures who inhabit it. Photograph by Patricia Saar.

EXTRAORDINARY ATTENTION has been given FOE's position on subsistence bowhead whaling by the Eskimo over the past few weeks. The resolution herewith was voted September 25 by our executive committee following several hours' discussion of varying views.

On September 8 we recommended to the Department of Commerce that the United States file an objection to the International Whaling Commission's resolution of June 1977 to delete the subsistence exemption granted to native peoples. This was, we thought, the least unhappy of various unhappy solutions. It recognized the need of the Inuit culture and the difficulty of protecting the bowhead unless the International Whaling Commission could also recognize and meet that need.

Since September 8, we learned of a new option. Since the IWC Scientific Committee meeting in November will be followed by a meeting of the IWC in December, further consideration of the subsistence ban would be possible. The IWC could allow a limited subsistence take of the bowhead if, upon receiving further evidence, the IWC were to see this transitional step as an enforceable method of protecting the whale.

Accordingly, we agreed that we would not support the filing of an objection at this time; that the United States should rapidly and sincerely move to see that the Eskimo be represented as part of the U.S. delegation at the November scientific committee meeting and at the December IWC meeting; and that the IWC should be asked to extend the deadline for filing an objection until after the December meeting.

It is our belief that the Eskimo's rights and perceived needs must be a part of any solution. Believing that this administration would now fully involve the Eskimo, and that the U.S. delegation in the November and December meetings would work vigorously for the protection of the Eskimo interests and that the IWC would accommodate them, we modified our position, reserving the right otherwise to urge our earlier position again.

We submit that the bowhead must be saved and the native culture allowed to evolve as the Eskimo, when provided bicultural education, sees fit. The cooperation of the Inuit community is essential to the long-term protection of the bowhead. The taking of bowhead may not prove to be essential to the Eskimo culture as it evolves. The rest of us need to hear the Eskimo out, and heed an older wisdom than our own.

This issue is vital to the Eskimo of Greenland, the Soviet Union, Canada, and the United States, and to the survival of subsistence aboriginal cultures around the world. Without their cooperation, the whales can hardly be saved. With it, they can be.

We sense a total accord among environmental organizations, and other global communities, as well, about the need to save the endangered great whales from extinction. Friends of the Earth shares that accord, and will continue to work for the ten-year moratorium on whaling we have supported assiduously since the United Nations Conference on the Human Environment in Stockholm in 1972. We hope that humanity's concern for the great whales will soon become unanimous, and we recognize the urgency attendant upon moving to save the seriously endangered bowhead before it is too late. The question that troubles us is whether the decision about methods is to be shared or imposed. We favor sharing, and reaching a decision that can be applied quickly and effectively and, because it is shared, be enforced.

We would further urge that the concern for the bowhead be broadened to include concern for the protection of habitat essential to the bowhead and the Eskimo. Threats to that habitat are being given too little heed in the present controversy. The next fifteen months are all the time that is left to provide maximum protection for the last great wilderness in the United States—Alaska's. That wilderness guarantees continuing productivity for indigenous people and wildlife on land and in the surrounding seas.

A threat fully as dangerous as uncontrolled subsistence whaling is uncontrolled corporate pressure for offshore oil exploration in the Beaufort Sea, home of the bowhead, and probably most vulnerable of all seas to the current push for rapid oil exhaustion and profits.

To save this wilderness and this sea will require the swift and inspired joint efforts of environmental and other public-interest organizations, and more importantly, cooperation between people in an old native culture and people in a highly exploitive transient culture.

The steps to assure bowhead survival are inseparable from this broader need. They ought not be perceived as a leap to disaster, coerced by righteous people overenamored of their newly acquired virtues. The steps ought to be manifestly reasonable to the necessary majority. Deliberate speed is in order.

***Not Man Apart,* October 1977**

"Deliberate speed," I should note, was not my phrase. The United States Supreme Court used it in recommending the speed with which racial integration should travel. The Eskimo-bowhead controversy raged on. *Not Man Apart* carried on too, in December 1977:

JOINING THE NATIONAL AUDUBON SOCIETY and the Sierra Club in withdrawing from a boycott Project Jonah never participated in—the boycott against Japanese and Russian products in protest against their whaling—FOE ended its part in the boycott by executive committee action on November 20. At the same time, FOE reaffirmed its support of a moratorium on commercial whaling.

Reasons for the action had been discussed at three earlier meetings, and communicated to other participants:

1. Boycotts are not friendly ways of doing environmental business, and secondary boycotts, within the U.S., are illegal—too much like the army's "company punishment," in which everyone in a company is restricted because of the unconfessed error of one. FOE was never happy about a secondary boycott of Japanese and Russian products, which does not mean that FOE was happy with Japanese and Russian whalers.

2. FOE has had problems in being part of the pot's calling the kettle black. Although the U.S. was very good about cutting out whaling, and the Japanese not so good, the opposite holds on certain emission and pesticide

controls, and in the export of nuclear technology and the spilling of nuclear wastes.

3. Whales could be threatened less by whalers than by the oil industry—drilling in the Beaufort Sea and on the outer continental shelf, and by careless shipping and spilling of oil, a lion's share of it for the most profligate oil-using country of all, our own. That profligacy is still out of control.

4. If the real point is not to be a paragon of virtue but to save whales, then it is not too wise, we suspect, to adopt a posture that prevents Japanese environmentalists from persuading their own government and fellow citizens to save whales. The boycott did inhibit them severely.

5. Small though whale protein may be in the Japanese diet and whale products in the economy, we are mindful that the cost of transition away from them is high and the U.S. government has hardly tried to share it. If, in Eastern religions, it is a sin to embarrass someone, we could concentrate not on embarrassment (in the form of a boycott), but on alternatives.

FOE has been looking for alternatives and we shall try harder. We are pleased to have been invited to be part of a Japanese-American Environmental Conference, planned to be held in Tokyo July 21-28, 1978.

For people who remain troubled about others who still practice the whaling we ourselves used to celebrate, there remains a pragmatic view of the boycott: between 1973 and 1976, we are told by the Whale Issue Committee of the Japanese American Citizens League, the volume of U.S.-Japan trade rose from $18 billion to $25.8 billion. And in 1977 the major problem confronting Japan, as reported by the *Manchester Guardian,* is how to reduce its mounting trade surplus.

It could not have been the loss of business that led Japan to accept reduced quotas on whaling, inasmuch as their problem in the face of the boycott was a too-rapid growth of exports (vodka exports probably didn't drop either). It is fair to assume that it was a different kind of pressure. Whatever function the boycott may have had, its time has passed, and the time has come to look for, and to help finance, alternatives to commercial whaling, and to do it in a friendly way.

While we are at it, we could look for alternatives to subsistence whaling, remembering that while we don't need it, some people on earth still believe they do. They may not particularly relish our trying to be wise all alone in telling them how to behave and survive. Better to spend our time trying to mitigate the damage we and other industrialized nations have been inflicting as we try to buy out the resources that subsistence cultures require to endure, leaving them inedible cash instead—and severing the crafts they have known so much longer than we have known ours.

There are many things we can teach. There is still quite a bit, conceivably, for us to learn.

***Not Man Apart,* December 1977**

One of the useful things FOE did for whales was to arouse the attention of William Curtsinger, a *National Geographic* photographer. He aroused my attention more dramatically than FOE had aroused his in his letter to me of December 17, 1976.

Would you be at all interested in doing a marine mammal book together? As I look over my photographic file of whales, seals, and dolphins, a book seems to me to be a very real possibility. My pictures cover the following (all taken in the wild):

[Bill included a chart displaying the type of photographs, color or black and white, surface or underwater, he had of the following: southern right whale, gray whale, fin whale, minke whale, humpback whale, narwhal, beluga, orca, false killer whale, pilot whale, dusky dolphin, bottlenose dolphin, California sea lion, South American fur seal, New Zealand fur seal, harp seal, hooded seal, southern elephant seal, crabeater seal, leopard seal, Weddell seal.]

I am a contractor; therefore all the photographs I take for the *Geographic* are returned to me except those actually published. I am leaving the first of the year for Argentina to begin fieldwork for a dolphin article for the *Geographic*. I have carte blanche to go and photograph blue whales, whenever a reasonable opportunity "surfaces." This year's fieldwork may also include monk seals.

I can't think of anyone else I would rather do this with. Would you and FOE be at all interested?

John McPhee told me many stories of you while we worked in the Pine Barrens of New Jersey together.

At the Portland airport, as soon as I could get there (a year later, he has reminded me!), Billy Curtsinger picked me up and took me to his home at Biddeford Pool, which reveals that I was in Maine, not Oregon. With the sound of Atlantic waves for background music, I looked at Billy's Kodachromes for hours, and heard his story. It took me no time to realize that his story needed an eloquent listener, one whom I knew very well—Kenneth Brower. Ken had been impressed enough with whales when he was only sixteen to write a piece about *Moby Dick* that I liked very much.

Ken had already become an important part of the Sierra Club and Friends of the Earth publishing effort. He was—and is—as good as anyone I know at seeing the natural world through others' eyes, and I thought he ought to try Billy's. The two of them put together FOE's most successful exhibit-format book, *Wake of the Whale*. As publisher I wrote a few words about it and spent many hours watching whales flow off the Mondadori

Editore press in Verona, probably the only whales that came near Verona's river. Let me borrow from Ken's introduction to *Wake*. It is the kind of writing I wish the father could learn from the son:

THE OCEAN HAS AN OLD ALLURE, a song to call her exiles back. The song is coeval with life on land. It preceded ears to hear, and cortices to understand. The early reptiles, obeying simple orders from the neuron clumps they used for brains, had scarcely begun their march inland when a few heard the silent notes, broke ranks, and dully faced about. They watched their footsteps lead them back through the tide wrack, across the sand, and to the water's edge. They waded in. Feet became fins again.

The returning reptiles swam off in all directions, diversifying, filling oceanic niches. By one hundred eighty million years ago, when dinosaurs had grown gigantic and were lumbering the land, ichthyosaurs had grown gigantic and were cruising the deep. Ichthyosaurs were a first attempt at dolphins and whales. They were nearly halfway there. In shape they were much like dolphins, but they lacked the dolphin's power of mind, the dolphin's social graces. The ichthyosaur, all savage teeth and tiny cranium, was a dolphin's nightmare of itself dreamed ages in advance.

Sixty million years ago, the hundred mammals, in their turn, began returning. The class Mammalia had just asserted its dominance of the land's fauna, when the sea called back certain family lines. We don't know what these first volunteers looked like. The fossil record has not revealed a trace, a common fate for missing links and a kindness perhaps. The volunteers were no doubt sorry-looking, like most transitional creatures. They were neither here nor there. They were fish impersonators, all dressed up in webbed feet and wet fur, the despair of their mothers, the laughingstock of the whole shore.

Yet by fifty million years ago, in the Eocene's "dawn of the recent," a time when, on land, the dawn horse, eohippus, was still the size of a terrier, sea mammals already amounted to something. The first whales, the archaeocetes, were snaking through the seas. They were creatures as outlandish as any in prehistory, but they were big.

Seas were warmer in the old days, but cruel all the same, and many lineages of sea mammals came to dead ends. For a while an oceangoing raccoon-dog paddled about, a brave experiment, but it sank without heirs. Other lineages prospered. The squalodonts, a family of primitive dolphins, were fruitful and multiplied. By fifteen million years ago, when horses had reached the size of sheep, and mastodons tramped the continents, the squalodonts had evolved skulls of a configuration close to that of modern dolphins. The ancestors of man still chattered in the trees. Newton's laws and Darwin's deductions were lowbrow grunts and leafy belches. The squalodonts boasted the best of what this planet had to offer then in the way of brains.

Modern marine mammals trace their descent—or *could* trace it, if they were the least interested in genealogy—back to six separate returns to the sea. The baleen whales, of which there are ten species, among them the blue, fin, right, humpback, and minke whales, are descended from a primitive hoofed mammal that was recalled to the sea sixty million years ago. The toothed whales, all sixty-four species, among them the sperm whale, various beaked whales, and the dolphins, are descended from another hoofed animal that wandered down to the ocean at about the same time—sixty million years before the present. The four species of sirenians—the manatees and dugongs—are descended from a third ungulate, which hoofed back fifty-five million years ago. The seventeen species of crawling seals, among them the harbor seal, ribbon seal, bearded seal, elephant seal, and harp seal, are descended from an otterlike carnivore that slipped into some embayment thirty million years ago. The fifteen species of walking seals—the sea lions, fur seals, and walruses—descend from a bearlike carnivore that splashed in about the same time. The sea otter, a single species, is descended from a land otter that came back five million years ago.

For warm-blooded animals, the great obstacle to the return, the ongoing problem of life in the sea, has been the cold. Thermal conductivity of water is more than twenty times that of air. Sea currents drain body heat much faster than land breezes, even in the tropics.

All sea mammals are sizable, for bulk conserves heat. For mammals, the lower weight limit for individual survival in the open sea seems to be about ten pounds.

Evolution will bring us no sea cats, then, nor sea mice. No sea rabbit will bound over the waves or snuffle along the bottom. Marine squirrels won't lay up stashes of cowries inside old wrecks or coral heads.

There won't be sea shrews. To keep home fires cheery, this tiniest of mammals must run around ceaselessly, perpetually irritable and overamped. In the sea, shrews would be insufferable.

Sea bears are possible, though. Indeed, in the polar bear, they may be in the process of becoming.

There is no law against a sea man.

If Bill Curtsinger is a transitional creature, a primate trying to become a seal, then he is caught in an early stage of transit. His posture is sometimes slouchy, and his eyes turn down at the outside corners, but he cannot properly be called sorry-looking, like the majority of those ambiguous animals fossilized on their way to someplace else. His eyes, blue and humorous, meet yours directly. His step on land is forthright. His skin is the thin, Nordic sort intended for use in high, temperate latitudes, and he has abused the warranty, immersing his epidermis under the sea ice of both poles, exposing it in small boats to the equatorial sun. His forehead and eyes are lined from squinting into scintillations. In a decade or so, his face will be a log of all the weather it's seen, a map of all the places.

For most of his career he has been a photographer of marine mammals. He doesn't know why. He did not plan things that way; he just slipped into it. Sometimes he photographs other animals—pelicans, herring, beaver—but he always seems to come back to those creatures of warm blood who preceded him home to the sea.

Bill slouches on his sofa in Maine. I sit more erect, my notebook open and resting on my knee. He has arranged it so I face inland and he faces the Atlantic. While we talk, Bill drums intermittently with a pencil on the wall behind him. He isn't interested in my questions, and in his answers he loses the thread.

For a month he has been home in Maine—an unusually long domestic interlude. He seems vaguely discouraged.

"Whenever I find myself growing grim about the mouth," says Ishmael, on the opening page of the greatest whale story of all, "whenever it is a damp, drizzly November in my soul; whenever I find myself involuntarily pausing before coffin warehouses, and bringing up the rear of every funeral I meet; and especially whenever my hypos get such an upper hand of me, that it requires a strong moral principle to prevent me from deliberately stepping into the street, and methodically knocking people's hats off—then, I account it high time to get to sea as soon as I can."

Bill drums on the wall, and his eyes wander away.

"What's the matter, Bill?" I ask.

"Huh? Nothing." He smiles sheepishly at me.

I don't let him off the hook. I fix him with a stare.

"Nothing," he repeats. "I don't know. Nothing."

He looks past me to the window. Outside, beyond the glass, the gray ocean sings him her primeval song.

Kenneth Brower, *Wake of the Whale,* 1979

O wad some Power the giftie gie us
To see oursels as ithers see us!

What did the Japanese, adamant hunters of whales, hear in this primeval song, or see in the gray ocean? In mid-1976, remembering the lines from Robert Burns that my father repeated to his children every few years, I had a chance to find out. In my own time I had looked askance at Japan, first for the miserable quality of the toys they made for us children, next and in spades, for Pearl Harbor, and after the war for the superb quality of the toys they made for us adults. When the U.S. Information Agency asked me to talk about pluralism in the United States in the cities of Tokyo,

Kamakura, Kyoto, Osaka, Fukuoka, Nagoya, and Sapporo, I leapt at the chance, looked up *pluralism,* opted for my usual environmental subjects, and had a chance to sample the Japanese view of America.

I learned, for example, how irritated the Japanese were by our insistence on dosing their citrus imports with pesticide poisons and dumping certain radioactive poisons from our nuclear ships that paused in the night in their harbors. It was suggested that I not dwell on Japanese fishing and whaling.

I did dwell, however, on the imminent malignancy of their exponential economic growth and its relation to their environment and that of the rest of the world. The English-language Japanese papers were quite happy about Japan's eight-percent annual growth in GNP, and they also lamented that all the world's forests combined could not fulfill Japan's need for wood products.

With such economic growth, I asked from city to city, where would Japan find thirty times as many resources as they were now using when a child born in 1976 reached voting age, and two hundred times as many when that child reached retirement age? If the world's forests were inadequate today, did they really want to find them two hundred times as inadequate then? And if, for example, they were already overstressing the world's fisheries and whale populations, did they really want to multiply that stress by any number, much less a huge one?

The usual reply was that the Japanese did not expect the eight-percent growth to continue indefinitely. My response was inevitably, "If you're going to stop growing sometime, why not stop while Japan is still beautiful and livable?" Or while the ocean still has whales in it, I said to myself.

They would smile, and I would move on to the next city, finally leaving Japan on July 1, my birthday, and arriving home the day before to celebrate it twice. In September there were other eyes to look through – the eyes of the subsistence hunters in the Eskimo village of Chivak. My host was another David – not David Brower of Point Barrow, for whom Friday came but once a week, but another David to whom it was an everyday occurrence because Friday was his last name.

"You'll think this plane is going to shake itself to pieces when we land, but it won't," the pilot told Jim Kowalski and me as we approached the so-called landing strip at Chivak; and we did but it didn't.

We were pleased to be alive and whole as we climbed out of the small craft, and wished it and its pilot a safe trip back to Bethel. We were delighted to feel welcomed – we hadn't quite expected a welcome – as we were led down the short path into the tiny outermost settlement on the Yukon-Kuskokwin Delta.

Deltas are supposed to be flat and this one was normal. A low range of hills to the north was the only relief on a horizon which here, unlike the rest of Alaska, was a straight line. Chivak itself did not break that line. It lay just below the gentle rise that held the airstrip and clung to the north bank of the river. One building, the recreation center, looked substantial. The houses didn't, including the house David Friday and his Eskimo family lived in.

Through Jim Kowalski, the Friends of the Earth representative in Alaska, David Friday had invited me to visit Chivak in 1975, and I was arriving a year late to get a taste of a native village. Jim had been working hard to build a rapport with the original settlers of the north country. We both knew how essential it was that we try to understand the people as well as the terrain. He was not at all sure, he told me, that he was being understood by the people. It was hard for me to imagine this because he looked so native himself. In height, heft, and hirsuteness he looked more like an Alaska brown bear than many of the bears did. He coupled this with the gentleness of the musician. Still, he was not prepared for David Friday's greeting—a good, solid hug. It was the first any native had bestowed on him, and Jim glowed.

Less substantial-looking than the rec hall, but far sturdier than the houses, were the oil tanks, perhaps fifteen feet high, that were Chivak's energy source. In front of several of the houses we passed were many dependents upon that energy source, the snowmobiles, in various stages of disrepair, that had replaced the huskies.

Like many others, David Friday's house echoed the heat-conserving design of the igloo. We had to stoop to get in the front entrance, but had plenty of stand-up room once we were inside. There I found that we had been preceded by the supersalesman of refrigerators. The kitchen portion of the main room contained a big one, not far from the color TV, and both were operating. I saw no way, even with the presence of the town's oil-fired electrical-generating system, that the electric clothes-washing machine in the entryway could operate. There was running water—but only that which ran off the roof into rain barrels. That problem received no further attention. I was too fascinated by the action within the house. Assorted children of the Chivak nuclear family dropped in without ceremony. The Friday home was theirs. "Star Trek" was being broadcast from Bethel, and the children were keeping up with it. I was entertained with color prints of various members of the immediate and surrogate families. I was fed and taken out on the river on a hunting or fishing expedition, whichever target presented itself first. (Neither did.) I noticed that the boat carried a spare motor and gasoline supply. There was no one to call if something went wrong, and my host knew how to fix things himself.

Back at the Fridays', when the time came, I was shown where the sanitary facility was—a chemical toilet separated from the sleeping portion of the room by curtains that isolated the toilet's corner and visibility, but nothing else. When night came I was granted David Friday's own bed; David would sleep on the sofa.

I settled down in the cooking part of the room, where David's mother—in her eighties, I thought, though he was only twenty-seven—was at work over the hot kitchen stove, having no trouble bending double to pick things off the floor and having no trouble unbending to see how well the seal meat was cooking. It was cooking all right, they said, but seemed to me to taste a bit fishy. Perhaps I just wasn't subsistent enough to relish it.

She and David's father, her contemporary, needed David's interpreting to understand the alien visitors. There were certain questions about ancestry that I did not feel compelled to ask. I could nevertheless ask stupid questions, and the first one came to my mind when I watched David's father eat blubber. He had once had more teeth than he was now using, and he assisted them by cutting the blubber into small pieces for easier mastication. While eating, he carried on a conversation with David in their Chivak dialect. I marveled at the subtlety of the sounds their words made.

"Suppose someone is a hundred yards away, and you are trying to make yourself understood," I asked. "Will the subtle sounds you speak be distinguishable that far away?"

"If someone is a hundred yards away," David replied, "you walk over and talk. There's plenty of time."

Somehow I was reminded of a Canadian Film Board production about the James Bay Project. In it one of the natives, whose village would be flooded out by the hydroelectric development, was, for the first time, in a city, courtroom, and witness chair, and given the question, "Do you promise to tell the truth, the whole truth, and nothing but the truth?"

I cannot forget his answer: "I can't tell you the truth. I can only say what I know."

In Chivak I wondered what a young Eskimo would know today. In the Chivak of old, without oil, snowmobiles, refrigerators, and "Star Trek," the entire village would be evacuated for part of each season. The entire village. The old ones and the babies, too. In the area appropriate for the season, they would make camp and hunt, fish, gather berries, or pursue whatever that season permitted. In succeeding years, they would choose a different area for each of the seasons, spreading their impact over time and space.

David, at twenty-seven, had learned the hunting and gathering skills needed for each of the seasons. His younger brother, at sixteen, was able to learn only about summer camp. The rest of the year his schooling was alien schooling, exported from the south. In it he learned the three R's, but not how Eskimos feed, clothe, and house themselves as people of all seasons.

That bothered me, and David's father too. He thought that young natives should be taught all they could learn about both cultures, then choose for themselves which one to live in and with.

That seemed reasonable to me at the time. But a Mohawk I met in Indian ceremonial country on Canada's Kootenay Plain led me to think again. The Mohawks, he said, want their children to learn their own culture first, and to learn it thoroughly before they let themselves be subject to admonishments from industrial addicts.

Ken Brower anticipated my experience by being with Eskimos on the North Slope just before the Prudhoe Bay oil discovery, shortly after his arduous crossing of the Brooks Range to Barter Island. He had special treatment from Eskimos respectful of his Brower surname. Ken wrote part of my concluding words in the Friends of the Earth book opposing the trans-Alaska oil pipeline—*Cry Crisis: Rehearsal in Alaska*.

"The North Slope, 1994. A lone caribou tries to pick its way through the maze of small feeder lines, gravel piles, drilling pads, old storage tanks, oil drums, and thawed tundra quagmire, all residue of the collecting net that drained the North Slope oil quickly, in the name of national security and self-sufficiency. The oil is gone, the wells have died. The 'poor boys' could not afford to stay in Alaska, much less shut the wells. A mile away, on the porch of an Arctic ghost town, an Eskimo man looks up from his newspaper to see the caribou against the skyline. He looks longingly after it. The Eskimo is youngish still and strong, though a little lean now, and with strangely vacant eyes. His small son sees the caribou, too, and watches the animal as it makes its way through the obstacle course.

"Scattered in the street below, rusting where they died, are the remains of snowmobiles. Across the street are the ruins of a filling station, with a sign posted on one of the pumps: 'Out of gas. Out of oil, too.' The paper on the Eskimo's lap, folded neatly to a back page, is the *Fairbanks News Miner,* very thin and two months old. (The plane does not call as often as it did.)

"The boy looks from the caribou to his father. The Eskimo feels his son's questioning eyes on him, but pretends not to. He is trying desperately to remember what he had heard from old people about hunting caribou. He cannot. He is as ignorant of that as he is of driving dog teams. It's all like one of those memories of a previous life." That was Ken's part. I carried on, full blast.

"The crisis contrivers may indeed have talked the gods of resources, the Big Banker in the Sky, into making one more loan. If so, it is secured by the unborn, who have no votes now but will soon bear the costs, with few resources to cash in and none to squander. To them, the unborn, it will seem that we did indeed burn books to get light, burn furniture to run air conditioners, and burn houses to warm ourselves. For a while, it worked. We did multiply and subdue the earth.

"As they credit us for all this, they must face the fact that the earth is not theirs to subdue, but theirs—and only in part theirs—to cherish. They will know what we began to profess: there is only one earth, and it had been beautiful. With no wildness left on it to inform them, they must go back where we ravaged their world, and bind up the wounds we inflicted. Each of them must use his or her head as we are not yet using ours, or the Four Horsemen will ride. They are saddling up now.

"This is the real crisis—a crisis we foist on our children unless we can be mature enough to shoulder our share. Old, tired, me-first thinking won't do it. There is still time for the contrivers in America to come up with a better answer before the harm is irreparable and costs us all too much. We need to help each other, however late we all are, in finding an alternative future our children can live in, and in it be proud of the parents they remember."

It was a good try, but failed. The drain has been operating and 1994, when Prudhoe Bay's bonanza is supposed to play out, is approaching rapidly.

Chivak has its recreation center, complete with jukebox, pool table, and a $2.50 Big Boy sandwich; it has refrigerators, cannibalized snowmobiles, and summer camp for the kids. But how much of the irreplaceable genius of people we in our ignorance choose to call primitive are we going to insist on drowning with cash? Never mind other people's ignorance. Just take my own. I can't light a fire without a match or a room without a switch. I might grow a vegetable or two, but children dependent upon my hunting ability would starve. Nor could I stand a chance of finding something in the wild to fix their headaches, or my own.

Just before I left Chivak, thirty hours after we had bumped our way to a stop at the airstrip, I was by the river's edge, admiring the metabolism of one of David's friends. Bare-armed, he took the north country's September chill with ease. As a parting shot I asked David to tell his father how much I admired the sweep of sky, neatly decorated with scattered cumulus, that covered the delta with that pleasant little interruption of low hills. The father took a good look at the sky and David interpreted his answer: "I went to Anchorage once," his father said, "but there was no place to look."

CHAPTER 12

ALASKA

OIL AND THE NORTHLANDS

PEOPLE WHO PREDICT A DISASTER ought not smile when it happens, especially when it happens to such a magnificent place as Alaska's Prince William Sound. They should not even let themselves say "I told you so." I am not smiling, but can't resist repeating a few words from a hearing before the U.S. House of Representatives Subcommittee on General Oversight and Alaska Lands in 1977: "In order to avoid needless damage to the land, streams, shores, wildlife, and original Alaskans, we should not hurry to exhaust the North Slope oil until: (a) We know the pipe is safe. We don't, and we tried to find out. (b) We know Valdez as a port, and its tankers, and their pilots, are also safe. We are by no means sure enough." I was testifying at that time as president of Friends of the Earth, having left the Sierra Club staff in 1969. Now I was again on the Sierra Club's board, and new threat to the North Slope was being pushed by the Reagan administration at the oil corporations' urging. The club's Washington staff urged me to testify against it before the Senate Committee on Energy and Natural Resources. On October 15, 1987, thirty-three years after my first testimony before the committee, I was at it again. I had seniority of sorts. None of the senators who had heard me the first time had survived. I remembered Wayne Aspinall's remark, "The longer I'm around here, the better I like seniority." There was a lot that I wanted to say and put in the record:

MR. CHAIRMAN, members of the committee, and staff:

Old mountaineers never die, and rarely fade away. When there were a lot of high places to get to first, I got to many of them. In World War II I had the opportunity to teach thousands of men how to get there in combat. After all that, thirty-five years ago, when I was a lad of forty, I first approached Capitol Hill. I have tried the Hill climb many times since, almost succeeding and often failing, and I have premonitions that this may be my last attempt. I hope that what I have to say will be useful to you soon, if not now, and ask your forbearance in letting an old mountaineer extend his time limit here. [The time limit was ten minutes, and I was allowed to go on for twenty.]

Thank you for the opportunity to appear here to make what suggestions I can about the Arctic National Wildlife Range and the proposed use of its oil resources. For my remarks I am drawing upon my experience with several organizations, but particularly with the Sierra Club, in which I have held various offices since 1933, except for a brief hiatus after I was asked to resign as executive director in 1969.

While serving in that office, I had the opportunity to help persuade Secretary of the Interior Fred A. Seaton to convince President Eisenhower to establish the Arctic Wildlife Range by proclamation. I well remember the resistance to that proclamation by an assistant secretary, Ted Stevens—resistance overcome in the last days of the Eisenhower administration by Clinton R. (Pink) Gutermuth. Day after day, as the president's last day grew closer, the proposal was stalled. Then Pink, in his own way, came into the secretary's office like a major storm from the Gulf of Alaska, starting gently and building into a rage. In final exasperation, he said in no uncertain terms, "All I want to say, Mr. Secretary, is this: Are you just sweet-talking us, or are we going to get this damned wildlife range proclaimed by the president?" Anyone who knew Pink Gutermuth then would know that it was easier to proclaim a refuge than to face the fury of a Gutermuth gale. Thanks in no small part to Pink, the proclamation was issued, and has been celebrated often, as it should be. It was President Eisenhower's greatest conservation achievement.

[I was not present at the meeting with the secretary, but I ran this account by Pink Gutermuth the evening before I testified. He was home and terminally ill. He told me my account was fair enough.]

Starting in 1950 with articles I helped to publish in the *Sierra Club Bulletin* (which I then edited), the club's interest in The Great Land was renewed with an article and a series of photographs by Ansel Adams, followed with articles by Lowell Sumner, Robert Rausch, and Starker Leopold, with skilled oversight by George Collins of the National Park Service. I also got to know Sir Frank Fraser Darling, a man I consider the Einstein of ecology.

It was natural for the club to be involved because its founder, John Muir, became concerned himself as a result of his travels in Alaska decades ago. Long before I had a chance to travel there, I accepted appointment as ringleader of the Arctic refuge proposal for many years at the annual North American Wildlife and Conservation Conferences. It was my duty to round up those attending from Alaska, together with un-Alaskans who cared for Alaska, to join sessions which Ira Gabrielson, the Mr. Conservation of his day, held in his conference command post. New assignments were made each year on behalf of the refuge for the ensuing year. Once the refuge had been proclaimed, the next item on the agenda was to persuade Canada to preserve the Porcupine caribou herd range, on its side of the border. The most devoted activist in this was Sigurd Olson. Now the shoe is on the other foot. Canada is doing its part, and the United States is waffling.

We all knew then about the Naval Petroleum Reserve, but not about forthcoming pressure to exploit it for civilian use rather than protect the caribou or the oil's security mission. The United States had not yet perfected its now-apparent determination to blow our vanishing resource of petroleum, key to so many future needs, out of industry's tall stacks and everybody's tail pipes, instead of treating it as a reserve. We did not fully appreciate the coming urge not to lock up, but to use up, this resource and thus deny it to future Americans and their security.

We had felt comfortable. Oil in Alaska seemed remote enough to be safe. Then came the discovery at Prudhoe Bay. I had just become executive director of the John Muir Institute for Environmental Studies, which had received generous contributions from Robert O. Anderson's (of Atlantic Richfield) foundation totaling eighty thousand dollars. These helped pay my salary and financed an important environmental conference at the Aspen Institute in 1969. John Ehrlichman attended to represent the Nixon administration—and for the first time heard about the greenhouse effect, which, according to San Francisco's water engineer, has raised the sea level six inches in the last decade. In 1896 scientists thought this earth warming would not be serious for a thousand years. It is serious now.

I was founder and president of Friends of the Earth as well. FOE was soon to join The Wilderness Society, the Environmental Defense Fund, and the Center for Law and Social Policy in a suit to require the proposed Alaska pipeline to meet the requirements of the National Environmental Policy Act.

You will recall Atlantic Richfield's interest in that pipeline. Our suit strained Bob Anderson's sense of humor and he sent no further grants our way. Years later I suggested to Thornton Bradshaw, then president of ARCO, that we were entitled to a major grant, thanks to the huge increase in oil revenue ARCO enjoyed because we had held up the pipeline long enough for the oil to sell at far more than ARCO had expected. FOE still deserves such a grant. The value of Alaska's oil can still rise by orders of magnitude—if you spare it.

You may also recall that we won our suit in court but lost it in Congress. Vice-President Spiro Agnew broke the tie vote in the Senate. This opened Alaska to a brief period of great wealth and to the subsequent hard times we were predicting. He also, by breaking the tie, reduced a great native culture that had been self-reliant for millennia to one the heritage of which may have been irretrievably eroded by a flash-in-the-pan bonanza of oil revenue. Congress let the trans-Alaska pipeline ignore the National Environmental Policy Act at a cost yet to be determined—a huge cost, I think, and the oil industry would like to forget it.

Secretary of the Interior Walter Hickel (whose confirmation I had opposed on the club's behalf) and I shared a platform twice shortly after our court loss in Congress, and both times we agreed. The first time he made himself unpopular with President Nixon by his opposition to the undeclared war in Vietnam. We next agreed that an oil railroad would have been preferable to an oil pipeline. For one thing, access could be controlled on a railroad, but not on a haul road. For another, a railroad could not spill as much oil as a pipeline could in a bad-case scenario. For a third, a railroad would have about one-fourth of a pipeline's capacity—the Prudhoe Bay oil would have been a boon to Alaska's economy four times as long—for nearly a century instead of two decades or so.

There was a fourth reason that we didn't discuss. A railroad would lead directly to the North American market by a secure route, and avoid a sea route that was not only perilous, but that also could easily end up in Japan—source of the pipe in the first place. You have all heard the renewed interest in selling Alaska oil to Japan to help our trade balance, if not our energy security. Why do we torture logic this way?

History can be dull, and perhaps what I have been reciting is dull to my audience if not to me. But one thing is axiomatic. If we do not learn from history, we are doomed to repeat it (I am paraphrasing a good authority). Let me quote here what is attributed to me in the National Aquarium, even though I don't remember when I said it: "We have not inherited the earth from our fathers; we are borrowing it from our children." This line also appears on the jacket of Lester Brown's important book, *Building a Sustainable Society*. It pinpoints what I think is the most important duty of this committee in dealing with this legislation.

If you borrow something with the intent of returning it or paying the loan back, that is ethical. If you have no intent to pay it back, or can't, then it is a form of stealing, which is supposed to be illegal. We cannot put used oil back. We cannot borrow it. We can steal it from America's future. Professor Charles Park, whom I encountered in John McPhee's book, *Encounters with the Archdruid,* told me that if this generation takes care of itself, the next generation can take care of its own self. He also told that to one of my Stanford classes I asked him to speak to. Although the class was polite to him, they did not buy that line. I have yet to encounter any audience that buys the idea that our obligation to the next generation is to take care of ourselves, then leave, waving good-bye and saying, "Lots of luck, kids." How many people here are urging you to do just that?

They should stop stealing from children. I am afraid that this is exactly what this legislation portends, and I therefore do not think you should approve it as presented here. In its present form there are too many important goals that the legislation cannot meet:

1. It cannot provide security for the caribou, as I think the caribou would let you know if they cared to speak.

2. It will not sustain the concept of preserving wilderness in perpetuity, a concept this nation has led much of the world to accept, and should not abandon now, especially for a trivial pursuit.

3. It is not capable of adding one iota to our national security, unless you believe in Strength Through Exhaustion—that the faster we find and use up the resources that are to sustain our future, the stronger we will be. This seems to have been our national energy policy for the past several administrations, including this one, and I think it is time to understand that every resource we exhaust strengthens our opponent, not us.

4. It fails to encourage the quest for a sustainable society, which is the only society that can conceivably be secure for more than the present moment. A sustainable society must depend upon renewable resources, which oil cannot be. It must recycle nonrenewable resources, and burned oil cannot be recycled. It needs to restore the base of renewable resources—our forests, soils, cities, and human minds. In this effort America needs to lead. We are in retreat.

There is oil off our shores and some within them, but not a great deal of it anymore. It is frontier oil, expensive to develop, and rapidly reaching the point where it will take more energy to get the oil to the people than the people will get out of the oil. We should use our generation's share, and no more than our share, of the oil that remains for services that oil renders best. We know that it is a building block for many things far more useful to us than automobile and stack exhaust. It can build things that do not lead to acid rain, the ominous warming of the atmosphere, and the thinning of the ozone barrier we all depend upon. As we use our share of oil, we should invest in ways to replace its energy. We don't. The ways exist, and this administration ignores them.

Yes, we need oil, but a lot less than we think. According to Professor Bartlett of the University of Colorado, if we were to reduce our use of oil a mere one percent per year, it would last forever. The day before forever we would be down to the last molecule, but we need not worry about that yet. Our present technology will enable us to reduce our per capita use of energy to far less than half of what it now is—something we know from the experience of such backward places as England, Sweden, and West Germany (and New York City as well). Their per capita use is half ours. They are cutting their use, and we can assume that they are doing so in the interest of building a sustainable society in their countries. We should be capable of doing better, and I urge that you require it. In my own fifty years' experience in the environmental movement, I have seen that most of the environmental damage, and of our stealing from children, that has turned me gray has come either from the mad dash for more energy or the thoughtless ways with which we waste what we find.

"Trend is not destiny," Rene Dubos said. If we keep following our present trend, we will indeed end up where we are headed. But that need not be our destiny. This nation has been steadily losing its former excellence in education, nutrition, public health, transportation, housing, technology, manufacturing, and world leadership. Too much of our talent is being directed to an arms race that no one can win. Our best efforts should be aimed not at eroding the American Dream, but in restoring it.

We need oil, but not this oil, not in our lifetime. We need energy conservation. We are not achieving it, and have abandoned the progressive steps we were making toward it. Energy efficiency and energy alternatives have been starved of support by this administration. Please, gentlemen, reverse this national retrogression!

North Slope oil will eventually be needed. Americans a few centuries hence may need it desperately. We surely do not. I hope that they will have perfected ways of getting it carefully, which we don't; of using it sparingly for its highest purpose, which we also don't; of cleaning up after themselves as we have not. I hope that we and they will restore the earth for the people and creatures who called it home before our industry intruded.

Moreover, I would urge that the United States, no matter what party controls it, not imperil one of the finest pieces of legislation produced in the Nixon administration—the National Environmental Policy Act. That act, of global importance, is becoming an endangered species, and we cannot afford to weaken it further. We ourselves are strong enough to meet its modest requirement that we look carefully before we leap. The Congress ought not preclude the opportunity for enough people to have their chance to look before they are shoved into a leap they don't need, and may very well not survive.

In conclusion: If, Mr. Chairman, the Arctic National Wildlife Range must yield its oil, please give a later generation a chance to make or defer that decision. We are not ordained to deny them that right. Join us in hoping that the people in dire need of oil then will have a sustainable national energy policy, that they will be exquisitely careful in how they take and use that oil; and that all the people who will be brief tenants on this planet between now and then will have an unspoiled Arctic National Wildlife Range for themselves, as part of what Wallace Stegner has identified as the geography of hope.

***Congressional Record* for October 15, 1987**

Thirty-five hundred words do not fit into twenty minutes. In my reading copy I made notes about where to take shortcuts, but the record included it all—and more.

Testimony before a congressional committee is little better than what one does with it afterward. The media will almost always have left the hearing before you got a chance to speak or be questioned. You hope the reporters will pick up a copy of your testimony and that you will have, in your accompanying press release, picked out your own best lines. But unless you do something about what new information is turned up in the question period, nothing will come of it. It will get printed in the hearing record and placed on a shelf. There the acid content of the paper will determine how long your work lasts. No one will read it. Unless the resulting legislation is litigated or unless someone has need for dissertation material.

Or you may go back to it yourself if anyone ever asks for your autobiography. It is perhaps for this reason that I tried to impress the senators and staff hearing me with the duration and intensity of the effort the Sierra Club and Friends of the Earth had put into the issue now again at hand. In a certain way, I was on a roll—a roll into the past. My current effort to help save Alaska's grandeur from the greed of Alaska's latter-day invasion was no flash-in-the-pan effort. It was beginning life again forty years later, in a septuagenarian. It was fun to dig up the literature to prove how right we were and still are, and to hope that by accident someone would take note. Or that avenues leading to possible success had been kept open for a moment.

To augment my testimony I gave the copying machine in the Sierra Club's Washington office an unconscionable amount of work—producing fifty copies, the number requested of all witnesses, of my more than one hundred backed-up pages of excerpts and photographs from publications and conferences relevant to Alaska. What amazed me is that all this was published in the record. The Sierra Club's interest in Alaska paid off.

Earth and the Great Weather

Earth and the Great Weather: The Brooks Range was about the northern rampart of Alaska, a range the size of California, about its people and their perils. Eliot Porter had wanted to do a book on the Brooks Range for the Sierra Club, but he lost interest in the Sierra Club as publisher in the course of the struggle to publish his two volumes on *Galapagos: The Flow of Wildness*. We did our best to find photographers who could lead people to fall in love with the range as Eliot would have. They did well, but there is only one Eliot Porter.

Friends of the Earth had hardly been incorporated before it became involved in Alaska, in large part because I had been drawn into the struggle for the Arctic Wildlife Range by George Collins and Lowell Sumner of the

National Park Service, who wanted it to be a national park, and Starker Leopold, who wanted it saved hell or high ice water.

Thanks to Max Linn, in public relations for the Sandia Corporation, assisted financially by Robert O. Anderson, most environmentally enlightened of the world's oil executives, I was employed by the John Muir Institute for Environmental Studies, which Max had founded with a little help from me. The institute was to be in part a center for the advanced study of ecosystems. The salary, far better than what the Sierra Club had intended to raise mine to, paid for part of my time. It was augmented by part of my honoraria for speaking and royalties for writing. I could volunteer the rest of my time to Friends of the Earth. JMI had been operating for more than a year. FOE had not yet been incorporated, but its role was fixed in several minds—Max's one of them. The other minds were of Alfred Forsyth, Stewart Ogilvy, and David Sive.

To make sure that ARCO's (Bob Anderson's) trans-Alaska pipeline was given the consideration required by the newly forged National Environmental Policy Act (NEPA, for short), we brought suit.

Friends of the Earth had no money, but did have people who cared deeply, including me. In enthusiasm bestowed on me by the organization I had just founded, I wired Michael McCloskey, my successor at the Sierra Club, and Stewart Brandborg, of The Wilderness Society, my principal ally in battle after battle, asking that FOE be allowed to join the suit. Brandy wired back, "Welcome aboard." Mike was silent, and the Sierra Club soon left the suit, believing, I think, that by being on an independent track it could work for other conservation projects in Alaska.

I still had hopes that there might be an accommodation, and that the counterpoint of text and image would help achieve it. I hoped, too, that the corporate mind, duly indoctrinated with the Philosophy of Limits, would somehow opt for the benign alternative.

HEADED TOWARD THE POLE on the direct route from Copenhagen to Anchorage, we watched the sun set for the first time that day at four in the afternoon and flew north into night. The captain announced our estimated time of arrival and I divided the distance by the hours and wrote on the airline map the times we would pass over principal points of interest. The map bore historical notes about the famous explorers and the successive dates on which their various expeditions got nearer and nearer the point from which everything else on earth was south. Before the light was gone on the last bleak land passing seven miles below us, a strong feeling of admiration for the explorers welled within me. For a quickly passing moment I wished I could have been there with them then.

I remembered my first polar-route flight, made memorable by what I was reading as I traveled across Greenland's icy mountains, over Baffin

Island and its own great mountains, then across Hudson Bay with a sweeping view north, whenever the cloud cover permitted, of the last great wilderness in North America. Loren Eiseley's *The Immense Journey* and the brilliance of his narrative of man's encounter with time alternated with the brilliance, out the starboard window, of the north country where man had looked hard at the limiting cold and had broken through that limit with his wits and his spirit.

But now I was reading what the *Economist* had to say about oil exploration in the Arctic and, once in that mood, began clipping what the *Times,* the *Observer,* and the *Financial Times* were saying about oil spills to add to my extensive collection on what tanker pilots didn't know about staying afloat. I was happy to have the stewardess change the subject by offering me a cocktail. Long before dinner it had got quite dark, and as we sped about nine miles per minute above the scene of arduous exploring long ago, I put on my headset and the movie began.

What the movie was I don't remember, because my headset was already off. I had glanced at my watch, saw that it was time to look below for the lights of Spitzbergen, and there they were. Far more diverting was the light in the sky, a display of the aurora borealis. My first view of an aurora was in 1939, when I saw it from the Sierra Nevada. In 1955 I saw one from Ellensburg, Washington; Kenneth Brower, then eleven, would not believe it was an aurora. For fifteen years I never saw it again. But here was a bold white light arched broadly over us, changing to a thin profile as we flew beneath its arch. There were not many passengers, so I could switch from port to starboard windows at will and did often, fascinated by the phenomenon. No one else seemed aware of it except a Japanese opposite me who kept his head to the window, a pillow alongside to exclude extraneous light. We exchanged glances of appreciation. "Isn't the captain going to announce this display?" I asked the stewardess, still excited by what I had seen only twice before in fifty-eight years. "No," she said, "the passengers would be annoyed to have the movie interrupted."

Later she woke those who wished to know when we were directly over the North Pole and I looked out again. The aurora was gone. The clouds concealing the Arctic Ocean were lit only by starlight. As dawn broke in the south, the cloud cover thinned and strange patterns emerged, a lacework of new leads and old in the ice pack. Ice patterns changed to polygons; permafrost was under the snow and our crossing of the Arctic Ocean was over. An airstrip showed faintly, Prudhoe Bay, I thought, but we passed too high and fast for me to spot landmarks I had seen there on the ground two months before, when the tundra world was green and the oil companies were showing conservationists their Prudhoe camp. We had learned about drilling pads, berms, life below zero, the care and feeding of tundra, the search for exotic grasses to heal scars. An Eskimo antilitter crew was out on the nearby tundra with big plastic bags. We learned that the oil company's ecologist thought caribou liked the pads and berms and would not be disturbed in their migration by the above-ground portions of the eight-hundred-mile proposed pipeline. We could marvel at the technology that allowed man to find oil in this icy desert and bring it to the surface. It was rather frightening to stand on a platform partway up a rig and watch an expert team slap pipe into the ground in a bit-changing operation. The rig, tower, platform, cables, winch drums, and engine shuddered and shrieked in violent surges and smashing stops that seemed about to tear the place apart. I resolved not to use gasoline again if it took this much trouble to get it.

If the technology for getting at the oil and bringing it to the surface was impressive, the technology for getting it to market was not. Looking at the miles of four-foot Japanese pipe piled on-site, I worried about the rush to get it there before enough was known about whether it would work or whether, if it worked, the Alaska environment could keep on working within range of it. I worried about the determination to get the oil out and used up fast, about the stubborn refusal to understand the long-term consequences of short-time exploitation.

I was worrying all over again now as our North Pole flight sped us toward the Brooks Range. I conjured up disjointed paragraphs of a letter I would send, were I chairman of the board of Atlantic Richfield or of British Petroleum, chief developers of Arctic Slope oil, to my directors and stockholders. It would explain how the company, out of corporate responsibility, must pause for breath in its dash for oil until a whole series of facts were in that were not yet available to anyone. The pause would cost everybody money; but if it were a pause that would help people live longer, part of the cost ought to be recoverable. The company was leading in a more rational approach to keeping the planet a tolerable one than corporations had previously thought necessary. The company did not think that the environmental crisis was a figment. Would the stockholders therefore be helpful and patient with the corporation in its deliberate choice to forego profits that might risk the environment excessively? And would stockholders who sincerely felt that costs to the corporation were more important than costs to the earth please sell their stock to someone who felt differently? A professional worrier could conceive the letter. But could a chairman send it, or a stockholder like it?

Alpenglow was now lighting the summits of the Brooks Range. Whether it was dawn or twilight, it would not reach the North Slope for months yet. Ahead, the sun broke the world's rim to the south of us and climbed feebly into a flaming sky as we flew over the tapestry of meanders of the Yukon. Shortly past Mount McKinley we started letting down. Ten hours out of Copenhagen we landed in Anchorage at two in the afternoon, two hours before we had departed Denmark, and half an hour later the sun set in the south for the second time that day; night came again and stayed this time. The show was over.

Crossing several meridians at jet speed is always upsetting. Being benighted twice in one day was more than my sidereal clock could handle. Another kind of double twilight, however, was far more disturbing, the twilight for exploration and for wilderness. The speed and ease of my travel took the exploration out of it and off the planet. I could ask, as Aldo Leopold did, "Of what avail are forty freedoms without a blank spot on the map?" The early explorers had earned a chance to see the blank spots of the Far North, but my fellow passengers and I had not. We could select from eight stereo channels as we looked down at where the blank spots had been.

Concurrently twilight was descending on wilderness. Just three years before my flights, Kenneth Brower, John Milton, and Steve Pearson were soaking up the Brooks Range wilderness experience that *Earth and the Great Weather* has much to say about. Three people had only themselves to depend upon, no source of resupply, unknown mountains, nameless valleys, rivers of stone, seas of grass, the ultimate wilderness. In three short years the oil stampede had put a civilized stamp on an area the size of Massachusetts in the remotest part of the North Slope. The civilizing had only begun to run its course. There is tension in the fabric of wilderness, and when it is cut it withdraws fast and far. The eight-hundred-mile pipeline, cut across the ultimate wilderness, was to be the second civilizing step in a series of no one could predict how many more steps. Already Ken, John, and Steve were deprived of knowing again the wildness they had known. Their route had lost the beyondness that counted very much. Where would their sons look for a chance to know wildness? "To be precious, the heritage of wilderness must be open only to those who can earn it again for themselves," Garrett Hardin has said. "The rest, since they cannot gain the genuine treasure by their own efforts, must relinquish the shadow of it." He quotes Goethe's "We must earn again for ourselves what we have inherited."

Earn it where? In whatever vestige of wilderness is left after this generation of brief tenants has glutted itself on conveniences, including a plethora of energy, no matter what it costs all who are to follow? Do the oil seekers and users intend to leave anything unspoiled? The extractors, seemingly the most efficient international organization yet put together, plan to double their all-time drain in the next decade, and to do so come what may and from wherever it may—the Arctic, western Pacific, continental shelf off Southeast Asia, the Middle East, South America, Algeria, the Gulf, Santa Barbara. The possibility of slowing the mad race, and of sparing a resource six hundred million years in the making and sixty years in the using, and of using it for purposes oil alone can serve, seems not to have entered any system of government's mind.

The oil people, finders and users, are the primary targets here because they are best organized of all in the unintended war to eradicate wilderness from the earth. They have plenty of company. Surely they must be on the verge of sensing that a planet too well oiled will, like a cormorant, die. Or are they? "The connection between the ability of civilization to protect wildness and the ability of civilization to survive is not so tenuous as we might wish," I said twelve years ago. "The kind of thinking that motivates the grab for what's left at the bottom of the barrel – the pitiful fragment of resources in the remaining wilderness – is the kind of thinking that has lost this country friends it cannot afford to lose." I said this at the North American Wildlife Conference in New York City. Between then and now mankind has used up as much oil as in all the preceding years, and the United States has gone far toward losing every friend it had. No one is proposing to send us another statue at the moment. And in March 1971 another North American Wildlife Conference, in Portland, was hearing an industry-dominated panel argue long, oblivious to alternative routes and schedules for development, that the oil should be hurried to market across the last great wilderness within U.S. borders and also across some of the most seismically active terrain within those borders or anyone else's. The oil-company representatives on the panel echoed the view of the Department of the Interior in its draft statement about the impact of North Slope oil development upon the environment: yes, there would probably be some damage, but demands for energy required forging ahead. National security would somehow be served. How depletion would serve national security was not explained; one who would strengthen the nation by using up its oil, a Friends of the Earth advertisement suggested, would probably burn his firewood before winter.

And when the final depletion comes, what kind of ghosts do we want in the Arctic or Northwest Passage ecosystems – still one of the greatest wildernesses on the planet? Voicing the concern of fellow Eskimos, "spirited pure lovers of that land who depend upon that land for a living," Willy Willoya puts a more cogent question: "When will the Caucasians let us rest and live peacefully? Where is the God they worship, when they destroy all our human rights and privileges? Where is the liberty and justice they proclaim to the entire world? Where are the wise, the strong, and the brave amongst the Americans who would be good to their brothers and their lands? And to the creatures and the islands and the waters and the meadows and the tundra and the caves and the mountains that are our home?"

Wilderness, in the days of popular concern about total environment and degradation, has had too quiet a voice speaking on its behalf. Pollution has been easier to herald because its impact is in nostrils, eyes, and genes everywhere. If what wilderness we have left is to serve its highest purpose – being there for itself and its indigenous life forms, being there as the outside to a world that is otherwise a cage, being there for its wholeness, its beauty, its truth—then those who understand it must speak again as lucidly and as persuasively as did Aldo Leopold, Robert Marshall, and Howard Zahniser. As Nancy Newhall put it beautifully thirteen years ago: "Wilderness holds answers to more questions than we have yet learned how to ask."

With no further effort at all, by merely letting our present momentum sweep us on with it, we can grind through the world's last wilderness. Just the undisciplined dash for energy can by itself obliterate wilderness. So dash on then, find the energy, and spend it! But what to do for an encore? The recoverable fossil fuels will be gone. The feasible dam sites will all have been built upon and will before too long be silted in. We will have run out of ways—once we find any—to dilute atomic waste from fission and will realize that fusion is better left in Pandora's box, remembering what came out last time we opened it. We will have endangered the flexibility of the atmosphere by probing the earth's fossil fires in geothermal experimentation. So we will use less energy, not more.

We will again get by with the energy the sun gives us each day instead of exploding and spilling our way through the energy capital the earth took four billion years to acquire.

Do we return to those ways while the world still has wilderness in it, or do we postpone the inevitable turning until we have severed outright and irrevocably those unbroken living connections to the beginning of life that the wilderness has so far preserved? Do we really want to repudiate the evolutionary force? These are questions rational people should not have much trouble answering if they pause to think them through.

Daniel Hudson Burnham (1846–1912) is credited with saying, "Make no little plans; they have no magic to stir men's blood." So why not a big plan? Blessed as we are with more data than were ever collected before, and confronted with an improving technology that might better serve us than direct us, we should prepare a plan not for a decade or a century, but a bolder plan to last a millennium, with option to renew.

A big, long-ranging plan of that order could lead to self-fulfilling predictions that are agreeable instead of the kind we have been getting lately. At a time when we see too many things wrong on the land and going wrong in the sea, why not contemplate a thousand good years instead of concocting sedatives [I should have said "drugs"] for 1984?

Unconventional though the thought may be, the United States could make it clear that we should like to see international leadership rotate peacefully a few times in the course of this thousand years. Such a relaxed attitude might give people, and the other mutually dependent creatures in the environment they are part of, a better chance at the succeeding thousand-year period. Perhaps we should not plan for a period beyond that, even though bristlecone pines do.

It is not the example of the bristlecone, however, that suggests a plan of this magnitude. It is the nuclear dilemma, the strange, self-centered behavior that allows us to deposit high-level radioactive waste (a term from the AEC's Honeybucket Glossary) in the global ecosystem, waste that some one hundred billion future people must take meticulous care of in order that a multitude of us today may enjoy our own brief pass at the planet with all the conveniences we are accustomed to. This waste is the dirtiest garbage of all. Forgetting its thermal pollution ("enrichment") for the moment, we know it is mutagenic, teratogenic, and damnably long-lived. We have already produced a great deal of it and this productivity is proliferating while we watch—or better, while we read ads calling it clean and look the other way. Our children must know where we left it and keep away. So must theirs, and *theirs,* by oral tradition if all other means fail. All this for at least a thousand years, with no fail-safe technique devised yet for the warehousing, no one putting up bond, no one prepared to write the insurance, no long-lasting Directions for Survivors chiseled in stone tablets, but with plenty of people willing to sell and install the machinery and merchandise the electrical power, and with all hands in the first, second, and third worlds eager to buy it without limit and without asking what it really costs.

The least we can do, if morality and ethics are still in our fiber, is to plan a thousand years of amenities for our progeny while they mind our nuclear garbage.

So a thousand good years, and an aim. Mere survival is not enough in the world we seek. Our institutions need to accommodate an optimistic vision of our future, to believe that if the golden rule is all right in religions, it should not be avoided in life.

A Thousand-year Plan for oil, with particular respect to the immediate foreground in Alaska, would recognize the contribution of those who discovered the North Slope oil resource, appropriately cover the costs they cannot cover, reward them, pay the state for storage underground, then record the oil reserve as part of the inventory to be budgeted to last a thousand years. The Plan would contemplate that oil may one day serve a more important purpose than fueling automobiles and supersonic transports. Precipitate exploitation would be discouraged and extravagant use would be prohibited. Studies of potential dangers of removing and transporting the oil in and across fragile ecosystems would be exhaustive and not an exercise in salvage ecology. The costs of perfecting spill-proof transportation would be met and development would await the meeting, the oil remaining safely stored underground until then, in situ. Whatever the costs were would be passed on to the user, who has always paid the costs anyway, although he has not always known it. If this materially raises the price, that increase in itself would make economically feasible the development of more efficient oil-using devices. We would pollute far less because pollution would be too wasteful and too expensive. This would be a residual advantage and a welcome one, since the Plan would not only expect oil to be available for a millennium, but also would expect the air to remain breathable for the duration. Applied to people, the Plan would celebrate and hold hard to the diversity that makes them strong, beautiful, and interesting. Applied to land use, it would obliterate laissez-faire. In forestry, it would eradicate monoculture. In agriculture, it would stop decimating organic diversity three billion years in the making. It would recognize that if population continues to grow at the present rate, humanity will outweigh the earth and there are better things to do with both.

Applied to pace, the Plan would encourage people to slow down and live, to take time to look for the real show, heeding Robinson Jeffers:

But look how noble the world is,
The lonely-flowing waters, the secret-keeping stones,
The flowing sky.

No one ought to have too little courage to try, for what is the alternative? Begun soon, the Thousand-year Plan should have rewards along the way. It should keep alive an orchestration of living things more beautiful than we now know, and perhaps even more beautiful than any of us remembers.

***Earth and the Great Weather*, 1971**

CRY CRISIS!

LET US JUST SAY that Hope didn't make it. Would Anger do better? In *Cry Crisis: Rehearsal in Alaska,* the anger of many contributors, including mine, sought to wake people up. We again tried a little of the symbiosis of image and text, something Ken Brower was getting very good at—hitting hard with beauty. Harvey Manning and I just hit hard, with Hugh Nash's blessing. If we had combined this with the mass-marketing genius of Ian Ballantine, we might just have turned the trick. But an edition size of twenty-five hundred or five thousand books can't do it alone. Nevertheless, as the disaster at Valdez has shown, we were right:

CRY CRISIS! probes a contrived crisis and stresses the real one. It tries not to be any more excited about what confronts America than Paul Revere was. Revere's role, vital though it was, is no more important than what needs to be done now. We would like *Cry Crisis!* to energize a battalion of Paul Reveres.

The energy shortage the nation is now being exposed to is, we believe, a contrived crisis designed to benefit a few. The real crisis lies largely in our failure to see where the true crisis lies.

Is it possible reasonably to conclude that the energy "crisis" just happened? We don't think so.

No international effort, the United Nations included, is more competent or better organized and financed than that which the oil-energy complex puts into action. The complex collectively monopolizes energy (except for solar and tidal capabilities and a few remaining forests), and energy is a major component of the world's principal currencies. The energy people know where the energy is, and in what quantities. They have computer programs, growth rates, demand rates, and discovery rates down cold. They know where and when they want to move capital. Theirs is not a world they will be surprised in, but it is a world full of surprises for us. In 1973 they were hard-selling oil in Europe while talking conservation to us. They can play wells and tank cars and storage tanks and tankers and refineries and pipelines like an organ's console.

Evidence of their contriving is circumstantial, and is likely to remain so. It is naïve to wait for some revelatory memo or tape. The chairman of the board of ARCO, an interviewer once wrote, carries no pencil with him to meetings. The caution and secrecy with which oil-industry deliberations are carried out is legendary. But the circumstantial evidence is compelling.

The energy crisis comes at a time of stiffening public resistance to offshore drilling, hurried oil-shale leasing, and reckless strip-mining. It comes at a time of growing public unease over the rush to open up one nuclear Pandora's box after another, a time of growing doubt over industry's pretense that nuclear power is clean and safe, when it is neither now, nor is it ever likely to be, safe enough. It comes just as long-fought-for pollution controls have finally been achieved, and it has already begun to eviscerate them. It comes at exactly the right moment to panic Congress into approving the Alaska pipeline and hamstringing the court's right to review the action.

The energy crisis has served big industry both as a vehicle for putting independent operators out of business, and as an armored car for attacking environmentalists. The environmentalists have long argued that the earth is a finite earth, that it imposes limits on growth, that there are severe penalties if we exceed the limits very long. They were the first group to predict energy shortages, and are now being blamed for them. The execution of the bearer of bad news is an old rite with modern applications. If the ringing of an alarm system bothers you, the energy-crisis creators have discovered, then call the ringers extremists, or doomsayers, or Cassandras, or even alarmists—and try to rip the alarm system out. The crisis serves still another function—moving an unprecedented amount of capital into energy-cartel control.

In short, if the energy crisis was not designed by the oil-energy complex, it certainly has been very profitable for them in a number of ways. If they did not dream it up, they should have.

Far from trying to get people to use less of a vanishing resource, the energy people are lobbying for supertankers, superports, and a frightfully hazardous liquefied-natural-gas transport combination that will use energy faster. They want enough electricity for two Americas by 1984. They have not lifted a finger to end the supersonic-transport program, which, were it operating as Mr. Nixon planned, would have required the equivalent of five new Prudhoe Bay discoveries by the year 2000, all to provide for the slight reduction in overall travel time that the plane would allow supersonic travelers. They have been tentative at best about influencing Detroit to be less wasteful of oil. They have been of no consequence in the effort to divert highway trust funds to good purpose, such as investing them in mass-transit systems that would move people and freight safely and well with far less energy. While talking about shortages and conservation, they flare two-thirds of the world's emerging natural gas at the well.

In September 1970 a show-me tour of the North Slope conducted for conservationists by the industry left many unconvinced. In Anchorage at the tour's conclusion, Phillip Berry, president of the Sierra Club, asked the president of Atlantic Richfield, "Isn't it possible for you in the oil industry to join the conservationists in persuading the public to stop its extravagant use of oil?"

"That's not our business," Thornton Bradshaw replied. It is oil-company business now, we are asked to believe—not by their deeds but by their ads.

The energy-crisis ploy seems to have begun following the Year of the Environment, 1970–71, when President Nixon said that environmental reform must come now or never. The energy industry saw their development and marketing customs were endangered. They could buy enormous amounts of advertising and, with it, buy the influence over editorial content that advertising-dependent media cannot resist, and still survive.

They could stage events, a requisite of sophisticated public relations.

On June 26, 1972, under the head "ENERGY CRISIS! THE INDUSTRY'S FRIGHT CAMPAIGN," Robert Sherrill asked in *The Nation:*

". . . Where did the energy crisis come from? To a large extent, it came out of the hats of the oil and gas industry's propagandists. Some are more candid than others in peddling their message, none more so than Wilbur Cross, senior editor on the publicity staff of Continental Oil Company. . . .

" 'Conoco was willing to go all the way,' " wrote Cross. 'We'll even do typing, editing, and proofing for you, if you like! And in certain instances we'll arrange transportation' on Conoco planes that happen to be going in the right direction. This ingenious proposal was first disclosed by Morton Mintz in the *Washington Post*. . . .

"Among the 'background texts, outlines, and subject ideas that we have been developing,' said Cross, 'was, you guessed it, the energy crisis.' "

It wasn't the time, however, to launch the array of "crisis" cover stories yet. But when the United States Supreme Court refused to review the environmentalists' lower-court victory blocking the Alaska pipeline, the industry was ready. Necessary legislation was drafted and the pressure to pass it began to build. A mild crisis occurred. Gasoline ran short at the pumps as the vote in the House neared. Stories hostile to the Canadian alternative appeared and stories friendly to it could not find space. The gentle ARCO ads pointing out how good the environment was made way for a strident full-pager in the *Washington Post* when it was time for the vote on an amendment requiring prompt study of the Canadian route. The Canadian alternative is not a substitute, the ad said. We need both pipelines. Let's get on with it!

The amendment was defeated and gasoline was back at the pumps. Aside from a few independent station operators who were forced to close, few suffered.

Noting well that the way to a man's heart was through his gas tank or a threat to his job, and with vaster battlegrounds than Alaska before it, the energy industry broadened its campaign.

The Explorers Club, with oil-company presidents and other explorers for energy prominent in its membership, sent out invitations June 15 to an "Energy Crisis Dinner" to be held November 28 – five months later – in the Grand Ballroom of the Waldorf Astoria, the invitees to be addressed by the President of Exxon, by Vice-President Agnew and science-journalist Jules Bergmann. Before the oil crisis developed, Mr. Agnew had one of his own.

But the plaster of the crisis had not hardened yet, even though a Middle East crisis was in the wind. On September 20 a *New York Times* story said: " 'The energy difficulties of the United States are not the result of any Arab oil squeeze, at least up to now,' John Lichtblau, head of the Petroleum Industry Research Foundation, said yesterday. 'For one thing, our dependence on Arab oil is very small.' "

That was a calm voice from industry. William E. Simon was still calm in the *Times* on October 15:

"The government released figures today showing that the United States could get along without Arab oil in the event of a cut-off of supplies due to the Arab-Israeli war.

"The figures showed that the United States imports about 1.1 million barrels a day of oil direct from the Arab countries. This is about 6 percent of the total daily consumption of 17 million barrels a day.

"William E. Simon, chairman of the President's Oil Policy Committee, said that the United States could reduce consumption by as much as 3 million barrels a day if it was willing to make the effort. . . .

"In addition to imports of oil from the Arab countries, the United States also imports about 2.7 million barrels a day from the Caribbean and

Latin America and 1.4 million barrels a day from Canada."

All the Arab oil did not stop coming when the Yom Kippur war broke out—indeed, many were to wonder how much really stopped coming, what with two sets of government figures in sharp disagreement. If it had all stopped coming, that would still be but a six-percent drop.

A mere six percent, however, would alarm no one. Canada supplied the U.S. more than that and could help further if asked, not ignored. But there was a new crisis. Watergate hearings and the suit by Common Cause were showing what an enormous contribution the oil companies had made to the Committee to Reelect the President. Many of the contributions were a violation of the Corrupt Practices Act. This brought a slap on the wrist. If you have given one hundred thousand dollars illegally, and the fine is only five thousand dollars, then you have given one hundred five thousand dollars. Who would notice the difference?

What else might be dug up? What contributions that were better camouflaged than those discovered so far? Not just for the 1972 elections, but for 1970, and 1968? What commitments did these bring, as for example, to forge ahead on the Alaska pipeline and damn the wildlife, wilderness, fisheries, Eskimos, the public, and national security? Watergate headlines were getting too much sensitive information too far out into the open. Soon the investigation might be of the Oilgate behind Watergate. Something dramatic was needed to change the headlines.

A president of the United States, with his power to command unequaled attention, could initiate a crisis of his choosing. Beef, milk, aspirin, whiskey. Couple a momentary delay in shipping schedules with a presidential announcement on all networks that a whiskey shortage is imminent, and the liquor-store shelves will be clear by nightfall. William F. Buckley, Jr., described the energy crisis as our having to get by with slightly more oil than we were using in 1970.

So the less-than-six-percent drop in Arabian crude led to the announcement of crisis and the request that the public cut fifteen percent. Let there be energy self-sufficiency, and let the environment come second.

Watergate embarrassment was off the front page immediately, and stayed off, with an exception of eighteen and a half minutes.

Then, almost as if the timing were masterminded, Americans could read full-page ads galore about how great a public resource huge oil-company profits were. In magazine after magazine, they saw Exxon's eight-page, four-color protestations of the innocence of offshore drilling. On one Exxon color spread was a map entitled, "The World of Known Oil Reserves." It showed fifty-three percent of the oil in the Middle East, sixteen percent in Africa, fifteen percent in the Soviet Union and other communist countries, five percent in the United States including Alaska, two percent in Canada, and nine percent in what's left of the world. For Exxon the map demonstrated the need for more offshore drilling. For President Nixon, too, apparently. The president and his oil-company advisors, after studying figures like those of the map, told the public in effect, "If we can use our oil up eight or more times as fast as the Arab countries will let us use their oil up, we will be self-sufficient." For how long? Not for very, but get it all under way before anyone figures that out. Conservationists saw a contrary message in the same map, but it was not their map to attach messages to, and they could not afford a competitive map of their own.

"Oil wells die, too. . . . When they do, they are shut in and disappear without a trace on the landscape," said a Mobil Oil ad in 1973. Above the words was a photograph of a simple rock cairn beneath Shiprock, New Mexico. This fabulous disappearance of oil wells—this simple tombstone—would have interested the millionaire rancher from Duval County, Texas, who visited the Friends of the Earth office in San Francisco in the same year. The rancher brought with him an album full of a different kind of photograph. In it were views of abandoned oil operations, bearing the signs of Mobil and most of the major oil companies—rusting tanks and pipes, thousands of acres of rangeland destroyed by saline pollution from oil wells, poisoned cattle, some pipes still leaking oil.

The rancher explained that when the profits of the major companies drop, the majors sell to the "poor boys," the small companies who squeeze the last drops of oil out of what the majors left behind, and who can't afford to clean up the mess the big boys made. The millionaire rancher had hundreds of color photographs of the damage to his land, he had made a film of it, and he had been to court, but the damage continued. He was only a millionaire, of course, and Friends of the Earth was considerably less than that. To give Mobil-ad circulation to a different tombstone, Duval County style ("Oil wells die, too. When they do, they bleed all over the landscape"), would have required more money than either Friends of the Earth or the rancher could spare. If millionaires cannot block damage to their holdings, what chance does an Eskimo stand, or other conservationists, unable to speak loudly enough to be heard in the din raised by the industry's campaign? We foresee a problem.

We would like to point out, too, when industry pledges anew its intention to sell its North Slope oil in the United States, that we see a catch or two.

For example: the oilman may really believe he can manage earthquakes and tidal waves in the land that displays these phenomena in their most frequent and frightful manifestations, but does he really believe he can manipulate his stockholders as easily? Suppose a stockholder wants his company's oil to go to Japan. The oilmen have variously denied that (any) (much) or (most) of Alaska's oil is destined for Japan, however much it might seem that just such a destination was nailed down with massive and premature shipment of Japanese pipe to be stacked along the Alaska route.

Japan needs outside oil far more than we, and she is conveniently close to the port of Valdez and to the heavy Japanese investment in her colonial Alaska. The Japanese proximity and the critical Japanese need for energy combine to make a most profitable market. For non-U.S. ships making an end run on the Jones Act (which requires that U.S.-to-U.S. marine shipments travel in U.S. bottoms), Tokyo would be a fine destination.

What happens, then, for all the oil-company denials, when shareholders of ARCO and other companies read Charles Chicchetti's clear analysis, published in a *Resources for the Future* book, of how the oil companies will clear an extra dollar per barrel by shipping the oil to Japan? This means an extra profit on the Prudhoe Bay reserve that has been proved so far of ten billion dollars. What happens when stockholders bring suit, as they are entitled to do, to force management to realize such profit—however piously management claimed it wished to forego the profit to please its domestic customers?

And if management means what it says about using Alaska oil in the U.S., why not a stockholder's suit to require that the oil come to the real market, the Midwest, by the least expensive, least hazardous route? On the score of initial expense alone, there would be nearly a three-billion-dollar advantage to bringing the Prudhoe reserve through Canada—using proved Arctic railroad technology for the Arctic portions of the route, and proved pipeline technology for the rest. Can a company afford to ignore such an economy and the resulting profit? And what about a Permanent Committee of Vigil, a cooperative pro bono effort by stockholders and environmentalists to check out, persuade, legislate against, or sue, everlastingly, every lapse on the part of those who unilaterally dreamed up the wrong route to the wrong place at the wrong time, if they adamantly persist in going ahead with it? What happens when the stockholders review some of the scenarios of disaster that spring easily to mind, but were omitted from the pipeline's environmental impact statement and operating criteria? What happens when the stockholders note, and thank the environmentalists for, the thirty-billion-dollar increase in value of the proved Prudhoe reserve? This increase has come from just leaving the oil in Alaska, rather than hastening to blow it out tail pipes in Japan and (or) the U.S. The price is climbing fast because oil-wise nations around the world are realizing that oil saved is a future resource earned, enhanced instead of squandered with unprecedented extravagance.

Perhaps a group of ARCO stockholders and British Petroleum shareholders might even like to suggest that their companies give the environmentalists a generous grant for sparing the companies from building an unsafe pipeline in the first place ("We didn't know how to build a safe pipeline then," the president of ARCO has said, in thanking environmentalists for delaying construction. Now the companies know, he thinks). They might offer a ten-percent finder's fee for the addition to real capital that safe leakproof storage in the Alaskan earth has brought about. This is a real capital gain for stockholders and for their neighbors, for Alaskans, for everyone's children. The environmentalists could use such financial support. It would enable them to keep their alarm systems operating in the public interest.

Perhaps the stockholders will do so. Until then, environmentalists will have to continue, as always, the struggle in the public interest at their own expense.

When Energy Czar William Simon, on the day of his appointment, announces that a second pipeline is necessary to bring the oil out of the North Slope faster – and he did – they will insist, as loudly as they can, that he is wrong on two counts. His is not just the second pipeline. Count them: (1) Trans-Alaska pipeline number one, ARCO et al. (2) Canada's proposed natural-gas pipeline through Canada. (3) ARCO's proposed line across Canada, which "would not be a substitute" for pipeline number one. (4) El Paso Natural Gas Company's proposed natural gas line across Alaska. (5) Secretary Morton's natural gas line across the Arctic National Wildlife Range. (6) Mr. Simon's "second" pipeline, its purpose to hurry the North Slope oil into automobiles, generators, furnaces, and human lungs. These six do not include the Canadian alternative, which Canada was willing to share, though her willingness to do so was kept secret from Congress by the Nixon administration. Simon's pipeline, if completed, would begin the realization of the environmentalists' worst fears. From the beginning, they worried that pipeline number one was just a camel's nose in the igloo. Then more pipelines and other exploitive corridors would multiply across the Great Land.

The count so far? To date, seven pipelines proposed.

Is that all? No. On December 6, 1973, the *Wall Street Journal* told briefly of still another, and on the following day the *San Francisco Chronicle* revealed further, and most alarming, details:

". . . Deputy Secretary of Defense William P. Clements, Jr., who has a $98-million investment in SEDCO Inc., an oil-drilling and pipeline construction company that serves the major international oil companies, has recommended in an internal Pentagon document the exploration and development of the vast Naval Petroleum Reserves, the largest untapped supply of oil in the United States.

"The recommendations suggest the possibility that private oil companies could develop the Navy's vast oil fields to fulfill military needs and sell what was left over to civilians. Many of these companies are SEDCO customers.

"Clements was unavailable for comment on the question of whether his recommendations constitute a conflict of interest because of his enormous personal investment in SEDCO, which is one of the largest offshore drilling companies in the world and one of the top five pipeline contracting firms in the nation. . . .

"In addition to being No. 2 man in the Pentagon, Clements is a member of President Nixon's cabinet-level Energy Emergency Group, which is formulating the administration's oil policy in the present fuel crisis and is managing the Defense Department's oil allocation program."

So Secretary Clements, then, and Secretary Morton, and Energy Czar Simon, and President Nixon, and Congress (telling the court to stay out of it) pursue the strange policy: Drain America First, and *Fast!* For self-sufficiency.

The industry's public relations campaign has indeed been persuasive. Oil has filled the vacuum the public leaves when it disdains participating in politics. The oil industry has hedged bets in the process, contributing to both the probable loser and the probable winner, thus creating the inevitable residue of obligation in both.

What the industry programed worked very well in 1973. Rising oil-company profits – the earnings for the top nine companies skyrocketed five billion dollars in the first nine months of 1973 – demonstrated their success. The companies succeeded in enthralling the Nixon administration, keeper of facts from Congress; they called the tune in Congress, which, in its approval of the pipeline, was willing to undercut the National Environmental Policy Act, its own finest environmental achievement; they demeaned the courts, whose role in protecting the public was compromised by Congress.

In June 1973, *The New Yorker* underscored the congressional default:

". . . The second event was the vote in the Senate last week approving the construction of an oil pipeline across Alaska – a vote that the *Times* called 'a shocking display of irresponsibility.' Every member of the Senate must know that the most pernicious financial pressure group in the United States is the oil lobby. . . . Moreover, on the same day that the Senate cast this crucial vote, the Federal Trade Commission charged the eight largest oil companies in the United States with having conspired for more than twenty years to eliminate competition, to keep prices artificially high, and to create shortages of oil and gas. "If the Watergate hearings have demonstrated anything, they have demonstrated the threat to the survival of our political system posed by the secret use of big money by unscrupulous people during political campaigns. . . . Approval of the pipeline bill by the Senate . . . suggests a readiness on the part of the bill's senatorial supporters to ignore charges, made after long study by independent government agencies, about practices that are in the business world exactly what the Watergate practices were in the political world. All in all it seems that the Senate has so far learned little from the appalling scandals it has uncovered."

The irresponsible vote was a tie vote. Broken the right way, it would have preserved the hard-won function of the National Environmental Policy Act and of the court. Then Vice-President Spiro T. Agnew, who had not yet been forced to resign, broke the tie—the wrong way.

The timidity of the Fourth Estate is the ultimate of default, the ultimate demonstration of Big Oil's success. The feeling of futility abroad in the land is the measure of that success, its source and its symbol.

With this feeling pervasive, it is all too easy to imagine election time 1976. The North Slope and other Arctic permits have been issued. The environmentalists and National Environmental Policy Act have been derailed. The oil-shale and strip-mine and offshore leases have been lobbied through by the same technique that worked so well in Alaska. The highway lobby, truckers, and airlines have exerted their pressure and have been permitted to resume their old habits. The supersonic-transport program is back out in the open where President Nixon wanted it to be when he withheld adverse information about it from Congress. Import quotas are diminished again to provide full protection of the domestic market for domestic producers. The depletion allowance has been raised. Nationalization of energy has been dismissed as radicalism. Financial-page headlines read: "WATERGATE COMMITTEE MEETS AGAIN."

Russell Baker, writing in the *New York Times* on December 2, 1973, saw it all more clearly:

"Here are pressing questions about the energy crisis and answers supplied by one who should know better.

"Q. What is the energy crisis?

"A. The energy crisis is the finest all-purpose alibi in America today. If you can't deliver the goods, it is because of the energy crisis. If you want to raise prices, it is necessitated by the energy crisis. If you want to cancel a visit with your wife's relatives, tell them, 'Sorry, it's the energy crisis.' . . . .

"Q. Wasn't anybody smart enough to notice until right now that we were running out of oil?

"A. Of course! Children of the 1930s—and they are running the government today—were aware of it. 'What will happen when we have used up all the oil?' they used to say. 'What a silly question!' their parents used to reply. 'Before that can happen science will come up with something new to replace oil.'

"Q. Why hasn't science come up with something new to replace oil?

"A. Because if it did, economic disaster would result. Oil companies would collapse. So would shipping and pipeline companies. Texas would become a disaster area and American taxpayers would have to put every sheik in Arabia on welfare. There would no longer be any reason to build the Alaska pipeline.

"Q. If the people running the government knew the energy crisis was coming, why didn't they stop construction years ago on the interstate highway system and use the money to build railroads?

"A. Because they knew the Interstate Highway System would be needed to help save gasoline when the energy crisis occurred. Without the Interstate Highways' capacity to move traffic at 70 miles an hour, it would be impossible to cut gasoline consumption by reducing the speed limit to 50 miles an hour.

"Q. Instead of going on daylight saving time to cut electricity usage a little at the end of the day, why not close down television after 9 o'clock so people will have to go to bed?

"A. If television shut down at 9 P.M., it would be the end of the 11 P.M. TV news shows all over the country. These shows are vital to fighting the energy crisis because they are often sponsored by gasoline companies whose commercials advise the audience how to cut gasoline consumption.

"Q. I have just bought a large car which uses a gallon of gasoline every eight miles. Since the people running the government knew the energy crisis was coming, why didn't they tell the auto makers, so the auto makers wouldn't have made this car and sold it to me?

"A. Because the people running the government were concerned about your safety. They did not want you to take your family onto turnpikes teeming with gigantic tractor-trailers unless you were all traveling in a vehicle much sturdier than the average tiny compact. . . .

"Q. Why was the energy crisis begun at this time, just when I was finally beginning to get interested in Watergate?

"A. The government reasoned that since fewer and fewer people believed anything the government said anymore it should hold the energy crisis right away while there were still a few people left to believe in it."

The real crisis is in the way we persistently read the wrong message into the energy shortage that confronts us. Instead of accepting the shortage as a warning to mend our ways, we see it as a challenge to race faster down our present ruinous path. Instead of being thankful for the reprieve, we are angry at the inconvenience. We see what the bottom of the cornucopia looks like, and would rather turn away.

On November 7, 1973, in his Energy Crisis Message, President Nixon told the nation that owing to the shortage of Arab oil, its citizens must lower speeds and thermostats, and dim lights. Fine. The president has a good grasp of the kind of conservation measures that will work in the home and the family car. But then he went on to say that we must open up our oil reserves. We must put reactors on the line faster and with less care. We must revive energy research and development (these were starved of funds by the president's withholding of them and his denigration of the role of science in government). We must put a growing economy ahead of a safe environment in our thinking. We must, by 1980, become self-sufficient in energy, dependent upon no other nation (as our five percent of the world's population increases its present disproportionate use of one-third of the world's energy). We must attain self-sufficiency by draining our own fossil-fuel resources first, and at an increasing rate.

In the president's scheme for the future, the conservation measures that work for the individual will not, for some reason, work for the nation. He would have citizens march in one direction, and industry race in the opposite. That our *national* energy consumption might be made to cease growing, or even to decrease, is not, to the president's mind, one of our options.

Industry's infatuation with growth is an old habit, difficult to break. But the time for overdrafts at the world's environmental bank has run out, we think, and sellers as well as buyers must realize that there will be no business at all on a dead planet.

People in industry have been slow to see the danger, but there are intimations of change. Robert O. Anderson is one of the few men in his august set to see the threat. He is chairman of the board of Atlantic Richfield. In 1972 I asked Anderson at the North American Wildlife Conference in Mexico City, "Cognizant as you are of the Club of Rome studies about limits to growth, cannot you and other leaders in the energy industry join in persuading the public to use less?" He answered: "That's a tough question. I just had lunch the other day with Professor Forrester (author of *World Dynamics*) and Dennis Meadows (of *Limits to Growth*). I know a lot of people think we ought to throw their books away. I think we're going to have to live with it."

We are indeed, and because we are, more leaders of the oil-energy complex should be lunching with the Forresters and the Meadowses, and letting a little of the new ethic rub off on them.

President, industry, and nation must be weaned soon from their recent dependence upon the Growth Ethic. The true message of the energy shortage, and of common sense, is that uncomfortably sooner, or inevitably and painfully later, we must redirect the growth that has let us prosper through the using up of everyone's resources.

The real crisis, then, is in the remorseless way we commit crimes against the future.

Thomas Jefferson once argued that no one generation has a right to encroach upon another generation's freedom. Today we need a new Jefferson as much as a new Paul Revere. There is a mentality abroad now that discounts children heavily and grandchildren almost totally, discounts their right to know the freedom of unspoiled places and the freedom of adequate energy. It is this same mentality that gives people of the other Americas—North, Central, South and Middle—no vote at all. This same mentality deems it somehow subhuman that Arab people might not wish to use up their oil for our purposes as fast as we wish them to.

***Cry Crisis!*, 1974**

ALASKA, THE WINTER of 1977–78 [or 1997–98].

The first of several of the planned trans-Alaska pipelines is now completed and two million barrels of oil pour through it every day. It is hot oil, at about one hundred sixty degrees. As often happens in winter in interior Alaska, the temperature outside the pipe is minus seventy degrees farenheit and dropping.

The two-hundred-forty-degree temperature difference is staggering, and the stress on the Japanese steel of the pipe exceeds what the builders anticipated. It was not their fault. The oil is at one hundred sixty degrees in part as an economy measure. Had the temperature been only thirty-two degrees so as to avoid permafrost melt, a threat not only to the pipe but also the ecosystem, then one hundred thousand more horsepower would have been required at the pumps.

The temperature differential is bad enough, but now a Richter 8.6 strikes, an earthquake a little rougher than the one that shook up Anchorage in 1964. That earthquake all but destroyed Valdez, at the pipeline's stormy supertanker-shuttle terminus in the tidal-wave-prone Gulf of Alaska. Secretaries of the Interior Walter J. Hickel and Rogers C. B. Morton glossed over warnings that seventy-five percent of the Alaska route was in major earthquake zones, whereas only three percent of the Canadian alternative route was. Engineers said they could handle earthquakes. Whatever they intended, the earthquake has slipped out of their grasp. The rupture is major.

"We will have delicate instruments to report on such events," the engineers said. They were right. The instruments report disaster. Now what?

It is very cold, there is a dense ice fog, and there is no way to get to the manual cutoff valves. The pumping stations are the only accessible control. They average sixty-five miles apart, with enough oil in the pipe between pairs of pumps to equal one hundred thirty Santa Barbara spill disasters. A torrent of oil is loose of a magnitude that was never dumped upon a major ecosystem in all the earth's history. One hundred thirty Santa Barbara spills gush swiftly into a major watershed and are headed for one of the world's major fisheries. There is no stopping the rush of black gold.

The engineers succeed in stopping the flow in the rest of the pipe: All the pumps are shut down, and the flow stops in all the other seven hundred miles of main pipe. It also stops in the several hundred miles of smaller feeder pipe that lace the North Slope.

The break is major. The stress of the temblor, added to the stress of the thermal gap, has split a great deal of pipe. Worse still, the weather and earthquake combined have caused general disruption of communications elsewhere in Alaska. The 1964 earthquake, at Richter 8.3, created an island thirty feet high in Valdez harbor, and the accompanying tidal wave mangled nearby oil tanks at Whittier. The new quake has added thirty-five feet to the island and has created a major rock slide, dumping massive amounts of talus – and many mangled oil tanks – into the harbor in spite of the engineers' expectations that the rock the tanks were on was more solid than Gibraltar's. The concurrent tsunami has beached and broken three supertankers loading in the harbor. Where the line crosses the Wrangell Mountains, a subsidiary earthquake has severely damaged the ice dam formed by a large glacier. The lake behind the glacier has just breached the ice dam and wiped out more pipeline in the torrent. There is already so much oil spilled from mangled tanks and broken supertankers that the harbor's fish do not notice the new supply as the river brings it in. They are already dead.

With herculean efforts, spurred by oil-company guilt at having so beset the Alaskan environment (congressional action and environmental suits and the faltering Japanese balance of payments already have impeded the Valdez-Tokyo tanker run), the Alyeska maintenance crews repair the breaks after a frantic thirty-seven-day effort. The oil that was at one hundred sixty degrees all along the pipe when the oil was moving has cooled to the ambient temperature. This varies widely along the line, sometimes rising briefly, then dropping again. It is time to start the pumps.

Start the pumps? The computer readout and all the delicate instruments make it perfectly clear that the cold oil is too viscous to move. If the oil could be warmed nearly one hundred degrees, the temperature at which ice would thaw, it would still take one hundred thousand horsepower more at the pumps to keep it moving, if it were moving. But there is all that inertia of viscous oil, dead in its tracks, and there is no way to raise its temperature to freezing. If you could raise it, it would make no difference anyway, for the necessary hundred thousand horses aren't there. The engineers knew the horsepower wouldn't be needed, because they knew about earthquakes, and no earthquake could trouble their pipe.

They share, they now realize, the fallibility of the engineers who designed the nuclear submarine *Thresher,* now imploded and irradiating the floor of the sea and whatever the unknown currents carry the radiation to. They share the fallibility of those who did not anticipate the leak in the oxygen system of *Apollo 13.* Of those who left the crescent wrench in the unhappy spot that three astronauts died for on an earlier *Apollo.* Of those who put the bad bolt on *Skylab.* They share the fallibility of the engineers of Westinghouse, a principal reactor builder, who built a thirty-five-million-dollar computer system that the Bay Area Rapid Transit (BART) people found too dangerous to use. Transportation engineers were fallible then.

Alaska pipeline engineers, it turns out now in 1978, have proved more disastrously fallible. You can always figure out another way, if you are an engineer, to get people across San Francisco Bay. But when your inadequate engineering spills a flood of oil that destroys wildlife, wilderness, and fisheries, you do not, as an engineer, have the foggiest idea how to replace these living things. Spilled oil will not even help the U.S. balance of payments.

How about the unspilled oil?

There is, still in the pipe, a viscous, immovable mass, and how are you supposed to get it moving again? By turning on heaters throughout more than seven hundred miles of pipe, four feet in diameter, filled with something slower than molasses in January? Were these heaters in the budget? With the energy crisis and all, can we afford to turn them on?

Operation Restart is not considered in the six-foot-high environmental impact statement. You don't like to ask tough questions of the people who put several million dollars in electoral campaigns. Tough questions would surely have been raised had Secretary Morton wished to hold public hearings on the revised impact statement. He must have known that the earlier statement was among the most ridiculous documents ever to issue from the government in the twentieth century. Perhaps he was not sure what the critics would think of the revision. No hearing, he ordered. It would be a circus, he said.

But how do the engineers move the oil again? What system, undisclosed, do they have up their sleeves? Where did they test it? Under what relevant conditions? Did it work? What would it cost? Is that cost included in the present pipeline estimate, an estimate that has risen from less than one billion dollars to more than four billion while the argument goes on?

Was the question about such a break asked at all? Was it asked and the asker silenced? Has something like this happened to others who did not like other parts of the Game Plan for the Gang Bang of Alaska—exploitation not just by oilmen, but by dammers, miners, pulpmakers, whale killers, fishmeal makers, and all others recently arrived in Alaska to see what they could take home from the state, letting the devil take the now hindmost who were there in the first place?

How move the chilled oil, then; or rather, to be charitable, *when?* Will they have to wait until summer?

"That is a good question," a geologist said. "I keep asking it, but I don't get any answers." Big Oil put the pressure on to move quickly, no matter how long-lasting the environmental cost. "A trade-off?" We've heard about trade-offs. Trading off our children's rights for our pleasures.

Footnote

The foregoing prediction can be prevented from becoming self-fulfilling, even at this late date—even until the pipe is laid and oil begins to flow through it. Wise counsel can still rule that the Alaska pipeline is wrong. Oil to the wrong place, at the wrong time, at the wrong rate, for the wrong reasons, benefiting the wrong people. At a time when wrongs need to be righted, rights are being wronged. The present pipeline decision is rampant cynicism: to hell with the consequences when campaign contributions of such munificence are at stake.

Concerning the postulation of wrecked tankers at Valdez: a look at the record, at the frequency of tsunamis there, would turn wise men pale. Did Interior look?

About the violent storms at Valdez, did anyone ask Pete Martin of Anchorage? He once stepped out of a Valdez hotel to mail a letter, and he did mail it; but he had to drop to all fours and crawl hard against a winter gale to get back to the hotel. Did anyone at Interior ask how loading supertankers would fare in such straits?

As for the one hundred thirty Santa Barbara disasters headed downstream for the mouth of the Yukon (or whatever river is Lucky Pierre): Who will clean up the ocean for the benefit of nonvoting whales and other marine creatures? At the *Pacem in Maribus* Convocation in Malta in 1970, it was pointed out that were there an oil spill anywhere off the coast of Africa, there would be no one on the entire Dark Continent trained to control it. Are the Eskimos better trained? Can they indeed handle what no one, on any continent, has yet been able to handle, except in public-relations fiction? Secretary Morton was present (as was I) at the Environmental Banquet of the Explorers Club when Thor Heyerdahl told of the forty-three days out of fifty-seven, on his second historic Atlantic crossing, that he spent in oil residue on what had been a clean ocean just ten years before. Did the Secretary hear and care? What is the trade-off for a dead ocean? Or can we clean it?

And who will clean up the land, heal the severing slash across the heart of our last great wilderness? What chance is there of adequate surveillance or even of a half-hearted beginning at cleaning up afterwards? The nearby few Alaska natives, Indian or Eskimo, have already had their wishes overridden. The Interior employees have already found how much healthier it is to remain silent, to rock no tankers or other boats. The conservationists have had to shift their thin ranks to protect what is still fairly pure. And can they afford the time, money, or people to monitor the massive destruction and specific operations that the raw power of Big Oil demanded and got? And even if the natives, the government employees, the latter Alaskans, and the conservationists worked together in unprecedented unison, would it make a difference? The Duval County answer is not reassuring. Looking on into the 1970s, we can send our protest, hoping they will now try very hard to do better, to Governor Egan, President Nixon, Secretary Morton, to Senators Stevens and Gravel, to ARCO and BP and Alyeska, and to all the other companies in Alaska. The Texas-oil mentality (with apologies to all Texans free of it) has brought destruction to the threshold of the Great Land—the potential of a carnage no one should wish to celebrate on the nation's two hundredth birthday.

Since most right-handed people read books from the back to the front, let us end the book with a letter of transmittal to whoever is here beginning to read it:

Cry Crisis! Rehearsal in Alaska is about what happens to people when they trade in their own new power for old used energy from other eons. The book is long, pithy, angry, kind, sometimes good-humored, always well-intended, and utterly and damned necessary.

As you will note, we would like to persuade some people we know to repent their sins against Alaska et al. We hope they will start to back-track a little very quickly, and discover how good it feels. *Cry Crisis!* names a few of the people and lists almost all their known sins. The worst sin of the most patriotic of them is that they want so desperately to drain America first.

The evil that all of us together can avoid is the cardinal sin: that this generation should want to drain the earth first.

That would be a sleazy bequest, even if the gift were tax deductible.

Can we help each other leave something better when we leave, and be brighter about enjoying a rather nice planet while we live?

Postscript: Our sin is that the book is so late. Only you can make it *too* late.

***Cry Crisis!*, 1974**

An Inner Voice

The Footnote had something to say about Valdez that ought to have been heeded, but was ignored instead, and the ignoring goes on.

At the last possible moment I listened myself to an inner voice. It happened this way.

When Ken, John, and Steve were off in the Brooks Range, ninety-pound packs and all, they expected six weeks in which there would be no contact with civilization. They were all in their early twenties, with some wilderness experience of course, John's having been particularly hairy in a Cutabereni jungle when he was hunted by people. So there they were, on the one hand, and here was I on the other. Climber of many peaks, trainer of many climbers, taught by others wiser than I to maintain and respect a margin of safety, to have some route of escape if a thing or two went wrong, but willing to accept the consequences if three or four things went wrong.

These innocent kids in an unknown wilderness! No prior planning on communication if a severe accident should happen. Not even signal panels to display if a bush pilot should happen to fly over.

That was it! We had developed this technique in the army and had used it well. I had even introduced it to Sierra Club High Trips. At least I could get some signal panels to them.

One of the things a battalion intelligence officer can do well is get on the telephone and find information. I got on and found the bush pilot who had taken the trio to Shrader Lake, from which point they were on their own. He knew their approximate route, and we made a deal.

Well into their trip the three men were camped by another lake, and a bush pilot circled and landed on it. "I'll bet my dad is on that plane," Ken said.

It's a wise child who knows his own father, to quote Shakespeare backwards, but Ken did not know I had achieved a high point in my life. I was not on that plane.

I had help from Anne, who suggested that wilderness and paternalism do not mix.

Ken was lucky. Look at what corporate paternalism has done for almost everybody else's wilderness!

CHAPTER 13

WILDERNESS AND YOU

SKIN IS THE HEAVIEST ORGAN of the body. It is also the thinnest, an arbitrary but fortunate boundary between what is within you and what isn't, the rest of the world. There is not as much wildness out there as I wish there were. There is more inside than you think. Taking this kind of inventory can be fun.

If you are my age, your heart has beat about three and a half billion times without any maintenance or replacement—a lot more if you are a jogger, which I am not. You have exhaled about four hundred million times, adding your bit to the atmosphere's burden of carbon dioxide. You have eaten seventeen tons of food, and would be better off if it had been four or five fewer. Your emanations have included about that many tons of perspiration, and that's not all. We won't go into sperm or egg counts. You have a bridge, arches, drums, and in all probability, a deviated septum. You have fully armed defensive forces, and trillions of cells, all of them properly fed most of the time, including the red cells running up and down your quiet wild streams bearing gifts. You also contain some islands—the islands of Langerhans, for example: "Any of the groups of small, angular cells, arranged in the form of anastomosing trabeculae among the gland tubules and alveoli of the pancreas, producing an internal secretion controlling the oxidation of sugar." Everyone knows that, and therefore has not given up white death. Or the island of Reil, "the central lobe of the cerebral hemisphere, situated deeply between the lips of the Sylvian fissure." You may very well not have known about these other lips, or who Sylvia is. Those are probably the lips that are sealed when television causes cerebral gridlock. Everywhere your cells go, mitochondria go, too, as Lewis Thomas has made perfectly and amazingly clear. They are with you but not of you, and without them you couldn't handle energy.

All these devices, and many many more, operate within—without your leave, and probably function far better than they would if you interfered. So do your nervous and circulatory systems, which are much too complicated to work. Equally unworkable are the intricacies of the wiring that gives your brain a chance to read and understand sound in stereo, and to tell where it comes from—whether from the right or left, above, below, or behind. The same is true of the one hundred twenty millions rods and cones in each retina, how they got placed where they belong, and how they react to motion and respond to color, coordinated as they are with your widely variable lens aperture, the great depth of your focusing capability, and your twin lubricating devices that operate automatically every few seconds. All this, and what you are able to do with what you see, is simply too much to believe, but it happens. It is also not possible, but happens, that you can remember whatever or whomever you have seen and paid attention to, and can run your own private videotape of either whenever you wish.

What else? Look up *Gray's Anatomy* and count the miracles for yourself. But you won't find there what I discovered one cloudy day when I had nothing better to do during my airline lunch than count the number of times I had to chew. Two thousand for lunch. That probably means at least five thousand chews per day unless you are on one of those horrible liquid weight-reducing diets. I became aware, while chewing, of what made it possible. It is absolutely necessary that your tongue, one of your softest, gentlest tissues, put the proper amount of food in between the hardest substance you own, your tooth enamel, not just on one side, but on both, and get the hell out of the way before you bite it. This is the tongue, mind you, that must go through thirty-two different motions to help you pronounce the English alphabet—this moistener of lips, this key to the kiss that counts, this seldom forked, often-civil organ. Let's hear it for the tongue!

There's so much to say about the wildness within you that I'll leave it to Lewis Thomas, with illustrations by Lennart Nilsson, and hope they collaborate. All I want to do here is remind you of your most important hidden assets. But how did they come to be?

You probably know, even though you do not remember all the details, that you began to take shape very soon after a bold vigorous sperm outraced millions of others and found a sirenlike egg, which was hardly moving at all, and there was a rendezvous, their first and only. The two of them contained all the essential information, each of them useless without the other, that could instruct the beginning and curtailing of every single cell and movement that was to become you and all your senses.

You must have known this already, but did you know something even more remarkable? The genetic material in the sperm and egg that was to be you—the very minimum, minus the packaging—multiplied by the approximately one hundred billion people who ever lived, would fit in a sphere one-sixth of an inch in diameter. That's a miracle in miniaturization. Hewlett-Packard can't equal it. And the development of that capability had nothing to do with civilization, because there wasn't any as the capability evolved. Your gene code remembers, in important ways, the day life began on earth. Everyone now living is directly connected with that day, some three and a half billion years ago. Many millions of species of plants and animals fell by the wayside as the megamillennia wore on. But none of your ancestors, whatever their shape, failed you. The baton of life was passed on perfectly in the ultimate relay race through time. It, not books, built your intuition, letting you know at a glance where this nettle, danger, lies between you and this flower, safety. And here you are, three and a half billion years old and hardly showing your age.

Why? Because your beginnings were honed in the pulling and tugging, the trial and error, the success and failure, the symbiotic relationships, the teamwork, the need for life if you will, in wilderness. Civilization is too new to have interfered with your becoming. What it has to do with your being is something else.

Put civilization aside for a moment and come with Anne, one or two of our children, and me to Tuolumne Meadows and on up toward Tioga Pass. After our first full view of Mount Dana and Mount Gibbs on the Sierra Crest, we'll drive a little farther to a vista point where a pond edged with grass reflects those peaks, rising three thousand feet above and beyond the pond's forest. Park here and bring some lunch with you, and some protection from sun, chill, and possibly a mosquito or two, unless it is August. Walk almost to the far end of the pond, counting the different flowers you see. Turn a little to the right and drop down through lodgepole pines to a long and narrow meadow. The stream that is usually in it may have given up by now, but no matter. Cross where it was, looking for gentians if it is late August, and walk toward an obvious enough saddle in the low ridge ahead of you, with a wonderful dead tree in it that you can't see yet. Look at the rainbow of colors in the little metamorphic rocks as you walk—remnants of the old roof pendant capping the Sierra's granite. But don't look for a trail. There isn't one. That's the beauty of it.

Just find your way down past the dead tree, follow a tiny stream to a larger one, ford it, and follow another meadow, heading south, until you find an easy way to pass through some more lodgepoles to hit the Dana Fork of the Tuolumne River. Take off your shoes and socks and, putting your shoes back on, carefully wade across. Drain your shoes, put socks back on, and head up the opposite bank. You will find an old deer trail with some young lodgepoles, twenty or thirty years old, growing right in the middle of it here and there. Bypass them, the way the deer now do. When you come to the first little tributary stream, follow its general course to its head. Going will be a bit rough here and there. Just take your time and try to remember where the good parts are so that you can find them on the way back down. Don't worry if you miss. Anne and I have never gone the same way twice, up or down. If you veer too far to the east, you get into cliffs that will require rock-climbing. If you try going up the middle of the slope, you get into a willow jungle. We've done that. We veered to the west once but Anne didn't like it. There were no woods or willows to tangle with, but there was talus and she doesn't prefer it. If you try passing over talus by climbing it, one block at a time, it is like trying to ride a bicycle at a standstill. It won't work. If you keep moving, it doesn't matter if one or two talus blocks are unstable. You have passed over them before they can move far enough out from under you to make a difference. If three or more are unstable in succession, you may be in trouble. Under the Devil's Crags, Hervey Voge and I found where a deer had got into that kind of trouble, and had left a foot behind. Don't worry. You won't be going that fast, and your feet are bigger than a deer's.

Our one-time veer to the west got us into a little rock-climbing, and Anne prefers meadows. I still have vestige enough of climbing ability left to enjoy a little scrambling, so long as it isn't too thin or exposed. Anne was rewarded, and so was I, by the discovery in some of the shaded rocky alcoves of beautiful groups of columbine that we had not seen on our other routes. There the only columbine was the red variety, near the stream, and we had to settle, for reward, on surprise discoveries, here and there, of white heather, the cassiope bells that were John Muir's favorite.

If you feel better on than off-trail (I hope you get over it), try our alternate goal for geriatrics in Yosemite—the Dana Plateau. From Tioga Lake there is a trail all the way up the left side of the stream that comes from the Dana Glacier. At the first meadow turn left and head uphill. We always turn too soon and miss a section of the trail, but it is too rocky anyway. It is more fun working your way up through the timberline *albicaulis*, the name I prefer for white-bark pine. Near the top of the steep slope you will find some neat portable lichens, if you like to collect them. Unportable lichens prevail, on rock too heavy to carry or dislodge, which is where they should have chosen to settle down in the first place, how many centuries ago?

Suddenly the slope relaxes, and you can begin your exploration of the Dana Plateau itself. Just head uphill along the gentle stream channel that formed in the ancestral Sierra. The plateau is an unglaciated remnant of the old easygoing hills that preceded the great Sierra uplift. The stream channel is dry, but not for long. Desolate and dry though the entire plateau looks, you will find spring-watered gardens halfway up, a good place to pause if you like the kind of Sierra detail Cedric Wright loved to photograph. Saunter beyond through the fascinating granite slabs on the old nivated slope, so gentle that most of the erosion has come from what the sun itself does. Marvel at the bathtubs it has created in the hollows of old stone and come up with your own theories about how they formed.

Slow down as you near the edge of the plateau, where your next step can be far too long. Here is where old glaciers gnawed at the plateau and gave it a sharp edge. Settle down safely alongside Marion Randall Parsons Point (my name for it, and unofficial) just out of the wind for your visual feast. The Mono Basin, Mono Lake, the Mono Craters, and the forever beyond spread out below you toward Nevada, where basins and ranges go on beyond forever. When you step back up into the wind, look back and there towers Mount Dana, sheltering its glacier. If you could look through Dana, you would see where we were when I digressed.

Are you still counting flowers, or just your pulse? Your pulse should be doing about ninety, and your flower count should be about half that by now—at which time I am usually counting my steps, estimating where I'll be by the next hundred. Anne goes uphill faster than I, probably because she knows better than to count steps. I go down faster, and am glad to offer her a hand at the tricky places. Chivalry is not dead. Besides, it stabilizes me.

Persevere, and soon the tangle of trees and rocks will ease, and so will the slope. You will be walking on glacier-polished granite, easy as a boulevard, or alternately on strips of meadow, with a few isolated, bold white-bark pines—I mean *albicaulis*—greeting you as you come to a little pass and drop a few feet in elevation to a long meadow with a stream meandering as you enter. You have arrived at what we modestly call Browers' Bench, with the apostrophe properly at the end. I have named it for all of us, with no authority whatsoever.

For the next half-mile or so you are on your own. Approach the meanders slowly and you will see trout. They are not very big. Neither is the meadow country they are in. They are just perfect, and so is it. Don't annoy them. Don't take them from their watery heaven. Let them enjoy it, and you enjoy them where and as they are.

Wander slowly up the stream that waters our lovely attenuated meadow. Look across at Gibbs and Dana, now hiding its plateau, or up above you to your right to where last winter's snow still brightens Mammoth Peak, and mosey along, like the stream, but in the other direction. Our stream has its own idea of where to pause and where to hurry. You can jump across it almost anywhere. The left bank, as in Paris, is more interesting. The important thing about the stream is the garden it waters. There are new flowers to count or to photograph, or just to remember. They are almost exactly where they were last year, and they'll be there next year with no one's help. Whether they are annuals, or perennials like the willow and *albicaulis,* they have something in common with you, especially if they are perennials.

The best-known Yosemite perennial was Ansel Adams, who never visited Browers' Bench. It is really more of a Cedric Wright or Eliot Porter place, because they liked to play Debussy with their cameras, while Ansel usually preferred Wagner. We found a Wagner for him there once, but never told him about it. We would not have found it had it not been for a Yosemite conference convened by the National Parks and Conservation Association to encourage the Park Service, park concessionaires, and environmentalists to compare notes. Anne and I were table companions of the superintendent of Yosemite National Park, so our conversation inevitably turned to our favorite place in Yosemite's High Sierra. We had always wanted to make a backpack camp on the bench, but it is off-limits to camping. Yosemite's high country doesn't need any more fire rings, or any further drain on trees that have died there and need to return to soil in their own slow way.

"Go ahead and camp there anyway," he said, and we did on our very next trip. No rangers threatened us that day—they would be highly unlikely to range to Browers' Bench anyway—but the sky was handsomely menacing. Heavy clouds kept us in shade all day, and the sun could do nothing about it until late, when it was low enough in the west to find us. I wasn't paying attention to it, being too busy smoothing out our bedsite and putting up a tarp just in case it chose to do what it never does, rain at night in the Sierra. Suddenly I looked eastward and exclaimed "Look at that!" with such vigor Anne thought I was frightened. We don't hear each other's words very well these days, but she let her eyes follow mine—and my pointed finger.

Mounts Dana and Gibbs were on fire, totally. The fire seemed to be burning within them. Their rock is a reddish metamorphic to begin with, but this was a serious red, all the more alarming because the sunset light was illuminating them and not the brooding sky above them. The sun's light had more to contend with than usual. El Chichon's eruption in Mexico had not got much press, but it put twenty times as much earth into the sky as had the eruption of Mount St. Helens, and so much higher in the sky that it couldn't get back down for more than a year. As a result, sunsets lasted much longer than normal (of course, there never was a normal sunset; you can't be unique and normal), and so did ours. The fire on the Sierra Crest simply would not burn out. Well into the evening, as the cloud cover began to thin, the world's best alpenglow in history lingered on Kuna Crest and its tiny glacier. We were too excited to care about sleep. Sleep would have been a gross waste of consciousness. We kept looking until there was nothing more to be looked at by diurnal creatures. Wagner had indeed visited our bench, and Ansel should have been there. He would not have cared for the color. Color was just something that got in the way of his tonal scale through which black descends on its way to being white. Ansel would have found tones enough. He might well have exceeded his *Moonrise, Hernandez, New Mexico*. But he was not there, and who knows what photographer will be fortunate enough to be there when El Chichon schedules another event and the Sierra skies have been cloudy all day. There was nothing perennial about what we saw.

We perennials do have something in common with the perennial willows that give us aspirin, and perennial *albicaulis*, which gave us shelter, and the perennial cassiope, which gives us more beauty than is necessary.

As part of his outreach program, Brower organized the Biennial Conference on the Fate of the Earth. The first one was held at the Cathedral of St. John the Divine in New York City, 1982.

But we have the same thing in common with annuals, the shooting star, the fireweed, and the whole dandelion family. We and all of them are alive, and one little submicroscopic part of each of them is, just like us, three and a half billion years old. They are this end of an old eternity. They are part of the wildness outside that is related, not too directly, to the wildness within us. We can create neither our wildness nor theirs. But remember, we can spare it and celebrate it. Come spare and celebrate it on the bench next time, or if you no longer can, rejoice that it is still there.

For our bench, and for your favorite places, and for the favorite places of other living things, too, will you try to make sure that wildness is still there?

Bibliography

Adams, Ansel. *My Camera in the National Parks*. Boston: Houghton Mifflin, 1950.

Albright, Horace M., and Taylor, Frank J. *Oh Ranger!* Stanford: Stanford University Press, 1928.

Atkinson, Brooks, and Olsen, W. Kent. *New England's White Mountains: At Home in the Wild*. San Francisco: Friends of the Earth, 1978.

Amory, Cleveland. *Man Kind?* New York: Harper and Row, 1974.

Barney, Gerald O., ed. *The Global 2000 Report to the President of the U.S.: Entering the 21st Century*. Vol. 1. New York, Pergamon Press, 1980.

Bates, Robert H., ed. *Five Miles High*. New York: Dodd, Mead and Company, 1939.

Bechtold, Fritz. *Nanga Parbat Adventure*. Translated by H. E. G. Tyndale. New York: E. P. Dutton and Company, 1936.

Bjornstad, Eric. *Desert Rock*. Denver: Chockstone Press, 1988.

Bradley, David. *No Place to Hide*. Boston: Little, Brown, and Company, 1948 and 1983.

Brooks, Paul. *The House of Life: Rachel Carson at Work*. Boston: Houghton Mifflin Company, 1972.

Brower, David R., ed. *Not Man Apart: The Big Sur Coast*. Lines by Robinson Jeffers. San Francisco: Sierra Club, 1965.

Brower, David R. *Environmental Activist, Publicist, and Prophet*. Interviewed by Susan Schrepfer, Sierra Club History Committee. Berkeley: Bancroft Library, University of California, 1979.

Brower, David R., ed. *Going Light—With Backpack or Burro*. San Francisco: Sierra Club, 1970.

Brower, David R. "It Couldn't Be Climbed." *The Saturday Evening Post*, February 1940.

Brower, David R., ed. *Manual of Ski Mountaineering*. San Francisco: Sierra Club, 1962. (Originally University of California Press, 1942.)

Brower, David R., ed. *The Meaning of Wilderness to Science*. San Francisco: Sierra Club, 1960.

Brower, David R. "Sierra High Trip." *National Geographic* 105 (June 1954):844-868.

Brower, David R., ed. *Wildlands in Our Civilization*. San Francisco: Sierra Club, 1964. Brower, Kenneth. *Earth and the Great Weather: The Brooks Range*. San Francisco: Friends of the Earth, 1971.

Brower, Kenneth, ed. Photographs by Eliot Porter. *Galapagos: The Flow of Wildness*. San Francisco: Sierra Club, 1968.

Brower, Kenneth. Photographs by Robert Wenkam. *Micronesia: Island Wilderness*. San Francisco: Friends of the Earth, 1975.

Brower, Kenneth. *The Starship and the Canoe*. New York: Holt, Rinehart, and Winston, 1978.

Brower, Kenneth. Photographs by William R. Curtsinger. *Wake of the Whale*. San Francisco: Friends of the Earth, 1979.

Brown, Harrison. *The Challenge of Man's Future*. New York: Viking Press, 1954.

Brown, Lester, et. al. *State of the World: A Worldwatch Institute Report on Progress Toward a Sustainable Society*. New York: W. W. Norton and Company, 1984, 1985, 1986, 1987, 1988, 1989.

Burgess, Thornton W. *The Adventures of Bobby Coon*. Boston: Little, Brown and Company, 1919.

Calef, George W. *Caribou and the barren-lands*. Ottawa, Ontario: Canadian Arctic Resources Committee, 1981.

Callison, Charles H. *America's Natural Resources*. New York: Ronald Press Co., 1967.

Carson, Rachel. *Silent Spring*. Boston: Houghton Mifflin, 1962.

Cohen, Michael P. *The History of the Sierra Club: 1892-1970*. San Francisco: Sierra Club Books, 1988.

Colorado River Storage Project: Congressional Subcommittee Hearings. Washington, D.C.: United States Government Printing Office, 1954.

The Commonwealth Club of California. "Should We Stop Building New Roads into California's High Mountains?" *The Commonwealth,* 1936.

Comstock, John Adams. *Butterflies of California*. Los Angeles: J. A. Comstock, 1927.

Cowles, Raymond B. *Zulu Journal: Field Notes of a Naturalist in South Africa*. Berkeley: University of California Press, 1959.

Daniel, John. *Common Ground*. Lewiston, Idaho: Confluence Press, 1988.

Dawson, William L. *The Birds of California*. San Diego: South Moulton Co., 1923.

Earle, Captain George F. *History of the 87th Mountain Infantry: Italy 1945.* San Antonio: Bradford-Robinson Printing, n.d.

Ehrlich, Paul R., and Ehrlich, Anne H. *The End of Affluence: A Blueprint for Your Future.* New York: Ballantine Books, 1974.

Eiseley, Loren. *Darwin's Century: Evolution and the Men Who Discovered It.* New York: Doubleday, 1958.

Eiseley, Loren. *The Immense Journey.* New York: Random House, Vintage edition, 1957.

Fowler, H. W. *A Dictionary of Modern English Usage.* 2nd ed. revised and edited by Sir Ernest Gowers. New York: Oxford University Press, 1965.

Fox, Stephen. *John Muir and His Legacy: The American Conservation Movement.* Boston: Little, Brown and Company, 1981.

Galbraith, John Kenneth. *The Affluent Society.* Boston: Houghton Mifflin, 1958.

Gary, Romain. *The Roots of Heaven.* New York: Simon and Schuster, 1958.

Gray, Henry. *Gray's Anatomy.* 35th rev. ed. London: Longman, 1973.

Gussow, Alan. *A Sense of Place: The Artist and the American Land.* San Francisco: Friends of the Earth, 1979.

Holland W. J. *Butterfly Book.* New York: Doubleday and McClure, 1916.

Hornbein, Thomas F. *Everest: The West Ridge.* San Francisco: Sierra Club, 1966.

Huxley, Aldous. *Brave New World Revisited.* New York: Harper and Row, 1958.

Jeffers, Robinson. *Not Man Apart.* San Francisco: Sierra Club Books, 1965.

Keats, John. *The Insolent Chariots.* New York: J. B. Lippincott, 1958.

Kidron, Michael, and Segal, Ronald. *The State of the World Atlas.* New York: Simon and Schuster, 1981.

King, Clarence. *Mountaineering in the Sierra Nevada.* 1871. 4th ed. New York: Charles Scribner's Sons, 1926.

Knight, Max. Photographs by Gerhard Klammet. *Return to the Alps.* San Francisco: Friends of the Earth/McCall Publishing Company, 1970.

Kroeber, Theodora. *Almost Ancestors.* San Francisco; Sierra Club Books, 1968.

Leopold, Aldo. *A Sand County Almanac: And Sketches Here and There.* New York: Oxford University Press, 1949.

Leopold, Aldo. *A Sand County Almanac, with Essays on Conservation from Round River*. New York: Oxford University Press, 1966.

Leydet, François. *The Last Redwoods*. San Francisco: Sierra Club, 1964.

Litton, Martin. *Oral History of Martin Litton*. Berkeley: Bancroft Library, University of California/Sierra Club, 1982.

Manning, Harvey. *Cry Crisis: Rehearsal in Alaska*. San Francisco: Friends of the Earth, 1974.

Manning, Harvey. *The Wild Cascades: Forgotten Parkland*. San Francisco: Sierra Club, 1965.

Meadows, Donella H., et. al. *The Limits to Growth*. London: Earth Island International, 1972.

Melville, Herman. *Moby Dick, or The Whale*. 1851. Commentary by Howard Mumford Jones. New York: W. W. Norton and Company, 1976.

McIntyre, Joan. *Mind in the Waters*. New York: Scribners/Sierra Club Books, 1974.

McPhee, John. *Encounters With the Archdruid*. New York: Farrar, Straus, and Giroux, 1971.

Muir, John. *Gentle Wilderness: The Sierra Nevada*. Photographs by Richard Kauffman. Edited by David R. Brower. San Francisco: Sierra Club Books, 1964.

Muir, John. *My First Summer in the Sierra*. Boston and New York: Houghton Mifflin, 1911.

Murray, W. H. *The Scottish Himalayan Expedition*. London: J. M. Dent and Sons, 1951.

Nash, Hugh, ed. *Progress As If Survival Mattered: A Handbook for a Conserver Society*. San Francisco: Friends of the Earth, 1981.

Nash, Roderick. *The American Environment: Readings in the History of Conservation*. Reading, Massachusetts: Addison Wesley Publishing Company, 1968.

Nash, Roderick, ed. *Grand Canyon of the Living Colorado*. San Francisco: Sierra Club, 1970. *National Wilderness Preservation Act: Senate Committee Hearings, Part 2*. Washington, D.C.: United States Government Printing Office, 1959.

Newhall, Nancy. Photographs by Ansel Adams, et. al. *This is the American Earth*. San Francisco: Sierra Club, 1960.

Packard, Vance. *The Status Seekers*. New York: David McKay Company, 1959.

Peattie, Roderick, ed. *The Sierra Nevada: The Range of Light*. New York: The Vanguard Press, 1947.

Phillips, David, and Nash, Hugh, eds. *The Condor Question: Captive or Forever Free?* San Francisco: Friends of the Earth, 1981.

Porter, Eliot. *The Place No One Knew: Glen Canyon on the Colorado*. San Francisco: Sierra Club/Ballantine, 1968. Reprinted by Gibbs Smith, Publisher, 1988.

Porter, Eliot. *In Wildness Is the Preservation of the World*. San Francisco: Sierra Club Books, 1962.

Powell, J. W. *The Exploration of the Colorado River and Its Canyons*. New York: Dover Publications, 1961. Republication of *Canyons of the Colorado*. Flood and Vincent, 1895.

The Primates. Time/Life Series. New York: Time Inc., 1965.

Reisner, Marc. *Cadillac Desert: The American West and Its Disappearing Water*. New York: Viking Penguin, 1986.

Rey, Guido. *Peaks and Precipices: Scrambles in the Dolomites and Savoy*. New York: Dodd, Mead and Company, 1914.

Robinson, Gordon. *Gordon Robinson: Forestry Consultant to the Sierra Club*. Interviewed by Harold K. Steen, Sierra Club History Committee. Berkeley: Bancroft Library, University of California, 1979.

Russell, Terry, and Russell, Renny. *On the Loose*. San Francisco: Sierra Club, 1967.

Sierra Club Bulletin. San Francisco: Sierra Club, 1893–1981.

Steffan, Jack. *The Gift of Wilderness*. New York: The John Day Company, 1960.

Stegner, Wallace Earle. *Beyond the Hundredth Meridian*. Boston: Houghton Mifflin, 1954.

Strand, Paul. *Time in New England*. Edited by Nancy Newhall. New York: Oxford University Press, 1950.

Whyte, William H., Jr. *The Organization Man*. New York: Simon and Schuster, 1956.

Wright, Cedric. *Words of the Earth*. San Francisco: Sierra Club, 1960.

Wolfe, Linnie Marsh. *Son of the Wilderness: The Life of John Muir*. New York: Alfred Knopf, 1945.

The World Commission on Environment and Development. *Our Common Future*. New York: Oxford University Press, 1987.

INDEX

true blueberry

delicious recipes for every meal

Linda Dannenberg

photographs by Zeva Oelbaum

stewart, tabori & chang
NEW YORK

Page 4: Low Bush blueberries
(Vaccinium Angustifolium)

Page 9: High Bush blueberry specimen
(Vaccinium Corymbosum)

Project editor: **Sandra Gilbert**
Production manager: **Kim Tyner**
Designer: **Pamela Geismar**
Photography assistants: **Effie Paroutsas** and **Emily Downard**
Models: **Amanda Romano, Claudio and Cal Cisneros**
Food stylist: **Sara Neumeier**
Cake plate (front cover and page 78) courtesy London Food Company, Montclair, New Jersey

The text of this book was composed in Memimas Medium, Eureka, and Avenir.

Published in 2005 by
Stewart, Tabori & Chang
115 West 18th Street
New York, NY 10011
www.abramsbooks.com

Canadian Distribution:
Canadian Manda Group
One Atlantic Avenue, Suite 105
Toronto, Ontario M6K 3E7
Canada

Library of Congress Cataloging-in-Publication Data
Dannenberg, Linda
True blueberry : delicious recipes for every meal / Linda Dannenberg ; photographs by Zeva Oelbaum.
p. cm.
Includes index.
ISBN 1-58479-417-8
1. Cookery (Blueberries) I. Title.
TX813.B5D36 2005
641.6'4737—dc22 2004062616

Printed in Singapore

10 9 8 7 6 5 4 3 2 1

First Printing

Stewart, Tabori & Chang is a subsidiary of La Martinière Groupe

LA MARTINIÈRE GROUPE

to Steve and Ben, with love

ACKNOWLEDGMENTS

I would like to express my deepest appreciation to all the innovative chefs and talented home cooks who so generously provided me with their wonderful blueberry recipes: Amy Albert, Dan Beck, Antoine Bouterin, Steven Carl, Page Dickey, Tom Douglas, Alain Ducasse, Brian Ellis, Pam Fletcher, Damon Gordon, Tom Gutow, Siggi Hall, Glenn Harris, Jeff Jackson, Maurice Leduc, François Payard, Debra Ponzek, the late Faye Porter, Joanna Pruess, Else Rhodes, Jeff Starr, Michael Stinchcomb, JoAnn DiRico Trautmann, and Patrice Yvon.

I am also extremely grateful to all the people who offered me advice, anecdotes, information, and blueberry samplers: Sandra Ables, Ann Davis at Jasper Wyman & Son, Rebecca Eggleton at Altamer Resort, Verne Gingerich, Craig Messmer, and Karen Van Winkle at Gingerich Farms, June Goldfinger at the Katonah General Store, Terry Gooch, Jennifer Hawkins at Hawkins International PR, Carrie Jeffcoat, Diane McIntyre at Häagen-Dazs, and Mary Medvedkov.

I would also like to express my warm appreciation, as ever, to my true-blue agent and friend, Gayle Benderoff, for her wise counsel and publishing expertise in making this book a reality.

The pleasure of doing this book was greatly enhanced by all the talented people who participated in its creation. I am so grateful to Leslie Stoker, my publisher, my gifted and patient editor, Sandy Gilbert, Zeva Oelbaum for her lovely and tantalizing photographs, Pamela Geismar for her creative design, and all the fine team at Stewart, Tabori & Chang: Dervla Kelly and Kim Tyner, and copyeditors Leda Scheintaub and Liana Fredley.

Finally, I would like to thank my great friends and neighbors—Alice Finley, Teresa and Leslie Scott, Polly Muller-Girard, Elise Symer, and Dan Farkas—who, along with my intrepid husband Steve and son Ben, tasted and critiqued many of the countless blueberry creations that came out of my kitchen. They approached each new dish with enthusiasm, and never got blueberried-out!

contents

introduction

"You ought to have seen what I saw on my way
To the village, through Mortenson's pasture to-day;
Blueberries as big as the end of your thumb,
Real sky-blue, and heavy, and ready to drum,
In the cavernous pail of the first one to come!
And all ripe together, not some of them green
And some of them ripe! You ought to have seen!"

— from "Blueberries," by Robert Frost, 1914

I have always loved blueberries, from as far back as I can remember. As a child, everything with blueberries was a treat for me, from the lattice-topped pies my mother used to bake, to the plump, sugar-topped muffins we used to buy at the old Boston department store Jordan Marsh, to a simple bowl of Cheerios scattered with fresh blueberries and dusted with sugar on a summer morning. Perhaps my affection for this little summer jewel was enhanced by kindergarten visits to the Waban village library, in the suburbs of Boston, where Miss Lyons, the librarian, would read our class Robert McCloskey's endearing classic *Blueberries for Sal*. A predecessor to McCloskey's immortal *Make Way for Ducklings*, *Blueberries for Sal* tells the story of a little girl, Little Sal, who sets off one August day in Maine to go blueberry-picking on Blueberry Hill with her mother. Their plan is to gather enough blueberries to see them through the winter. But the little tin pail into which Little Sal drops her plucked harvest—"*Kuplink, Kuplank, Kuplunk!*"—never fills because Little Sal can't resist eating all her blueberries. On Blueberry Hill, Little Sal and her mother separately encounter a mother bear and her playful cub, Little Bear, who finds blueberries as irresistible as Little Sal does. A bit of confusion ensues when Little Sal and Little Bear briefly tramp along after the wrong mothers, but all ends well and happily, with blueberries aplenty for all.

It would, in fact, be hard not to love the blueberry. Tiny, compact, gorgeously blue in a variety of hues, with a smooth skin bunched into a ruffled crown on top, the blueberry has a subtle, sweet flavor that is totally transformed and intensified by the alchemy of heat. Common and accessible though it may be, the blueberry is a rare fruit indeed. Rare, that is, in its attributes and powers. Not only does this adaptable berry add vibrant color and delicate, distinctive flavor and texture to everything from salads to soups, main courses to scrumptious desserts, but it is increasingly being hailed as phenomenally nutritious and beneficial to your health. Studies have shown that this amazing "wash and ready" fruit—no peeling, seeding, or chopping required—is capable of helping to prevent certain cancers, lower blood pressure, diminish cholesterol, avert and perhaps reverse age-related short-term memory loss, impede urinary tract infections, reduce the inflammation of arthritis, and improve vision. This tiny fruit is looking more and more like nature's cure-all.

A Bit of History

Blueberries have grown wild in Europe, Canada, and the United States for thousands of years. In Europe the berry is known as the whortleberry or the myrtille, or the bilberry, a very close relation. Wild blueberries grow in a multitude of varieties with flavors ranging from tangy and sour to exquisitely sweet. They are commonly called low-bush blueberries, because they grow low to the ground, sprawling around and across rocks and blanketing sandy "barrens" and sunny stretches bordering pastureland. Scrubby but thriving in acidic soil, they grow just a foot or two tall. Their berries are harvested with narrow-toothed hand rakes in an annual late-summer ritual of back-wearying work. The Native American tribes of New England enjoyed fresh, dried, and smoked blueberries in their diet, and used the root to brew a soothing tea. In the early seventeenth century the tribes sold or traded bushels of fresh, sun-dried, and smoked blueberries to the English colonists, who added them to their traditional puddings in place of currants. The Native Americans and the early colonists called them "starberries" because their ruffled tops resembled a five-pointed star.

The cultivation of blueberries began in North America in the early twentieth century, with breeders, notably Dr. Frederick V. Coville, a USDA botanist from Maryland, and a pioneer grower named Elizabeth C. White from New Jersey, developing hybrids from wild high-bush blueberries in the Northeast. A hearty blueberry variety called rabbit-eye was cultivated primarily in the deep South. These hybrids were able to thrive in areas where blueberries were not originally grown. Cultivated blueberries are commonly known as high-bush blueberries, because they grow into tall, treelike shrubs, some six feet tall. High-bush blueberries, larger and more uniform in flavor, are the berries that are most widely available fresh in the produce sections of supermarkets nationwide. But only half or less of the national crop of cultivated blueberries is sold fresh; the rest is processed in one form or another, mainly frozen. The great majority of the wild blueberry crop (98 percent of which is grown in Maine) is processed as well, primarily flash-frozen or pressed into juice and sold throughout the year. In processed form, the blueberry is slowly making inroads around the world. Japan imports a significant portion of U.S. and Canadian production, and the little berry has even made an appearance in Taiwan, when McDonald's introduced a blueberry pie at outlets in Taipei.

The time has come for a cookbook devoted entirely to the blueberry. The recent health news alone makes the blueberry—high in fiber, loaded with vitamins A and C, low in calories and sodium, and, of course, fat free—a riveting and deserving subject. "If there is one food I would recommend that my patients eat every day," Dr. Sanjay Gupta wrote in his column, "Your Health," in the October 7, 2002, issue of *Time*, "it is blueberries."

Health News

- Reporting at a meeting of the American Chemical Society, Dr. James Joseph, chief of the USDA Human Nutrition Research Center on Aging at Tufts University in Boston, said, "The blueberry has emerged as a very powerful food in the aging battle. Given the possibility that blueberries may reverse short-term memory loss and forestall other effects of aging, their potential may be very great." Dr. Joseph's studies measured the antioxidant activity of more than forty commercially available fruits and vegetables, and ranked blueberries number one. Dr. Joseph is also the author of a fascinating book, *The Color Code*, which explores the importance of various naturally occurring pigments in our food. According to Dr. Joseph, we should all be eating not only "blues" every day, but something deep green (spinach, broccoli, watercress . . .), yellow-orange (pumpkin, acorn squash, apricots . . .), and red (tomatoes, strawberries . . .) as well.

- In a research study conducted by Dr. Amy Howell at the Blueberry Cranberry Research Center of Rutgers University, and published in the *New England Journal of Medicine*, blueberries were found to help promote urinary tract health by preventing E. coli bacteria from attaching to the bladder wall.

- A new study at the USDA is focusing on the ability of blueberries to prevent age-related macular degeneration, a disease of the retina. As a result of reports of this study, in Japan blueberries have been dubbed "vision fruit," and sales of blueberries have skyrocketed.

- In his weekly health column in the *Connecticut Post*, Yale plastic surgeon Dr. James Lyons wrote, "I always tell my patients to eat blueberries and melons for their skin."

- As part of their "Thrive" campaign, Kaiser-Permanente, the country's oldest

HMO, erected a huge billboard in the heart of San Francisco displaying a dramatic cluster of gigantic blueberries and the words "Be Pro-Antioxidant."

- Dr. Agnes M. Rimando, a research chemist with the USDA's Agricultural Research Service, states in a study presented to the annual meeting of the American Chemical Society that a compound naturally occurring in blueberries called pterostilbene might help guard against heart disease by lowering cholesterol. The stilbenes in blueberries, which include the chemicals resveratrol and piceatannol, "known to be strong antioxidants with chemo-preventive activity," says Dr. Rimando's report, could also be a "potent weapon in the battle against obesity and heart disease through their cholesterol reducing potential."

The positive news about blueberries is simply overwhelming. A half-cup to a cup a day may indeed keep the doctor away.

Blueberries in the Kitchen

In choosing and developing recipes for True Blueberry, I explored a wide array of blueberry products. Among them are, of course, fresh blueberries, both cultivated and wild; air-or heat-dried blueberries that resemble raisins or currants; freeze-dried blueberries that are delicately crunchy and lighter than air; and canned sweetened blueberries and canned unsweetened blueberries. All but the last two feature in my recipes; with the abundance of frozen blueberries available even when fresh ones are not (or when they are exorbitantly expensive out of season), I didn't see the need for the canned varieties, although they are fine for preparing sauces. In most of the recipes, cultivated and wild blueberries are interchangeable, except in a few cases where the chefs specify wild. The mild, large, juicy cultivated blueberries, which can grow to the size of a marble, and the small, concentrated wild blueberries, which can be as tiny as a baby pea, will yield a slightly different flavor and presentation in a recipe, but in general both work nicely. Look for berries that are smooth, firm, and deep indigo with a silvery cast in color, with no wetness or mushiness apparent in the box.

When I come across boxes of beautiful fresh berries on sale in August, I put aside a pint or two, unwashed, in the refrigerator in self-seal plastic bags or Tupperware-style containers. They keep well for a week or so. They should be washed just before eating. The rest of the bounty I freeze or dry. (Freezing and slow, gentle drying do not interfere with the berries' antioxidant properties.) To freeze, you simply spread the berries (after rinsing and patting them dry) in a single layer on a small baking sheet or narrow tray, then put them in the freezer overnight. The next morning, store them in self-seal plastic bags or in Tupperware-style containers in the freezer until ready to use. They are ready to pop into a recipe, frozen, straight from the bag, or to be thawed and drained, then added to a recipe. (You can also freeze the berries unwashed. You just have to be sure you defrost and rinse them, draining well, before you use them in a recipe.) First frozen individually, the berries should not stick together when placed in the bags. They last well for several months. (Some people with freezers better than mine say they keep frozen berries up to a year, at a constant 0°F.) Frozen blueberries sometimes remain a bit wetter than you'd like after thawing and draining. To prevent discoloration of the batter when you bake with thawed blueberries, toss the berries first with a couple of teaspoons of flour to lightly coat just before adding to the batter.

To oven-dry blueberries, creating raisinlike little nuggets, spread the berries (previously washed and patted dry) in a single layer on a baking sheet. Place in the center of a very low oven (150°F to 170°F), and bake for about five hours, until the berries are shriveled and resemble raisins. Cool, then store in sealed plastic bags or sealed glass jars. I love the dried blueberries in scones, coffee cakes, and tea breads.

Out, Out, Darned Spot!

In preparing hundreds of blueberry recipes during the preparation of this book, working morning, noon, and night with blueberries in every form and at every temperature, I encountered certainly more than my share of blueberry stains. My wooden utensils took on a permanent pale purple cast. The grout of my tile floors was stained before serious scrubbing with bleach-enhanced detergents made them disappear, and, of course, whatever I was wearing ended up spotted with blue. I tried several forms of stain removal, from old-fashioned vinegar- and sour milk–soaking remedies to cascades of boiling water, to dabs of odiferous carpet-cleaning solvent. (All on washable garments; on dry-clean-only clothes, I rest the fabric over an absorbent cotton cloth, dab off the offending spot with cold water, then take the piece ASAP to the dry cleaner.) Time is of the essence when removing the blueberry stain; getting to it before it dries is critical. What I found works best is to dab off the stain with a dry cloth as soon as you're spotted. Then, heat a pot of water to boiling, lay the fabric over a bowl, and carefully pour the boiling water in a thin stream over the stain. You may still have a "ghost" of the stain on the fabric. Saturate this with a laundry stain stick like Spray 'n Wash or stain gel like Shout, and wash in the machine on warm with a detergent such as Tide with Bleach Alternative. A second round of stain stick and machine washing may be required to entirely remove the stain. The alternative to all this time spent removing red, indigo, green, and purple stains is to invest in a dark-blue wardrobe for your blueberry-cooking and blueberry-eating activities.

About the Recipes

The recipes in *True Blueberry* span half the world, from northern California to Iceland, and hail from such unexpected places as Grand Cayman Island and the island of Anguilla in the Caribbean. Some of the recipes, such as the Parisian Blueberry Tart, the Blueberry Buttermilk Biscuits, the Blueberry Maple Syrup, and the Blueberry-Beet Borscht, are old favorites of mine. Others are dazzling and unexpected discoveries. I would never have imagined, for example, tender chunks of lobster dipped in blueberry glaze and served on a bed of baby arugula, a recipe that chef Tom Gutow sent me from the Castine Inn in Maine; or the blueberry-cilantro-cured gravlax that Brian Ellis, chef of Manhattan's Jane restaurant, developed on a trip to Alaska. And then there were new twists on old classics that I loved, among them Roast Marinated Duck with Blueberry Sauce, from French-born Manhattan chef Antoine Bouterin, and the splendid Blueberry Gingerbread from David Daniels, executive chef at the Federalist, the elegant restaurant in Boston's XV Beacon Hotel. And, finally, there was the thrill of experimenting with these beautiful little berries, and coming up with recipes that were new, different, and really good, such as the Juicy Blue-Burger (it works; ask my son!) and the amethyst-hued Blueberry Martini.

This book was an enormous pleasure to produce, and a large part of that pleasure was sharing all of these recipes with family, friends, and neighbors, my gentle tasters and critics. Blueberries in every form—from a handful straight from the picking pail to a sophisticated dessert from a three-star chef—seem to spread joy, evoke comfort, and impart a healthy glow whenever and wherever they are served. After all the testing and tasting, and tasting some more, I have a new mantra: "Be happy—get the blues!"

chapter 1

breakfast and brunch

blueberry-corn muffins

Rich, moist, and slightly sweet, these bright yellow, blue-studded muffins are a delectable treat warm from the oven at breakfast time. Makes 6 Texas-size jumbo muffins, or 12 standard-size muffins

- 5 tablespoons unsalted butter, melted, plus some for greasing the tin
- 1½ cups all-purpose flour
- 2½ teaspoons baking powder
- ¾ teaspoon salt
- 1 cup yellow cornmeal
- 1 cup sugar
- 1 cup milk
- 1 large egg
- 1 cup fresh, frozen, or dried blueberries

Preheat the oven to 400°F. Grease a large 6-hole or standard 12-hole muffin tin and set aside.

Sift the flour, baking powder, and salt together into a large bowl. Add the cornmeal and ⅔ cup of the sugar, then whisk until well mixed. Set aside. In a separate bowl, combine the milk and egg and beat to blend. Add the wet ingredients to the dry and stir with a wooden spoon just until the mixture is moistened. Do not overmix. Add the blueberries and gently fold them in. Spoon the batter into the muffin tin. Sprinkle the muffin tops with the remaining ⅓ cup sugar. Bake in the center of the oven for 25 to 28 minutes for Texas-size jumbo muffins, 20 to 24 minutes for standard-size muffins, until the muffins are golden brown. Gently loosen the muffins around the sides with a knife before taking them out.

blueberry crumb muffins

These wonderful blueberry muffins with their generous, crunchy crumb topping are a favorite morning treat at the home of Debra Ponzek, the acclaimed chef formerly at the helm of New York's Montrachet restaurant, and today president of her own catering company, Aux Délices Foods in Stamford and Greenwich, Connecticut. "These muffins are a perennial best-seller at our shops," says Debra, "and I also make them often at home for my family." Warning: They are addictively delicious. Makes 12 Texas-size jumbo muffins, or 24 standard-size muffins

FOR THE CRUMB TOPPING:

1½ sticks (12 tablespoons) unsalted butter, chilled and cut into small pieces

2 cups all-purpose flour

1 cup granulated sugar

1 cup loosely packed dark brown sugar

½ teaspoon ground cinnamon

½ teaspoon salt

FOR THE MUFFINS:

1 cup canola oil, plus some for greasing the tins

5½ cups all-purpose flour

1½ cups sugar

3 tablespoons plus 1½ teaspoons baking powder

½ teaspoon salt

3 large eggs

2½ cups milk

3 cups fresh blueberries

To make the crumb topping: In the bowl of an electric mixer fitted with a paddle attachment, or in the bowl of a food processor, combine all of the ingredients. Mix, or process, until the mixture is well combined and begins to stick to the sides of the bowl and form crumbs.

Set aside.

To make the muffins: Preheat the oven to 350°F. Grease a large 12-hole or 2 standard 12-hole muffin tins and set aside.

In a large bowl, combine the flour, sugar, baking powder, and salt and set aside. In a separate bowl, combine the eggs, milk, and oil and whisk or beat to blend. Add the egg mixture to the dry ingredients and stir with a wooden spoon or fork just until the ingredients are combined and moist; the batter should not be smooth. Add the blueberries and gently fold them in with a spatula or large spoon. Spoon the batter into the muffin tin, filling each hole two thirds full. Top the muffins with the crumb mixture.

Bake in the center of the oven for 30 to 35 minutes for Texas-size jumbo muffins, 20 to 25 minutes for standard-size muffins, until the muffins are lightly browned and a toothpick inserted into the center of a muffin comes out clean. Transfer the tin to a wire rack to cool. Gently loosen the muffins around the sides with a knife before taking them out.

blueberry butter

Easy to make, this rich, sweet blueberry butter is lovely to have on hand to spread on English muffins, toast, or waffles. Make a tasty variation of this recipe—blueberry-honey butter—by substituting 3 tablespoons honey for the confectioners' sugar. Makes about 2 cups

- 2 sticks (16 tablespoons) unsalted butter, slightly softened
- ⅔ cup fresh blueberries, coarsely chopped
- 3 tablespoons confectioners' sugar

In the bowl of a small food processor, combine the butter, blueberries, and sugar and process, scraping down the sides 2 or 3 times, until the mixture is well blended and fluffy. Transfer to a crockery butter bell or small ceramic bowl, cover, and chill before serving. Store in the refrigerator.

passover blueberry muffins

Made without baking powder, baking soda, or yeast, these light and flavorful Passover morning treats get their loft from the fluffy beaten egg whites. Makes 8 to 10 standard-size muffins

- ½ cup canola or other vegetable oil, plus some for greasing the tin
- 3 large eggs, separated
- 1 cup sugar
- ½ cup matzo cake meal or fine matzo meal
- ½ cup potato starch
- ½ teaspoon salt
- 1 cup fresh, frozen (thawed and drained), or freeze-dried blueberries
- ½ teaspoon ground cinnamon

Preheat the oven to 350°F. Grease a standard 12-hole muffin tin and set aside.

In a large bowl, combine the egg yolks, ¾ cup of the sugar, and the oil and beat well with a whisk until the mixture is lemony yellow and smooth. Set aside. In another bowl, combine the matzo meal, potato starch, and salt and whisk together until well blended. Set aside. In the bowl of an electric mixer, fitted with a whisk attachment if available, beat the egg whites on medium speed until they are glossy and hold stiff peaks. Fold one third of the egg whites into the egg yolk mixture. Add the rest of the egg whites and gently fold them in, working to maintain as much volume as possible as you fold all the ingredients in. Sprinkle on one third of the matzo meal mixture and gently fold it in, and repeat with the remaining two thirds of the mixture. Add the blueberries and gently fold them in. Spoon the batter into the muffin tin, filling each hole three quarters full. (If there are any empty muffin holes, fill each with ½ inch of water so the tin won't burn.) Combine the remaining ¼ cup sugar with the cinnamon and sprinkle each muffin top with about 1 teaspoon of the mixture. Bake for about 30 minutes, until the muffins are golden brown. Transfer the tin to a wire rack to cool completely. Slide a sharp knife around the edges of the muffins to loosen them, then remove and serve.

moody's blueberry-raspberry muffins

Moody's Diner in Waldboro, Maine, has been a beacon for travelers heading north up Maine's Route 1 for seventy-seven years. Although they offer a large menu of diner specialties, Moody's long ago grew famous for their assortment of fresh pies and their blueberry muffins. These blueberry-raspberry muffins, a delicious variation baked by Moody's veteran pastry chef, Ethelynn Barbour, are a summertime treat when raspberries come into season. Ethelynn suggests that you sugar the tops of only those muffins you plan to consume immediately, since the sugared tops tend to become damp after sitting or being stored. Makes 12 standard-size muffins

- Scant ½ cup canola or other vegetable oil, plus some for greasing the tin
- 2¼ cups plus 1 tablespoon all-purpose flour
- 1 tablespoon baking powder
- 1 teaspoon salt
- ⅔ cup plus 2 tablespoons sugar
- 2 large eggs
- 1 cup plus 2 tablespoons milk
- 1 teaspoon vanilla extract
- ½ cup fresh blueberries
- ½ cup fresh raspberries

Preheat the oven to 375°F. Grease a standard 12-hole muffin tin and set aside.

Sift 2¼ cups of the flour, the baking powder, and salt together into a large bowl. Set aside. In the bowl of an electric mixer, combine ⅔ cup of the sugar, the oil, and eggs and beat on high until creamy and lemony in color, about 30 seconds. Reduce the speed to the lowest setting, add the milk and vanilla, and mix just until blended. Add the sugar mixture to the flour mixture and, using a wooden spoon, stir until just combined; the batter should still be a little lumpy. Toss the berries with the remaining 1 tablespoon flour to coat, then add them to the batter and very gently fold them in. Ladle the batter into the muffin tin, filling each hole almost to the top. Make sure each hole has a share of berries. Sprinkle the muffin tops with the remaining 2 tablespoons sugar. Bake for 20 to 25 minutes, until the muffins are a light golden brown. Set the pan aside to cool. Gently loosen the muffins around the sides with a knife before taking them out.

jordan marsh blueberry muffins

Jordan Marsh's blueberry muffins were almost as famous a culinary specialty as Boston's classic baked beans when I was growing up in the Boston suburbs in the 1950s and 1960s. No trip to this esteemed old department store was complete without a visit to their renowned bakery to stock up on the delicious sugar-topped muffins for the next morning's breakfast. Recently a good friend and fellow Massachusetts native, JoAnn DiRico Trautmann, revealed that she actually had a recipe for these marvelous muffins. The recipe came courtesy of an old neighbor, Mrs. Champagne, who, sometime in the mid-1960s, asked for, and received, the recipe from Jordan Marsh's Framingham store. Jordan Marsh went out of business in 1983, but their muffins, happily, live on. Makes 12 standard-size muffins

- 2 cups all-purpose flour
- 2 teaspoons baking powder
- ½ teaspoon salt
- 1 stick (8 tablespoons) lightly salted butter, softened
- 1½ cups sugar
- 2 large eggs
- ½ cup milk
- 2½ cups fresh or frozen blueberries

Preheat the oven to 350°F. Grease a standard 12-hole muffin tin and set aside.

Sift the flour, baking powder and salt together into a medium bowl. Set aside.

In the bowl of an electric mixer, combine the butter and 1¼ cups of sugar and cream at low speed until the mixture is smoothly blended. At low speed, add the eggs, one at a time, and blend. Add the flour mixture and the milk a little at a time, alternating one with the other, and beat until blended, then remove the bowl from the mixer. Add ½ cup of the blueberries and gently fold them in with a large wooden spoon or spatula. Add the rest of the berries and gently fold them in. Ladle the batter into the muffin tins, filling each hole almost to the top. Sprinkle the remaining ¼ cup sugar over the muffin tops, then bake in the center of the oven for 25 to 30 minutes, until the muffins are puffy and golden brown. Remove to a wire rack and cool in the tins for 1 hour before serving. Gently loosen the muffins around the sides with a knife before taking them out.

blueberry-orange coffee cake

Delicate citrus flavors accent the mild sweetness of the blueberries in this delicious sugar-topped cake perfect for brunch or afternoon tea. Serves 6 to 8

FOR THE CAKE:

- 1 stick (8 tablespoons) unsalted butter, softened, plus some for greasing the pan
- 2½ cups all-purpose flour
- 2½ teaspoons baking powder
- 1 teaspoon baking soda
- ¾ teaspoon salt
- 1 cup granulated sugar
- 1 large egg
- 1 large egg white
- ¼ cup fresh orange juice
- ½ cup milk
- 1½ teaspoons vanilla extract
- 1 teaspoon finely grated lemon zest
- 2 cups fresh blueberries
- ⅓ cup turbinado (golden-brown, natural crystallized) sugar
- 1 teaspoon ground cinnamon

FOR THE TOPPING:

- ¾ cup sour cream
- ¾ cup plain yogurt
- 3 tablespoons confectioners' sugar
- ½ teaspoon vanilla extract
- ¼ cup fresh blueberries, for garnish

To make the cake: Preheat the oven to 350°F.

Line the bottom of a 10-inch springform pan or a 12 by 8-inch baking dish with parchment paper. Butter the bottom and sides and set aside. Sift the flour, baking powder, baking soda, and salt together into a large bowl and set aside.

In the bowl of an electric mixer, ideally fitted with a whisk attachment, combine the butter and granulated sugar and cream on medium-high speed until smooth and pale yellow, about 4 minutes. Add the egg and egg white and beat until smoothly blended. Add about ½ cup of the flour mixture, beat to blend, then add the orange juice, about half cup of the milk, the vanilla, and the lemon zest and beat to blend. Repeat, alternating the flour mixture and the milk, beating after each addition, until smoothly blended. Scrape the batter into the prepared pan. In a small bowl, combine the turbinado sugar and cinnamon, stir to combine, then sprinkle evenly on top of the batter. Bake in the center of the oven for 45 to 55 minutes (baking in the 10-inch pan will take a little longer), until a toothpick inserted into the center of the cake comes out clean.

Cool on a wire rack for 1 hour. Unmold the cake from the springform pan onto a serving plate. If using the rectangular baking dish, cut the cake into 12 squares.

To make the topping: In a large bowl, combine the sour cream, yogurt, confectioners' sugar, and vanilla and whisk until well blended and airy. Serve the cake garnished with a spoonful of the sour cream mixture and a few scattered blueberries.

blueberry pain perdu—blueberry french toast pudding

This is a rich and luscious variation of French toast that is a treat at a weekend brunch or as a dessert. Blueberries are sandwiched between two layers of batter-soaked challah, the mixture refrigerated for at least 8 hours, then baked just before serving. A blueberry sauce, satiny with a touch of butter, accompanies the confection. The recipe calls for cream cheese but works nicely without it as well, if you wish to shave a few calories off this dish. Serves 8

FOR THE PAIN PERDU PUDDING:

6 large eggs

1 cup milk

1 teaspoon vanilla extract

½ teaspoon salt

1 teaspoon ground cinnamon

½ cup maple syrup

1½ pounds challah or other egg bread, crusts removed, cut into 1-inch cubes (to yield about 8 cups)

1 cup fresh blueberries

1 cup (8 ounces) cream cheese, cut into small bits

FOR THE BLUEBERRY SAUCE:

1 cup fresh blueberries

½ cup sugar

3 tablespoons water

1 tablespoon cornstarch

1 tablespoon unsalted butter

To make the pain perdu pudding: In a large bowl, combine the eggs, milk, vanilla, salt, cinnamon, and maple syrup. With a whisk, beat until smoothly blended. Set aside. Spread half of the bread cubes over a 13 by 9-inch baking dish. Scatter the blueberries over the bread. Scatter the cream cheese bits over the blueberries. Top with the remaining bread cubes. Pour the egg mixture carefully over the top layer of bread cubes so that they are evenly covered. Seal the baking dish with plastic wrap and refrigerate for at least 8 hours, or overnight.

Preheat the oven to 350°F.

Remove the baking dish from the refrigerator 30 minutes before baking. Remove the plastic wrap and cover the dish with aluminum foil. Bake in the center of the oven for 30 minutes. Uncover the dish and bake for about 30 minutes more, until the top is golden brown. Set aside on a wire rack for about 15 minutes to cool slightly.

continued . . .

To make the blueberry sauce: In a small saucepan, combine the blueberries, sugar, and 2 tablespoons of the water and bring to a boil over medium-high heat, stirring frequently. Lower the heat to medium-low and simmer for about 8 minutes, until the berries soften and begin to release their juice. In a small cup, combine the cornstarch with the remaining 1 tablespoon water and stir to dissolve. Add to the blueberry mixture and stir to blend. Cook for 1 minute, stirring constantly, until the sauce thickens. Remove from the heat, add the butter, and stir until melted and blended.

Serve the Blueberry Pain Perdu warm, spooned into individual serving bowls and drizzled with the blueberry sauce.

blueberry maple syrup

Simple to make, this berry-enhanced maple syrup is delicious with pancakes. It also works nicely using raspberries instead of blueberries. Makes 2½ cups

1½ cups maple syrup

½ cup fresh blueberries

In a small saucepan, combine the maple syrup and the blueberries. Heat over medium-high heat, stirring occasionally, until the mixture just starts to boil. Reduce the heat to medium-low, cover, and simmer, stirring occasionally, for about 5 minutes, until the berries burst and release their juice. Set aside, covered, until ready to serve.

multigrain buttermilk pancakes with blueberries

These hearty and healthy griddlecakes, with great texture from the cornmeal and the oat flakes, are a cross between classic pancakes and rib-sticking corn flapjacks. Serves 4 to 6

- 1⅔ cups all-purpose flour
- 1 tablespoon baking powder
- 1 teaspoon baking soda
- 1 teaspoon salt
- ⅓ cup yellow cornmeal
- ⅓ cup rolled oats
- 3 tablespoons sugar
- 1½ cups buttermilk
- 2 large eggs, lightly beaten
- ½ stick (4 tablespoons) unsalted butter, melted
- ½ cup fresh blueberries
- 2 to 3 tablespoons vegetable oil

Sift the flour, baking powder, baking soda, and salt together into a large bowl. Add the cornmeal, oats, and sugar and whisk to combine. Add the buttermilk, eggs, and butter and mix to combine. Add the blueberries and gently fold them in. In a skillet or a griddle, heat 2 tablespoons of the oil over medium-high heat until hot.

Ladle in ½-cupfuls of batter for each pancake. When the tops bubble and the edges dry, turn the pancakes and cook until the bottoms are browned. Add a little more oil as needed for each batch. Serve immediately, or keep warm (but not for too long!) in a low oven.

blueberry-sweet potato bread

This prizewinning recipe from Odessa, Texas, comes wrapped up in a wonderful story. Back in 1996, the state of Texas inaugurated a recipe contest as part of the festivities celebrating the fiftieth anniversary of the National School Lunch Program. The winner in the Totally Texas category was Faye Porter, the pastry chef at Ector Junior High School in Odessa. Faye, a beloved fixture in the local school communities who passed away in 2002 at the age of seventy-five, developed the Blueberry–Sweet Potato Bread from a family recipe offered by Vico Aguirre, her friend and colleague in the Odessa Schools Food Services Department. As another friend, Sandra Ables, a supervisor in the department tells it, "Faye and Vico took the recipe to Austin, and Faye prepared it for the judges. Of course, it won first place, and she later prepared and served the Blueberry Sweet Potato Bread to our then state governor, George W. Bush. He not only loved the bread, but loved Faye, and invited her back to go fishing with him and his dad. Before she could do that, Governor Bush was elected President of the United States." This nutritious and flavorful bread is now a fixture on school breakfast and lunch programs nationwide. As a variation, Faye sometimes would prepare the bread as a dessert, as she did for George Bush at a luncheon at the governor's mansion, dressing it up with a blueberry sauce and crème anglaise. Serves 14 to 16 (Makes two 9 by 5-inch loaves)

- 2 to 3 large unpeeled sweet potatoes
- ½ cup vegetable oil, plus some for greasing the pans
- 4 cups all-purpose flour
- 2 tablespoons baking powder
- ½ teaspoon baking soda
- 1 tablespoon ground cinnamon
- 1 teaspoon freshly grated nutmeg
- 2 cups sugar
- 2 large eggs, beaten
- 2 cups frozen blueberries, thawed

Place a large pot of water over high heat and bring to a boil. Add the sweet potatoes, making sure there is sufficient water to cover them, reduce the heat to medium, cover the pot, and cook about 25 minutes, until the sweet potatoes are soft. Drain, reserving ¼ cup of the liquid. Peel the sweet potatoes, then mash enough to measure 2 cups. Set aside.

Preheat the oven to 350°F. Grease two 9 by 5-inch loaf pans and set aside.

Sift the flour, baking powder, baking soda, cinnamon, and nutmeg into a large bowl. Set aside. In another large bowl, combine the mashed sweet potatoes, reserved 1/4 cup cooking liquid, the sugar, eggs, and oil. Stir by hand to blend, leaving the batter with all ingredients incorporated but still a little lumpy. Add the flour mixture and stir just until the ingredients are moistened; the batter will be quite thick. Add the blueberries (if they are moist, first toss them with a sprinkling of flour to coat), and gently fold them in. Scrape the mixture into the loaf pans and bake in the center of the oven for about 1 hour, until the tops are browned and a toothpick or skewer inserted into the centers comes out clean. Transfer the pans to wire racks to cool. Serve warm or at room temperature.

lemon-ricotta pancakes with blueberry-peach compote

These light and lemony pancakes are the creation of Jeff Jackson, executive chef at A R Valentien, the Arts and Crafts–style dining room of the Lodge at Torrey Pines resort in La Jolla, California. The batter is very similar to a soufflé batter, with a small amount of flour and lots of eggs, the whites used to give the pancakes their loft. In fact, I used this same recipe to make individual soufflés—baked in 4-inch buttered and sugared ramekins for about 18 minutes—and they were fabulous. The blueberry-peach compote, which calls for both fresh and dried blueberries, has the intense flavor and pleasing texture of a relish. Serves 4 to 6

FOR THE BLUEBERRY-PEACH COMPOTE:

½ cup sugar

½ cup water

2 cups fresh blueberries

1 cup dried blueberries

2 peaches

FOR THE LEMON-RICOTTA PANCAKES:

6 large eggs, separated

½ cup sugar

3 tablespoons finely grated lemon zest

½ cup flour

½ teaspoon salt

1½ cups ricotta

1 stick (8 tablespoons) unsalted butter, melted

2 to 3 tablespoons vegetable oil

To make the blueberry-peach compote: In a heavy-bottomed saucepan, combine the sugar and water and bring to a boil over medium-high heat. Add the fresh and dried blueberries and stir to combine. Turn the heat down to low and simmer for 20 minutes, stirring once or twice. Remove from the heat and set aside. Meanwhile, bring a small pot of water to a rolling boil and lower in the peaches. Cook for several minutes, just until the skins split. Remove and immediately plunge them into an ice-water bath. Peel the peaches, remove the pits, and, working over a dish to retain the juices, cut the peaches into small chunks. Fold the peaches and juice into the blueberry mixture. Cover and set aside until ready to serve.

To make the lemon-ricotta pancakes: In the bowl of an electric mixer, combine the egg yolks, sugar, and lemon

continued . . .

zest and mix at medium speed for about 3 minutes, until the mixture is satiny and pale yellow. Add the flour and salt and mix for 2 minutes. Add the ricotta and butter and mix until incorporated. Set aside. In another bowl, whip the egg whites until they hold stiff peaks. Fold one third of the egg whites into the yolk mixture. Add the remaining egg white mixture and gently fold it in, working to maintain as much volume as possible.

Heat 2 tablespoons of the oil in a large skillet or griddle over high heat. When hot, reduce the heat to medium-high. Ladle the batter into the skillet, about ½ cup per pancake. Flip when the edges just start to turn brown and little bubbles begin to form in the pancake. Cook just until lightly browned on the other side. Add a little bit more oil as needed for each batch. Serve immediately, accompanied by the Blueberry-Peach Compote served in a sauceboat or bowl at the table.

lemon-ricotta scones with blueberries

These moist, rich scones were created by pastry chef Else Rhodes at the Ocean Edge Resort in Brewster, Massachusetts, where they are part of a delightful breakfast served overlooking Cape Cod Bay. The scones are denser and more tangy than classic scones, from the addition of ricotta, buttermilk, and lemon zest. They are made without eggs, which leaves the crumb with a lovely ivory hue. The recipe works well with either fresh or dried blueberries.

Serves 6 to 8

- 1 stick (8 tablespoons) unsalted butter, cut into small pieces, plus some for greasing the baking sheet
- 1½ cups all-purpose flour
- ½ cup sugar
- 2 tablespoons baking powder
- ½ teaspoon salt
- ½ cup buttermilk
- ½ cup ricotta
- ½ cup 2% milk
- Finely grated zest of 1 lemon
- 1 cup fresh blueberries, or ½ cup dried blueberries
- ½ cup heavy cream
- ½ cup sugar

Preheat the oven to 400°F. Grease a baking sheet and set aside.

In the bowl of a food processor, combine the flour, sugar, baking powder, salt, and butter. Process for about 10 seconds, until the mixture has the texture of coarse cornmeal. Transfer to a large bowl and set aside. In the bowl of an electric mixer, combine the buttermilk, ricotta, milk, and lemon zest. Mix on medium speed until blended, about 1 minute. Add the buttermilk mixture to the dry ingredients and stir with a wooden spoon or fork until the ingredients are just moistened. Do not over-mix. Add the blueberries and gently fold them in. Drop the batter by heaping tablespoons onto the baking sheet about 2 inches apart. Brush the tops of the scones with the cream, then sprinkle each one with a heaping teaspoon of sugar. Bake in the center of the oven for 12 to 16 minutes, until the scones are a pale golden brown. Serve warm, or transfer to a wire rack to cool and serve at room temperature.

easy blueberry jam

Requiring only three ingredients and about twenty minutes of cooking time, this blueberry jam is a breeze to make. It works well with both fresh and frozen blueberries, so it's a condiment that can grace your breakfast table all year round. If you use frozen blueberries, use them straight from the freezer without thawing. Makes about 3 cups

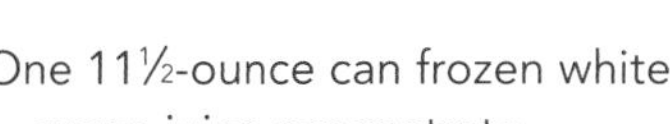

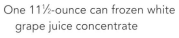

- One 11½-ounce can frozen white grape juice concentrate
- 1 teaspoon finely grated lemon zest
- 3 cups fresh or frozen blueberries

In a large saucepan, combine the grape juice concentrate, lemon zest, and blueberries and bring to a boil over medium-high heat. Reduce the heat to medium and cook, stirring frequently to prevent the berries from sticking or burning, until the mixture jells, about 25 minutes. To test the consistency of the mixture, place a tablespoon of it in a small cup and cool to room temperature. Lightly touch the mixture to see if it has a jellied consistency. If it is still too liquidy, cook for about 5 more minutes. Remove from the heat, cover, and set aside for 1 hour. Ladle the mixture into 2 sterilized pint jars, cover, and refrigerate. You can store the jam for about 1 month.

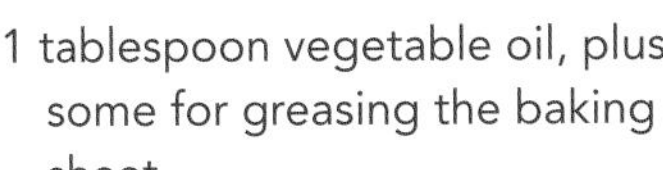

blueberry buttermilk biscuits

Fluffy and melt-in-your-mouth tender, these buttermilk biscuits studded with freeze-dried blueberries are quick and easy to make. Tasty for brunch or teatime, they are also a fine accompaniment to a roast chicken or Southern-fried chicken. In this recipe, the blueberries take on the consistency of raisins.

Makes 10 to 12 biscuits

- 1 tablespoon vegetable oil, plus some for greasing the baking sheet
- 2½ cups all-purpose flour
- 1 tablespoon baking powder
- ½ teaspoon baking soda
- ½ teaspoon salt
- ½ cup sugar
- 1 cup whole buttermilk (if you can only find reduced-fat buttermilk, substitute ⅓ cup heavy cream for ⅓ cup of the buttermilk)
- 1 teaspoon vanilla extract
- ¾ cup freeze-dried blueberries

Preheat the oven to 425°F. Grease a baking sheet and set aside.

In a large bowl, combine the flour, baking powder, baking soda, salt, and sugar and stir to combine. Add the buttermilk, oil, and vanilla and stir gently with a fork just until the ingredients are moistened. Be careful not to overmix; too many turns can make the biscuits tough. Add the blueberries and gently fold in. With floured hands, gather the dough into a ball, and then press gently against the sides and bottom of the bowl to pick up any loose bits. Drop the dough by heaping tablespoons onto the baking sheet 2 inches apart.

Bake for about 10 minutes, until the biscuits are a pale golden brown. Serve immediately.

chapter 2

soups and salads

blueberry-beet borscht

For those who love classic, deli-style cold beet borscht, this variation with blueberries enhancing the beets will be a happy discovery. I love blueberries and I love beet borscht, and I thought the two flavors would complement each other, so one summer day when I was making cold borscht for lunch with friends, I added blueberries, and a new soup was born. The flavor is very intense, so a soup cup, rather than a bowl, with a generous dollop of sour cream, is all you need for a perfect summer starter. Serves 4 to 6

- 3 cups water
- 1 pound (about 4 medium) beets, peeled and cut into matchstick strips
- 1 cup fresh blueberries
- 2 tablespoons fresh lemon juice
- 1 tablespoon sugar
- 2 teaspoons salt
- Freshly ground black pepper to taste
- Sour cream, for garnish
- 2 tablespoons chopped fresh dill, optional, for garnish

In a large saucepan or medium soup pot, combine the water, beets, blueberries, lemon juice, sugar, salt, and several turns of the pepper mill and stir to combine. Bring to a boil over medium-high heat, then reduce the heat to medium-low and simmer for 25 to 30 minutes, until the beets are tender. Cool to room temperature, then transfer the soup to a storage container, cover, and refrigerate.

Serve chilled, in soup cups garnished with a spoonful of sour cream and, if you wish, a sprinkling of dill.

chilled blueberry-pinot noir soup

Blueberries and wine bring out the best in each other. In this soup, different wines will add their own distinctive flavor and character to the soup. I like to use a dry but fruity red wine such as Pinot Noir, but you can give the soup a totally different, sweeter, rounder character with white wines such as Riesling, a spicy, sweet Gewürztraminer, or an opulent Sauternes. Serves 6 to 8

- 2 cups water
- ¼ cup sugar
- 3 cups fresh or frozen blueberries
- 1 cup Pinot Noir wine
- 1 tablespoon fresh lemon juice
- ½ teaspoon salt
- 2 to 3 tablespoons crème fraîche or sour cream

In a large saucepan over medium-high heat, combine the water and sugar. Cook until the sugar dissolves. Add the blueberries and bring to a boil. Reduce the heat to a simmer and cook, stirring often, for about 10 minutes, until the blueberries soften and burst. Add the wine, lemon juice, and salt, stir to combine, then cook, stirring occasionally, for 5 minutes.

Set the pan aside and let the mixture cool. Transfer to the bowl of a food processor or a blender and puree for about 30 seconds, until smooth. For a very smooth soup, strain the mixture into a bowl. If you like a soup with more body, omit the straining and transfer the soup to a bowl. Chill well in the refrigerator for at least 2 hours. Ladle into serving bowls, add a rounded teaspoon of crème fraîche in the center of each, and serve immediately.

blueberry vinegar

Simple and delicately aromatic, blueberry vinegar adds a fragrant touch to dressings and salads. You can use the vinegar after just a day, but it gets more intense and flavorful the longer it sits. The recipe calls for fresh blueberries, but you can also make it with freeze-dried blueberries. Makes 1½ cups

½ cup fresh blueberries, halved
1 cup white wine vinegar
1 tablespoon crème de cassis

In a small glass bowl, combine the berries, vinegar, and crème de cassis. Cover with plastic wrap and set aside at room temperature to macerate for 24 hours. Transfer to a 12-ounce jar, seal, and store in the refrigerator for up to 2 months.

blueberry vinaigrette

This recipe for a luscious vinaigrette comes from fellow food writer Joanna Pruess, who devised it to complement the wild rice and turkey salad that follows. Joanna also uses this dressing over sliced avocados or a shredded green cabbage salad with caraway seeds. Makes about 1½ cups

⅓ cup Blueberry Vinegar (see above)
1 teaspoon salt, or to taste
1 tablespoon honey
2 teaspoons Dijon mustard
1 small clove garlic
1 cup vegetable oil
Freshly ground black pepper to taste

In a small bowl, combine the vinegar and salt and stir to dissolve the salt. Add the honey and mustard and stir to blend. Transfer the mixture to the bowl of a blender or food processor. Add the garlic, oil, and several turns of the pepper mill, and puree until smooth. Use immediately, or cover and refrigerate for up to 3 days.

wild rice and turkey salad with blueberry vinaigrette

Serves 4

3 cups cooked wild rice

½ pound cooked turkey breast, cut into ½-inch cubes

½ cup coarsely chopped walnuts, lightly toasted

½ cup thinly sliced scallions

½ cup Blueberry Vinaigrette (page 39)

1 to 2 tablespoons minced tarragon, optional

Freshly ground black pepper to taste

Bibb or Boston lettuce leaves, to line the plates

½ cup dried blueberries

In a large bowl, combine the wild rice, turkey, walnuts, and scallions. Add the vinaigrette, tarragon, if using, and several turns of the pepper mill and toss again. Line 4 serving plates with the lettuce leaves, then divide the salad among the plates. Scatter on the dried blueberries and serve.

red, white, and blueberry potato salad

This festive salad is the perfect patriotic addition to a Fourth of July or Bastille Day (July 14) picnic or barbecue. The blueberries harmonize with the sweetness of the potatoes, while the red peppers and the celery add crunch and contrast. I like to serve it in a clear glass salad bowl. Serves 6

- 2½ pounds small red potatoes
- 1½ teaspoons salt
- 2 tablespoons red wine vinegar
- ½ teaspoon sugar
- ¾ cup mayonnaise
- ½ teaspoon freshly ground black pepper
- 1 cup plus 2 tablespoons fresh blueberries
- 1 small red bell pepper, diced (reserve 2 tablespoons for garnish)
- ½ cup diced celery
- 1 small red onion, diced
- ½ cup chopped scallions

In a large pot, combine the potatoes with enough water to just cover and 1 teaspoon of the salt. Bring to a boil over high heat, cover, and cook for 25 minutes, or until the potatoes are cooked through but still firm. Drain and set aside to cool.

Meanwhile, in a medium bowl, combine the vinegar with the remaining ½ teaspoon salt and the sugar and stir until the salt and sugar dissolve. Add the mayonnaise and black pepper and whisk to blend. Chill until ready to use.

Cut the potatoes into quarters and place them in a large bowl along with 1 cup of the blueberries, red pepper, celery, onion, and scallions. Add the chilled mayonnaise dressing and toss very gently, taking care not to crush the blueberries. Check the seasoning, adding more salt and pepper to taste. Cover and chill for about 2 hours to allow the flavors to meld. Just before serving, toss the salad gently and transfer to a clear glass or other clean salad bowl. Scatter the remaining 2 tablespoons blueberries and the reserved 2 tablespoons red pepper over the top and serve.

blueberry balsamic vinaigrette

This intriguing recipe comes from the U.S. Highbush Blueberry Council in El Dorado Hills, California. The distinctive flavor of blueberries marries beautifully with the slightly caramelized flavor of balsamic vinegar. The touch of lime adds a bright note of citrus, and the cinnamon stick a hint of spice. A flavorful, aromatic vinegar such as this is ideal for a very simple vinaigrette dressing, composed only of olive oil, salt, pepper, and the vinegar. The vinegar alone adds a savory—and dietetic—accent to grilled pork or chicken, while the vinaigrette is perfect for a salad of mesclun greens or baby romaine. Makes 2 cups of vinegar; makes ⅔ cups of vinaigrette

FOR THE VINEGAR:

1 cup fresh or frozen (thawed and drained) blueberries

1 cup balsamic vinegar

½ cup sugar

Peel of ½ lime, green part only, cut with very sharp knife into thin strips

One 3-inch cinnamon stick

FOR THE VINAIGRETTE:

3 tablespoons blueberry balsamic vinegar (see above)

½ teaspoon salt

Freshly ground black pepper to taste

½ cup extra-virgin olive oil

To make the vinegar: In a medium nonreactive saucepan—stainless steel or enameled—crush the blueberries with a potato masher. Add the vinegar, sugar, lime peel, and cinnamon stick and bring to a boil over medium-high heat. Reduce the heat to low and simmer, covered, for 20 minutes. Remove from the heat and set aside for 1 hour to cool. Transfer to a bowl, cover with plastic wrap, and refrigerate for 2 days to steep, so that the rich, interesting flavors can blend. Using a fine mesh sieve, strain the mixture into a bowl, pressing out as much liquid as possible with the back of a wooden spoon. Discard the solids. Pour the vinegar into clean glass jars, seal tightly, and refrigerate for up to 2 months.

To make the vinaigrette: In a small bowl, combine the vinegar, salt, and several turns of the pepper mill and whisk to dissolve the salt. Add the oil and whisk briskly to blend.

Drizzle over ½ pound salad greens, to serve 4, and toss lightly to coat.

lobster salad with blueberry-beet sauce, and cucumber salad garnish

At the Castine Inn, on the coast of Maine just south of Bar Harbor, owner/chef Tom Gutow's guests have come to expect dazzling, innovative lobster dishes. Tom was recently honored by the Governor's Great Taste of Maine Culinary competition as "Lobster Chef of the Year." This dish, an appetizer in which the lobster is glazed with a reduction sauce of blueberries, beets, and orange, is garnished with a cucumber salad dressed with fresh vanilla yogurt. The composition exemplifies Tom's culinary philosophy of creating dishes with multiple layers of concentrated flavors and contrasting textures. Tom makes his own vanilla vinegar, used in the sauce, by adding used vanilla beans to a bottle of white wine–tarragon vinegar. You can also find vanilla vinegar in some gourmet shops. This recipe demands time and effort. Save it for a dinner when you want to impress your friends. Note that you must start preparations (the vanilla yogurt, the vanilla vinegar) a day ahead. This unusual dish demands a very particular wine, light with a touch of sweetness. Tom recommends a Vouvray from the Loire Valley, or a southern Rhône white featuring the Viognier grape.

Serves 6

FOR THE VANILLA YOGURT:

¼ cup milk

¼ cup sugar

½ vanilla bean, split, seeds scraped out

2 cups plain yogurt

FOR THE BLUEBERRY CARAMEL:

1 cup sugar

¼ cup cold water

2 cups fresh blueberries, or frozen blueberries, thawed, pureed

FOR THE BLUEBERRY-BEET SAUCE:

¼ cup white wine–tarragon vinegar

¼ vanilla bean, split

1 cup fresh orange juice

1 cup fresh peeled and diced beets

1 cup blueberry caramel (see above)

1 long seedless cucumber, peeled, thinly sliced, patted dry

6 ounces baby arugula

Three 1½-pound lobsters, boiled, meat picked out

To make the vanilla yogurt: In a small saucepan, combine the milk and the sugar and stir to dissolve. Bring just to a boil over medium-high heat, stirring frequently, then remove immediately from the heat. Add the vanilla bean and scraped seeds and set the pan aside to cool. Transfer the mixture to a small bowl, cover with plastic wrap, and refrigerate overnight. In a medium bowl, combine the vanilla milk with the yogurt and stir well to blend. Strain the mixture through a fine-mesh sieve and chill until ready to use.

To make the blueberry caramel: In a medium saucepan, combine the sugar with the water. Set the pan over low heat, stirring until the sugar dissolves. Scrape down any sugar crystals that cling to the side of the pan, as these can sometimes cause sudden crystallization after the sugar liquefies. Increase the heat to medium and bring to a boil without stirring (sugar will crystallize if you stir it after it begins to boil). Cook until the temperature on a warmed candy thermometer dipped into the syrup reaches 250°F, or until the mixture is bubbling with large bubbles and turns a light honey color. (Caramelizing sugar can be tricky. The sugar can suddenly crystallize and turn grainy after it looks lovely and syrupy. If this happens, return the syrup to the heat, add a bit more water, and bring the mixture back to 250°F.) Remove from the heat and add the blueberries, whisking briskly to blend. Return to the heat briefly, whisking constantly to make sure the mixture is completely melted and smooth. Set aside to cool.

To make the blueberry-beet sauce: Several hours or a day ahead, combine the vinegar and the vanilla bean in a small bowl and set aside to infuse.

In a medium saucepan over medium-high heat, combine the orange juice and beets. Bring the mixture to a boil, stirring frequently, then reduce the heat to a low simmer and slowly poach the beets until they are soft and almost all of the liquid has evaporated (there should be about 3 tablespoons of liquid remaining). Remove from the heat and set the pan aside to cool. Transfer the mixture to the bowl of a powerful blender or a food processor and blend or process until the mixture forms a fine, satiny puree. While processing, add the vanilla vinegar. Strain the mixture through a sieve. In a large bowl, combine the blueberry-beet mixture with about ⅓ cup of the blueberry caramel and whisk to combine. Taste to see if the mixture has a good balance between sweet and acidic flavors. If a bit more sweetness is needed, add a few more tablespoons of the blueberry caramel and whisk to blend. Set aside or refrigerate until ready to serve. (Save any blueberry caramel to top ice cream and pound cake.)

continued . . .

To assemble the lobster salad: In a medium bowl, combine the cucumbers with ½ cup of the vanilla yogurt (save the rest of the yogurt for another use) and stir to coat. Arrange a line of cucumber slices along one side of each of 6 salad plates. Place a small handful of arugula on the other side of each plate. Divide the lobster meat into six portions, half a lobster per person, making sure that each serving gets 1 claw, half a tail, and a bit of the knuckle meat. Dip each portion of the lobster meat into the blueberry-beet glaze so it is well coated. Shake off the excess—the lobster shouldn't be dripping with glaze—and arrange each portion of lobster on top of the bed of arugula on the salad plate. Serve immediately.

pineapple-blueberry Jell-O mold fruit salad

This is a light, fruity retro dessert that may bring back childhood memories, as it does for me. Serve it plain, or accompanied by a big dollop of whipped cream. Serves 6 to 8

- Two 3-ounce packages black-cherry Jell-O or other gelatin
- 2 cups water
- One 20-ounce can crushed pineapple in its own juice, drained (reserve the juice)
- 1 cup cranberry juice
- 1 cup fresh blueberries
- 1 cup fresh strawberries

Place the gelatin in a large Pyrex dish and set aside. Bring the water to a boil, then pour it over the gelatin in the dish and stir to dissolve. Add the reserved pineapple juice and the cranberry juice and stir to blend. Set aside for 1½ to 2 hours to partially set. Add the pineapple, blueberries, and strawberries and stir to combine. Pour the gelatin mixture into a ring mold or other decorative mold and refrigerate for at least 4 hours to set and chill completely. To unmold, lower the mold into a large pan of hot water for a few seconds, just until the gelatin loosens from the sides and bottom. Place a large plate on the top of the mold and reverse in one smooth movement so the gelatin mold transfers to the plate. Serve immediately.

blueberry-sour cream dressing with trio of bitter greens salad

This salad is a delicious study in contrasts—sweet and salty; bitter and sweet; acidic and creamy—with a delicate spicy note of pepper. It awakens all your taste buds, and is a perfect light starter for any meal, especially one that does not include cream in the main course. The subtle sweetness of the blueberries is a perfect foil for the bitter flavor of the watercress, endives, and arugula. Start the dressing two hours ahead of serving. Serves 4

FOR THE DRESSING:

½ cup white wine vinegar

2 teaspoons sugar

1 teaspoon salt

½ cup fresh blueberries, halved

½ cup sour cream

Freshly ground black pepper to taste

FOR THE SALAD:

1 bunch (about 1 cup firmly packed) watercress, leaves and delicate stems only

2 Belgian endives, cut into 1-inch pieces

½ cup baby arugula

4 tablespoons fresh blueberries, for garnish

To make the dressing: In a medium glass or ceramic bowl, combine the vinegar, sugar, salt, and blueberries, stir gently until the sugar and salt dissolve, and set aside for 2 hours.

Transfer the blueberry mixture to a blender or food processor and puree for about 10 seconds. In a medium bowl, combine the blueberry mixture with the sour cream and pepper and whisk well to blend.

To make the salad: In a salad bowl, combine the watercress, endives, and baby arugula and toss to combine. Add the blueberry–sour cream dressing and toss to combine. Divide the salad among 4 serving plates, garnish each serving with 1 tablespoon of the blueberries, and serve.

fennel, arugula, orange, and blueberry salad

This is an amazingly flavorful salad with lots of color and crunch. It offers a melange of bitter, sweet, and acidic flavors, plus the deep, distinctive anise notes from the fennel, which play off each other deliciously. The blueberries are the salad's punctuation marks that add visual allure and small, subtle bursts of sweetness. To slice the fennel and the onion, I use a mandolin slicer. An essential tool in many restaurants, and available in most houseware and gourmet shops, a mandolin can cut the vegetables into slices that are almost translucent. Serves 4 to 6

1 large fennel bulb, base and branches trimmed, delicate fernlike leaves reserved

½ small red onion, thinly sliced

1 seedless navel orange, peeled, thinly sliced, segments separated (reserve as much juice as possible)

½ pound (about 4 cups loosely packed) baby arugula

1 cup fresh blueberries

1 tablespoon sherry vinegar

½ teaspoon salt

½ cup canola or other light vegetable oil

1 teaspoon Dijon mustard

Freshly ground black pepper to taste

Using a mandolin slicer or a very sharp knife, slice the fennel, starting from the base up, into very thin slices. In a salad bowl, combine the fennel with the onion, orange, arugula, and ½ cup of the blueberries and toss lightly to combine. Set aside. In a small bowl, combine the vinegar and salt and stir until the salt dissolves. Add the oil, mustard, and several turns of the pepper mill and whisk, or stir rapidly with a fork, to blend, ideally until the mixture emulsifies and looks creamy. Drizzle over the salad, then toss lightly to combine. Garnish with the remaining ½ cup blueberries and the reserved fennel leaves and serve.

minted blueberry-melon fruit salad

Blueberries and melons, especially orange-fleshed melon, have a special affinity, their sweet but distinctive flavors bringing out the best in each other. In this recipe, mint enters the mix, adding its distinctive menthol essence and a slight peppery note to the creamy dressing. Serves 4 to 6

- 1 large ripe orange-fleshed melon, skin removed, seeded, and cut into bite-size pieces
- 2 cups fresh blueberries
- ¼ cup fresh orange juice
- ¼ cup dry (fino or manzanilla) sherry
- ⅔ cup crème fraîche
- 1 bunch mint

In a large glass or ceramic bowl, combine the melon, 1¾ cups of the blueberries, the orange juice, sherry, and crème fraîche. Stir gently to combine. Add 5 mint sprigs, stir gently to combine, then cover the bowl with plastic wrap and refrigerate for at least 4 hours or overnight. Remove and discard the mint, stir, then spoon the melon mixture into serving bowls. Garnish each serving with some of the remaining ¼ cup blueberries and a sprig of mint, and serve.

chapter 3

appetizers and main courses

king salmon tartare with blueberries

A yachting trip to the wilds of Alaska yielded not only adventure and a dramatic change of pace for Glenn Harris, chef of Manhattan's Neptune Room Restaurant on the Upper West Side, but also some intriguing and delicious recipes. "I was looking for new ways to use some of the great salmon we were catching, as well as some of the other local products we found on the trip." One recipe is this delicious salmon tartare with blueberries, tossed in a Dijon vinaigrette, now served at the Neptune Room. Another recipe, which follows, Blueberry-Cured Salmon Gravlax, is a visually striking appetizer, cured with salt, herbs, wild blueberries, and cilantro. "The gravlax was concocted by one of my companions on the trip, Brian Ellis, chef of Jane in downtown Manhattan," says Glenn. "It's absolutely gorgeous when you cut into it—a strip of deep purple on the outside, bright orange on the inside." Serves 4

½ pound sushi-grade wild king salmon, skinned and cut into ½-inch pieces

1 cup fresh blueberries

2 tablespoons Dijon mustard

1 tablespoon fresh lemon juice

1 teaspoon chopped fresh dill

Salt to taste

Freshly ground black pepper to taste

1 to 2 teaspoons extra-virgin olive oil

In a large bowl, combine the salmon and blueberries. Set aside.

In a small bowl, combine the mustard, lemon juice, dill, a generous pinch of salt, and several turns of the pepper mill. Whisk to blend. Pour the dressing over the salmon mixture and stir gently to combine. Top with a drizzle of the oil. Chef Harris suggests serving the tartare in small bowls set over ice.

blueberry-cured salmon gravlax

Traditional gravlax employs sugar, kosher salt, and dill for curing. This unique version from Brian Ellis, the chef at the helm of the restaurant Jane, in New York's Tribeca district, uses the sugar and salt, of course, with mint, cilantro, and blueberries replacing the dill to delicious effect. A honey-mustard sauce is a traditional pairing with gravlax. To make, combine 5 tablespoons of honey mustard, 3 tablespoons of Dijon mustard, and 1 tablespoon of chopped fresh dill. Serves 8

- One 2½-pound side of salmon fillet
- 1 cup kosher salt, or coarse sea salt
- 1 cup granulated sugar
- 2 cups fresh or frozen, thawed and drained wild blueberries
- 1 bunch cilantro, stems removed
- 1 bunch mint, stems removed
- 2 tablespoons freshly ground black pepper

Generously cover a large platter with plastic wrap, leaving enough runover to eventually cover the salmon. Rinse the salmon and pat it dry, then place it on the platter skin side down and set aside.

In the bowl of a food processor, combine the salt, sugar, blueberries, cilantro, mint, and pepper and process to a coarse puree, 8 to 10 seconds. Transfer the mixture to a sieve set over a bowl and let it sit for about 10 minutes to remove excess liquid. Spread the mixture over the salmon, covering all exposed flesh. Cover snugly with plastic wrap, weight with a large plate and perhaps a can of soup on top, and refrigerate for 48 to 72 hours, draining the platter from time to time as necessary, if liquid seeps out.

Before serving, unwrap the salmon and wipe or scrape off the blueberry mixture coating with a clean damp cloth or dinner knife. Using a long, thin, very sharp knife, slice on a sharp diagonal starting about 3 inches in from one end and slicing toward that end. After the first slice—the end piece—slices should have just a small edge of deep blue border around the succulent salmon flesh. Serve with thin slices of rye bread and honey-mustard sauce.

cornmeal-crusted snapper with spicy blueberry compote

On the serene and sophisticated Caribbean island of Grand Cayman, executive chef Steven Carl, originally from Rhode Island, commands the kitchens of the Hyatt Regency Resort overlooking Seven Mile Beach. His dishes fuse a passion for Caribbean cuisine with a background of regional American cooking. In this unique recipe, a typically Caribbean fish—red snapper—teams up with blueberries reminiscent of Carl's native New England. "I like the sweetness of the blueberries with the mild flavor of the snapper. I added lemon zest for a bit of tartness, cornmeal for crunch, and jalapeño chiles for a traditionally Caribbean touch of heat." For those who prefer their food without too much heat, the sauce is also delicious without the peppers. This recipe requires a bit of chef-style preparation, such as infusing the cooking oil with aromatic spices, but the results are worth it. Chef Carl suggests serving the fish with roasted sweet potatoes, either quartered or mashed, with a bit of butter and salt.

Serves 4

FOR THE BLUEBERRY COMPOTE:

2 lemons

5 teaspoons sugar

¼ cup olive oil

1 teaspoon whole coriander seeds

½ teaspoon whole black peppercorns

1 cinnamon stick

2 pieces star anise

1 bay leaf

½ teaspoon mustard seeds

2 shallots, finely sliced

1 small jalapeño chile, seeds and pith removed, finely julienned

2 cups fresh or frozen, thawed and drained blueberries

3 tablespoons beef or chicken stock

Salt to taste

FOR THE SNAPPER:

4 red snapper fillets, skin on, 4 to 5 ounces each

Salt to taste

Freshly ground black pepper to taste

¼ cup cornmeal

4 tablespoons olive oil

4 sprigs fresh thyme or mint, for garnish, optional

To make the blueberry compote: Finely grate the zest of 1 lemon. Place in a small, fine-mesh sieve and set aside. Juice both lemons and set the juice aside. In a small bowl, combine 4 or 5 ice cubes and 1½ cups water. In a small skillet, combine 1½ cups water with 3 teaspoons of the sugar and bring to a boil over high heat. Lower the lemon zest in the strainer into the boiling sugar water for 15 seconds, then shock it in the ice bath. Repeat 2 more times, then set the zest aside in the strainer. (This procedure takes the bitterness out of the zest.)

In a medium skillet, heat the oil over medium heat. Add the coriander seeds, peppercorns, cinnamon stick, star anise, bay leaf, and mustard seeds and stir to combine. Cook for 5 to 6 minutes, until the seeds begin to sizzle and pop and the spices begin to release their aromatic flavors. Remove from the heat and set the pan aside to cool for 10 minutes. Strain the oil, discard the spices, and return the oil to the pan. Heat the oil over medium heat, then add the shallots. Sauté for 3 to 4 minutes, stirring frequently, until the shallots soften and start to look translucent but not browned. Add the lemon zest and jalapeño, stir to combine, then sauté for about 2 minutes, or until soft. Add the lemon juice and blueberries, stir to combine, then cook, stirring occasionally, for 5 minutes. Add the stock, a generous pinch of salt, and the remaining 2 teaspoons sugar and stir to combine. Cook, stirring occasionally, for 5 minutes, or until the blueberries are cooked through and softened but still retain their shape. Adjust the seasoning, then set aside on a warm corner of the stove until ready to serve.

To cook the snapper: Season the flesh side of the fillets with salt and pepper, then sprinkle each with about 1 tablespoon of the cornmeal, making sure that all the flesh is generously covered. Set aside. In a large skillet, heat the oil over high heat until almost smoking. Place the fillets in the skillet skin side down and cook for 2 minutes. Using a large spatula, carefully turn the fillets over and cook for 4 to 5 minutes, until the fillets are cooked through.

Spoon a small pool of sauce in the center of each serving plate and arrange the fillets over the sauce. Garnish the servings with a sprig of thyme or mint atop each fillet, if you wish. Serve immediately, with extra sauce passed at the table in a sauceboat.

corn and blueberry relish

This easy, colorful condiment, actually a cross between a relish and a salad, is a delicious garnish for grilled salmon, a juicy sautéed pork chop, or seared scallops. Its creator, Seattle star chef Tom Douglas, calls it a "rapid relish," one of several he uses in his four innovative Seattle restaurants, including the original, Dahlia Lounge, and the latest, Lola. "I like using simple fruit or vegetable relishes instead of heavy sauces, especially with fish," says Tom. He suggests several variations on the recipe, depending on your mood and what's available in the market. "Instead of blanching the corn, you could cook it on the cob on the grill first, and then cut the slightly charred kernels from the cob," he says. "Instead of using mâche (sometimes called corn salad or lamb's lettuce), you could use baby arugula or baby spinach. You could also try replacing the mint with basil leaves." Serves 6

FOR THE VINAIGRETTE:

2 teaspoons champagne vinegar (or other mild vinegar)

1 teaspoon fresh lemon juice

2 teaspoons minced shallots

2 tablespoons extra-virgin olive oil

Fleur de sel or kosher salt to taste

Freshly ground black pepper to taste

FOR THE RELISH:

Salt

1 cup corn kernels cut from the cob

5 cups loosely packed trimmed mâche, baby arugula, or spinach leaves

1 cup fresh blueberries

3 tablespoons mint leaves torn into pieces

1 tablespoon thinly sliced chives

To make the vinaigrette: In a small bowl, combine the vinegar, lemon juice, and shallots. Slowly whisk in the oil. Season with fleur de sel and pepper. Set aside.

To make the relish: Bring a small pot of salted water to a boil and set up a bowl of ice water. Add the corn to the pot and cook for 2 minutes. Drain the corn and immediately plunge it into the bowl of ice water. Drain the corn. In a medium bowl, combine the corn, mâche, blueberries, mint, chives, and vinaigrette and toss gently to coat.

Serve immediately, mounded over grilled salmon or pork chops, or mounded in the center of a plate, surrounded by seared scallops.

blueberry-sage turkey loaves

Dried blueberries work best in this succulent turkey meat loaf, since they add texture and distinctive flavor without discoloring the white meat. The sweet and tangy sauce contrasts nicely with the loaves, but the loaves are also tasty all by themselves. Serve with mashed potatoes or buttered rice and a green salad. Serves 4

FOR THE TURKEY LOAVES:

1½ pounds ground turkey

½ cup dried blueberries

4 slim stalks celery, trimmed, outside fibers peeled, and finely chopped

½ cup finely chopped fresh parsley

1 tablespoon fleur de sel or kosher salt

1 tablespoon celery seed

2 teaspoons dried sage

1 medium shallot, finely minced

3 tablespoons vegetable oil

Freshly ground black pepper to taste

FOR THE SAUCE:

½ cup white vermouth

½ cup chicken stock

1 tablespoon brown sugar

1 tablespoon Dijon mustard

½ teaspoon salt

Freshly ground black pepper to taste

To make the turkey loaves: Preheat the oven to 350°F.

In a large bowl, combine the turkey, blueberries, celery, parsley, fleur de sel, celery seed, sage, shallot, oil, and several turns of the pepper mill. Using your hands or a wooden spoon, mix until well blended. Divide the turkey mixture into 4 equal oval patties, about 1½ inches thick in the center. Place in a 9 by 13-inch enameled heavy-bottomed baking dish. Bake for about 30 minutes, until firm to the touch in the center and lightly browned. Using a spatula, transfer the patties to a large dish and set aside to rest for about 5 minutes.

Make the sauce: Set the baking dish over high heat. Add the vermouth and deglaze the dish, scraping up any brown bits sticking to the bottom. Add the stock, brown sugar, mustard, salt, and several turns of the pepper mill and stir to incorporate. Reduce the heat and simmer, stirring frequently, for 4 minutes.

Transfer the turkey loaves to individual plates, spoon the sauce equally over each, and serve.

roast stuffed turkey breast with red wine-blueberry sauce

A festive and economical main course, this roast stuffed turkey breast would make a perfect alternative to a whole turkey on Thanksgiving or Christmas for a gathering of eight or so friends and family. Serves 8

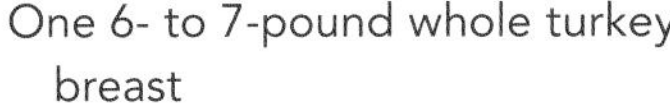

- One 6- to 7-pound whole turkey breast
- Salt to taste
- Freshly ground black pepper to taste
- 1 recipe Cornbread Stuffing with Sweet Onion and Wild Blueberries (page 60)
- 1 tablespoon unsalted butter, softened
- 1 small onion, coarsely chopped
- 2 stalks celery, coarsely chopped
- 2 ounces pancetta, coarsely chopped
- 2 sprigs fresh thyme, or ½ teaspoon dried
- 1 sprig fresh rosemary, or ½ teaspoon dried
- 2½ cups chicken stock
- 1½ cups Pinot Noir or other dry red wine
- 1 cup fresh or frozen blueberries, preferably wild

Preheat the oven to 425°F. Rinse the turkey breast with cold water and thoroughly pat it dry. Generously season the breast cavity of the turkey breast with salt and pepper. Fill the breast cavity and the small cavity under the flap of skin at the neck with the stuffing. Spread the skin with the butter, then season with salt and pepper. Set in a roasting pan skin side up. Scatter the onion, celery, pancetta, thyme, and rosemary around the breast. Roast in the center of the oven (the top of the turkey should be at least 4 inches from the heating element) for 20 minutes. Reduce heat to 350°F and roast, basting with the stock every 20 minutes or so, for about 2 hours and 20 minutes, until the juices run clear when pierced deeply with a small skewer or fork. If you have an instant-read meat thermometer, the internal temperature should register 160°F. Baste one last time 10 minutes before removing from the oven, using all the remaining stock. Remove from the oven and transfer the turkey breast to a serving platter and let rest 15 minutes.

Meanwhile, prepare the gravy: Place the roasting pan across two burners at medium-high heat. Bring the juices to a boil, then add the wine and deglaze the pan, scraping up the brown bits on the bottom and sides of the pan. Add the blueberries and stir to combine. Reduce the heat to medium-low and simmer for 10 minutes, stirring and scraping frequently. Set a sieve or fine colander over a large bowl and strain the sauce into the bowl, pressing down with the back of a wooden spoon to squeeze out all the juices. Adjust the seasonings to taste. Transfer the sauce to a warmed gravy boat. Carve the turkey breast, spoon out the stuffing, and drizzle each serving with the red wine–blueberry sauce. Pass the rest at the table.

cornbread stuffing with sweet onion and wild blueberries

This is a wonderful stuffing for almost any kind of mild-flavored bird you can think of—a roaster, capon, Cornish hens, or turkey. I like to use dried wild blueberries when I can find them, but you can also substitute dried cranberries or golden raisins. The mixture will generously stuff an 8- to 10-pound bird. I often use this stuffing for the Roast Stuffed Turkey Breast with Red Wine–Blueberry Sauce that follows. Makes about 5 cups

- 2 tablespoons unsalted butter
- 2 tablespoons olive oil
- 1 medium Vidalia or other sweet onion, finely diced
- 1 small clove garlic, minced
- 3 medium stalks celery, diced
- 1 cup crumbled day-old or fresh cornbread, air-dried for several hours
- 3 cups day-old soft white-bread crumbs, air-dried for several hours
- ¾ cup dried wild blueberries
- ½ teaspoon dried sage
- 2 tablespoons chopped parsley
- Pinch of freshly grated nutmeg
- ¾ teaspoon dried thyme, or 1½ teaspoons minced fresh
- 1 teaspoon salt
- ½ teaspoon freshly ground black pepper
- ⅔ cup chicken stock, warmed

In a large skillet over medium heat, heat the butter and oil until the butter starts to bubble. Add the onion, garlic, and celery and stir to combine. Cook for 4 to 6 minutes, until the mixture softens and begin to turn translucent, but not brown. Add the cornbread, bread crumbs, blueberries, sage, parsley, nutmeg, thyme, salt, and pepper and stir to combine.

Remove from the heat and transfer the mixture to a large bowl. Add the stock and, using a wooden spoon or—if the mixture is cool enough—your hands, mix until all the ingredients are moistened. Use to stuff a bird, or transfer to a buttered baking dish and bake, covered, at 350°F for 25 minutes, and serve as a side dish.

zesty blueberry barbecue sauce

This succulent barbecue sauce, zesty with the punch of chopped jalapeños, is the creation of Chef Debra Ponzek, founder of Aux Délices Foods catering company in Stamford and Greenwich, Connecticut. The sauce is a wonderful accompaniment to grilled chicken or duck breasts. Makes about 1½ cups

- 2 tablespoons olive oil
- 3 medium shallots, finely chopped
- 1 small jalapeño, seeded and finely chopped
- 2 cups fresh blueberries
- 2 tablespoons champagne vinegar
- 2 tablespoons brown sugar
- 1 tablespoon Dijon mustard
- ½ cup water

In a medium skillet, heat the oil over medium-high heat. Add the shallots and the jalapeño, reduce the heat to medium, and sauté, stirring frequently, until the shallots soften and start to look translucent, about 4 minutes. Add the blueberries, vinegar, brown sugar, mustard, and water, stir to combine, then simmer, stirring occasionally, until the sauce is glossy and slightly thickened, about 15 minutes. Set aside to cool, then transfer to a food processor and puree until smooth. Use to baste chicken or duck breasts on the grill.

roast marinated duck with blueberry sauce

Antoine Bouterin, whose restaurant, Bouterin, is a Manhattan favorite, offers this succulent duck dish to his Upper East Side clientele. A native of Provence, where he rarely encountered blueberries, Bouterin was inspired to create this variation of a classic duck with fruit sauce (normally prepared with oranges or cherries) by the abundance of beautiful local blueberries that appear in New York markets in July and August. The blueberry reduction sauce is somewhat time-consuming but is absolutely fabulous. Serve the duck with a mixture of wild and long-grain rice and perhaps a sweet potato puree, both of which are delicious with the sauce. Serves 2

FOR THE DUCK:

2 cups port wine

2 cups water

¼ cup sugar

¼ cup honey

One 4- to 4½-pound duck, wing tips removed

Salt to taste

Freshly ground black pepper to taste

FOR THE BLUEBERRY SAUCE:

2 tablespoons olive oil

⅓ cup diced shallots

½ cup sugar

½ cup cider vinegar

½ cup brandy

1¼ cups fresh blueberries

1½ teaspoons chopped fresh tarragon

2 cups duck or chicken stock

Salt to taste

Freshly ground black pepper to taste

To make the duck: In a pot large enough to hold the duck, combine the port, water, sugar, and honey and stir to blend. Place over high heat and bring to a boil. As soon as the mixture comes to a boil, remove the pot from the heat. Meanwhile, season the duck cavity with generous pinches of salt and pepper, and truss. Place the duck in the pot and marinate at room temperature, turning occasionally, for 20 minutes.

Preheat the oven to 450°F. Transfer the duck to a rack set in a shallow roasting pan. Place the duck in the center of the oven, lower the oven temperature to 350°F, and roast for about 1½ hours, or until the duck is browned and crisp. If you have a meat thermometer, the internal temperature should be 185°F.

Meanwhile, prepare the blueberry sauce: In a medium skillet, heat the oil over medium heat. Add the shallots, stir to combine, then cook, stirring frequently, until the shallots are soft and translucent but not browned, 4 to 5 minutes. Reduce the heat to low. Add the sugar, stir to combine, and cook, stirring frequently, until the sugar caramelizes to a golden brown, 10 to 14 minutes. Add the vinegar, brandy, 1 cup of the blueberries, and the tarragon and stir to combine. Raise the heat to medium-high and cook until the blueberries soften, about 5 minutes. Add the stock, bring to a boil, and cook, stirring frequently and maintaining a low boil, until the mixture is reduced by half, 20 to 25 minutes. Season with salt and pepper. Set aside until ready to serve.

Carve the duck, dividing it between 2 serving plates. Spoon the sauce over the duck and garnish each plate with 2 tablespoons fresh blueberries. Serve immediately, with any extra blueberry sauce in a sauceboat on the side.

blueberry-lime salsa

Spicy, sassy, and succulent, this berry salsa is a lively enhancement to grilled chicken, pork, or duck. You can make it up to a day ahead and store it, covered, in the refrigerator. When grilling chicken breasts to serve with this salsa, I marinate them for about 30 minutes in lime juice, a clove of coarsely chopped garlic, and coarse salt. Serves 6 to 8

- 1 small jalapeño
- 2½ cups fresh blueberries
- ½ small red onion
- ½ small red bell pepper, cored and seeded
- 3 tablespoons fresh lime juice
- ½ teaspoon coarse sea salt
- ½ cup loosely packed finely julienned fresh basil
- ⅓ cup loosely packed coarsely chopped cilantro
- 1 tablespoon extra-virgin olive oil
- ½ teaspoon freshly grated ginger
- Freshly ground black pepper to taste

Preheat the broiler. Place the jalapeño under the broiler and char on all sides. Remove, place in a brown paper bag, close, and set aside. In the bowl of a food processor, combine 2 cups of the blueberries, the onion, and red pepper. Process until the mixture is coarsely chopped. Transfer to a bowl and add the lime juice and salt and stir to combine. Set aside.

Using a paper towel or rubber gloves to protect your skin if it is sensitive to hot peppers, trim the stem and peel off the skin of the jalapeño. Slice it in half, remove and discard the seeds (unless you like your salsa really hot), and finely chop the jalapeño. Add the jalapeño to the blueberry mixture, along with the basil, cilantro, the remaining ½ cup blueberries, the oil, ginger, and several turns of the pepper mill, and stir well to combine. Set aside for about 1 hour to allow the flavors to blend. Spoon a little bit over individual portions of grilled chicken, pork, or duck, and serve the rest in a bowl, passed at the table.

juicy blue-burger

When I prepared these blueberry-laced hamburgers for lunch for the first time, my husband, Steve, and my 21-year-old son, Ben, the cheeseburger maven, approached them with less than enthusiasm. One might even say with trepidation. But the verdict from both was overwhelmingly positive. My husband, who had the burger plain, pronounced it "really good." My son, who ate his with melted cheddar cheese on top, proclaimed it "excellent." He even went on to say that they could use even a few more blueberries. I have made these burgers with a variety of blueberry products—fresh, freeze-dried, and dried (like raisins). I think they are most successful with the freeze-dried varieties, since they do not have all the water of fresh blueberries and add the subtle flavor and health benefits of blueberries without changing the basic texture of the burgers. My second choice would be dried blueberries. Makes 4 burgers

½ cup freeze-dried blueberries

1 pound ground beef (preferably Black Angus chuck)

½ teaspoon salt

Freshly ground black pepper to taste

4 slices sharp cheddar cheese, optional, for cheeseburgers

Place the blueberries in the bowl of a food processor and pulse until powdered. In a large bowl, combine the blueberries with the beef, salt, and several turns of the pepper mill. With your hands or a wooden spoon, mix and knead the beef until all the ingredients are evenly incorporated. Form into 4 burgers. Pan-fry or grill according to your taste. If you're making cheeseburgers, add the cheese about 2 minutes before the end of the cooking time. Place the burgers on buns and serve with ketchup or chili sauce.

savory blueberry steak sauce

This tasty steak sauce, with sweet and sour notes, is particularly good with steaks grilled on the barbecue. My favorite cuts for grilling are New York strips and porterhouse. Serves 6 to 8

- 3 tablespoons unsalted butter or margarine
- 2 small or 1 medium shallot, finely chopped
- 2 tablespoons all-purpose flour
- ¼ cup sherry vinegar
- ¼ cup ketchup
- 3 tablespoons Dijon mustard
- ¼ cup orange juice
- ¼ cup molasses
- ½ teaspoon dried thyme, or ¾ teaspoon fresh, crushed
- ¼ teaspoon dried sage, crushed
- 2 cups fresh or frozen blueberries, preferably wild
- Salt to taste
- Freshly ground black pepper to taste

Melt the butter in a large skillet over medium heat. Add the shallots and sauté for 3 to 4 minutes, until the shallots are soft and translucent, but not browned. Sprinkle in the flour, stir to blend, and cook, stirring constantly, until the mixture begins to bubble. Add the vinegar, ketchup, mustard, orange juice, molasses, thyme, and sage and stir to combine. Add the blueberries and stir to combine. Raise the heat to medium-high and bring to a boil. Reduce the heat to a simmer and cook, stirring often, for about 15 minutes, until the mixture is thickened and glossy. Season with salt and pepper to taste. Cool, then transfer the mixture to the bowl of a food processor or blender and puree for 30 to 40 seconds, until very smooth. Serve warm in a sauceboat.

icelandic rack of lamb with wild blueberry-wild thyme sauce

This superb recipe comes all the way from Iceland, created by Reykjavik chef Siggi Hall. Siggi is Iceland's most celebrated chef, proprietor of his eponymous restaurant, Siggi Hall, at Odinsveum, and for many years host of a popular television cooking show. The restaurant, renowned for innovative dishes featuring local seafood, game, and organic lamb, has been included on Condé Nast *Traveler* magazine's list of the world's Top 100 Hot Tables. Siggi, who created this dish for the fiftieth anniversary of Icelandic independence, waxes poetic when describing the ingredients. "There is great harmony in this dish," he says. "The Icelandic lamb, born in the spring, are completely free range, grazing in the hills, valleys, and mountains. And the blueberries and thyme grow wild in the pure, clean Icelandic heathers and hillsides, where the sun shines twenty-four hours a day in our long Arctic summers. Our blueberries, especially from the northern part of the island, are beautiful, small, some dark blue, some almost black." Make an effort to find wild blueberries for this recipe. Siggi suggests serving this lamb with mashed potatoes and steamed, buttered organic vegetables. I've also accompanied this lamb with tiny haricots verts tossed with shallot butter. Serves 4

1 cup fresh or frozen wild blueberries

2 tablespoons fresh thyme leaves, lightly crushed

¾ cup ruby port wine

Two 2- to 2½-pound racks of lamb, fat trimmed (leave about a ½-inch line of fat on the top of the rack)

Sea salt to taste

Freshly ground white pepper to taste

2 cups lamb stock, or top-quality beef stock

1 tablespoon unsalted butter, cut into bits

4 fresh thyme sprigs, for garnish, optional

In a large bowl, combine the blueberries, thyme, and port. Set aside to steep at room temperature for 1 hour. Preheat the oven to 425°F. Heat a large, heavy ovenproof skillet over high heat. Place the lamb in the center, fat side down, and sear until the fat has melted and the side of the rack is deep golden brown. Transfer the skillet to the center of the oven and roast for 15 (for rare) to 20 (for medium-rare) minutes. If you use a meat thermometer, the temperature, measured at the thickest part of the rack, should read 125°F for rare, 130°F for medium-rare. Using tongs, transfer the lamb to a serving platter, sprinkle with pinches of salt and white pepper, then cover loosely with aluminum foil and set aside to rest until the sauce is ready.

Meanwhile, pour out excess fat from the skillet and place the skillet over medium-high heat. Add the blueberry mixture and stir to deglaze the pan, scraping up all the brown bits stuck to the bottom and sides of the pan. Cook, stirring frequently, until the port is reduced by half, about 5 minutes. Add the stock, stir to combine, then cook until the liquid is reduced by about two thirds, about 10 minutes. Add the butter and stir to blend. Season with salt and white pepper, then transfer the sauce to a warmed sauceboat. Slice the lamb between the ribs, dividing the little chops among 4 warmed serving plates. Spoon a bit of sauce over each serving and garnish, if you wish, with a sprig of thyme. Serve with mashed potatoes, buttered steamed vegetables, and the rest of the sauce passed at the table.

blueberry chutney

This fabulous spicy and pungent chutney was created by Jeff Starr, culinary director and executive chef for Trinchero Family Estates, one of California's premier wineries. Jeff serves his chutney with rack of lamb, and accompanies the dish with a Trinchero Family Merlot, a lovely wine with blueberry notes that compliment the chutney and lamb. The chutney also is delicious paired with baked ham or roasted duck. Makes about 3 cups

- 1 cup fresh orange juice
- ¾ cup champagne vinegar
- 1 cup water
- ½ cup sugar
- 1 cinnamon stick, crushed
- 3 pieces star anise, crushed
- 4 whole cloves
- ½ vanilla bean, split, seeds scraped out
- 1 teaspoon salt
- 1 teaspoon red chile flakes
- 2 cups dried blueberries
- 1 teaspoon cornstarch dissolved in ¼ cup water

In a large, heavy-bottomed nonreactive saucepan or casserole, combine the orange juice, vinegar, water, sugar, cinnamon, star anise, cloves, vanilla bean scrapings, salt, and chile flakes.

Cook at a simmer over medium heat for 30 minutes. Strain out the solids and return to medium heat. Add the blueberries and the cornstarch mixture and stir to combine. Simmer for 30 minutes. Cool in the pan for about 30 minutes, then transfer to a glass or ceramic bowl, cover lightly, and refrigerate until ready to serve. Serve lightly chilled.

baked acorn squash with blueberry filling

This colorful and delicious squash dish, offered to me by my friend Michael Stinchcomb, makes a festive addition to a holiday table. Michael serves the squash as one of several side dishes to accompany a roast turkey or baked ham at his home in Southampton, New York. "I love the flavors of the squash and the blueberries together," he says, "and the colors are dazzling." Serves 6

- 3 acorn squash, halved, seeds and strings removed
- Salt
- Freshly ground black pepper
- 4 tablespoons unsalted butter
- 1¾ cups fresh blueberries
- 2 tablespoons brown sugar

Preheat the oven to 350°F. Sprinkle the insides of the squash with a pinch of salt and pepper. Place a sheet of parchment paper over a baking sheet and spread 1 tablespoon of the butter over it. Place the squash cut side down on the baking sheet and bake in the center of the oven for 35 minutes, until the squash is firm-tender.

Meanwhile, in a medium saucepan, combine 1 cup of the blueberries with the remaining 3 tablespoons butter and the brown sugar and set over medium-high heat. Cook for about 6 minutes, stirring occasionally, until the mixture is bubbling and slightly thickened. Add a pinch of salt and stir to blend. Set aside in the pan.

Remove the squash from the oven. Using a sharp knife, slice a small disk from the bottom of each piece (taking care not to cut into the bottom of the cavity) so the squash will be able to sit straight on the baking sheet when turned over. Turn the squash over so they're cut side up, and spoon the blueberry mixture equally into the cavities. Spoon the remaining fresh blueberries, about 2 tablespoons per squash half, on top of the blueberry mixture. Return to the oven and bake for 15 to 20 minutes, until the filling bubbles and the squash is tender. Serve immediately.

sautéed red cabbage with blueberries and mushrooms

Joanna Pruess, a food writer and good friend, found inspiration years ago in the life and work of a renowned chef, teacher, and writer from Brittany named Josephine Araldo. A Cordon Bleu–trained chef who had a sixty-five-year career in both France and the United States, Josephine was teaching in San Francisco when Joanna, who was a student at Berkeley in the 1960s, met her. "Josephine loved to juxtapose fruits and vegetables in the same dish," says Joanna. This savory red cabbage and blueberry dish, created by Josephine many years ago and prepared often by Joanna at her home, is a prime example. Serves 6

- ½ stick plus 1 tablespoon (5 tablespoons) unsalted butter
- 2 tablespoons rendered bacon fat
- 1 medium onion, thinly sliced
- 1 small red cabbage, shredded
- ½ cup dry red wine
- Salt to taste
- ½ pound white mushrooms, thinly sliced
- Freshly ground black pepper to taste
- 1 small clove garlic, minced
- 4 tablespoons finely chopped fresh parsley
- 1 cup fresh blueberries

In a large, heavy-bottomed pot or casserole, heat 2 tablespoons of the butter and the bacon fat over medium-high heat. Add the onion and sauté until lightly browned, 6 to 7 minutes. Add the cabbage, wine, and a pinch of salt and stir to combine. Cover and cook over low heat, stirring occasionally to prevent burning, for 20 to 30 minutes, until the cabbage is tender.

Meanwhile, melt 2 tablespoons of the butter in a hot skillet over medium-high heat. Add the mushrooms and sauté, stirring frequently, until just soft, without letting them render their water, about 4 minutes. Season with salt and pepper. Combine the garlic and parsley, then add them to the mushroom mixture and stir to incorporate. Set aside.

Reduce the heat under the cabbage mixture to low, add the mushroom mixture, and stir to combine. When warmed through, add the blueberries and toss with the remaining 1 tablespoon butter. Adjust the seasonings and serve.

chapter 4

desserts

last-minute blueberry-raspberry tarts

Prepared just before serving, this is an easy tart that makes a great impression. It can be made with other fruits as well—pears or apples work very nicely—but it is particularly delicious with berries. You can top each with a small scoop of rich vanilla ice cream, but the tart is wonderful all on its own. To make four tarts, divide the recipe in half. Serves 8

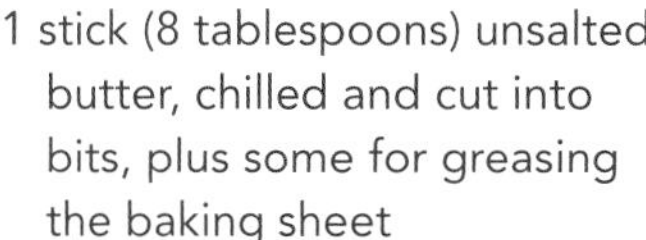

- 1 stick (8 tablespoons) unsalted butter, chilled and cut into bits, plus some for greasing the baking sheet
- One 17-ounce package frozen puff pastry, defrosted for 30 minutes
- ¾ cup sugar
- 4 cups fresh blueberries
- 1 cup fresh raspberries

Preheat the oven to 400°F. Lightly grease a baking sheet.

Spread the 2 pastry sheets flat, cut each into quarters, then transfer to the baking sheet. Turn up the edges of each piece ½ inch all around to form a border. Sprinkle the bottom of each piece with 1 teaspoon of the sugar. In a large bowl, combine the blueberries, raspberries, and ⅓ cup of the sugar and toss gently to coat the berries. Spoon the berry mixture equally over each pastry shell. Scatter 1 tablespoon of the butter over each tart, then sprinkle the remaining sugar equally over the 8 tarts. Bake in the center of the oven for 17 to 20 minutes, until the pastry is golden brown and the fruit is softened and bubbly. Serve immediately.

parisian blueberry tart

I discovered this luscious, French-style tart with blueberries dotting a browned, custardy base in a little bistro called Au Pont Marie on the Ile St. Louis in Paris. Sadly, the bistro closed a couple of years back, but this tart remains a lovely culinary souvenir of a romantic Paris dining experience. Serves 8

FOR THE CRUST:

1¾ cups all-purpose flour, plus some for rolling out the dough

1 stick (8 tablespoons) unsalted butter, chilled and cut into bits, plus some for greasing the pan

½ cup sugar

⅛ teaspoon salt

1 large egg, beaten

4 tablespoons water

FOR THE FILLING:

2 large eggs

2 tablespoons all-purpose flour

5 tablespoons granulated sugar

1 teaspoon baking powder

3 cups fresh blueberries

2 tablespoons confectioners' sugar

To make the crust: In the bowl of a food processor or in a mixing bowl, combine the flour, butter, sugar, and salt and process for 10 to 12 seconds, or mash with your fingertips, until the mixture has a dry, crumbly texture resembling coarse cornmeal. Add the egg and water and pulse 12 to 14 times, or mix, just until the dough begins to come together in a mass, but before it forms into a ball. (The dough can become tough if it is processed even a few seconds too long.) Remove the dough from the bowl, knead it for several seconds between your hands, then transfer it to a sheet of plastic wrap or waxed paper. Flatten the dough into a flat disk, wrap, and refrigerate for at least 1 hour.

Preheat the oven to 375°F. Lightly butter a 10½-inch removable-bottom tart pan.

On a floured work surface, roll out the dough with a floured rolling pin into a 13-inch circle. Transfer to the tart pan and press the dough gently into the bottom and fluted sides. Fold the overhang over onto itself, reinforcing the sides, so that just ½ inch extends over the rim. Flute the edges between your thumb and forefinger, or gently crimp with the tines of a fork.

To make the filling: In a large bowl, beat the eggs, flour, 2 tablespoons of the granulated sugar, and the baking powder together until light and creamy. Add the blueberries and gently stir to coat. Spoon the mixture into the prepared tart shell and sprinkle with the remaining 3 tablespoons granulated sugar. Bake in the center of the oven for 35 to 40 minutes, until the filling is well browned. Transfer the pan to a wire rack to cool completely. Remove the sides from the tart pan, sprinkle the top of the tart with confectioners' sugar, and serve.

mixed berries in wine and lime sauce

A light, refreshing, and easy way to serve fresh berries in season. Splashed with a bit of sweet, fruity white wine, lime juice, and sugar, the berries here have the starring role. I love to make this with the lush, plummy Alsatian white wine called Gewürztraminer. Serves 6 to 8

- 2 cups fresh blueberries
- 2 cups fresh raspberries
- 1 cup small to medium strawberries, halved
- ⅔ cup Gewürztraminer wine, white Zinfandel, or other sweet, fruity white wine
- 1 tablespoon fresh lime juice
- 2 tablespoons sugar
- Mint sprigs, for garnish

In a large bowl, combine the blueberries, raspberries, strawberries, wine, lime juice, and sugar and toss gently until the sugar dissolves the berries are well coated with sauce. Cover with plastic wrap and chill for 1 to 2 hours. Toss once more just before serving. Spoon the berries and sauce into individual bowls, garnish each serving with a sprig of mint, and serve.

blueberry-rhubarb pie

Sweet with a subtle hint of tartness, this is a delicious variation on the classic blueberry pie. I make it with a flaky, sweetened short-crust pastry. You can prepare this pie with a classic lattice-top woven crust, but I like to make a more whimsical topping, cutting out the top-crust dough with a cookie cutter into cute shapes to fit the occasion—perhaps stars for a Fourth of July picnic, or daisies for a dinner with friends. Serves 6 to 8

FOR THE CRUST:

2 cups all-purpose flour, plus some for rolling out the dough

10 tablespoons (1 stick plus 2 tablespoons) unsalted butter, chilled and cut into bits, plus some for greasing the pan

½ teaspoon salt

½ teaspoon baking powder

½ cup sugar

⅓ cup cold milk

FOR THE FILLING:

2 tablespoons cornstarch

⅓ cup water

1 pound thin to medium rhubarb stalks (about 5), cut into 1-inch pieces

½ cup plus 2 tablespoons sugar

½ teaspoon finely grated lemon zest

½ teaspoon ground cinnamon

⅛ teaspoon salt

1½ cups fresh blueberries

2 tablespoons unsalted butter

1 egg, beaten

To make the crust: In the bowl of a food processor or in a large bowl, combine the flour, butter, salt, baking powder, and sugar and process 10 to 12 seconds, or mash with your fingertips, until the mixture has the dry, crumbly texture of coarse cornmeal. Add the milk and pulse 10 to 12 times, or work together with your fingertips, just until the dough comes together in a smooth mass, but before it forms into a ball. If the dough is too dry, add another tablespoon of milk and pulse or mix for another few seconds. Remove the dough from the bowl and work it into a ball with your hands. If the dough is very sticky, coat your palms with flour once or twice and work it into the dough. The dough should be malleable but should not stick to your hands. Divide the dough in half and transfer onto 2 pieces of plastic wrap or waxed paper, press the dough into flat disks, wrap well, and refrigerate for at least 1 hour.

continued . . .

To make the filling: In a medium saucepan, combine the cornstarch with the water and stir to dissolve. Add the rhubarb, ½ cup of the sugar, the lemon zest, cinnamon, and salt and cook over medium-high heat, stirring frequently, for 3 minutes. Remove from the heat, cool for 5 minutes, then add the blueberries and stir to combine. Set aside.

Preheat the oven to 425°F. Lightly butter a 10½-inch tart pan. On a floured work surface, roll out the dough with a floured rolling pin into two 13-inch circles. Transfer 1 circle to the tart pan and press the dough gently into the bottom and sides. Fold the overhang over onto itself so that just ½ inch extends over the rim. Flute the edges between your thumb and forefinger, or gently crimp with the tines of a fork. Using a cookie cutter in the shape of your choice, cut shapes from the remaining circle of dough. Spoon the filling into the pie crust and dot with the butter. Arrange the cut-out dough over the top of the filling, with the pieces touching but not overlapping. Brush the rim of the bottom crust and the cut-out dough on top with the egg and sprinkle with the remaining 2 tablespoons sugar.

Bake in the center of the oven for about 40 minutes, until the crust is golden brown.

Set aside on a wire rack to cool.

rhubarb, raspberry, and blueberry crisp

Rhubarb, blueberries, and raspberries comprise a dashing trio, the tartness of the rhubarb and the raspberries contrasting subtly with the mild sweetness of the blueberries. Like most crisps, this recipe is quick and easy to prepare, just a combination of the warmed rhubarb with the other filling ingredients, crowned with the sweet, crumbly topping and baked. Serves 8

FOR THE FILLING:

2 tablespoons cornstarch

⅓ cup water

1 pound thin rhubarb stalks, cut into 1-inch pieces

1 teaspoon fresh lemon juice

½ cup sugar

⅛ teaspoon salt

1 cup fresh blueberries

1 cup fresh raspberries

FOR THE TOPPING:

½ stick (4 tablespoons) unsalted butter, slightly softened

1 cup brown sugar

1½ cups all-purpose flour

⅛ teaspoon salt

1 teaspoon ground cinnamon

1 cup rolled oats

Preheat the oven to 350°F.

To make the filling: In a small bowl, combine the cornstarch and water and stir to blend. In a medium saucepan, combine the cornstarch mixture with the rhubarb, lemon juice, sugar, and salt and bring to a boil over medium-high heat. Reduce the heat immediately to medium and cook for about 3 minutes, until the mixture is bubbling and softened. Remove from the heat, add the blueberries and raspberries, and gently stir to combine. Pour into a 9 by 13-inch glass baking dish and set aside.

To make the topping: In a large bowl or the bowl of an electric mixer, cream the butter with the brown sugar until blended. Add the flour, salt, and cinnamon and stir to combine. Add the oats and stir to incorporate. Using your hands, knead the mixture against the sides of the bowl, then squeeze and crumble through your fingers to give the topping a crumblike texture. Sprinkle the crumbs over the rhubarb mixture. Bake in the center of the oven for 35 to 40 minutes, until the top is browned and bubbling. Serve warm or at room temperature.

passover blueberry tart

This is a tempting and beautiful tart to serve to your guests over the Passover holidays. The crust is created from matzo meal and pressed into the pan as you would with a graham-cracker crust, and the vanilla pastry cream is thickened with potato starch. As a variation, use an assortment of blueberries, raspberries, blackberries, and strawberries instead of the blueberries alone. Serves 6 to 8

FOR THE MATZO MEAL CRUST:

- 1 stick (8 tablespoons) unsalted butter, chilled and cut into bits, plus some for greasing the pan
- 3 tablespoons potato starch, plus some for dusting the pan
- 1½ cups matzo meal
- ¼ cup sugar
- ⅛ teaspoon salt
- 1 large egg
- 2 tablespoons cold water

FOR THE FILLING:

- 1½ cups milk
- ½ vanilla bean, split, or 1 teaspoon vanilla extract
- 3 large egg yolks
- ¼ cup sugar
- 2 tablespoons potato starch
- 3 cups fresh blueberries or mixed berries
- ½ cup red currant jelly
- 1 tablespoon water

To make the matzo meal crust: Preheat the oven to 375°F. Butter a 10½-inch tart pan well and dust with potato starch.

In a food processor, combine the matzo meal, sugar, potato starch, butter, and salt and process for 12 to 14 seconds, until the mixture has the texture of coarse cornmeal. Add the egg and water and pulse several times, until the mixture starts to come together, but before it forms a ball. Remove the dough from the bowl and knead between your hands for about 10 seconds. If the dough is sticky, you may want to flour your hands with a bit of potato starch. Press the dough evenly into the bottom and sides of the tart pan. Make sure that enough of the dough comes up the sides to form a border on top of the rim. Prick the bottom and sides with a fork. Bake in the center of the oven for about 15 minutes, until the crust is lightly browned. Transfer the pan to a wire rack to cool completely.

To make the filling: In a heavy-bottomed saucepan, bring the milk just to a boil over medium heat. If you are using a vanilla bean, add it now, cover the pan, remove it from the heat, and set aside. Combine the egg yolks and sugar in a large glass or ceramic bowl, then whisk briskly for about 2 minutes, until the mixture is thick and pale yellow. Add the potato starch and whisk to blend. Remove the vanilla bean, if used, from the milk. If a skin has formed over the milk, remove it. Slowly pour the milk into the egg mixture, whisking until blended and smooth.

Return the mixture to the saucepan and bring to a boil, whisking constantly over medium heat. Reduce the heat to low and cook at a simmer, whisking constantly so that the bottom won't burn, for 1 to 2 minutes, until thick, smooth, and pale yellow. Remove from the heat. If you are using vanilla extract, stir it in now.

Cover the cream with a sheet of plastic wrap placed directly on the surface of the cream to prevent a skin from forming. Cool, then refrigerate the cream for at least 1 hour, or even overnight.

To assemble the tart, spread the pastry cream over the bottom of the tart shell. Gently spread the berries evenly over the top of the pastry cream. Set aside. In a small saucepan, melt the jelly over medium heat, stirring occasionally. Remove from the heat and whisk in the water until the mixture is blended. Allow to cool for 1 to 2 minutes, then, using a pastry brush, spread the glaze over the berries and any exposed pastry cream. Also brush the rim of the crust with the glaze. Chill for 1 hour before serving.

brioche-topped apple-blueberry galette

In traditional French cooking, a galette is a round, flat cake or tart, often topped with a pastry cream or finely sliced fruit. In the French countryside, you can also find savory galettes, like the crisp, golden potato galette sometimes served with lamb. In this recipe, a round of puff pastry is covered by concentric circles of apple and dried blueberries, and crowned by a crumbly topping made from fresh brioche. Serve on its own, or with crème fraîche, whipped cream, or ice cream. Serves 6 to 8

- All-purpose flour for rolling out the dough
- One 9 by 9-inch square of commercial puff pastry, at room temperature
- 3 tablespoons granulated sugar
- ⅛ teaspoon ground cinnamon
- 3 medium Granny Smith apples, peeled, quartered, cored, and very thinly sliced
- ⅓ cup dried blueberries
- 6 tablespoons unsalted butter, chilled and cut into bits
- 2 fresh brioche, about 6 ounces total, chopped into coarse crumbs
- 2 tablespoons brown sugar

Preheat the oven to 375°F.

On a floured work surface, working with a lightly floured rolling pin, roll out the puff pastry to a square roughly 20 percent larger than the original, about 11 inches square. Using the bottom of a 10½-inch removable-bottom tart pan as a guide, cut out a 10½-inch circle. Reassemble the removable-bottom tart pan. Using a pastry brush, lightly moisten the bottom and sides of the pan with water. Carefully transfer the circle of puff pastry dough to the tart pan (one easy way to do this is to lay the dough partially over the rolling pin and lift it over to the pan). In a small cup, combine the granulated sugar with the cinnamon, sprinkle the pastry with 1 tablespoon of the mixture, and set both aside.

Starting at the outside edge of the tart, spread the apples in overlapping concentric circles, working toward the center and covering all the pastry. Scatter the blueberries evenly over the apples. Dot the fruit with 2 tablespoons of the butter bits, sprinkle with the remaining sugar-cinnamon mixture, and set aside.

In the bowl of a food processor, or in a large bowl, combine the brioche crumbs, brown sugar, and the remaining 4 tablespoons butter. Pulse, or mash with a fork or pastry cutter, until the ingredients are incorporated but still coarse; you don't want to pulverize the mixture. Scatter the crumbs evenly over the fruit. Bake in the center of the oven for about 35 minutes, until the pastry has puffed and the brioche topping is well browned. Transfer to a wire rack to cool, then remove the sides of the pan and place the tart on a large plate to serve.

fresh spiced blueberries

So simple it hardly qualifies as a recipe, this is a wonderful last-minute way to jazz up fresh blueberries. A touch of sugar, a dash of cinnamon, a pinch of clove, flecks of fresh basil, and a dollop of sour cream do the trick. Serves 4

3 tablespoons sugar

¼ teaspoon ground cinnamon

Pinch of ground cloves

3 cups fresh blueberries

3 fresh basil leaves, finely julienned

½ cup sour cream

4 baby basil sprigs, for garnish, optional

In a small bowl, combine the sugar, cinnamon, and cloves and stir well to combine. In a large bowl, combine the blueberries with the sugar mixture and the basil and stir gently to combine. Divide among 4 individual bowls, spoon about 2 tablespoons of the sour cream onto each serving, and garnish, if you wish, with a tiny sprig of basil.

provençal blueberry tart

This dessert is an adaptation of a lovely berry tart created at the Château du Domaine St. Martin in the sun-washed Provençal countryside of Vence. What is unusual about this tart, but typical of Provençal fare, even desserts, is that it includes a light touch of olive oil in both the crust and the flanlike filling.

Serves 6

FOR THE CRUST:

- 1½ cups all-purpose flour, plus some for rolling out the dough
- 1 stick (8 tablespoons) unsalted butter, chilled and cut into bits, plus some for greasing the pan
- ½ cup sugar
- ½ teaspoon salt
- 1 large egg
- 1 tablespoon extra-light olive oil

FOR THE FILLING:

- 2 cups fresh blueberries
- 1 cup sugar
- Finely grated zest of 1 lemon
- 1 teaspoon baking powder
- 1 cup all-purpose flour
- 1 cup half-and-half
- ½ cup extra-light olive oil
- 2 large eggs
- 3 tablespoons melted butter
- ½ cup confectioners' sugar

To make the crust: In a food processor or a medium bowl, combine the flour, butter, sugar, and salt. Process for about 15 seconds, or mash with your fingertips, until the mixture is dry and crumbly, resembling coarse cornmeal. Add the egg and oil and pulse 10 or 12 times, or mix, until the dough comes together but before it forms a ball. Remove the dough from the bowl, and, with lightly floured hands, knead between your palms for about 1 minute. Press flat into a disk, wrap with plastic wrap, and refrigerate for at least 1 hour.

Butter a 9½-inch removable-bottom tart pan. On a well-floured work surface, roll out the dough to a 12-inch circle, about ⅛ inch thick. Transfer the pastry to the tart pan and press into the bottom and fluted sides, leaving ½ inch excess dough extending above the rim; fold this ½ inch of dough over onto itself, creating a doubled ½-inch border. Flute the edges with your thumb and forefinger. Prick the bottom of the shell, cover with plastic wrap, and refrigerate for 30 minutes.

Preheat the oven to 375°F. Remove the shell from the refrigerator, discard the plastic wrap, and cover with aluminum foil. Fill the shell with baking weights such as dried beans or rice, then bake in the center of the oven for 8 minutes. Remove the weights and aluminum foil and bake for another 5 minutes, until the crust is completely dry but not browned. Set on a wire rack to cool.

To make the filling: In a small bowl, combine the blueberries and ½ cup of the sugar, toss gently to coat the berries, and set aside. In the bowl of an electric mixer, combine the remaining ½ cup sugar, the lemon zest, baking powder, and flour. Mix on low to blend. Add the half-and-half and oil and mix on medium to blend. Add the eggs and butter and mix on medium until the ingredients form a smooth batter.

Spread the blueberries evenly in the bottom of the baked shell. Pour in the batter and fill to ½ inch below the top of the shell. Bake in the center of the oven for about 35 minutes, until the filling just starts to brown and the center of the tart is firm when the pan is jiggled. Remove from the oven and sprinkle with the confectioners' sugar. Cool and serve at room temperature.

assorted berry gratin

This light and lovely gratin, a traditional French baked dish with a golden crust, is prepared with fromage blanc, the versatile low-fat or fat-free creamy French-style fresh cheese that visually resembles a cross between sour cream and yogurt. The fluffy gratin topping is a cross between a meringue and a soufflé.

Serves 6

1 teaspoon unsalted butter, softened

12 ounces (1½ cups) fromage blanc

9 tablespoons granulated sugar

⅓ cup heavy cream

1 teaspoon vanilla extract

2 large eggs, separated

2 tablespoons all-purpose flour

Pinch of salt

4 cups fresh blueberries

2 cups fresh raspberries

1 cup fresh blackberries

1 tablespoon fresh lemon juice

3 tablespoons confectioners' sugar

Preheat the oven to 425°F. Lightly butter an 8- or 9-inch square or oval baking dish and set aside.

In a large bowl, lightly whip the fromage blanc with a whisk until it is aerated and smooth, about 1 minute. Add 6 tablespoons of the granulated sugar, the cream, vanilla, egg yolks, and flour and whisk until the mixture is smooth and fluffy. Set aside.

In the bowl of an electric mixer, combine the egg whites and salt. Beat until the mixture holds soft peaks. Do not overbeat. Gradually and gently fold the egg whites into the fromage blanc mixture until smoothly blended but still very airy. Set aside.

In a large bowl, combine the blueberries, raspberries, and blackberries. Place ⅔ cup of the fruit mixture in a bowl and set aside. Add the remaining 3 tablespoons of the granulated sugar and the lemon juice to the remaining fruit and stir to combine. Transfer the fruit mixture to the baking dish. Spoon on the fromage blanc mixture, spreading it smoothly and evenly over the fruit. Bake in the center of the oven for 25 to 30 minutes, until the fromage blanc topping is puffy and nicely browned. Remove from the oven and sprinkle with half of the confectioners' sugar. Garnish with the reserved berries, placing them in the cracks of the crust. Dust with the remaining confectioners' sugar and serve immediately.

blueberry gingerbread

When I served this cake at a Sunday lunch, my guests proclaimed it "off the charts" in deliciousness. Rich with the harmonious flavors of molasses, freshly grated ginger, spices, and wild blueberries, the cake is the masterly creation of David Daniels, executive chef of the Federalist, the restaurant at Boston's elegant Fifteen Beacon Hotel. If you cannot find wild Maine or other wild blueberries, use ½ cup dried blueberries. Serves 8 to 10

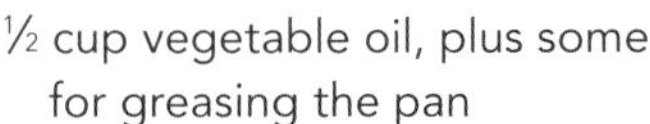

- ½ cup vegetable oil, plus some for greasing the pan
- 2½ cups all-purpose flour, plus some for dusting the pan
- 1 cup plus 2 tablespoons sugar
- ½ teaspoon salt
- 3 tablespoons molasses
- 1 large egg
- 1 teaspoon freshly grated ginger
- 1 teaspoon ground cinnamon
- ½ teaspoon freshly grated nutmeg
- 1½ teaspoons baking soda
- 1½ cups fresh wild Maine blueberries
- 1 cup buttermilk

Preheat the oven to 350°F. Grease a 12 by 7-inch baking pan and dust with flour.

In the bowl of an electric mixer, ideally fitted with a whisk attachment, beat together the oil, 1 cup of the sugar, the salt, and molasses until blended. Add the egg and ginger and beat to blend. Set aside. In a separate bowl, sift together the flour, cinnamon, nutmeg, and baking soda. In a small bowl, combine 2 tablespoons of this mixture with the blueberries and toss to coat. Add one third of the remaining flour mixture to the oil mixture and mix to blend. Add half of the buttermilk and mix to blend. Repeat this procedure with the flour and the buttermilk, finishing with the final third of the flour mixture, mixing to blend. Add the blueberries and gently fold them in.

Pour the batter into the baking pan. Sprinkle the top with the remaining 2 tablespoons sugar. Bake in the center of the oven for 35 to 40 minutes, until the center is firm and a toothpick inserted into the center comes out dry.

Transfer the pan to a wire rack to cool. Serve slightly warm or at room temperature, cutting into squares and plating directly from the pan.

glazed blueberries with ricotta-mascarpone swirl

Many fruits and cheeses partner each other beautifully—think pears and Roquefort, apples and cheddar, cream cheese and dates. Blueberries have a special affinity for soft, fresh white cheeses such as ricotta, farmer's cheese, and mascarpone. A case in point is blueberry blintzes, in which farmer's cheese marries perfectly with the blueberries either (or both) inside and outside the blintz. Another delicious example is this recipe, in which glazed blueberries, shining with a jellied crème de cassis coating, swirl in a base of sweetened ricotta mixed with rich mascarpone, a mixture similar to cannoli filling. Serves 6

FOR THE GLAZED BLUEBERRIES:

1 cup strawberry or red currant jelly

2 tablespoons crème de cassis

3 cups fresh blueberries

FOR THE RICOTTA-MASCARPONE BASE:

2 cups whole-milk ricotta

1 cup marscapone cheese

1 cup heavy cream

½ cup confectioners' sugar

3 tablespoons finely grated lemon zest

To make the glazed blueberries: In a microwave-safe bowl or Pyrex measuring cup, heat the jelly in the microwave oven on high for about 25 seconds. Stir and return to the microwave oven for another few seconds until completely melted. Add the crème de cassis and stir to blend. In a medium bowl, combine the jelly mixture with the blueberries and stir gently with a wooden spoon or a spatula until the berries are well coated. Set aside until ready to use. If you make this several hours ahead, refrigerate, but bring to room temperature 30 minutes before assembling the dessert.

To make the ricotta-mascarpone base: In the bowl of an electric mixer, fitted with a paddle attachment if available, combine the ricotta, mascarpone, cream, confectioners' sugar, and lemon zest. Beat on medium until the mixture is well blended and slightly increases in volume, about 3 minutes. Refrigerate until ready to serve.

To assemble the dessert: Spoon the ricotta mixture into 6 individual serving bowls or parfait glasses. Make a small indentation in the center of each serving. Place 2 heaping tablespoons of the blueberry mixture in each indentation. Using a small, dull knife such as a butter knife, gently swirl the blueberry mixture into the ricotta mixture so that the two elements look just slightly marbleized; do not blend. If you are serving in a parfait glass, you can also spoon the ricotta mixture and the blueberry mixture into the glass in alternate layers, starting with a layer of the ricotta mixture. Serve immediately.

mixed berry coulis

A fresh fruit coulis is a bare-bones sauce created from a puree of fresh fruit and sugar. A combination of blueberries and raspberries makes a lovely coulis for ice cream or to drizzle on cake or over pancakes. Raspberries or strawberries alone, or even ripe peaches, also make a fine coulis. Makes 2 cups

- 2 cups fresh blueberries
- 2 cups fresh raspberries
- 1 cup superfine or granulated sugar

In the bowl of a food processor, combine the blueberries, raspberries, and ½ cup of the sugar. Pulse for about 4 seconds, scrape down the sides, then process for several more seconds, slowly pouring in the remaining ½ cup sugar through the feed tube as the machine is processing, until the mixture is a smooth puree. Cover and chill until ready to serve.

poppy seed angel food cake with glacéed blueberries

This elegant and imaginative dessert was created by Else Rhodes, the executive pastry chef of the Ocean Edge Resort on Cape Cod in Brewster, Massachusetts. It's a colorful, "red, white, and blue" dessert with a harmony of interesting flavors—orange, blueberry, raspberry, and poppy seed. The preparation of the blueberries is an unusual one; the berries are actually caramelized in the sugar. You can make the sauce several hours, or even a day, ahead. Any leftover sauce is delicious on vanilla ice cream or drizzled on pancakes. Serves 8 to 10

FOR THE GLACÉED BLUEBERRIES:

2 cups sugar

½ cup water

½ cup orange juice

2 teaspoons finely grated orange zest

4 cups fresh or frozen blueberries

FOR THE POPPY SEED ANGEL FOOD CAKE:

1 cup (about 7) egg whites

1 teaspoon cream of tartar

½ teaspoon salt

½ cup sugar

½ cup all-purpose flour

1 tablespoon poppy seeds

One to two 1-pint containers raspberry sorbet

Sprigs of fresh mint or fresh lavender flowers, for garnish, optional

To make the glacéed blueberries: In a large saucepan, combine the sugar, water, orange juice, and orange zest and bring to a boil over medium heat. Reduce the heat to medium and boil, without stirring, for about 10 minutes, until the sugar mixture is golden brown and caramelized. Remove from the heat, add the blueberries and stir quickly and constantly until the berries are incorporated with the sugar mixture. Return to the heat and cook for about 3 minutes, until the mixture is well blended and all hardened sugar is dissolved. (When you first add the blueberries, they may harden instantly with the caramelized sugar, but when you keep stirring, the sugar mixture and blueberries will soften into a satiny sauce.) Set aside.

To make the poppy seed angel food cake: Preheat the oven to 375°F.

In the bowl of an electric mixer, fitted with a whisk attachment if available, combine the egg whites and cream of tartar and beat at medium speed until mixture holds soft peaks. While beating, slowly add the salt and sugar and continue to beat until the mixture can form and hold stiff peaks. Sift the flour onto the egg white mixture and gently fold it in, working to maintain as much volume as possible. Sprinkle on the poppy seeds and gently fold them in. Transfer the batter to a removable-bottom Bundt pan or an angel food cake pan. Bake for about 12 minutes, until the top of the cake is golden brown. Remove the pan from the oven and invert it onto a sturdy, long-necked glass bottle, such as a large beer bottle or wine bottle, and set aside to cool.

To serve, spoon about ½ cup of the glacéed blueberries into the bottom of individual shallow bowls. Place a slice of angel food cake on top, and crown with a scoop of raspberry sorbet. Garnish, if you wish, with a sprig of mint or lavender, and serve.

blueberry-peach delight

This lush, low-fat frozen dessert, easy to whip up in a flash, was devised in the Häagen-Dazs test kitchens by those lucky souls whose job it is to dream up new, fanciful ways to use ice cream. Blueberry-Peach Delight makes a cool and pleasing summer dessert. Serves 2 or 3

- 1 cup low-fat milk
- 1 large frozen banana, cut into 1-inch slices
- ½ cup plus 2 tablespoons frozen blueberries
- 1 cup Häagen-Dazs Vanilla frozen yogurt
- 1 cup Häagen-Dazs Orchard Peach sorbet
- ½ ripe peach, pitted and thinly sliced, optional
- 2 to 3 fresh mint sprigs, optional

In the bowl of a blender or small food processor, combine the milk, banana, ½ cup of the blueberries, the frozen yogurt, and the sorbet. Blend on high speed until the mixture is smooth.

Spoon into 2 or 3 glass parfait dishes. Garnish with the remaining 2 tablespoons blueberries and, if you wish, the peaches and mint. Serve immediately.

busy girl's angel-cake and mixed berry torte

Nobody has to know how easy this impressive and yummy dessert is to make. Food purists may cringe at the store-bought or mix-based angel cake at the heart of the recipe, but there are days when you just want something simple, fast, fresh, and attractive to serve as a festive dessert. This three-layered angel cake, filled with whipped cream and fruit, fits the bill. It's a favorite of a blue-berry-loving Westchester friend, Pam Fletcher, who kindly gave me her recipe, and recommends Duncan Hines Angel Cake if you are going to use a mix.

Serves 8 to 10

- 1 store-bought angel cake, or angel cake prepared from a mix according to package directions
- 2 cups sliced fresh strawberries
- 2 cups plus 2 tablespoons fresh blueberries
- 2 tablespoons granulated sugar
- 2 cups heavy cream
- 4 tablespoons confectioners' sugar
- 2 teaspoons vanilla extract
- 1½ cups plain yogurt
- 4 whole fresh strawberries
- 1 fresh mint sprig, optional

Using a long, flat, sharp knife with a serrated edge, carefully slice the angel cake horizontally into 3 equal layers. Set aside.

In a large bowl, combine the sliced strawberries, 2 cups of the blueberries, and the granulated sugar and stir to combine. Set aside.

In the bowl of an electric mixer, combine the cream, confectioners' sugar, and vanilla. Beat on medium until the mixture forms soft peaks. Remove the bowl from the mixer. Whisk the yogurt until it is light and airy, then gently fold it into the whipped cream.

Place the bottom layer of the angel cake on a cake plate and spread one third of the whipped cream mixture over the top. Spoon half of the strawberry-blueberry mixture evenly over the cream mixture. Place the second layer of the cake over the berries and repeat with one third of the whipped cream mixture and the remaining half of the fruit. Place the remaining layer of cake over the fruit and spread the remaining third of the whipped cream mixture on top. Garnish with the whole strawberries, the remaining 2 tablespoons blueberries, and, if you wish, the mint sprig. Keep chilled until ready to serve.

caribbean blueberry-coconut bread pudding

Blueberries are truly ubiquitous, making their way even to the tiny Caribbean island of Anguilla, just off Saint Martin in the West Indies. There, at the exclusive luxury villa resort of Altamer, chef Maurice Leduc serves this luscious, blueberry-dotted bread pudding, prepared from lightly toasted bread, flavored with a splash of rum, and crowned with a crunchy sugar and coconut topping. Serves 6

Unsalted butter for greasing the pan

4 slices white country bread (about 6 ounces), crusts on, cut into small chunks

4 large eggs

1¼ cups whole milk

¼ cup dark rum

1 teaspoon vanilla extract

3 tablespoons granulated sugar

1¾ cups blueberries

½ cup sweetened shredded coconut

¼ cup turbinado (golden-brown, natural crystallized) sugar

Preheat the oven to 375°F.

Butter a small baking dish (a 9-inch oval works well) and set aside.

Spread the bread pieces over a small baking sheet. Bake in the center of the oven until the bread is lightly browned, about 5 minutes. Set aside.

In a large bowl, combine the eggs, milk, rum, vanilla, and granulated sugar. Beat until well blended. Add the blueberries and gently fold them in. Arrange the browned bread pieces in the bottom of the baking dish. Pour the egg mixture over the bread and let it soak for about 20 minutes. Gently press the bread down into the egg mixture so that all pieces are moistened. Sprinkle the top with the coconut and turbinado sugar, then bake in the center of the oven for 35 to 40 minutes, until the pudding is set and the top is golden brown. Serve warm or at room temperature.

blueberry crumble

I love crumbles—fruit-based desserts with sweet, crunchy, crumbly toppings. I especially love the crumbly part, so whenever I make a crumble, the topping is very generous. This easy blueberry crumble, wonderful with vanilla ice cream, is a prime example. Serves 4 to 6

FOR THE FILLING:

3 cups fresh blueberries

¼ cup sugar

1 teaspoon cornstarch

1 tablespoon fresh lemon juice

FOR THE TOPPING:

1½ cups all-purpose flour

½ cup light brown sugar

¼ teaspoon salt

¼ cup finely chopped pecans or almonds, optional

1 stick (8 tablespoons) unsalted butter, chilled and cut into bits

Preheat the oven to 350°F.

To make the filling: In a large bowl, combine the blueberries, sugar, cornstarch, and lemon juice and stir to coat the berries. Transfer the mixture to a 2-quart shallow baking dish or an 8- or 9-inch square baking pan. Set aside.

To make the topping: In a large bowl, combine the flour, brown sugar, salt, pecans if you wish, and the butter.

Using a fork, a pastry blender, or your fingertips, mash the ingredients together until the mixture resembles coarse crumbs.

Sprinkle the topping mixture over the berry mixture, covering the berries evenly. Bake in the center of the oven for 30 to 40 minutes, until the topping is nicely browned and the berries are bubbling. Serve warm or at room temperature.

oatmeal-blueberry cookies

This recipe calls for dried blueberries, which resemble currants in size and texture, but have a bit more flavor and chewiness. The cookie is a variation on the classic oatmeal-raisin cookie, with a little more spice. For those on a low-cholesterol diet, a vegetable-oil-based spread such as Benecol or Take Control (Regular, not the Light versions, which don't work for cooking) can be substituted for the butter or margarine. Makes about 24 three-inch cookies

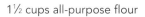

- 1½ cups all-purpose flour
- 1 teaspoon baking soda
- 1 teaspoon baking powder
- 1 teaspoon ground cinnamon
- ½ teaspoon ground ginger
- ¼ teaspoon ground cloves
- ½ teaspoon freshly grated nutmeg (or ¼ teaspoon dried ground nutmeg)
- ½ teaspoon salt
- 2 sticks (1 cup) unsalted butter or margarine, softened
- 1½ cups firmly packed brown sugar
- 2 large eggs
- 1 teaspoon vanilla extract
- 3 cups quick-cooking or old-fashioned rolled oats
- 1 cup dried blueberries
- ½ cup chopped pecans, optional

Preheat the oven to 350°F.

Sift the flour, baking soda, baking powder, cinnamon, ginger, cloves, nutmeg, and salt together into a large bowl and whisk to blend. Set aside.

In the bowl of an electric mixer, combine the butter and brown sugar. Beat on medium speed until the mixture is creamed and fluffy. Add the eggs and vanilla and beat until smoothly blended. Add the flour mixture and mix until combined. Remove the bowl from the mixer and add the oats, blueberries, and pecans and stir in with a wooden spoon.

Drop by rounded tablespoonfuls onto an ungreased cookie sheet, about 1½ inches apart. Bake in the center of the oven for 10 to 12 minutes, or until golden brown and crisp around the edges. Cool for 2 minutes on the baking sheet, then transfer to a wire rack to cool completely.

blueberry-pumpkin tea loaf with streusel topping

Spicy, moist, and irresistible, this tea loaf can also be made into muffins. Substitute a buttered 12-hole muffin pan for the loaf pan and bake for about 40 minutes. Serves 8 to10 as a loaf, or makes 12 standard-size muffins

FOR THE TEA LOAF:

- Unsalted butter for greasing the pan
- 1¾ cups plus 1 tablespoon all-purpose flour
- 1 teaspoon baking soda
- ½ teaspoon baking powder
- 1 teaspoon salt
- 1 teaspoon ground cinnamon
- ½ teaspoon ground ginger
- ¼ teaspoon ground cloves
- ½ teaspoon freshly grated nutmeg (or ¼ teaspoon ground dried nutmeg)
- 1 cup cooked or canned pumpkin puree
- ¼ cup milk
- ⅓ cup soft shortening
- ⅔ cup granulated sugar
- ⅓ cup light brown sugar
- 2 large eggs
- 1 cup fresh blueberries

FOR THE TOPPING:

- ⅓ cup all-purpose flour
- ⅓ cup sugar
- ½ teaspoon ground cinnamon
- 3 tablespoons unsalted butter, cut into bits

To make the tea loaf: Preheat the oven to 350°F.

Butter a 9 by 5-inch loaf pan and set aside. Sift 1¾ cups of the flour, the baking soda, baking powder, salt, cinnamon, ginger, cloves, and nutmeg together into a large bowl. Set aside.

In a small bowl, combine the pumpkin and milk and whisk until smoothly blended. Set aside.

In the bowl of an electric mixer, combine the shortening, granulated sugar, and brown sugar and beat on medium-high until smooth and creamy, about 4 minutes. Add 1 egg, beat to blend, then add the second egg and beat until the mixture is smooth and creamy.

Add about one quarter of the flour mixture and beat to blend. Add about one quarter of the pumpkin mixture and beat to blend. Repeat 3 more times, beating well after each addition. Remove the mixing bowl from the mixer. Toss the blueberries with the remaining 1 tablespoon of the flour, then add them to the batter and gently fold them in. Pour the batter into the loaf pan and set aside.

To make the topping: In a small bowl, combine the flour, sugar, and cinnamon and stir to blend. Add the butter and, using a fork, mash it into the flour mixture until it forms large crumbs. Sprinkle the topping evenly over the batter in the loaf pan, then place it in the center of the oven. Bake for 1 hour and 15 minutes to 1 hour and 20 minutes, until a toothpick inserted into the center of the cake comes out clean.

Cool in the pan on a wire rack for about 1 hour. Serve slightly warm or at room temperature.

wild blueberry-cassis sauce

This is a very quick and easy sauce to make, with crème de cassis—black currant liqueur—adding pizzazz to the wild blueberries. (You can use cultivated blueberries instead, but the taste won't be quite as intense.) I like to serve it with vanilla ice cream, or topping a trio of bright sorbets—perhaps raspberry, coconut, and mango. Makes about 1½ cups

- 2 cups fresh or frozen wild blueberries
- ½ cup crème de cassis
- 1 tablespoon confectioners' sugar

Combine all the ingredients in a blender or in the bowl of a food processor. Puree for 10 to 15 seconds, until smooth. Spoon over ice cream or sorbet.

blueberry-lemon curd tart

My friend, food writer Joanna Pruess, has been making this wonderful tart for years, to the acclaim of family and friends. The tartness of the curd contrasts deliciously with the mild sweetness of the blueberries and the crunchy sweetness of the crust. "If I have leftover pastry crust dough," says Joanna, "I roll it out and cut out lemon shapes, bake them in a pan alongside the crust (a few minutes less), glaze them with a bit of the lemon curd, and then decorate the top of the tart with them before serving. I garnish each lemon shape with a sprig of mint for the "leaves." To save time, Joanna notes, you can use a purchased pie crust or rolled-out purchased puff pastry for the crust. Serves 8

FOR THE LEMON CURD FILLING:

- 2 large eggs
- ⅔ cup sugar
- 5 tablespoons plus 1 teaspoon unsalted butter, melted
- ½ cup fresh lemon juice (from 3 to 4 lemons)
- Finely grated zest of 3 lemons

FOR THE PASTRY:

- 1¾ cups all-purpose flour, plus some for rolling out the dough
- 1 stick (8 tablespoons) unsalted butter, chilled and cut into bits, plus some for greasing the pan
- ½ cup sugar
- ⅛ teaspoon salt
- 1 large egg, beaten
- 4 tablespoons water

FOR THE TOPPING:

- 3 cups fresh blueberries
- 3 tablespoons confectioners' sugar
- Cut-out cookie shapes, for decoration, optional
- Fresh mint leaves, for decoration, optional

To make the lemon curd filling: In a heavy medium saucepan, whisk the eggs and sugar together until the mixture is airy and pale yellow. Add the butter and lemon juice and whisk to blend. Set the pan over medium-low heat and cook, whisking continuously, until the mixture is thickened and coats the back of a spoon, 6 to 8 minutes. Be very careful not to cook this mixture too quickly, or you will end up with scrambled eggs. Slow, gentle, and patient are the watchwords of this recipe. Remove from the heat and stir in the lemon zest. Transfer the lemon curd to a glass or ceramic bowl and cool slightly, then cover and refrigerate until the mixture is completely chilled, at least 2 hours. (You can prepare the lemon curd a day ahead.)

To make the pastry: In the bowl of a food processor, or in a large bowl, combine the flour, butter, sugar, and salt and process for 10 to 12 seconds, or mash with your fingertips, until the mixture has a dry, crumbly texture resembling coarse cornmeal. Add the egg and water and pulse 12 to 14 times, or mix, just until the dough begins to come together in a mass, but before it forms into a ball. (The dough can become tough if it is processed even a few seconds too long.) Remove the dough from the bowl, knead it for several seconds between your hands, then transfer it to a sheet of plastic wrap or waxed paper. Flatten the dough into a flat disk, wrap, and refrigerate for at least 1 hour.

Preheat the oven to 375°F.

On a floured work surface, roll out the dough with a floured rolling pin into a 13-inch circle. Transfer to a buttered 10½-inch removable-bottom tart pan and press the dough gently into the bottom and fluted sides. Fold the overhang over onto itself, reinforcing the sides, so that just ½ inch extends over the rim. Prick the bottom of the pastry several times with a fork. Flute the edges between your thumb and forefinger, or gently crimp with the tines of a fork. Line the tart shell with aluminum foil and fill almost to the top with baking weights or dried beans. Gently press the weights or beans into the edges to prevent shrinkage. Bake in the center of the oven for 10 minutes, then remove the weights and foil and bake for about 15 minutes, just until the crust is light golden brown. Transfer the pan to a wire rack and cool completely.

To assemble the tart: Scrape the chilled lemon curd into the tart shell. Spoon the blueberries over the lemon curd, spreading them evenly over the top. Gently press the berries just slightly into the lemon curd. Dust with the confectioners' sugar (a fine strainer or sieve works well for this task), and decorate, if you wish, with cut-out cookie shapes and mint leaves. Set aside for 1 hour, or refrigerate for 2 hours or so, so that the filling can slightly soften the crust.

blueberry ice cream

With an intense blueberry flavor and a wonderful royal purple hue, this rich ice cream exemplifies the essence of the blueberry. Serve it alone or garnished with an assortment of red berries. Makes about 1½ quarts

- 3 cups fresh or frozen blueberries
- 1 cup sugar
- ⅓ cup fresh lemon juice
- ½ cup water
- 2 cups heavy cream
- ½ teaspoon vanilla extract

In a large saucepan, combine the blueberries, sugar, lemon juice, and water and heat over medium-high heat until the mixture comes to a boil. Reduce the heat to medium-low and simmer, stirring occasionally, until the blueberries release their juice and the mixture thickens slightly, about 12 minutes. Remove from the heat and set aside to cool completely. Add the cream and vanilla and stir to blend. Pour the mixture into the canister of an ice cream maker and freeze according to the manufacturer's directions.

blueberry sorbet

The rich blueberry flavor of this beautiful sorbet is enhanced by the little splash of Alsatian framboise eau de vie, a fragrant raspberry brandy. The sorbet is delightful without the brandy as well. Makes 1 quart

- 3 cups fresh or frozen blueberries
- ½ cup water
- 3 tablespoons fresh lemon juice
- ½ cup sugar
- 2 tablespoons framboise eau de vie, raspberry brandy, or kirsch

Combine the blueberries, water, and lemon juice in the bowl of a food processor and puree for about 2 minutes, until smooth. Transfer to a large glass or metal bowl. Add the sugar and eau de vie and stir well, until all the sugar is dissolved. Refrigerate for 1 to 3 hours to chill. Pour the mixture into the canister of an ice cream maker and freeze according to the manufacturer's instructions.

classic hot blueberry sauce

There are many variations of hot blueberry sauce, but this is one I've found to be most versatile and pleasing. The touch of lemon zest adds a bright, sprightly note to the flavor. The hint of lemon works in a subtle counterpoint to the rich, sweet desserts that this sauce often garnishes. Serve over ice cream, puddings, flans, and cheese blintzes. Makes 1½ cups

2 cups fresh blueberries
⅓ cup sugar
2 tablespoons fresh lemon juice
1 teaspoon finely grated lemon zest
Pinch of ground cinnamon
1 tablespoon water
1½ teaspoons cornstarch

In a medium saucepan, combine the blueberries, sugar, lemon juice, lemon zest, and cinnamon and stir to combine. Cook over medium-high heat for 5 to 7 minutes, until the berries soften and begin to release their juice. Reduce the heat to medium and stir until the mixture is smooth and no berries remain intact. In a small cup, combine the water and cornstarch and stir to blend. Add to the blueberry mixture and stir to blend. Cook for about 1 more minute, until the mixture thickens. Remove from the heat and set aside to cool for about 2 minutes, then serve.

To store, let cool, cover, and refrigerate for up to 3 days. Reheat for a few seconds in a microwave oven or in a saucepan over low heat.

blueberry potato cake with glazed blueberry sauce

Tom Gutow, chef-owner of the Castine Inn in Castine, Maine, is a passionate supporter of local producers and local ingredients in the creation of his cuisine. It is only natural, then, that in one of his dishes the blueberry and the potato would find each other. For this recipe, Tom, who trained with the late, great Burgundian chef Bernard Loiseau, adapted a classic dessert from the south of Burgundy—a cake made from a puree of potatoes—adding a generous sprinkling of Maine blueberries. Tom makes his cakes using small ring molds set on a baking sheet covered with kitchen parchment. Since many home cooks don't have ring molds handy, here I call for baking the cakes in a pan of individual mini-heart molds, or in ramekins. At the Castine Inn, the Blueberry Potato Cakes are served drizzled with glazed blueberries. Serves 8

FOR THE BLUEBERRY POTATO CAKE:

2 medium russet potatoes

Salt

6 tablespoons unsalted butter, melted

3 large eggs, separated

⅓ cup plus 2 tablespoons mascarpone cheese

2½ tablespoons all-purpose flour

¾ teaspoon baking powder

½ vanilla bean, split, seeds scraped out

½ cup sugar

½ cup fresh blueberries

FOR THE GLAZED BLUEBERRY SAUCE:

1 cup sugar

¼ cup cold water

1 cup fresh blueberries

In a large saucepan, combine the potatoes with enough cold water to cover and a pinch of salt. Bring to a boil over high heat, partially cover the pan, reduce the heat to medium, and cook until tender, about 25 minutes. Drain, peel, and mash the potatoes until very smooth, either with a potato ricer or a potato masher. Measure out 1 cup of mashed potatoes and set aside; save any leftover potato for another use.

In the bowl of an electric mixer, ideally equipped with a paddle attachment, combine the potatoes, butter, egg yolks, and mascarpone and mix at medium speed until well combined. Sift the flour and baking powder into the potato mixture and mix to blend.

Transfer to a large bowl and set aside.

Preheat the oven to 350°F. In the bowl of the electric mixer, this time ideally equipped with a whisk attachment, combine the egg whites and the vanilla bean seeds. Beat at medium speed until the whites become light and frothy. While beating, slowly sprinkle in the sugar and beat until the whites form stiff, shiny peaks. Gently fold the egg white mixture into the potato mixture, adding about one third at a time, and working in a circular motion from the bottom of the bowl to the top. Add the blueberries and gently fold them in. Spoon the batter into a 6-hole mini-heart mold lightly brushed with melted butter (you will have a little bit left over, to cook in a couple of ramekins or individual tart pans), or into eight 4-inch ramekins lightly brushed with melted butter. Bake in the center of the oven until the tops are golden brown and a toothpick or little skewer inserted into the center of the cakes comes out clean, 25 to 30 minutes. Transfer the pan or ramekins to a wire rack to cool slightly. Serve slightly warm accompanied by glazed blueberry sauce.

To make the glazed blueberry sauce: In a medium saucepan, combine the sugar and water. Set the pan over low heat, stirring until the sugar dissolves. Scrape down any sugar crystals that cling to the side of the pan, as these can sometimes cause sudden crystallization after the sugar liquefies. Increase the heat to medium and bring to a boil without stirring (sugar will crystallize if you stir it after it begins to boil). Cook until the temperature on a warmed candy thermometer dipped into the syrup reaches 250°F, or until the mixture is bubbling with large bubbles and turns a light honey color. (Caramelizing sugar can be tricky. The sugar can suddenly crystallize and turn grainy after it looks lovely and syrupy. If this happens, return the syrup to the heat, add a bit more water, and bring the mixture back to 250°F.) Remove from the heat to cool for 1 to 2 minutes, then add the blueberries, stirring briskly to coat. The mixture may crystallize briefly, but will liquefy again as the berries release their juice. Serve over the cakes, slightly warm or at room temperature.

blueberry rolypoly

This is a lovely, simple summer dessert recipe from my neighbor, the garden writer Page Dickey. The recipe is a souvenir of many family summers spent in northern Maine, where wild blueberries blanket the landscape in late July and August. "I'll always remember," says Page, "the smell of blueberry bushes hugging the rocks in the summer sun." The original recipe, created by Page's Aunt Helen, whom Page recalls as a wonderful country cook, called for the biscuit dough to be rolled out, the uncooked blueberries spooned on, and then the ensemble rolled up like a jellyroll and baked in a pan. This adaptation evolved, Page explains, because "with four small children I ran out of steam after a time, and began to just spoon the dough on the berries, and bake it like a cobbler." Serve with vanilla ice cream. Serves 4 to 6

FOR THE FILLING:

2 cups fresh wild blueberries

½ cup sugar

⅛ teaspoon ground cinnamon

1 tablespoon fresh lemon juice (omit if berries are very tart)

FOR THE TOPPING:

1 cup all-purpose flour, preferably unbleached

½ teaspoon salt

1 teaspoon baking powder

2 tablespoons sugar

3 tablespoons unsalted butter, chilled and cut into bits

⅓ cup milk

Preheat the oven to 400°F. In a small casserole or soufflé dish, combine the blueberries, sugar, cinnamon, and lemon juice. Bake in the center of the oven for 10 minutes, until the blueberries are heated through and just begin to bubble.

Meanwhile, in a large bowl, sift together the flour, salt, baking powder, and sugar. Add the butter and, using a pastry blender or a fork, cut it into the flour mixture. Add the milk and stir just enough to moisten the ingredients. Spoon the dough across the top of the berries and bake in the center of the oven for about 30 minutes, until the top is golden brown and the berries are bubbling through. Serve warm or at room temperature.

blueberries with crème anglaise

Blueberries are so perfect all by themselves that many people like to serve them with just a slight gilding of the lily. "I just love plain blueberries," says my colleague and fellow villager, Amy Albert, an editor with *Fine Cooking* magazine." They taste like the color blue to me! When I serve them for company, I like to present the blueberries by themselves in a bowl, and accompany them with a crème anglaise sauce on the side." Crème anglaise, literally "English cream," is a classic recipe in the repertory of French cuisine. It is traditionally flavored with vanilla, but you can substitute 2 tablespoons of rum or Grand Marnier for the teaspoon of vanilla if you like. Blueberries with this simple French cream sauce are delectable. Serves 6

FOR THE CRÈME ANGLAISE:

5 large egg yolks

½ cup sugar

2 cups milk

1 teaspoon vanilla extract

4½ cups fresh blueberries

In a large saucepan, whisk together the egg yolks and sugar. In another saucepan, heat the milk over medium heat until hot but not boiling. Pour the hot milk into the yolk mixture, stirring constantly. Set over medium heat and stir constantly until the sauce thickens and coats the back of a spoon. Do not let the sauce come to a boil or it will curdle. Remove from the heat, pour the mixture through a fine-mesh sieve into a bowl, then add the vanilla and stir to blend. Place plastic wrap directly on the surface of the sauce to prevent a skin from forming. Cool to room temperature and serve, or cover and refrigerate if not serving immediately.

Divide the blueberries among 6 serving bowls, and pass the crème anglaise in a sauceboat at the table.

gratin of blueberries with vanilla

The humble blueberry, with all of its newly publicized attributes capturing headlines coast to coast, has begun to gain the attention of some of the world's greatest chefs, among them the celebrated Alain Ducasse. Chef Ducasse, whose restaurants in Monaco, Paris, Provence, New York, and throughout the world have garnered him acclaim, and more Michelin stars than any other living chef, did not, by his own admission, pay much attention to the blueberry until recently. In France, the berry, known as the myrtille, he explains, is not used as often in desserts as it is in America. "I had no recipes for an exclusively blueberry dessert until recently," says Mr. Ducasse. "With the help of Damon Gordon, the executive chef at my restaurant Mix, in Manhattan, we created this simple yet impressive gratin of blueberries. It's not a completely traditional gratin, but I think you'll enjoy it." You can prepare the compote and sabayon portions of the recipe several hours ahead of time, and keep them refrigerated until you're ready to assemble and serve the dessert. Serves 4

FOR THE BLUEBERRY COMPOTE:

4 cups fresh blueberries

2 tablespoons unsalted butter

1 teaspoon sugar

½ vanilla bean, split, seeds scraped out

3 fresh mint leaves

1 tablespoon crème de cassis

FOR THE SABAYON:

4 large egg yolks

1 tablespoon red Vermouth

1 teaspoon sugar

1 vanilla bean, split, seeds scraped out

FOR THE WHIPPED CREAM:

¼ cup heavy cream

Confectioners' sugar, for dusting the top

To make the blueberry compote: Place the blueberries in a colander and gently rinse them under cold water; shake out excess water. Melt the butter in a medium saucepan over medium-low heat. Add the sugar, vanilla bean and seeds, mint, crème de cassis, and blueberries. Cook slowly, stirring occasionally, until the blueberries soften and begin to release their juice, about 7 minutes. Transfer the mixture to an ovenproof gratin dish and set aside to cool. If making ahead of time, refrigerate until ready to use.

To make the sabayon: In the top of a double boiler set over gently simmering water (water at too high a boil will curdle the eggs), whisk the egg yolks to combine. Add the vermouth, sugar, and seeds from the vanilla bean and whisk continuously until the mixture doubles in volume. Remove from the heat and set aside to cool. If making ahead, cool, then cover and refrigerate until ready to use.

To make the whipped cream: In the chilled bowl of an electric mixer, ideally equipped with a whisk attachment, or in a chilled bowl, beat or whisk the cream until it holds soft peaks. Set aside, or refrigerate until ready to use.

To prepare the gratin: Preheat the broiler. Gently fold the whipped cream into the cooled sabayon, working in a circular motion from the bottom of the bowl to the top. Spread the mixture over the berry mixture, then dust the top with a couple tablespoons of confectioners' sugar (a fine-mesh sieve works well for this task). Set under the broiler, watching carefully, until the top is lightly browned. Serve immediately.

blueberry mousse

This lovely lavender mousse is the creation of Patrice Yvon, my favorite local French pâtissier, whose shop, L'Anjou Pâtisserie, in Bedford Hills, New York, keeps me supplied—too well!—with croissants, tarts, exquisite gateaux, and crisp baguettes. When I asked Patrice what specialties he offered using blueberries, he told me tarts, of course, but that was about it. Then he started to think for a bit about this versatile berry. "Well," he said, "maybe I could try a blueberry mousse. That might work very nicely." And, voilà. It does indeed. Here is Patrice's confection. Serves 8

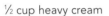

- ½ cup heavy cream
- 1 tablespoon confectioners' sugar
- ½ cup large egg whites (3 to 4 egg whites)
- 1 cup granulated sugar
- One 7-gram packet unflavored gelatin
- 1¼ cups fresh blueberries, pureed until smooth
- 8 fresh mint sprigs, for garnish, optional
- 3 tablespoons fresh whole blueberries, for garnish, optional

In the bowl of an electric mixer, ideally equipped with a whisk attachment, combine the cream and confectioners' sugar. Beat on medium speed until the mixture forms firm but not stiff peaks. Refrigerate until ready to use.

In a clean bowl of the electric mixer, ideally equipped with the whisk attachment, beat the egg whites at medium speed until they form soft peaks. Gradually add ¼ cup of the granulated sugar and continue to beat until the whites are stiff but not dry.

Meanwhile, in a medium saucepan, combine the remaining ¾ cups granulated sugar with 3 tablespoons of water. Set the pan over low heat, stirring until the sugar dissolves. Scrape down any sugar crystals that cling to the side of the pan, as these can sometimes cause sudden crystallization after the sugar liquefies. Increase the heat to medium and bring to a boil without stirring (sugar will crystallize if you stir it after it begins to boil). Cook until the temperature on a warmed candy thermometer dipped into the syrup reaches 250°F, or until the mixture is bubbling with large bubbles and turns a light honey color. (Caramelizing sugar can be tricky. The sugar can suddenly crystallize and turn grainy after it looks lovely and syrupy. If this happens, return the syrup to the heat, add a bit more water, and bring the mixture back to 250°F.) Remove from the heat to cool for 1 to 2 minutes. Then, as the mixer is beating the egg white mixture, pour in the caramelized sugar in a thin stream; try to avoid getting the syrup on the side of the mixing bowl, where it will stick. Beat constantly until the mixture cools, 10 to 15 minutes.

Meanwhile, put 1/4 cup cold water in a small bowl and sprinkle the gelatin over it, wait several minutes, then stir to dissolve. Add the gelatin mixture to the cooled egg white mixture and continue beating for about 5 minutes. Add the blueberry puree and beat for 2 minutes. Remove from the mixer. Add about one third of the whipped cream and gently fold it in, working in a circular motion from the bottom of the bowl to the top. Repeat with the remaining whipped cream, adding one third at a time and gently folding it in. Fold until the whipped cream is completely incorporated, with no white flecks remaining. Transfer to a 2- to 3-quart soufflé dish or other round bowl and refrigerate for at least 2 hours. Serve chilled, each serving garnished, if you wish, with a mint sprig and a few artistically placed berries.

blueberry pavlova

MERINGUES FILLED WITH BLUEBERRY SORBET AND WHIPPED CREAM ON A POOL OF BLUEBERRY SAUCE

This dazzling, elegant dessert is the creation of François Payard, one of New York's premier pastry chefs. Named after the Russian ballerina Anna Pavlova, this seasonal dish is on the summer menu at the Bistro Payard on Lexington Avenue in Manhattan. The recipe takes time and care to prepare, with several separate components demanding attention, so save it for a special occasion. It will wow your guests! Meringues can be temperamental, and will work best on a day that is not too humid. The whipped cream, blueberry sauce, and blueberry sorbet can all be made a day ahead. (If you have a few extra meringues, they make great fat-free cookies; store them in a dry place.) Serves 8

FOR THE MERINGUES:

½ cup egg whites (about 4 egg whites)

½ cup granulated sugar

1 cup confectioners' sugar

FOR THE WHIPPED CREAM:

2 cups heavy cream

¼ cup vanilla sugar (or ¼ cup sugar and 1 teaspoon vanilla extract)

FOR THE BLUEBERRY SAUCE:

3 cups fresh blueberries

3 tablespoons crème de cassis

1 recipe Blueberry Sorbet (page 104)

2 to 3 tablespoons confectioners' sugar, for dusting

To make the meringues: Preheat the oven to 200°F. Place the egg whites in the bowl of an electric mixer, ideally equipped with a whisk attachment. Beat until they form soft peaks. Continue beating and sprinkle on the granulated sugar. Beat until the mixture forms firm peaks. Remove from the mixer. Sift on the confectioners' sugar a little at a time and gently fold it in, working in big strokes from the bottom to the top of the bowl until the confectioners' sugar is blended. Cover a large baking sheet (or 2 if they are medium-size) with a sheet of parchment paper. Spoon the meringue mixture onto the baking sheet(s), creating 16 meringues that are 3 inches in diameter, leaving about 1 inch between the meringues. The meringues should be about 1 inch high. Finish the tops of 8 meringues with a little swirl; smooth the top of the remaining 8 meringues to a flat surface with a spatula. Bake in the center of the oven for 2 hours. The meringues should not brown but simply harden to a crisp shell. Set aside to cool.

To make the whipped cream: Combine the cream and the vanilla sugar in the bowl (preferably chilled) of an electric mixer. Beat until the mixture forms gentle peaks.

Refrigerate until ready to serve.

To make the blueberry sauce: In a medium saucepan over medium-low heat, combine the blueberries and the crème de cassis. Cook, stirring occasionally, for 15 to 20 minutes, until the mixture thickens and reduces slightly. Cool slightly, then puree until smooth in a food processor or blender. Set aside to cool, or refrigerate until ready to serve.

To assemble the Pavlova: Spoon a small pool of the blueberry sauce in the center of each of 8 dessert plates. Spread a ½-inch layer of whipped cream over the top of each flat meringue and the bottom of each swirled meringue. Place a flat meringue over the blueberry sauce on each plate. Place a small scoop of blueberry sorbet on top, pressing it gently to slightly flatten it. Cover each scoop with a swirled meringue. Dust each serving with confectioners' sugar and serve immediately.

blueberry-lemon pound cake

Among the perennial favorites at Payard Pâtisserie in New York, where stellar French pastry chef François Payard commands the kitchens, are his luscious pound cakes, lemon, chocolate-pistachio, and raisin-apricot among them. This recipe, with blueberries, is a tempting variation on François's classic lemon pound cake. Serves 8 to 10

- Unsalted butter for greasing the pan
- 1 cup all-purpose flour, plus some for flouring the pan, and perhaps the blueberries
- ⅛ teaspoon baking powder
- 2 large eggs
- ⅔ cup sugar
- Pinch of salt
- Finely grated zest of 1 lemon
- ⅓ cup heavy cream
- ½ stick (4 tablespoons) unsalted butter, melted, at room temperature
- 1 cup fresh blueberries

Preheat the oven to 325°F. Butter and flour a 9 by-5-inch loaf pan. Set aside.

Sift the flour and the baking powder together into a large bowl and set aside.

In the bowl of an electric mixer equipped with a whisk attachment, combine the eggs, sugar, and salt and beat until the mixture is frothy and pale yellow in color. Add about one third of the flour mixture and the lemon zest and beat to combine. Add about one third of the cream and beat to combine. Repeat until all the flour mixture and cream are combined and the batter is smooth. Beat in the butter in a thin stream. Remove from the mixer. If the blueberries are at all moist (after washing or refrigeration), toss them with a tablespoon of flour to coat. Scatter the blueberries over the top of the batter and gently fold them in. Pour the batter into the prepared pan and bake in the center of the oven for 55 to 60 minutes, until the top is golden brown and a toothpick or thin knife inserted into the center of the cake comes out clean. Transfer the pan to a wire rack to cool. Serve warm or at room temperature.

chapter 5

drinks

blueberry-orange wake-up cocktail

In this tempting, lavender-hued drink, the tartness of the orange juice is smoothed by the mild sweetness of the blueberries. The concoction makes a beautiful breakfast or brunch beverage. Serves 2

- 1½ cups well-chilled orange juice
- ¾ cup chilled fresh blueberries
- 2 teaspoons honey
- 2 fresh mint sprigs

In a blender or small food processor, combine the orange juice, blueberries, and honey and blend until very smooth. Pour into two 8-ounce glasses, garnish with mint, and serve.

blueberry energy booster shake

Full of blueberries as well as a cornucopia of other berries and fruit, this afternoon pick-me-up will brighten your eyes, clear away the cobwebs, and give you the energy to finish the day on a high note. As a variation, you can use this recipe to create a fresh fruit sauce for sorbets or pound cake by reducing the cranberry juice to 1 cup, adding 2 to 3 tablespoons of shredded sweetened coconut, pureeing, then chilling until ready to serve. Serves 4

- 2 cups cranberry juice
- 1 cup fresh blueberries
- ½ red apple, such as Gala or Fuji
- ½ banana
- ½ cup fresh pineapple chunks, or ¼ cup pineapple juice
- ¼ cup fresh blackberries
- 2 tablespoons honey or maple syrup

In a blender or food processor, combine all the ingredients. Blend until very smooth. Pour over ice into 4 tall glasses and serve.

blueberry iced tea

This is a lovely variation on classic iced tea, refreshing on a hot summer afternoon. The fragrance of the blueberries enhances the aroma of good tea such as Darjeeling, Ceylon, or English breakfast tea. To add a further blueberry note, make ice cubes with 3 or 4 blueberries in each cube. Serves 4

- 4 Darjeeling, Ceylon, or English breakfast tea bags
- 4 cups water
- ½ cup fresh blueberries
- 4 to 8 teaspoons sugar
- 4 fresh mint sprigs

Place the tea bags in a teapot and set aside. Boil the water, wait just until it comes off the boil (no more bubbles), then pour it into the teapot. Add the blueberries, then set the pot aside to steep for about 5 minutes. Swirl the teabags around, then remove from the pot and discard. Let the tea with the blueberries cool for about 2 hours. Pour the tea into 4 tall glasses filled with ice, keeping the blueberries in the pot. Add sugar to taste, garnish each glass with a sprig of mint, and serve.

blueberry martini

This drink glows with the color of a fine amethyst, as beautiful to serve as it is to imbibe. The blueberry-infused vodka functions as the traditional vermouth would in the drink; in other words, just a touch of it added to straight vodka gives this Martini its flavor and glow. The splash of lime and dash of triple sec give the drink the flair of a Cosmo. The blueberry-infused vodka will make 8 to 10 drinks. The Martini recipe serves 2

FOR THE BLUEBERRY-INFUSED VODKA:

- 1 cup vodka
- ½ cup sugar
- 2 tablespoons crème de cassis
- ½ cup whole fresh or frozen blueberries
- ½ cup fresh or frozen blueberries, coarsely mashed

FOR THE BLUEBERRY MARTINI:

- ¼ cup (4 ounces) vodka
- 2 tablespoons blueberry-infused vodka (see above)
- 2 teaspoons fresh lime juice
- 1 tablespoon triple sec
- 4 or 5 ice cubes

To make the blueberry-infused vodka: In a 16-ounce glass jar, combine the vodka, sugar, and crème de cassis and stir until the sugar dissolves. Add the whole and mashed blueberries and stir gently to combine. Seal tightly and set aside at room temperature. Let the mixture sit for at least a day, but the longer it macerates the better, with more infused blueberry flavor. Two weeks is ideal. From time to time, gently turn the jar upside down, then right side up, to blend the berry and vodka components. Refrigerate after 2 weeks.

To make the blueberry Martini: In a small shaker or pitcher, combine all the ingredients and stir to blend. Strain into a chilled martini glass. Spoon in 3 whole berries from the blueberry-vodka mix, and serve.

blueberry-banana frappe

Call it a frappe (as I, a Boston native, do) or call it a milkshake, this frothy, violet-hued little confection is just yummy. You can make it with frozen yogurt or rich vanilla ice cream, depending upon your dietary concerns. While I usually make my frappes with frozen yogurt, occasionally I splurge on the real thing, since nothing compares to the lusciousness of great high-fat-content ice cream. Serves 2

1 cup frozen or fresh blueberries

1 medium banana, cut into small pieces

1 cup milk

1 cup vanilla frozen yogurt or vanilla ice cream

½ teaspoon vanilla extract

3 cracked ice cubes

In a blender or food processor, combine all the ingredients. Blend or process for about 1 minute, until the mixture is smooth and frothy. Pour into tall chilled glasses and serve immediately.

blueberry-pineapple smoothie

This bright and tangy beverage is an eye-opener at breakfast time, or a perfect afternoon pick-me-up. You can make it either with freeze-dried blueberries, which makes the flavor more intense, or fresh blueberries. Serves 2

¾ cup (6 ounces) pineapple juice

¾ cup freeze-dried blueberries, or 1 cup fresh blueberries

1 cup crushed ice

In a blender or food processor, combine all the ingredients and puree until smoothly blended. Serve immediately.

appendix

resources

To experience in person the cuisine of the restaurants, hotels, inns, pastry shops, and the winery whose recipes appear in this book, contact them at the following addresses:

AR Valentien
The Lodge at Torrey Pines
11480 North Torrey Pines Road
La Jolla, CA 92037
Tel.: 858-453-4420

Aux Délices Foods by Debra Ponzek
3 West Elm Street
Greenwich, CT 06830
Tel.: 203-622-6644
and
1075 East Putnam Avenue
Riverside, CT 06878
Tel.: 203-698-1066
www.auxdelicesfoods.com

Bouterin
420 East 59th Street
New York, NY 10022
Tel.: 212-758-0323
www.bouterin.com

The Castine Inn
P.O. Box 41
Main Street
Castine, ME 04421
Tel.: 207-326-4365
www.castineinn.com

Château du Domaine Saint-Martin
Route Coursegoules
06140 Vence, France
Tel.: 011-33-4-93-58-02-02
www.chateau-st-martin.com

Dahlia Lounge
2001 Fourth Avenue
Seattle, WA 98121
Tel.: 206-682-4142
www.dahlialounge.com

Hyatt Regency Resort Grand Cayman
Seven Mile Beach
Grand Cayman
West Indies
Tel.: 345-949-1234
www.grandcayman.hyatt.com

Jane
100 West Houston Street
New York, NY 10012
Tel.: 212-254-7000
www.janerestaurant.com

L'Anjou Pâtisserie
130 North Bedford Road
Mount Kisco, NY 10549
Tel.: 914-242-4929

Mix
68 West 58th Street
New York, NY 10019
Tel.: 212-583-0300
www.mixny.com

The Neptune Room
511 Amsterdam Avenue
New York, NY 10024
Tel.: 212-496-4100
www.theneptuneroom.com

Payard Pâtisserie and Bistro
1032 Lexington Avenue
New York, NY 10021
Tel.: 212-717-5252
www.payard.com

Siggi Hall Restaurant
Hotel Odinsvé
Thorsgata 1
112 Reykjavik, Iceland
Tel.: 011-354-511-6677
www.siggihall.is

Trinchero Family Estates
P.O. Box 248
St. Helena, CA 94574
Tel.: 707-963-3104
www.trincherofamily-estates.com

mail-order blueberries and blueberry products

For plump, big, cultivated blueberries—fresh, frozen, and dehydrated—as well as blueberry syrup and gifts packs:
Gingerich Farms Products
P.O. Box 910
Canby, OR 97013
Tel.: 503-651-3742
www.gingerich.com

For an array of wild Maine blueberry products, including quick-frozen blueberries, wild blueberry juice, canned wild blueberries, and information on local retailers in your area:
Jasper Wyman & Son
P.O. Box 100
Milbridge, ME 04658
Tel.: 800-341-1758
www.wymans.com

For crisp, organic, deep blue, sweet freeze-dried blueberries that make great trail snacks and also plump up nicely in cooking (also other tasty freeze-dried fruits and veggies):
Just Tomatoes Etc!
P.O. Box 807
Westley, CA 95387
Tel.: 209-894-5371
www.justtomatoes.com

For delectable chocolate-covered blueberries—dried blueberries coated with milk chocolate and robed in a bright blue sugar shell—in elegant gold packaging:
Chicago Chocolate Company
P.O. Box 13063
Chicago, IL 60613
Tel.: 888-568-1733
www.chicagochocolate.com

For high-quality blueberry bushes (Vaccinium corymbosum), as well as information on planting, fertilizing, pruning, and harvesting:
White Flower Farm
P.O. Box 50
Route 63
Litchfield, CT 06759
Tel.: 800-503-9624
www.whiteflowerfarm.com

For Duke, Bluecrop, and Elliot varieties from a small, family-run blueberry farm:
Waters Blueberry Farm
925 Bainbridge Road
Smithville, MO 64089
Tel.: 816-532-3473
www.watersblueberryfarm.com

For a wide variety of blueberries, including Bluecrops, Bluerays, Darrows, Earliblues, Jerseys, Patriots, Sunshine Blues, and Misty Blues, from a venerable company founded in 1816:
Stark Bro's Nurseries and Orchards
11523 Highway NN
Louisiana, MO 63353
Tel.: 800-325-4180
www.starkbros.com

For lovely, elegantly crafted jewelry by artist Michael Michaud in a range of blueberry designs—brooches, necklaces, bracelets, even picture frames—created from hand-patinaed bronze and set with blue coral:
Four Seasons Design Group
2400 Merrick Road
Bellmore, NY 11710
Tel.: 800-295-6784
www.fourseasonsdesigngroup.com
Check out the site for local stores selling Michael Michaud's jewelry and decorative objects.

For salt-glaze pottery jugs, crocks, pitchers, even bean-pot-style ceramic lamps, all decorated with blue-glazed blueberry motifs:
Salmon Falls Stoneware
The Coastal Shop
Route One
York, ME 03909
Tel.: 207-351-2588
www.salmonfallsstoneware.com

For a variety of blueberry products, gifts, and collectibles, such as gourmet blueberry coffee, pancake and scone mixes, and glazed pottery from rural Maine:
The Blueberry Basket
P.O. Box 130
Alfred, ME 04002
Tel.: 207-490-3919
www.blueberrybasket.com

selected websites

www.wildblueberries.com
The website of the Wild Blueberry Association of North America, with wild blueberry news, research, the latest health and nutrition information, product information, and recipes.

www.blueberry.org/ushbc-news.htm
The website of the U.S. Highbush Blueberry Council, an organization of the cultivated blueberry industry, offering the latest blueberry news, history, growing information, research, nutrition facts, and recipes.

www.nabcblues.org
This website of the North American Blueberry Council, an organization of members of the high-bush blueberry industry, offers a link—"U-Pick Blueberries Farms"—that helps you find blueberry farms in your area where you can go and pick your own cultivated blueberries.

selected bibliography

Camp, Wendell H., Victor B. Boswell, and John R. Magness. *The World in Your Garden* Washington, D.C.: National Geographic Society, 1957.

Hibler, Janie. *The Berry Bible,* New York: William Morrow, 2004.

Joseph, James A., Daniel A. Nadeau, M.D., and Anne Underwood. *The Color Code: A Revolutionary Eating Plan for Optimum Health,* New York: Hyperion, 2002.

McCloskey, Robert. *Blueberries for Sal,* New York: Viking Press, 1948.

Seymour, E.L.D. *The New Garden Encyclopedia,* Wm. H. Wise & Co., 1946.

index

Page numbers in italics refer to illustrations.